Call first! Not because we ~~...~~ but because every element ~~...~~ changed since we've hung u~~...~~

Info Lines & Services T~~...~~ site, www.damron.com, we e~~...~~ as well as services like the state tourism board or the personal guide with a limo.

Accommodations Most accommodations (especially B&Bs) require advance reservations. It's a good idea to request a brochure ahead of time, and to be clear about deposit and cancellation policies when making reservations.

Bars & Nightclubs Many codes apply only a few nights a week, especially when we've noted "theme nights." You should call the bar to verify what is scheduled for which nights. Bars coded **BW** (beer/wine) might not serve both.

Restaurants All restaurants listed are gay-friendly; those with mostly gay/lesbian clientele are coded **MW**.

Cafes are casual hangouts serving coffee and pastries, but not full menus.

Entertainment & Recreation Something touristy, maybe a little kitschy, unusual, or commonly overlooked, that even your friends who've lived there all their lives won't mind doing with you.

Publications If you want to know what's new, get one when you get to town. They're usually free and distributed in many of the locations we list. Your best bet, however, is to go right to the local LGBT or alternative bookstore to get the latest issue and/or lowdown.

Gyms are workout facilities, not bathhouses. They're mostly straight, unless coded **MW** or **MO**.

Men's Clubs include sex clubs, bathhouses, playspaces, and sex-oriented groups.

Men's Services are mostly telephone-dating services.

Cruisy Areas In many cities, you're more likely to meet vice cops than partners at public grounds. Try the local bar or bathhouse instead if you're bent on picking up. To avoid entrapment, read the notice about "Cruisy Areas," page 4.

Unconfirmed means we've called, several times, but no one answered. The phone still works but everything else may be different. Definitely call first.

Events Calendar Lists those "can't-miss" events for the upcoming year — from circuit parties to bear jamborees to street fairs and festivals.

Tour Operators A brief description of what kinds of tours the tour operator offers.

As Damron has done since 1964, we reward the best letters (those packed with new info of openings and closings we haven't already found) with a *FREE COPY* of next year's edition.

Table of Contents

United States of America

Table of Contents

Who we are

In 1964, a businessman published a book of all the gay bars he knew from his constant travels across the United States. This book could fit comfortably in the palm of your hand. Despite its small size, it was an impressive accomplishment. Each one of the listings he had visited himself. Every last copy of that book he sold himself. The name of this pioneering businessman—Bob Damron.

Almost fifty years later, his little book, the Damron Men's Travel Guide (originally *Bob Damron's Address Book*), is still a bestseller. And it has remained the model for the countless gay travel guides to follow in its wake. Today, Damron's ever-expanding list of titles includes: the *Damron Women's Traveller* for lesbians; the *Damron City Guide*, a full-color map guide; and *Damron Accommodations*, with thousands of expanded B&B listings and color photos.

How we maintain the accuracy of our listings

Our editors contact every single listing in our database annually, usually by phone, fax, or email. They also receive updated information directly from business owners and you, our readers. If you send in new, verifiably correct information, Damron will send you a free copy of the next edition as our way of saying a very sincere "thank you" for your help.

PLEASE READ THIS NOTICE ABOUT "CRUISY AREAS"

Certain locations are categorized as "Cruisy Areas." These areas include but are not limited to parks, rest stops, and beaches. Information regarding these areas is furnished to Damron by various sources and, due to time and other constraints, Damron is unable to investigate these areas. Areas marked as "AYOR" (At Your Own Risk) may involve risk and the reader should proceed with caution. However, the absence of an AYOR rating does not guarantee the safety or security of any area. Therefore, Damron makes no warranty or representation as to the safety, security, or status of those areas marked as cruisy areas. Damron urges readers to avoid sexual activity within Cruisy Areas.

BEWARE — MOST POLICE DEPARTMENTS IN THE USA HAVE COPIES OF THE MEN'S TRAVEL GUIDE.

Publisher	**Damron Company**
President	
& Editor-in-Chief	**Gina M. Gatta**
Managing Editor	**Erika O'Connor**
Roving Editor	**Ian Philips**
Cover Photo	
& Design	**Mary Burroughs**

Board of Directors

Gina M. Gatta, Edward Gatta, Jr., Louise Mock

In Memory of Bob Damron and Dan Delbex

How to Contact Us

Mail: PO Box 422458, San Francisco, CA 94142-2458
Web: www.damron.com
Phone: 415/255-0404 & 800/462-6654
        [9am-5pm (PST) Mon-Fri]
Fax: 415/703-9049

A WHOLE NEW KIND OF CRUISING.

No matter which way you go, you're always
headed in the right direction in Key West.

Key West

Close To Perfect · Far From Normal

FIND YOUR STORY

frameline 37

SAN FRANCISCO INTERNATIONAL
LGBT FILM FESTIVAL JUNE 20 - 30, 2013

frameline.org

hope
healing
remembrance

Photo: Mike Shriver

Honor a Life Touched by AIDS by Engraving a Name in the Circle of Friends

NATIONAL
· A I D S ·
MEMORIAL
G R O V E

In 1996, Congress and the President of the United States designated the AIDS Memorial Grove as a national memorial to commemorate all lives touched by AIDS. Located in San Francisco's Golden Gate Park, the National AIDS Memorial Grove is a place of natural beauty and serenity, and home to the Circle of Friends.

The Circle of Friends, engraved in a flagstone terrace near the eastern entrance to the Grove, is surrounded by redwood trees and flowering dogwoods. It is a special place – a place of remembrance. Like the Vietnam Veterans Memorial, the Circle of Friends offers a testament to the individual lives touched by AIDS, making permanent a personal message of love and loss.

By engraving a name in the Circle of Friends, your own, that of someone you honor, love, or miss, you tell the world that this global tragedy must never be forgotten, and that everyone lost to AIDS will be remembered always.

Names are inscribed in November annually, prior to our World AIDS Day national observance on December 1st.

For more information, please call 415-765-0497, or visit www.aidsmemorial.org.

do you speak **SONOMA?**

{ **Sonomads:** *n.* People who embrace the wanderlust of Sonoma Wine Country.

**Speak a little Sonoma
and you'll feel like a local.**

Because you're more than a visitor,
you're a new friend.

**Learn by immersion and win a savory
Sonoma County experience!**

SonomaCounty.com/gay   1-800-576-6662

SONOMA
C O U N T Y

Plan your next trip with

myGayTrip.com

Idan, 23
4 travels
8 reviews

GRAN CANARIA
TEL AVIV
BARCELONA
STOCKHOLM
PARIS
MYKONOS
BERLIN
MIAMI

Idan by
Nimrod Kapeluto

myGayTrip.com: meet gay travelers and find your next destination. Hotels, bars, restaurants, bathhouses, beaches... Get all the right places !

Join us on
40,000+ fans
facebook.com/myGayTrip

Follow us on
twitter.com/myGayTrip

IT'S SO MIAMI.

So someone tried to describe to you how Miami's so different,
so exciting and so party perfect. Know this. No tweet, snapshot or
posting will ever be enough. You so have to visit to get it. **MiamiLGBT.com**

MIAMI
GREATER MIAMI AND THE BEACHES

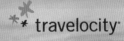

USA

ALABAMA

Statewide

■PUBLICATIONS

➤**Ambush Mag** 504/522-8049
LGBT newspaper for the Gulf South (TX through FL)

Anniston

■CRUISY AREAS

Cheaha Park [AYOR] Cheaha Scenic Dr
early evenings, head toward the walking trail (beware of cops!)

Auburn

■ACCOMMODATIONS

Black Bear Camp Men's Retreat
[MO,R,SW,N,NS,WI,WC,GO] 10565 US Hwy
280 W, Waverly 334/887-5152 *hot tub, kitchen*

■CRUISY AREAS

Rest Area [AYOR] Hwy 280 (30 miles E of Alexander City & 5 miles W of Auburn) *evenings*

Birmingham

■ACCOMMODATIONS

Hamton Inn [GF,WI,WC] 2021 Park Pl N
(at 21st St N) 205/322-2100 *also restaurant & lounge*

■BARS

The Garage Cafe [GF,F,E] 2304 10th
Terrace S (at 23rd St S) 205/322-3220
11am-close, from 3pm Sun-Mon, great sandwiches, live music

Our Place [M,NH,V,GO] 205/715-0077
4pm-midnight, till 2am Fri-Sat

Wine Loft [GF] 2200 1st Ave N
205/323-8228 *5pm-close, clsd Sun-Mon, wine bar, light food served*

■NIGHTCLUBS

Al's on 7th [MW,NH,D,DS,18+] 2627 7th
Ave S (at 27th St) 205/321-2812
theme nights

The Quest Club [M,D,DS,PC,WC,$] 416
24th St S (at 5th Ave S)
205/251-4313 *24hrs, [19+] Wed-Sun, patio*

Steel Urban Lounge [GF,D] 2300 1st
Ave N (at 23rd St) 205/324-0666
6pm-close, from 8pm wknds, upscale lounge

■CAFES

Chez Lulu [E] 1909 Cahaba Rd
205/870-7011 *lunch & dinner Tue-Sun, Sun brunch, clsd Mon, plenty veggie, also bakery*

■RESTAURANTS

Bottega Cafe & Restaurant [WC]
2240 Highland Ave S (btwn 22nd &
23rd) 205/939-1000 *5:30pm-10pm, clsd Sun, full bar*

The Bottletree 3719 3rd Ave S (at 37th
St S) 205/533-6288 *3pm-close, from
11am wknds, vegetarian/ vegan, also bar,
live music venue*

Highlands Bar & Grill [WC] 2011 11th
Ave S (at 20th St) 205/939-1400
5:30pm-10pm, clsd Sun-Mon

John's City Diner [WC] 112 21st St N
(btwn 1st & 2nd Ave N)
205/322-6014 *lunch weekdays &
dinner Mon-Sat, clsd Sun, full bar*

Rojo 2921 Highland Ave S (at 30th St)
205/328-4733 *11am-10pm, clsd Mon,
wknd brunch, Latin & American cuisine*

Silvertron Cafe 3813 Clairmont Ave S
(at 39th St S) 205/591-3707 *11am-
9pm, from 8am Sat, also full bar, more
gay Mon*

Taj India 2226 Highland Ave S
205/939-3805 *lunch & dinner, Indian,
plenty veggie*

■ENTERTAINMENT & RECREATION

Terrific New Theatre 2821 2nd Ave S
(in Dr Pepper Design Complex)
205/328-0868

■MEN'S SERVICES

➤**MegaMates** 205/595-3388 *Call to
hook up with HOT local men. FREE to
listen & respond to ads. Use FREE code
DAMRON. MegaMates.com.*

Alabama • *USA*

▪EROTICA

Alabama Adult Books 801 3rd Ave N (at 8th) **205/322-7323** *super-arcade*

Birmingham Adult Books [★] 7610 1st Ave N (at 76th St) **205/836-1580** *booths*

The Downtown Bookstore 2731 Rev Abraham Woods Jr Blvd (at 28th St) **205/328-5525** *arcade, booths*

Pleasure Books 7606 1st Ave N (at 76th St N) **205/836-7379** *arcade, booths*

▪CRUISY AREAS

Cahaba River Rd Park [AYOR] at Jefferson/ Shelby county line (on Hwy 280 E, exit before Cahaba River bridge & turn left) *follow trail; noon & late afternoon popular*

Cullman

▪CRUISY AREAS

Heritage Park [AYOR] Cherokee Ave *hospital side of park*

Daphne

▪CRUISY AREAS

Spanish Fort Overlook [AYOR] scenic overlook, off Hwy 98 (from I-10, exit at Daphne/ Spanish Fort at Hwy 98) *great view of Mobile Bay (beware of cops!)*

Decatur

▪RESTAURANTS

The Waffle House 710 6th Ave NE (btwn Layfayette & Walnut) **256/355-2871** *24hrs, popular after-hours*

Dothan

▪NIGHTCLUBS

Club Imagination [MW,D,TG,K,DS,18+,PC] 4129 Ross Clark Circle NW (off Hwy 431 N) **334/792-6555** *6pm-4am, clsd Sun-Tue*

Dothan Dance Club [GF,DS,MR,C,PC,GO] 2563 Ross Clark Circle (at Hwy 52 West) **334/792-5166** *11pm Fri, from 6pm Sat-Sun, clsd Mon-Th*

Eufaula

▪CRUISY AREAS

Rest Area [AYOR] southbound on Hwy 431 (S of town) *busier evenings*

Fairhope

▪CRUISY AREAS

Wilson Park [AYOR] downtown (next to post office) *late nights, street cruising w/ cars circling park*

Geneva

▪ACCOMMODATIONS

Spring Creek Campground & Resort [M,SW,N,WI,GO] 163 Campground Rd (at Spring Creek Rd) **334/684-3891** *some theme wknds w/ DJ, day passes*

Gulf Shores

▪CRUISY AREAS

Bon Secour Wildlife Refuge [AYOR] on Hwy 180, mile marker 12 (turn left on Mobile St Dr & take to beach) *walk right 1 mile, nude beach & dunes past beach homes*

Huntsville

▪BARS

Partners [MW,D,F,E,K,WC,GO] 256/ **539-0975** *5pm-2am, from 6pm wknds*

Vieux Carre [MW,NH,D,E,DS,WC] 1204 Posey (at Larkin) **256/534-5970** *7pm-2am, clsd Mon*

▪CRUISY AREAS

Monte Sano Scenic Overlook [AYOR] Governors Dr (on left before Monte Sano Blvd)

Jacksonville

▪CRUISY AREAS

Germania Springs Park [AYOR] off N Hwy 21 (Pelham Rd) (past JSU campus) *afternoons (beware cops!)*

Mobile

see also Pensacola, Florida

▪INFO LINES & SERVICES

Pink Triangle AA Group 251/ **479-9994** (AA#), 251/438-7080 (church) *7pm Tue, Th & Sat, call for loc*

■ACCOMMODATIONS

Berney/ Fly B&B [GF,21+,SW,NS,WI,WC]
1118 Government St **251/405-0949**
Victorian B&B, full brkfst, near downtown

■BARS

Gabriel's Downtown [MW,K,V,PC] 55 S
Joachim St (off Government)
251/432-4900 *7pm-close, patio*

Midtown Pub [MW,NH,D,F,K] 153 S
Florida St (at Emogene) **251/450-1555**
noon-2am

■NIGHTCLUBS

B-Bob's Downtown [M,D,B,DS,P,WC]
213 Conti St (at Joachim)
251/433-2262 *6pm-close, from 7pm
Sat, 2-level multi-venue club, home den
of Gulf Coast Bears, also gift shop*

■RESTAURANTS

True Midtown Kitchen 1104 Dauphin
St **251/433-2253** *lunch & dinner,
brunch only Sun, full bar, soul food*

Montgomery

■ACCOMMODATIONS

The Lattice Inn [GS,SW,WI,WC,GO] 1414
S Hull St (at Clanton) **334/262-3388**

■NIGHTCLUBS

Club 322 [MW,D,DS] 322 N Lawrence St
334/263-4322 *8pm-close, clsd Mon*

■MEN'S SERVICES

▶**MegaMates 334/414-9500** *Call to
hook up with HOT local men. FREE to
listen & respond to ads. Use FREE code
DAMRON. MegaMates.com.*

■CRUISY AREAS

Woodmere Park [AYOR] Woodmere
Blvd (at Eastern)

Steele

■ACCOMMODATIONS

Bluff Creek Falls [M,SW,PC,WI,GO]
1125 Loop Rd **256/538-0678,
205/515-7882** *secluded campground,
50 minutes from Birmingham*

Sylacauga

■CRUISY AREAS

Noble Park [AYOR] N Broadway Ave
after dark, park near pavilions

Tuscaloosa

■NIGHTCLUBS

Icon [M,D,DS] 516 Greensboro Ave
9pm-2am, clsd Sun-Mon

■MEN'S SERVICES

MegaMates 205/535-3200 *Call to
hook up with HOT local men. FREE to
listen & respond to ads. Use FREE code
DAMRON. MegaMates.com.*

■CRUISY AREAS

Bowers Park [AYOR] from McFarland
Blvd turn E onto 37th St, then turn N
onto Bowers Park Dr

Jack Warner Pkwy Parks [AYOR] along
Black Warrior River *formerly River Rd
Parks, check out 4th park near boat
ramp*

ALASKA

Statewide

■ENTERTAINMENT &
RECREATION

Out in Alaska [★] PO Box 82096,
Fairbanks 99708 **877/374-9958,
907/374-9958** *adventure travel
throughout Alaska for LGBT travelers*

Anchorage

■INFO LINES & SERVICES

AA Gay/ Lesbian 336 E 5th Ave (at
Community Center) **907/929-4528**
6pm Mon

Gay/ Lesbian Helpline 1300 East St
907/258-4777, 888/901-9876
(outside Anchorage) *6pm-11pm*

Identity, Inc 336 E 5th Ave
907/929-4528 *community center,
newsletter*

■ACCOMMODATIONS

A Wildflower Inn B&B [GS,NS,WI,GO]
1239 I St (at 13th) **907/274-1239,
877/693-1239** *convenient, downtown
location*

Alaska • *USA*

Alaska Heavenly Lodge [GF,NS] 34950 Blakely Rd (at Mile 49 Sterling Hwy), Cooper Landing **907/595-2012, 866/595-2012** *hot tub, cedar sauna*

Alaska's North Country Castle B&B [GF,NS] 14600 Joanne Cir **907/345-7296** *ocean & mtn views, full brkfst*

Anchorage Jewel Lake B&B [GS,NS,WI,GO] 8125 Jewel Lake Rd **907/245-7321, 877/245-7321** *full brkfst, kids ok*

Arctic Fox Inn [GS,GO] 327 E 2nd Ct **907/272-4818, 877/693-1239** *also apts*

City Garden B&B [GS,NS,WI,GO] 1352 W 10th Ave (at N St) **907/276-8686** *beautiful views of Mt McKinley, 10-minute walk to downtown area*

Copper Whale Inn [GS,WI,NS,WC,GO] 440 L St (at 5th Ave) **907/258-7999, 866/258-7999** *downtown*

Eagle Nest Guest House [MO,WI,GO] 25411 Crystal Creek Dr, Eagle River **907/903-1828**

Earth B&B & Tours [GF,NS,WI] 1001 W 12th Ave **907/279-9907** *close to downtown*

Gallery B&B [GS,WC,GO] 1229 G St (at 12th) **907/274-2567** *lesbian-owned*

Inlet Tower Hotel & Suites [GS,WI,WC] 1200 L St (at 12th) **907/276-0110, 800/544-0786** *also bar & restaurant*

Renfro's Lakeside Retreat [GF,WI,GO] 27177 Seward Hwy, Seward **907/288-5059, 877/288-5059** *log cabins on Kenai Lake, seasonal*

■BARS

Bernie's Bungalow Lounge [GF,F] 626 D St (at W 5th Ave) **907/276-8808** *cocktail lounge, patio, food served*

Kodiak Bar [MW,D,F] 225 E 5th Ave (btwn Cordova & Barrow) **907/258-5233, 907/865-8978** *3pm-2:30am, till 5am Fri-Sat*

Mad Myrna's [MW,NH,D,F,K,DS] 530 E 5th Ave (at Fairbanks) **907/276-9762** *4pm-2:30am, till 3am Fri-Sat*

Raven [MW,NH,WC] 708 E 4th Ave **907/276-9672** *1pm-2:30am, till 3am wknds*

■RESTAURANTS

Bear Tooth Theatre Pub & Grill 1230 W 27th Ave **907/276-4200** *movie theater, pub & grill all in one*

China Lights 12110 Business Blvd, Eagle River **907/694-8080** *11:30am-10pm, till 10:30pm wknds*

Club Paris 417 W 5th Ave **907/277-6332** *11am-midnight, from 4pm Sun, perhaps the finest restaurant in town*

Garcia's 11901 Business Blvd #104 (next to Safeway), Eagle River **907/694-8600** *11am-midnight, from noon wknds, Mexican*

Ginger 425 W 5th Ave (at D St) **907/929-3680** *lunch Mon-Fri, dinner nightly, bar from 3pm, Pacific Rim/ Asian*

Marx Brothers Cafe 627 W 3rd Ave **907/278-2133** *5:30pm-10pm, clsd Sun-Mon, great food & views*

Simon & Seafort's 420 L St (btwn 4th & 5th) **907/274-3502** *lunch week-days, dinner nightly, great view, full bar*

Snow City Cafe [★BW,WI] 1034 W 4th Ave (at L St) **907/272-2489** *7am-3pm, till 4pm wknds*

■ENTERTAINMENT & RECREATION

Out North 3800 DeBarr Rd **907/279-3800, 907/279-8099** *community-based & visiting-artist exhibits, screenings & performances*

■BOOKSTORES

Title Wave Books 1360 W Northern Lights Blvd **907/278-9283, 888/598-9283** *10am-8pm, till 9pm Fri-Sat, 11am-7pm Sun, LGBT section; also at 415 W 5th Ave, 907/258-9283*

■PUBLICATIONS

Anchorage Press 907/561-7737 *alternative paper*

■EROTICA

Le Shop 305 W Diamond Blvd (at C St) **907/522-1987** *8am-1am*

Fairbanks

■ACCOMMODATIONS

All Seasons B&B Inn [GF,NS,WI,WC] 763 7th Ave (at Barnette St) 907/451-6649, 888/451-6649 *full brkfst*

Billie's Backpackers Hostel [GF,F] 2895 Mack Blvd 907/479-2034, 907/799-6120

■CAFES

Hot Licks Ice Cream 3453 College Rd 907/479-7813 *seasonal*

Haines

■ACCOMMODATIONS

The Guardhouse Boarding House [MW,NS,WI,GO] 15 Fort Seward Dr 907/766-2566, 866/290-7445 *in former jail of Fort William H. Seward*

Homer

■ACCOMMODATIONS

Sadie Cove Wilderness Lodge [GF,NS] Kachemak Bay State Park 907/235-2350, 888/283-7234 *tree planted for every guest to offset carbon emission, 3 full meals a day*

■CAFES

Spit Sister Cafe [GS,WI] Homer Spit Rd (at Harbor View Boardwalk #5) 907/235-4921 (summer), 907/299-6868/ 6767 (winter) *5am-4pm*

■ENTERTAINMENT & RECREATION

Alaska Fantastic Fishing Charters 800/478-7777 *deluxe cabin cruiser for big-game fishing (halibut)*

Juneau

■ACCOMMODATIONS

Pearson's Pond Luxury Suites & Adventure Spa [GF,NS,WI] 4541 Sawa Circle 907/789-3772, 888/658-6328 *B&B resort & spa*

The Silverbow Inn [GF,NS,WI] 120 Second St 907/586-4146, 800/586-4146

■RESTAURANTS

Hangar on the Wharf 2 Marine Way Ste 106 907/586-5018 *lunch & dinner, full bar, great fish & chips*

■CRUISY AREAS

Cope Park [AYOR] *mornings & afternoons (summers)*

Ketchikan

■ACCOMMODATIONS

Anchor Inn by the Sea [GF,NS,WI] 4672 S Tongass Hwy 907/247-7117, 800/928-3308

■ENTERTAINMENT & RECREATION

Southeast Sea Kayaks [GF] 3 Salmon Landing 907/225-1258, 800/287-1607

McCarthy

■ACCOMMODATIONS

McCarthy Lodge & Ma Johnson's Hotel [GF,F,NS] 907/554-4402 *inside Wrangell St Elias nat'l park*

Palmer

■ACCOMMODATIONS

Alaska Garden Gate B&B [GS,NS,WI,GO] 950 S Trunk Rd 907/746-2333 *full brkfst, hot tub, lesbian-owned*

Seward

■ENTERTAINMENT & RECREATION

Puffin Fishing Charters [GS] PO Box 606, 99664 907/224-4653, 800/978-3346 *day fishing trips*

Sitka

■CAFES

Backdoor Cafe 104 Barracks St (behind Old Harbor Books on Lincoln St, no street sign) 907/747-8856 *6:30am-5pm, till 2pm Sat, clsd Sun*

■ENTERTAINMENT & RECREATION

Esther G Sea Taxi 215 Shotgun Alley 907/738-6481, 907/747-6481 *marine wildlife tours, transportation service*

ARIZONA

Bisbee

ACCOMMODATIONS

Casa de San Pedro B&B
[GF,SW,NS,WI,WC,GO] 8933 S Yell Ln (at Hwy 92 & Palominas Rd), Hereford **520/366-1300, 888/257-2050** *full brkfst*

Copper Queen Hotel [GF,SW,NS,WC] 11 Howell Ave **520/432-2216** *restored historic landmark, restaurant*

➤**David's Oasis Camping Resort** [MW,21+,SW,WI,GO] 5311 W Double Adobe Rd, McNeal **520/979-6650** *bar & internet cafe*

Doublejack Guesthouse [M,NS,WI] **520/559-6708**

Eldorado Suites [GF,NS,WI] 55 OK St **520/432-6679**

Sleepy Dog Guest House [GF,NS,WI] 212A Opera Dr **520/432-3057, 520/234-8166** (cell) *reclaimed miner's cabin*

BARS

Copper Rainbow Bistro
[MW,BW,K,PC,WC] 5311 W Double Adobe Rd, McNeal **520/979-6650** *5pm-10pm Fri-Sat, 2pm-7pm Sun*

St Elmo's [GF,E] 36 Brewery Ave **520/432-5578** *10am-2am, live bands Fri-Sat*

Bullhead City

includes Laughlin, Nevada

BARS

The Lariat Saloon [MW,NH,MR,WC] 1161 Hancock Rd (at 95) **928/704-1969** *3pm-close, patio*

CRUISY AREAS

Adult Theater Hwy 95 (S of town) *bookstores w/ arcade*

Karen's Adult Bookstore Hwy 95 (near Mohave Jct, S of town)

Flagstaff

■ACCOMMODATIONS

Abineau Lodge [GS,NS,WI,GO] 1080 Mountainaire Rd 928/525-6212, 888/715-6386

The Historic Hotel Monte Vista [GF,E,NS] 100 N San Francisco St (at Aspen) 928/779-6971, 800/545-3068 *full bar*

Inn at 410 [GF,WI,WC] 410 N Leroux St 928/774-0088, 800/774-2008

Motel in the Pines [GF,WC] 80 W Pinewood Blvd (exit 322), Pinewood 928/286-9699, 800/574-5080 *20 miles from Flagstaff*

Starlight Pines B&B [GS,NS,WI,GO] 3380 E Lockett Rd (at Fanning) 928/527-1912, 800/752-1912 *full brkfst*

■BARS

Charly's Pub & Grill [GF,F,E,WC] 23 N Leroux St (at Weatherford Hotel) 928/779-1919 *8am-2am*

Monte Vista Lounge [GF,D,E,K] 100 N San Francisco St (at Hotel Monte Vista) 928/774-2403 *noon-2am, from 11am Fri-Sun*

■CAFES

Macy's European Coffee House [F] 14 S Beaver St 928/774-2243 *6am-10pm, vegetarian/ vegan bakey*

■RESTAURANTS

Cafe Olé [BW,WC] 119 S San Francisco St (at Butler) 928/774-8272 *lunch & dinner, clsd Sun, Mexican*

Granny's Closet 218 S Milton Rd 928/774-8331 *lunch & dinner, also sports bar*

Pasto [BW,WC] 19 E Aspen (at San Francisco) 928/779-1937 *lunch & dinner, clsd Sun*

■CRUISY AREAS

Rest Area [AYOR] off I-40 (17 miles W of Flagstaff)

Thorpe Park [AYOR]

Golden Valley

■EROTICA

Pleasure Palace Adult Bookstore 4150 US Hwy 68 (at Houck Rd) 928/565-5600

Grand Canyon

■ACCOMMODATIONS

Grand Canyon Lodge North [GF,F] end of Hwy 67, North Rim 877/386-4383 *at the North Rim of the Grand Canyon*

Grand Canyon Lodges [GF,F] 928/638-2631 *the only "in-park" lodging at the South Rim*

Jerome

■ACCOMMODATIONS

The Cottage Inn Jerome [GS,GO] 928/634-0701, 928/649-6759 *full brkfst*

Mile High Grill & Inn [GF,GO] 309 Main St 928/634-5094 *cool hotel, also restaurant*

■RESTAURANTS

Quince Grill & Cantina [WC] 363 S Main St 928/634-7087 *8am-5pm, 7am-9pm Th-Sun*

Kingman

■ACCOMMODATIONS

Kings Inn Best Western [GF,F,SW,WI,WC] 2930 E Andy Devine Ave 928/753-6101, 800/750-6101

Lake Havasu City

■INFO LINES & SERVICES

Lake Havasu City AA 877/652-9005

■ACCOMMODATIONS

Nautical Inn [GF,SW,WI] 1000 McCulloch Blvd N 928/855-2141, 800/892-2141

Lake Powell

■ACCOMMODATIONS

Dreamkatchers Lake Powell B&B [GS,WI,GO] 435/675-5828

Phoenix

see also Scottsdale & Tempe

■ INFO LINES & SERVICES

1 Voice LGBT Community Center
4442 North 7th Ave **602/712-0111**
noon-7pm, clsd Sun

Lambda Phoenix Center 2622 N 16th
St (at Virginia Ave) **602/635-2090**
space for many 12-step programs

■ ACCOMMODATIONS

Arizona Royal Villa Complex
[MO,SW,N,NS,WI,GO] 4312 N 12th St
602/266-6883, 888/266-6884 hot
tub

➤**Arizona Sunburst Inn**
[MO,R,SW,N,NS,WI,GO] 6245 N 12th Pl
(at Rose Ln) **602/274-1474,**
800/974-1474 hot tub

Clarendon Hotel & Suites
[GS,SW,WI,WC,GO] 401 W Clarendon Ave
(at 3rd Ave) **602/252-7363**

FireSky Resort & Spa [GF,SW,WI,WC]
4925 N Scottsdale Rd, Scottsdale
480/945-7666, 800/528-7867

Hotel San Carlos [GF,F,SW,WI] 202 N
Central Ave **602/253-4121,**
866/253-4121 boutique hotel, rooftop
pool, restaurant

Maricopa Manor B&B Inn
[GS,SW,WI,WC,GO] 15 W Pasadena Ave
602/274-6302, 800/292-6403

Orange Blossom Hacienda
[GF,SW,WI,GO] 3914 E Sunnydale Dr
(btwn Recker & Hunt Hwy), Gilbert
480/755-4346, 888/920-2803

Rainbow Casita [M,SW,N,NS,WI,GO]
2707 N 20th Ave (at Thomas Rd)
602/628-5781

The Saguaro Hotel [GF,SW,NS] 7353 E
Indian School Rd, Scottsdale
480/308-1100, 800/808-2440 hip
boutique hotel

The Saguaro Scottsdale [GS,SW]
4000 N Drinkwater Blvd, Scottsdale
480/308-1100

Scottsdale Thunderbird Suites
[GF,SW,NS,WI,WC] 7515 E Butherus Dr
(at Scottsdale Rd), Scottsdale
480/951-4000, 800/951-1288 full
brkfst, gym, hot tub, full bar

ZenYard [GS,SW,NS,WI,GO] 830 E
Maryland Ave **602/845-0830,**
866/594-0242

■ BARS

Amsterdam [MW,F,E,K] 718 N Central
Ave (btwn Roosevelt & Fillmore)
602/258-6122 4pm-2am, till 4am
wknds, also Club Miami [D]

Anvil [M,D,L,S] 2303 E Indian School Rd
602/956-2885 1pm-2am

Apollo's [M,D,NH,E,K,S,WI] 5749 N 7th
St (S of Bethany Home) **602/277-9373** 11am-2am

Bar 1 [M,NH,K,WI] 3702 N 16th St (at E
Clarendon) **602/266-9001** 10am-2am

Bar Smith [GS,D,F] **602/229-1265**
9pm-2am, till 3am Sat, clsd Sun

BS West [MW,D,K,V,WC] 7125 E 5th Ave
(in pedestrian mall), Scottsdale
480/945-9028 2pm-2am

The Bunkhouse Saloon [M,NH,K] 4428
N 7th Ave (at Indian School)
602/200-9154 8am-2am, from 10am
Sun, patio

Cash Inn Country [W,D,CW,K,WI,WC]
2140 E McDowell Rd (at 22nd St)
602/244-9943 2pm-close, from noon
wknds

Charlie's [★M,D,CW,DS,WC] 727 W
Camelback Rd (at 7th Ave)
602/265-0224 2pm-2am, noon-4am
Fri-Sat

Claude's Lounge [M,NH,K,S,V,WI] 4132
E McDowell Rd (at 41st St)
602/388-4030 2pm-2am

Club 24 [M,D,WC] 2424 E Thomas Rd
(at 24th St) **602/682-5088** 3pm-2am
Wed-Sun

Cruisin' 7th [M,DS,K,TG,WC] 3702 N 7th
St (near Indian School) **602/212-9888**
6am-2am, from 10am Sun, hustlers

Dick's Cabaret [M,D,S,18+] 3432 E Illini
(off University, behind Radisson Hotel)
602/274-3425 7pm-2am, till 3am Fri-
Sat, "all male nude review," no alcohol

Friends [M,NH,B,F,K,S,GO] 1028 E Indian
School Rd (at N 10th Pl)
602/277-7729 8am-2am, from 10am
Sun

Arizona • USA

Ice Pics [MW,V] 3108 E McDowell Rd (at 32nd St) 602/267-8707 *10pm-2am, from 2pm Sun*

Kobalt [MW,K,E] 3110 N Central Ave 602/264-5307 *11am-2am*

Lush Lounge [GS,D,F,K] 2050 N Alma School Rd #8, Chandler 480/857-9444 *11am-2am, clsd Mon*

Nu Towne Saloon [★M,NH,WC] 5002 E Van Buren (at 48th St) 602/267-9959 *noon-2am, patio, cruisy*

Oz [MW,NH,V,WI,WC] 1804 W Bethany Home Rd (at 19th) 602/242-5114 *6am-2am*

Plazma [MW,NH,K,V] 1560 E Osborn Rd (at N 16th St) 602/266-0477 *2pm-close, from noon wknds*

Rainbow Cactus [MW,NH] 15615 N Cave Creek Rd (btwn Greenway Pkwy & Greenway Rd) 602/867-2463 *3pm-2am*

The Rock/ La Roca [MW,NH,E,DS,TG,K] 4129 N 7th Ave (at Indian School) 602/248-8559 *2pm-2am, from 11am wknds*

Roscoe's on 7th [MW,F] 4531 N 7th St (at Minnezona) 602/285-0833 *2pm-2am, from 10am wknds, sports bar*

◼ NIGHTCLUBS

Club Zarape [M,DS,MR-L] 1730 McDowell Rd 602/413-5159 *9:30pm-close Fri-Sat, Latino drag bar*

Karamba [★M,D,MR-L,DS,WC] 1724 E McDowell (at 16th St) 602/254-0231 *9pm-close, clsd Mon-Wed, Latin wknds*

◼ CAFES

Copper Star Coffee [WI] 4220 N 7th Ave (at Indian School) 602/266-2136 *6am-9pm, till 11pm Fri-Sat, coffee in a converted gas station*

◼ RESTAURANTS

Alexi's [WC] 3550 N Central Ave #129 (in Valley Bank Bldg) 602/279-0982 *lunch Mon-Fri, dinner nightly, clsd Sun, int'l, full bar, patio*

AZ/88 7553 E Scottsdale Mall, Scottsdale 480/994-4576 *11:30am-1am, from 5pm wknds, bar popular w/ gay men Fri-Sat evenings*

Barrio Cafe [E,GO] 2814 N 16th St 602/636-0240 *lunch Tue-Fri, dinner Tue-Sun, Sun brunch, clsd Mon, Mexican, live music*

Cheuvront Restaurant & Wine Bar [GS] 1326 N Central Ave (at McDowell) 602/307-0022 *11am-10pm, till midnight Fri-Sat, 4pm-9pm Sun*

Coronado Cafe 2201 N 7th St 602/258-5149 *lunch Mon-Sat, dinner Tue-Sat, clsd Sun*

Durant's 2611 N Central Ave 602/264-5967 *lunch Mon-Fri, dinner nightly, American*

FEZ 3815 N Central Ave (S of Clarendon) 602/287-8700 *11am-midnight, from 8:30am wknds, Moroccan influence, full bar, patio*

Green 2240 N Scottsdale Rd #8, Tempe 480/941-9003 *11am-9pm, clsd Sun, vegetarian/ vegan*

Harley's Bistro [MW] 4221 N 7th Ave (N of Indian School) 602/234-0333 *lunch Tue-Fri, dinner nightly, clsd Mon, Italian*

Los Dos Molinos 8684 S Central Ave 602/243-9113 *lunch & dinner, clsd Sun-Mon, Mexican*

MacAlpines's Soda Fountain 2303 N 7th St 602/262-5545 *11am-7pm, till 8pm Fri-Sat, great milkshakes*

Malee's 7131 E Main, Scottsdale 480/947-6042 *lunch & dinner, Thai, full bar*

Mi Patio 3347 N 7th Ave 602/277-4831 *10am-10pm, Mexican*

Persian Garden Cafe [WI] 1335 W Thomas Rd (at N 15th Ave) 602/263-1915 *lunch & dinner, dinner only Sat, clsd Sun-Mon*

Portland's 105 W Portland St (at Central Ave) 602/795-7480 *lunch Tue-Fri, dinner Mon-Sat, clsd Sun, also wine bar*

Restaurant Mexico 423 S Mill Ave, Tempe 480/967-3280 *11am-9pm, till 10pm Fri-Sat, clsd Sun*

Rose & Crown 628 E Adams St 602/256-0223 *11am-2am, British pub*

Arizona • USA

Switch [WI] 2603 N Central Ave **602/264-2295** *11am-midnight, from 10am wknds, full bar*

Ticoz [WI] 5114 N 7th St (N of Camelback) **602/200-0160** *11am-midnight, Latin cuisine, full bar*

Vincent on Camelback [WC] 3930 E Camelback Rd (at 40th St) **602/224-0225** *dinner Mon-Sat, clsd Sun, Southwestern*

▉ ENTERTAINMENT & RECREATION

Soul Invictus 1022 NW Grand Ave (near W Van Buren St) **602/214-4344** *queer-friendly art gallery & cabaret*

Stray Cat Theatre 132 E 6th St (at Performing Arts Ctr), Tempe **480/634-6435** *off-the-beaten-path productions*

▉ BOOKSTORES

Changing Hands 6428 S McClintock Dr, Tempe **480/730-0205** *new & used, LGBT section*

▉ RETAIL SHOPS

➤Off Chute Too 4111 N 7th Ave (at Indian School Rd) **602/274-1429** *9am-9pm, till 10pm Fri-Sat, 10am-6pm Sun, LGBT gift shop in Melrose District*

Root Seller Gallery 3343 N 7th St **602/265-7668** *10am-7pm, 11am-5pm Sun, LGBT books & gifts*

▉ PUBLICATIONS

Echo Magazine **602/266-0550, 888/324-6624** *bi-weekly LGBT newsmagazine*

Ion Arizona Magazine **602/308-4662** *entertainment guide for the AZ gay community*

'N Touch Magazine **602/373-9490** *LGBT newsmagazine*

▉ GYMS & HEALTH CLUBS

Pulse Fitness [GF] 18221 N Pima Rd #H-130, Scottsdale **480/907-5900**

▉ MEN'S CLUBS

➤Chute [MO,B,L,V,18+] 1440 E Indian School Rd **602/234-1654** *24hrs, private rooms, gym, steam room*

Flex Complex [SW,PC] 1517 S Black Canyon Hwy (btwn 19th Ave & I-17) **602/271-9011** *24hrs*

▉ MEN'S SERVICES

➤MegaMates **602/993-4567** *Call to hook up with HOT local men. FREE to listen & respond to ads. Use FREE code DAMRON. MegaMates.com.*

▉ EROTICA

Adult Shoppe 111 S 24th St (at Jefferson) **602/306-1130** *24hrs; several locations*

Castle Megastore 300 E Camelback (at Central) **602/266-3348** *also 5501 E Washington, 8802 N Black Canyon Fwy, 8315 E Apache Tr*

Fascinations 10242 N 19th Ave #1-7 **602/943-5859** *many locations*

International Bookstore 3640 E Thomas Rd (at 36th St) **602/955-2000**

Modern World 1812 E Apache (at McClintock Dr), Tempe **480/967-9052** *24hrs*

Pleasure World/ Book Cellar [V] 4029 E Washington (at 40th St) **602/275-0015** *also 1838 NW Grand Ave & 6527 N 59th Ave*

Zorba's Adult Book Shop 2924 N Scottsdale Rd (N of Thomas), Scottsdale **480/941-9891** *24hrs, video rentals & arcade .*

▉ CRUISY AREAS

Dreamy Draw Park [AYOR] Squaw Peak Pkwy (Hwy 51) (off Northern) *go E along the driveway to the back—popular w/ 9-5ers; be alert—major crackdown on cruising in Phoenix!*

Papago Park [AYOR] Galvin Pkwy (btwn McDowell Rd & Van Buren St) *be alert—major crackdown on cruising in Phoenix!*

Washington Park [AYOR] 21st Ave (at Glendale) *nights; be alert—major crackdown on cruising in Phoenix!*

Prescott

■ACCOMMODATIONS

The Motor Lodge [GF,WI,GO] 503 S Montezuma St (at Leroux) 928/717-0157

■CRUISY AREAS

Heritage Park [AYOR] Willow Creek Rd (3 miles S of Hwy 89)

Sedona

■ACCOMMODATIONS

Apple Orchard Inn [GF,SW,NS,WC] 656 Jordan Rd 928/282-5328, 800/663-6968 *full brkfst*

El Portal Sedona [GF,NS,F,WI,WC] 95 Portal Ln 928/203-9405, 800/313-0017

The Lodge at Sedona—A Luxury B&B Inn [GS,SW,NS,WI] 125 Kallof Pl 928/204-1942, 800/619-4467

Sedona Rouge Hotel & Spa [GF,SW,NS,WI,WC] 2250 W Hwy 89-A 928/203-4111, 866/312-4111 *restaurant & bar*

Southwest Inn at Sedona [GF,SW,NS,WI] 3250 W Hwy 89-A 928/282-3344, 800/483-7422

■CAFES

Old Town Red Rooster Cafe 901 N Main St, Cottonwood 928/649-8100 *10am-4pm, 8am-2pm Sun*

■RESTAURANTS

Judi's 40 Soldiers Pass Rd 928/282-4449 *lunch & dinner, clsd Sun, full bar*

Piñon Bistro [WC,GO] 1075 S State Rte 260 (Rte 89-A), Cottonwood 928/649-0234 *dinner Th-Sun only, lesbian-owned*

■RETAIL SHOPS

Sedona Green Gallery & Gifts 273 N Hwy 89A #F (btwn Jordan & Mesquite) 928/239-5353 *10-15% discount to self-identifying gay & lesbian customers*

Tucson

■INFO LINES & SERVICES

AA Gay/ Lesbian 3269 N Mountain Ave 520/624-4183 *many mtgs*

Wingspan, Southern Arizona's LGBT Community Center 430 E 7th St 520/624-1779, 800/553-9387 *11am-2pm, resources, youth support (3pm-8pm Mon-Fri)*

■ACCOMMODATIONS

Armory Park Guesthouse [GF,GO] 219 S 5th Ave 520/206-9252

Catalina Park Inn [GS,NS,WI,GO] 309 E 1st St 520/792-4541, 800/792-4885

Desert Trails B&B [GF,SW,NS] 12851 E Speedway Blvd 520/885-7295, 877/758-3284 *adobe hacienda on 3 acres bordering Saguaro Nat'l Park, also guesthouse*

Hotel Congress [GS,F,E,WI] 311 E Congress St 520/622-8848, 800/722-8848 *cafe, full bar & club*

La Casita Del Sol [GS,NS,WI,GO] 407 N Meyer Ave (btwn Church Ave & Franklin Ave) 520/623-8882 *1880s adobe guesthouse*

Natural B&B & Retreat [GS,NS,WI,GO] 520/881-4582, 888/295-8500 *nonallergenic, full brkfst, massage available*

Royal Elizabeth B&B Inn [GS,SW,NS,WI,GO] 204 S Scott Ave (at Broadway) 520/670-9022, 877/670-9022 *historic 1878 downtown mansion*

■BARS

Club Congress/ The Tap Room [GF,NH,D,E,K] 311 E Congress (at Hotel Congress) 520/622-8848 *11am-2am, dance club from 9pm*

IBT's (It's About Time) [MW,D,K,S,WC] 616 N 4th Ave (at University) 520/882-3053 *noon-2am*

New Moon [MW,D,F,K,WI] 915 W Prince Rd 520/293-7339 *4pm-close, clsd Mon*

Venture-N [M,L,WI] 1239 N 6th Ave (at Stone) 520/882-8224 *9am-2am, Sun BBQ, patio*

Arizona • USA

Woody's [M,K,V,WC] 3710 N Oracle Rd (at W Thurber Rd) 520/292-6702 11am-2am

■CAFES

Revolutionary Grounds [F,WI] 606 N 4th Ave (at E 5th St) 520/620-1770 8am-8pm, till 11pm Fri-Sat, noon-7pm Sun, also leftist bookstore

■RESTAURANTS

Blue Willow 2616 N Campbell Ave (at Grant) 520/327-7577 7am-9pm, from 8am wknds, brkfst served all day

Cafe Poca Cosa 110 E Pennington St 520/622-6400 11am-9pm, till 10pm Fri-Sat, clsd Sun-Mon, Mexican-influenced bistro, patio

Colors Food & Spirits [MW,DS] 5305 E Speedway 520/323-1840, 520/323-1877 2pm-10pm, open later Fri-Sat, 11am-7pm Sun

The Grill on Congress 100 E Congress St (at Scott) 520/623-7621 24hrs, full bar

■ENTERTAINMENT & RECREATION

The Loft Cinema [F,BW] 3233 E Speedway Blvd 520/795-0844, 520/322-5638 Tucson's independent art house

■BOOKSTORES

Antigone Books [WC] 411 N 4th Ave (at 7th St) 520/792-3715 10am-7pm, till 9pm Fri-Sat, 11am-5pm Sun, LGBT

■PUBLICATIONS

'N Touch Magazine LGBT newsmagazine

■MEN'S SERVICES

➤**MegaMates** 520/791-2345 Call to hook up with HOT local men. FREE to listen & respond to ads. Use FREE code DAMRON. MegaMates.com.

■EROTICA

The Bookstore Southwest 5754 E Speedway Blvd 520/790-1550

Caesar's Adult Shop 2540 N Oracle Rd (btwn Glen & Grant) 520/622-9479

Continental Book Shop 2655 N Campbell Ave (at Grant) 520/327-8402 private rooms, arcade

Hydra 145 E Congress (at 6th) 520/791-3711 vinyl, leather, toys, shoes

■CRUISY AREAS

Tanque Verde Falls/ Reddington Pass upper Tanque Verde Falls, clothing-optional, gay area is beyond straight area

ARKANSAS

Batesville

■CRUISY AREAS

Riverside Park [AYOR]

Crosses

■CAFES

Crosses Grocery & Cafe [★GO] 4223 Hwy 16 (E of Elkins, outside Fayetteville) 479/643-3307 6am-8:30pm, on the Pig Trail

Eureka Springs

■ACCOMMODATIONS

A Byrds Eye View [GS,NS,WI,GO] 36 N Main (at Douglas) 479/253-0200, 888/210-8401 in heart of downtown, porch

The Grand TreeHouse Resort [GS,WI,GO] 350 W Van Buren (at Pivot Rock Rd) 479/253-8733

Heart of the Hills Inn [GS,NS,GO] 5 Summit St (on Historic Loop) 479/253-7468, 800/253-7468

Lookout Lodge [GF,NS,WI] 3098 E Van Buren 479/253-9335, 877/253-9335

Magnetic Valley Resort [M,SW,WI,GO] 597 Magnetic Rd (at Passion Play Rd) 479/244-6821, 888/210-8401

Mount Victoria [GF,WI] 28 Fairmount St 479/253-7979, 888/408-7979 full brkfst & dinner

Out on Main [GS,NS,WI,GO] 269 N Main St (at Magnetic Rd) 479/253-8449 3-room cottage, full kitchen

Palace Hotel & Bath House [GF,NS,WI] 135 Spring St 479/253-7474, 866/946-0572 historic bathhouse open to all

Pond Mountain Lodge & Resort [GS,SW,NS,WC,GO] 479/253-5877, 800/583-8043 *mtntop inn on 150 acres*

Red Bud Manor Inn [GF,WI,WO] 7 Kingshighway 479/253-9649, 866/253-9649

Roadrunner Inn [GF,R,NS,WI] 3034 Mundell Rd 479/253-8166, 888/253-8166 *guestrooms & log cabins, lake views*

Texaco Bungalow [GS,GO] 77 Mountain St 888/253-8093

The Woods Resort [MW,NS,GO] 50 Wall St (off Hwy 62) 479/253-8281 *cottages, jacuzzis, kitchens, treehouse hot tub*

■ Bars

Chelsea's Corner Cafe [GF,E,D,WI] 10 Mountain St (at Center St) 479/253-6723 *11am-2am, till 10pm Sun, patio*

Eureka Live [GS,D,F,K] 35 N Main 479/253-7020 *11am-1:30am, clsd Mon-Tue*

Henri's Just One More [GS,NH,F,E,WI] 19 1/2 Spring St 479/253-5795 *noon-2am, clsd Tue, gay night Wed from 5pm*

The Lumberyard Saloon & Steakhouse [GS,F,E,K,WI] 105 E Van Buren 479/253-0400 *2pm-2am, till midnight Sun, live bands*

Pied Piper Pub & Inn [GF,F,V] 82 Armstrong (at Main St) 479/363-9976, 866/363-9976 *noon-midnight, also restaurant & hotel*

■ Cafes

Mud Street Cafe 22G S Main St 479/253-6732 *8am-3pm, clsd Tue-Wed*

■ Restaurants

Autumn Breeze [NS] 190 Huntsville Rd (1/2 mile off Hwy 62) 479/253-7734 *5pm-9pm, clsd Sun, hrs vary in winter*

Caribe Restaurant & Cantina 309 W Van Buren 479/253-8102 *4pm-9pm, clsd Tue, from noon wknds, also bar*

Cottage Inn 450 Hwy 62 W 479/253-5282 *5pm-9pm, clsd Mon-Wed, Mediterranean, full bar*

Ermilio's 26 White St 479/253-8806 *5pm-9pm, Italian, full bar*

Gaskins Cabin Steak House [GS,BW,R] 2883 Hwy 23 N (Hwy 187) 479/253-5466 *5pm-9pm, till 8pm Sun, clsd Mon-Tue*

■ Entertainment & Recreation

Diversity Pride Events 479/253-2555 *produces events during Valentine's & Spring, Summer, Fall Diversity Wknds & more*

Fayetteville

■ Info Lines & Services

AA Gay/ Lesbian 568 W Sycamore 479/443-6366 (AA#)

■ Accommodations

Hilton Garden Inn Bentonville [GF,SW,WI,WC] 2204 SE Walton Blvd (Exit 85, off I-540), Bentonville 479/464-7300, 877/782-9444

■ Nightclubs

Club Push [MW,D,K,DS,18+] 21 N Block Ave 479/443-4600 *9pm-2am, clsd Sun-Tue*

Speakeasy [M,D,WC] 509 W Spring St (at West St) 479/443-3279 *5pm-2am, clsd Sun-Tue*

■ Cafes

The Common Grounds 412 W Dickson St (at West) 479/442-3515 *7am-midnight, full bar, also restaurant*

■ Restaurants

Bordinos 310 W Dickson St 479/527-6795 *dinner nightly, lunch Tue-Fri, clsd Sun, full bar*

Hugo's 25 1/2 N Block Ave 479/521-7585 *11am-10pm, clsd Sun*

■ Bookstores

Hastings Bookstore 2999 N College Ave (Fiesta Square Shopping Center) 479/521-0244 *9am-10pm, till 11pm Fri-Sat, 9am-11pm Sun*

■ Publications

Out on the Town Magazine 479/244-0578 *GLBT magazine covering the Deep South*

Arkansas • USA

■ CRUISY AREAS

Flat Rock Beach [AYOR] 10 miles W of town *nude beach*

Fort Smith

■ BARS

Kinkead's [GS,NH,D,DS,K,WI,GO] 1004 1/2 Garrison Ave **479/226-3144** *5pm-2am, from 7pm Fri-Sat, clsd Mon*

Helena

■ ACCOMMODATIONS

The Edwardian Inn [GF,NS,WI] 317 Biscoe **870/338-9155, 800/598-4749** *60 miles from Memphis*

Hot Springs

■ ACCOMMODATIONS

The B Inn [GS,WI,GO] 316 Park Ave (at Cental Ave) **501/547-7172**

Park Hotel of Hot Springs [GS,WI] 211 Fountain St (at Central Ave) **501/624-5323, 800/895-7275**

The Rose Cottage [GF] 218 Court St (at Exchange St) **501/623-6449**

■ CRUISY AREAS

Degray Lake [AYOR] lakeside area *afternoon in the woods*

Rest Area [AYOR] off Hwy 70 (btwn Hot Springs & I-30)

Jonesboro

■ CRUISY AREAS

Craighead Forest Park [AYOR] *seasonal (beware of cops!)*

Little Rock

■ ACCOMMODATIONS

Legacy Hotel & Suites [★GF,WI,WC] 625 W Capitol Ave (at Gaines) **501/374-0100, 888/456-3669** *nat'l historic property in downtown area*

■ BARS

Discovery [GS,D,DS,S,V,PC,WC] 1021 Jessie Rd (btwn Cantrell & Riverfront) **501/664-4784** *9pm-5am Sat only*

Miss Kitty's [MW,K] 307 W 7th St (at Center St) **501/374-4699** *9pm-2am Fri-Sat*

Trax [M,NH,CW,B,L,OC,WI,WC] 415 Main St, North Little Rock **501/244-0444** *5pm-2am, also restaurant*

Triniti Nightclub [MW,D,DS,S,V,18+,PC,WC] 1021 Jessie Rd (btwn Cantrell & Riverfront) **501/664-2744** *9pm-5am Fri only*

■ RESTAURANTS

Bossa Nova 2701 Kavanaugh Blvd (at Ash St) **501/614-6682** *lunch & dinner, Sun brunch, clsd Mon, Brazilian, plenty veggie*

Juanita's [E,R] 614 President Clinton (at River Market) **501/372-1228** *11am-close, clsd Sun, Mexican, also live music*

La Hacienda 3024 Cantrell Rd **501/661-0600** *lunch & dinner, Mexican*

Lilly's Dim Sum, Then Some/ B-Side [GO] 11121 N Rodney Parham Rd **501/716-2700** *11am-9pm, till 10pm Fri-Sat, clsd Sun, contemporary Asian, plenty veggie, lesbian-owned*

Vino's Pizza [BW] 923 W 7th St (at Chester) **501/375-8466** *11am-close*

■ ENTERTAINMENT & RECREATION

The Weekend Theater [GO] 1001 W 7th St (at Chester) **501/374-3761** *plays & musicals on wknds*

■ BOOKSTORES

Wordsworth Books & Co 5920 R St **501/663-9198** *9am-7pm, till 6pm Fri-Sat, noon-5pm Sun, independent*

■ RETAIL SHOPS

A Twisted Gift Shop 1007 W 7th St (at Chester) **501/376-7723** *noon-midnight, gift shop*

Inz & Outz [WC] 6115 W Markham #103 **501/296-9484** *10am-8pm, noon-6pm Sun, pride items, books*

■ EROTICA

Adult Video 2923 W 65th St (off I-30 W) **501/562-4282** *24hrs, arcade*

Cupids 3920 W 65th St (off I-30, exit 135) **501/565-2020** *24hrs, arcade*

■ CRUISY AREAS

Reservoir Park [AYOR] Cantrell Rd (2 miles E of I-430, exit 9)

Texarkana

■BARS

The Chute [MW,D,K,DS] 714 Laurel St
870/772-6900 *7pm-2am Th-Sat*

CALIFORNIA

Amador City

■ACCOMMODATIONS

Imperial Hotel [GF,NS] 14202 Hwy 49
(at Water St) **209/267-9172** *B&B,
brick Victorian hotel, full brkfst, restaurant & bar*

Anaheim

see Orange County

■MEN'S SERVICES

➤**MegaMates** 714/905-0050 *Call to
hook up with HOT local men. FREE to
listen & respond to ads. Use FREE code
DAMRON. MegaMates.com.*

Angeles Nat'l Forest

■CRUISY AREAS

**Beach in the Upper Big Tujunga
Canyon (UBTC)** [AYOR] Hwy 2, exit
Angeles Crest Hwy, head N, turn left to
UBTC Rd, turn right (btwn marker 4.5 &
4.8) *little nude beach along creek*

Angels Camp

■ACCOMMODATIONS

Cooper House B&B Inn [GS,WI,GO]
1184 Church St (at Raspberry Ln)
209/736-2145, 888/330-3764

Antelope Valley

see Lancaster

Arcata

see also Eureka

■INFO LINES & SERVICES

Queer Humboldt PO Box 45, 95518-
0045 **707/834-4839** *"Humboldt
County's online resource for the LGBT
community," includes links & events
calendar, check out www.queerhumboldt.org*

■BARS

The Alibi [MW,NH,F,E,YC] 744 9th St
707/822-3731 *cocktail lounge w/ live
music, also restaurant (8am-midnight)*

■CAFES

Cafe Mokka [E] 495 J St (at 5th)
707/822-2228 *from noon, coffee &
soups (bread bowls), live music, also
Finnish sauna & hot tubs*

North Coast Co-op [WI] 811 I St
707/822-5947 *6am-9pm*

■RESTAURANTS

Wildflower Bakery & Cafe [★BW]
1604 G St **707/822-0360** *8am-8pm,
till 9pm Th-Sat, vegetarian*

■BOOKSTORES

Northtown Books 957 H St
707/822-2834 *10am-7pm, till 9pm
Fri-Sat, noon-5pm Sun, LGBT section*

■EROTICA

Pleasure Center 1731 G St #D
707/826-1708

■CRUISY AREAS

Aldergrove Marsh [AYOR] Alder Grove
Rd (off West End Rd) *parking lot on left
after Ericson Way*

Azalea State Reserve [AYOR] along
Mad River (on N Bank Rd) *6 miles N of
Arcata*

Arnold

■ACCOMMODATIONS

Dorrington Inn at Big Trees [GS]
3450 Hwy 4 (at Boards Crossing),
Dorrington **209/795-2164,
877/795-2164** *cottages & suites*

Atascadero

■EROTICA

Diamond Adult World 7253 El
Camino Real **805/462-0404**

■CRUISY AREAS

Atascadero Lake Park & Zoo [AYOR]
off Rte 41 *parking lot*

California • *USA*

Bakersfield

■INFO LINES & SERVICES
Gay AA 1001 34th St 661/322-4025 (AA#), 661/324-0371 (Alano Club #) 7:30pm Mon

■BARS
The Mint [GS,A,E] 1207 19th St (at M) 661/325-4048 *6am-2am, live music*

■NIGHTCLUBS
The Casablanca Club [GS,NH,D,E,C,DS,V,WC] 1825 N St (at 19th St) 661/324-0661 *9pm-2am, clsd Mon-Wed*

■BOOKSTORES
Russo's Books 9000 Ming Ave #1-4 661/665-4686 *10am-8pm*

■EROTICA
Cinema 19 [★] 1224 19th St (btwn L & M Sts, across from The Mint) 661/323-7711 *cruisy, arcade & theater*

Deja Vu 1524 Golden State Ave (at Chester Ave) 661/322-7300 *noon-2am, arcade*

■CRUISY AREAS
Gordon's Ferry [AYOR] Round Mountain Rd (at China Grade Loop), Oildale

Yokuts Park [AYOR] W of Hwy 99 (at Beach Park) *take W Truxtun Ave to Empire Dr entrance*

Benicia
see Vallejo

Berkeley
see East Bay

Big Bear Lake

■ACCOMMODATIONS
Alpine Retreats [GS,NS,GO] 433 Edgemoor (at Big Bear Blvd) 909/725-4192, 909/878-4155 (reservations) *3 cottages*

Grey Squirrel Resort [GS,SW,WI,GO] 39372 Big Bear Blvd 909/866-4335, 800/381-5569

Knickerbocker Mansion Country Inn [GS,NS,WI,WC,GO] 869 Knickerbocker Rd 909/878-9190, 877/423-1180 *full brkfst*

Rainbow View Lodge [GS,NS] 2726 View Dr (at Hilltop), Running Springs 909/867-1810, 888/868-1810

Switzerland Haus [GF,NS] 41829 Switzerland Dr 909/866-3729, 800/335-3729

Big Sur

■ACCOMMODATIONS
Eagle's Nest [GF,NS,WI,GO] Pfeiffer Ridge #10 831/667-2587, 888/742-9321 *deck w/ views of Pfeiffer Ridge & ocean, full kitchen*

Lucia Lodge [GF,NS,WI] 62400 Hwy 1 831/688-4884, 866/424-4787 *oceanview cabins, also restaurant & lounge*

■CRUISY AREAS
Julia Pfeifer Burns State Park [AYOR] 20 miles S of Big Sur *sunrise to sunset*

Bishop

■CRUISY AREAS
Keough Hot Springs [AYOR] Hwy 395 (6 miles S of Bishop) *take Keough Hot Springs Rd exit, go W a half mile, turn right & continue 50 yds*

Burlingame
see San Francisco

Cambria

■ACCOMMODATIONS
El Colobri [GF,WI] 5620 Moonstone Beach Dr 805/924-3003

The J Patrick House B&B [GF,NS,WI] 2990 Burton Dr (1/2 mile off Hwy 1) 805/927-3812, 800/341-5258

Sea Otter Inn [GF,SW,NS,WI,WC] 6656 Moonstone Beach Dr 805/927-5888, 800/966-6490

■BARS
Mozzi's Saloon [GF,E] 2262 Main St 805/927-4767 *1pm-2am, from 11am Sat-Sun, cowboy bar*

■CRUISY AREAS

Fiscalini Ranch Preserve

Moonstone Beach Boardwalk

Capistrano Beach

■ACCOMMODATIONS

Capistrano Seaside Inn [GF,WC] 34862 Pacific Coast Hwy **949/496-1399, 800/252-3224** (reservations only) *outdoor jacuzzi, ocean views, across from beach*

Carmel

see also Monterey

■ACCOMMODATIONS

Best Western Carmel Mission Inn [GF,SW,NS] 3665 Rio Rd **831/624-1841, 800/348-9090** *pets ok, also restaurant & lounge*

Carmel Resort Inn [GF,NS,WI] Carpenter Ave (btwn 1st & 2nd Ave) **831/293-8390**

Carmel River Inn [GF,SW,NS] Hwy 1 at Carmel River Bridge **831/624-1575**

Cypress Inn [GF,WI] Lincoln & 7th **831/624-3871, 800/443-7443** *pets very welcome, owned by Doris Day*

■RESTAURANTS

Flaherty's Seafood Grill & Oyster Bar [WC] 6th Ave (btwn Dolores and San Carlos) **831/625-1500** *open daily 11am*

Rio Grill 101 Crossroads Blvd **831/625-5436** *lunch & dinner, full bar*

■CRUISY AREAS

Garland Ranch Regional Park [AYOR] Rte G16 (9 miles E of Carmel), Carmel Valley

Garrapata State Beach [AYOR] 10 miles S of crossroads (on right side of Hwy 1) *nude sunbathing*

Chico

■INFO LINES & SERVICES

Stonewall Alliance Center 358 E 6th St (at Flume) **530/893-3336** *HIV testing & counseling, recorded info, meetings*

■CRUISY AREAS

Deer Pens [AYOR] 8th & Forest Sts

Chino

■RESTAURANTS

Riverside Grill 5258 Riverside Dr (at Central) **909/627-4144** *8am-9pm*

Chula Vista

see also San Diego

■MEN'S SERVICES

►**MegaMates** 619/734-1110 *Call to hook up with HOT local men. FREE to listen & respond to ads. Use FREE code DAMRON. MegaMates.com.*

■EROTICA

F St Bookstore [WC] 1141 3rd Ave (btwn Naples & Oxford) **619/585-3314**

Clearlake

includes major towns of Lake County

■ACCOMMODATIONS

Blue Fish Cove Resort [GF,SW] 10573 E Hwy 20, Clearlake Oaks **707/998-1769** *lakeside resort cottages, boat facilities & rentals*

Edgewater Resort [SW,NS,WI,GO] 6420 Soda Bay Rd (at Hohape Rd), Kelseyville **707/279-0208, 800/396-6224**

Featherbed Railroad B&B [GF,SW,WI] 2870 Lakeshore Blvd, Nice **707/274-8378**

Sea Breeze Resort [GS,SW,NS,WI,WC,GO] 9595 Harbor Dr, Glenhaven **707/998-3327** *lakefront cottages*

Cloverdale

see also Healdsburg

■ACCOMMODATIONS

Vintage Towers B&B [GF,NS,WI] 302 N Main St (at 3rd) **707/894-4535, 888/886-9377** *Queen Anne mansion, full brkfst*

■RESTAURANTS

Hamburger Ranch & Bar-B-Que [BW] 31195 N Redwood Hwy **707/894-5616** *7am-9pm, patio*

California • *USA*

Concord

see East Bay

■MEN'S SERVICES
➤MegaMates 925/695-1100 *Call to hook up with HOT local men. FREE to listen & respond to ads. Use FREE code DAMRON. MegaMates.com.*

Corning

■CRUISY AREAS
Woodson Bridge State Recreational Area [AYOR] 5 miles E of Corning (on Sacramento River)

Costa Mesa

see Orange County

Cupertino

■ACCOMMODATIONS
Cypress Hotel [GF,SW,WI,NS] 10050 S De Anza Blvd **408/253-8900, 800/499-1408**

■CRUISY AREAS
Stevens Creek Canyon Park [AYOR] Foothill Blvd *at first road, turn left below the dam, go down, then go up to the top parking area on the right*

Dana Point

see Orange County

Danville

see East Bay

Davis

see also Sacramento

■INFO LINES & SERVICES
LGBT Resource Center [WI,WC] University House Annex **530/752-2452** *9am-5pm, clsd wknds, info, referrals, meetings, library*

■CAFES
Mishka's Cafe [★] 610 2nd St **530/759-0811** *7:30am-11pm*

■BOOKSTORES
The Avid Reader 617 2nd St **530/758-4040** *10am-10pm*

■MEN'S SERVICES
➤MegaMates 530/760-1011 *Call to hook up with HOT local men. FREE to listen & respond to ads. Use FREE code DAMRON. MegaMates.com.*

Desert Hot Springs

see Palm Springs & Joshua Tree Nat'l Park

East Bay

includes major cities of Alameda and Contra Costa Counties: Alameda, Antioch, Berkeley, Concord, Danville, Fremont, Hayward, Lafayette, Newark, Oakland, Pleasant Hill, Richmond, San Leandro, Walnut Creek

■INFO LINES & SERVICES
East Bay AA 510/839-8900 (AA#) *variety of LGBT-friendly mtgs*

La Peña Cultural Center [NS,WC] 3105 Shattuck Ave, Berkeley **510/849-2568** *multicultural center & cafe, hosts meetings, dances, performance art, events*

Lighthouse Community Center 1217 A St (near 2nd St), Hayward **510/881-8167** *LGBT support groups & social events*

Pacific Center for Human Growth [WC] 2712 Telegraph Ave (at Derby), Berkeley **510/548-8283** *10am-8pm Mon-Fri*

Rainbow Community Center of Contra Costa County 3024 Willow Pass Rd #200 (btwn Parkside & Esperanza), Concord **925/692-0090** *10am-5pm Mon-Fri*

■ACCOMMODATIONS
Hotel Durant [GS,F,NS,WI] 2600 Durant Ave, Berkeley **510/845-8981, 800/238-7268**

Washington Inn [GF,NS,WC] 495 10th St (at Broadway), Oakland **510/452-1776** *historic boutique hotel, also restaurant*

Waterfront Hotel [GF,SW,NS,WI,WC] 10 Washington St, Oakland **510/836-3800, 888/842-5333**

■ BARS

The Alley [GS,P] 3325 Grand Ave (btwn Lake Park & Elwood Aves), Oakland **510/444-8505** *4pm-2am, camptastic sing-along piano bar from 9pm, more gay Th, also restaurant*

Bench & Bar [★M,D,K,DS,P,S,YC,WC] 510 17th St, Oakland **510/444-2266** *4pm-2am*

Cafe Van Kleef [GF,E,$] 1621 Telegraph Ave (at Broadway), Oakland **510/763-7711** *4pm-2am, clsd Sun, eclectic crowd & live-music scene—from cabaret to blue grass to jazz*

Club 21 [M,D,MR-L] 2111 Franklin St (at 21st St), Oakland **510/268-9425** *theme nights*

Easy Lounge [GF,NH,D,V] 3255 Lakeshore Ave, Oakland **510/338-4911** *4:30pm-2am, from 2pm Sat, cool lounge w/ theme nights*

White Horse [MW,D,K,WC] 6551 Telegraph Ave (at 66th), Oakland **510/652-3820** *3pm-2am, from 1pm wknds, popular wknds (also Sun beer bust)*

World Famous Turf Club [MW,D,K,DS,WC] 22519 Main St (at A St), Hayward **510/881-9877** *4pm-2am, from noon Sat-Sun, huge patio*

■ NIGHTCLUBS

Club 1220 [MW,D,CW,K,WI,WC] 1220 Pine St (at Civic Dr), Walnut Creek **925/938-4550** *4pm-2am, theme nights*

■ CAFES

Au Coquelet Cafe [F,BW] 2000 University Ave, Berkeley **510/845-0433** *6am-2am*

Bittersweet 5427 College Ave (in Rockridge District), Oakland **510/654-7159** *9am-7pm, till 9pm Fri-Sat*

Caffe Strada [★WC] 2300 College Ave (btwn Way & Durant), Berkeley **510/843-5282** *6am-midnight, students, great patio*

Cole Coffee 6255 College Ave (btwn 62nd & 63rd Sts), Oakland **510/985-1958** *7am-7pm, hip hideaway in lovely Rockridge*

Raw Energy [GO] 2050 Addison St (btwn Shattuck & Milvia), Berkeley **510/665-9464** *7:30am-7pm, 11am-4pm Sat, clsd Sun, organic juice cafe*

■ RESTAURANTS

Arizmendi Bakery & Pizzeria 4301 San Pablo Ave (at 43rd St), Emeryville **510/547-0550** *7am-7pm, till 3pm Mon, clsd Sun, excellent pastries, breads & pizzas*

Banh Cuon Tay Ho [TG,BW] 344-B 12th St (at Webster), Oakland **510/836-6388** *10am-9pm, till 8pm Sun, clsd Sun*

Cactus Taqueria 5642 College Ave (at Shafter, in Rockridge), Oakland **510/658-6180** *11am-10pm, till 9pm Sun*

César [★] 4039 Piedmont, Oakland **510/883-0222** *noon-11pm, Spanish tapas, full bar till midnight*

Connie's Cantina [★] 3340 Grand Ave (btwn Lake Park Ave & Mandana Blvd), Oakland **510/839-4986** *10:30am-9pm, clsd Sun, delicious homemade Mexican food, plenty veggie, patio*

Dopo [★] 4293 Piedmont Ave (btwn Glenwood & Echo), Oakland **510/652-3676** *lunch Mon-Th, dinner nightly, clsd Sun, Italian, worth the wait*

Le Cheval [★BW,WC] 1007 Clay St, Oakland **510/763-8495** *11am-9:30pm, from 5pm Sun, Vietnamese*

Lois the Pie Queen [★] 851 60th St (off Martin Luther King Jr Hwy), Oakland **510/658-5616** *8am-2pm, 7am-3pm wknds, Southern homecooking & killer desserts*

Mama's Royal Cafe [★BW,WC] 4012 Broadway (at 40th), Oakland **510/547-7600** *7am-2:30pm, from 8am wknds, come early for excellent wknd brunch*

Rockridge Cafe [★] 5492 College Ave (at Forest), Oakland **510/653-1567** *7:30am-3pm, great brkfsts, plenty veggie*

Zachary's Chicago Pizza [★BW] 5801 College Ave, Oakland **510/655-6385** *11am-10pm, pizza that is worth the crowds & the long wait!*

California • USA

■ENTERTAINMENT & RECREATION
Oakland East Bay Gay Men's Chorus 800/706-2389

■BOOKSTORES
Black Oak Books 2618 San Pablo Ave, Berkeley 510/486-0698 *11am-7pm*

Diesel, A Bookstore 5433 College Avenue, Oakland 510/653-9965 *10am-9pm, till 10pm Fri-Sat, till 6pm Sun, independent*

Laurel Book Store [WC,GO] 4100 MacArthur Blvd (at 39th Ave, 2 blks from High St), Oakland 510/531-2073 *10am-7pm, till 6pm Sat, 11am-5pm, general, LGBT section, readings, lesbian-owned*

Pendragon Books 5560 College Ave (at Oceanview), Oakland 510/652-6259 *9am-10pm, from 10am Sun, used books, great to browse while waiting for a table in Rockridge*

■RETAIL SHOPS
Collectors Realm 3 2566 Telegraph Ave (btwn Parker & Dwight), Berkeley 510/540-1182 *2pm-8pm, from noon wknds, vintage gay porn*

■MEN'S CLUBS
Steamworks [★WI,PC] 2107 4th St (at Addison), Berkeley 510/845-8992 *24hrs, call for recorded info*

■EROTICA
Golden Gate Books/ El Cerrito Secrets 10601 San Pablo Ave (at Moeser Ln), El Cerrito 510/528-1569 *8am-1am, arcade*

Good Vibrations [★WC] 2504 San Pablo Ave (at Dwight Wy), Berkeley 510/841-8987 *11am-8pm, 10am-6pm Fri-Sat*

Good Vibrations [★] 3219 Lakeshore Ave, Oakland 510/788-2389 *10am-9pm*

Not Too Naughty 15670 E 14th St, San Leandro 510/278-4944 *arcade*

■CRUISY AREAS
Aquatic Park [AYOR] Bolivar Dr (off I-80, at Ashby Ave exit), Berkeley

Bushrod Park [AYOR] Shattuck Ave (btwn 59th & 60th Sts), Oakland *near tennis courts*

Central Park (aka Lake Elizabeth) [AYOR] Paseo Padre Ave & Stevenson Blvd, Fremont *trails right of lake & parking lot*

Gateway Exit [AYOR] Hwy 24, first exit after Caldecott Tunnel (if coming from Oakland), Orinda *stay right, parking lot & woods ahead*

Heather Farm Park [AYOR] Ygnacio Valley Rd, Walnut Creek *take Ygnacio Valley Rd for 2 miles E of Hwy 680, turn right into park on San Carlos Rd*

Hillcrest Park [AYOR] off Larkspur Dr, Antioch *take Hillcrest exit off Hwy 4, take left off Hillcrest Rd onto Larkspur Rd, park is on right after 6 blocks*

Keller Beach [AYOR] Miller-Knox Regional Park, Richmond *take Garrard Blvd exit of Hwy 580 after tunnel on Dornan Dr*

Lake Temescal Park [AYOR] Broadway Ave (at State Hwy 13), Oakland *afternoons*

Oyster Bay Park [AYOR] btwn San Leandro Marina & Oakland Airport (along the bay), San Leandro *take Doolittle to Williams, go W toward bay & make right when Williams ends*

El Cajon

■MEN'S SERVICES
▶**MegaMates** 619/387-0383 *Call to hook up with HOT local men. FREE to listen & respond to ads. Use FREE code DAMRON. MegaMates.com.*

Elk

■RESTAURANTS
Queenie's Roadhouse Cafe [GO] 6061 S Hwy 1 707/877-3285 *8am-3pm, clsd Tue-Wed, fabulous all-day brkfsts*

Elk Grove

■CRUISY AREAS
Elk Grove Park [AYOR] *take Hwy 99 to Elk Grove Blvd exit, head E & turn right at East Stockton, rear entrance to park is on left*

Escondido

■Men's Services

➤**MegaMates** 760/708-0800 *Call to hook up with HOT local men. FREE to listen & respond to ads. Use FREE code DAMRON. MegaMates.com.*

Eureka

see also Arcata

■Accommodations

Abigail's Elegant Victorian Mansion [GF,NS] 1406 C St (at 14th St) 707/444-3144 *1878 nat'l historic landmark, sauna*

Carter House Inns [GF,NS,WC] 301 L St 707/444-8062, 800/404-1390 *enclave of 4 unique inns, full brkfst, restaurant, wine shop*

Trinidad Bay B&B [GF,NS,WI,GO] 560 Edwards St (at Trinity), Trinidad 707/677-0840 *full brkfst*

Trinidad Escape [MW,WI] 707/677-3457

■Bars

Lost Coast Brewery [GF,F,BW,WI,WC] 617 4th St (btwn G & H Sts) 707/445-4480 *11am-1am, kitchen open till midnight*

The Shanty [GS,NH,GO] 213 3rd St (at C St) 707/444-2053 *noon-2am*

■Nightclubs

Where's Queer Bill [MW,D,TG] 707/832-4785 *monthly queer events, wheresqueerbill.com*

■Cafes

The Boathouse Espresso Bar & Eatery [WI,WC,GO] 1125 King Salmon Ave 707/441-1454

North Coast Co-op 25 4th St (at B St) 707/443-6027 *6am-9pm, co-op store w/ bakery, deli & espresso cafe*

Ramone's Cafe & Bakery 209 E St (Old Town) 707/445-2923 *7am-6pm*

■Restaurants

Chalet House of Omelettes [WC] 1935 5th St (at U St) 707/442-0333 *6am-3pm, brkfst & lunch*

Folie Douce [BW,R,WC] 1551 G St, Arcata 707/822-1042 *dinner only, clsd Sun-Mon, bistro*

Hurricane Kate's 511 2nd St (Old Town) 707/444-1405 *lunch & dinner, clsd Sun-Mon*

■Bookstores

Booklegger [WC] 402 2nd St (at E St) 707/445-1344 *10am-5:30pm, 11am-4pm Sun*

■Erotica

Good Relations [WC] 223 2nd St 707/441-9570, 888/485-5063 *queer-owned/ run*

■Cruisy Areas

Hilfiker Reserve [AYOR] off Hilfiker Ln *last parking lot & wood trails*

Fairfield

see Vacaville

Fort Bragg

see also Mendocino

■Accommodations

The Cleone Gardens Inn [GF,NS,WI,WC] 24600 N Hwy 1 707/964-2788, 800/400-2189 (N CA only) *country garden retreat on 2.5 acres, cottages, hot tub*

The Weller House Inn [GF,NS,WI] 524 Stewart St (at Pine) 707/964-4415, 877/893-5537 *1886 Victorian, full brkfst*

■Restaurants

Cowlick's 250B N Main St 707/962-9271 *delicious homemade ice cream, including mushroom ice cream (in-season)—it's actually quite good!*

Purple Rose [WC] 24300 N Hwy 1 707/964-6507 *5pm-9pm, clsd Sun-Mon, Mexican*

■Entertainment & Recreation

Skunk Train California Western foot of Laurel St 707/964-6371, 866/457-5865

California • USA

■BOOKSTORES

Windsong Books & Records 324 N Main St (at Redwood Ave) **707/964-2050** *10am-5:30pm, till 4pm Sun, mostly used*

Fountain Valley

see Orange County

Fremont

see East Bay

■MEN'S SERVICES

➤**MegaMates** 510/401-0101 *Call to hook up with HOT local men. FREE to listen & respond to ads. Use FREE code DAMRON. MegaMates.com.*

Fresno

■INFO LINES & SERVICES

Community Link 559/266-5465 *LGBT support, also publishes Newslink*

Fresno AA 559/221-6907 *call or check website (www.fresnoaa.org) for meetings*

■ACCOMMODATIONS

The San Joaquin Hotel [GF,SW,WI,WC] 1309 W Shaw Ave (at Fruit) **559/225-1309, 800/775-1309**

■BARS

The Phoenix [M,NH,CW,B,L,MR,V,OC] 4538 E Belmont Ave (at Maple) **559/252-2899** *5pm-2am, patio, popular beer busts & other events*

Red Lantern [M,NH,CW,MR-L,WI,WC] 4618 E Belmont Ave (at Maple) **559/251-5898** *2pm-2am, Latin night Sat very popular, patio*

■NIGHTCLUBS

Club Legends [MW,D,DS] 3075 N Maroa Ave **559/222-2271** *8pm-2am, from 6pm Fri, from 9pm Sat, from 4pm Sun*

Express [★M,D,DS,V,GO,$] 708 N Blackstone (btwn Olive & Belmont, on Bremer) **559/445-0878** *9pm-2am, from 6pm Sun, clsd Mon-Wed, theme nights, patio*

North Tower Circle [MW,D,DS] 2777 N Maroa Ave (at E Princeton Ave) **559/229-4188** *7pm-2am*

■RESTAURANTS

Cafe Rousseau 568 E Olive Ave (in Tower District) **559/445-1536** *lunch Tue-Fri, dinner from 5:30pm, clsd Sun-Mon, cont'l, also wine bar*

Don Pepe's 4582 N Blackstone Ave (at Gettysburg) **559/224-1431** *9am-9pm, Mexican*

Irene's Cafe [BW] 747 E Olive Ave (in Tower District) **559/237-9919** *8am-9pm, some veggie, popular hamburgers*

Sequoia Brewing Company [E] 777 E Olive Ave (in Tower District) **559/264-5521** *11am-10pm, till midnight Fri-Sat, till 9pm Sun, micro-brewery w/ restaurant, live music*

Veni Vidi Vici [E,R] 1116 N Fulton (S of Olive Ave, in Tower District) **559/266-5510** *California fine dining, nightclub later*

■MEN'S CLUBS

The Bunker [MO,PC] 2592 S Railroad Ave (at E Jensen) **559/486-3100** *10am-10pm, till 11pm wknds, clsd Mon*

■MEN'S SERVICES

➤**MegaMates** 559/261-2221 *Call to hook up with HOT local men. FREE to listen & respond to ads. Use FREE code DAMRON. MegaMates.com.*

■EROTICA

Suzie's Adult Superstores 1267 N Blackstone Ave **559/497-9613** *24hrs*

Wildcat Book Store 1535 Fresno St (at G St) **559/237-4525** *video arcade*

■CRUISY AREAS

LA-SF Time Out [AYOR] US 99 (at Kingsburg, S of Fresno) *go to cheap motel next to rest area; rest stop activity discouraged*

Garden Grove

see Orange County

■MEN'S SERVICES

➤**MegaMates** 714/467-9991 *Call to hook up with HOT local men. FREE to listen & respond to ads. Use FREE code DAMRON. MegaMates.com.*

Gaviota

■CRUISY AREAS
Vista Point [AYOR] Hwy 101 S (1/2 S of Gaviota Beach) *parking lot & nearby woods*

Grass Valley

see Nevada City

Gualala

■ACCOMMODATIONS
Breakers Inn [GS] 39300 S Hwy 1 707/884-3200

North Coast Country Inn [GF,NS] 34591 S Hwy 1 707/884-4537, 800/959-4537 *hot tub*

■BOOKSTORES
The Four-Eyed Frog 39138 Ocean Dr (in Cypress Village) 707/884-1333

Half Moon Bay

■ACCOMMODATIONS
Mill Rose Inn [GF,NS,WI] 615 Mill St 650/726-8750, 800/900-7673 *classic European elegance by the sea, full brkfst, hot tub*

■RESTAURANTS
Moss Beach Distillery [★WC] 140 Beach Wy (at Ocean) 650/728-5595 *lunch & dinner, Sun brunch, steak & seafood, patio, even own ghost*

Pasta Moon [E,WC] 315 Main St (at Mill) 650/726-5125 *lunch & dinner, Italian, full bar*

Hayward

see East Bay

■MEN'S SERVICES
➤**MegaMates** 510/342-2122 *Call to hook up with HOT local men. FREE to listen & respond to ads. Use FREE code DAMRON. MegaMates.com.*

Healdsburg

see Russian River & Sonoma County

Hemet

■CRUISY AREAS
Gibbel Park [AYOR] 2500 W Florida Ave (at Kirby, enter here) *very discreet*

Huntington Beach

see Orange County

Idyllwild

■ACCOMMODATIONS
The Heritage House Inn [GF] 25880 Cedar St 951/659-5150, 877/659-4789 *inn & cabins*

Quiet Creek Inn & Vacation Rentals [GF,NS,WI,GO] 26345 Delano Dr (at Toll Gate Rd) 951/659-6110, 800/450-6110 *vacation rentals*

The Rainbow Inn [GS,NS,WI,GO] 54420 S Circle Dr 951/659-0111 *full brkfst, patio, also conference center*

Strawberry Creek Inn B&B [GF,NS,WC,GO] 26370 Hwy 243 (at S Cir Dr) 951/659-3202, 800/262-8969 *relaxing getaway w/ sundeck, garden & hammocks*

■RESTAURANTS
Cafe Aroma [E] 54750 North Circle 951/659-5212 *7am-10pm, great ambience & food*

Irvine

see Orange County

Joshua Tree Nat'l Park

includes Twentynine Palms

■ACCOMMODATIONS
The Desert Lily [GF,WI] PO Box 139, 92252-0800 760/366-4676, 877/887-7370 *artist-owned adobe-style B&B on 5 acres; clsd July-Aug*

Desert Wonderland & The Tile House [GS,GO] 805/452-4898 *in high desert near Joshua Tree Nat'l Park*

Joshua Tree Highlands Houses [GS,NS,WI,WC,GO] 760/366-3636 *private, fully equipped rentals*

Moon Way Lodge [GS,SW,WI,NS,GO] 760/835-9369

California • *USA*

Sacred Sands [GS,NS,WI,GO] HC1 Box 1071 A, 63155 Quail Springs Rd (at Desert Shadows), Joshua Tree 760/424-6407

Spin & Margie's Desert Hideaway [GF] 64491 29 Palms Hwy 760/366-9124 *hacienda-style B&B, suites w/ private patios*

Starland Retreat [M,N,18+] Yucca Valley 760/364-2069

■RESTAURANTS

The Crossroads Cafe & Tavern 61715 29 Palms Hwy 760/366-5414 *7am-8pm, till 9pm Fri-Sat, clsd Wed*

Kernville

■ACCOMMODATIONS

River View Lodge [GS,NS,GO] 2 Sirretta St 760/376-6019 *resort on Kern River, jacuzzi*

La Mirada

■RESTAURANTS

Mexico 1900 11531 La Mirada Blvd 562/941-2016 *lunch & dinner, Mexican*

Laguna Beach

see Orange County

Lake Tahoe

see also Lake Tahoe, Nevada

■ACCOMMODATIONS

Alpine Inn & Spa [GS,SW] 920 Stateline Ave (Lake Ave/ Hwy 50), South Lake Tahoe 530/544-3340, 800/826-8885

Black Bear Inn [GS,NS,WI,GO] 530/544-4451, 877/232-7466 *full brkfst, hot tub, fireplaces*

The Cedar House Sport Hotel [GF,WI] 10918 Brockway Rd, Truckee 530/582-5655, 866/582-5655

Spruce Grove Cabins [GF,NS] 3599-3605 Spruce Ave, South Lake Tahoe 530/544-0549, 800/777-0914

Tahoe Valley Lodge [GF,SW,NS,WI] 2241 Lake Tahoe Blvd (at Tahoe Keys Blvd), South Lake Tahoe 530/541-0353, 800/669-7544 *motel*

■RESTAURANTS

Driftwood Cafe [WC] 1001 Heavenly Village Way #1A 530/544-6545 *7am-3pm, homecooking*

Passaretti's [BW] 1181 Emerald Bay Rd/ Hwy 50, South Lake Tahoe 530/541-3433 *11am-9pm, Italian*

■CRUISY AREAS

El Dorado Beach [AYOR] btwn Rufus Allen Blvd & Lakeview, South Lake Tahoe

Private Beach [AYOR] off Pine St (near Park), South Lake Tahoe *private beach behind resorts*

Livermore

see East Bay

Lodi

■EROTICA

Intimates & Adult Superstore [AYOR] 203 N Houston Ln 209/369-6191 *also arcade*

Long Beach

■INFO LINES & SERVICES

AA Gay/ Lesbian 2017 E 4th St (at Cherry, at Gay & Lesbian Center) 562/434-4455 *7pm Mon [MW] & 7pm Fri [M]*

The Gay & Lesbian Center of Greater Long Beach 2017 E 4th St (at Cherry) 562/434-4455 *9am-9pm, by appt Sat, activities & support groups, HIV testing*

■ACCOMMODATIONS

Beachrunners' Inn [GS,NS] 231 Kennebec Ave (at Junipero & Broadway) 562/856-0202, 866/221-0001 *B&B, near beach, hot tub*

Dockside Boat & Bed [GF] Dock 5, Rainbow Harbor (at Pine Ave Pier) 562/436-3111 *spend the night on a yacht, views of Queen Mary*

Hotel Current [GS,SW,WI,WC] 5325 E Pacific Coast Hwy 562/597-1341, 800/990-9991

Hotel Maya [GS] 700 Queensway Dr 562/435-7676

Queen Mary [GF,NS,WC] 1126 Queens Hwy **877/342-0742** *historic ocean liner*

The Varden Hotel [GS,WI,NS,WC] 335 Pacific Ave (at 3rd St) **562/432-8950, 877/382-7336**

▌BARS

The Brit [M,NH,WC] 1744 E Broadway (at Cherry) **562/432-9742** *10am-2am, patio*

The Broadway [MW,NH,K,WC] 1100 E Broadway (at Cerritos) **562/432-3646** *10am-2am, [K] Fri-Sat*

The Crest [M] 5935 Cherry Ave (at South) **562/423-6650** *2pm-2am, from noon wknds*

The Falcon [M,NH,WC] 1435 E Broadway (at Falcon) **562/432-4146** *7am-2am, from 6am wknds*

Flux [MW,NH,WI] 17817 Lakewood Blvd (at Artesia), Bellflower **562/633-6394** *noon-2am, patio, theme nights*

Liquid Lounge [GS,NH,F,E,K,GO] 3522 E Anaheim St **562/494-7564** *11am-1am, till 2am Fri-Sat, [K] Fri-Sat, patio*

Mineshaft [★M,B] 1720 E Broadway (btwn Gaviota & Hermosa) **562/436-2433** *10am-2am*

Paradise Piano Bar & Restaurant [MW,NH,F,E,P] 1800 E Broadway Blvd (at Hermosa) **562/590-8773** *3pm-1am, from 10am Sat-Sun, live entertainment*

Pistons [M,B,L] 2020 E Artesia (at Cherry) **562/422-1928** *2pm-2am patio*

Que Será [GS,D,A,E] 1923 E 7th St (at Cherry) **562/599-6170** *9pm-2am Tue, from 5pm Wed-Sat, from 3pm Sun, clsd Mon, theme nights, [$] after 9pm*

Silver Fox [M,K,V,WC] 411 Redondo (at 4th) **562/439-6343** *4pm-2am, from noon wknds, popular happy hour, [K] Wed & Sun*

Sweetwater Saloon [M,NH,WC] 1201 E Broadway (at Orange) **562/432-7044** *10am-2am, popular days, cruisy*

▌NIGHTCLUBS

The Basement Lounge [GS,D,E] 149 Linden Ave (at E Broadway) **562/901-9090** *also restaurant*

Boy's Room [M,D,E,S,WC] 3428 E Pacific Coast Hwy (at Redondo, at the Executive Suite) **562/597-3884** *9pm-2am Fri only*

Club Ripples [★M,D,MR,F,E,K,DS,S,V,YC] 5101 E Ocean (at Granada) **562/433-0357** *noon-2am, patio, theme nights, T-dance Sun, Bear Bar every 2nd Sat*

Executive Suite [★MW,D,E,WC] 3428 E Pacific Coast Hwy (at Redondo) **562/597-3884** *1pm-2am, from noon wknds*

The Powder Room [W,D,E] 525 E Broadway (at Bliss 525) **562/495-7252**

▌CAFES

Hot Java [WI] 2101 E Broadway Ave **562/433-0688** *6am-11pm, till midnight Fri-Sat, also soups, sandwiches, salads*

The Library [WI] 3418 E Broadway **562/433-2393** *6am-midnight, till 1am Fri-Sat, from 7am wknds*

▌RESTAURANTS

212 Degrees Bistro 2708 E 4th St **562/439-8822** *8am-2pm, clsd Mon, Mexican-inspired*

Cafe Sevilla 140 Pine St **562/495-1111** *dinner only, Sun brunch, Spanish, also music & dancing*

Hamburger Mary's [MW,D] 740 E Broadway (at Alamitos) **562/436-7900** *11am-2am, full bar w/ theme nights*

Omelette Inn 318 Pine Ave **562/437-5625** *7am-4pm*

Open Sesame 5215 E 2nd St **562/621-1698** *lunch & dinner, Middle Eastern*

Original Park Pantry [WC] 2104 E Broadway (at Junipero) **562/434-0451** *6am-10pm, till 11pm Fri-Sat, int'l*

Two Umbrellas Cafe [GO] 1538 E Broadway (btwn Gaviota & Falcon) **562/495-2323** *8am-2pm, clsd Mon*

Utopia 445 E 1st St **562/432-6888** *lunch Mon-Fri, dinner nightly, clsd Sun, seafood, California cuisine, plenty veggie*

California • *USA*

■BOOKSTORES

Open 2226 E 4th St (btwn Cherry & Junipero, in heart of Retro Row) 562/499-6736 *11am-7pm, till 8pm Sat, till 6pm Sun, clsd Mon, general; also films, art & events*

■RETAIL SHOPS

Hot Stuff [GO] 2121 E Broadway (at Junipero) 562/433-0692 *11am-7pm, 10am-6pm Sat, noon-5pm Sun, cards, gifts & adult novelties, serving community since 1980*

■MEN'S CLUBS

1350 Club [18+] 510 W Anaheim St (at Neptune), Wilmington 310/830-4784 *24hrs*

■MEN'S SERVICES

➤**MegaMates** 562/485-4008 *Call to hook up with HOT local men. FREE to listen & respond to ads. Use FREE code DAMRON. MegaMates.com.*

■EROTICA

The Crypt on Broadway 1712 E Broadway (btwn Cherry & Falcon) 562/983-6560 *10am-midnight, leather, toys*

The RubberTree 5018 E 2nd St (at Granada) 562/434-0027 *gifts for lovers, women-owned*

■CRUISY AREAS

Please Note: All cruisy areas for Long Beach have been removed by request of various LGBT community organizations.

LOS ANGELES

Los Angeles is divided into 8 geographical areas:
LA—Overview
LA—West Hollywood
LA—Hollywood
LA—West LA & Santa Monica
LA—Silverlake
LA—Midtown
LA—Valley
LA—East LA & South Central

LA—Overview

■INFO LINES & SERVICES

Alcoholics Anonymous 323/936-4343 & 735-2089 (en español), 800/923-8722 *call or check web (www.lacooa.org) for meetings*

Crystal Meth Anonymous 877/262-6691 *call or check website (www.crystalmeth.org) for meetings in LA County*

LA Gay & Lesbian Center 1625 N Schrader Blvd (McDonald/Wright Building) 323/993-7400 *9am-9pm, till 1pm Sat, clsd Sun, wide variety of services*

LA Gay & Lesbian Center's Village at Ed Gould Plaza 1125 N McCadden Pl (at Santa Monica) 323/860-7302 *9am-9pm, clsd Sun, cybercenter, cafe, theaters, library*

■ENTERTAINMENT & RECREATION

The Celebration Theatre 7051 Santa Monica Blvd (at La Brea) 323/957-1884 *LGBT theater, call for more info*

The Ellen DeGeneres Show *you know you want to dance w/ Ellen! check out ellen.warnerbros.com for tickets*

The Gay Mafia Comedy Group [MW,GO] *improv/ sketch comedy*

The Getty Center 1200 Getty Center Dr, Brentwood 310/440-7300 *10am-6pm, till 9pm Fri-Sat, clsd Mon, LA's shining city on a hill & world-class museum; of course, it's still in LA so you'll need to make reservations for parking (!)*

Griffith Observatory enter on N Vermont St (in Griffith Park) 213/473-0800 *noon-10pm, from 10am wknds, clsd Mon*

Highways 1651 18th St (at the 18th Street Arts Center), Santa Monica 310/315-1459 *"full-service performance center"*

IMRU Gay Radio KPFK LA 90.7 FM *7pm Mon*

Outfest 213/480-7088 *LGBT media arts foundation that sponsors the annual LGBT film festival each July (see listing in Film Festival Calendar)*

The source to gay nightlife, music, photos and beauty.

ODYSSEY

odysseymagazine.net

Photo courtesy of Cockyboys, Mason Star

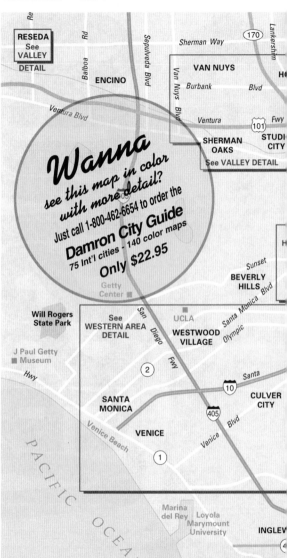

RESEDA
See
VALLEY
DETAIL

Sherman Way

(170)

Lankershm

Sepulveda Blvd

Balboa

Rd

Van Nuys Blvd

VAN NUYS

Burbank

Blvd

H

ENCINO

Ventura Blvd

Ventura

(101) Fwy

STUDI

CITY

SHERMAN
OAKS
See VALLEY DETAIL

Wanna
see this map in color
with more detail?
Just call 1-800-462-6654 to order the
Damron City Guide
75 Int'l cities - 140 color maps
Only $22.95

Getty
Center ■

H

Sunset

BEVERLY
HILLS

Santa Monica Blvd

Will Rogers
State Park

J Paul Getty
■ Museum

Hwy

See
WESTERN AREA
DETAIL

San Diego

Fwy

UCLA ■

WESTWOOD
VILLAGE

Santa Monica

Olympic

(2)

Santa

(10)

CULVER
CITY

SANTA
MONICA

(405)

VENICE

Venice Beach

Venice

Blvd

(1)

PACIFIC

Marina
del Rey

Loyola
Marymount
University

INGLEV

OCEA

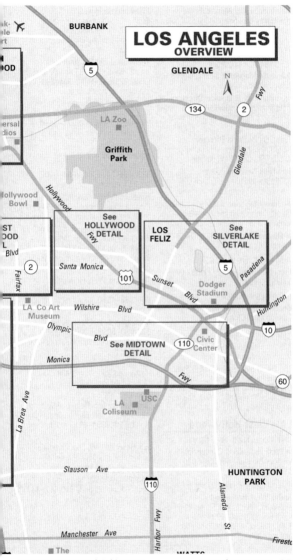

LOS ANGELES
OVERVIEW

BURBANK

GLENDALE

N

LA Zoo

Griffith
Park

Hollywood Bowl ■

Hollywood

See
HOLLYWOOD
DETAIL

LOS
FELIZ

See
SILVERLAKE
DETAIL

Pasadena

Santa Monica

Sunset

Dodger
Stadium

Blvd

Huntington

LA Co Art
Museum

Wilshire

Blvd

Olympic

Blvd

See MIDTOWN
DETAIL

Civic
Center

Monica

Fwy

LA
Coliseum

USC

Slauson Ave

HUNTINGTON
PARK

Manchester Ave

Alameda
St

Firesto

Harbor Fwy

WATTS

■ The

La Brea Ave

Fairfax

Glendale Fwy

Rainbow Skate/ Moonlight Rollerway Gay Skate [MW] 5110 San Fernando Rd (N of W Colorado St, near LA Zoo), Glendale **818/241-3630** *8pm Wed only*

▰PUBLICATIONS

Adelante Magazine 323/256-6639 *bilingual LGBT magazine*

Essential Gay & Lesbian Directory 310/841-2800, 866/718-GAYS *business directory serving the LGBT community*

Frontiers Business Directory 323/930-3220 *annual survival guide to LGBT Southern CA & Bay Area*

Frontiers Newsmagazine 323/930-3220 *huge LGBT newsmagazine w/ listings for everything*

➤**Gloss Magazine** 510/451-2090 *CA arts/ entertainment magazine, biweekly*

➤**Odyssey Magazine** 323/874-8788 *dish on LA's club scene*

▰MEN'S SERVICES

Escort Guys 44-(0) 7722/062 077, 571/527-1022

▰CRUISY AREAS

Beach in the Upper Big Tujunga Canyon (UBTC) [AYOR] Hwy 2, exit Angeles Crest Hwy, head N, turn left to UBTC Rd, turn right (btwn marker 4.5 & 4.8), Angeles Nat'l Forest *little nude beach along creek*

The Usual Suspects: Griffith Park, Elysian Park, Echo Park, Santa Fe Dam Regional Park, Whitsett Park [AYOR] *don't bother: LAPD & the rangers are waiting for you*

LA—West Hollywood

▰INFO LINES & SERVICES

➤**West Hollywood Convention & Visitors Bureau** 800/368-6020, 310/289-2525

▰ACCOMMODATIONS

Andaz West Hollywood [GS,SW,NS,WI,WC] 8401 Sunset Blvd (at Kings Rd) **323/656-1234, 800/233-1234** *on the Sunset Strip, rooftop pool*

Chamberlain [★GS,SW,WC] 1000 Westmount Dr (near Holloway) **310/657-7400, 800/201-9652** *boutique hotel, rooftop pool, restaurant & lounge*

The Elan Hotel Los Angeles [GS,NS,WI,WC,GO] 8435 Beverly Blvd (at Croft) **323/658-6663, 866/203-2212** *hip & trendy, fitness room*

The Grafton on Sunset [GS,SW,WC] 8462 W Sunset Blvd (at La Cienega) **323/654-4600, 800/821-3660** *sundeck, panoramic views, located in heart of Sunset Strip*

Holloway Motel [GS,NS] 8465 Santa Monica Blvd (at La Cienega) **323/654-2454, 888/654-6400** *centrally located*

Hotel Le Petit [GF,SW,WC] 8822 Cynthia St (at Larrabee) **310/854-1114** *all-suite hotel, hot tub*

Le Parc Suite Hotel [★GF,F,SW,WC] 733 N West Knoll Dr (at Melrose) **310/855-8888, 800/578-4837** *deluxe-class all-suite hotel, tennis courts, also restaurant*

The London West Hollywood [GF,SW,WI] 1020 N San Vicente Blvd **866/282-4560** *luxury hotel including dining in Gordon Ramsay's restaurant*

Mondrian [GF] 8440 Sunset Blvd **323/650-8999, 800/697-1791** *home of trendy Skybar & Asia de Cuba restaurant*

Ramada Plaza Hotel—West Hollywood [GF,F,SW,WC] 8585 Santa Monica Blvd (at La Cienega) **310/652-6400**

San Vicente Inn-Resort [M,SW,N,GO] 845 N San Vicente Blvd (at Santa Monica) **310/854-6915** *hot tub, steam room, cruisy*

SLS Hotel [GF] 465 S La Cienega Blvd (at San Vicente) **310/247-0400**

Sunset Marquis Hotel & Villas [GS,SW,WI,WC] 1200 Alta Loma Rd (1/2 block S of Sunset Blvd) **310/657-1333** *full brkfst, sauna, hot tub*

Join the jet-set

west hollywood

California • *USA*

■BARS

The Abbey [★MW,F,WC] 692 N Robertson Blvd (at Santa Monica) 310/289-8410 *8am-2am, also restaurant, patio*

Comedy Store [GF] 8433 Sunset Blvd (at La Cienega) 323/650-6268 *8pm-2am, legendary stand-up club*

Fiesta Cantina [MW,F] 8865 Santa Monica Blvd (at San Vicente) 310/652-8865 *noon-2am, raucous Mexican restaurant & bar*

Fubar [★M,D,K,S] 7994 Santa Monica Blvd (at Crescent Hts) 323/654-0396 *4pm-2am, theme nights, [K] Tue, [D,$] Fri-Sun, go-go boys Sat*

Gold Coast [★M,NH,WC] 8228 Santa Monica Blvd (at La Jolla) 323/656-4879 *11am-2am, from 10am wknds*

Gym Sports Bar [GS,NH,WC] 8737 Santa Monica Blvd (at Hancock) 310/659-2004 *4pm-2am, from noon wknds*

Here Lounge [MW,P] 696 N Robertson Blvd (at Santa Monica) 310/360-8455 *4pm-2am*

Improv [GF,F] 8162 Melrose Ave (at Crescent Heights) 323/651-2583 *stand-up comedy, also restaurant*

Micky's [★M,D,F,V,YC,GO] 8857 Santa Monica Blvd (at San Vicente) 310/657-1176 *noon-2am, after-hours wknds, patio*

Mother Lode [★M,NH,K,WC] 8944 Santa Monica Blvd (at Robertson) 310/659-9700 *3pm-2am, beer bust Sun*

Revolver [★M] 8851 Santa Monica Blvd (at San Vicente) 310/694-0430 *4pm-2am, from noon wknds, a WeHo institution*

Trunks [M,NH,V,YC] 8809 Santa Monica Blvd (at Larrabee) 310/652-1015 *1pm-2am*

■NIGHTCLUBS

Cherry Pop [M,D] 661 N Robertson Blvd (at Santa Monica, at Ultra Suede) 9pm *Sat only*

Club Papi Los Angeles [M,D,MR-L] 652 N La Peer Dr 323/692-9573 *9pm-4am, monthly party, call for dates*

Eleven Restaurant & Nightclub 8811 Santa Monica Blvd (at Larrabee St) 310/855-0800 *lunch & dinner, more gay for the bar atmosphere till 2am*

The Factory [★M,D,V,$] 652 N La Peer Dr (at Santa Monica) 310/659-4551 *9pm-2am Fri-Sat, theme nights*

Hype Fridays [M,D] 652 La Peer (at Santa Monica, at Factory) *9:30pm Fri only*

Plaza [M,D,MR-L,DS,$] 739 N La Brea Ave (at Melrose) 323/939-0703 *9pm-2am, from 8pm Fri-Sat, clsd Tue, shows nightly at 10:15pm & midnight*

Rage [★M,D,F,DS,V,18+,YC,WC] 8911 Santa Monica Blvd (at San Vicente) 310/652-7055 *noon-2am*

Ultra Suede [GS,D,A,E] 661 N Robertson Blvd (at Santa Monica) 310/659-4551 *10pm-2am Wed-Sat, theme nights*

■CAFES

Champagne French Bakery & Cafe [F] 8917-9 Santa Monica Blvd 310/657-4051 *6:30am-9pm, till 11pm Fri-Sat, coffees & pastries as well as brkfst, lunch & dinner, some outdoor seating*

Grind House Cafe [WI] 1051 N Havenhurst Dr 323/650-7717 *6:30am-10pm, coffeehouse*

Urth Caffe [F] 8565 Melrose Ave (btwn Robertson & La Cienega) 310/659-0628 *6:30am-midnight, organic coffees, teas & treats, plenty veggie & vegan, patio*

■RESTAURANTS

AOC 8022 W Third St (at Crescent Heights Blvd) 323/653-6359 *dinner nightly, wine bar, eclectic, upscale*

Basix Cafe 8333 Santa Monica Blvd (at Flores) 323/848-2460 *7am-11pm, outdoor seating*

Bite [BW,WC] 8807 Santa Monica Blvd (at San Vicente) 310/659-3663 *11:30am-11:30pm, plenty veggie*

Bossa Nova [BW,WC] 685 N Robertson Blvd (at Santa Monica) **310/657-5070** *11am-midnight, Brazilian, patio*

Cafe La Boheme [WC] 8400 Santa Monica Blvd (btwn Benecia Ave & Fox Hills Dr) **323/848-2360** *5pm-10pm Fri-Sat, till 11pm Sun-Th, eclectic Californian, full bar, patio*

Canter's Deli [WC] 419 N Fairfax (btwn Melrose & Beverly) **323/651-2030** *24hrs, hip after-hours, Jewish/American, full bar*

Eat Well [★] 8252 Santa Monica Blvd (at La Jolla) **323/656-1383** *7am-9:30pm, 8am-3pm wknds, comfort food diner*

Falcon [GS] 7213 Sunset Blvd (btwn Poinsettia & Formosa) **323/850-5350** *dinner Wed-Sat, California/cont'l fusion*

Hamburger Mary's Bar & Grill [MW,TG,E,K,DS,S,V,GO] 8288 Santa Monica Blvd **323/654-3800** *11am-1am, till 2am Fri-Sat*

Hedley's 640 N Robertson Blvd **310/659-2009** *lunch & dinner, also wknd brunch, clsd Sun night & Mon*

The Hudson 1114 N Crescent Heights Blvd **323/654-6686** *4pm-2am, from 10am Sat-Sun*

Il Piccolino Trattoria [WC] 350 N Robertson Blvd (btwn Melrose & Beverly) **310/659-2220** *lunch & dinner, clsd Sun, patio*

Joey's Cafe 8301 Santa Monica Blvd **323/822-0671** *8am-10pm, a little bit coffeehouse, a little bit diner, popular at lunch*

Kokomo Cafe [WC] 7385 Beverly Blvd (between La Brea Ave & Fairfax Ave) **323/933-0773** *8am-4pm, diner*

Koo Koo Roo [BW,WC] 8520 Santa Monica Blvd (at La Cienega Blvd) **310/657-3300** *11am-11pm, till 10pm Sun, lots of healthy chicken dishes*

Lola's 945 N Fairfax Ave (at Santa Monica) **323/654-5652** *5:30pm-2am, great martinis*

Louise's Trattoria [BW] 7505 Melrose Ave (at Gardner) **323/651-3880** *11am-10pm, Italian, great foccacia bread, patio*

Lucques [WC] 8474 Melrose Ave (at La Cienega) **323/655-6277** *lunch Tue-Sat, dinner nightly, French, full bar, patio*

Marix Tex Mex [MW,WC] 1108 N Flores (btwn La Cienega & Fairfax) **323/656-8800** *11:30am-11pm, from 11am wknds, great margaritas, patio*

Nyala 1076 S Fairfax (at Whitworth Dr) **323/936-5918** *many Ethiopian, Nigerian & other African restaurants to choose from on this block*

Real Food Daily [★BW,WC] 414 N La Cienega (btwn Beverly & Melrose) **310/289-9910** *11:30am-10pm, till 11pm Fri-Sat, Sun brunch 10am-3pm, organic vegan, patio*

St Felix 8945 Santa Monica Blvd (at Hilldale) **310/275-4428** *4pm-2am, small plates*

Tart 115 S Fairfax Ave (at Farmer's Daughter Hotel) **323/937-3930, 800/334-1658** *7am-midnight, Southern*

Taste 8454 Melrose Ave (at La Cienega) **323/852-6888** *lunch & dinner, wknd brunch, upscale eclectic, full bar*

Versailles 1415 S La Cienega (at W Pico) **310/289-0392** *lunch & dinner, Cuban*

■BOOKSTORES

Book Soup 8818 W Sunset Blvd (at Larrabee) **310/659-3110** *9am-10pm, till 7pm Sun, LGBT section*

■RETAIL SHOPS

665 Leather 8722 Santa Monica Blvd (at Huntley Dr) **310/854-7276** *noon-8pm, till 10pm Fri-Sat, custom leather & neoprene, also accessories & toys*

Marginalized Tattoo [GO] 4228 Melrose Ave (at Vermont) **213/422-4801** *featuring Dave Davenport (aka "Dogspunk"), named best gay tattoo artist by Frontiers*

■GYMS & HEALTH CLUBS

24 Hour Fitness 8612 Santa Monica Blvd, West Hollywood **310/652-7440** *recently renovated, tres gay*

The Easton Gym [GF] 8053 Beverly Blvd (at Crescent Hts) **323/651-3636**

California • USA

The Fitness Factory [★] 650 N La Peer Dr (at Santa Monica) 310/358-1838 6am-9pm, till 8pm Fri, 7am-5pm Sat, 8am-1pm Sun

■ MEN'S CLUBS

Melrose Spa [★18+,PC] 7269 Melrose Ave (at Poinsettia) 323/937-2122 24hrs

Slammer [18+,PC] 3688 Beverly Blvd (2 blocks E of Vermont) 213/388-8040 8pm-4am, from 2pm wknds

■ MEN'S SERVICES

▶**MegaMates** 323/648-3999 Call to hook up with HOT local men. FREE to listen & respond to ads. Use FREE code DAMRON. MegaMates.com.

■ EROTICA

Chi Chi LaRue's 8932 Santa Monica Blvd (at San Vicente) 323/337-9555 10am-midnight, till 2am Th-Sun

Circus of Books 8230 Santa Monica Blvd (at La Jolla) 323/656-6533 6am-2am

The New Unicorn Bookstore 8940 Santa Monica Blvd (at Robertson Blvd) 310/652-6253

Pleasure Chest 7733 Santa Monica Blvd (at Genesee), N Hollywood 323/650-1022 10am-midnight, till 1am Th-Sat

Studs Theatre 7734 Santa Monica Blvd (at the Legendary Pussycat Theatre) 949/436-1036 9am-3am, till 5am Fri-Sat

LA—Hollywood

■ ACCOMMODATIONS

Coral Sands Motel [GS,SW,WI] 1730 N Western Ave (at Hollywood Blvd) 323/467-5141

Hilton Garden Inn [GF,F,SW,WI,WC] 2005 N Highland (at Franklin) 323/876-8600 exercise room, jacuzzi

Hollywood Hotel – The Hotel of Hollywood [GF,SW,NS,WI,WC] 1160 N Vermont Ave (at Santa Monica) 323/315-1800, 800/800-9733

■ BARS

Boardner's [GS,D,F,K] 1652 N Cherokee Ave 323/462-9621 4pm-2am, "a Hollywood legend & best-kept secret since 1942", theme nights

Faultline [★M,B,L,V,WC] 4216 Melrose Ave (at Vermont) 323/660-0889 5pm-2am, from 2pm wknds, clsd Mon-Tue, patio

■ NIGHTCLUBS

Arena/ Circus Disco [★M,D,MR-L,S,V] 6655 Santa Monica Blvd (at Seward, Circus behind Arena) 323/810-6993 9pm-2am Tue-Wed & Fri-Sat, theme nights

Avalon [GS,D,$] 1735 Vine St (at Hollywood Blvd) 323/462-8900 one of LA's best dance music clubs, call for events

Club Tranzit [TG] 1775 N Ivar (at Joseph's Cafe), Hollywood 818/761-9472 10pm Th only

Mr Black LA [MW,D] 1737 N Vine St (at Hollywood Blvd, at Bardot) 323/462-8900 Tue only

Tempo [M,D,MR-L,E,S] 5520 Santa Monica Blvd (at Western) 323/466-1094 9pm-2am, 7pm-3am Th-Sat, from 2pm Sun, live bands Sat, beer bust Sun

TigerHeat [GS,D,TG,E,DS,V,18+,$] 1735 Vine (at Avalon) 323/467-4571 9:30pm-3am Th only

■ RESTAURANTS

101 Coffee Shop 6145 Franklin Ave 323/467-1175 7am-3am, diner

La Poubelle [WC] 5907 Franklin Ave (at Bronson) 323/465-0807 5:30pm-midnight, French/ Italian, full bar

Lucy's Cafe El Adobe 5536 Melrose Ave (near Gower St) 323/462-9421 11:30am-11pm, clsd Sun, Mexican, patio

Musso & Frank Grill 6667 Hollywood Blvd (near Las Palmas) 323/467-5123 11am-11pm, clsd Sun-Mon, the grand-dame diner/ steak house of Hollywood: great pancakes, potpies & martinis!

Off Vine [BW] 6263 Leland Wy (at Vine) 323/962-1900 lunch & dinner, wknd brunch

California • *USA*

Prado [WC] 244 N Larchmont Blvd (at Beverly) 323/467-3871 *lunch & dinner, dinner only Sun, Caribbean*

Quality [WC] 8030 W 3rd St (at Laurel) 323/658-5959 *8am-3:30pm, home-style brkfst*

Rockwell VT 1714 N Vermont Ave (at Prospect, enter in alley) 323/669-1550 *5pm-2am, brunch wknds*

Roscoe's House of Chicken & Waffles 1514 N Gower (at Sunset) 323/466-7453 *8:30am-midnight, till 4am Fri-Sat*

Sushi Hiroba 776 N Vine St 323/962-7237 *lunch Mon-Fri, dinner nightly*

▓ BOOKSTORES

Skylight Books [★] 1818 N Vermont Ave (at Melbourne Ave) 323/660-1175 *10am-10pm, way cool independent in Los Feliz, great fiction & alt-lit sections*

▓ GYMS & HEALTH CLUBS

Gold's Gym [GF] 1016 N Cole Ave (near Santa Monica & Vine) 323/462-7012 *5am-midnight, 7am-9pm Sat-Sun*

▓ MEN'S CLUBS

Flex [SW] 4424 Melrose Ave (btwn Normandie & Vermont) 323/663-7786 *24hrs, patio, steam*

►Hollywood Spa [★PC] 1650 N Ivar (near Hollywood & Vine) 323/463-5169, 800/772-2582 *24hrs*

The Zone [PC] 1037 N Sycamore Ave (at Santa Monica) 323/472-6495 *8pm-dawn, from 2pm Sun*

▓ EROTICA

X Spot 6775 Santa Monica Blvd (at Highland) 323/463-0295 *24hrs*

LA—West LA & Santa Monica

▓ ACCOMMODATIONS

Casa Malibu [GF,F,WI] 22752 Pacific Coast Hwy, Malibu 310/456-2219

The Georgian Hotel [GF,F,WI,WC] 1415 Ocean Ave (btwn Santa Monica & Broadway), Santa Monica 310/395-9945, 800/538-8147

Hotel Angeleno [GS,SW,NS,WI] 170 N Church Ln (at Hwy 405) 310/476-6411, 866/264-3536 *boutique hotel w/ landmark circular shape, gym*

Hotel Erwin [GS] 1697 Pacific Ave (at Venice Way), Venice Beach 310/452-1111, 800/786-7789

Hotel Palomar [GS,SW,WC] 310/475-8711, 800/472-8556

The Inn at Venice Beach [GF,WI,WC] 327 Washington Blvd (at Via Dolce), Marina Del Rey 310/821-2557, 800/828-0688 *European-style inn*

The Linnington [MW,GO] 310/422-8825 *B&B, jacuzzi, lesbian-owned*

Shutters on the Beach [GF,SW,WI] 1 Pico Blvd, Santa Monica 310/458-0030, 800/334-9000

W Los Angeles [GF,F,SW] 930 Hilgard Ave (at Le Conte) 310/208-8765, 800/421-2317 *suites, gym, day spa*

▓ BARS

The Dolphin [MW,NH,K,WC] 1995 Artesia Blvd (at Green Ln), Redondo Beach 310/318-3339 *7pm-2am, patio, [D] Tue & Fri-Sat, [K] Sun, Tue & Th*

Roosterfish [★M,NH] 1302 Abbot Kinney Blvd (at Cadiz), Venice 310/392-2123 *11am-2am, patio*

▓ CAFES

The Novel Cafe 2507 Main St, Santa Monica 310/396-7700 *7am-1am, from 8am Sat, 8am-midnight Sun, also used bookstore*

▓ RESTAURANTS

12 Washington 12 Washington Blvd (at Pacific), Marina Del Rey 310/822-5566 *5pm-10pm, till 11pm Fri-Sun, cont'd*

Axe 1009 Abbot Kinney, Venice 310/664-9787 *lunch & dinner, clsd Mon, healthy, plenty veggie*

Baja Cantina 311 Washington Blvd (at Sanborn), Marina Del Rey 310/821-2252 *10:30am-1am, also brunch wknds, full bar*

Border Grill [★] 1445 4th St (at Broadway), Santa Monica 310/451-1655 *lunch & dinner from famous "Two Hot Tamales" chefs, Mexican*

Cantalini's Salerno Beach Restaurant [★E,BW] 193 Culver Blvd (at Vista del Mar), Playa del Rey 310/821-0018 *lunch Mon-Fri, dinner nightly, Italian, homemade pastas, live music Sun nights*

Cora's Coffee Shoppe 1802 Ocean Ave (N of Pico Blvd), Santa Monica 310/451-9562 *7am-3pm, from 7am wknds, clsd Mon, organic*

Drago [WC] 410 N Canon, Beverly Hills 310/786-8236 *lunch Mon-Sat, dinner nightly, Sicilian Italian*

Gjelina [BW] 1429 Abbot Kinney Blvd, Venice 310/450-1429 *pizzas & small plates*

Golden Bull 170 W Channel Rd (at Pacific Coast Hwy), Santa Monica 310/230-0402 *4:30pm-10pm, till 11pm wknds, Sun brunch, American, full bar*

Hamburger Habit [★] 11223 National Blvd (at Sepulveda) 310/478-5000 *10am-11pm, till midnight Fri-Sat*

Joe's 1023 Abbot Kinney Blvd, Venice 310/399-5811 *lunch Tue-Fri, dinner nightly, wknd brunch, clsd Mon, French/ Californian*

Real Food Daily [BW,WC] 514 Santa Monica Blvd (btwn 5th & 6th), Santa Monica 310/451-7544 *11:30am-10pm, organic vegan*

Seed Bistro 11917 Wilshire Blvd 310/477-7070 *lunch Mon-Fri, dinner nightly, clsd Sun, vegan*

Wokcano 1413 5th St, Santa Monica 310/458-3080 *11am-12:30am, till 1:30am Fri-Sat, sushi bar & Chinese cafe*

▪ENTERTAINMENT & RECREATION

Muscle Beach Ocean Front Walk, Venice Beach *LOTS to see at this popular Venice Boardwalk beach!*

Santa Monica Pier Ocean Ave (at Colorado Ave), Santa Monica

Will Rogers State Beach Pacific Coast Hwy (at Temescal Canyon Rd) *gay beach*

▪BOOKSTORES

Diesel, A Bookstore 23410 Civic Center Way, Malibu 310/456-9961 *10am-7pm, till 9pm Fri-Sat, till 6pm Sun, independent*

▪RETAIL SHOPS

David Aden Gallery 361 Vernon #8 (at 4th Ave), Venice Beach 310/396-2949 *9am-5pm or by appt, large collection of male fine-art photography*

▪MEN'S CLUBS

Roman Holiday 12814 Venice Blvd (at Beethoven) 310/391-0200 *24hrs*

▪MEN'S SERVICES

▶**MegaMates** 310/883-2299 *Call to hook up with HOT local men. FREE to listen & respond to ads. Use FREE code DAMRON. MegaMates.com.*

▪EROTICA

Pleasure Island 18426 Hawthorne Blvd (btwn Artesia & 190th), Torrance 310/793-9477 *11am-midnight, till 2am Fri-Sat*

LA—Silverlake

▪ACCOMMODATIONS

Sanborn GuestHouse [GS,NS,WI,GO] 1005 1/2 Sanborn Ave (near Sunset) 323/666-3947 *private unit w/ kitchen*

▪BARS

4100 Bar [GS,NH] 4100 Sunset Blvd (at Manzanita) 323/666-4460 *8pm-2am*

AKBar [★GS,NH,D,WC] 4356 W Sunset Blvd (at Fountain) 323/665-6810 *7pm-2am, hip Silverlake hangout*

Cavern Club Theater 1920 Hyperion Ave (at Casita Del Campo) 323/969-2530, 323/662-4255 *wide variety of shows, Wed-Sat nights*

Cha Cha Lounge [GF,NH,GO] 2375 Glendale Blvd (at Silverlake) 323/660-7595 *5pm-2am, hipster lounge*

Club Nur [★MW,D] 2810 Hyperion Ave (at Rowena, at MJ's) 323/660-1503 *Th only, Middle Eastern night*

California • *USA*

Eagle LA [★M,L,WC] 4219 Santa Monica Blvd (at Hoover) 323/669-9472 *4pm-2am, from 2pm wknds, uniform bar*

Good Luck Bar [GF] 1514 Hillhurst Ave (nr Hollywood Blvd) 323/666-3524 *7pm-2am, from 8pm wknds, stylish dive bar*

Little Joy [GS,NH,MR-L] 1477 W Sunset Blvd (at Portia) 213/250-3417 *6pm-2am, from 1pm wknds*

MJ's [★M,NH,D,B,L,WC] 2810 Hyperion Ave (at Rowena) 323/660-1503 *4pm-2am, from 2pm Fri- Sun, theme nights*

The Other Side/ Flying Leap Cafe [M,NH,E,P,OC] 2538 Hyperion Ave (at Griffith Park) 323/661-0618 *noon-2am*

Silverlake Lounge [GS,E,DS] 2906 Sunset Blvd (at Silver Lake Blvd) 323/663-9636 *3pm-2am, rock 'n' roll club, drag shows wknds*

■ NIGHTCLUBS

A Club Called Rhonda [GS,D] 213/482-2313 *monthly party, "house, disco, & polysexual hard partying," check www.rhondasays.net for info*

Dragstrip 66 [★GS,D,A,DS,$] 1154 Glendale Blvd (btwn W Sunset & Park Ave, at the Echoplex) 323/969-2596 *occasional events, trashy pansexual rock 'n' roll drag club*

The Echo [GS,D,E] 1822 W Sunset Blvd (at Glendale Blvd) 213/413-8200

Full Frontal Disco [GS,D,TG] 4356 W Sunset Blvd (at Fountain) 213/626-2285 *last Sun only, '70s-'80s disco party*

■ RESTAURANTS

Casita Del Campo [★] 1920 Hyperion Ave 323/662-4255 *11am-midnight, till 2am Fri-Sat, Mexican, patio*

Cha Cha Cha [MW,WC] 656 N Virgil Ave (at Melrose) 323/664-7723 *lunch & dinner, Caribbean, plenty veggie*

Cliff's Edge 3626 Sunset Blvd (at Griffith Park Blvd) 323/666-6116 *dinner only, wknd brunch, plenty veggie, romantic, outdoor seating*

Cru 1521 Griffith Park Blvd 323/667-1551 *noon-4pm & 6pm-10pm, vegan*

El Conquistador [BW] 3701 W Sunset Blvd (at Lucille) 323/666-5136 *lunch Tue-Sun, dinner nightly, Mexican, patio*

The Good Microbrew & Grill 3725 Sunset Blvd (at Lucille) 323/660-3645 *11am-10pm, till 11pm Fri, 9am-10pm wknds, plenty veggie*

Home 1760 Hillhurst Ave, Los Feliz 323/669-0211 *9am-10pm, patio*

The Kitchen [GO] 4348 Fountain Ave (at Sunset Blvd) 323/664-3663 *5pm-1am, from 11am Sat, till 10pm Sun, cozy diner*

Michelangelo Pizzeria Ristorante 2742 Rowena 323/660-4843 *lunch & dinner*

Square One Dining 4854 Fountain Ave (at Vermont Ave) 323/661-1109 *8am-3pm, great brkfst*

Vermont Restaurant & Bar [GO] 1714 N Vermont Ave 323/661-6163 *lunch Mon-Fri, dnner nightly, clsd Sun*

■ BOOKSTORES

Serifos 3814 W Sunset Blvd 323/660-7467 *independent book-store, gifts*

■ RETAIL SHOPS

Rough Trade Gear 3915 Sunset Blvd 323/660-7956 *noon-10pm, 10am-midnight Fri-Sat, till 8pm Sun*

Syren 2809 1/2 W Sunset Blvd 213/289-0334 *noon-10pm, clsd Mon, leather & latex*

■ GYMS & HEALTH CLUBS

Body Builders [GF] 2516 Hyperion Ave (at Tracy) 323/668-0802

■ EROTICA

Circus of Books 4001 Sunset Blvd (at Sanborn) 323/666-1304 *6am-2am*

Romantix Adult Superstore 3147 N San Fernando Rd 323/258-2867 *24hrs*

LA—Midtown

■ACCOMMODATIONS

O Hotel [GS,F,WI] 819 S Flower St
213/623-9904

The Standard, Downtown LA
[GS,SW,F,WI] 550 S Flower St
213/892-8080

■BARS

Cafe Club Fais Do-Do [GF,F,E] 5257 W
Adams Blvd (btwn Fairfax & La Brea)
323/931-4636 *8pm-2am, live music,
also Cajun restaurant*

■NIGHTCLUBS

Bordello [GF,C,F] 901 E 1st St (at S
Vignes St) 213/687-3766 *burlesque
shows, also restaurant*

Coco Bongo [W,D,MR-L,DS,S,18+] 3311
S Main St 818/233-5322 *9pm-2am,
clsd Mon-Wed*

Critter Control [MW,D,A,DS,TG] *queer
dance parties in downtown LA*

Jewel's Catch One Disco [GS,D,A,WC]
4067 W Pico Blvd (at Norton)
323/734-8849 (hotline),
323/737-1159 *call for hours, clsd
Wed-Th, theme nights*

Mustache Mondays [MW,D,TG,A] 336 S
Hill St (at W 4th St, at La Cita bar)
213/687-7111 *9pm Mon only, queer
fashionistas*

■RESTAURANTS

Bar & Kitchen LA 819 S Flower St (at
O Hotel) 213/784-3048 *new-
American*

Border Grill Downtown [E,WC] 445 S
Figueroa St (at 5th St) 213/486-5171
lunch & dinner, late-night cocktails

Cassell's 3266 W 6th St (at Vermont)
213/480-5000 *10:30am-4pm, clsd
Sun, great burgers*

Doughboys Cafe 8136 W 3rd St
323/852-1020 *7am-10pm*

■MEN'S CLUBS

Klyt [MR-L] 132 E 4th St
213/972-9145 *24hrs, steam room &
dry sauna*

Midtowne Spa—Los Angeles [SW] 615
S Kohler (at Central) 213/680-1838
24hrs

LA—Valley

**includes San Fernando & San
Gabriel Valleys**

■BARS

The Bullet [M,L,WC] 10522 Burbank
Blvd (at Cahuenga), North Hollywood
818/762-8890 *noon-2am, patio*

Cobra [★M,D,MR-L,WC] 10937 Burbank
Blvd (1 block E of Vineland), North
Hollywood 818/760-9798 *4pm-9pm,
till 2am Wed-Sun*

Silver Rail [MW,NH] 11518 Burbank
Blvd (btwn Colfax & Lankershim)
818/980-8310 *4pm-2am, from noon
wknds*

■NIGHTCLUBS

C Frenz [★MW,NH,D,MR,K,C,S,WC,GO]
7026 Reseda Blvd (at Sherman Way),
Reseda 818/996-2976 *3pm-2am, till
3am Sat, patio, theme nights, beer bust
Sun*

Club Coco Bongo [MW,D,MR-
L,DS,S,18+] 19655 Sherman Wy (at
Corbin Ave), Reseda 818/233-5322
9pm-2am, clsd Mon-Wed

Oil Can Harry's [M,D,CW,S] 11502
Ventura Blvd (at Tujunga & Colfax),
Studio City 818/760-9749 *7:30pm-
2am, from 9pm Fri, from 8pm Sat, clsd
Sun-Mon & Wed, dance lessons Tue &
Th, classic disco Sat*

Rain [MW,D] 12215 Ventura Blvd,
Studio City 818/755-9596 *5pm-2am*

■CAFES

Aroma 4360 Tujunga Ave, Studio City
818/508-0677 *6am-11pm, from 7am
Sun, coffeehouse w/ small bookstore*

■RESTAURANTS

Du-Par's 12036 Ventura Blvd (at Laurel
Canyon), Studio City 818/766-4437
*24hrs, plush diner schmoozing; also 75
W Thousand Oaks Blvd, Thousand Oaks*

Firefly Studio City 11720 Ventura
Blvd, Studio City 818/762-1833 *5pm-
2am, till midnight Sun, great beer
braised mussels, full bar*

California • *USA*

Gourmet 88 230 N San Fernando Blvd, Burbank **818/848-8688** *11:30am-10pm, till 11pm Fri-Sat, Mandarin*

■GYMS & HEALTH CLUBS

Gold's Gym 6233 N Laurel Canyon Blvd (at Oxnard), North Hollywood **818/506-4600**

■MEN'S CLUBS

Eros Station 15164 Oxnard St (rear entrance), Van Nuys **818/994-6200** *2pm-2am Sat, till 1am Sun*

➤**The North Hollywood Spa** [V] 5636 Vineland (at Burbank) **818/760-6969, 800/772-2582** *24hrs, no membership required*

Roman Holiday [MO] 14435 Victory Blvd, Van Nuys **818/780-1320** *open 24hrs*

■MEN'S SERVICES

➤**MegaMates** 818/996-7000 *Call to hook up with HOT local men. FREE to listen & respond to ads. Use FREE code DAMRON. MegaMates.com.*

■EROTICA

Diamond Adult World 6406 Van Nuys Blvd (at Victory), Van Nuys **818/997-3665** *24hrs*

Eros Station 15164 Oxnard St, Van Nuys **818/994-6100** *10am-1am, videos & toys*

Romantix Adult Superstore 21625 Sherman Wy (at Nelson), Canoga Park **818/992-9801**

■CRUISY AREAS

Chatsworth Park South [AYOR] 22360 Devonshire St, Chatsworth *parking lot & nearby woods*

LA—East LA & South Central

■BARS

Chico Bar [★M,D,MR-L,S] 2915 W Beverly Blvd (at Garfield), Montebello **323/721-3403** *9pm-2am, theme nights*

Manhattan Beach

see also LA—West LA & Santa Monica

■ACCOMMODATIONS

Sea View Inn at the Beach [GF,SW,NS,WI] 3400 Highland Ave **310/545-1504**

■RESTAURANTS

The Local Yolk [WI,WC] 3414 Highland Ave (at Rosecranz) **310/546-4407** *6:30am-2pm*

Marin County

includes Corte Madera, Mill Valley, San Anselmo, San Rafael, Sausalito, Tiburon

■INFO LINES & SERVICES

AA Gay/ Lesbian 415/499-0400 *check www.aasf.org for meeting times*

Spectrum LGBT Center of the North Bay [WC] 30 N San Pedro Rd # 160, San Rafael **415/472-1945** *drop-in hours: 11am-5pm Mon-Fri*

■ACCOMMODATIONS

Acqua Hotel [GF,NS,WI,WC] 555 Redwood Hwy, Mill Valley **415/380-0400, 888/662-9555**

Casa Madrona Hotel & Spa [GF,F] 801 Bridgeway, Sausalito **415/332-0502, 800/288-0502** *overlooks SF skyline*

Larkspur Hotel [GF,SW,NS,WI] 160 Shoreline Hwy, Mill Valley **415/332-5700, 866/823-4669**

The Lodge at Tiburon [GF,SW,NS,WI] 1651 Tiburon Blvd, Tiburon **415/435-3133, 866/823-4669** *also restaurant & bar*

Waters Edge Hotel [GS,NS,WI,WC] 25 Main St, Tiburon **415/789-5999**

■RESTAURANTS

Guaymas 5 Main St (at ferry dock), Tiburon **415/435-6300** *gourmet Mexican, great views of the Bay*

ENTERTAINMENT & RECREATION

Black Sand Beach heading to San Francisco: take last exit before Golden Gate Bridge, go right on Outlook Rd, look for dirt parking lot, Golden Gate Nat'l Rec Area *popular nude beach, look for trail*

BOOKSTORES

Book Passage [★] 51 Tamal Vista Blvd, Corte Madera 415/927-0960, 800/999-7909 *9am-9pm, beloved independent which draws the biggest names to read*

The Depot Bookshop & Cafe 87 Throckmorton, Mill Valley 415/383-2665 *7am-7pm, independent, also cafe w/ patio*

RETAIL SHOPS

Cowgirl Creamery 80 4th St (at Tomales Bay Foods), Pt Reyes Station 415/663-9335 *10am-6pm Wed-Sun, handmade cheeses, picnic lunches to go*

Mendocino

see also Fort Bragg

ACCOMMODATIONS

Agate Cove Inn [GF,NS] 11201 N Lansing St 707/937-0551, 800/527-3111 *full brkfst, fireplaces*

The Alegria Quartet & Oceanfront Inn Cottages [GF,NS,WI] 44781 Main St 707/937-5150, 800/780-7905 *in the village, ocean views*

Blair House & Cottage [GF,NS] 45110 Little Lake St (at Ford St) 707/937-1800, 800/699-9296 *in former "home" of Jessica Fletcher of Murder, She Wrote*

Brewery Gulch Inn [GS,NS,WI] 9401 N Hwy 1 707/937-4752, 800/578-4454 *oceanview B&B made of eco-salvaged redwood*

Dennen's Victorian Farmhouse [GF,NS,WI] 7001 N Hwy 1 (at Hwy 128) 707/937-0697, 800/264-4723 *full brkfst*

Glendeven Inn [GF,NS,WI] 8205 N Hwy 1 (1.7 miles S of Mendocino), Little River 707/937-0083, 800/822-4536 *full brkfst & wine bar, farmhouse on the coast*

Hill House Inn [GS] 10701 Palette Dr 707/937-0554, 800/422-0554 *also restaurant*

The Inn at Schoolhouse Creek [GS,NS,WI,WC] 7051 N Hwy 1, Little River 707/937-5525, 800/731-5525 *B&B w/ cottages & suites, full brkfst, hot tub, fireplaces*

John Dougherty House [GF,NS,GO] 571 Ukiah St (at Kasten St) 707/937-5266, 800/486-2104

Little River Inn Resort & Spa [GF,F,NS,WI] 7901 N Hwy 1, Little River 707/937-5942, 888/466-5683 *resort w/ spectacular ocean views*

MacCallum House Inn [GS,NS,WI,WC] 45020 Albion St (at Lansing) 707/937-0289, 800/609-0492 *also restaurant & Grey Whale bar & cafe*

Orr Hot Springs [GF,R,SW,N] 13201 Orr Springs Rd, Ukiah 707/462-6277 *mineral hot springs, hostel-style cabins, private cottages & campsites, clothing-optional, no food provided*

Packard House [GF,NS,WI,GO] 45170 Little Lake St (at Kasten St) 707/937-2677, 888/453-2677 *full brkfst*

Sea Gull Inn [GF,NS,WI,WC] 44960 Albion St 707/937-5204, 888/937-5204

Stanford Inn by the Sea [GF,SW,NS,WI,WC] Coast Hwy 1 & Comptche-Ukiah Rd 707/937-5615, 800/331-8884 *full brkfst, fireplaces*

Stevenswood Resort & Spa [GS,WI,WC,GO] 8211 N Hwy 1 707/937-2810, 800/421-2810

RESTAURANTS

Cafe Beaujolais [R,WC] 961 Ukiah St 707/937-5614 *lunch & dinner*

ENTERTAINMENT & RECREATION

Tour Mendocino Wines [GO] 798 Maple Ave, Ukiah 707/849-2700 *wine tour company that offers custom built tours for our guests, in Mendocino, Sonoma & Napa*

■BOOKSTORES

Gallery Bookshop Main & Kasten St S
707/937-2665 *9:30am-6pm, independent*

Menlo Park

see Palo Alto

Mill Valley

see Marin County

Modesto

see also Stockton

■ACCOMMODATIONS

Rodeway Inn [GF,SW,WI] 936 McHenry
Ave (at Roseburg Ave) **209/523-7701**

■BARS

Brave Bull [MW,D,MR-L,E,K,S] 701 S 9th
St **209/529-6712** *7pm-2am, clsd
Mon, [K] Wed, Latin Night Th [DS,S]*

Tiki Lounge [MW,NH,D,MR,TG,K] 932
McHenry Ave (at Roseburg Ave)
209/577-9969 *5:30pm-2am*

■CAFES

Deva Cafe [F,E,WC] 1202 J St
209/572-3382 *7am-3pm, 8am-noon
Sun, patio*

Queen Bean 1126 14th St
209/521-8000 *7am-8pm, till 11pm
wknds*

■RESTAURANTS

Minnie's Restaurant 107 McHenry Ave
209/524-4621 *lunch Tue-Fri, dinner
Tue-Sun, clsd Mon, full bar*

■RETAIL SHOPS

Mystical Body 121 McHenry Ave
209/527-1163 *noon-8pm, clsd Sun-
Mon, body piercing*

■EROTICA

L'Amour Shoppe 1507-B 9th St
209/521-7987

Liberty Adult Book Store 1030
Kansas Ave **209/524-7603**

Suzie's Adult Superstores 115
McHenry Ave (at Needham)
209/529-5546 *8am-midnight, arcade*

■CRUISY AREAS

McHenry Ave Recreation Area
[AYOR] River Rd (N of Modesto) *go N on
McHenry to River Rd & turn left*

Tuolumne River Regional Park [AYOR]
S Santa Cruz Ave *parking lot & nearby
woods*

Monterey

■ACCOMMODATIONS

Asilomar Conference Grounds
[GF,F,SW,NS,WI] 800 Asilomar Blvd,
Pacific Grove **831/372-8016,
888/635-5310** *Arts & Crafts-style
buildings designed by Julia Morgan*

Gosby House Inn [GF,NS,WC] 643
Lighthouse Ave (at 18th), Pacific Grove
831/375-1287, 800/527-8828

Monterey Fireside Lodge [GF,NS,WI]
1131 10th St **831/373-4172,
800/722-2624**

The Monterey Hotel [GF,WI] 406
Alvarado St **831/375-3184,
800/966-6490**

■NIGHTCLUBS

Franco's Club [MW,D,MR-L] 10639
Merritt St, Castroville **831/633-2090**
10pm-2am Sat only

■RESTAURANTS

Old Fisherman's Grotto 39
Fisherman's Wharf #1 **831/375-4604**
11am-10pm

Tarpy's Roadhouse 2999 Monterey
Salinas Hwy (at Canyon Dr)
831/647-1444 *lunch & dinner, Sun
brunch, patios & gardens, full bar*

■ENTERTAINMENT & RECREATION

Ag Venture Tours [GF] PO Box 2634,
93942 **831/761-8463**

Monterey Bay Aquarium 886 Cannery
Row **831/648-4800** *come for the
otters, stay for the day*

Morro Bay

see San Luis Obispo

Mountain View

■ MEN'S SERVICES

➤MegaMates 650/210-4300 *Call to hook up with HOT local men. FREE to listen & respond to ads. Use FREE code DAMRON. MegaMates.com.*

Napa Valley

■ ACCOMMODATIONS

Beazley House B&B Inn [GF,NS,WI,WC] 1910 First St, Napa 707/257-1649, 800/559-1649 *historic inn, full brkfst, pet-friendly*

Brannan Cottage Inn [GF,NS,WI] 109 Wapoo Ave, Calistoga 707/942-4200 *B&B in Victorian cottage, full brkfst*

The Chablis Inn [GF,SW,NS,WC] 3360 Solano Ave (Redwood Rd at Hwy 29), Napa 707/257-1944, 800/443-3490 *stylish motel*

The Chanric Inn [GS,SW,NS,WI,GO] 1805 Foothill Blvd, Calistoga 707/942-4535, 877/281-3671 *full brkfst*

Chateau de Vie [GS,SW,WI,NS,GO] 3250 Hwy 128, Calistoga 707/942-6446, 877/558-2513 *chateau w/ gardens, full brkfst, hot tub*

The Ink House B&B [GF,NS,WI] 1575 St Helena Hwy S, St Helena 707/963-3890 *Italianate Victorian, full brkfst*

The Inn on First [GS,WI,GO] 1938 1st St, Napa 707/253-1331, 866/253-1331

Luxe Calistoga [GF,NS] 1139 Lincoln Ave (at Myrtle), Calistoga 707/942-9797 *on historic main street*

Meadowlark Country House [GS,SW,N,NS,WI,GO] 601 Petrified Forest Rd, Calistoga 707/942-5651, 800/942-5651 *clothing-optional mineral pool, sauna & hot tub*

Napa River Inn [GF,WI] 500 Main St (at 5th), Napa 707/251-8500, 877/251-8500 *luxury boutique hotel w/ spa, located in historic Napa Mill*

Yountville Inn [GF,SW,NS] 6462 Washington St, Yountville 707/944-5600, 888/366-8166 *alongside Hopper Creek, spa, private patios*

■ RESTAURANTS

Brannan's [GO] 1374 Lincoln Ave (at Washington), Calistoga 707/942-2233 *lunch & dinner, brunch wknds, full bar, live jazz wknds*

Cindy's Backstreet Kitchen 1327 Railroad Ave, St Helena 707/963-1200 *11:30am-9:30pm*

Flat Iron Grill [GO] 1440 Lincoln Ave (at Washington), Calistoga 707/942-1220 *dinner & seasonal wknd lunches*

Redd [R] 6480 Washington St, Yountville 707/944-2222 *lunch Mon-Sat, dinner nightly, Sun brunch, American*

SolBar 755 Silverado Trail (at the Solage Hotel), Calistoga 707/226-0850 *soul-food*

Tra Vigne [R] 1050 Charter Oak Ave (Hwy 29), St Helena 707/963-4444 *11:30am-10pm, also wine bar*

■ ENTERTAINMENT & RECREATION

Harbin Hot Springs [★GF] 18424 Harbin Springs Rd, Middletown 707/987-2477, 800/622-2477 (CA only) *retreat & workshop center, massage, some sundecks clothing-optional*

Lavender Hill Spa 1015 Foothill Blvd (at Lincoln Ave), Calistoga 707/942-4495, 800/528-4772 *9am-9pm*

■ BOOKSTORES

Copperfield's Books 1330 Lincoln Ave, Calistoga 707/942-1616 *9am-7pm, till 9pm Fri-Sat, 10am- 6pm Sun*

■ MEN'S SERVICES

➤MegaMates 707/266-2021 *Call to hook up with HOT local men. FREE to listen & respond to ads. Use FREE code DAMRON. MegaMates.com.*

California • USA

CRUISY AREAS

Red Rock Beach [AYOR] Stinson Beach *nude beach 1 mile S of Stinson Beach, off Hwy 1*

Vista Point [AYOR] Rte 12/121 bridge over Napa River, Napa *parking lot & nearby woods N of bridge on E side*

Nevada City

ACCOMMODATIONS

The Flume's End B&B [GS] 317 S Pine St 530/265-9665 *creekside Victorian, full brkfst*

CAFES

Java John's 306 Broad St 530/265-3653 *6:30am-5pm*

RESTAURANTS

Friar Tuck's [E,WC] 111 N Pine St (at Commercial) 530/265-9093 *dinner from 5pm, American/ fondue, full bar*

CRUISY AREAS

Hoyt's Crossing [AYOR] Hwy 49 *take to Hoyt Trail & follow till crosses Yuba River, near upstream end of Miner's Tunnel, nude sunbathing*

Newport Beach

see Orange County

Oakland

see East Bay

Oceanside

MEN'S SERVICES

►**MegaMates** 760/405-4005 *Call to hook up with HOT local men. FREE to listen & respond to ads. Use FREE code DAMRON. MegaMates.com.*

Orange County

includes Anaheim, Costa Mesa, Garden Grove, Huntington Beach, Irvine, Laguna Beach, Newport Beach, Santa Ana

INFO LINES & SERVICES

AA Gay/ Lesbian Laguna Beach 714/556-4555 (AA#) *call or visit www.oc-aa.org for meeting times*

The Center Orange County 1605 N Spurgeon St, Santa Ana 714/953-5428 *9am-5pm Mon-Fri or by appt or event*

ACCOMMODATIONS

Best Western Plus Plus Laguna Brisas Spa Hotel [GS,SW,NS,WI,WC] 1600 S Coast Hwy (at Bluebird), Laguna Beach 949/494-7272, 888/296-6834 *resort hotel*

Best Western Raffles Inn & Suites [GF,SW,WI] 2040 S Harbor Blvd, Anaheim 714/750-6100, 800/308 -5278 *walk to Disneyland*

Casa Laguna Inn & Spa [GF,SW,WI,NS,GO] 2510 S Coast Hwy, Laguna Beach 949/494-2996, 800/233-0449 *inn & cottages overlooking the Pacific*

Fairfield Inn Placentia [GF,SW,WI,WC] 710 W Kimberly Ave, Placentia 714/996-4410, 800/308-5286

Holiday Inn & Suites Anaheim [GF,SW,WI,WC] 1240 S Walnut, Anaheim 714/535-0300, 800/308-5312 *walk to Disneyland, also restaurant*

The Hotel Hanford [GF,SW,WI,WC] 3131 S Bristol St (at Baker St), Costa Mesa 714/557-3000, 877/426-3673

Laguna Cliffs Inn [GF,SW,NS,WI,WC] 475 N Coast Hwy, Laguna Beach 949/497-6645, 800/297-0007 *hot tub, easy beach access*

Laguna Cliffs Marriott Resort & Spa [GF,SW,WI] 25135 Park Lantern, Dana Point 949/661-5000, 800/533-9748

The St Regis Monarch Beach [GF,F,SW,NS,WI,WC] One Monarch Beach Resort, Dana Point 949/234-3200

Surf & Sand Resort [GF,F,SW,WI] 949/497-4477, 888/869-7569

BARS

Club Bounce [MW,D,E,K] 1460 S Coast Hwy, Laguna Beach 949/494-0056 *2pm-2am, upstairs dance bar Fri-Sat*

Frat House [★MW,D,MR,DS,S,YC,WC] 8112 Garden Grove Blvd (at Beach Blvd), Garden Grove 714/373-3728 *3pm-2am*

Ibiza Bar & Nightclub [GF,NH,D,WC] 18528 Beach Blvd **714/963-7744** *noon-2am, from 4pm Mon, from 2pm Sun*

Tin Lizzie Saloon [M,NH,WC] 752 St Clair (at Bristol), Costa Mesa **714/966-2029** *11:30am-2am*

Velvet Lounge [MW,D,F,K] 416 W 4th St, Santa Ana **714/232-8727** *11:30am-2am*

NIGHTCLUBS

Bravo [GS,D,A,MR-L,F,DS,S] 1490 S Anaheim Blvd, Anaheim **714/533-2291** *Latin music Wed & Fri-Sat, more gay Th & Sat night, goth & electronica Sun*

Club Lucky Presents [★M,D,E,S,18+,$] **949/551-2998** *check www.clubluck-ypresents.com for weekly parties in OC*

El Calor [GF,D,MR-L,DS] 2916 W Lincoln Ave (at E Beach Blvd), Anaheim **714/527-8873** *8pm-2am, Latin music, also restaurant*

Lions Den [MW,D,K,DS,YC] 719 W 19th St (at Pomona Ave), Costa Mesa **949/645-3830** *9pm-2am, clsd Mon, only gay Fri for Fiesta Latino*

CAFES

Avanti Cafe [F,BW] 259 E 17th St (at Westminster), Costa Mesa **949/548-2224** *11am-10pm, till 8pm Sun, brkfst, lunch & dinner, veggie & vegan*

The Koffee Klatch [WI] 1440 S Coast Hwy (btwn Mountain & Pacific Coast Hwy), Laguna Beach **949/376-6867** *7am-11pm, till midnight Fri-Sat*

Zinc Cafe [BW,WC] 350 Ocean Ave (at Broadway), Laguna Beach **949/494-6302** *7am-4pm, also market till 6pm, patio*

RESTAURANTS

Cafe Zoolu [BW,WC] 860 Glenneyre St, Laguna Beach **949/494-6825** *5pm-10pm, clsd Mon*

The Cottage 308 N Coast Hwy (at Aster), Laguna Beach **949/494-3023** *brkfst, lunch & dinner, homestyle cooking, some veggie*

Dizz's As Is 2794 S Coast Hwy (at Nyes Pl), Laguna Beach **949/494-5250** *open 5:30pm clsd Mon, full bar, patio*

Madison Square & Garden Cafe 320 N Coast Hwy, Laguna Beach **949/494-0137** *8am-3pm, clsd Tue, dog-friendly*

Nirvana Grille 303 Broadway St, Laguna Beach **949/497-0027** *dinner nightly, seasonal rooftop deck*

Sundried Tomato Cafe [GO] 361 Forest Ave #103, Laguna Beach **949/494-3312** *lunch & dinner, full bar*

Three Seventy Common 370 Glenneyre St, Laguna Beach **949/494-8686** *dinner only, upscale American bistro & martini bar*

ENTERTAINMENT & RECREATION

San Onofre State Beach on I-5, S of San Clemente (exit at Basilone Rd), Laguna Beach

West St Beach Laguna Beach

MEN'S SERVICES

▶**MegaMates** **714/594-0400** *Call to hook up with HOT local men. FREE to listen & respond to ads. Use FREE code DAMRON. MegaMates.com.*

EROTICA

A-Z Bookstore 8192 Garden Grove Blvd (at Beach), Garden Grove **714/534-9349**

Garden of Eden 12061 Garden Grove Blvd, Garden Grove **714/534-9805** *24hrs*

Pink Kitty [GO] 17955 Sky Park Cir, Ste A, Irvine **949/660-4990** *10am-6pm*

CRUISY AREAS

Calafia State Beach [AYOR] to the left, off the fwy (from Hwy 5 S), San Clemente

Eisenhower Park [AYOR] Orange

Fairview Park [AYOR] Costa Mesa

Fullerton Dam [AYOR] on Harbor Blvd, Fullerton area

Heisler Park [AYOR] N side of park, Laguna Beach *also take path to the ocean, then climb over the rocks to the right; beware cops (!)*

California • USA

Santiago Park [AYOR] off I-5 (at Main St), Santa Ana *parking lot & nearby woods, early evenings*

William Mason Regional Park [AYOR] Culver St & University Ave, Irvine

Oroville

■CAFES

Mug Shots [WI,GO] 2040 Montgomery St 530/538-8342 *6am-6pm, 8am-3pm Sun*

Oxnard

■MEN'S SERVICES

➤**MegaMates** 805/200-0299 *Call to hook up with HOT local men. FREE to listen & respond to ads. Use FREE code DAMRON. MegaMates.com.*

■CRUISY AREAS

Oxnard Shores Beach [AYOR] 5th St (past Harbor Blvd) *head to sand dunes*

Pacifica

■CRUISY AREAS

Grey Whale Cove Beach [AYOR] Hwy 1 *3 miles S of Pacifica on Devil's Slide, large parking lot on left, nude beach*

San Pedro Mountain Park [AYOR] Linda Mar & Odstaad Dr

Palm Springs

■INFO LINES & SERVICES

AA Gay/ Lesbian 760/324-4880 (AA#) *call for meeting schedule*

The Center 611 S Palm Canyon #201 760/416-7790 *programs & services, 12-step meetings*

■ACCOMMODATIONS

Ace Hotel Palm Springs [GS,SW,F,WI] 701 E Palm Canyon Dr 760/325-9900

All Worlds Resort [★M,SW,N,WI] 526 S Warm Sands Dr (at Ramon) 760/323-7505 *4 hot properties, rooms for all budgets*

The Bearfoot Inn [MO,B,N,WI] 888 N Indian Canyon Dr (at El Alameda) 888/871-2327

Caliente Tropics Resort [GS,F,SW,NS,WC,GO] 411 E Palm Canyon Dr 760/327-1391, 888/277-0999 *pet-friendly motor hotel, jacuzzi*

Calla Lily Inn [GF,SW,NS,WI] 350 S Belardo Rd (at Baristo) 760/323-3654, 888/888-5787 *"a tranquil oasis"*

Calmada Boutique Hotel [MW,SW,WI] 3569 Calmada Rd, Pioneertown 760/228-3141 *resort 30 min from Palm Springs*

Canyon Club Hotel [M,SW,N,WI,GO] 960 N Palm Canyon Dr (btwn Tachevah & El Alameda) 760/778-8042, 877/258-2887 *clothing-optional, kitchens, hot tub & patios*

Casa Ocotillo [★M,SW,NS,V,N,WI,GO] 240 E Ocotillo Ave 760/327-6110, 800/996-4108 *intimate & elegant resort-style accommodations in a 1934 Mexican hacienda—"the ultimate getaway for the discriminating traveler"*

➤**CCBC Resort Hotel** [★M,SW,N,WC,GO] 68300 Gay Resort Dr (btwn Melrose & Palo Verde), Cathedral City 760/324-1350, 800/472-0836 *mention Damron for 25% off (holidays not included, JocKuzzi Spa, steam room, saltwater pool, waterfall & cave, jail & dungeon*

Century Palm Springs [★M,SW,N,WI] 598 Grenfall Rd (btwn Ramon & Sunny Dunes) 760/323-9966, 800/475-5188 *'50s guesthouse w/ sleek retro style*

Chaps Inn [M,SW,WI,WC,GO] 312 E Camino Monte Vista 760/327-8222, 800/445-8916 *catering to leather & bears mostly*

Desert Eclipse Resort [M,SW,N,WI,WC,GO] 537 Grenfall Rd (at Ramon) 760/325-0655, 800/798-0655 *studios, hot tub*

Desert Paradise Resort Hotel [M,SW,N,NS,WI,GO] 615 Warm Sands Dr (at Parocela) 760/320-5650, 800/342-7635

Desert Star Hotel [GF,SW,NS,WI] 1611 S Calle Palo Fierro 800/399-1006 *boutique hotel of bungalows w/ full kitchens*

California • *USA*

The East Canyon Hotel & Spa
[★M,SW,NS,WI,GO] 288 E Camino Monte
Vista 760/320-1928, 877/324-6835
boutique hotel, day spa

El Mirasol Villas [M,SW,N,NS,WI,GO]
525 Warm Sands Dr (at Ramon)
760/327-5913, 800/327-2985
*newly renovated bungalows in a garden
setting, steam room & jacuzzi*

Escape [M,SW,N,NS,WI,GO] 641 E San
Lorenzo Rd (at Random)
760/325-5269, 800/621-6973 *hot
tub*

The Hacienda at Warm Sands
[★M,V,SW,N,NS,WI,WC,GO] 586 Warm
Sands Dr (at Parocela) 760/327-8111,
800/359-2007 *brkfst & catered lunch*

Helios Resort [★M,SW,N,NS,WI,WC,GO]
280 East Mel Ave 877/435-4677
resort, hot tub

The Horizon Hotel [GF,SW,WI] 1050 E
Palm Canyon Dr 760/323-1858,
800/377-7855

Hotel Zoso [GF,SW,WI] 150 S Indian
Canyon Dr 760/325-9676 *4-acre
resort, restaurant & bar, spa*

Hyatt Regency Suites Palm Springs
[GF,SW,WI] 285 N Palm Canyon Dr
760/322-9000, 800/554-9288 *also
restaurant & bar*

➤Inn Exile [★M,F,SW,N,WI,GO] 545
Warm Sands Dr (at Ramon)
760/327-6413, 800/962-0186
resort, hot tub, gym, steam

INNdulge Palm Springs
[★M,SW,N,NS,WI,GO] 601 Grenfall Rd (at
Parocela) **760/327-1408,
800/833-5675** *hot tub, Out &
About-rated 5 Palms*

La Dolce Vita Resort
[M,SW,N,NS,WI,WC,GO] 1491 S Via
Soledad (at Sonora & S Palm Canyon)
760/325-2686, 877/644-4111 *full
brkfst, jacuzzi*

Mojave [GF,SW,NS,WC] 73721 Shadow
Mountain Dr, Palm Desert
800/391-1104 *boutique hotel, hot tub,
spa services*

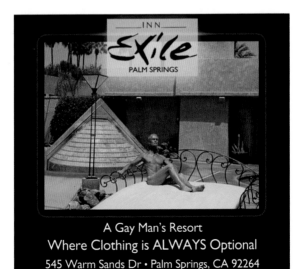

INN
Exile
PALM SPRINGS

A Gay Man's Resort
Where Clothing is ALWAYS Optional
545 Warm Sands Dr • Palm Springs, CA 92264
1-800-962-0186 • www.innexile.com

PALM SPRINGS · SINCE 1933
DESERT HOSPITALITY AT ITS BEST

28 UNIQUE GUESTROOMS

HEATED POOL/SPA & OUTDOOR MISTING SYSTEM

CONTINENTAL BREAKFAST & EVENING SOCIAL HOUR

WIRELESS INTERNET ACCESS

CLOTHING OPTIONAL

WEEKLY AND MIDWEEK DISCOUNTS

WARMSANDSVILLAS.COM
1 800 357 5695

California • USA

Pura Vida Resorts [M,SW,WI,WC,GO] 589 S Grenfall St (at Parocela) 760/832-6438, 877/786-0519

Rendezvous [GF,SW,WI] 1420 N Indian Canyon Dr 760/320-1178, 800/485-2808 '50s chic

Ruby Montana's Coral Sands Inn [GS,SW,WI,WC,GO] 210 W Stevens Rd (at N Palm Canyon) 760/325-4900, 866/820-8302 resort, kitschy 1950s chic

Santiago Resort [M,SW,N,NS,WI,GO] 650 San Lorenzo Rd (at Mesquite) 760/322-1300, 800/710-7729 brkfst & lunch included

Tortuga del Sol [M,SW,N,NS,WI,GO] 715 San Lorenzo 760/416-3111, 888/541-3777 resort, jacuzzi

Triangle Inn Palm Springs [★M,SW,N,GO] 555 San Lorenzo Rd (at Random Rd) 760/322-7993, 800/732-7555 hot tub, 2 sundecks

Villa Mykonos [MW,SW,WI] 67-590 Jones Rd (at Cree), Cathedral City 800/471-4753 timeshare condos & rental units

Villa Royale [★GF,SW] 1620 Indian Trail 760/327-2314, 800/245-2314 jacuzzi, also Europa restaurant

▶**Warm Sands Villas** [★M,SW,N,NS,WI,GO] 555 Warm Sands Dr (at Ramon) 760/323-3005, 800/357-5695 hot tub

■BARS

Azul [MW,NH,V] 369 N Palm Canyon Dr 760/325-5533 11am-close, from 10am Sun, also restaurant

The Barracks [M,L] 67-625 E Palm Canyon Dr (at Canyon Plaza), Cathedral City 760/321-9688 2pm-2am, cruisy

DiGS [MW,NH,CW,K] 36-737 Cathedral Canyon Dr (at 111), Cathedral City 760/321-0031 2pm-2am, from 10am Sun, patio

Georgie's Alibi [M,NH,F,V] 369 N Palm Canyon Dr 760/325-5533 11am-close, from 10am Sun

Hunter's Video Bar [★M,D,V] 302 E Arenas Rd (at Calle Encilia) 760/323-0700 10am-2am, go-go boys Fri, theme nights

Score [M,NH,V] 301 E Arenas Rd 760/327-0753 6am-2am

SpurLine [M,NH,K,V] 200 S Indian Canyon Dr (at Arenas) 760/778-4326 noon-2am, from 2pm Mon-Tue, lounge

Streetbar [★M,NH,E,K,WC] 224 E Arenas Rd (at Calle Encilia) 760/320-1266 10am-2am, patio

Tool Shed [M,NH,L] 600 E Sunny Dunes Rd (at Palm Canyon) 760/320-3299 10am-2am, from 8am wknds, cruise bar

Toucan's Tiki Lounge [MW,D,E,DS,S] 2100 N Palm Canyon Dr (at Via Escuela) 760/416-7584 noon-2am, [E] Mon, [DS] Wed & Sun, go-go dancers wknds

■CAFES

Palm Springs Koffi [★WI,GO] 515 N Palm Canyon Dr (at Alejo) 760/416-2244 5:30am-8pm

▓▓■RESTAURANTS

Amici 71380 Hwy 111, Rancho Mirage 760/341-0738 lunch & dinner, clsd Sun, Italian, patio, also full bar

Bangkok Five 70-026 Hwy 111, Rancho Mirage 760/770-9508 dinner nightly, Thai

Billy Reed's [WC] 1800 N Palm Canyon Dr (at Vista Chino) 760/325-1946 7am-9pm, till 10pm Fri-Sat

Blue Coyote Grill 445 N Palm Canyon Dr 760/327-1196 11am-10pm, till 11pm Fri-Sat, Southwestern

Bongo Johnny's 214 E Arenas Rd 760/866-1905 8am-10pm, till 11pm Fri-Sat, burgers & sandwiches

Cafe Palette [E,GO] 315 E Arenas 760/322-9264 11am-10pm, also delivers

The Chop House [R] 262 S Palm Canyon Dr 760/320-4500 from 5pm, steak

Copley's 621 N Palm Canyon Dr (btwn E Tamarisk Rd & E Granvia Valmonte) 760/327-9555 6pm-10pm, contemporary American, full bar

Davey's Hideaway [P] 292 E Palm Canyon Dr 760/320-4480 from 5pm, steak, seafood & pasta, patio, full bar

El Gallito [BW] 68820 Grove St (at Palm Canyon), Cathedral City 760/328-7794 *10am-9pm, home-made Mexican*

Hamburger Mary's 415 N Palm Canyon Dr 760/778-6279 *11am-close, full bar*

Jake's 664 N Palm Canyon Dr 760/327-4400 *lunch & dinner, wknd brunch, clsd Sun night & Mon, American bistro*

Las Casuelas 368 N Palm Canyon Dr (btwn Amado & Alejo) 760/325-3213 *11am-10pm, Mexican*

Mango Restaurant & Ultra Lounge 2080 Palm Canyon Dr 760/327-7676 *lunch & dinner, swank lounge*

Matchbox 155 S Palm Canyon Dr (in Mercado Plaza, 2nd level) 760/778-6000 *4pm-11pm, till 1am Fri-Sat pizza*

Nature's Health Food & Cafe 555 S Sunrise Way #301 760/323-9487 *8am-7pm, 9am-5pm wknds, vegan/vegetarian*

Peppers Thai Cuisine 396 N Palm Canyon Dr 760/322-1259 *lunch & dinner*

Pinocchio in the Desert 134 E Tahquitz Canyon Way 760/322-3776 *7:30am-2pm, outdoor seating*

Pomme Frite 256 S Palm Canyon Dr 760/778-3727 *dinner nightly, lunch wknds, clsd Tue, Belgian beer & French food*

Rick's Restaurant 1973 N Palm Canyon Dr 760/416-0090 *6am-3pm, Cuban/American*

Rio Azul 350 S Indian Canyon Dr 760/992-5641 *dinner nightly, open for lunch wknds, Mexican*

Rock Garden Cafe 777 S Palm Canyon Dr 760/327-8840 *8am-10pm, Greek, patio*

Shame on the Moon [R,WC] 69-950 Frank Sinatra Dr (at Hwy 111), Rancho Mirage 760/324-5515 *5pm-9:30pm, cont'l, full bar, patio*

Sherman's Deli & Bakery 401 E Tahquitz Canyon Wy 760/325-1199 *7am-9pm, kosher-style deli*

Spencer's Restaurant [R] 701 W Baristo Rd 760/327-3446 *9am-2:30pm & 5pm-10pm, Sun brunch, upscale contemporary*

Tootie's Texas Barbeque 68-703 Perez Rd, Cathedral City 760/202-6963 *11am-8pm, clsd Sun, the name says it all*

Towne Center Cafe 44491 Town Center Wy, Palm Desert 760/346-2120 *6am-8pm, Greek diner*

Trio 707 N Palm Canyon Dr 760/864-8746 *dinner nightly, also lounge*

Wang's in the Desert 424 S Indian Canyon Dr (at E Saturnino Rd) 760/325-9264 *from 5:30pm, Chinese, full bar*

Zin American Bistro 198 S Palm Canyon (at Arenas) 760/322-6300 *lunch & dinner*

▰ENTERTAINMENT & RECREATION

The Living Desert Zoo & Gardens [$] 47-900 Portola Ave, Palm Desert 760/346-5694 *9am-5pm (8am-1pm June-Aug), zoo & endangered species conservation center*

Ruddy's 1930s General Store Museum 221 S Palm Canyon Dr 760/327-2156 *10am-4pm Th-Sun, clsd summers, "the most you can spend is 95¢"*

▰BOOKSTORES

Q Trading Company 606 E Sunny Dunes Rd (at Indian Canyon) 760/416-7150, 800/756-2290 *10am-6pm, LGBT, also cards, gifts, videos*

▰RETAIL SHOPS

Bear Wear Etc 319 E Arenas Rd 760/323-8940 *11am-6pm, till 10pm Th-Sat, noon-6pm Sun, men's clothing, leather & resort wear*

GayMartUSA 305 E Arenas Rd (at Indian Canyon) 760/416-6436 *10am-midnight*

Mischief 210 E Arenas Rd (at Indian Canyon) 760/322-8555

Off Ramp Leathers 650 E Sunny Dunes Rd #3 760/778-2798 *custom motorcycle leathers*

California • USA

PUBLICATIONS

The Bottom Line/ Pulp
760/323-0552 *the desert's LGBT bar guide & classifieds*

Desert Daily Guide 760/320-3237 *LGBT weekly*

►**Odyssey Magazine** 323/874-8788 *dish on L.A. & Palm Springs' club scene*

GYMS & HEALTH CLUBS

Gold's Gym [GF] 4070 Airport Center Dr (at Ramon) 760/322-4653

WorkOUT Gym [GO] 2100 N Palm Canyon Way #C100 760/325-4600

►**World Gym Palm Springs** [M,WC,GO] 1751 N Sunrise Way (at Vista Chino) 760/327-7100 *5am-10pm, 6am-8pm wknds, day passes available, steam & sauna, club-quality sound system*

MEN'S SERVICES

►**MegaMates** 760/406-8222 *Call to hook up with HOT local men. FREE to listen & respond to ads. Use FREE code DAMRON. MegaMates.com.*

EROTICA

Gear Leather & Fetish 650 E Sunny Dunes #1 (at S Calle Palo Fierro) 760/322-3363 *noon-7pm, till midnight Fri-Sat, leather, fetish & piercing*

Hidden Joy Book Shop 68-424 Commercial (at Cathedral Canyon), Cathedral City 760/328-1694 *arcade*

Perez Images 68-366 Perez Rd, Cathedral City 760/321-1033 *24hrs*

CRUISY AREAS

Cahuilla Hills Park [AYOR] Palm Desert

Palmdale

see Lancaster

Palo Alto

ACCOMMODATIONS

Creekside Inn [GS,SW,NS,WI,WC] 3400 El Camino Real (at Page Mill Rd) 650/493-2411, 800/492-7335 *restaurant & lounge*

Hotel Avante [GS,SW,NS,WI] 860 E El Camino Real, Mountain View 650/940-1000, 800/538-1600

■ BOOKSTORES
Books Inc 855 El Camino Real 650/321-0600 *9am-8pm*

■ MEN'S SERVICES
➤**MegaMates** 650/223-0505 *Call to hook up with HOT local men. FREE to listen & respond to ads. Use FREE code DAMRON. MegaMates.com.*

Pasadena

■ BARS
The 35er [GS,NH,F] 626 /356-9315 *3pm-1am, from 12:30pm Fri-Sun*

The Boulevard Bar [M,NH,K,P] 3199 E Foothill Blvd (at Sierra Madre Villa) 626/356-9304 *4pm-2am, from 3pm Fri-Sun*

■ RESTAURANTS
Kings Row 20 E Colorado Blvd 626/793-3010 *4pm-midnight, till 2am wknds, gastropub*

Lanna Thai [WC] 400 S Arroyo Pkwy 626/577-6599 *11am-10:30pm, Thai, full bar*

■ ENTERTAINMENT & RECREATION
The Huntington 1151 Oxford Rd, San Marino 626/405-2100 *art collection, botanical gardens*

■ MEN'S SERVICES
➤**MegaMates** 626/720-2999 *Call to hook up with HOT local men. FREE to listen & respond to ads. Use FREE code DAMRON. MegaMates.com.*

■ EROTICA
Romantix Adult Superstore 45 E Colorado Blvd (at Raymond) 626/683-9468

Paso Robles

■ ACCOMMODATIONS
Asuncion Ridge Vineyards & Inn [GF,WI,GO] 805/461-0675

Hotel Cheval [GF,WI] 1021 Pine St 805/226-9995, 866/522-6999

■ ENTERTAINMENT & RECREATION
River Oaks Hot Springs Spa 800 Clubhouse Dr 805/238-4600 *9am-9pm, clsd Mon*

Petaluma

■ RESTAURANTS
Brixx [★E] 16 Kentucky St (in Lanmart Bldg) 707/766-8162 *dinner from 5pm, handmade pizzas, paninis*

■ BOOKSTORES
Copperfield's Books 140 Kentucky St (btwn Western & Washington, downtown) 707/762-0563 *9am-9pm, 10am-6pm Sun*

■ CRUISY AREAS
Lucchesi Park [AYOR]

Placerville

■ ACCOMMODATIONS
Albert Shafsky House B&B [GF,NS,WI,GO] 2942 Coloma St (at Spring St/ Hwy 49) 530/642-2776, 877/262-4667 *full brkfst, lesbian-owned*

Rancho Cicada Retreat [M,SW,N,GO] 10001 Bell Rd, Plymouth 209/245-4841, 877/553-9481 *riverside retreat, campsites, tents & cabins*

■ CRUISY AREAS
Lumsden Park [AYOR] Wiltse Rd *parking lots & woods*

Pleasant Hill

see East Bay

Point Reyes

■ CRUISY AREAS
Hagmire Pond [AYOR] Hwy 1 (at milepost 20.53) *nude sunbathing & woods; walk right across meadow & look for pond on the right, walk up hill to right of pond*

California • USA

Pomona

■BARS

Alibi East & Back Alley Bar [M,D,K]
225 S San Antonio Ave (at 2nd)
909/623–9422 *noon-2am, till 3am Fri, smoking patio*

The Hookup [MW,F,K,V,WC,GO] 1047 E
2nd St (at Pico) **909/620–2844** *noon-2am, beer bust Sun*

■NIGHTCLUBS

340 [MW,D,F,DS] 340 S Thomas St
909/865–9340 *7pm-4am, 6pm-2am Sun, clsd Mon-Th*

Redding

■NIGHTCLUBS

Club 501 [MW,D,YC] 1244 California St
(at Center & Division, enter rear)
530/243–7869 *6pm-2am, from noon Sun*

■EROTICA

Secrets, Hilltop Books 2131 Hilltop Dr
530/223–2675

■CRUISY AREAS

Clear Creek Rd [AYOR] 13 miles W of
Hwy 273 (4 miles W of old 99) *nude beach, summers*

Redlands

■CRUISY AREAS

Ford Park [AYOR] Ford St (at Parkford
Dr) *take I-10 E & exit at Ford St, turn right & first street you come to
(Prospect) turn right again; park begins where street stops; take sidewalk adjacent to tennis court that goes up hill*

Sylvan Park [AYOR] 601 N University St
(exit 10 E at University St) *make left when going under bridge; weekdays only*

Redondo Beach

see also Los Angeles—West LA &
Santa Monica

■ACCOMMODATIONS

Best Western Sunrise Hotel
[GF,SW,WI] 400 N Harbor Dr
310/376–0746, 800/334–7384 *hot tub, kids ok*

Palos Verdes Inn [GF,F,SW,NS,WI,WC]
1700 S Pacific Coast Hwy
310/316–4211, 800/421–9241
jacuzzi

Riverside

see also San Bernardino

■NIGHTCLUBS

Menagerie [MW,D,K,DS,WC] 3581
University Ave (at Orange)
951/788–8000 *4pm-2am*

VIP Nightclub & Restaurant
[MW,D,F,K,DS,18+] 3673 Merrill Ave (at
Magnolia) **951/784–2370** *5pm-2am*

■MEN'S SERVICES

▶**MegaMates** 951/530–9991 *Call to hook up with HOT local men. FREE to listen & respond to ads. Use FREE code DAMRON. MegaMates.com.*

■CRUISY AREAS

Fairmount Park [AYOR] off Rte 60 (at
Market St exit)

Riverton

■CRUISY AREAS

Bull Creek Rd [AYOR] off Hwy 50 *trail along river*

Russian River

includes Cazadero, Forestville,
Guerneville, Monte Rio, Occidental
& Sebastopol

■INFO LINES & SERVICES

AA Meetings in Sonoma County
707/544–1300 (AA#),
800/224–1300 *call for meeting times*

**Russian River Chamber of
Commerce & Visitors Center** 16209
First St (on the plaza), Guerneville
707/869–9000 *10am-5pm, till 4pm Sun*

▶**Sonoma County Tourism Bureau**
800/576–6662

■ACCOMMODATIONS

Applewood Inn [GF,F,SW,NS,WI,WC,GO]
13555 Hwy 116 (at Mays Canyon),
Guerneville **707/869–9093,
800/555–8509**

boon hotel & spa [GS,SW,NS,WI,GO] 14711 Armstrong Woods Rd, Guerneville **707/869-2721**

Fern Grove Cottages [GF,SW,NS,WI] 16650 River Rd, Guerneville **888/243-2674**

Guerneville Lodge [GS,NS,WI] 15905 River Rd (at Hwy 116), Guerneville **707/869-0102** *camping*

Highland Dell Resort [GF,F,WI] 21050 River Blvd (at Bohemian Hwy), Monte Rio **707/865-2300**

Highlands Resort [MW,SW,N] 14000 Woodland Dr, Guerneville **707/869-0333** *country retreat on 4 wooded acres, hot tub*

Inn at Occidental [GF,NS,WC] 3657 Church St, Occidental **707/874-1047, 800/522-6324**

➤**r3 Hotel** [MW,E,F,V,SW,N,WC,GO] 16390 4th St (at Mill), Guerneville **707/869-8399** *bar & restaurant*

Rio Villa Beach Resort [GF,NS,WI,GO] 20292 Hwy 116 (at Bohemian Hwy), Monte Rio **707/865-1143, 877/746-8455**

Village Inn & Restaurant [GS,NS,WC,WI,GO] 20822 River Blvd, Monte Rio **707/865-2304** *historic inn w/ restaurant & full bar*

West Sonoma Inn & Spa [GS,SW,NS,WI,WC] 14100 Brookside Ln (at Main St), Guerneville **707/869-2470, 800/551-1881** *6-acre resort*

The Woods Resort [★M,SW,N,NS,WI,WC,GO] 16484 4th St (at Mill St), Guerneville **707/869-0600, 877/887-9218** *cottages, guest cabins & suites*

■BARS

Mc T's Bullpen [GS,NH,K,E,WI,WC] 16246 First St (at Church), Guerneville **707/869-3377** *10am-2am, sports bar, patio*

Rainbow Cattle Co [★GS,NH] 16220 Main St (at Armstrong Woods Rd), Guerneville **707/869-0206** *6am-2am, DJ Bruce Sat*

Whitetail Winebar [GO] 16230 Main St, Guerneville **707/604-7449** *4pm-10pm, 3pm-11pm Fri-Sat, till 9pm Sun, clsd Tue*

■CAFES

Coffee Bazaar [★WI] 14045 Armstrong Woods Rd (at River Rd), Guerneville **707/869-9706** *6am-8pm, soups, salads & sandwiches*

Coffee Catz [E,WI,WC] 6761 Sebastopol Ave (at Hwy 116), Sebastopol **707/829-6600** *7am-6pm, till 8pm Th, till 10pm Wed & Fri-Sat*

Roasters Espresso Bar [E,WI] 6656 Front St (Hwy 116), Forestville **707/887-1632** *6am-6pm, from 7am Sat-Sun*

■RESTAURANTS

boon eat + drink [BW] 16248 Main St (at Hwy 116), Guerneville **707/869-0780** *lunch & dinner, clsd Tue-Wed, American*

Cape Fear Cafe [WC] 25191 Main St, Duncans Mills **707/865-9246** *9am-2:30pm & 5pm-9pm (clsd Wed & Th off-season)*

Chef Patrick [BW,WC] 16337 Main St (at Hwy 116), Guerneville **707/869-9161** *dinner nightly*

Farmhouse Inn Restaurant [BW] 7871 River Rd, Forestville **707/887-3300, 800/464-6642** *dinner, clsd Tue-Wed*

Garden Grill 17132 Hwy 116, Guerneville **707/869-3922** *8am-8pm, great burgers & sandwiches, some veggie, patio*

Main Street Station [C,BW] 16280 Main St (at Church St), Guerneville **707/869-0501** *11am-7pm, Italian restaurant & pizzeria*

River Inn Grill [★WC] 16141 Main St, Guerneville **707/869-0481** *8am-3pm, local favorite*

Tahoe Chinese Restaurant 6492 Mirabel Rd, Forestville **707/887-9772** *lunch & dinner Mon-Fri, dinner only Sat-Sun*

Underwood Bar & Bistro 9113 Graton Rd, Graton **707/823-7023** *lunch & dinner, clsd Mon*

Willow Wood Market Cafe [★] 9020 Graton Rd, Graton **707/823-0233** *8am-9pm, from 9am Sat, brunch 9am-3pm Sun*

■ENTERTAINMENT & RECREATION

The Nude Beach [AYOR] on Russian River at Wohler Bridge, Guerneville

Pegasus Theater Co [WC] **707/583-2343** *classic to contemporary plays*

■BOOKSTORES

River Reader [WC] 16355 Main St (at Mill), Guerneville **707/869-2240** *10am-6pm, extended summer hours*

■RETAIL SHOPS

Bruce's Barber Shop 16190 Main St #C (in the Russian River Realty Bldg), Guerneville *11am-5:30pm, Tue till 5pm, Fri till 6pm, 9am-2pm Sat, clsd Sun-Mon*

Sonoma Nesting Company [GO] 16151 Main St, Guerneville **707/869-3434** *antiques & home decorating*

Up the River 16212 Main St (at Armstrong Woods Rd), Guerneville **707/869-3167** *cards, gifts, T-shirts & more*

■CRUISY AREAS

Steelhead Beach Regional Park [AYOR] 9000 River Rd, Forestville *beach & woods*

Sacramento

■INFO LINES & SERVICES

Gay AA **916/454-1100**

Sacramento Gay & Lesbian Center 1927 L St **916/442-0185** *noon-6pm Mon-Fri*

■ACCOMMODATIONS

Citizen Hotel [GF,NS,WI,WC] 926 J Street **916/447-2700**

Governors Inn [GF,SW,NS,WI] 210 Richards Blvd (at I-5) **916/448-7224, 800/999-6689** *internet, hot tub, exercise room*

The Greens Hotel [GS,SW,WI,WC] 1700 Del Paso Blvd (at Arden) **707/365-5905**

Inn & Spa at Parkside [GS,WI,WC,GO] 2116 6th St (at U St) **916/658-1818, 800/995-7275** *full brkfst, jacuzzi, also full-service spa*

■BARS

The Bolt [M,NH,B,L] 2560 Boxwood St (at El Camino) **916/649-8420** *5pm-2am, from 2pm wknds, patio, volleyball in summer*

The Depot [★M,NH,TG,E,S,V,WC] 2001 K St **916/441-6823** *4pm-2am, till 4am Fri-Sat, from 2pm wknds*

Dive Bar [★GS] 1016 K St **916/737-5999** *4pm-2am, super cool water tank*

The Mercantile Saloon [★M,NH,WC] 1928 L St (at 20th St) **916/447-0792** *10am-2am*

■NIGHTCLUBS

Badlands [M,D,S,V] 2003 K St **916/448-8790** *6pm-2am, from 2pm Fri-Sat, from 4pm Sun*

Club 21 [GS,D,F,MR,V,GO,WC,$] 1119 21st St (btwn K & L Sts) **916/443-1537** *Mexican restaurant by day, Club Bojangles gay night Wed & Sun (18+)*

Club Papi Sacramento [M,D,MR-L] 2000 K St (at Faces) **415/675-9763** *monthly party from 9pm-3am, call for dates*

➤**Faces** [★MW,D,K] 2000 K St (at 20th St) **916/448-7798** *4pm-2am, 3 bars w/ various theme nights, patio*

Head Hunters Video Lounge & Grill [MW,E,F] 1930 K St (at 20th Street) **916/492-2922** *dinner Tue-Sun, Sun brunch, bar open till 2am*

■CAFES

Mondo Bizarro [E,WI] 1827 I St **916/443-6133** *7am-7pm, from 8am Sun*

N Street Cafe [WI,WC] 2022 N Street **916/491-4008** *6am-6pm, 8am-3pm Sat-Sun*

Largest Gay Bar In Northern California!

Celebrating Over 27 Years In Business!

15 Bar Stations

3 Dance Floors

4 Smoking Patios

State Of The Art Lighting & Sound

VIP Mezzanine With Bottle Service

And Yes We Have A Pool!

California • *USA*

■RESTAURANTS

Chops 1117 11th St (at L St, across from State Capitol Building) **916/447-8900** *lunch Mon-Fri, dinner nightly, steak & seafood, full bar*

Ernesto's 1901 16th St **916/441-5850** *Mexican*

Hamburger Patties [K,DS,WC] 1630 J St (at 17th) **916/441-4340** *11am-10pm, from 10am wknds, full bar*

Hot Rod's Burgers 2007 K St **916/443-7637** *11am-2am, till 3am Fri-Sat*

Ink Eats & Drinks 2730 N St (at 28th) **916/456-2800** *lunch, dinner, late-night brkfst, wknd brunch, full bar, DJ wknds*

Jack's Urban Eats 1230 20th St (at Capitol Ave) **916/444-0307** *11am-8pm, till 9pm Wed-Sat*

Paesanos 1806 Capitol Ave (at 18th) **916/447-8646** *11:30am-9:30pm, from noon wknds, Italian, funky artwork, patio, full bar; also 8519 Bond Rd, 916/690-8646*

Pizza Rock [★] 1020 K St **916/737-5777** *11am-10pm, till midnight Wed-Th, till 3am Fri-Sat*

Rick's Dessert Diner 2322 K St (btwn 23rd & 24th) **916/444-0969** *10am-midnight, till 1am wknds, from noon Sun*

Thai Palace 3262 J St (33rd St) **916/447-5353** *lunch & dinner*

Zócalo 1801 Capitol Ave (at 18th Ave) **916/441-0303** *11am-10pm, Mexican, full bar*

■ENTERTAINMENT & RECREATION

Lavender Library, Archives & Cultural Exchange of Sacramento 1414 21st St **916/492-0558** *4:30pm-8pm Th-Fri, noon-6pm wknds, clsd Mon-Wed*

■PUBLICATIONS

➤**Gloss Magazine** 510/451-2090 *CA arts/ entertainment magazine, bi-weekly*

Outword Magazine 916/329-9280 *statewide LGBT newspaper*

■MEN'S CLUBS

Folsom Park Sauna [MO,$] 9261 Folsom Blvd #400 **916/363-1247** *10am-10pm*

The Sacs4men Men's Club near Watt & Elkhorn, Rio Linda **916/879-4611, 916/410-6550 (info line)** *call for info & location; also overnight room rentals*

■MEN'S SERVICES

➤**MegaMates** 916/340-1414 *Call to hook up with HOT local men. FREE to listen & respond to ads. Use FREE code DAMRON. MegaMates.com.*

■EROTICA

G Spot [★GO] 2009 K St (at 20th) **916/441-3200**

Goldie's I 201 N 12th St (at North B St) **916/447-5860**

Kiss-N-Tell 4201 Sunrise Blvd (at Fair Oaks) **916/966-5477** *clean, well-lighted erotica store; also 2401 Arden Wy, 916/920-5477*

L'Amour Shoppe 2531 Broadway (at 26th) **916/736-3467**

■CRUISY AREAS

American River Access [AYOR] off La Rivera Dr, near Howe Ave & Watt Ave

Beach & levee on American River [AYOR] at end of N 10th St, off Richards Blvd

San Bernardino

see also Riverside

■INFO LINES & SERVICES

AA Gay/ Lesbian 897 Via Lata, Colton **909/825-4700** *call or visit www.inlandempireaa.org for times*

■MEN'S SERVICES

➤**MegaMates** 909/663-0300 *Call to hook up with HOT local men. FREE to listen & respond to ads. Use FREE code DAMRON. MegaMates.com.*

■EROTICA

Bearfacts Book Store 1434 E Baseline St **909/885-9176** *24hrs, arcade*

Le Sex Shoppe 304 W Highland Ave **909/881-3583** *arcade*

CRUISY AREAS

Cajon Pass [AYOR] Cajon Pass (off Rte 138, W of I-15, in San Bernardino Nat'l Forest), Cajon Junction *parking lot & nearby woods*

San Clemente

see Orange County

San Diego

INFO LINES & SERVICES

Live & Let Live Alano Club 1730 Monroe Ave 619/298-8008 *10:30am-10pm, from 8:30am wknds, see www.lllac.org for meetings*

San Diego LGBT Community Center 3909 Centre St (at University) 619/692-2077 *9am-10pm, till 7pm Sat, clsd Sun*

ACCOMMODATIONS

Balboa Park Inn [GF,NS] 3402 Park Blvd (at Upas) 619/298-0823, 800/938-8181

Beach Area B&B/ Elsbree House [GF,NS] 5054 Narragansett Ave (at Sunset Cliffs Blvd) 619/226-4133, 800/607-4133 *B&B & 3-bdrm condo near beach*

The Bristol Hotel [GS,WI,WC] 1055 First Ave 619/232-6141, 800/662-4477 *restaurant & bar, great collection of pop art*

Handlery Hotel & Resort [GF,SW,NS,WI,WC] 950 Hotel Circle N 619/298-0511, 800/676-6567

Inn at the Park [GF,WI] 525 Spruce St (btwn 5th & 6th) 619/291-0999, 877/499-7163 *1926 hotel, bar [P] & 2 restaurants, popular Fri happy hour*

Keating House [GF,NS,WI,GO] 2331 2nd Ave (at Juniper) 619/239-8585, 800/995-8644 *Victorian B&B, full brkfst*

Kings Inn Hotel [GS,SW,WI,NS,WC] 1333 Hotel Circle S (Bachman St) 619/297-2231, 800/785-4647

Lafayette Hotel & Suites [GF,F,SW,NS,WI,WC] 2223 El Cajon Blvd (btwn Louisiana & Mississippi) 619/296-2101, 800/468-3531 *also restaurant*

Mike's Place [M,WI,GO] 1252 Lincoln Ave (at Washington St) 619/992-7466 *private guest cottage*

Ocean Inn [GF,WI,WC] 1444 N Hwy 101, Encinitas 760/436-1988, 800/546-1598 *30 min from downtown San Diego*

The Sofia Hotel [GS,WC] 150 W Broadway 619/234-9200, 800/826-0009

Sunburst Court Inn [GS,NS,WI,GO] 4086 Alabama St (at Polk) 619/294-9665, 866/217-5490 *all-suite inn*

W San Diego [GF,SW,NS,WI,WC] 421 W B St 619/398-3100, 888/625-5144 *rooftop bar, also restaurant*

BARS

Bourbon Street [★M,E,V] 4612 Park Blvd (at Adams) 619/291-4043 *4pm-2am, front bar, lounge & patio*

The Brass Rail [MW,D,WC] 3796 5th Ave (at Robinson) 619/298-2233 *7pm-2am, from 2pm Fri-Sun, clsd Tue, theme nights, Latin night Sat*

The Caliph [M,E,K,P,OC,WC] 3100 5th Ave (at Redwood) 619/298-9495 *11am-2am, from noon wknds, piano bar*

Cheers [M,NH] 1839 Adams Ave (at Park) 619/298-3269 *11am-2am, patio*

El Camino [GF,D,F,YC] 2400 India St (at Kalmia, in Little Italy) 619/685-3881 *dinner nightly, Sun brunch, kitschy Mexican, live music, full bar*

Fiesta Cantina [F] 142 University Ave 619/298-2500 *noon-2am, from 10am wknds*

The Flame [★GS,D] 3780 Park Blvd (at University) 619/795-8578 *clsd Mon-Wed, goth Sat, patio*

Flicks [★M,K,V,YC] 1017 University Ave (at 10th Ave) 619/297-2056 *2pm-2am*

Gossip Grill [W,F,WC,GO] 1440 University Ave (at Normal) 619/260-8023 *2pm-close, also restaurant*

The Hole [M,NH,L] 2820 Lytton St (at Rosecrans) 619/226-9019 *4pm-close, from noon wknds, tropical patio*

California • *USA*

Kickers [★MW,D,CW,WC] 308 University Ave (at 3rd Ave, at Urban Mo's) 619/491-0400 *Th only, also dance lessons*

The Loft [M,NH,WC] 3610 5th Ave (at Brookes) 619/296-6407 *11am-2am*

No 1 Fifth Ave (no sign) [M,NH,V] 3845 5th Ave (at University) 619/299-1911 *noon-2am, patio*

Pecs [M,NH,B,L,WC] 2046 University Ave (at Alabama) 619/296-0889 *noon-2am, from 10am Sun, patio, cruisy*

Redwing Bar & Grill [M,NH] 4012 30th St (at Lincoln, North Park) 619/281-8700 *11am-2am, patio*

San Diego Eagle [M,NH,L,WC] 3040 North Park Wy (at 30th) 619/295-8072 *4pm-2am, from 2pm Fri-Sun*

SRO Lounge [M,NH,TG,OC] 1807 5th Ave (btwn Elm & Fir) 619/232-1886 *10am-2am, cocktail lounge*

■NIGHTCLUBS

Bear Night [M,D,B] 3811 Park Blvd (btwn University & Richmond, at Numbers) *9pm 1st Sat only*

Eden [GS,D] 1202 University (at Vermont) 619/269-3336 *also lounge & restaurant*

Numbers [★MW,D,S,V,WC] 3811 Park Blvd (at University) 619/294-7583 *patio, bear night 1st Sat*

Rich's [★M,D,V,S,YC] 1051 University Ave (at Vermont) 619/295-2195 *open Wed-Sun, theme nights, L.L. Bear [B,L] 3rd Sat*

■CAFES

Babycakes [BW] 3766 5th Ave (at Robinson) 619/296-4173 *9am-11pm, till midnight Fri-Sat, patio*

The Big Kitchen [WC] 3003 Grape St (at 30th) 619/234-5789 *8am-2pm*

Claire de Lune 2906 University Ave 619/688-9845 *6am-10pm, till midnight Fri-Sat*

Espresso Roma UCSD Price Center #76 (at Voight), La Jolla 858/450-2141 *7am-10pm, 8am-4pm wknds*

Extraordinary Desserts 2929 5th Ave 619/294-2132 *also store in Little Italy: 1430 Union, 619/249-7001, the name says it all*

Gelato Vero [WI] 3753 India St 619/295-9269 *7am-midnight, great desserts (yes, the gelato is truly delicious) & coffee*

Twiggs 4590 Park Blvd (at Madison Ave, University Heights) 619/296-0616 *7am-11pm*

Urban Grind [★GO,WI] 3797 Park Blvd (at University) 619/299-4763 *7am-10pm*

■RESTAURANTS

Adams Avenue Grill [BW,WC,GO] 2201 Adams Ave (at Mississippi) 619/298-8440 *brkfst, lunch & dinner, bistro*

Arrivederci 3845 4th Ave 619/299-6282 *lunch & dinner*

Bai Yook Thai 1260 University Ave 619/296-2700 *lunch & dinner, dinner only Sun*

Baja Betty's [★MW,WC] 1421 University Ave (at Normal St) 619/269-8510 *11am-midnight, till 1am Fri-Sat, Mexican, patio*

Bamboo Lounge 1475 University Ave (at Herbert St) 619/291-8221 *4pm-midnight, till 1am wknds, sushi*

Bangkok Thai Bistro 540 University Ave 619/269-9209 *11am-10pm, till 11pm Fri-Sat*

Brian's American Eatery [B,BW] 1451 Washington St 619/296-8268 *6:30am-10pm, 24hrs Fri-Sat*

Cafe 222 222 Island Ave 619/236-9902 *7am-2pm, great brkfst*

Celadon 3671 5th Ave (at Pennsylvania) 619/297-8424 *lunch & dinner, upscale Thai*

Cody's La Jolla [E,R] 8030 Girard Ave (at Coast Blvd S), La Jolla 858/459-0040 *brkfst & lunch daily, contemporary California cuisine, live music*

The Cottage 7702 Fay (at Klein), La Jolla 858/454-8409 *7:30am-3pm, dinner June-Sept*

Crazee Burger [BW] 4201 30th St (at Howard) 619/282-6044 *11am-9pm, till 11pm Fri-Sat*

Crest Cafe [WC] 425 Robinson (btwn 4th & 5th) 619/295-2510 *7am-midnight*

Hash House A Go Go 3628 5th Ave 619/298-4646 *brkfst, lunch & dinner, clsd Mon, great brkfst*

Hillcrest Brewing Company [MW] 1458 University Ave 619/491-0400 *first gay brewery in California*

Inn at the Park [★M] 525 Spruce St (btwn 5th & 6th) 619/296-0057 *dinner nightly, also bar* [P]

Jimmy Carter's Mexican Cafe 3172 5th Ave (at Spruce) 619/295-2070 *7am-9pm*

Kous Kous 3940 4th Ave, Ste 110 (beneath Martinis on Fourth) 619/295-5560 *5pm-11pm, Moroccan*

Lips [DS] 3036 El Cajon Blvd 619/295-7900 *5pm-close, Sun gospel brunch, clsd Mon, "the ultimate in drag dining," Bitchy Bingo Wed, celeb impersonation Th, DJ wknds*

Luna Grill 350 University 619/296-5862 *11am-10pm, Near East & Mediterranean, plenty veggie/ vegan*

Martinis Above Fourth [C,P,GO] 3940 4th Ave, Ste 200 (btwn Washington & University) 619/400-4500 *open 5pm, from 4pm Fri-Sat, clsd Sun*

The Mission 3795 Mission Blvd (at San Jose), Mission Beach 858/488-9060 *7am-3pm*

Ono Sushi 1236 University Ave (at Richmond) 619/298-0616 *lunch wknds, dinner nightly*

The Prado 1549 El Prado (in Balboa Park) 619/557-9441 *lunch & dinner, Latin/ Italian fusion*

The Range 1263 University Ave 619/269-1222 *lunch & dinner, brkfst wknds*

Roberto's 3202 Mission Blvd 858/488-1610 *open 24hrs, the best rolled tacos & guacamole, multiple locations*

Rudford's [★] 2900 El Cajon Blvd (at Kansas St) 619/282-8423 *24hrs, homestyle cooking*

Saigon on Fifth 3900 5th Ave, Ste 120 619/220-8828 *11am-3am, Vietnamese*

South Park Abbey [E] 1946 Fern St (at Grape St) 619/696-0096 *3pm-1:30am, from 9am Sat-Sun, till midnight Sun-Mon, clsd Tue*

Terra 3900 block of Vermont St (at 10th Ave) 619/293-7088 *lunch & dinner, clsd for dinner*

Urban Mo's [★MW,D,E,WC] 308 University Ave (at 3rd) 619/491-0400 *9am-2am, 10am-midnight Sun, 3 full bars (Club Mo's), patio*

Veg N Out 3442 30th St (North Park) 619/546-8411 *11am-9pm, from noon Sun, vegetarian/ vegan*

Waffle Spot 1333 Hotel Circle S (at King's Inn) 619/297-2231 *7am-2pm*

West Coast Tavern 2895 University Ave 619/295-1688 *lunch & dinner, upscale, also lounge*

■ ENTERTAINMENT & RECREATION

Diversionary Theatre 4545 Park Blvd #101 (at Madison) 619/220-0097 (box office #), 619/220-6830 *LGBT theater*

Ocean Beach I-8 West to Sunset Cliffs Blvd *very dog-friendly*

Torrey Pines Beach State Park ("Blacks Beach") *popular nude beach*

■ BOOKSTORES

Traveler's Depot 1655 Garnet Ave (btwn Jewell & Ingraham) 858/483-1421 *10am-6pm, 11am-5pm wknds, guides, maps & more*

■ RETAIL SHOPS

Auntie Helen's [WC] 4028 30th St (at Lincoln) 619/584-8438 *10am-6pm, 11am-5pm Sun-Mon, thrift shop benefits PWAs*

Babette Schwartz [GO] 421 University Ave (at 5th Ave) 619/220-7048 *11am-9pm, till 5pm Sun, campy novelties & gifts*

VULCAN

-STEAM AND SAUNA-

steam room
sauna
whirlpool
patio sundeck
private rooms
community rooms
bunkroom
lockers
4 tv lounges
open 24 hours

619.238.1980
805 W. Cedar St.
San Diego, CA 92101

downtown
across from the trolley

Flesh Skin Grafix 1155 Palm Ave, Imperial Beach **619/424-8983** *tattoos & piercing*

House Boi [GO] 1435 University Ave **619/298-5200** *noon-8pm, 11am-7pm Sun, clsd Mon, clothing, house furnishings*

Mankind 3425 5th Ave (at Upas St) **619/497-1970** *11am-10pm, noon-6pm Sun*

Obelisk the Bookstore [★WC] 1029 University Ave (at 10th) **619/297-4171** *10am-9pm, till 10pm wknds, LGBT*

▬PUBLICATIONS

Blade California 562/314-7674

The Bottomline 3314 4th Ave **619/291-6690** *bi-weekly, news, entertainment & listings, covers San Diego & Palm Springs*

LGBT Weekly 1850 5th Ave **619/450-4288**

San Diego PIX 1010 University Ave **877/727-5446**

▬GYMS & HEALTH CLUBS

Urbanbody Gym 3148 University Ave (at Iowa St, North Park) **619/795-9712**

▬MEN'S CLUBS

Club San Diego [★PC] 3955 4th Ave (btwn Washington & University) **619/295-0850** *24hrs*

▶**Vulcan Steam & Sauna** [★PC] 805 W Cedar St (at Pacific Hwy) **619/238-1980** *24hrs*

▬MEN'S SERVICES

▶**MegaMates** **619/308-0800** *Call to hook up with HOT local men. FREE to listen & respond to ads. Use FREE code DAMRON. MegaMates.com.*

▬EROTICA

Adult Emporium [GO] 3576 Main St (at San Diego) **619/239-1878** *24hrs*

Barnett Ave Adult Superstore 3610 Barnett Ave (near intersection of Barnett & Jessop Ln) **619/224-0187** *24hrs*

The Crypt 3847 Park Blvd (at University) **619/692-9499**

Gemini Adult Books [WC] 5265 University Ave (at 52nd) 619/287-1402

Pleasures & Treasures Adult/Leather Shop [GO] 2228 University Ave (at Mississippi St) **619/822-4280** *clsd Tue*

Romantix Adult Superstore 1407 University Ave (at Richmond) **619/299-7186**

▬CRUISY AREAS

Please Note: All cruisy areas for San Diego have been removed because the SDPD aggressively polices these areas.

SAN FRANCISCO

San Francisco is divided into 7 geographical areas:
SF—Overview
SF—Castro & Noe Valley
SF—South of Market
SF—Polk Street Area
SF—Downtown & North Beach
SF—Mission District
SF—Haight, Fillmore, Hayes Valley

SF—Overview

▬INFO LINES & SERVICES

AA Gay/ Lesbian 1821 Sacramento St 415/674-1821 *check www.aasf.org for meeting times*

The Center for Sex & Culture 1349 Mission St (btwn 10th & 11th St) 415/902-2071 *very queer-friendly classes, workshops, gatherings, events, readings & more*

Crystal Meth Anonymous 415/835-4747

GLBT Hotline of San Francisco 415/355-0999 *5pm-9pm Mon-Fri, peer-counseling, info*

LYRIC (Lavender Youth Recreation/Information Center) 127 Collingwood (btwn 18th & 19th) 415/703-6150 *peer-run support line for LGBT youth under 24*

Magnet [★] 4122 18th St 415/581-1600 *center for gay men's health*

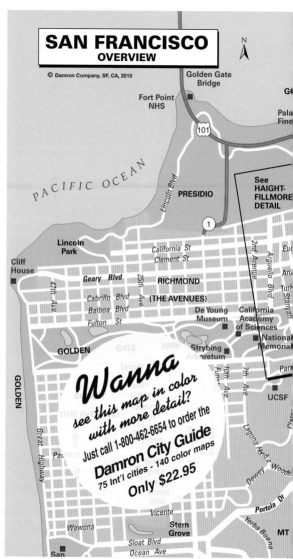

SAN FRANCISCO
OVERVIEW

© Damron Company, SF, CA, 2010

N

Golden Gate
Bridge

Fort Point
NHS

Pala
Fine

G

101

PACIFIC OCEAN

Lincoln Blvd

PRESIDIO

1

See
HAIGHT-
FILLMORE
DETAIL

Lincoln
Park

California St

Clement St

2nd Avenue

Arguello Blvd

Euc

Cliff
House

Geary Blvd

25th Ave

RICHMOND
(THE AVENUES)

47th Ave

Cabrillo Blvd

Balboa Blvd

Fulton St

De Young
Museum

California
Academy
of Sciences

An

Turk

Stanyan

National
Memorial

GOLDEN

GATE

PARK

Strybing
Arboretum

10th Ave

7th Ave

Par

UCSF

GOLDEN

Great Highway

Wanna
*see this map in color
with more detail?*
Just call 1-800-462-6654 to order the
Damron City Guide
75 Int'l cities - 140 color maps
Only $22.95

Laguna Honda

Dewey Woods

Portola Dr

Yerba Buena

Vicente

Wawona

Stern
Grove

Sloat Blvd

Ocean Ave

MT

San

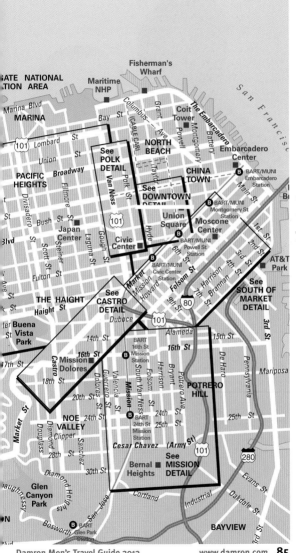

AFTER
SHOCK

the official after hours of folsom street fair™

friscodisco
events

in san francisco

California • USA

The San Francisco LGBT Community
Center 1800 Market St (at Octavia)
415/865-5555 *noon-10pm, from 9am Sat, clsd Sun, cybercenter, cafe, classes & more*

■ NIGHTCLUBS

➤**Frisco Disco Events** [★M,D] *gay dance events in San Francisco*

Gus Presents [★M,D] *popular parties in San Francisco*

Trannyshack [★M,D,TG,E,GO] *occasional events, check trannyshack.com for info*

■ RESTAURANTS

Beach Chalet Brewery & Restaurant [E] 1000 Great Hwy (at Fulton St)
415/386-8439

■ ENTERTAINMENT & RECREATION

Baker Beach Lincoln Blvd at Bowley, in the Presidio *popular nude beach*

Black Sand Beach first exit past Golden Gate Bridge (Alexander) (go left under fwy, right on Outlook Rd, look for dirt parking lot), Golden Gate Nat'l Rec Area *popular nude beach, look for trail*

Castro Theatre 429 Castro (at Market)
415/621-6120 *art house cinema, many LGBT & cult classics, live organ evenings*

Cruisin' the Castro Tours tour meets at the rainbow flag at Harvey Milk Plaza (corner of Castro & Market)
415/255-1821 *"a TOP city tour & walking w/ pride since 1989! Diverse, fun, informative & NO hills!"*

Femina Potens 415/864-1558 *nonprofit art & performance promoting women & transfolk in the arts*

➤**Frameline** [★] **415/703-8650** *LGBT media arts foundation that sponsors annual SF Int'l LGBT Film Festival in June*

Golden Gate Bridge Beach/ Marshall Beach, aka "Nasty Boy Beach" [M,N,AYOR] Lincoln Blvd at Langdon Ct, in the Presidio *can get very crowded!*

The Intersection for the Arts [GF] 925 Mission St #109 415/626-2787 *San Francisco's oldest alternative arts space (since 1965!) w/ plays, art exhibitions, live jazz, literary series, performance art & much more*

Local Tastes of the City Tours [GO]
415/665-0480, 888/358-8687 *explore history & culture of local neighborhoods as "we eat our way through San Francisco"*

The Marsh 1062 Valencia (at 22nd St)
415/826-5750, 415/282-3055 *queer-positive theater*

➤**National AIDS Memorial Grove** [WC] Golden Gate Park (on corner of Middle Drive East & Bowling Green Dr)
415/765-0497, 888/294-7683 *guided tours available 9am-noon every 3rd Sat*

New Conservatory Theatre Center 25 Van Ness Ave, Lower Lobby (at Market) **415/861-8972** *LGBT theater in historic Masonic Bldg*

QComedy Gay Comedy Showcase [★MW,$] 415/533-9133 *see www.qcomedy.com for location*

San Francisco Pride 1800 Market St, PMB #Q31 94102 415/864-3733

Steve Silver's Beach Blanket Babylon [★] 678 Beach Blanket Babylon Ave (formerly Green St) (btwn Powell & Columbus, in Club Fugazi)
415/421-4222 *the USA's longest running musical revue & wigs that must be seen to be believed; also restaurant & full bar*

Thanks Babs, the Day Tripper [GO] 702/370-6961

Theatre Rhinoceros 1360 Mission St #200 800/838-3006, 415/552-4100 *LGBT theater*

Victorian Home Walks [GO]
415/252-9485 *custom-tailored walking tours w/ San Francisco resident*

Yerba Buena Center for the Arts [GF] 701 Mission St (at 3rd St)
415/978-2787 (box office) *annual season includes wide variety of contemporary dance, theater & music, also film theater & gallery*

California • *USA*

■PUBLICATIONS

BAR (Bay Area Reporter)
415/861-5019 *the weekly LGBT newspaper*

Bay Times 415/503-1386 *bi-weekly, good Bay Area resource listings*

➤**Gloss Magazine** 510/451-2090 *CA arts/ entertainment magazine, bi-weekly*

■MEN'S CLUBS

SF Jacks 415/267-6999 *2nd & 4th Mon, doors open 7:30pm-8:30pm only, mandatory clothes check, call hotline for location*

Steamworks [★PC] 2107 4th St (at Addison), Berkeley 510/845-8992 *24hrs, live DJ Fri-Sat*

■MEN'S SERVICES

➤**MegaMates** 415/430-1199 *Call to hook up with HOT local men. FREE to listen & respond to ads. Use FREE code DAMRON. MegaMates.com.*

SF—Castro & Noe Valley

■ACCOMMODATIONS

24 Henry & Village House [M,NS,WI,GO] 24 Henry St (btwn Sanchez & Noe) 415/864-5686, 800/900-5686 *B&B, some shared baths, 1-bdrm apt also available*

Andrew Whelan House [GS,NS,WI,GO] 415/621-7736 *Victorian home & garden, shared baths*

Beck's Motor Lodge [GF,WC] 2222 Market St (at Sanchez) 415/621-8212 *in the heart of the Castro (ie, cruisy)*

➤**Belvedere House** [★MW,NS,WI,GO] 598 Belvedere St (at 17th St) 415/731-6654, 877/226-3273 *wall-to-wall books, art & style*

Casa Buena Vista [GF,NS,WI] Corona Heights (near Market & Castro) 916/974-7409, 916/813-3119 (cell) *rental apts*

Castillo Inn [WI] 48 Henry St (at Noe) 415/864-5111, 800/865-5112

BELVEDERE HOUSE
San Francisco's #1 Gay Bed & Breakfast

www.GayBedAndBreakfast.net
toll free   1.877 B and B SF

598 Belvedere Street (at 17th Street)
we're right above the Castro

... just a short distance to the bars,
shops, restaurants, all the fun
... great views of Pacific Ocean +
Golden Gate Bridge + GG Park

Six stylish, cozy guestrooms

cable TV with DVD + CD

personal refrigerators
FREE refreshments
breakfast buffet till noon
FREE fruit + pastries all day
FREE wireless internet

special treats on big gay days

California • *USA*

Castro Suites [GS,NS,WI,GO] 927 14th St (at Noe) **415/437-1783** *furnished apts, kitchen*

Edwardian San Francisco [GF,NS] 1668 Market St (btwn Franklin & Gough) **415/864-1271, 888/864-8070** *some shared baths, hot tub, jacuzzi*

Inn on Castro [MW,NS,WI,GO] 321 Castro St (btwn 16th & 17th) **415/861-0321** *full brkfst*

The Parker Guest House [★M,NS,WI,GO] 520 Church St (at 17th) **415/621-3222, 888/520-7275** *guesthouse complex w/ gardens, steam spa*

Tom's Place [M,L,WI,NS,GO] 4510 18th St (at Douglass) **415/861-0516** *slinged play area*

Travelodge Central [GF] 1707 Market St (at Valencia) **415/621-6775, 800/578-7878 (reservations)** *nonsmoking rooms available, close to LGBT center*

▶**The Willows Inn** [MW,NS,WI,GO] 710 14th St (at Church) **415/431-4770, 800/431-0277** *"amenities, comfort, great location"*

■ BARS

440 Castro [★M,NH,B,L] 440 Castro St **415/621-8732** *noon-2am, very cruisy*

Blackbird [GS,NH,GO] 2124 Market St **415/503-0630**

Boy Bar [M,D] 2369 Market St (at Castro, at the Cafe) *Fri only*

The Cafe [MW,D,YC] 2369 Market St (at Castro) **415/861-3846** *5pm-2am, from 3pm Sat-Sun*

Cafe du Nord [GF,A,F,E] 2170 Market St (at Sanchez) **415/861-5016** *live music, theme nights*

The Edge [M,NH,L] 4149 18th St **415/863-4027** *noon-2am, classic cruise bar*

Harvey's [★MW,NH,E,DS,WC] 500 Castro St **415/431-4278** *11am-11pm, 9am-2am wknds, also restaurant*

Hi Tops 2247 Market St *the Castro's gay sports bar*

Last Call Bar [M,NH] 3988 18th St 415/861-1310 *noon-2am*

The Lookout [M,F] 3600 16th St (at Market) 415/431-0306 *3:30pm-2am, from 12:30pm wknds*

Martuni's [GS,NH,P] 4 Valencia St (at Market) 415/241-0205 *4pm-2am, lounge, great martinis*

Midnight Sun [★M,V] 4067 18th St (at Castro) 415/861-4186 *2pm-2am, from 1pm Sat-Sun*

The Mint [MW,K] 1942 Market St (at Buchanan) 415/626-4726 *noon-2am, popular karaoke bar nights, also sushi restaurant*

The Mix [M,NH] 4086 18th St 415/431-8616 *3pm-2am, from 8am wknds, heated patio*

Moby Dick [M,NH,V] 4049 18th St (at Hartford) *2pm-2am, from noon wknds*

Pan Dulce [MW,D,MR-L] 2369 Market St (at the Cafe) 415/861-3846 *9pm-2am Th only, "The Castro's Biggest Latino Party!"*

Pilsner Inn [★M,NH,YC] 225 Church St (at Market) 415/621-7058 *10am-2am, great patio*

Q Bar [★M,NH,D,WC] 456 Castro St 415/864-2877 *4pm-2am, from 2pm wknds, sidewalk patio*

Rebel [M,D] 1760 Market St (at Valencia) 415/431-4202 *4pm-3am, noon-4am wknds*

SF Badlands [★M,NH,D,V,WC] 4121 18th St (at Castro) 415/626-9320 *2pm-2am, Sun beer bust*

Swirl [GF] 572 Castro St (at 19th) 415/864-2262 *1pm-8pm, till 9pm Fri-Sat, wine bar & wine store, tastings & events*

Twin Peaks Tavern [M,OC] 401 Castro St (at Market & 17th) 415/864-9470 *noon-2am, from 8am Th-Sun*

■ CAFES

Cafe Flore [★MW,WI] 2298 Market St (at Noe) 415/621-8579 *7am-2am, full bar, great patio to see & be seen, come early for a seat*

Caffe Trieste [★E] 1667 Market St (at Gough) 415/551-1000 *7am-8pm, great coffee, live music*

Duboce Park Cafe [F] 2 Sanchez St (at Duboce) 415/621-1108 *7am-8pm, outdoor seating*

Jumpin' Java [WI] 139 Noe St (at 14th St) 415/431-5282 *6:30am-7:30pm, 7am-8pm wknds*

Lovejoy's Tea Room [★] 1351 Church St (at Clipper) 415/648-5895 *11am-6pm, clsd Mon-Tue, for a tea party fit for a queen*

Orbit Room Cafe 1900 Market St (at Laguna) 415/252-9525 *4pm-2am, till midnight Sun, also bar*

Philz Coffee 4023 18th (at Noe) 415/875-9656 *6am-8pm*

Samovar Tea Lounge 498 Sanchez St (at 18th St) 415/626-4700 *10am-10pm*

Starbucks [B] 4094 18th St (at Castro) 415/626-6263 *always a bear jamboree*

Sweet Inspiration [F] 2239 Market St 415/621-8664 *8am-11pm, till 12:30am Fri-Sat, fabulous desserts*

■ RESTAURANTS

Anchor Oyster Bar [MW,BW] 579 Castro St (at 19th) 415/431-3990 *11:30am-10pm, from 4pm Sun*

Bisou 2367 Market St (at 17th) 415/556-6200 *dinner nightly, Sun brunch, clsd Mon, French*

Blue [★BW] 2337 Market St (btwn Castro & Noe) 415/863-2583 *11:30am-11pm, wknd brunch from 10:30am, homecooking served w/ style*

Catch [E] 2362 Market St 415/431-5000 *lunch & dinner [R], wknd brunch, seafood*

Chloe's [★] 1399 Church St (at 26th St) 415/648-4116 *8am-4pm, come early for wknd brunch*

Chow [★] 215 Church St (at Market) 415/552-2469 *8am-11pm, till midnight wknds, patio*

Cove Cafe [MW,WC] 434 Castro St 415/626-0462 *8am-9pm, till 10pm Fri-Sat*

California • USA

Eric's Chinese Restaurant [★] 1500 Church St (at 27th St) **415/282-0919** *11am-9pm*

Eureka Restaurant & Lounge 4063 18th St (at Hartford) **415/431-6000** *dinner nightly, lounge upstairs*

Firewood Cafe 4248 18th St (at Diamond St) **415/252-0999** *11am-11pm, rotisserie chicken, pastas, oven-fired pizzas, salads*

Hot Cookie 407 Castro St **415/621-2350** *11am-1am, hot cookies!*

Ike's Place 89 16th St (at Sanchez) **415/553-6888** *10am-7pm, amazing sandwiches, plenty veggie/ vegan, long wait*

It's Tops 1801 Market St (at Octavia) **415/431-6395** *8am-3pm daily, 8pm-3am Wed-Sat, vintage diner*

Jake's on Market [WC] 2223 Market St **415/431-0692** *dinner, wknd brunch, full bar*

Kasa Indian Eatery 4001 18th St (at Noe) **415/621-6940** *11am-10pm, till 11pm Fri-Sat, plenty veggie*

La Mediterranée [BW] 288 Noe (at Market) **415/431-7210** *11am-10pm, till 11pm Sat-Sun*

Orphan Andy's [GO] 3991 17th St **415/864-9795** *24hrs, diner*

Poesia Osteria Italiana 4072 18th St (at Collingwood) **415/252-9325** *dinner nighly, Italian, great food, full bar*

The Sausage Factory [MW,BW] 517 Castro St **415/626-1250** *11:30am-midnight, pizza & pasta*

Sparky's 242 Church St (at Market) **415/626-8666** *24hrs, diner, popular after-hours*

Squat & Gobble 3600 16th St **415/552-2125** *8am-10pm, popular wknds for brkfst, outdoor seating*

Takara Sushi [MW] 4243 18th St (at Diamond) **415/626-7864** *lunch & dinner, clsd Tue, cont'l/ Japanese*

Thailand Restaurant 438-A Castro St **415/863-6868** *11am-10pm, plenty veggie*

Woodhouse Fish Co 2073 Market St (at 14th) **415/437-2722** *noon-9:30pm, New England clam shack-style seafood*

Zuni Cafe [★] 1658 Market St (at Franklin) **415/552-2522** *lunch & dinner, clsd Mon, upscale cont'l/ Mediterranean, full bar*

■ENTERTAINMENT & RECREATION

Castro Country Club [MW] 4058 18th St (at Hartford) **415/552-6102** *alcohol- & drug-free space, cafe*

GLBT History Museum 4127 18th St (at Castro) **415/621-1107** *11am-7pm, noon-5pm Sun, clsd Tue*

Pink Triangle Park near Market & Castro *"in remembrance of LGBT victims of the Nazi regime"*

■BOOKSTORES

Aardvark Books 227 Church St **415/552-6733** *10:30am-10:30pm, mostly used, good LGBT section*

Books, Inc [WC] 2275 Market St **415/864-6777** *10am-10pm, LGBT section, readings*

■RETAIL SHOPS

Best in Show 545 Castro St (btwn 18th & 19th) **415/864-7387** *11am-8pm, 11am-7pm Sat, 11am-6pm Sun*

De La Sole Footwear 549 Castro St (btwn 18th & 19th) **415/255-3140** *11am-7pm, till 8pm Sat*

HRC Action Center & Store 575 Castro St **415/431-2200** *10am-9pm, till 10pm wknds, Human Rights Campaign merchandise & info*

Kenneth Wingard 2319 Market St (btwn Noe & Castro) **415/431-6900**

Rolo 2351 Market St **415/431-4545** *11am-8pm, till 7pm Sun, designer labels*

■GYMS & HEALTH CLUBS

SF Fitness 2301 Market St **415/626-4488** *day passes available*

►Sun Days Tanning Center 3985 17th St (at Market & Castro Sts) **415/626-8222** *8am-10pm, 10am-6pm Sun*

Tan Line Optional.

Photo by: Cliff Baker

Open:
Mon-Sat 8am-10pm
Sun 10am-6pm

CONVENIENT LOCATION IN
the Castro
3985 17th Street (at Castro)
(415) 626-8222

Sun-Days
TANNING CENTERS

■MEN'S CLUBS

➤**Eros** [PC] 2051 Market St (btwn Church & Dolores) **415/864-3767** *noon-midnight, till 3am Fri-Sat, safer-sex club, theme nights, massage available, day passes*

■EROTICA

Auto-Erotica 4077-A 18th St, 2nd flr **415/861-5787** *"purveyor of vintage porn & fine dildos"*

Chaps 4057 18th St (btwn Castro & Hartford) **415/863-1699** *10am-11pm, till midnight Fri-Sat*

Rock Hard 518 Castro St (at 18th St) **415/437-2430** *9:30am-11pm, till midnight Fri-Sat, toys, DVDs, lube, leather, cockrings & more*

■CRUISY AREAS

Collingwood Park [AYOR] (btwn 18th & 19th Sts) *Castro merry-go-round, after bars close*

SF—South of Market

■ACCOMMODATIONS

Americania Hotel [GF,SW,NS,WC] 121 7th St (at Mission) **415/626-0200, 800/444-5816**

Holiday Inn Civic Center [GF,SW,WI,WC] 50 8th St (at Market) **415/626-6103, 877/252-1169**

Hotel Whitcomb [GF,WI,WC] 1231 Market St (btwn 8th & 9th) **415/626-8000** *landmark hotel on Pride route, also restaurant & Starbucks on-site*

The Mosser Hotel [GS,NS] 54 4th St (btwn Market & Mission) **415/986-4400, 800/227-3804** *1913 landmark, also restaurant & full bar*

➤**Renoir Hotel** [GS,NS,WI,WC] 45 McAllister St (at Market St) **415/626-5200, 800/576-3388** *1909 historical landmark building, lounge, restaurant, convenient location for public transit*

Vagabond Inn San Francisco
[GS,WI,WC] 385 9th St (at Harrison)
415/431-5131, 800/522-1555
motel, close to SOMA bars

The Westin San Francisco Market Street [GF,NS] 50 3rd St
415/974-6400, 888/627-8561
sauna

■BARS

Dada SF Studio [GS,GO] 86 2nd St
(btwn Market & Mission)
415/357-1367 4pm-midnight, till
2am Th-Sat, from 8pm Sat, clsd Sun, art
gallery

Hole in the Wall Saloon [★M,NH,L]
1369 Folsom (btwn 9th & 10th)
415/431-4695 noon-2am, "a nasty
little biker bar"

Kok Bar [★M,L] 1225 Folsom St (at 8th)
415/255-2427 5pm-2am, from 3pm
Sun, cruisy

Lone Star Saloon [★M,B,L] 1354
Harrison St (btwn 9th & 10th)
415/863-9999 noon-2am, from 9am
wknds, patio, bear bar, beer bust wknds

Powerhouse [M,NH,L] 1347 Folsom St
(at Dore Alley) **415/552-8689** 4pm-
2am, theme nights, popular wknds w/
DJ, patio, cruisy

SF Eagle [★M,NH,L] 398 12th St (at
Harrison)

■NIGHTCLUBS

1015 Folsom [★GS,D,$] 1015 Folsom St
(at 6th) **415/431-1200** 10pm-close
Fri-Sat, call for events

Asia SF [★GS,D,MR-A,S,$] 201 9th St (at
Howard) **415/255-2742** 10pm-close
Wed-Sat, theme nights, go-go boys, also
Cal-Asian restaurant w/ en-drag dinner
service

Bearracuda [M,D,B] 1151 Folsom St (at
Eight) 9pm 1st Sat only

Beat Box [GS,D] 314 11th St theme
nights

Standard Rooms $89-$159 Suites $175-$350

- Gay-friendly boutique hotel in historic landmark building
- Near cable cars, Union Square, theaters and shopping
- Walking distance to Folsom St., SOMA bars/clubs, Castro 15 min.
- 130 rooms, with private bath/shower, safe and WiFi. Valet parking available
- Best views of SF Pride Parade from Market Street rooms and suites (last Sunday June)
- Ideal for Up Your Alley and Folsom Street Fair
- New restaurant open 7 days/wk; New bar open 6 days/wk

Renoir Hotel
San Francisco

45 McAllister At Market St., San Francisco, CA 94102
www.renoirhotel.com • 800-576-3388 • Fax 415-626-0916 IGLTA

California • *USA*

Bootie SF [★GF,D,E,$] 375 11th St (at Harrison, at DNA Lounge) **415/626-1409 (DNA info line)** *9pm-3am Sat, mashups, bootlegs, bastard pop*

Cat Club [GS,D] 1190 Folsom St (at 8th) **415/703-8965** *hosts many one-night clubs & events*

Club Papi SF [M,D,MR-L] 525 Harrison (at The Factory) **415/675-9763** *monthly party from 10pm-4am, call for dates*

The Crib SF [MW,D,V,18+,$] 715 Harrison St (at 3rd) *9:30pm-2am Th only*

Endup [GS,D,MR] 401 6th St (at Harrison) **415/646-0999 (info line)**, **415/357-0827** *theme nights, popular Sun mornings*

Fever [M,D] 401 6th St (at Harrison, at Endup) *11pm-11am Fri only*

Flourish [W,D] *quarterly fancy queer party, dress to impress!*

GusPresents.com *The host w/ the most—Gus is always throwing one hell of a party for the boys!*

Honey Soundsystem [M,D,B] 1535 Folsom St (at Holy Cow) *Sun only, local DJ collective*

Industry [M,D] 525 Harrison St (at 1st) *monthly party*

Mezzanine [GS,D,MR,TG,E,WC,$] 444 Jessie (at Mint) **415/625-8880** *9pm-close, live music, big name DJs, call for events*

The Stud [★MW,D,YC] 399 9th St (at Harrison) **415/863-6623** *5pm-2am, theme nights*

■Cafes

Brain Wash [★E,BW] 1122 Folsom St (at 7th St) **415/861-3663, 415/431-9274** *7am-11pm, 8am-10pm Sun, laundromat & cafe*

■Restaurants

Ame [R] 689 Mission St (at 3rd St, in St Regis Hotel) **415/284-4040** *lunch & dinner, full bar*

Ananda Fuara 1298 Market St (at 9th) **415/621-1994** *8am-8pm, till 3pm Wed, clsd Sun, vegetarian*

Anchor & Hope 83 Minna St (at 2nd St) **415/501-9100** *lunch Mon-Fri, dinner nightly, seafood*

Butter 354 11th St (btwn Folsom & Harrison) **415/863-5964** *6pm-2am, clsd Mon, "white trash bistro," full bar, theme nights*

Don Ramon's Mexican Restaurant 225 11th St (btwn Howard & Folsom) **415/864-2700** *lunch Tue-Fri, dinner nightly, clsd Mon, some veggie, full bar*

Fringale [WC] 570 4th St (btwn Bryant & Brannan) **415/543-0573** *lunch Tue-Fri & dinner nightly, French bistro*

Heaven's Dog 1148 Mission St (at 7th) **415/863-6008** *5pm-1am, till 9pm Sun, Chinese*

Rocco's Cafe [★] 1131 Folsom St (at 7th) **415/554-0522** *brkfst & lunch daily, dinner Wed-Sat only*

The Slanted Door [★R] 1 Ferry Building #3 **415/861-8032** *lunch & dinner, Vietnamese, full bar*

Supperclub [E] 657 Harrison St (btwn 2nd & 3rd) **415/348-0900** *6:30pm-close, live performance art & acrobatics, also full bar & nightclub*

Ted's 1530 Howard St (at 11th) **415/552-0309** *6am-6pm, 8am-5pm wknds, excellent deli sandwiches*

Tu Lan 8 6th St (at Market) **415/626-0927** *lunch & dinner, clsd Sun, Vietnamese, dicey neighborhood but delicious (& cheap) food*

Woodward's Garden [WC] 1700 Mission St (at Duboce) **415/621-7122** *dinner from 6pm, clsd Sun-Mon*

Yank Sing [★] 101 Spear St (at Mission, at One Rincon Center) **415/781-1111** *11am-3pm Mon-Fri, 10am-4pm wknds, dim-sum heaven!*

■Entertainment & Recreation

111 Minna Gallery [GS,D,E] 111 Minna St (at 2nd St) **415/974-1719** *also art gallery, call for events*

■Retail Shops

Dandelion [GO] 55 Potrero Ave (at Alameda St) **415/436-9500, 888/548-1968** *10am-7pm, till 6pm Fri-Sat, noon-5pm Sun*

Mr S Leather & Fetters USA San Francisco 385 8th St (at Harrison) **415/863-7764, 800/746-7677** *11am-7pm, erotic goods, custom leather & latex*

Stompers 323 10th St (at Folsom) **415/255-6422, 888/BOOTMAN** *11am-6pm, noon-4pm Sun, clsd Mon, boots, cigars & gloves*

■GYMS & HEALTH CLUBS

SF Fitness [★] 1001 Brannan St (at 9th) **415/552-4653** *day passes available*

■MEN'S CLUBS

►Blow Buddies [★MO,L,V,PC,GO] 933 Harrison (btwn 5th & 6th) **415/777-4323** *open late Wed-Sun, clsd Mon-Tue*

Mack Folsom Prison [MO,L,PC] 1285 Folsom (at 9th) **415/252-1221** *6pm-6am, 24hrs wknds, fetish parties*

Playspace [MO] 962 Folsom St *open Th-Sun, the ideal hook-up location*

■EROTICA

Folsom Gulch 947 Folsom (btwn 5th & 6th) **415/495-6402** *10am-2am, 24hrs Fri-Sat, hot arcade action, serving the gay community for over 25 years!*

Good Vibrations [★W,WC] 899 Mission St (at 5th St) **415/513-1635, 800/289-8423** *10am-9pm, till 10pm Fri-Sat, clean, well-lighted sex toy store*

Pop Sex 960 960 Folsom St (btwn 5th & 6th) **415/543-2124** *10am-2am, 24hrs wknds, the best in adult entertainment*

■CRUISY AREAS

Folsom St [AYOR] btwn 5th & 6th *late*

SF—Polk Street Area

■ACCOMMODATIONS

Inn On Broadway [GF,WI,WC] 2201 Van Ness Ave (at Broadway) **415/776-7900, 800/727-6239** *motel close to Fisherman's Wharf*

California • *USA*

The Monarch Hotel [GF] 1015 Geary St (at Polk) 415/673-5232, 800/777-3210 *Edwardian boutique-style hotel*

Nob Hill Motor Inn [GF,NS,WI,WC] 1630 Pacific Ave (at Van Ness Ave) 415/775-8160, 800/343-6900 *hotel*

The Phoenix Hotel [★GF,SW,WI] 601 Eddy St (at Larkin) 415/776-1380, 800/248-9466 *1950s-style motor lodge, fave of celebrity rockers*

Radisson Hotel Fisherman's Wharf [GF,SW,WI,WC] 250 Beach St (at Hyde) 415/392-6700

San Francisco City Center Hostel [GF,NS,WI] 685 Ellis St (at Larkin) 415/474-5721 *hostel, shared & private rooms available, free brkfst, kids ok*

■BARS

The Cinch [M,NH,WI,WC] 1723 Polk St (at Clay) 415/776-4162 *9am-2am, patio, lots of pool tables & no attitude, [D] Th-Sat, [DS] Fri*

Edinburgh Castle [GF,NH,E] 950 Geary St (at Polk) 415/885-4074 *5pm-2am, Scottish pub w/ single malts & authentic fish & chips*

Gangway [M,NH] 841 Larkin St (btwn Geary & O'Farrell) 415/776-6828 *8am-2am*

Lush Lounge [★GS,NH,WC] 1092 Post (at Polk) 415/771-2022 *3pm-2am, from noon wknds*

■NIGHTCLUBS

Divas [M,NH,D,TG,DS] 1081 Post St (at Larkin) 415/474-3482 *7am-2am, TS/TVs & their admirers*

Go BANG! [MW,D] 510 Larkin (at Turk, at Deco Lounge) *4th Sat only, underground '70s-'80s disco*

■CAFES

La Boulange de Polk 2310 Polk St (at Green St) 415/345-1107 *7am-7pm, French bakery & cafe, outdoor seating, Parisian down to the attitude*

Quetzal Internet Cafe [★E,V,BW,WI] 1234 Polk St (at Sutter) 415/673-4181 *6:30am-10pm, roasts own coffee*

■RESTAURANTS

Grubstake II [MW,BW] 1525 Pine St (at Polk) 415/673-8268 *5pm-4am, from 10am wknds, diner/ Portuguese*

Rex Cafe 2323 Polk St 415/441-2244 *dinner from 5:30pm, brunch 10am-3pm wknds, American, full bar*

Street 2141 Polk St (btwn Broadway & Vallejo) 415/775-1055 *dinner, clsd Mon, incredible hamburgers*

■BOOKSTORES

Books Inc Opera Plaza [★] 601 Van Ness Ave (at Turk) 415/776-1111 *8:30am-9pm, general, LGBT section, readings*

■EROTICA

Frenchy's 1020 Geary St (at Polk) 415/776-5940 *24hrs*

Glass Kandi 569 Geary St (at Taylor) 415/931-2256 *4pm-9pm, noon-9pm Sat, till 7pm Sun, glass dildos*

Good Vibrations [★W] 1620 Polk St (btwn Sacramento & Clay) 415/345-0400

■CRUISY AREAS

Polk St [AYOR] btwn Geary & California Sts *hustlers*

SF—Downtown & North Beach

■ACCOMMODATIONS

Adante Hotel [GS,NS,WC] 610 Geary St (at Jones) 415/673-9221, 888/423-0083 *in Union Square/ Theater District, kids ok*

Andrews Hotel [GF,NS,WI] 624 Post St (btwn Taylor & Jones) 415/563-6877, 800/926-3739 *Victorian hotel, also Italian restaurant*

Argonaut Hotel [GF,NS,WC] 495 Jefferson St (at Hyde) 415/563-0800, 800/790-1415 *boutique hotel in Fisherman's Wharf*

Dakota Hotel/ Hostel [GF,WI] 606 Post St (at Taylor) 415/931-7475 *near Union Square*

Executive Hotel Vintage Court [GF,NS,WI,WC] 650 Bush St (at Powell) **415/392-4666, 888/388-3932** *also world-famous 5-star Masa's restaurant, French*

Galleria Park Hotel [GS,WI,NS,WC] 191 Sutter St (at Kearny) **415/781-3060, 800/792-9639** *boutique hotel*

Grand Hyatt San Francisco [GF,WI] 345 Stockton St (at Sutter) **415/398-1234** *restaurant & lounge, gym*

Halcyon Hotel [GF,NS,WI] 649 Jones St (at Post) **415/929-8033, 800/627-2396**

Handlery Union Square Hotel [GF,SW,WI,WC] 351 Geary St **415/781-7800, 800/995-4874** *steps from Union Square*

Harbor Court Hotel [GF,SW,WI,WC] 165 Steuart St (btwn Howard & Mission) **415/882-1300, 866/792-6283** *in the heart of the Financial District, gym*

Hilton San Francisco Financial District [GS] 750 Kearny St (at Clay) **415/433-6600, 800/424-8292**

Hotel Abri [GF,WI] 127 Ellis St (at Powell) **415/392-8800, 866/778-6169** *boutique hotel*

Hotel Adagio [GF,WC] 550 Geary St (at Shannon) **415/775-5000, 800/228-8830**

Hotel Bijou [GS,NS,WI,WC] 111 Mason St (at Eddy) **415/771-1200, 800/771-1022**

The Hotel California [GF,NS] 580 Geary St (at Jones) **415/441-2700, 800/227-4223** *also popular Millennium gourmet vegetarian restaurant & bar*

Hotel Carlton [GF] 1075 Sutter (at Larkin) **415/673-0242, 800/922-7586** *also Saha restaurant, Arabic-fusion*

Hotel Diva [GF,NS,WI] 440 Geary (at Mason) **415/885-0200, 800/553-1900** *hip hotel, gym*

California • *USA*

The Hotel Frank [GS,WC] 386 Geary St (at Mason) 415/986-2000, 877/828-4478 *1908 art deco masterpiece, full brkfst*

Hotel Fusion [GS,NS,WI,WC] 140 Ellis St (at Powell St) 415/568-2525, 866/753-4244

Hotel Griffon [GS,WI,WC] 155 Steuart St (at Mission) 415/495-2100, 800/321-2201 *also restaurant, bistro/cont'l*

Hotel Mark Twain [GF,WI,WC] 345 Taylor St (at Ellis) 415/673-2332, 877/854-4106 *also Fish & Farm restaurant*

Hotel Metropolis [GF,WI,NS] 25 Mason St (at Eddy) 415/775-4600, 877/628-4412 *near Union Square shopping*

Hotel Monaco [GF] 501 Geary St (at Taylor) 415/292-0100, 866/622-5284 *pets ok, also Grand Cafe restaurant, French*

Hotel Nikko San Francisco [GF,SW,NS,WC] 222 Mason St (at Ellis) 415/394-1111, 866/645-5673 *health club & spa, also ANZU restaurant*

Hotel Palomar [GS,WI] 12 4th St (at Market) 415/348-1111, 866/373-4941 *boutique hotel*

The Hotel Rex [GF,WC] 562 Sutter St (at Powell) 415/433-4434, 800/433-4434 *full bar*

Hotel Triton [GF,WI,WC] 342 Grant Ave (at Bush) 415/394-0500, 800/800-1299 *designer theme rooms*

Hotel Union Square [GF,WI] 114 Powell St (at Ellis) 415/397-3000, 800/553-1900 *1930s art deco lobby*

Hotel Vitale [GF,NS,WI,WC] 8 Mission St (at Steuart) 415/278-3700, 888/890-8688 *4-star, full-service waterfront luxury hotel, rooftop spa, restaurant & bar*

Hyatt Regency San Francisco [GF,NS,WI] 5 Embarcadero Center (at California) 415/788-1234, 800/233-1234 *luxury waterfront hotel*

The Inn at Union Square [GF,NS,WI] 440 Post St (at Powell) 415/397-3510, 800/288-4346 *complimentary brkfst & wine & cheese daily*

JW Marriott Hotel San Francisco [GF,NS,WI,WC] 500 Post St (at Mason) 415/771-8600, 888/236-2427

Kensington Park Hotel [GF,NS,WI] 450 Post St 415/788-6400 *on Union Square, also Farallon Restaurant*

King George Hotel [GS,F,WI,WC] 334 Mason St (at Geary) 415/781-5050

Larkspur Hotel [GF,WI,NS] 524 Sutter St (at Powell) 415/421-2865, 866/823-4669 *B&B-inn on Union Square, afternoon tea, wine hour*

Luz Hotel [GS] 725 Geary St (at Leavenworth) 415/928-1917 *clothing-optional jacuzzi*

Nob Hill Hotel [GS,NS,WC] 835 Hyde St (btwn Bush & Sutter) 415/885-2987, 877/662-4455 *European-style hotel, jacuzzi*

Petite Auberge [GF,NS] 863 Bush St (at Taylor) 415/928-6000, 800/365-3004

Prescott Hotel [GF,NS,WI] 545 Post St (btwn Taylor & Mason) 415/563-0303, 866/271-3632 *small luxury hotel*

San Francisco Downtown Hostel [GS,WI,WC] 312 Mason St (at O'Farrell) 415/788-5604 *hostel, shared baths, open kitchen*

San Remo Hotel [GS,NS,WI] 2237 Mason St (btwn Chestnut & Francisco) 415/776-8688, 800/352-7366 *1906 Italianate pensione, shared baths*

Serrano Hotel [GF,WI,WC] 405 Taylor St (at O'Farrell) 415/885-2500, 866/289-6561 *in Theater District*

Sir Francis Drake Hotel [GF,WI] 450 Powell St (at Sutter) 415/392-7755, 800/795-7129 *1928 landmark, also restaurant & Starlight Room*

The Stratford Hotel [GS,WI,WC] 242 Powell St (at Geary) 415/397-7080, 866/688-0038 *near Union Square*

The Touchstone Hotel [GF,WC] 480 Geary St (btwn Mason & Taylor) 415/771-1600 *in Theater District, full brkfst*

Tuscan Inn [GF,WC] 425 N Point St (at Mason) **415/561-1100, 888/648-4626**

Union Square Plaza Hotel [GF] 432 Geary St (at Mason) **415/776-7585, 800/841-3135** *1 block from Union Square*

Vertigo Hotel [GS,NS,WI,WC] 940 Sutter St (at Leavenworth) **415/885-6800, 888/444-4605** *boutique hotel*

Villa Florence Hotel [GF,WI] 225 Powell St (at Geary) **415/397-7700, 866/823-4669** *Union Square boutique hotel, also Kuleto's restaurant, Italian*

■BARS

Aunt Charlie's Lounge [M,NH,DS] 133 Turk St (at Taylor) **415/441-2922** *10am-midnight, till 2am Fri- Sat*

Bourbon & Branch [GS,R] 501 Jones St (at O'Farrell) **415/931-7292** *in Prohibition-era speakeasy, drinks are worth the price*

■NIGHTCLUBS

Hero [★M,D,$] 420 Mason (at Geary, at Ruby Skye) *occasional Sun T-dance, check local listings for dates*

■CAFES

Caffe Trieste [★] 601 Vallejo St **415/392-6739** *get a taste of the real North Beach (past & present)*

Sugar Cafe [F,WI] 679 Sutter St (at Taylor) **415/441-5678** *10am-2am, from 8am wknds, cafe by day, cocktails by night*

■RESTAURANTS

Ar Roi 643 Post St (at Jones) **415/771-5146** *lunch & dinner, clsd Sun, Thai*

The Buena Vista 2765 Hyde St (at Beach) **415/474-5044** *9am-2am, from 8am wknds, the restaurant that introduced Irish coffee to America*

Cafe Claude [E,BW] 7 Claude Ln (near Bush & Kearny) **415/392-3515** *11:30am-10:30pm, from 5:30pm Sun, as close to Paris as you can get in SF*

Canteen **415/928-8870** *dinner nightly, brkfst wknds*

Le Colonial 20 Cosmo Pl (btwn Taylor & Jones) **415/931-3600** *dinner nightly, wknd brunch, Vietnamese, full bar*

Dottie's True Blue Cafe [GO] 522 Jones St (at Geary) **415/885-2767** *7:30am-3pm, clsd Tue, great brkfst*

Golden Era [★] 572 O'Farrell St **415/673-3136** *11am-9pm, clsd Tue, vegetarian/ vegan*

Mario's Bohemian Cigar Store Cafe [BW,WI] 566 Columbus Ave (at Union) **415/362-0536** *10am-close, great foccacia sandwiches*

Millennium 580 Geary St (at Jones) **415/345-3900** *dinner only, Euro-Mediterranean, upscale vegetarian*

■ENTERTAINMENT & RECREATION

Rrazz Room [★GS,C,WC] 222 Mason (at Nikko Hotel) **415/394-1189, 800/380-3095** *cabaret w/ world-class performers*

Sunday's A Drag@The Starlight Room [MW,E,$] 450 Mason St (at Powell) **415/395-8595** *Sun brunch, noon & 2:30pm drag shows*

■BOOKSTORES

Book Passage 1 Ferry Bldg #42 **415/835-1020** *10am-8pm, from 8am Sat, 10am-7pm Sun-Mon, independent*

City Lights Bookstore 261 Columbus Ave (at Pacific) **415/362-8193** *10am-midnight, historic beatnik bookstore, many progressive titles, LGBT section, whole floor dedicated to poetry*

■SEX CLUBS

Power Exchange [GS] 220 Jones St **415/487-9944**

■EROTICA

Nob Hill Adult Theatre [MO,$] 729 Bush St (at Powell) **415/781-9468** *9am-2:30am, male dancers, over 25 shows daily*

Video Secrets 389 Bay St (at Mason) **415/391-9349**

California • USA

SF—Mission District
includes Bernal Heights

■ ACCOMMODATIONS

Elements [★GS,F,WI] 2515 Mission St (at 21st St) 415/647-4100, 866/327-8407 *hostel w/ private or shared rooms*

▶**The Inn San Francisco** [GF,NS,WI] 943 S Van Ness Ave (btwn 20th & 21st) 415/641-0188, 800/359-0913 *Victorian mansion, hot tub*

Noe's Nest B&B [GF,NS] 1257 Guerrero St (btwn 24th & 25th Sts) 415/821-0751 *kitchens, fireplace*

■ BARS

El Rio [★GS,NH,MR,E] 3158 Mission St (at Cesar Chavez) 415/282-3325 *5pm-close Mon-Th, from 3pm wknds, patio*

Esta Noche [M,D,MR-L,TG,S] 3079 16th St (at Mission) 415/861-5757 *1pm-2am, salsa & disco in a classic Tijuana dive*

Lexington Club [★W,NH,GO] 3464 19th St (btwn Mission & Valencia) 415/863-2052 *5pm-2am, from 3pm Fri-Sun*

Lone Palm [GS] 3394 22nd St (at Guerrero) 415/648-0109 *4pm-2am, a bar for grown ups (we know you're out there)*

Nihon [GS,D,F] 1779 Folsom St (at 14th St) 415/552-4400 *6pm-close, clsd Sun, whiskey lounge, also Japanese restaurant*

Phone Booth [MW,NH] 1398 S Van Ness Ave (at 25th) 415/648-4683 *1pm-2am*

Pop's Bar [GS,NH,WC] 2800 24th St (btwn York & Bryant) 415/401-7677 *4pm-2am, photobooth*

Stray Bar [GS,NH,GO] 309 Cortland Ave, Bernal Heights (at Bocana) 415/821-9263 *4pm-2am, from 2pm wknds*

Truck Bar [MW,NH,F,GO] 1900 Folsom St (at 15th) 415/252-0306 *11pm-2am, from 4pm Sat, from 2pm Sun*

Wild Side West [GS,WC] 424 Cortland, Bernal Heights (at Wool) 415/647-3099 *1pm-2am, patio, magic garden*

Zeitgeist [★GS,F] 199 Valencia St (at Duboce) 415/255-7505 *9am-2am, divey biker bar & beer garden*

■ NIGHTCLUBS

Hard French [MW,D,MR,F,$] 3158 Mission (at El Rio) *3pm-8pm 1st Sat only, soul dance party*

The Make-Out Room [GS,D,E] 3225 22nd St (at Mission) 415/647-2888 *6pm-2am*

Mighty [GF,D] 119 Utah St (at 15th St) 415/762-0151

Stay Gold [MW,D] 161 Erie St (at Mission, at Public Works) *10:30pm last Wed only*

Sundance Saloon [★MW,D,CW,GO,$] 550 Barneveld Ave (at space5050, 2 blocks off Bayshore Blvd at Industrial) 415/820-1403 *5pm-10:30pm Sun (lessons at 5:30pm) & 6:30pm-10:30pm Th (lessons at 7pm)*

Thee Parkside [GF,E] 1600 17th St (at Wisconsin, Potrero Hill) 415/252-1330 *live bands & events*

■ CAFES

Dolores Park Cafe [★F,E] 501 Dolores St (at 18th St) 415/621-2936 *7am-8pm, outdoor seating overlooking Dolores Park, live music Fri*

Farleys [E] 1315 18th St (at Texas St, Potrero Hill) 415/648-1545 *6:30am-10pm, from 7:30am Sat & 8am Sun*

The Revolution Cafe [E] 3248 22nd St (btwn Mission & Bartlett) 415/642-0474 *9am-1am*

Tartine Bakery [★] 600 Guerrero St (at 18th St) 415/487-2600 *8am-7pm, from 9am Sun, French bakery w/ a line out the door*

■ RESTAURANTS

Aslam's Rasoi 1037 Valencia St (at 21st) 415/695-0599 *5pm-11pm, Indian & Pakistani*

Boogaloos [★] 3296 22nd St (at Valencia) 415/824-4088 *8am-3pm, worth the wait*

Circolo 500 Florida St (at Mariposa) 415/553-8560 *5pm-close, clsd Mon, Latin-Asian fusion, full bar*

Delfina [★R] 3621 18th St (at Dolores) 415/552-4055 *5:30pm-10pm, Tuscan cuisine, full bar, patio (summers)*

El Farolito [★] 2779 Mission St (at 24th) 415/824-7877 *10am-3am, delicious, cheap burritos & more*

Farina 3560 18th St (at Guerrero) 415/565-0360 *dinner nightly, Sun brunch, Italian*

Just For You [★MW] 722 22nd St (at 3rd St) 415/647-3033 *7:30am-3pm, Southern brkfst*

Luna Park 694 Valencia St (at 18th) 415/553-8584 *lunch & dinner, wknd brunch*

Maverick 3316 17th St (btwn Mission & Valencia) 415/863-3061 *dinner nightly, also wknd brunch, upscale American, great wine selection*

Medjool [★WC] 2522 Mission St (at 21st St) 415/550-9055 *5pm-10pm, till 11pm Fri-Sat, clsd Sun, tapas, also cafe, lounge & rooftop bar*

Moki's Sushi & Pacific Grill 615 Cortland Ave (at Moultine) 415/970-9336 *dinner nightly*

Pauline's Pizza Pie [★MW,BW] 260 Valencia St (btwn 14th & Duboce) 415/552-2050 *5pm-10pm, clsd Sun-Mon, gourmet pizza*

Picaro [BW,WC] 3120 16th St (at Valencia) 415/431-4089 *5pm-10pm, from 9:30am wknds, Spanish tapas bar*

Pork Store Cafe [★BW] 3122 16th St (at Valencia) 415/626-5523 *8am-4pm daily & 7pm-3am Fri-Sat, American/ diner food, great breakfasts; also 1451 Haight St, 415/864-6981*

Range [★] 842 Valencia St (btwn 19th & 20th Sts) 415/282-8283 *dinner nightly, California contemporary, full bar*

California • USA

Slow Club [WC] 2501 Mariposa (at Hampshire) **415/241-9390** *lunch Mon-Fri, dinner Mon-Sat, wknd brunch, full bar*

■ENTERTAINMENT & RECREATION

Dolores "Beach" Church & 19th St (at the top corner of Dolores Park) *popular "beach" in Dolores Park, crowded on sunny days*

Metronome Ballroom [GS,$] 1830 17th St (at De Haro) **415/252-9000** *dance lessons, salsa to swing, dance parties wknds, call for events*

■BOOKSTORES

Dog Eared Books 900 Valencia St (at 20th) **415/282-1901** *10am-10pm, till 8pm Sun, new & used, good LGBT section*

Modern Times Bookstore [WC] 2919 24th St (at Alabama) **415/282-9246**

■RETAIL SHOPS

Black & Blue Tattoo [★W] 381 Guerrero (at 16th St) **415/626-0770**

Body Manipulations 3234 16th St (btwn Guerrero & Dolores) **415/621-0408** *noon-7pm, from 2pm Mon-Th, piercing (walk-in basis), jewelry*

■EROTICA

Good Vibrations [★W,WC] 603 Valencia St (at 17th St) **415/522-5460, 800/289-8423** *11am-7pm, till 8pm Th, till 9pm Fri-Sat, clean, well-lighted sex toy store*

Mission St News 2086 Mission St (at 17th) **415/626-0309** *24hrs*

SF—Haight, Fillmore, Hayes Valley

■ACCOMMODATIONS

The Chateau Tivoli B&B [GF,NS,WI] 1057 Steiner St (at Golden Gate) **415/776-5462, 800/228-1647** *historic SF B&B*

Hayes Valley Inn [GS,NS,WI] 417 Gough St (at Hayes) **415/431-9131, 800/930-7999** *European-style pension, shared baths*

Hotel Del Sol [★GS,NS,SW,WI,WC] 3100 Webster St (at Greenwich) **415/921-5520, 877/433-5765**

Hotel Drisco [GF,NS] 2901 Pacific Ave (at Broderick) **415/346-2880, 800/634-7277**

Hotel Kabuki [GF,WC] 1625 Post St (at Laguna) **415/922-3200, 800/533-4567** *in Japantown*

Hotel Majestic [GF,NS,WI,WC] 1500 Sutter St (at Gough) **415/441-1100, 800/869-8966** *one of SF's earliest grand hotels, also restaurant, full bar*

Hotel Tomo [GF,NS,WI] 1800 Sutter St (at Buchanan) **415/921-4000, 888/822-8666** *in Japantown, restaurant & bar*

Inn at the Opera [GF,NS,WI,WC] 333 Fulton St (at Franklin) **415/863-8400, 866/729-7182**

Jackson Court [GF,NS,WI] 2198 Jackson St (at Buchanan) **415/929-7670**

The Laurel Inn [GF,NS] 444 Presidio Ave (at Sacramento) **415/567-8467, 800/552-8735**

Metro Hotel [GF,WI] 319 Divisadero St (at Haight) **415/861-5364** *European-style pension*

Queen Anne Hotel [GF,NS,WI,GO] 1590 Sutter St (at Octavia) **415/441-2828, 800/227-3970**

San Francisco Fisherman's Wharf Hostel [GS,F,WI,NS,WC] Fort Mason, Bldg 240 (at Franklin) **415/771-7277** *hostel, shared baths*

Shannon-Kavanaugh Guest House [GF,NS,GO] 722 Steiner St (at Hayes) **415/563-2727** *1-bdrm garden apt in house on SF's famous "Postcard Row"*

Stanyan Park Hotel [GF,NS,WC] 750 Stanyan St (at Waller) **415/751-1000** *historic Victorian*

■BARS

Marlena's [M,NH,DS,P,WC] 488 Hayes St (at Octavia) **415/864-6672** *noon-2am, [DS] Sat, Cheers for drag queens (a friendly oasis in hip & het Hayes Valley)*

Rickshaw Stop [★GF,F,E] 155 Fell St (btwn Van Ness & Franklin) **415/861-2011** *Wed-Sat only, hipster bar, nightclub (many bands) & restaurant*

Trax [M,NH] 1437 Haight St (at Masonic) **415/864-4213** *noon-2am*

▓ NIGHTCLUBS

Cockblock [MW,D,MR] 155 Fell St (at Rickshaw Shop) *10pm-2am 2nd Sat*

Cockfight [M,D,A] 424 Haight St (at Webster, at Underground SF) **415/864-7386** *9pm 1st Sat only*

Underground SF [GS,D,A] 424 Haight St (at Webster) **415/551-1590** *5:30pm-2am, clsd Mon, theme nights, call for events, more gay Sat*

▓ CAFES

Blue Bottle Coffee Company [★] 315 Linden St (at Gough St) **415/252-7535** *7am-5pm, from 8am wknds, organic coffee & treats from kiosk in front of artists' workshop— wonderful hidden treat*

▓ RESTAURANTS

Absinthe Brasserie & Bar 398 Hayes St (at Gough) **415/551-1590** *lunch & dinner, bar till 2am Fri-Sat, clsd Mon*

Alamo Square Seafood Grill 803 Fillmore (at Grove) **415/440-2828** *dinner only*

Burma Superstar [★] 309 Clement St **415/387-2147** *lunch & dinner, Burmese food that will rock your world*

Cheese Steak Shop 1716 Divisadero St (btwn Bush & Sutter) **415/346-3712** *9am-10pm, from 11am Sun, from 10am Mon, best cheese steak outside Philly, also veggie versions*

Eliza's [★] 2877 California (at Broderick) **415/621-4819** *lunch Mon-Wed, dinner nightly, excellent Chinese food*

Ella's 500 Presidio Ave (at California) **415/441-5669** *brkfst & lunch Mon-Fri, popular wknd brunch*

Garibaldi's [WC,GO] 347 Presidio Ave (at Sacramento) **415/563-8841** *lunch weekdays, dinner nightly, Mediterranean, full bar*

Greens [★] Fort Mason, Bldg A (near Van Ness & Bay) **415/771-6222** *lunch Tue-Sat, dinner Mon-Sat, Sun brunch, gourmet vegetarian, spectacular view of the Golden Gate Bridge*

Little Star Pizza [★BW] 846 Divisadero St (btwn Fulton & McAllister Sts) **415/441-1118** *5pm-10pm, till 11pm Fri-Sat, clsd Mon, Chicago-style deep dish pizza*

Memphis Minnie's BBQ [★] 576 Haight St **415/864-7675** *11am-10pm, till 9pm Sun, clsd Mon*

Nopa 560 Divisadero St (at Hayes) **415/864-8643** *dinner 6pm-1am, bar from 5pm, urban rustic*

Park Chow [★] 1238 9th Ave (btwn Irving & Lincoln) **415/665-9912** *11am-10pm, brunch from 10am wknds, eclectic & affordable*

Patxi's Chicago Pizza 511 Hayes St (at Octavia) **415/558-9991** *11am-10pm, clsd Mon, Chicago-style deep dish pizza, also thin crust*

Pluto's Fresh Food for a Hungry Universe 627 Irving St (btwn 7th & 8th Aves) **415/753-8867** *11am-10pm, design your own sandwiches*

Suppenküche [BW,GO] 601 Hayes (at Laguna) **415/252-9289** *dinner, Sun brunch, German cuisine served at communal tables*

Thep-Phanom [★BW] 400 Waller St (at Fillmore) **415/431-2526** *5:30pm-10:30pm, excellent Thai food, worth the wait!*

▓ BOOKSTORES

Bibliohead Bookstore [GO] 334 Gough St (at Hayes) **415/621-6772** *eclectic used books, queer stock*

The Booksmith 1644 Haight St **415/863-8688** *cool independent, big-name author readings*

▓ RETAIL SHOPS

Cold Steel America 1783 Haight St **415/621-7233** *noon-8pm, piercing & tattoo studio*

Flight 001 525 Hayes St (btwn Octavia & Laguna) **415/487-1001, 877/354-4481** *11am-7pm, till 6pm Sun, way cool travel gear*

Timbuk 2 Store 506 Hayes St **415/252-9860** *11am-7pm, noon-6pm Sun, messenger-style bags & backpacks*

California • *USA*

■GYMS & HEALTH CLUBS
Kabuki Springs & Spa 1750 Geary Blvd (at Fillmore) 415/922-6000 *10am-9:45pm, traditional Japanese bath w/ extensive menu of spa sevices*

■CRUISY AREAS
Buena Vista Park [AYOR] Haight St (btwn Baker & Central) *evenings in northern & highest part*

Land's End [AYOR] NW tip of SF *inquire locally*

San Jose

includes Campbell & Los Gatos; see also Cupertino, Santa Clara & Sunnyvale

■INFO LINES & SERVICES
AA Gay/ Lesbian 274 E Hamilton Ave, Ste D, Campbell 408/374-8511 *24hr helpline, check www.aasanjose.org for meetings*

Billy DeFrank LGBT Community Center [WC] 938 The Alameda 408/293-3040 *3pm-9pm, from 10am Wed, clsd Sat-Mon*

■ACCOMMODATIONS
Hotel De Anza [GF,F,E,WC,NS] 233 W Santa Clara St 408/286-1000, 800/843-3700 *art deco gem*

Moorpark Hotel [GF,SW,WC] 4241 Moorpark Ave 408/864-0300, 877/740-6622 *also bar & restaurant*

■BARS
Brix [MW,NH,D,MR,TG,K,V,WC] 349 S 1st St (at San Salvadore) 408/947-1975 *6pm-2am, from 4pm Sun*

Mac's Club [M,NH] 39 Post St (btwn 1st & Market) 408/288-8221 *noon-2am, patio*

Renegades [M,NH,B,L] 501 W Taylor St (at Coleman Ave) 408/275-9902 *2pm-2am, patio*

■NIGHTCLUBS
Splash [M,D,K,DS,V,GO] 65 Post St (at 1st) 408/292-2222 *9pm-2am Th-Sat, theme nights*

■RESTAURANTS
Eulipia Restaurant & Bar 374 S 1st St (at San Carlos) 408/280-6161 *dinner only, clsd Mon*

Pasta Pomodoro 1205 The Alameda (at Race) 408/292-9929 *Italian*

Vin Santo 1346 Lincoln Ave 408/920-2508 *dinner nightly, clsd Mon, Northern Italian, wine bar*

■ENTERTAINMENT & RECREATION
Tech Museum of Innovation 201 S Market St (at Park Ave) 408/294-8324 *10am-5pm, IMAX Dome Theater, a must-see for digital junkies*

■MEN'S CLUBS
Watergarden [★WI,18+,PC] 1010 The Alameda 408/275-1215 *24hrs, great outdoor patio & jacuzzi, Latino Th*

■MEN'S SERVICES
➤**MegaMates** 408/514-1111 *Call to hook up with HOT local men. FREE to listen & respond to ads. Use FREE code DAMRON. MegaMates.com.*

■EROTICA
Leather Masters 969 Park Ave (at Race St) 408/293-7660 *noon-8pm, clsd Sun-Mon, fetish clothes, toys, etc*

Party Time 1456 W San Carlos St 408/998-0925 *arcade*

San Luis Obispo

■INFO LINES & SERVICES
GALA/ Gay & Lesbian Alliance of the Central Coast 1060 Palm St (at Santa Rosa St) 805/541-4252 *9am-6pm, clsd wknds*

■ACCOMMODATIONS
The Madonna Inn [GF,F,SW] 100 Madonna Rd 805/543-3000, 800/543-9666 *one-of-a-kind theme rooms*

The Palomar Inn [GS,NS,WI] 1601 Shell Beach Rd, Shell Beach 888/384-4004 *motel*

Sycamore Mineral Springs Resort [GF] 1215 Avila Beach Dr 805/595-7302, 800/234-5831 *hot mineral spring spa, integrative retreat center, also restaurant*

■BARS
Fuel Dock [GF] 900 Main St, Morro Bay 805/772-8478

Gaslight Lounge [GF] 2143 Broad St 805/543-4262 *dive bar*

Legends [GF] 899 Main St, Morro Bay 805/772-2525

The Library [GF,D,WC] 723 Higuera St 805/542-0199

■CAFES

Linnaea's Cafe [E,WI] 1110 Garden St (near Marsh) 805/541-5888 *6:30am-11pm*

Outspoken Cafe [GO] 1422 Monterey St (at California) 805/788-0885 *7am-5pm, clsd wknds, cafe & juice bar*

West End Espresso & Tea [GO] 670 Higuera St #A (at Nipomo) 805/543-4902, 805/544-3581 *6:30am-7pm, till 9pm Th, till 8pm Fri-Sat, outdoor seating*

■RESTAURANTS

Big Sky Cafe 1121 Broad St (btwn Higuera & Marsh Sts) 805/545-5401 *7am-10pm, 8am-9pm Sun-Th, plenty veggie/ vegan*

High Street Deli 350 High St 805/541-4738 *7am-7pm, 8am-3pm Sun*

Novo 726 Higuera St 805/543-3986 *lunch & dinner*

Vieni Vai 690 Higuera St 805/544-5282 *lunch & dinner, Sun brunch, Italian*

■ENTERTAINMENT & RECREATION

Pirate's Cove Beach [GS,N,AYOR] 404 Front St, Avila Beach

■BOOKSTORES

Coalesce Bookstore 845 Main St, Morro Bay 805/772-2880 *10am-5:30pm, 11am-4pm Sun*

Volumes of Pleasure [WC,GO] 1016 Los Osos Valley Rd, Los Osos 805/528-5565 *10am-6pm, clsd Sun-Mon*

■PUBLICATIONS

GALA News & Reviews 805/541-4252 *news & events for Central California coast*

■CRUISY AREAS

Embarcadero Boat Ramp [AYOR] Tidelands Park

Morro Bay Rock [AYOR] Coleman Dr

San Rafael

see Marin County

San Ramon

see East Bay

Santa Ana

see Orange County

Santa Barbara

see also Ventura

■INFO LINES & SERVICES

Pacific Pride Foundation 126 E Haley St #A-11 805/963-3636 *9am-5pm Mon-Fri*

■ACCOMMODATIONS

Canary Hotel [GF] 31 W Carrillo 805/884-0300, 866/999-5401

Inn of the Spanish Garden [GF,SW,NS,WC] 915 Garden St (at Carrillo) 805/564-4700, 866/564-4700 *luxury hotel*

Old Yacht Club Inn [GF,NS,WI] 431 Corona Del Mar Dr 805/962-1277, 800/676-1676 *only B&B on beach*

The Orchid Inn at Santa Barbara [GS,NS,WI,WC,GO] 420 W Montecito St 805/965-2333, 800/427-2156 *1900s Victorian*

White Jasmine Inn [GS,NS,WI] 1327 Bath St (at Sola) 805/966-0589 *cottages, full brkfst, fireplaces*

■BARS

Reds Wine Bar [GS,F,E,WI] 211 Helena Ave 805/966-5906 *2pm-10pm, till 2am Th-Sat, clsd Mon*

■NIGHTCLUBS

Wildcat Lounge [★GS,D] 15 W Ortega St 805/962-7970 *more gay Sun*

■CAFES

Our Daily Bread 831 Santa Barbara St 805/966-3894 *6am-5:30pm, 7am-4pm Sat, clsd Sun, bakery/ cafe*

California • USA

Santa Barbara (continued)

■RESTAURANTS

Joe's Cafe 536 State St
805/966-4638 *7:30am-11pm*

The Natural Cafe 508 State St
805/962-9494 *11am-9pm*

Opal Restaurant & Bar 1325 State St
(at Sola St) 805/966-9676 *lunch
(Mon-Sat) & dinner nightly, full bar*

Sojourner Cafe [BW,WC] 134 E Canon
Perdido (at Santa Barbara)
805/965-7922 *11am-11pm*

■ENTERTAINMENT & RECREATION

Santa Barbara Mission 2201 Laguna
St 805/682-4713 *the "queen of the
missions"; take a self-guided tour btwn
9am-4:30pm*

■BOOKSTORES

Chaucer's Books [★] 3321 State St (at
Las Positas Rd, Loreto Plaza)
805/682-6787 *9am-9pm, till 6pm
Sun*

■EROTICA

For Adults Only 223 Anacapa St
805/963-9922 *24hrs*

The Riviera Adult Superstore 4135
State St (at Hwy 154 intersection)
805/967-8282 *10am-midnight, pride
items, community resources*

Santa Clara

■ACCOMMODATIONS

Avatar Hotel [GS,WI,NS,WC] 4200 Great
America Pkwy 408/235-8900,
800/586-5691

Biltmore Hotel & Suites [GF,SW,NS,WI]
2151 Laurelwood Rd (at Montague
Expwy) 408/988-8411,
800/255-9925

■NIGHTCLUBS

A Tinker's Damn (TD's) [M,D,DS] 46 N
Saratoga Ave (at Stevens Creek)
408/243-4595 *3pm-2am, from 1pm
wknds*

■EROTICA

Hot Stuff 56 Saratoga Ave
408/241-9971 *arcade*

L'Amour Shoppe 2329 El Camino Real
408/296-7076 *24hrs, arcade*

Santa Cruz

■INFO LINES & SERVICES

AA Gay/ Lesbian 5732 Soquel Dr,
Soquel 831/475-5782 (AA#) *call or
visit www.aasantacruz.org for meetings*

The Diversity Center [WI] 1117 Soquel
Ave (at Cayuga) 831/425-5422 *open
daily, call for events*

■ACCOMMODATIONS

Chaminade Resort & Spa
[GF,SW,NS,WC] 1 Chaminade Ln (at
Soquel Ave) 831/475-5600,
800/283-6569

Dream Inn [GS,F,SW,WI] 175 W Cliff Dr
831/426-4330, 866/774-7735

■BARS

Mad House [GS,NH,D,DS,GO] 529
Seabright Ave (at Murray St)
831/425-2900 *4pm-2am, clsd Mon,
more gay Th*

■NIGHTCLUBS

Blue Lagoon [GF,D,A,E,TG,V,WC] 923
Pacific Ave 831/423-7117 *3:30pm-
2am, theme nights, live bands*

■RESTAURANTS

Betty Burgers 505 Seabright Ave (at
Murray) 831/423-8190 *10am-10pm,
retro burger joint, outdoor seating*

Cafe Limelight [TG,WC,GO] 1016 Cedar
St (at Locust St) 831/425-7873 *lunch
& dinner, clsd Mon, European*

Cilantros Mexican Restaurant 1934
Main St (in Town Center strip mall),
Watsonville 831/761-2161 *lunch &
dinner*

Crêpe Place [E,WC] 1134 Soquel Ave (at
Seabright, across from Rio Theater)
831/429-6994 *11am-midnight, from
9am Sat-Sun, full bar, garden patio*

Saturn Cafe [GO] 145 Laurel St (at
Pacific) 831/429-8505 *10am-3am,
vegetarian diner*

Silver Spur 2650 Soquel Dr
831/475-2725 *6am-3pm, clsd Sun*

■ENTERTAINMENT & RECREATION

Bonny Doon Beach [GS,N,AYOR] Hwy 1 at Bonny Doon Rd (at milepost 27.6, N of Santa Cruz) *park in paved parking lot; nude side of beach to the north*

■BOOKSTORES

Bookshop Santa Cruz [WC] 1520 Pacific Ave 831/423-0900 *9am-10pm*

■GYMS & HEALTH CLUBS

Kiva Retreat House Spa 702 Water St (at Ocean) 831/429-1142 *noon-11pm, till midnight Fri-Sat, check for women-only & men-only hours*

■MEN'S SERVICES

➤**MegaMates** 831/515-1020 *Call to hook up with HOT local men. FREE to listen & respond to ads. Use FREE code DAMRON. MegaMates.com.*

■EROTICA

Frenchy's Cruzin Books & Video 3960 Portola Dr (at 41st Ave) 831/475-9221 *arcade*

■CRUISY AREAS

Laguna Creek Beach [AYOR] 7 miles N of town

Santa Rosa

see Sonoma County

Saratoga

■RETAIL SHOPS

Vine Life 14572-A Big Basin Way 408/872-1500 *11am-5pm, wine, cards & gifts*

Sausalito

see Marin County

Sebastopol

see Russian River & Sonoma County

Sonoma County

see also Russian River

■INFO LINES & SERVICES

AA Meetings in Sonoma County 707/544-1300 (AA#), 800/224-1300 *call or visit www.sonomacountyaa.org for meetings*

➤**Sonoma County Tourism Bureau** 707/522-5800, 800/576-6662 *see ad in front color section*

■ACCOMMODATIONS

An Inn 2 Remember [GF,NS,WI,GS] 171 W Spain St (at First St W), Sonoma 707/938-2909 *located in Wine Country, whirlpool baths & fireplaces, free use of bikes*

Beltane Ranch [GF] 11775 Sonoma Hwy (Hwy 12), Glen Ellen 707/996-6501 *1892 New Orleans-style ranch house*

Best Western Dry Creek Inn [GS,SW,WI] 198 Dry Creek Rd, Healdsburg 707/433-0300, 800/222-5784

Camellia Inn [GF,SW,NS,WI] 211 North St (at Fitch), Healdsburg 707/433-8182, 800/727-8182 *Italianate Victorian, full brkfst*

The Gaige House [GF,SW,WI] 13540 Arnold Dr, Glen Ellen 707/935-0237, 800/935-0237 *in the Wine Country*

Grape Leaf Inn [GF,WI] 539 Johnson St, Healdsburg 707/433-8140, 866/433-8140 *Queen Anne Victorian, full brkfst*

Hyatt Vineyard Creek Hotel [GF,SW,WI,WC] 170 Railroad St (at Third St), Santa Rosa 707/284-1234 *resort, seafood restaurant*

Les Petites Maisons [GF,WI] 1190 E Napa St (at 8th St E), Sonoma 707/933-0340, 800/291-8962

Madrona Manor [GF,F,SW,NS,WC] 1001 Westside Rd, Healdsburg 707/433-4231, 800/258-4003 *also restaurant*

Magliulo's Rose Garden Inn [GF,WI,WC] 681 Broadway (at Andrieux), Sonoma 707/996-1031

Sonoma Chalet [GF] 18935 5th St W, Sonoma 707/938-3129, 800/938-3129

■CAFES

A' Roma Roasters [MW,E,WC,GO] 95 5th St (Railroad Square), Santa Rosa 707/576-7765 *6am-close, from 7am Sat-Sun*

California • *USA*

Coffee Catz [E,WI] 6761 Sebastopol Ave #300 (in Gravenstein Station), Sebastopol **707/829-6600** *7am-6pm, till 10pm Wed (open mic), till 10pm Fri-Sat (live bands), garden*

Screamin' Mimi's 6902 Sebastopol Ave (intersection of Hwy 12 & 116), Sebastopol **707/823-5902** *espresso drinks & homemade ice cream*

Sonoma's Best 1190 E Napa St (at 8th St E), Sonoma **707/996-7600** *7am-6pm, 8am-5pm Sun, local products—cheese, wine, olive oils & more—under one roof*

■RESTAURANTS

Cafe 522 [BW,GO] 522 Broadway, Sonoma **707/938-7373** *lunch & dinner, wknd brunch, clsd Mon, local & sustainably raised produce & meat*

Estate 400 W Spain St, Sonoma **707/933-3663** *lunch & dinner, Sun brunch, clsd Mon, Italian*

Fig Cafe & Wine Bar 13690 Arnold Dr, Glen Ellen **707/938-2130** *dinner nightly, Sun brunch*

Mom's Apple Pie 4550 Gravenstein Hwy N, Sebastopol **707/823-8330** *pie worth stopping for on your way to & from Russian River!*

Singletree Inn [GO] 165 Healdsburg Ave, Healdsburg **707/433-8263** *7am-3pm, good brkfsts, famous BBQ sandwiches, some veggie, local wines, outdoor seating*

Slice of Life 6970 McKinley St, Sebastopol **707/829-6627** *11am-9pm, from 9am Sat-Sun, clsd Mon, vegan & vegetarian*

Syrah Bistro 205 5th St (at Davis), Santa Rosa **707/568-4002** *dinner nightly, California/ French*

■ENTERTAINMENT & RECREATION

Out In The Vineyard [GO] **707/495-9732** *tours of the wine country*

River's Edge Kayak & Canoe Company [GO] **707/433-7247** *river excursions*

■RETAIL SHOPS

Grower's Collective Tasting Room **707/996-1364** *noon-5:30pm, clsd Tue-Th, open wknds only in winter*

■MEN'S SERVICES

➤**MegaMates** **707/583-1112** *Call to hook up with HOT local men. FREE to listen & respond to ads. Use FREE code DAMRON. MegaMates.com.*

■EROTICA

Secrets Santa Rosa 3301 Santa Rosa Ave (at Todd), Santa Rosa **707/542-8248**

Springville

■ACCOMMODATIONS

Great Energy [MW,SW,NS] PO Box 473, 93265 **559/539-2382** *retreat in foothills of Sierra Nevada mtns*

Stockton

see also Modesto

■NIGHTCLUBS

Paradise Club [MW,D,E,V,YC] 10100 N Lower Sacramento Rd (near Grider) **209/477-4724** *6pm-2am, from 3pm Sun*

■EROTICA

Suzie's Adult Superstores 3126 E Hammer Ln **209/952-6900** *24hrs, arcade*

■CRUISY AREAS

Oak Park [AYOR] Alpine Ave

Sunnyvale

see also San Jose

■ACCOMMODATIONS

Wild Palms Hotel [GF,SW,WI,WC] 910 E Fremont Ave (at Wolfe Ave) **408/738-0500, 800/538-1600** *hot tub*

■MEN'S SERVICES

➤**MegaMates** **408/331-7400** *Call to hook up with HOT local men. FREE to listen & respond to ads. Use FREE code DAMRON. MegaMates.com.*

Sutter Creek

■ACCOMMODATIONS

The Foxes Inn of Sutter Creek
[GF,NS,WI,GO] 77 Main St (at Keys St)
209/267-5882, 800/987-3344 *full brkfst*

Temecula

■NIGHTCLUBS

Aloha J's [MW,D,F] 27497 Ynez Rd
951/506-9889 *gay/ straight, more gay Wed*

Club Velocity [MW,D,F] 27725 Jefferson Ave Ste 101 (at Johnny G's)
951/506-0399 *9pm Sun only; also Wed at Aloha J's*

Tiburon

see Marin County

Twentynine Palms

see Joshua Tree Nat'l Park

Ukiah

■BARS

Perkins St Lounge [GF,D,E,K] 228 E
Perkins St 707/462-0327 *3pm-2am*

Upland

■NIGHTCLUBS

Oasis [M,D,F,DS,WC] 1386 E Foothill Blvd #H (at Grove) 909/920-9590 *6pm-2am Wed-Sat, from 8pm Sun*

■EROTICA

Sensations Love Boutique 1656 W
Foothill Blvd (at Mountain)
909/985-1654

The Toy Box 1999 W Arrow Rte (at Central) 909/920-1115 *24hrs*

Vacaville

■INFO LINES & SERVICES

Solano Pride Center 1125 Missouri St #203-D, Fairfield 707/398-3463 *call for meeting times*

■EROTICA

Secrets Adult Super Store 564 Parker Rd (at Union Ave), Fairfield
707/437-9297 *arcade*

■CRUISY AREAS

Lee Bell Park [AYOR] Travis Blvd (at Union Ave), Fairfield

Vallejo

includes Benicia

■BARS

Town House Cocktail Lounge
[GS,NH,GO] 401-A Georgia St (at Marin)
707/553-9109 *1pm-midnight, from 10am Sat-Sun*

■BOOKSTORES

Bookshop Benicia [WC] 856
Southampton Rd, Benicia
707/747-5155 *10am-7pm, till 6pm wknds*

Van Nuys

■MEN'S SERVICES

►**MegaMates 818/465-0500** *Call to hook up with HOT local men. FREE to listen & respond to ads. Use FREE code DAMRON. MegaMates.com.*

Ventura

see also Santa Barbara

■INFO LINES & SERVICES

AA Gay/ Lesbian 805/389-1444
(AA#), 800/990-7750

■BARS

Paddy McDermott's [MW,D,F,E,K] 2 W
Main St (at Ventura) 805/652-1071
2pm-2am, beer busts

■EROTICA

Three Star Books 359 E Main St
805/653-9068 *24hrs*

■CRUISY AREAS

Surfers Point [AYOR] N of the Ventura Pier (btwn fairgrounds & Ocean) *go N along beach to Hobo's Jungle*

Victorville

■BARS

Ricky's [GS,D,F,K,DS,WC] 13728 Hesperia Rd #12 760/951-5400 *6pm-2am, clsd Mon*

California • *USA*

■EROTICA

Oasis Adult Dept Store 14949 Palmdale Rd **760/241-0788** *arcade*

■CRUISY AREAS

Deep Creek Hot Springs [AYOR] Apple Valley *from I-15, take Bear Valley Cutoff & turn right onto Central Rd; go left onto Ocotillo Rd for 2 miles & turn right onto Bowen Ranch Rd (unmarked dirt road)*

Grady Trammel Park [AYOR] 3/4 mile N of West Side 15 bar (on Stoddard Wells Rd) *watch out for rangers (!)*

Walnut Creek

see East Bay

■MEN'S SERVICES

➤**MegaMates** 925/300-9999 *Call to hook up with HOT local men. FREE to listen & respond to ads. Use FREE code DAMRON. MegaMates.com.*

Yosemite Nat'l Park

■ACCOMMODATIONS

The Ahwahnee Hotel [GF,F,SW,NS] Yosemite Valley Floor **866/875-8456** **(reservations)** *incredibly dramatic & expensive grand fortress*

Highland House B&B [GF,WI] 3125 Wild Dove Ln (at Jerseydale Rd), Mariposa **209/966-3737**

The Homestead [GF,NS,WI] 41110 Rd 600, Ahwahnee **559/683-0495, 800/483-0495** *cottages & 2-bdrm house*

June Lake Villager [GF,WI] 2640 Hwy 158 (2.5 miles W of Hwy 395), June Lake **760/648-7712, 800/655-6545**

Narrow Gauge Inn [GF,SW,NS] 48571 Hwy 41, Fish Camp **559/683-7720, 888/644-9050**

Queen's Inn by the River [GS,NS,WI,WC,GO] 41139 Hwy 41, Oakhurst **559/683-4354** *garden w/ river view, lesbian-owned*

Tenaya Lodge at Yosemite [GF,F,SW] 1122 Hwy 41, Fish Camp **559/683-6555, 888/514-2167**

The Yosemite Bug Rustic Mountain Resort [GF,F,SW,NS,WI,WC] 6979 Hwy 140, Midpines **209/966-6666, 866/826-7108** *hostel w/ dorms, cabins, private rooms & tents*

Yosemite View Lodge [GF,SW,WC] 11136 Hwy 140, El Portal **209/379-2681, 888/742-4371** *3 pools, 2 restaurants & lounge*

Yosemite's Apple Blossom Inn B&B [GF,NS,WC] 559/642-2001, **888/687-4281** *20 minutes from S entrance to Yosemite, hot tub*

■CRUISY AREAS

Rest Stop [AYOR] at turn to Glacier Point on road to valley

COLORADO

Statewide

■PUBLICATIONS

➤**Out Front Colorado** 303/778-7900 *statewide LGBT newspaper*

Aspen

■ACCOMMODATIONS

Aspen Mountain Lodge [GF,SW,NS] 311 W Main St **970/925-7650, 800/362-7736**

Hotel Aspen [GF,SW,NS,WI] 110 W Main St **970/925-3441, 800/527-7369** *hot tub, après-ski wine & cheese*

Hotel Lenado [GF] 200 S Aspen St **970/925-6246, 800/321-3457**

St Moritz Lodge [GF,SW,NS,WI,GO] 334 W Hyman Ave **970/925-3220, 800/817-2069**

■RESTAURANTS

Jimmy's 205 S Mill St (at Hopkins) **970/925-6020** *5:30pm-11pm, Sun brunch, also from 4:30pm, patio*

Syzygy [E,WC] 308 E Hopkins Ave **970/925-3700** *seasonal, 6pm-10pm, bar till 2am*

■BOOKSTORES

Explore Booksellers & Bistro [F,WI,WC] 221 E Main St (at Aspen) **970/925-5336, 800/562-7323** *10am-10pm, also vegetarian restaurant*

Beaver Creek

■ACCOMMODATIONS

Beaver Creek Lodge [GF,SW,NS,WI,WC]
26 Avondale Ln (at Village Rd)
970/845-9800, 800/525-7280 *also restaurant, mtn chic, steam room, gym*

Boulder

■INFO LINES & SERVICES

Out Boulder 2132 14th St (at Pine)
303/499-5777 *LGBT resource center*

■ACCOMMODATIONS

The Briar Rose B&B [GF,NS,WI] 2151
Arapahoe Ave (at 22nd St)
303/442-3007, 888/786-8440 *full organic brkfst*

■CAFES

Walnut Cafe [★WC] 3073 Walnut St
(at 30th) 303/447-2315 *7am-3:30pm, patio*

■ENTERTAINMENT & RECREATION

Boulder Area Bicycle Adventures
[GO] 303/494-7062 *bike tours of Boulder & annual LGBT ride in June*

■BOOKSTORES

Left Hand Books 1200 Pearl St #10 (E
of Broadway) 303/443-8252 *10am-9pm, noon-6pm Sun*

■RETAIL SHOPS

Enchanted Ink [GO] 1200 Pearl St #35
(at Broadway) 303/440-6611 *tattoos, piercing, henna*

■CRUISY AREAS

Dream Canyon [SW,N] Lost Angel Rd
(off Sugarloaf Mtn Rd) *inquire locally for detailed directions*

Breckenridge

■ACCOMMODATIONS

Valdoro Mountain Lodge
[GS,SW,NS,WI,WC] 500 Village Rd
970/453-4880, 800/436-6780
condos w/ access to pool, massage facilities & outdoor hot tub

Colorado Springs

(includes Manitou Springs)

■INFO LINES & SERVICES

Colorado Springs Pride Center [WI]
719/471-4429 *noon-5pm*

■ACCOMMODATIONS

Blue Skies Inn B&B [GS,NS,WI,WC] 402
Manitou Ave (at Mayfair), Manitou
Springs 719/685-3899,
800/398-7949 *Gothic Revival, full brkfst*

Old Town Guesthouse [GF,NS,WI,WC]
115 S 26th St 719/632-9194,
888/375-4210 *full brkfst, hot tub*

Pikes Peak Paradise [GF,NS,WI,GO] 236
Pinecrest Rd, Woodland Park
719/687-6656, 800/728-8282 *full brkfst, hot tub, mansion w/ view of Pikes Peak*

Two Sisters Inn—A B&B [★GF,NS]
10 Otoe Pl, Manitou Springs
719/685-9684, 800/274-7466

■BARS

Bubbles [MW,D,K,DS,S,WC] 1110 E
Filmore St (at Nevada) 719/473-0177
6pm-2am, till 4am Fri-Sat, clsd Mon

Club Q [★M,NH,D,F,E,K,S,18+,WC,GO]
3430 N Academy Blvd (at N Carefree)
719/570-1429 *6pm-2am, till 4am Sat, clsd Mon*

Underground [M,NH,D,F,K,GO] 110 N
Nevada Ave (at Kiowa St)
719/578-7771 *4pm-2am, from 2pm Sun*

■CAFES

**Spice of Life an Ingredients
Emporium** [WI] 727 Manitou Ave,
Manitou Springs 719/685-5284 *7am-6pm*

■RESTAURANTS

Dale Street Bistro Cafe 115 E Dale (at
Nevada) 719/578-9898 *lunch & dinner, brunch wknds*

■MEN'S CLUBS

Buddies [MO,MR,V,18+,N,PC,GO] 3430 N
Academy Blvd (N Carefree)
719/591-7660 *3pm-4am, clsd Mon-Tue, beer bust Sun*

Colorado • USA

▰MEN'S SERVICES

►MegaMates 719/520-9797 *Call to hook up with HOT local men. FREE to listen & respond to ads. Use FREE code DAMRON. MegaMates.com.*

▰EROTICA

First Amendment Adult Bookstore
220 E Fillmore St (at Nevada)
719/630-7676

XXX-Treme Mature Fantasy Store
620 Peterson Rd (Platte -Hwy 24)
719/638-0200

▰CRUISY AREAS

Palmer Park [AYOR] *many undercover cops*

Denver

▰INFO LINES & SERVICES

Gay/ Lesbian AA 303/322-4440

The GLBT Center of Colorado (The Center) [WC] 1301 E Colfax
303/733-7743 *10am-8pm Mon-Fri, from noon Sat, extensive resources & support groups*

Sketchin' OUT (Crystal Meth Anonymous) [WC] 1301 E Colfax
303/733-7743 *7pm Fri; also Ray of Light (Narcotics Anonymous) 7pm Wed*

▰ACCOMMODATIONS

The Brown Palace [GF,WI] 321 17th St (at N Broadway) 303/297-3111, 800/321-2599 *sun in every room, also restaurant & spa*

Capitol Hill Mansion B&B [GF,NS,WI] 1207 Pennsylvania St (at 12th)
303/839-5221, 800/839-9329 *full brkfst, hot tub*

Castle Marne B&B [GF,WI] 1572 Race St (at 16th Ave) 303/331-0621, 800/926-2763 *hot tubs on private balconies*

The Curtis [GF,SW,WI] 1405 Curtis St
303/571-0300, 800/525-6651 *hip hotel, restaurant*

The Gregory Inn, LoDo [GF,NS,WI] 2500 Arapahoe St (at 25th)
303/295-6570, 800/925-6570 *full brkfst, jacuzzis*

Hotel Monaco [GF,NS,WI] 1717 Champa St (at 17th) 303/296-1717, 800/990-1303 *gym, spa, also Italian restaurant*

Hotel Teatro [GF,NS,WI] 1100 14th St
303/228-1100, 888/727-1200 *luxury boutique hotel, 2 restaurants*

The Oxford Hotel [GF,F,WI] 1600 17th St 303/628-5400, 800/228-5838 *health club & spa, also restaurant & art deco lounge*

▰BARS

Aqua Lounge [MW,E,V,WI] 1417 Krameria (btwn 14th & Colfax)
720/287-0584 *4pm-2am, piano bar*

Barker Lounge [M,NH] 475 Santa Fe Dr (at 5th St) 303/778-0545 *noon-2am, also large patio w/ bar, dogs welcome*

The Beauty Bar [GS,D,E]
720/542-8024 *5pm-10pm, 7pm-2am Sat, clsd Sun-Mon*

Bender's Tavern [GF,F,E,K] 314 E 13th Ave (at Grant) 303/861-7070 *4pm-2am, from 7pm Mon-Wed, clsd Sun, live bands*

Black Crown Piano Lounge [M,F,E] 1446 S Broadway 720/353-4701 *4pm-midnight, till 2am Fri-Sat, from 11am Sat-Sun*

Boyztown [M,NH,S,WI] 117 Broadway (btwn 1st & 2nd Aves) 303/722-7373 *3pm-2am, from noon wknds, male dancers Tue-Sun*

Broadways [M,NH,WI] 1027 Broadway (at 11th Ave) 303/623-0700 *2pm-2am, from noon Sat-Sun, cool mix of folk*

Charlie's [★M,D,CW,K,DS,WC] 900 E Colfax Ave (at Emerson)
303/839-8890 *11am-2am, 2 clubs, also restaurant*

The Compound/Basix [★M,NH,D] 145 Broadway (at 2nd Ave) 303/722-7977 *7am-2am, [D] Fri-Sat*

Dazzle [GF,F,E] 930 Lincoln St (btwn 9th & 10th Aves) 303/839-5100 *from 4pm Sun-Th, from 11am Fri, also Sun brunch, jazz club & restaurant*

Denver Eagle [M,NH,B,L,WC,GO] 3600 Blake St (at 36th) 303/291-0250 *4pm-2am, from 2pm wknds, clsd Mon*

Chronicling our struggles and our victories. NOW THE FIRST AND THIRD WEDNESDAY OF EACH MONTH and online 24/7 at
OutFrontONLINE.com
facebook.com/outfrontcolorado.com
twitter.com/outfrontco

Colorado • USA

The Denver Wrangler [M,B,WC] 1700 Logan St (at 17th Ave) **303/837-1075** 11am-2am, levi/ bear bar, popular Sun beer bust

Eden [W,F,E] 3090 Downing St (at 31st Ave) **303/832-5482** 4pm-2am, from 11am Sun (brunch till 4pm)

El Chapultepec [★GF,F,E,$] 1962 Market St (at 20th) **303/295-9126** 9am-2am, live jazz & blues, 1-drink minimum per set

El Potrero [GS,MR-L,E,F] 320 S Birch St (at Leetsdale Dr), Glendale **303/388-8889** Mexican restaurant early, Latino gay bar late (Wed, Sat-Sun)

R&R Denver [MW,NH] 4958 E Colfax Ave (at Elm St) **303/320-9337** 3pm-2am, from 1pm Fri, from 11am wknds

Rock Bar [GS] 3015 E Colfax (at Milwaukee) **303/322-4444** 5pm-2am, dive bar, theme nights

There Urban Whiskey Bar [MW,WI,WC,GO] 1526 E Colfax (btwn Humboldt & Franklin) **303/830-8437** 11am-2am

X Bar [MW,D,F] 629 E Colfax Ave **303/832-2687** 2pm-2am, from 10am wknds

■NIGHTCLUBS

Beta Nightclub [GS,D,$] 1909 Blake St (btwn 19th & 20th) **303/383-1909** more gay Th

Climax Sunday at Club Vinyl [MW,D] 1082 Broadway **303/832-8628** 4pm-2am Sun, great rooftop patio

La Rumba [GF,D,E,$] 99 W 9th Ave (at Broadway) **303/572-8006** salsa dancing Et lessons Th & Sat, more gay Fri for Lipgloss (Brit-pop & indie music)

Lannie's Clocktower Cabaret [GF,F,E,C] 16th St Mall at Arapahoe (in historic D&F Tower) **303/293-0075** upscale cabaret w/ variety of acts weekly, including drag & burlesque

Tracks [GS,D,DS,MR] 3500 Walnut St (at 36th) **303/863-7326** 9pm-2am, clsd Sun-Wed, 2 rooms, theme nights

■CAFES

City, O City 206 E 13th Ave (at Sherman) **303/831-6443** 7am-2am, from 8am wknds, vegetarian/ vegan, also bar

Common Grounds [WI] 3484 W 32nd Ave (Lowell) **303/458-5248** also also at 17th & Wazee

Dazbog [WI] 1201 E 9th Ave (at Downing) **303/837-1275** 6am-10pm, from 7am Sun, outdoor seating w/ heated patio

Geez Louise [F,GO] 4924 E Colfax Ave (E of Colorado Blvd) **303/322-3833** 6am-4pm, from 7am wknds, till 2pm Mon

The Market at Larimer Square 1445 Larimer Sq (btwn 14th & 15th) **303/534-5140** 6am-11pm, till midnight Fri-Sat, till 10pm Sun

Paris on the Platte [E,WI] 1553 Platte St (at 15th) **303/455-2451** 7am-2am, soups, salads, sandwiches, live music

■RESTAURANTS

Annie's Cafe & Bar [★] 3100 E Colfax (at St Paul) **303/355-8197** 7am-10pm, from 8am Sat, diner

The Avenue Grill 630 E 17th Ave (at Washington) **303/861-2820** 11am-11pm, till midnight Fri-Sat, till 10pm Sun

Banzai Sushi 6655 Leetsdale Dr (E of Colorado Blvd) **303/329-3366** lunch Mon-Fri, dinner nightly

Barricuda's 1076 Ogden St (at E 11th) **303/860-8353** 10am-2am, also dive bar

Beatrice & Woodsley [R] 38 S Broadway **303/777-3505** one of America's top restaurants

Benny's Restaurante y Tequila Bar 301 E 7th Ave (at Grant St) **303/894-0788** lunch & dinner, patio

The Corner Office Restaurant & Martini Bar 1405 Curtis St (at Curtis Hotel) **303/825-6500** 6am-midnight, till 2am Fri-Sat, groovy Sun disco brunch

Devil's Food 1020 S Gaylord St (at E Tennessee) **303/733-7448** 7am-10pm, till 3pm wknds, yummy desserts

Duo 2413 W 32nd Ave (at Zuni) **303/477-4141** *dinner nightly, wknd brunch, hip, organic, creative American, full bar*

Euclid Hall Bar & Kitchen 1317 14th St **303/595-4255** *11:30am-1am, till 2am Fri-Sat, American tavern, pub food*

Fruition 1313 E 6th Ave **303/831-1962** *5pm-10pm, till 8pm Sun, contemporary French*

Hamburger Mary's/ Club M [★GS,D,K,DS] 700 E 17th Ave (at Washington St, across from JR's bar) **303/832-1333** *11am-2am, from 10am Sun*

Il Vicino 550 Broadway **303/861-0801** *11am-10pm, pizza*

Jelly Cafe 600 E 13th Ave (at Pearl) **303/831-6301** *7am-3pm, a whole lotta Jelly-filled fun*

Las Margaritas Uptown [★GO] 1035 E 17th Ave (at Downing) **303/830-2199** *11am-1am, Mexican, also bar*

Pete's Kitchen [★] 1962 E Colfax Ave **303/321-3139** *24hrs, diner, popular after bars close*

Racine's 650 Sherman St (at 6th Ave) **303/595-0418** *brkfst, lunch, dinner, late night & Sun brunch, full bar*

Sexy Pizza 1018 E 11th Ave **303/830-8111**

Steuben's 523 E 17th Ave **303/830-1001** *11am-11pm, American comfort food served up hip, patio, full bar*

Sunny Gardens 6460 E Yale Avenue **303/691-8830** *Chinese, plenty veggie/ vegan*

Thai Pot Cafe 1550 S Colorado Blvd (at E Florida) **303/639-6200** *lunch & dinner*

Tom's Home Cookin' [WC,GO] **303/388-8035** *11am-3pm, clsd Sat-Sun, Southern comfort food*

Vesta Dipping Grill 1822 Blake St (near 18th St) **303/296-1970** *5pm-10pm Sun-Th, till 11pm Fri-Sat, upscale*

WaterCourse Foods 837 E 17th Ave (at Clarkson) **303/832-7313** *7am-9pm, till 10pm Fri-Sat, vegetarian/ vegan*

Wazee Supper Club [WC] 1600 15th St (at Wazee) **303/623-9518, 303/825-3199 (pizza delivery)** *11am-2am, noon-midnight Sun, classic comfort food, full bar*

■ENTERTAINMENT & RECREATION

Mercury Cafe [F,E] 2199 California St **303/294-9281** *5:30pm-close, swing, tango, salsa dancing, live shows, also restaurant, dinner Tue-Sun, wknd brunch*

Rocky Mountain Rainbeaus **303/863-7739** *all-inclusive, all-levels, high-energy square dance club*

■BOOKSTORES

Tattered Cover Book Store [WC] 2526 Colfax Ave (at Elizabeth St) **303/322-7727, 800/833-9327** *9am-9pm, 10am-6pm Sun, independent, cafe; also 1628 16th St, 303/ 436-1070*

■RETAIL SHOPS

Bound By Design 1332 E Colfax Ave (at Humboldt) **303/830-7272, 303/832-TAT2** *piercing & tattoos*

CJ's Leather 116 S Broadway (btwn Alameda & Virginia) **303/733-6212, 866/690-1157** *11am-5pm, clsd Sun-Mon*

Heaven Sent Me [WC] 116 S Broadway (btwn Alameda & Virginia) **303/733-9900** *11am-7pm, pride items, clothing, gifts*

Rockmount Ranch Wear 1626 Wazee St **303/629-7777, 800/776-2566** *8am-6pm, from 11am wknds, makers of the shirts worn in Brokeback Mountain*

■PUBLICATIONS

Gayzette 720/435-8914 *LGBT monthly publication*

▶**Out Front Colorado** **303/778-7900** *statewide bi-weekly LGBT newspaper, since 1976*

■GYMS & HEALTH CLUBS

Pura Vida Fitness & Spa 2955 E 1st Ave #200 **303/321-7872**

■MEN'S CLUBS

CCC (Community Country Club) [V,PC] 2151 Lawrence St (at 21st) **303/297-2601**

Colorado • *USA*

Denver Swim Club [★MO,V,YC,SW,PC] 6923 E Colfax Ave (at Olive) 303/322-4023

Midtowne Spa—Denver [PC] 2935 Zuni St (at 29th) **303/458-8902** *24hrs*

■MEN'S SERVICES

▶**MegaMates** 303/433-6789 *Call to hook up with HOT local men. FREE to listen & respond to ads. Use FREE code DAMRON. MegaMates.com.*

■EROTICA

Circus Cinema 5580 N Federal Blvd 303/455-3144 *24hrs*

Crypt Adult Entertainment 139 Broadway (btwn 1st & 2nd) 303/778-6584 *10am-2am, all-male theaters & arcades*

The Crypt on Broadway 8 Broadway (at Ellsworth) **303/733-3112** *11am-11pm, leather, clubwear & more*

Dove Theater 3480 W Colfax (at King St) 303/893-0037 *8:30am-12:30am, 24hrs wknds*

Pleasure Entertainment Center 127 S Broadway (at Bayaud) **303/722-5852** *open 23hrs; also* 3250 W Alameda, 303/934-2373 & 3490 W Colfax, 303/825-6505

Romantix Adult Superstore 633 E Colfax Ave (at Washington) 303/831-8319

■CRUISY AREAS

Cheesman Park [AYOR] *near Pavilion beware of undercover cops!*

Durango

■ACCOMMODATIONS

Leland House B&B [GF,NS,WI,WC] 721 E 2nd Ave 970/385-1920

Mesa Verde Far View Lodge [GF,NS,WI] 1 Navajo Hill, Mesa Verde National Park **602/331-5210, 800/449-2288** *inside nat'l park*

Rochester Hotel [★GF,NS,WC] 721 E 2nd Ave **800/664-1920** *Western-style house, full brkfst*

■RESTAURANTS

Palace Restaurant [WC,GO] 505 Main Ave (at 5th St) **970/247-2018** *11am-10pm, clsd Sun (in winter), full bar, patio*

Estes Park

■ACCOMMODATIONS

Mountain Sage Inn [GF,NS] 553 W Elkhorn Ave 970/586-2833, 800/552-2833

Stanley Hotel [GF,SW,WI] 333 Wonderview Ave 800/976-1377, 970/577-4000 *the inspiration for Stephen King's The Shining*

Fort Collins

■ACCOMMODATIONS

Archer's Poudre River Resort [GF,GO] 33021 Poudre Canyon Hwy, Bellvue 970/881-2139, 888/822-0588

■BARS

Choice City Shots [MW,NH,D,K,S,WC,GO] 124 LaPorte Ave (at College) 970/221-4333 *6:30pm-midnight, till 1:30am Th-Sat*

Grand Junction

■RESTAURANTS

Leon's Taqueria 505 30th Rd 970/242-1388 *11am-9pm*

■EROTICA

24 Road Video Exchange 639 24 Rd (at Mesa Mall) 970/243-4112 *10am-11pm*

Junction News 754 North Ave (at 7th St) 970/242-9702 *24hrs, till midnight Sun-Mon*

■CRUISY AREAS

Hawthorne Park [AYOR]

Walker Wildlife Area [AYOR] Hwy 6/50 W, past Mesa Mall (near the CO River) *in the woods*

Hotchkiss

■ACCOMMODATIONS

Leroux Creek Inn & Vineyards [GF] 12388 3100 Rd 970/872-4746

■RESTAURANTS

North Fork Valley Restaurant & Thirsty Parrot Pub [E] 140 W Bridge St 970/872-4215 *11am-8pm, American/Mexican*

Pueblo

BARS

Pirate's Cove [MW,NH,WC] 105 Central Plaza (off 1st & Union) 719/543-2683 4pm-2am, call for Sun hrs, clsd Mon

CRUISY AREAS

City Park Pueblo Blvd & Thatcher *N side near gazebo*

Stratton

ACCOMMODATIONS

Claremont Inn [GS,F,WI,GO] 800 Claremont St (off exit 419, I-70) 719/348-5125, 888/291-8910 *2 hours from Denver, full brkfst*

Vail

RESTAURANTS

Larkspur Restaurant & Market [WC] 458 Vail Valley Dr (in the Golden Peak Lodge) 970/754-8050 *lunch & dinner, fine dining, also bar, patio, ski-in/ out*

Sweet Basil [WC] 193 E Gore Creek Dr 970/476-0125 *lunch & dinner, bar*

CONNECTICUT

Statewide

PUBLICATIONS

➤**Metroline** 860/231-8334 *regional newspaper & entertainment guide, covers CT, RI & MA*

Bethel

CAFES

Molten Java [E,GO] 213 Greenwood Ave 203/739-0313 *6am-9pm, till 10pm Fri-Sat, 8am-8pm Sat-Sun*

RESTAURANTS

Bethel Pizza House 206 Greenwood Ave 203/748-1427 *11am-11pm, till midnight Fri-Sat*

Bridgeport

RESTAURANTS

Bloodroot Restaurant & Bookstore 85 Ferris St (at Harbor Ave) 203/576-9168 *lunch Tue & Th-Sat, dinner Tue-Sat, brunch only Sun, clsd Mon, vegetarian*

MEN'S SERVICES

➤**MegaMates** 203/612-9962 *Call to hook up with HOT local men. FREE to listen & respond to ads. Use FREE code DAMRON. MegaMates.com.*

EROTICA

Boston Book & Video 2053 Boston Ave 203/335-9705 *open till 2am*

Romantix Adult Superstore 410 North Ave 203/332-7129

Bristol

EROTICA

Amazing Superstore 167 Farmington Ave 860/582-9000

CRUISY AREAS

Rockwell Park [AYOR] Rte 72

Colebrook

ACCOMMODATIONS

Rock Hall Luxe Lodging [GS,SW,NS,WI] 19 Rock Hall Rd 860/379-2230

Danbury

ACCOMMODATIONS

Maron Hotel & Suites [GF,WI,WC] 42 Lake Ave Extension (off I-84) 203/791-2200, 866/811-2582 *kids/ pets ok*

BARS

Triangles Cafe [★MW,D,K,DS,V,GO] 66 Sugar Hollow Rd, Rte 7 203/798-6996 *5pm-1am, till 2am Fri-Sat, patio*

RESTAURANTS

Sesame Seed 68 W Wooster St 203/743-9850 *lunch & dinner, clsd Sun, Mediterranean/ Italian*

Thang Long [BYOB] 56 Padanaram Rd (near North Street Shopping Center) 203/743-6049 *lunch & dinner, Vietnamese*

Enfield

EROTICA

Bookends 44 Enfield St/ Rte 5 860/745-3988

Connecticut • USA

Groton

◼EROTICA
Amazing 591 Rte 12 #8
860/448-0787

Hartford

◼INFO LINES & SERVICES
Hartford Gay & Lesbian Health Collective 1841 Broad St (at New Britain Ave) 860/278-4163 *9am-5pm, till 9pm Th, clsd wknds*

True Colors 576 Farmington Ave 860/232-0050, 888/565-5551 *support & mentoring for LGBT youth*

◼ACCOMMODATIONS
Butternut Farm [GS,NS,WI] 1654 Main St, Glastonbury 860/633-7197 *full brkfst*

Inn at Kent Falls [GS,SW,NS,WI,WC,GO] 107 Kent Cornwall Rd, Kent 860/927-3197 *1 hr from Hartford*

The Mansion Inn [GF] 139 Hartford Rd (at Main St), Manchester 860/646-0453

◼BARS
Chez Est [★MW,D,F,K,DS] 458 Wethersfield Ave (at Main St) 860/525-3243 *3pm-1am, till 2am Fri-Sat*

Polo [MW,D,E,K,DS,S] 678 Maple Ave (btwn Preston & Mapleton) 860/278-3333 *9pm-1am, till 2am Fri-Sat, clsd Sun-Wed*

◼CAFES
Tisane Tea & Coffee Bar [F,K,WI] 537 Farmington Ave (at Kenyon) 860/523-5417 *8am-1am, till 2am Sat, also bar, men's night Tue*

◼RESTAURANTS
Arugula [R,WC] 953 Farmington Ave, West Hartford 860/561-4888 *lunch & dinner, clsd Mon, Mediterranean*

Firebox 539 Broad St 860/246-1222 *11:30am-10:30pm, 4:30pm-8:30pm Sun, contemporary American, also farmers market Th (April-Oct)*

Peppercorns Grill 357 Main St 860/547-1714 *lunch Mon-Fri, dinner nightly, clsd Sun, Northern Italian*

Pond House Cafe [BYOB,WC] 1555 Asylum Ave, W Hartford 860/231-8823 *lunch & dinner Tue-Sat, wknd brunch, patio*

Trumbull Kitchen 150 Trumbull St (at Pearl St) 860/493-7417 *lunch Mon-Sat dinner nightly, global cuisine/ tapas*

◼ENTERTAINMENT & RECREATION
Real Art Ways [WI] 56 Arbor St 860/232-1006 *contemporary art, cinema, performance, also lounge*

◼RETAIL SHOPS
➤**MetroStore** 493 Farmington Ave (at Sisson Ave) 860/231-8845 *8:30am-8pm, till 5:30pm Tue, Wed & Sat, clsd Sun, magazines, travel guides, leather, DVD rentals & more*

◼PUBLICATIONS
➤**Metroline** 860/233-8334 *regional newspaper & entertainment guide, covers CT, RI & MA*

◼MEN'S SERVICES
➤**MegaMates** 860/242-3600 *Call to hook up with HOT local men. FREE to listen & respond to ads. Use FREE code DAMRON. MegaMates.com.*

◼EROTICA
Erotic Zone [AYOR] 35 W Service Rd (at Hwy 91 N) 860/549-1896 *8am-6pm*

Very Intimate Pleasures 100 Brainard Rd (exit 27, off I-91) 860/246-1875

◼CRUISY AREAS
Bushnell Park [AYOR] S of Asylum Ave (downtown exit off I-84)

Meriden

◼CRUISY AREAS
Hubbard Park [AYOR]

Middletown

◼ENTERTAINMENT & RECREATION
Wednesday Night Supper Club [M,B,F,GO] 825 Saybrook Rd (at Tommy's Restaurant) 860/346-8686 *6:30pm-close Wed only*

Connecticut • USA

Mystic

▪ACCOMMODATIONS

House of 1833 B&B Resort
[GF,SW,NS,WI,GO] 72 N Stonington Rd
860/536-6325, 800/367-1833

The Mare's Inn B&B [GF,NS,WC,GO]
333 Colonel Ledyard Hwy, Ledyard
860/572-7556

Mermaid Inn of Mystic
[MW,WI,NS,GO] 2 Broadway
860/536-6223, 877/692-2632 *B&B
w/ village location & river views, full
brkfst, lesbian-owned*

The Old Mystic Inn [GF,NS,WI,GO] 52
Main St (at Rte 27), Old Mystic
860/572-9422

New Britain

▪CRUISY AREAS

Martha Hart Park [AYOR] off Corbin
Ave

New Haven

▪INFO LINES & SERVICES

New Haven Pride Center [WC] 14
Gilbert St, West Haven **203/387-2252**

▪ACCOMMODATIONS

Linden Point House [GF,WI] 30 Linden
Point Rd, Stony Creek **203/481-0472**

Omni New Haven Hotel at Yale
[GF,WI,WC] 155 Temple St (at Chapel)
203/772-6664, 800/843-6664

▪BARS

168 York St Cafe [MW,F,GO] 168 York
St **203/789-1915** *3pm-1am, till 2am
Fri-Sat, also restaurant, dinner Mon-Sat,
Sun brunch, patio*

The Bar [GS,D,E,F,WC] 254 Crown St (at
College) **203/495-8924** *11:30am-
1am, from 5pm Mon-Tue, more gay Tue*

Partners [MW,D,L,K,DS] 365 Crown St
(at Park St) **203/776-1014** *5pm-1am,
till 2am Fri-Sat, from 8pm Mon-Tue &
Sat-Sun*

▪NIGHTCLUBS

Gotham Citi Cafe [★GS,D,DS,18+,WC]
169 East St **203/498-2484** *9pm-4am,
clsd Sun-Wed, more gay Sat*

▪CAFES

Atticus Bookstore/ Cafe 1082 Chapel
St (at York St) **203/776-4040** *7am-
9pm*

▪RESTAURANTS

116 Crown 116 Crown St
203/777-3116 *upscale tapas, great
mixed drinks*

Beachhead [E] 3 Cosey Beach Ave,
East Haven **203/469-5450** *4pm-close,
from 1pm Sun, seafood, Italian, patio*

Bentara 76 Orange St **203/562-2511**
*lunch Mon-Sat, dinner nightly,
Malaysian, plenty veggie*

Claire's Corner Copia [WI,WC] 1000
Chapel St (at College St)
203/562-3888 *8am-9pm, till 10pm
Fri-Sat, vegetarian*

Mezcal 14 Mechanic St (at Lawrence)
203/782-4828 *lunch Tue-Sun, dinner
nightly, authentic Mexican*

Miya Sushi 58 Howe St (at Chapel St)
203/777-9760 *lunch & dinner, clsd
Sun-Mon*

Soul de Cuba 238 Crown St
203/498-2822 *lunch & dinner, full bar*

▪EROTICA

Fairmount Theatre 33 Main St Annex
203/467-3832

Very Intimate Pleasures 170 Boston
Post Rd, Orange **203/799-7040**

▪CRUISY AREAS

East Rock State Park [AYOR] lower
parking lot *days*

New London

▪BARS

Frank's Place [M,D,F,E,K,WI,WC] 9 Tilley
St (at Bank) **860/442-2782** *4pm-1am,
till 2am Fri-Sun, patio*

O'Neill's Brass Rail [M,K,DS,WI] 52
Bank St **860/443-6203** *noon-1am, till
2am Fri-Sat*

Norwalk

▪INFO LINES & SERVICES

Triangle Community Center 16 River
St (at Wall St) **203/853-0600** *call for
info*

■CRUISY AREAS

Merritt Pkwy Park & Ride [AYOR] Rte 15, exit 38 (Rte 123, New Canaan Ave) *main lot, turn right*

Ridgefield

■RESTAURANTS

Caputo's East Ridge Cafe 5 Grove St 203/894-1940 *11:30am-10pm, also mellow, upscale bar*

■CRUISY AREAS

Riverside on Rte 7 [AYOR] opposite Ridgefield Motor Inn

Stamford

■CRUISY AREAS

Cove Island Park [AYOR] intersection of Cove Rd & Weed Ave

Uncasville

■NIGHTCLUBS

Mohegan SunDayz [MW,D,E] 1 Mohegan Sun Blvd 888/777-7922 *8pm Sun only at Mohegan Sun casino & resort*

Waterbury

■EROTICA

Video Book of Waterbury 90 S Main St 203/573-1066

■CRUISY AREAS

Lakewood Park/ Twin Lakes Annex [AYOR] Farmwood Rd *days*

Westport

■ENTERTAINMENT & RECREATION

Sherwood Island State Park Beach *left to gay area*

Willimantic

■EROTICA

Dan's Adult World 1110 Main St 860/456-3780

DELAWARE

New Castle

■EROTICA

Bob's Discount Books 174 S DuPont Hwy (near 13/40 split) 302/328-4812 *clsd Sun, arcade*

Rehoboth Beach

■INFO LINES & SERVICES

Camp Rehoboth Community Center 37 Baltimore Ave 302/227-5620 *9am-5:30pm Mon-Fri, 10am-4pm wknds, community center, HIV testing & counseling, also magazine*

Gay & Lesbian AA 302/856-6452 *noon Th*

Narcotics Anonymous 37 Baltimore Ave (at Camp Rehoboth center) 302/227-5620 *5:30pm Sun*

■ACCOMMODATIONS

At Melissa's B&B [GS,NS,WI] 36 Delaware Ave (btwn 1st & 2nd) 302/227-5504, 800/396-8090

Bellmoor Inn [GF,SW,WI] 6 Christian St (at Delaware) 866/227-5800, 800/425-2355 *upscale inn & spa*

Bewitched & BEDazzled B&B [GS,NS,WI,WC,GO] 67 Lake Ave (at Rehoboth Ave) 302/226-3900, 866/732-9482

Breakers Hotel & Suites [GF,SW,WC] 105 2nd St (at Olive) 302/227-6688, 800/441-8009

Cabana Gardens B&B [GS,SW,NS,GO] 20 Lake Ave (at 3rd St) 302/227-5429

Canalside Inn [GS,SW,NS,WI,WC,GO] Canal at 6th 302/226-2006, 866/412-2625

Delaware Inn B&B [GF,SW,GO] 55 Delaware Ave (at Bayard Ave) 302/227-6031, 800/246-5244

The Homestead at Rehoboth B&B [GF,NS,WI,WC,GO] 35060 Warrington Rd (at Old Landing Rd) 302/226-7625

Lazy L at Willow Creek [GS,SW,WI,GO] 16061 Willow Creek Rd (at Hwy 1), Lewes 302/644-7220

The Lighthouse Inn B&B
[GS,NS,WI,GO] 20 Delaware Ave (at 1st St) **302/226-0407**

The Ram's Head [MO,SW,N,GO] 35006 Warrington Rd (at John J Williams Hwy) **302/226-9171**

Rehoboth Guest House
[MW,NS,WI,GO] 40 Maryland Ave (btwn 1st & 2nd Sts) **302/227-4117, 800/564-0493**

The Royal Rose Inn [GS,GO] 41 Baltimore Ave (at 1st St) **302/226-2535**

Shore Inn at Rehoboth [MO,WI,N,GO] 37239 Rehoboth Ave (across from Double L Bar) **302/227-8487**

Silver Lake Guest House
[MW,NS,WI,GO] 20388 Silver Lake Dr (at Robinson Dr) **302/226-2115, 800/842-2115** *near Poodle Beach*

Summer Place Hotel [GS] 30 Olive Ave (at 1st) **302/226-0766, 800/815-3925**

■ BARS

The Blue Moon [★MW,E,DS,K] 35 Baltimore Ave (btwn 1st & 2nd) **302/227-6515** *6pm-2am, clsd Jan, also restaurant*

Dogfish Head Brewings & Eats
[GF,F,E] 320 Rehoboth Ave (at 4th) **302/226-2739**

Double L Bar [M,D,L,B,D,E] 622 Rehoboth Ave (at Church) **302/227-0818** *4pm-2am, patio*

Finbar Pub & Grill [GF,F,E] 316-318 Rehoboth Ave (at 4th) **302/227-1873** *from 3pm, from noon Fri-Sun, popular happy hour*

Frogg Pond [GF,NH,F,E,K] 3 S 1st St (near Rehoboth Ave) **302/227-2234** *11am-1am, popular happy hour*

Rigby's Bar & Grill [GS,F,E,K] 404 Rehoboth Ave (at State St) **302/227-6080** *3pm-1am, from 10am Sun*

■ CAFES

The Coffee Mill [WI,GO] 127B Rehoboth Ave **302/227-7530** *7am-11pm, till 5pm (off-season)*

Lori's Cafe [GO] 39 Baltimore Ave (at 1st) **302/226-3066** *seasonal, call for hours, courtyard*

■ RESTAURANTS

Aqua Grill [E] 57 Baltimore Ave **302/226-9001** *seasonal, deck, full bar*

Back Porch Cafe 59 Rehoboth Ave **302/227-3674** *lunch & dinner, Sun brunch, seasonal*

Big Sissies Bar & Grill 37385 Rehoboth Ave **302/226-7600** *3pm-1am*

Buttery [R] 102 2nd St, Lewes **302/645-7755** *lunch, dinner, Sun brunch*

Cafe Sole 44 Baltimore Ave **302/227-7107** *lunch daily, dinner Wed-Sun, patio, also full bar*

Cloud 9 [D,WC] 234 Rehoboth Ave (at 2nd) **302/226-1999** *4pm-2am, Sun brunch from 11am, also bar*

The Cultured Pearl 301 Rehoboth Ave (2nd flr) **302/227-8493** *dinner only, pan-Asian/ sushi, cocktail lounge*

Dos Locos [★] 208 Rehoboth Ave (across from Fire Company) **302/227-3353** *11:30am-10pm, till 11pm Fri-Sat, Mexican*

Eden [★WC] 23 Baltimore Ave **302/227-3330** *dinner Tue-Sat, seasonal, wine list & martini bar*

Espuma 28 Wilmington Ave **302/227-4199** *6pm-10pm, clsd Mon, full bar from 5pm*

Fins 243 Rehoboth Ave **302/226-3467** *dinner nightly, lunch Sat-Sun, fish house & raw bar*

Go Fish! 24 Rehoboth Ave **302/226-1044** *11:30am-9:30pm (in-season), authentic British fish & chips*

Hobo's Restaurant & Bar 56 Baltimore Ave **302/226-2226** *from 11am (in-season)*

Iguana Grill 52 Baltimore Ave **302/227-5273** *lunch & dinner (summers), Southwestern, full bar, patio*

JD's Filling Station 329 Savannah Rd, Lewes **302/644-8400** *7:30am-9pm*

Jerry's Seafood 108 2nd St, Lewes **302/645-6611** *lunch & dinner daily, "home of the crab bomb"*

Mariachi [WC] **302/227-0115** *11am-9pm, till 11pm Fri-Sat, Mexican-Latin American*

Planet X Cafe 35 Wilmington Ave **302/226-1928** *seasonal, lunch, dinner, Sun brunch*

Purple Parrot Grill [K,DS,WC] 134 Rehoboth Ave **302/226-1139** *lunch & dinner daily, brunch Sun, karaoke & drag shows wknds*

Seafood Shack [K] 42 1/2 Baltimore Ave (at 1st St) **302/227-5881** *patio seating, live music wknds*

■ENTERTAINMENT & RECREATION

Cape Henlopen State Park Beach 42 Cape Henlopen Dr, Lewes **302/645-8983** *8am-sunset*

Poodle Beach S of boardwalk at Queen St *popular gay beach*

■BOOKSTORES

Proud Bookstore 149 Rehoboth Ave (at Village of the Sea Shops) **302/227-6969**

■RETAIL SHOPS

Leather Central 36983 Rehoboth Ave **302/227-0700** *leather uniforms, toys, accessories*

■PUBLICATIONS

Letters from Camp Rehoboth **302/227-5620** *newsmagazine w/ events & entertainment listings*

■GYMS & HEALTH CLUBS

Body Shop 1st Ave (at Wilmington) **302/226-0920** *8am-7pm, till 6pm Sun, on the beach, $12 day pass*

Midway Fitness 34823 Derrickson Dr **302/645-0407**

Wilmington

■NIGHTCLUBS

Crimson Moon Tavern [M,D,DS,V] 1909 W 6th St (at Union St) **302/654-9099** *6pm-2am, from 7pm Sat, clsd Sun-Tue*

■RESTAURANTS

Eclipse 1020 Union St **302/658-1588** *lunch Mon-Fri, dinner nightly, upscale*

The Green Room [E] 11th & Market St (at Hotel Dupont) **302/594-3154** *brkfst, lunch & dinner, Sun brunch, full bar*

Mrs Robino's [WC] 520 N Union St (at Pennsylvania) **302/652-9223** *11am-9pm, till 10pm Fri-Sat, family-style Italian, full bar*

■MEN'S SERVICES

➤**MegaMates** **302/397-0111** *Call to hook up with HOT local men. FREE to listen & respond to ads. Use FREE code DAMRON. MegaMates.com.*

DISTRICT OF COLUMBIA

Washington

■INFO LINES & SERVICES

➤**Kasper's Livery Service** [GO] 201 Eye St SW **202/554-2471, 800/455-2471** *limousine service serving DC, MD & VA*

Triangle Club **202/659-8641** *various 12-Step groups, call for times*

■ACCOMMODATIONS

Beacon Hotel & Corporate Quarters [GF,F,WC] 1615 Rhode Island Ave NW (at 17th) **202/296-2100, 800/821-4367**

➤**The Bed & Breakfast at the William Lewis House** [★M,GO] 1309 R St NW (at 13th) **202/462-7574, 800/465-7574** *turn-of-the-century, hot tub, full brkfst wknds*

The Carlyle Suites Hotel [GS,F,WI,WC] 1731 New Hampshire Ave NW (btwn R & S Sts) **202/234-3200, 800/964-5377** *art deco, gay Sun brunch*

Donovan House [GS] 1155 14th St NW (at Massachusetts Ave NW) **202/737-1200, 800/383-6900** *stylish hotel, rooftop bar*

Embassy Suites Hotel at the Chevy Chase Pavilion [GF,SW,WC] 4300 Military Rd NW (at Wisconsin) **202/362-9300**

Grand Hyatt Washington [GF,SW,NS,WI,WC] 1000 H St NW **202/582-1234**

Hamilton Crowne Plaza Hotel [GF,NS,WC] 14th & K St NW 202/682-0111, 800/263-9802

Hotel George [GF,WI] 15 E St NW 202/347-4200, 800/546-7866

Hotel Helix [GF,WC,NS,WI] 1430 Rhode Island Ave NW 202/462-9001, 800/706-1202 *full-service boutique hotel, also Helix Lounge*

Hotel Monaco Washington DC [GF,WC,WI] 700 F St NW (at 7th) 202/628-7177, 800/649-1202 *boutique hotel*

Hotel Palomar [GF,F,SW,WI,WC] 2121 P St NW (at 21st St) 202/448-1800, 866/866-3070 *in Dupont Circle*

Hotel Rouge [GF,WI,WC] 1315 16th St NW (at Rhode Island) 202/232-8000, 800/738-1202 *also restaurant & bar*

Kalorama Guest House [GS,NS,WI] 2700 Cathedral Ave NW (off Connecticut Ave) 202/328-0860, 800/974-9101

Madison Hotel [GF,WI] 1177 15th St NW (at M St NW) 202/862-1600, 800/424-8577 *luxury hotel, also restaurant & spa*

Morrison-Clark Historic Hotel & Restaurant [GF,WI] 1015 L St NW (at Massachusetts Ave NW) 202/898-1200, 800/322-7898 *hotel in 2 Victorian town houses w/ very popular restaurant*

The River Inn [GF,WI,WC] 924 25th St NW (at K St) 202/337-7600, 888/874-0100 *also Dish + Drinks restaurant*

Savoy Suites Hotel [GF,WI,WC] 2505 Wisconsin Ave NW (at Calvert, in Georgetown) 202/337-9700, 800/944-5377 *also restaurant*

Topaz Hotel [GF,WI,WC] 1733 N St NW (at Massachusetts Ave NW) 202/393-3000, 800/775-1202 *also restaurant & bar*

You are *always* welcome at the
Bed and Breakfast at the

WILLIAM LEWIS

HOUSE

Washington's Finest
(202) 462~7574
(800) 465~7574

Warm, Cozy, Convenient
Close to 17th St.
Close to Dupont Circle
Close to Gay Attractions
Minutes from the Mall
Close to Metro
Great Restaurants Nearby
Perfect for Business
Great for Sightseeing
Friendly, Affordable, First Class
Accommodations

Visa, Mastercard, American Express and
Discover Accepted
Smoking Permitted in the Garden
Reservations Recommended
Off Street Parking Available
E~mail: Info@WLewisHous.com
Web: Http://www.WLewisHous.com
Fax (202)462~1608

Gay Owned and Operated

District of Columbia • *USA*

■BARS

Back Door Pub [M,MR-AF,S,WC] 1104 8th St SE, 2nd flr (at L St) **202/546-5979** *5pm-2am, till 3am Fri-Sat*

The Black Cat [GS,D,E,WC] 1811 14th St NW (at the Black Cat) **202/667-4490** *many queer events, live music, dance parties, also cafe*

DC Bear Crue [M,D,B,K] *Fri nights and Sun beer bust, check dcbearcrue.com for details*

DC Eagle [★M,L,WC] 639 New York Ave NW (btwn 6th & 7th) **202/347-6025** *4pm-2am, till 3am Fri-Sat, 2pm-2am Sun*

DIK Bar/ Windows [M,D,K,OC] 1637 17th St NW (at R St NW, upstairs) **202/328-0100** *4pm-2am, aka Dupont Italian Kitchen*

The Fireplace [M,NH,MR,V,WC] 2161 P St NW (at 22nd St) **202/293-1293** *1pm-2am, till 3am Fri-Sat*

Green Lantern [M,NH,D,B,K,V,WC] 1335 Green Court NW (in alley L St, btwn 13th & 14th) **202/347-4533** *4pm-2am, till 3am wknds*

JR's [★M,NH,F,V,YC] 1519 17th St NW (at Church) **202/328-0090** *2pm-2am, till 3am Fri, 1pm-2am Sun, cruisy, hot cocktail hour*

Larry's Lounge [MW,NH,F,WC,GO] 1840 18th St NW (at T St) **202/483-1483** *4pm-1am, till 2am Fri-Sat, patio*

Mova [M] 2204 14 St NW **202/797-9730** *5pm-2am, till 3am Fri-Sat*

Mr Henry's Capitol Hill [GF,MR,E,NS,WC] 601 Pennsylvania Ave SE (at 6th St) **202/546-8412** *11:30am-11:30pm, also restaurant*

Nellie's Sports Bar [M,NH] 900 U St NW (at 9th) **202/332-6355** *5pm-midnight, 3pm-2am Fri, from 11am wknds*

Number Nine [MW,NH] 1435 P St NW (at 15th St NW) **202/986-0999** *5pm-close*

Omega [★M,D,MR,K,DS,S,WI] 2122 P St NW (enter rear) **202/223-4917** *4pm-2am, from 8pm Sat, from 7pm Sun*

POV Roof Terrace Bar [GF,F] 515 15th Street NW (at Alexander Hamilton Pl) **202/661-2400** *11am-2am, pricey cocktails; superior views of the White House & Lincoln Memorial*

Remington's [★MW,D,CW,K,DS,V] 639 Pennsylvania Ave SE (btwn 6th & 7th) **202/543-3113** *4pm-2am, till 3am Fri-Sat, 6pm-2am Sun, CW dance lessons Wed*

Wisdom [GS,F] 1432 Pennsylvania Ave SE **202/543-2323** *5pm-2am, till 3am Fri-Sat*

■NIGHTCLUBS

Bachelors Mill [★M,D,MR-AF,K,S,WC] 1104 8th St SE (downstairs at Back Door Pub) **202/546-5979** *11pm-3am Th-Sat only*

Blowoff [★M,D,S] 815 V St NW (at 9th, at 9:30 Club) *10:30pm-3am monthly, varying Sat*

Chief Ike's Mambo Room [GF,D,E,WC] 1725 Columbia Rd NW (at Ontario Rd) **202/332-2211** *4pm-2am, till 3am Fri, 6pm-3am Sat*

Cobalt/ 30 Degrees Lounge [★M,D,E,DS] 1639 R St NW (at 17th) **202/232-4416** *5pm-2am, till 3am Fri-Sat*

Delta Elite [MW,D,MR-AF] 3734 10th St NE (at Perry St NE, in Brookland) **202/529-0626** *midnight-4am Fri-Sat only, ladies night Fri, men's night Sat till 5am*

Mixtape [MW,D] *2nd Sat only, alternative queer dance party, check mixtapedc.com for info*

She Rex [W,D,E,WC] 1725 Columbia Rd NW (at Ontario Rd, at Chief Ike's) **202/332-2211**

Town Danceboutique [★M,D,DS,18+] 2009 8th St NW (at U St NW) **202/234-8696** *9pm-4am Fri-Sat, 18+ Fri*

Ziegfeld's/ Secrets [M,D,DS,S] 1824 Half St SW **202/863-0670** *9pm-close Wed-Sun, [DS] downstairs, strippers upstairs*

■CAFES

Cosi [★WI] 1647 20th St NW **202/332-6364** *7am-11pm, till midnight Fri-Sat, 8am-10pm Sun, full bar from 4pm, make your own s'mores*

Hello Cupcake 1361 Connecticut Avenue NW 202/861-2253 *10am-7pm, till 9pm Fri-Sat, 11am-6pm Sun, cupcakes!*

Jolt 'n' Bolt [★] 1918 18th St NW (at Florida) 202/232-0077 *7am- 8:30pm, patio*

Soho Tea & Coffee [F,WI,WC] 2150 P St NW (at 21st St) 202/463-7646 *7am-1am, till 2am wknds, patio*

■ Restaurants

18th & U Duplex Diner [GS] 2004 18th St NW (at Ave U) 202/265-7828 *6pm-11pm, till 12:30am Tue-Wed, till 1:30am Fri-Sat, comfort food, full bar*

2 Amys Pizza [WC] 3715 Macomb St NW 202/885-5700 *lunch & dinner Tue-Sun, dinner only Mon*

Acadiana [R] 901 New York Ave NW 202/408-8848 *lunch Mon-Fri, dinner nightly, brunch Sun, Cajun, great bourbon selection*

Annie's Paramount Steak House [★WC] 1609 17th St NW (at Corcoran) 202/232-0395 *10am-11:30pm, till 1am Th & Sun, 24hrs Fri-Sat, full bar*

Banana Cafe & Piano Bar [E,P,GO] 500 8th St SE (at E St) 202/543-5906 *11am-10:30pm, till 11pm Fri-Sat, Puerto Rican/ Cuban, famous margaritas*

Bar Pilar 1833 14th St NW (at Swann St) 202/265-1751 *dinner nightly, Sun brunch, new American*

Beacon Bar & Grill [★] 1615 Rhode Island Ave NW (at 17th, at Beacon Hotel) 202/872-1126 *brkfst, lunch & dinner, popular Sun brunch, patio*

Busboys & Poets [E,WI,WC] 2021 14th St NW (at V St) 202/387-7638 *8am-midnight, till 2am Fri-Sat, 10am-midnight Sun, also bookstore, live jazz & poetry*

Cafe Green 1513 17th St NW 202/234-0505 *11am-10pm, 10am-4pm Sun, clsd Mon, plenty veggie/ vegan*

Cafe Japoné [★MR-A,K] 2032 P St NW (at 21st) 202/223-1573 *6pm-1:30am, till 2:30am Fri-Sat, Japanese, full bar, live jazz*

Cafe La Ruche 1039 31st St 202/965-2684 *dinner, Sun brunch, French, patio*

Cafe Luna [★MW] 1633 P St NW (at 17th) 202/387-4005 *10am-11pm, till midnight wknds*

Cafe Saint Ex/ Gate 54 1847 14th St NW 202/265-7839 *lunch, dinner, Sun brunch, modern American, also Gate 54 club downstairs, popular Th* [GF,D]

Dupont Italian Kitchen & Bar [WC] 1637 17th St NW (at R St) 202/328-3222, 202/328-0100 *11am-11pm, bar 4pm-2am*

Firefly 1310 New Hampshire Ave NW 202/861-1310 *lunch & dinner, wknd brunch, plenty veggie*

Floriana [GO] 1602 17th St NW (at Q St NW) 202/667-5937 *dinner nightly, Italian, full bar, patio*

Food For Thought [WC] 1811 14th St NW (at the Black Cat) 202/667-4490 *8pm-1am, 7pm-2am Fri-Sat, mostly vegan/ veggie, indie/ punk music shows, readings*

Guapo's [WC] 4515 Wisconsin Ave NW (at Albemarle) 202/686-3588 *lunch & dinner, Mexican, full bar*

Jaleo [E,WC] 480 7th St NW (at E St) 202/628-7949 *lunch & dinner, tapas, full bar, Sevillanas dancers Wed*

Java Green Eco Cafe 1020 19th St NW 202/775-8899 *8am-8pm, 10am-6pm Sat, clsd Sun, organic cafe, plenty veggie/ vegan*

Level One 1639 R St NW (at 17th) 202/745-0025 *dinner nightly, wknd brunch*

Logan Tavern [GO] 1423 P St NW 202/332-3710 *lunch & dinner, wknd brunch, American comfort food, also bar*

Occidental Grill 1475 Pennsylvania Ave NW (btwn 14th & 15th) 202/783-1475 *lunch Mon-Sat, dinner nightly, clsd Sun, upscale, political player hangout*

Perry's 1811 Columbia Rd NW (at 18th) 202/234-6218 *5:30pm-11:30pm, popular drag Sun brunch, contemporary American & sushi, full bar*

Pizza Paradiso 2003 P Street NW 202/223-1245 *11am-11pm, till midnight wknds,Gluten-Free Crust*

Posto 1515 14th St NW 202/332-8613 *dinner nightly, Italian*

District of Columbia • *USA*

Rasika [WC] 633 D St NW
202/637-1222 *lunch Mon-Fri, dinner Mon-Sat, clsd Sun, Indian*

Rice 1608 14th St NW (at 'Q')
202/234-2400 *lunch & dinner, Thai*

Rocklands 2418 Wisconsin Ave NW (at Calvert) 202/333-2558 *11am-10pm, till 9pm Sun, BBQ & take-out*

Sala Thai 1301 U St NW (at 13th)
202/462-1333 *lunch & dinner*

Skewers [★E] 1633 P St NW (at 17th)
202/387-7400 *11am-11pm, noon-midnight wknds, Middle Eastern, belly dancing Sat, full bar*

Smoke & Barrell [E] 2471 18th St NW
202/319-9353 *beer, bbq & bourbon*

Soul Vegetarian Exodus 2606 Georgia Ave NW 202/328-7685 *11am-9pm, till 3pm Sun (brunch), all-vegan menu, no frills*

Thaitanic 1326 14th St NW (at Rhode Island Ave) 202/588-1795 *lunch & dinner, Thai, plenty veggie*

Trio [WC] 1537 17th St NW (at Q St NW) 202/232-6305 *8am-midnight, American, full bar, sidewalk cafe*

Zaytinia 701 9th Street NW (at G St)
202/638-0800 *lunch & dinner, Greek/ Mediterranean*

■ENTERTAINMENT & RECREATION

Anecdotal History Tours [GF]
301/294-9514 *guided tours, by appt only*

Bike & Roll Washington DC [GF] 1100 Pennsylvania Ave NW (off 12th St, at Old Post Office Pavilion)
202/842-2453

Capital Bikeshare 877/430-2453 *look for the red bikes at parking stations around the city; join for 24hrs or longer*

Hillwood Museum & Gardens [R]
4155 Linnean Ave NW (at Tilden St NW)
202/686-5807 *10am-5pm Tue-Sat, Fabergé, porcelain, furniture & more*

Phillips Collection 1600 21st St NW (at Q St) 202/387-2151 *clsd Mon, America's first museum of modern art, near Dupont Circle*

■BOOKSTORES

G Books [GO] 1520 U St NW, BSMT (btwn 15th St & U St) 202/986-9697 *4pm-10pm, used gay books, mags, movies, pride items*

Kramerbooks & Afterwords Cafe & Grill [E,F,WC] 1517 Connecticut Ave NW (at Q St) 202/387-1400 *7:30am-1am, 24hrs wknds, also cafe & bar*

■RETAIL SHOPS

HRC Action Center & Store 1640 Connecticut Avenue NW
202/232-8621 *10am-9pm, till 10pm wknds, Human Rights Campaign merchandise & info*

Leather Rack 1723 Connecticut Ave NW (btwn R & S Sts) 202/797-7401

Pulp 1803 14th St NW 202/462-7857 *11am-7pm, till 5pm Sun, cards, gifts*

Universal Gear 1529 14th St NW (btwn P & Q) 202/319-0136 *11am-10pm, till midnight Fri-Sat, casual, club, athletic & designer clothing*

■PUBLICATIONS

Metro Weekly 202/638-6830 *LGBT newsmagazine, extensive club listings*

Washington Blade 202/747-2077 *LGBT newspaper*

■GYMS & HEALTH CLUBS

Washington Sports Club 1835 Connecticut Ave NW (at Columbia & Florida) 202/332-0100

■MEN'S CLUBS

Crew Club 1321 14th St NW (at Rhode Island) 202/319-1333 *24hrs*

Glorious Health Club [MO] 2120 West Virginia Ave NE 202/269-0226

■MEN'S SERVICES

▶**MegaMates** 202/822-1666 *Call to hook up with HOT local men. FREE to listen & respond to ads. Use FREE code DAMRON. MegaMates.com.*

■EROTICA

Pleasure Place [WC] 1063 Wisconsin Ave NW, Georgetown (btwn M & K Sts)
800/386-2386

■CRUISY AREAS

Rock Creek Park [AYOR] Beach Dr N of Military Rd *behind Francis swimming pool*

FLORIDA

Statewide

■ PUBLICATIONS

➤ **Ambush Mag** 504/522-8047
LGBT newspaper for the Gulf South (TX through FL)

HOTSPOTS! Magazine
954/928-1862 *"South Florida's largest gay publication"*

Amelia Island

■ ACCOMMODATIONS

The Hoyt House [GF,SW,WI,WC,GO]
804 Atlantic Ave 904/277-4300,
800/432-2085 *full brkfst*

■ RESTAURANTS

Beech Street Grill [E] 801 Beech St (at 8th St), Fernandina Beach
904/277-3662 *5:30pm-9pm, lunch Wed-Fri, Sun brunch*

Brett's Waterway Cafe 1 S Front St 904/261-2660 *lunch & dinner, seafood*

■ CRUISY AREAS

Burney Park [AYOR] off A1A

Bonifay

■ CRUISY AREAS

Wayside Park Hwy 79 *parking lot & woods 6 miles N of Bonifay at Holmes Creek bridge*

Boynton Beach

see West Palm Beach

Bradenton

see also Sarasota

■ MEN'S SERVICES

➤ **MegaMates** 941/527-0527 *Call to hook up with HOT local men. FREE to listen & respond to ads. Use FREE code DAMRON. MegaMates.com.*

Cape Coral

see Fort Myers

Clearwater

see also Dunedin, New Port Richey, Port Richey & St Petersburg

■ ACCOMMODATIONS

Holiday Inn Select [GF,F,SW,WI,WC]
3535 Ulmerton Rd (Rte 688 W)
727/577-9100, 888/465-4329

■ BARS

Pro Shop Pub [★M,NH,B,GO] 840
Cleveland St (at Prospect)
727/447-4259 *1pm-2am*

■ RETAIL SHOPS

Skinz 2027 Gulf to Bay Blvd (aka State Rd 60, at Hercules Rd) 727/441-8789
10am-6pm, clsd Sun

■ MEN'S SERVICES

➤ **MegaMates** 727/230-0030 *Call to hook up with HOT local men. FREE to listen & respond to ads. Use FREE code DAMRON. MegaMates.com.*

Cocoa

■ BARS

The Ultra Lounge [M,NH] 407 Brevard Ave, Cocoa Village 321/690-0096
6pm-2am

Cross City

■ ACCOMMODATIONS

Southern Comfort Campground
[M,SW,NS,WI,WC,GO] 50 SE 74th Ave (at Hwy 19) 352/498-0490,
352/210-6953

Daytona Beach

■ ACCOMMODATIONS

The August Seven Inn [GF,NS,WI,GO]
1209 S Peninsula Dr (at Silver Beach)
386/248-8420 *1 block from ocean*

Mayan Inn [GF,SW,WI,WC,GO] 103 S Ocean Ave 386/252-2378, 800/329-8622

The Villa B&B [GF,SW,N,NS,WI,GO] 801
N Peninsula Dr 386/248-2020,
888/248-7060

■ BARS

Streamline Lounge [GF,D,E,WI] 140 S
Atlantic Ave (at Streamline Hotel)
386/258-6937 *11am-3am, penthouse lounge*

■NIGHTCLUBS

Savoy Daytona [MW,NH,D,V,WC,GO] 546 Seabreeze Blvd (at Atlantic Ave) **386/226-5600** *5pm-2:30am, from 3pm Sun*

■CAFES

Java Joint & Eatery 2201-E N Oceanshore Blvd, Flagler Beach **386/439-1013** *7am-4pm*

■RESTAURANTS

Anna's Trattoria [BW] 304 Seabreeze Blvd **386/239-9624** *5pm-10pm, clsd Sun-Mon, Italian*

The Clubhouse 600 Wilder Blvd (at Daytona Beach Golf & Country Club) **386/257-0727** *6am-7:30pm*

Frappes North [E,WC] 123 W Granada Blvd (at S Yonge St), Ormond Beach **386/615-4888** *lunch Tue-Fri, dinner nightly, clsd Sun*

Sapporo 501 Seabreeze Ave **386/257-4477**

■PUBLICATIONS

Watermark **407/481-2243** *bi-weekly LGBT newspaper for Central FL*

■EROTICA

The Banned Bookstore 701 N Ridgewood Ave **386/248-0072**

X-Mart Boutique 2591 W International Speedway Blvd **386/252-8707** *24hrs*

Delray Beach

■BARS

Tag Bar [M,D,DS] 25 NE 2nd Ave **954/801-3247** *4pm-2am*

Dunedin

see also St Petersburg

■NIGHTCLUBS

Blur Nighclub [M,D,K,DS] 325 Main St **727/736-0206** *8pm-2am, clsd Sun-Mon*

■CRUISY AREAS

Honeymoon Island State Recreation Area [AYOR] end of Causeway Blvd *nude sunbathing & beach*

Fort Lauderdale

■INFO LINES & SERVICES

Greater Fort Lauderdale Convention & Visitors Bureau 100 E Broward Blvd, Ste 200 **800/227-8669 (code 187)**, **954/765-4466**

Lambda South Inc [WC] 1306 E Las Olas Blvd **954/761-9072** *meeting space for LGBT in recovery*

The Pride Center at Equality Park [WC] 2040 N Dixie Hwy, Wilton Manors **954/463-9005** *10am-10pm, noon-5pm wknds, outreach*

■ACCOMMODATIONS

15 FTL Guesthouse [M,SW,N,WI,WC,GO] 908 NE 15th Ave (at Sunrise) **954/523-7829**, **888/234-5494** *Key West-style guesthouse*

Alcazar Resort [MO,SW,N,NS,WI,GO] 555 N Birch Rd (at Terramar) **954/567-2525, 888/830-9931** *at the beach*

Bungalow Six Guesthouse [M,SW,WI,GO] 2726 NE 6th Ln (at 27th St), Wilton Manors **954/561-5454, 877/210-6317**

The Cabanas [★M,SW,NS,WI,GO] 2209 NE 26th St **954/564-7764, 866/564-7764** *riverfront, kayaks available, clothing-optional jacuzzi, spa*

Cheston House [MO,SW,N,NS,WI,GO] 520 N Birch Rd (at Viramar) **954/566-7950, 866/566-7950** *on beach*

►**Coconut Cove Guesthouse** [MO,SW,N,NS,WI,GO] 3012 Granada St (at Birch St & A1A) **954/523-3226, 888/414-3226** *courtyard gardens*

Coral Reef Guesthouse [MO,SW,N,NS,WI,WC,GO] 2609 NE 13th Ct (off Sunrise Blvd) **954/568-0292, 888/365-6948** *very secluded*

Ed Lugo Resort [GF,SW,WI,GO] 2404 NE 8th Ave (Wilton Manors) **954/275-8299**

Florida • USA

Elysium Resort [MO,SW,N,NS,WI,GO]
552 N Birch Rd (at Terramar)
954/564-9601, 800/533-4744
sundeck, near beach

The Flamingo—Inn Amongst the Flowers [MO,SW,N,NS,WI,GO] 2727
Terramar St (near Birch)
954/561-4658, 888/286-8218

The Grand Resort & Spa
[MO,SW,N,NS,WI,WC,GO] 539 N Birch Rd
(at Windamar) 954/630-3000,
800/818-1211 *sundeck, spa, gym, clothing-optional courtyard, gay-owned*

Hotel Lush Royale [MO,SW,NS,WI]
2835 Terramar St (at Orton)
954/564-6442

▶Inn Leather Guesthouse
[★MO,L,SW,N,WI,GO] 610 SE 19th St (at
SW 1st Ave) 954/467-1444,
877/532-7729 *sling in each room & dungeon*

Liberty Apartment & Garden Suites
[MO,SW,WI,WC,GO] 1501 SW 2nd Ave (at
Sheridan), Dania Beach
954/927-0090, 877/927-0090

Manor Inn [MO,SW,N,NS,WI,GO] 2408
NE 6th Ave (at NE 24th St), Wilton
Manors 954/566-8223,
866/682-7456

Mary's Resort [M,SW,NS,WI,GO] 1115
Tequesta St (at 11th Ave)
954/523-3500, 866/805-6570

Palm Plaza Resort
[MO,L,SW,N,WI,WC,GO] 2801 Riomar St
(at Birch) 954/630-3000

Pineapple Point Guest House
[★MO,SW,N,NS,WI,WC,GO] 315 NE 16th
Terr (at NE 3rd Ct) 954/527-0094,
888/844-7295 *luxury guesthouse, gym*

The Royal Palms Resort & Spa
[★M,F,SW,NS,WI,GO] 717 Breakers Ave
954/564-6444, 800/237-7256

▶The Schubert Resort
[★MO,SW,NS,WI,WC,GO] 855 NE 20th
Ave 954/763-7434, 866/763-7435

Sea Grape House Inn
[M,SW,N,NS,WI,GO] 1109 NE 16th Pl (at
Dixie Hwy) 954/525-6586,
800/377-8802

Florida • USA

Villa Venice Men's Resort [MO,SW,NS,WI,WC,GO] 2900 Terramar St (at Orton) **954/564-7855, 877/591-5127** *2 blocks to beach*

Windamar Beach Resort [M,SW,N,WI,GO] 543 Breakers Ave (near Bayshore) **954/561-0039, 866/554-6816** *just steps from the gay beach*

▶**The Worthington Guest House** [MO,SW,NS,WI,GO] 543 N Birch Rd (at Terramar) **954/563-6819, 800/445-7036** *resort, clothing-optional hot tub*

■BARS

Andy's Lounge [GS,NH,CW] 12450 W State Rd 84, Davie **954/472-7081** *3pm-8am, Sun gay night*

Bill's [M,NH,DS,K,WC] 2209 Wilton Dr (off NE 23rd St) **954/567-5978** *2pm-2am, till 3am Fri-Sat, from noon Sat-Sun*

Boardwalk [★M,NH,S,18+] 1721 N Andrews Ave **954/463-6969** *3pm-2am, till 3am Fri-Sat, strippers from 5pm*

Cubby Hole [M,NH,B,F,WI] 823 N Federal Hwy (at 8th St) **954/728-9001** *11am-2am, till 3am Fri-Sat*

The Depot [M,NH,F,E,K,SW] 2935 N Federal Hwy **954/537-7076** *noon-2am, till 3am Fri-Sat*

Georgie's Alibi [M,F,V,NS,WI,WC] 2266 Wilton Dr (at NE 4th Ave) **954/565-2526** *11am-2am*

Jackhammer in Exile [★M,D,B,L,WC] 2232 Wilton Dr (at Boom, in Wilton Manors) **954/630-3556** *Sun only T-dance*

Johnny's/ Club 11 [M,NH,F,S,WC] 1116 W Broward Blvd (at 11th Ave) **954/522-5931** *2pm-2am, from noon Sun, male dancers nightly*

The Manor Complex [MW,D,F,E,C] 2345 Wilton Dr, Wilton Manors **954/626-0082** *11am-11pm, also Epic nightclub, also restaurant & cafe*

Matty's on the Drive [M,NH,F,WC] 2426 Wilton Dr, Wilton Manors **954/564-1799** *11am-2am, till 3am Fri-Sat*

Mona's [M,NH,K] 502 E Sunrise Blvd (at 5th Ave) **954/525-6662** *noon-2am, till 3am wknds*

Monkey Business [M,NH,C,DS] 2740 N Andrews Ave **954/514-7819** *9am-2am, till 3am wknds*

Naked Grape [GF] 2163 Wilton Dr (at NE 20th St), Wilton Manors **954/563-5631** *4pm-midnight, 2pm-1am Fri-Sat, clsd Sun-Mon, wine bar*

Noche Latina Saturday [M,D,E,MR] 2345 Wilton Dr (at Manor Complex), Wilton Manors **954/626-0082** *11pm Sat at Ivy nightclub*

PJ's Corner Pocket [M,NH,MR-A,V] 924 N Flagler Dr **954/533-0257** *4pm-2am, from 7pm Sat, clsd Wed*

Ramrod [★M,B,L] 1508 NE 4th Ave (at 16th St) **954/763-8219** *3pm-2am, till 3am wknds, cruisy, patio, also LeatherWerks leather store*

Scandals [M,D,CW,B,E,F,K,OC,WC] 3073 NE 6th Ave, Wilton Manors **954/567-2432** *noon-2am, patio*

Shannon & Anthony's Corner Pub [GS,NH,GO] 1915 N Andrews Ave **954/564-7335** *11am-2am*

Sidelines Sports Bar [★MW,NH] 2031 Wilton St, Wilton Manors **954/563-8001** *2pm-2am, from noon wknds*

Smarty Pants [★M,NH,F,E,K,DS,WC] 3038 N Federal Hwy (at Oakland Park Blvd) **954/561-1724** *9am-2am, till 3am Sat, noon-2am Sun*

The Stable Bar [M,NH,DS] 205 E Oakland Park Blvd (at Andrews) **954/565-4506** *2pm-2am, noon-3am Fri-Sat*

■NIGHTCLUBS

Boom [★M,D,E,K,DS,V,GO] 2232 Wilton Dr, Wilton Manors **954/630-3556** *3pm-2am, till 3am wknds, T-dance Sun*

Dudes Bar [MO,E,P,S,V] 3270 NE 33rd St **954/568-7777** *2pm-2am, till 3am Fri-Sat*

Living Room [M,D] 300 SW 1st Ave (at Brickell) **888/992-7555** *gay Fri only*

Torpedo [M,D,S] 2829 W Broward Blvd (at 28th Ave) **954/587-2500** *10pm-dawn*

CAFES

Cafe Emunah [F] 3558 N Ocean Blvd 954/561-6411 *11am-10pm, clsd Fri, sunset-1am Sat*

Gelato Station [GO] 2031 Wilton Dr 954/567-5930 *noon-11pm, till 2am Fri-Sat*

Java Boys [★WI] 2230 Wilton Dr, Wilton Manors 954/564-8828 *7am-11pm*

Jimmies Chocolates & Cafe 148 N Federal Hwy, Dania Beach 954/921-0688 *bistro w/ fresh fare & wine*

Storks [WC] 2505 NE 15th Ave (at NE 26th St, Wilton Manors) 954/567-3220 *6:30am-midnight, bear night Th*

RESTAURANTS

La Bonne Crêpe 815 E Las Olas Blvd 954/761-1515 *7am-9:30pm, till 11:30pm Fri-Sat, patio*

Canyon 1818 E Sunrise Blvd 954/765-1950 *Southwestern, full bar*

Courtyard Cafe [GO] 2211 Wilton Dr 954/563-2499 *7am-11pm, 24hrs Th-Sat*

Flip Flops 3051 NE 32nd Ave 954/567-1672 *11am-9pm, till 10pm Fri-Sat, casual waterfront dining*

The Floridian [WC] 1410 E Las Olas Blvd 954/463-4041 *24hr diner*

Fuego Latino Cuban [BW] 1417 E Commercial Blvd 954/351-7754 *11am-10pm, till 11pm Fri-Sat, from noon Sun*

Galanga 2389 Wilton Dr, Wilton Manors 954/202-0000 *dinner nightly, lunch weekdays, Thai, also sushi*

Hi-Life Cafe [R] 3000 N Federal Hwy (at Oakland Park Blvd, in the Plaza 3000) 954/563-1395 *dinner, clsd Mon*

Humpy's 2244 Wilton Dr, Wilton Manors 954/566-2722 *11am-10pm, till 2am Th-Sat, pizza & panini*

J Marks Restaurant [GO] 1245 N Federal Hwy 954/390-0770 *11am-10pm, till 11pm Fri-Sat, full bar*

Kitchenetta [WC] 2850 N Federal Hwy 954/567-3333 *dinner nightly, clsd Mon*

La Bamba [WC] 4245 N Federal Hwy 954/568-5662 *more gay Mon night*

Lester's Diner [★WC] 250 State Rd 84 954/525-5641 *24hrs, more gay late nights*

Lips [K,DS] 1421 E Oakland Park Blvd (at Dixie Hwy) 954/567-0987 *6pm-close, from noon Sun, clsd Mon, "the ultimate in drag dining"*

Mason Jar Cafe [GO] 2980 N Federal Hwy 954/568-4100 *11:30am-3pm Mon-Fri, dinner nightly, upscale comfort food*

Mojo [E] 4140 N Federal Hwy 954/568-4443 *open 4pm, clsd Sun, full bar*

Le Patio [GO] 2401 NE 11th Ave 954/530-4641

PL8 Kitchen 210 SW 2nd St 954/524-1818 *lunch & dinner, till 2am wknds, small plates*

Portia's [WC,GO] 199 E Oakland Park Blvd 954/616-8107 *11am-9pm, Southern style*

Rosie's Bar & Grill [★] 2449 Wilton Dr, Wilton Manors 954/563-0123 *11am-11pm*

SAIA [WI] 999 N Fort Lauderdale Beach Blvd 954/302-5252 *authentic Asian cuisine*

Simply Delish Cafe [WC] 2287 Wilton Dr, Wilton Manors 954/565-8646 *8am-2pm, clsd Mon*

Sublime 1431 N Federal Hwy 954/539-9000 *5:30pm-10pm, clsd Mon, vegan/ vegetarian*

Tequila Sunrise Mexican Grill [E] 4711 N Dixie Hwy 954/938-4473 *11:30am-10pm, till 11pm Th-Sat, 1pm-10pm Sun*

Victoria Park Diner 1730 E Sunrise Blvd 954/759-0022 *6:30am-9pm*

BOOKSTORES

Pride Factory 850 NE 13th St 954/463-6600 *10am-9pm, 11am-7pm Sun*

Florida • USA

▓RETAIL SHOPS

GayMartUSA 2240 Wilton Dr (at NE 6th Ave) **954/630-0360** *10am-midnight*

J Miles 831 N Federal Hwy **954/463-3988** *clsd Tue-Wed & summers*

LeatherWerks [L,18+,GO] 1226 NE 4th Ave (at 13th St) **954/761-1236** *11am-8pm, noon-6pm Sun, leatherwear & gear, adult toys; also inside the Ramrod (8pm-close)*

Mix [GO] 2258 Wilton Dr (in Shoppes of Wilton Manors), Wilton Manors **954/566-9166** *11am-9pm, till 11pm Th-Sat, designer men's apparel*

Out of the Closet 2097 Wilton Dr, Wilton Manors **954/358-5580** *10am-7pm, till 6pm Sun*

The Outlet 2031 Wilton Dr **954/396-3383** *10am-11pm, clubwear*

The Poverello Center 2056 N Dixie Hwy **954/561-3663** *thrift store to support the purchase of food for people living w/ HIV/AIDS in Broward County*

To The Moon [GO] 2205 Wilton Dr (at 6th Ave), Wilton Manors **954/564-2987** *10am-11pm, pride gifts, cards & candy candy candy!*

▓PUBLICATIONS

Genre Latino/ Latin Boys Magazine *get the dirt on Latin nights & clubs in Southern FL*

What's Happening Magazine **407/690-0809** *statewide LGBT entertainment & lifestyle magazine*

▓GYMS & HEALTH CLUBS

Island City Health & Fitness 2270 Wilton Dr, Wilton Manors **954/318-3900** *5am-11pm, 8am-8pm wknds*

▓MEN'S CLUBS

Club Fort Lauderdale [★SW,18+,PC] 110 NW 5th Ave (at Broward) **954/525-3344** *24hrs*

Clubhouse II [V,PC] 2650 E Oakland Park Blvd **954/566-6750** *24hrs, gym, [L] Tue*

Slammer [MO,BYOB,PC] 321 W Sunrise Blvd **954/524-2625** *8pm-close*

▓MEN'S SERVICES

➤**MegaMates** **954/761-7070** *Call to hook up with HOT local men. FREE to listen & respond to ads. Use FREE code DAMRON. MegaMates.com.*

▓EROTICA

Fetish Factory 855 E Oakland Park Blvd **954/563-5777** *11am-9pm, noon-6pm Sun*

Rock Hard 2301 Wilton Dr, Wilton Manors **954/318-7625**

Secrets of Romance 10145 NW 46th St, Sunrise **954/748-5855** *10am-2pm, clsd Sun, cross dressing store*

Tropixxx Video 1514 NE 4th Ave (at NE16th St), Wilton Manors **888/464-5988**

▓CRUISY AREAS

Beach at Sebastian St [AYOR]

Fort Lauderdale Beach [★AYOR] opposite 18th St NE (btwn Oakland Park & Sunrise Blvds) *dune area cruisy all night & gay beach during the day*

Holiday Park [AYOR] Sunrise Blvd (on right side at Federal Hwy) *exit I-95 at Sunrise Blvd & head E toward beach, open 5am-midnight*

Pompano Beach [AYOR] 16th St & A1A (N of Atlantic)

Fort Myers

▓INFO LINES & SERVICES

Gay AA Lambda Drummers [WC] 3049 McGregor Blvd (at St John the Apostle MCC) **239/275-5111 (AA#)** *8pm Tue & Sat in social hall*

▓ACCOMMODATIONS

The Hibiscus House B&B [GF,NS,WI,WC] 2135 McGregor Blvd **239/332-2651**

Lighthouse Resort Inn & Suites [★GF,SW,NS,WI,WC] 1051 5th St, Fort Myers Beach **239/463-9392, 800/778-7748**

▓BARS

The Office Pub [M,NH,B] 3704 Cleveland Ave (at Grove) **239/936-3212** *noon-2am, theme nights*

■NIGHTCLUBS

The Bottom Line (TBL)
[MW,D,K,DS,V,WC] 3090 Evans Ave (at Hanson) **239/337-7292** *2pm-2am*

■RESTAURANTS

McGregor Grill [GO] 15675 McGregor Blvd, Ste 24 **239/437-3499** *11:30am-2am, from 4pm Sun, pub fare, some outdoor dining*

The Oasis [BW,WC] 2260 Dr Martin Luther King Blvd **239/334-1566** *breakfast, lunch & dinner*

■MEN'S SERVICES

▶**MegaMates 239/337-3100** *Call to hook up with HOT local men. FREE to listen & respond to ads. Use FREE code DAMRON. MegaMates.com.*

■CRUISY AREAS

Bowditch Point Recreational Park [AYOR] 50 Estero Blvd (at end of street), Fort Myers Beach

Bunche Beach [AYOR] John Morris Pkwy *S end of beach*

Horton Park [AYOR] Everest Pkwy (go E on Del Prado to end), Cape Coral *open sunrise to sunset*

Fort Pierce

■EROTICA

The Lion's Den Adult Superstore 7100 Okeechobee Rd (exit 129 off I-95) **772/466-6323**

Gainesville

■INFO LINES & SERVICES

Free to Be AA 3131 NW 13th St (The Pride Center) **352/372-8091** (AA#) *7:30pm Sun, LGBT AA group*

Pride Community Center 3131 NW 13th St #62 **352/377-8915** *3pm-7pm, noon-4pm Sat, clsd Sun*

■BARS

Spikes [MW,NH,WC] 4130 NW 6th St **352/376-3772** *5pm-2am, till 11pm Sun*

The University Club [★MW,D,K,DS,S,YC,WC] 18 E University Ave (enter rear) **352/378-6814** *5pm-2am, from 9pm Sat, till 11pm Sun, 3 levels, patio*

■ENTERTAINMENT & RECREATION

Ponte Vedra LGBT Beach *Go N from Gainesville on Waldo Rd to N 301, then E on I-10. I-10 becomes 95. Go S on 95, then take a left. Go E onto Butler Blvd, which ends at A1A. Turn right onto A1A & then drive 5 to 7 minutes looking for Guana Boat Landing parking lot on the right.*

■BOOKSTORES

Wild Iris Books [TG,E,WC] 802 W University Ave (at 8th St) **352/375-7477** *1pm-9pm, till 5pm Sat, clsd Sun-Mon*

■CRUISY AREAS

Bolen's Bluff Dock [AYOR] US 441 S (past Praynes Prairie, on the right) *days*

Hollywood

■ACCOMMODATIONS

Rooftop Resort [GS,SW,N,WI] 1215 N Ocean Dr **954/925-0301** *the premier nudist swinger resort hotel in S Florida*

■NIGHTCLUBS

The Castle Lounge [M,DS] 1322 N Dixie Hwy **954/840-9683**

■MEN'S SERVICES

▶**MegaMates 954/342-0342** *Call to hook up with HOT local men. FREE to listen & respond to ads. Use FREE code DAMRON. MegaMates.com.*

■EROTICA

Hollywood Spice 600 N State Rd 7 (btwn Hollywood Blvd & Johnson St) **954/983-4687** *arcade*

Pleasure Emporium 1321 S 30th Ave **954/927-8181**

Sensations Video 106 S State Rd 7 **954/894-7701** *arcade*

■CRUISY AREAS

Holland Park [AYOR] Johnson St (at Intracoastal)

Florida • USA

Inverness

ACCOMMODATIONS

Camp David [MO,SW,N] 2000 S Bishop Point Rd 352/344-3445 *camping/ RV retreat, membership req'd*

Thousand Palms Resort [GF,SW,WI,GO] 6545 W State Rt 44 352/748-2237

Islamorada

ACCOMMODATIONS

Casa Morada [GF,SW] 136 Madeira Rd 305/664-0044, 888/881-3030 *luxury all-suite hotel w/ private island*

Lookout Lodge Resort [GF,NS,WI] 87770 Overseas Hwy (at Plantation Blvd) 305/852-9915, 800/870-1772 *waterfront resort*

Jacksonville

INFO LINES & SERVICES

Free to Be LGBT AA 634 Lomax St 904/399-8535 (AA#) *6:30pm Mon*

ACCOMMODATIONS

Comfort Inn Oceanfront [GF,F,F,SW,WC] 1515 N 1st St, Jacksonville Beach 904/241-2311, 800/654-8776

Hilton Garden Inn Jacksonville JTB/ Deerwood Park [GF,SW,WI,WC] 9745 Gate Pkwy (at Southside Blvd) 904/997-6600, 877/782-9444

Spring Hill Suites Jacksonville [GF,SW,NS,WI] 4385 Southside Blvd (at J Turner Butler Blvd) 904/997-6650, 888/287-9400

BARS

616 Bar [MW,NH,B,K] 616 Park St (at I-95) 904/358-6969 *4pm-2am, patio*

AJ's Bar & Grill [W,D,F,E,DS,WC] 10244 Atlantic Blvd (in Regency Walk Shopping Center) 904/805-9060 *4pm-2am, clsd Mon, men very welcome*

Bo's Coral Reef [MW,NH,D,DS] 201 5th Ave N (at 2nd St), Jacksonville Beach 904/246-9874 *2pm-2am*

In Cahoots [M,D,A,MR,E,K,DS,V,WC] 711 Edison Ave (btwn Riverside & Park) 904/353-6316 *8pm-2am, from 4pm Sun, clsd Mon-Tue*

The Metro [★MW,D,DS,P,S,V,18+,WC] 859 Willow Branch Ave 904/388-8719 *2pm-2am, till 4am Fri-Sat*

The New Boot Rack Saloon [M,CW,K,BW,WI,WC] 4751 Lenox Ave (at Cassat Ave) 904/384-7090 *3pm-2am, patio*

Park Place Lounge [MW,NH,D,WC] 931 King St (at Post) 904/389-6616 *noon-2am*

NIGHTCLUBS

The Pearl [GS,D] 1101 N Main St (E 1st St) 904/791-4499 *9pm-2am, clsd Sun-Wed*

RESTAURANTS

Al's Pizza 1620 Margaret St, Ste 201 904/388-8384 *in Riverside/ Little 5 Points area*

Biscotti's [★] 3556 Saint Johns Ave (Talbot Ave) 904/387-2060 *10:30am-10pm, till midnight Fri-Sat, from 8am Sat-Sun*

Bistro Aix 1440 San Marco Blvd 904/398-1949 *11am-10pm, till 11pm Fri, 5pm-11pm Sat, 5pm-9pm Sun*

European Street Cafe [★BW,WC,GO] 2753 Park St (at King) 904/384-9999 *10am-10pm, deli, patio*

Mossfire Grill 1537 Margaret St 904/355-4434 *lunch & dinner, full bar*

RETAIL SHOPS

Metro Gift Shop 859 Willow Branch Ave (inside The Metro) 904/388-8719 *2pm-2am Fri-Sat only*

Rainbows & Stars 1046 Park St (in historic 5 Points) 904/356-7702 *10am-7pm Wed-Fri, noon-7pm Sat, noon-5pm Sun, clsd Mon-Tue*

MEN'S CLUBS

Club Jacksonville [★SW,PC] 1939 Hendricks Ave (at Atlantic) 904/398-7451 *24hrs*

MEN'S SERVICES

▶**MegaMates** 904/721-9999 *Call to hook up with HOT local men. FREE to listen & respond to ads. Use FREE code DAMRON. MegaMates.com.*

CRUISY AREAS

Willowbranch Park [AYOR] Park St (btwn Willow Branch Ave & Cherry St) *take Roosevelt Blvd to McDuff Ave & head toward river*

Key Biscayne

CRUISY AREAS

Bear Cut Park [AYOR] in Crandon Beach Park *head W on beach; beware cops (even undercover)!*

Key West

INFO LINES & SERVICES

Gay & Lesbian Community Center [WI] 513 Truman Ave 305/292-3223 *many meetings & groups*

Keep It Simple (Gay/ Lesbian AA) 305/296-8654 (AA #) *8pm Mon-Sat, 5:30pm Sun*

➤**Key West Business Guild** 305/294-4603, 800/535-7797 *see ad in front color section*

ACCOMMODATIONS

Alexander Palms Court [GF,SW,WC,GO] 715 South St (at Vernon) 305/296-6413, 800/858-1943

Alexander's Guest House [★MW,SW,N,WI,WC,GO] 1118 Fleming St (at Frances) 305/294-9919, 800/654-9919

Ambrosia House Tropical Lodging [GF,SW,WI,WC] 615 & 618-622 Fleming St (at Simonton) 305/296-9838

Andrews Inn [GF,SW,NS,WI] Zero Whalton Ln (at Duval) 305/294-7730, 888/263-7393

The Artist House [GS,NS,WI] 534 Eaton St (at Duval) 305/296-3977, 800/582-7882

Avalon B&B [GF,SW,WI] 1317 Duval St (at United) 305/294-8233, 800/848-1317

Big Ruby's Guesthouse [M,SW,N,WI,NS,WC,GO] 409 Appelrouth Ln (at Duval & Whitehead) 305/296-2323, 800/477-7829

Curry House [GS,SW,NS,WI] 806 Fleming St (at William) 305/294-6777, 800/633-7439

Cypress House & Guest Studios [GF,SW,NS,WI,WC] 601 Caroline (at Simonton) 305/294-6969, 800/525-2488

Equator Guest House [MO,SW,N,NS,WI,WC,GO] 818 Fleming St (at William) 305/294-7775, 800/278-4552

The Grand Guesthouse [MW,WI,NS,GO] 1116 Grinnell St 305/294-0590, 888/947-2630

Heartbreak Hotel [GS,GO] 716 Duval St (near Petronia) 305/296-5558

Heron House Court [GF,SW,NS,WI,WC] 412 Frances St (at Eaton) 800/932-9119

Island House [MO,F,SW,N,NS,WI,GO] 1129 Fleming St (at White) 305/294-6284, 800/890-6284 *cafe & bar, very cruisy*

Key West Harbor Inn B&B [GS,SW,NS,WI] 219 Elizabeth St (at Greene) 305/296-2978, 800/608-6569

Knowles House B&B [GS,SW,N,NS,GO] 1004 Eaton St (at Grinnell) 305/296-8132, 800/352-4414

La Te Da [★MW,S,21+,SW,WI,WC,GO] 1125 Duval St (at Catherine) 305/296-6706, 877/528-3320

Marquesa Hotel [★GF,SW,NS,WI,WC] 600 Fleming St (at Simonton) 305/292-1919, 800/869-4631 *also Cafe Marquesa 6pm-10:30pm, full bar*

The Mermaid & the Alligator–A Key West B&B [GS,SW,NS,WI,GO] 729 Truman Ave (at Windsor Ln) 305/294-1894, 800/773-1894

Florida • *USA*

The New Orleans House Guesthouse
[M,SW,N,WI,GO] 724 Duval St, upstairs
(at Petronia) 305/293-9800,
888/293-9893 sundeck, hot tub,
garden bar, play areas

Pearl's Key West
[★GS,SW,NS,WI,WC,GO] 525 United St
(at Duval) 305/292-1450,
800/749-6696 all-welcome historic
inn offering guesthouse ambiance &
resort amenities; breakfast, 2 pools, 2
hot tubs, gym, poolside bar & grill

Pilot House Guest House
[GS,SW,N,NS,WI,WC] 414 Simonton St (at
Eaton) 305/293-6600,
800/648-3780

Seascape Inn [GF,SW,NS,WI] 420 Olivia
St (at Duval) 305/296-7776,
800/765-6438

**Simonton Court Historic Inn &
Cottages** [GF,SW,NS,WI] 320 Simonton
St (at Caroline) 305/294-6386,
800/944-2687

Tropical Inn [GF,SW,WI] 812 Duval St
(at Petronia) 305/294-9977,
888/611-6510 hot tub, sundeck

■BARS

The 801 Bourbon Bar
[★MW,NH,D,K,C,DS,P,S] 801 Duval St (at
Petronia) 305/294-4737 10am-4am,
from noon Sun, also Saloon One [M,L]

Bobby's Monkey Bar [M,NH,E,K,WI,WC]
900 Simonton St (at Olivia)
305/294-2655 noon-4am

Bourbon Street Pub [★M,S,V,SW,WC]
724 Duval St (at Petronia)
305/293-9800 11am-4am, from noon
Sun, popular daytime bar

Garden of Eden [GS,D,E,N] 224 Duval
St 305/296-4565 10am-4am, from
noon Sun

Hog's Breath Saloon [GF,F,E] 400 Front
St 305/296-4222

La Te Da [★MW,F,C,P,WC,GO] 1125
Duval St (at Catherine) 305/296-6706

Virgilio's [GS,D,F,E] 524 Duval St (at
Fleming in La Trattoria) 305/296-8118
7pm-4am, martini bar, garden

■NIGHTCLUBS

Aqua [★MW,D,E,K,DS,V,WC] 711 Duval St
305/294-0555 3pm-2am

Bottle Cap Lounge [GS,D]
305/296-2807 noon-4am

■CAFES

Croissants de France [BW] 816 Duval
St 305/294-2624 bakery 7:30am-
6pm, restaurant open till 10pm, patio

■RESTAURANTS

Antonia's Restaurant [★] 615 Duval
St (at Southard) 305/294-6565 lunch
& dinner, Italian, full bar

Azur 425 Grinnell St 305/292-2987
Mediterranean

Blue Heaven [E] 729 Thomas St
305/296-8666 great brkfst, also lunch
& dinner

Bo's Fish Wagon [★] 801 Caroline (at
William) 305/294-9272 lunch &
dinner, "seafood & eat it"

Cafe Sole 1029 Southard St (at
Frances) 305/294-0230 dinner
nightly, Sun brunch, romantic, candlelit
backyard

Camille's 1202 Simonton (at Catherine)
305/296-4811 brkfst, lunch & dinner,
bistro, hearty brkfst

El Meson de Pepe [E] 410 Wall St (in
Mallory Sq) 305/295-2620 lunch &
dinner, Cuban

The Flaming Buoy Filet Co [WC] 1100
Packer St (at Virginia) 305/295-7970
lunch & dinner

Grand Cafe Key West 314 Duval St
305/292-4740 lunch & dinner

Half Shell Raw Bar 231 Margaret St
305/294-7496 11am-10pm, waterfront

Hurricane Hole 305/294-8025,
305/294-0200 10am-10pm, dockside
bar

Jack Flats [WC] 509 Duval St
305/294-7955 11am-2am

**Kelly's Caribbean Bar Grill &
Brewery** 301 Whitehead St (at Caroline)
305/293-8484 lunch & dinner, owned
by actress Kelly McGillis

La Trattoria Venezia 524 Duval St (at
Fleming) 305/296-1075 5pm-
10:30pm

Lobos Mixed Grill [BW] 5 Key Lime Sq (south of Southard St) 305/296-5303 *11am-6pm*

Louie's Backyard [★] 700 Waddell Ave (at Vernon) 305/294-1061 *11:30am-1am, deck*

Mangia Mangia [BW] 900 Southard St (at Margaret St) 305/294-2469 *dinner only, fresh pasta, patio*

Mangoes [WC] 700 Duval St (at Angela) 305/292-4606 *lunch & dinner, bar till 1am, "Floribbean" cuisine, full bar*

Michaels 532 Margaret St 305/295-1300 *dinner only, steakhouse*

New York Pasta Garden 1075 Duval St (Duval Square) 305/292-1991 *11am-10pm*

Nine One Five 915 Duval St 305/296-0669 *dinner only, tapas, full bar*

Salsa Loca 618 Duval St (in Cowboy Bills) 305/292-1865 *clsd Mon, tasty, inexpensive Mexican*

Sarabeth's 530 Simonton St 305/293-8181 *8am-9pm, American*

Seven Fish [★] 632 Olivia St (at Elizabeth) 305/296-2777 *6pm-10pm, clsd Tue*

Square One [WC] 1075 Duval St (at Truman) 305/296-4300 *lunch & dinner, dinner only Mon*

Sweet Tea's 1114 Duval St 305/509-7451 *11am-10pm*

Upper Crust 611 Duval St 305/293-8890 *noon-11pm, excellent pizza*

ENTERTAINMENT & RECREATION

BluQ Sailing [M,GO] 200 Margaret St 305/923-7245 *all-gay sails*

Fort Zachary Taylor Beach *more gay to the right*

Gay & Lesbian Trolley Tour 305/294-4603

SkinnyDipperCruises.com Garrison Bight Marina (Palm Ave) 305/240-0517 *clothing-optional chartered cruises*

Venus Charters [★GO] Garrison Bight Marina 305/304-1181

BOOKSTORES

Key West Island Books 513 Fleming St (at Duval) 305/294-2904 *10am-9pm, till 6pm Sun*

RETAIL SHOPS

Fast Buck Freddie's [WC] 500 Duval St (at Fleming) 305/294-2007

Fausto's Food Palace 522 Fleming St (at Duval) 305/296-5663 *8am-8pm, till 7pm Sun, cruisy grocery store*

Frank's In Touch 706-A Duval St (at Angela) 305/294-1995 *9am-9pm, gay gifts*

GYMS & HEALTH CLUBS

Key West Island Gym [GO] 1119 White St 305/295-8222

MEN'S SERVICES

▶**MegaMates** 305/390-0390 *Call to hook up with HOT local men. FREE to listen & respond to ads. Use FREE code DAMRON. MegaMates.com.*

EROTICA

Fairvilla Megastore 520 Front St 305/292-0448

Leather Master 418 Appelrouth Ln 305/292-5051 *11am-10pm, noon-8pm Sun*

Truman Adult Books & Video 922 Truman Ave 305/295-0120 *arcade*

CRUISY AREAS

Higgs Beach [AYOR] on White St

Little Hamaca Park [AYOR] on Government Rd *from downtown, go E on Flagler Rd, turn right on Government, follow past airport to park at end of road*

Lake Worth

see also West Palm Beach

INFO LINES & SERVICES

Compass LGBT Community Center [WC] 201 N Dixie Hwy 561/533-9699 *9am-9pm, till 7pm Fri, 3pm-7pm Sat, clsd Sun*

BARS

The Bar [MW,NH,D,K,GO] 2211 N Dixie Hwy 561/370-3954 *2pm-2am, noon-midnight Sun*

The Mad Hatter Bar & Grill
[M,NH,V,OC,GO] 1532 N Dixie Hwy (16th Ave) **561/547-8860** *1pm-2am, noon-midnight Sun*

Mara [M,D] 1132 N Dixie Hwy **561/827-6468** *7pm-2am Wed, 10pm-2am Th-Fri, till 5am Sat, from 6pm Sun*

■**CAFES**

Mother Earth Coffee & Gifts [E,GO] **561/460-8647** *8am-7pm, till 10pm Fri-Sat*

■**RESTAURANTS**

The Cottage [WC] 522 Lucerne Ave **561/586-0080** *dinner only, also bar*

Lakeland

■**BARS**

Pulse [M,D,TG,DS,S,WC] 1030 E Main St **863/688-9463** *6pm-2am, till midnight Sun*

■**MEN'S SERVICES**

►**MegaMates** 863/248-0100 *Call to hook up with HOT local men. FREE to listen & respond to ads. Use FREE code DAMRON. MegaMates.com.*

■**CRUISY AREAS**

Lake Morton [AYOR] *beware cops (including undercover)!*

Largo

■**BARS**

Christopher Street Bar [M,D,DS,S,WI] 13344 66th St N (at Ulmerton Rd) **727/538-0660, 727/520-4111** (info line) *2pm-2am*

■**EROTICA**

Buddies of Largo 13801 66th St **727/539-7979**

Madison

■**ACCOMMODATIONS**

The Mystic Lake Manor [MO,R,SW,N,WI,WC,GO] **850/973-8435** *full brkfst, hot tub*

Marathon

■**ACCOMMODATIONS**

Tropical Cottages [GF,V,NS] 243 61st St Gulf **305/743-6048**

■**ENTERTAINMENT & RECREATION**

Bahia Honda State Park & Beach 12 miles S of Marathon

Melbourne

■**ACCOMMODATIONS**

Beach Bungalow [GF,NS,WI] 312 Wavecrest Ave, Indialantic by the Sea **321/984-1330, 888/414-5314**

Crane Creek Inn B&B [GS,SW,NS,WI] 907 E Melbourne Ave **321/768-6416**

■**BARS**

Cold Keg [MW,D,C,DS,18+,WC] 4060 W New Haven Ave (1/2 mile E of I-95) **321/724-1510** *4pm-2am, clsd Sun*

■**EROTICA**

Hot Flixx 3369 Sarno Rd (Bldg A) **321/752-8805**

MIAMI

Miami is divided into 3 geographical areas:
Miami—Overview
Miami—Greater Miami
Miami—Miami Beach/ South Beach

Miami—Overview

■**INFO LINES & SERVICES**

►**Greater Miami CVB** 305/539-3000, 800/933-8448 *see ad in front color section*

Switchboard of Miami **305/358-1640** *24hrs, gay-friendly info & referrals for Dade County*

■**ENTERTAINMENT & RECREATION**

Sailboat Charters of Miami [MW] 3400 Pan American Dr (at S Bayshore Dr) **305/772-4221** *private sailing charters aboard all-teakwood 46-foot clipper to Bahamas & the Keys*

■**PUBLICATIONS**

Genre Latino/ Latin Boys Magazine *get the dirt on Latin nights & clubs in Southern FL*

What's Happening Magazine **407/690-0809** *statewide LGBT entertainment & lifestyle magazine*

Miami—Greater Miami

■ BARS

The Dugout [M] 3215 NE 2nd Ave (at NE 32nd St) **305/438-1117** *4pm-3am, from 6pm Sat-Sun*

Eros Lounge [M,NH,K,DS] 8201 Biscayne Blvd **305/754-3444** *4pm-3am, till midnight Sun-Mon*

Jamboree [M,NH,DS] 7005 Biscayne Blvd (at NE 70th) **305/759-0066** *7pm-2am, dive bar, patio*

■ NIGHTCLUBS

Club Boi [M,D,MR,18+] 1060 NE 79th St **305/836-8995** *11pm-close Tue & Fri-Sat*

Club Sugar [MW,D,MR-L,DS] 2301 SW 32nd Ave (at Coral Wy) **305/443-7657** *10:30pm-5am Th-Sat, 8pm-3am Sun, clsd Mon-Wed*

Discotekka [M,D,18+] 950 NE 2nd Ave (at Metropolis Nightclub) **305/371-3773** *after hours Sat only*

House [GS,D] Wynwood Arts District

Johnny's Miami [M,D,S] 62 NE 14th St **305/640-8749** *5pm-5am, stripper bar*

Kaffe Krystal [GF,D,MR-L] 10855 SW 72nd St (at SW 107th Ave) **305/274-1112** *clsd Mon-Tue*

Space Miami [GF,D] 34 NE 11th St (at NE 1st Ave) **305/375-0001** *popular club w/ int'l visiting DJs*

Swinging Richard's [M,S,$] 17450 Biscayne Blvd **954/357-2532** *6:30pm-close, clsd Sun-Mon, gay strip club, nude dancers*

■ CAFES

Gourmet Station 7601 Biscayne Blvd (at NE 71st St) **305/762-7229** *8am-9pm, till 8pm Fri, clsd Sat-Sun*

■ RESTAURANTS

Area 31 [WC] 270 Biscayne Blvd Way (at the Epic Hotel) **305/424-5234** *brkfst, lunch & dinner, amazing view*

Cafeina 297 NW 23rd St (W of Miami Ave) **305/438-0792** *5pm-3am Th-Fri, from 9pm Sat, clsd Sun-Wed, tapas, also gallery, bands, events*

Habibi's Grill 93 SE 2nd St (at NE 1st Ave) **786/425-2699** *11am-8pm, clsd Sun, Lebanese/ Mediterranean*

Jimmy's East Side Diner [WC] 7201 Biscayne Blvd **305/754-3692** *7am-4pm*

Joey's 2506 NW 2nd Ave **305/438-0488** *lunch & dinner, clsd Sun, Italian, patio*

The Magnum Lounge & Restaurant [★NH,E,P,R] 709 NE 79th St **305/757-3368** *6pm-midnight, bar open 5pm-2am, clsd Mon*

Michy's 6927 Biscayne Blvd (at NE 69th) **305/759-2001** *dinner only, "luxurious comfort food"*

Ortanique on the Mile 278 Miracle Mile (at Salzedo), Coral Gables **305/446-7710** *Caribbean, full bar*

Ristorante Fratelli Milano [WC] 213 SE 1st St (at 2nd Ave) **305/373-2300** *11am-10pm*

Royal Bavarian Schnitzel Haus 1085 NE 79th St **305/754-8002** *5pm-11pm, German fare*

Soyka 5556 NE 4th Ct **305/759-3117** *lunch & dinner, wknd brunch, full bar*

UVA 69 6900 Biscayne Blvd (at NE 69th) **305/754-9022** *11am-11pm, full bar, patio*

Wynwood Kitchen & Bar 2550 NW 2nd Ave **305/722-8959** *5:30pm-midnight, Latin, great art*

■ ENTERTAINMENT & RECREATION

Awarehouse Miami 550 NW 29th St **305/576-4004** *artsy venue w/ live music, art shows & more*

Roam Rides 888/760-7626 *Vespa scooter rental, delivered to your hotel; also guided tours of Wynwood neighborhood art murals*

■ BOOKSTORES

Lambda Passages Bookstore 7545 Biscayne Blvd (at NE 76th) **305/754-6900** *11am-9pm, noon-6pm Sun, LGBT/ feminist*

■ RETAIL SHOPS

Creative Male 222 NE 25th St #116 **305/573-3080** *noon-8pm, till 6pm Sun*

◼MEN'S CLUBS

Club Aqua Miami [MO,SW,PC] 2991 Coral Wy (at S Red Rd) 305/448-2214 *24hrs*

◼CRUISY AREAS

Matheson Hammock Beach [AYOR] on Old Cutler Rd (S of Kendall Dr) *also Indian Hammocks Park on 117 Ave in Kendall*

Miami—Miami Beach/ South Beach

◼ACCOMMODATIONS

The Angler's [GS,SW,WI] 660 Washington Ave 305/534-9600, 866/729-8800 *restaurant & lounge*

Aqua Hotel & Lounge [GS,WI] 1530 Collins Ave 305/538-4361 *boutique hotel*

Beachcomber Hotel [GF,NS,WI] 1340 Collins Ave (at 13th St) 305/531-3755, 888/305-4683

Blue Moon Hotel [GF,SW,WI] 944 Collins Ave 305/673-2262

Bresaro Suites at the Mantell Plaza [GS,SW,GO] 255 W 24th St 305/772-5665

The Cardozo Hotel [GF,F,WI,WC] 1300 Ocean Dr 305/535-6500, 800/782-6500

The Century [GF,F,NS,WI,WC] 140 Ocean Dr 305/674-8855, 877/659-8855

Chesterfield Hotel, Suites & Day Spa [GS] 855 Collins Ave 305/531-5831, 877/762-3477

Circa 39 Hotel [GF,SW,NS,WI,WC] 3900 Collins Ave (at 39th St) 305/538-4900, 877/824-7223

The Colony Hotel [GF,F,WI,WC] 736 Ocean Dr (at 7th St) 305/673-0088

Delano Hotel [GF,F,SW,WI,WC] 1685 Collins Ave 305/672-2000, 800/697-1791

The European Guesthouse [MW,SWWI,GO] 721 Michigan Ave (btwn 7th & 8th) 305/673-6665

The Hotel [GF,F,SW,NS,WI,WC] 801 Collins Ave 305/531-2222, 877/843-4683

Hotel Ocean [GS,F,WI,WC] 1230-38 Ocean Dr 305/672-2579

Island House South Beach [GS,GO] 1428 Collins Ave 305/864-2422, 800/382-2422

The King & Grove Tides [GS,F,SW,WI] 1220 Ocean Dr (at 12th St) 305/604-5070, 305/503-3268 *private beach area, also La Marea restaurant*

Lords of South Beach [M,F,SW,NS,WC] 1120 Collins Ave 305/674-7800, 877/448-4754

The National Hotel [GS,F,SW,WI,WC] 1677 Collins Ave 305/532-2311, 800/327-8370 *luxury hotel on the beach*

North Beach Guest House [M,WI] 7996 Crespi Blvd (at 80th St) 305/807-7819

Penguin Hotel [MW,F,WI,WC] 1418 Ocean Dr 305/534-9334

The Raleigh, Miami Beach [GF,SW,WI,WC] 1775 Collins Ave (at Ocean Front) 305/534-6300, 800/848-1775

South Seas [GF,F,SW,WI] 1751 Collins Ave 305/538-1411, 800/345-2678

The Winterhaven [GS,WI,WC] 1400 Ocean Dr 305/531-5571

◼BARS

Buck15 Lounge [GS,E] 437 Lincoln Ln 305/538-3815 *10pm-5am, clsd Sun-Mon, more gay Th*

Creme Lounge [MW,NH,D] 725 Lincoln Ln N (upstairs from Score) 305/535-1163 *open Tue & Th-Sat*

Palace Bar & Grill [MW,F,DS,GO] 1200 Ocean Dr (at 12th St) 305/531-7234 *10am-1am, till 2am Fri-Sat*

◼NIGHTCLUBS

Mova [MW] 1625 Michigan Ave 305/534-8181 *3pm-3am, from noon Sun, lounge w/ DJ wknds*

Score [★M,D,K,DS,V] 727 Lincoln Rd (at Meridian) 305/535-1111 *lounge opens 3pm, dance club 10pm-5am Tue & Th-Sat*

Twist [★M,D,K,DS,V,WC] 1057 Washington Ave (at 11th) 305/538-9478 *1pm-5am*

CAFES

News Cafe 800 Ocean Dr (at 8th St) 305/538-6397 *24hrs, bookstore & bar*

RESTAURANTS

11th Street Diner 1065 Washington (at 11th) 305/534-6373 *24hrs, full bar*

8 Oz Burger Bar 1080 Alton Rd (at 11th St) 305/397-8246 *11am-3am, till 5am Th-Sat, also bar*

B&B: Burger & Beer Joint 1766 Bay Rd (at 18th St) 305/672-3287 *lunch & dinner*

Balans 1022 Lincoln Rd (btwn Michigan & Lennox) 305/534-9191 *8am-midnight*

Big Pink 157 Collins (at 2nd St) 305/532-4700 *8am-midnight, open late wknds*

David's Cafe II 1654 Meridian Ave 305/672-8707 *24hrs, Cuban*

Juice & Java [WC] 1346 Washington Ave (at 14th St) 305/531-6675 *9am-9pm, clsd Sun, healthy fast food*

Larios on the Beach [WC] 820 Ocean Dr (at 8th) 305/532-9577 *11:30am-midnight, Cuban*

Nexxt Cafe 700 Lincoln Rd (at Euclid Ave) 305/532-6643 *11:30am-11pm*

Spiga 1228 Collins Ave (at 12th St) 305/534-0079

Sushi Rock Cafe [★] 1351 Collins Ave (at 14th) 305/532-2133 *noon-midnight*

Tiramesu 721 Lincoln Rd 305/532-4538 *lunch & dinner, Italian*

ENTERTAINMENT & RECREATION

Beach Scooter Rentals 1341 Washington Ave 305/604-1414

Fritz's Skate & Bike 1620 Washington Ave 305/532-1954

The Gay Beach/ 12th St Beach 12th St & Ocean *where the boys are*

Lincoln Rd Lincoln Rd (btwn Bay Rd & Collins Aves) *pedestrian mall*

South Beach Bike Tours [GO] 305/673-2002

RETAIL SHOPS

Pink Palm 723 Lincoln Rd (at Meridian Ave) 305/397-8097 *10am-11pm*

GYMS & HEALTH CLUBS

Crunch 1259 Washington Ave 305/674-8222

David Barton Gym 2323 Collins Ave 305/534-1660

MEN'S SERVICES

➤**MegaMates** 305/250-9909 *Call to hook up with HOT local men. FREE to listen & respond to ads. Use FREE code DAMRON. MegaMates.com.*

EROTICA

Pleasure Boutique 1019 5th St 305/673-3311

Sensations Video 1317 Washington Ave 305/534-2330 *24hrs*

X Spot 19800 S Dixie Hwy 305/255-2190 *24hrs*

CRUISY AREAS

Haulover Beach Park [AYOR] North Miami Beach *popular nude beach, N of station #27; beware of cops (even undercover)!*

Mt Dora

ACCOMMODATIONS

Adora Inn [GS,NS,WI,GO] 352/735-3110 *full brkfst*

Naples

see also Fort Myers

BARS

Bambusa Bar & Grill [GF,NH,F,V,GO] 600 Goodlette Rd N (at 5th Ave N) 239/649-5657 *4pm-midnight*

CAFES

Sunburst Cafe [WC] 2340 Pine Ridge Rd (at Airport Pulling Rd) 239/263-3123 *7am-3pm*

RESTAURANTS

Caffe dell'Amore [BW,WC] 1400 Gulf Shore Blvd N (at Banyan Blvd) 239/261-1389 *dinner only, clsd Sun-Mon in summer, Italian*

Patric's [GS,E] 1485 Pine Ridge Rd #3 239/304-9754 *11am-10pm*

Florida • *USA*

The Real Macaw 3275 Bayshore Dr
239/732-1188 *occasionally have gay events*

New Port Richey

■Bars

Chill Chamber [MW,D,E,WC] 3501 Universal Plaza (at Moog Rd & US 19) **727/844-3474** *2pm-2am*

Ocala

■Bars

Copa/ Tropix [M,D,DS,F] 2330 S Pine Ave **352/351-5721** *2pm-2am*

The Pub [M,NH] 14 NW 5th St **352/857-7256** *8pm-2am*

Orlando

■Info Lines & Services

GLBT Community Center of Central Florida 946 N Mills Ave **407/228-8272** *9am-9pm, noon-5pm Sat-Sun*

■Accommodations

Eo Inn & Spa [GS,F,NS,WI] 227 N Eola Dr (at Robinson) **407/481-8485, 888/481-8488** *boutique hotel, rooftop terrace, hot tub, cafe on-site*

Four Points by Sheraton Studio City [GF,SW,WI,WC] 5905 International Dr (at Kirkman) **407/351-2100, 866/716-8105** *bar & restaurant*

Grand Bohemian Hotel Orlando [GF,SW,NS,WI,WC] 325 S Orange Ave **407/313-9000, 888/213-9110**

Hyatt Residency Grand Cypress [GF,SW,WI,WC] 1 Grand Cypress Blvd **407/239-1234**

Parliament House Resort [★MW,D,MR,F,S,YC,SW,WC,GO] 410 N Orange Blossom Tr **407/425-7571** *also 6 bars (open at 8pm)*

Rick's B&B [M,N,SW,WI,GO] PO Box 22318, 32830 **407/396-7751, 407/414-7751 (cell)** *full brkfst, patio, near Walt Disney World*

Wyndham Orlando Resort [GF,SW,WC] 8001 International Dr **407/351-2420**

■Bars

Bar Codes [M,NH,B,L,BW] 4453 Edgewater Dr (at Thistledown Dr) **407/412-6917** *noon-2am, patio*

Bear's Den [M,B] 410 N Orange Blossom Tr (at Parliament House) **407/425-7571** *6pm-2am, from noon wknds, also restaurant*

Copper Rocket [GF,BW,WC] 106 Lake Ave (at 17-92), Maitland **407/645-0069** *4pm-2am, also restaurant*

Hank's [M,NH,BW,WC] 5026 Edgewater Dr (at Lee Rd) **407/291-2399** *noon-2am, patio*

Jungle Sundays [M,D,DS] 26 Wall St Plaza (upstairs at Monkey Bar) **407/481-1199** *4pm-2am Sun only (seasonal)*

The New Phoenix [MW,NH,D,E,K,DS] 7124 Aloma Ave (at Forsythe), Winter Park **407/678-9070** *6pm-2am, from 4pm Th-Sat*

Paradise [M,NH,K,WI,GO] 1300 N Mills Ave (btwn Virginia & Colonial) **407/898-0090** *4pm-2am, from noon wknds*

The Peacock Room [GF,NH,E] 1321 N Mills Ave (at Montana) **407/228-0048** *4:30pm-2am, from 8pm wknds, art shows, live music*

Savoy [M,S] 1913 N Orange Ave (at Berkshire) **407/898-6766** *5pm-2am, male dancers nightly*

Sip Orlando [GS,NH,K,WI] 724 Virginia Dr (at Dauphin Ln) **407/894-4747** *4pm-midnight, till 2am Fri-Sat, from 7pm Sat, 3pm-midnight Sun, art openings every 2nd Th*

Stonewall Bar [M,D,F,K,S,WC,GO] 741 W Church St (at Glenn Ln) **407/373-0888** *5pm-2am*

Wylde's [MW,NH,WI] 3530 S Orange Ave (at Suddath Dr) **407/852-0612** *5pm-2am, underwear Sat*

■Nightclubs

Parliament House Resort [★MW,D,MR,F,S,V,18+,SW,WC,GO] 410 N Orange Blossom Tr (at South St) **407/425-7571** *10:30am-3am, 6 bars*

Pulse Orlando [M,D,DS,18+] 1912 S Orange Ave (at Kaley St) **407/649-3888** *9pm-2am, clsd Sun*

Revolution [MW,D,MR,DS,S,V,18+,WC] 375 S Bumby Ave (at South St) **407/228-9900** *4pm-close, from 10pm Sun, go-go dancers, patio*

■ CAFES

Pom Pom's 67 N Bumby Ave **407/894-0865** *11am-5am, 24hrs Fri-Sat, tea & sandwiches*

White Wolf Cafe & Antique Shop [E,BW,WC] 1829 N Orange Ave (at Princeton) **407/895-9911** *7am-9pm, till 10pm Fri-Sat, 8am-3pm Sun*

■ RESTAURANTS

Dandelion Communitea Cafe [BW] 618 N Thornton Ave (at Colonial) **407/362-1864** *11am-10pm, till 3pm Mon, till 5pm Sun, vegetarian/ vegan*

Dexter's Thornton Park [E] 808 E Washington St **407/648-2777** *lunch & dinner, also Winter Park & Lake Mary locations*

Ethos Vegan Kitchen [WI,WC] 601-B New York Ave (at Fairbanks) **407/228-3898** *11am-10pm, 10am-3pm Sun*

Funky Monkey Wine Company [DS] **407/427-1447** *5pm-11pm, sushi*

Garden Cafe [WC] 810 W Colonial Dr (at Westmoreland) **407/999-9799** *11am-10pm, clsd Mon, vegetarian Chinese*

Hamburger Mary's Orlando [E,K,V,WC,GO] 110 W Church St (at Garland) **321/319-0600** *11am-midnight, till 1am Th-Sat, full bar*

Houston's [WC] 215 South Orlando Ave, Winter Park **407/740-4005** *lunch & dinner*

Hue 629 E Central Blvd (at N Summerlin Ave) **407/849-1800** *lunch & dinner, full bar*

Loving Hut [WC] 2101 E Colonial Dr (at Palm Dr) **407/894-5673** *11am-9pm, from 3pm Sun, clsd Tue, vegetarian/ vegan*

The Rainbow Cafe [MW] at Parliament House **407/425-7571** *7am-11pm, till 3am Fri-Sun*

■ BOOKSTORES

Mojo 930 N Mills Ave (at E Marks St) **407/896-0204** *1pm-8pm, 3pm-6pm Sun, LGBT*

■ RETAIL SHOPS

A Comic Shop 114 South Semoran Blvd, Winter Park **407/332-9636** *11am-7pm, till 9pm Wed, till midnight Fri-Sat*

The Back Room [GO] 5026 Edgewater Dr (outside Hanks Bar) **407/298-2802** *6pm-midnight, till 1:30am Fri-Sat, cards, erotica, etc*

Fairvilla's Sexy Things 7631 International Blvd **407/826-1627** *gifts, adult toys*

Twisted Tom's 410 N Orange Blossom Tr (at Parliament House) **407/425-7571 x127**

■ PUBLICATIONS

Hotspots 954/928-1862 *weekly entertainment guide*

Watermark PO Box 533655 32853 **407/481-2243** *bi-weekly LGBT newspaper for Central FL*

What's Happening Magazine **407/690-0809** *statewide LGBT entertainment & lifestyle magazine*

■ MEN'S CLUBS

Club Orlando [SW,PC] 450 E Compton St (at Delaney Ave) **407/425-5005** *24hrs*

■ MEN'S SERVICES

▶**MegaMates** **407/657-4500** *Call to hook up with HOT local men. FREE to listen & respond to ads. Use FREE code DAMRON. MegaMates.com.*

■ EROTICA

Fairvilla Megastore 1740 N Orange Blossom Tr **407/425-6005** *9am-2am*

Midnight News at Parliament House **407/425-7571** *6pm-2am*

■ CRUISY AREAS

Mead Botanical Gardens [AYOR] Denning Rd & Garden St, Winter Park *take I-4 to Fairbanks exit & go E to Denning Rd, turn right & go 1 mile, on left*

Florida • *USA*

Split Oak Park [AYOR] Narcoossee Rd *Take Narcoossee Rd, 5 miles S of 417, to Clapp Sims Duda Rd & turn left. Go for 1.5 miles to park.*

Turkey Lake Rest Area [AYOR] *take FL Turnpike N from I-4 to milepost 263 btwn exits 259 & 265*

Palm Beach

■ACCOMMODATIONS

The Chesterfield Hotel [GF,SW] 363 Coconut Row **561/659-5800**

■RESTAURANTS

Ta-boo [WC] 221 Worth Ave **561/835-3500** *11:30am-10pm, till 11pm Fri-Sat, cont'l*

■EROTICA

Adult Video Warehouse 501 Northlake Blvd, North Palm Beach **561/863-9997**

Panama City

■ACCOMMODATIONS

Casa de Playa [MW,SW,NS,GO] 20304 Front Beach Rd, Panama City Beach **850/236-8436** *guesthouse, steps from Gulf of Mexico, jacuzzi, patios*

Wisteria Inn [GS,SW,NS] 20404 Front Beach Rd, Panama City Beach **850/234-0557** *tropical inn, hot tub*

■BARS

La Royale Lounge & Liquor Store [MW,NH,WC] 100 Harrison (at Beach Dr) **850/763-1755** *3pm-3am, till 4am Fri-Sat, from 7pm Sun, courtyard*

Splash Bar [M,NH,DS,S,V,18+,YC,WC,GO] 6520 Thomas Dr, Panama City Beach **850/236-3450** *6pm-2am, till 4am Th-Sat, also pride shop*

■NIGHTCLUBS

Fiesta Room [MW,D,DS,WC] 110 Harrison Ave (at Beach Dr) **850/763-1755** *3pm-3am*

■CRUISY AREAS

Tyndall Bridge [AYOR] on Tyndall Pkwy (toward Air Force base) *parking lot*

Pensacola

■INFO LINES & SERVICES

GLBT AA Group 716 9th Ave (at Jackson) **850/433-4191 (AA#)** *6pm Sun*

■ACCOMMODATIONS

The Compound Campground [M,SW,N,WI,PC,GO] 7962 Hickory Hammock Rd (at Ward Basin Rd), Milton **850/221-2289, 901/481-5000** *21+, hot tub, shower/ bath facilities, tent & RV camping, cabins, day passes*

■BARS

The Cabaret [MW,E,K,WC] 101 S Jefferson St **850/607-2020** *3pm-2:30am*

The Round-Up [★M,NH,B,L,V,WC] 560 E Heinberg St **850/433-8482** *2pm-3am, patio*

■NIGHTCLUBS

Emerald City [★MW,D,DS,S,18+,WC] 406 E Wright St (at Alcaniz) **850/433-9491** *3pm-3am, clsd Tue, patio*

■CAFES

End of the Line Cafe [★E,WI,WC] 610 E Wright St **850/429-0336** *10am-10pm, 11am-5pm Sun, clsd Mon, vegetarian; also live music & art*

■CRUISY AREAS

The Bluffs [AYOR] Scenic Dr *beware of cops!*

Pompano Beach

■RESTAURANTS

J Marks Restaurant [E,WC,GO] 1490 NE 23rd St (at Federal Hwy/ US1) **954/782-7000** *11am-10pm, till 11pm Fri-Sat, full bar*

Port St Lucie

■NIGHTCLUBS

Rebar [MW,NH,D,V,WC,GO] 8283 S Federal Hwy (at Prima Vista) **772/340-7777** *4pm-2am, till midnight Sun, video bar*

Sarasota

INFO LINES & SERVICES

Gay AA 7225 N Lockwood Ridge Rd (in Pierce Hall, Church of the Trinity MCC) **941/355-0847 (church #)** *7pm Sun & 7pm Th*

ACCOMMODATIONS

The Cypress [GF,NS,WI] 621 Gulfstream Ave S **941/955-4683**

Turtle Beach Resort [GF,SW,WI,WC] 9049 Midnight Pass Rd **941/349-4554**

NIGHTCLUBS

Throb [M,D,DS,GO] 2201 Industrial Blvd **941/358-6969** *2pm-2am, theme nights*

RESTAURANTS

Caragiulos 69 S Palm Ave **941/951-0866** *lunch & dinner, Italian-American*

PUBLICATIONS

What's Happening Magazine 407/690-0809 *statewide LGBT entertainment & lifestyle magazine*

MEN'S SERVICES

▶**MegaMates** 941/870-0800 *Call to hook up with HOT local men. FREE to listen & respond to ads. Use FREE code DAMRON. MegaMates.com.*

EROTICA

Romantix Tamiami Books 7338 S Tamiami Tr **941/923-7626**

CRUISY AREAS

Gravel Pit Lake [AYOR] Honore Ave (N of 17th St at Cooper Creek Park) *road has no sign, turn right after passing power lines*

South Beach

see Miami Beach/ South Beach

St Augustine

see also Jacksonville

ACCOMMODATIONS

Alexander Homestead [GF,NS,WI] 14 Sevilla St **904/826-4147, 888/292-4147**

Casa Monica [GF,SW,NS,WC] 95 Cordova St **904/827-1888, 888/213-8903**

The Inn at Camachee Harbor [GF,F,WI] 201 Yacht Club Dr (at May St) **904/825-0003, 800/688-5379**

Our House B&B [GS,WI,GO] 7 Cincinnati Ave **904/347-6260**

RESTAURANTS

Collage [★R] 60 Hypolita St **904/829-0055** *dinner nightly, "artful global dining"*

CRUISY AREAS

Riverdale Park [AYOR] CR 13 (at SR 207) *take Hwy 207 to CR 305, follow through Racey Point & then Riverdale, days*

Vilano Beach Walkway [AYOR] *go N on A1A 2 miles, 2nd crosswalk over A1A, beachside*

St Petersburg

see also Tampa

ACCOMMODATIONS

Bay Palms Waterfront Resort [GF,SW,NS,WI,GO] 4237 Gulf Blvd, St Petersburg Beach **727/360-7642, 800/257-8998**

Dicken's House B&B [GS,WI,GO] 335 8th Ave NE **727/822-8622, 800/381-2022**

Flamingo [MW,E,SW,F,WI,WC] 4601 34th St South **727/321-5000**

GayStPete House [M,SW,N,NS,WI,WC,GO] 4505 5th Ave N (at 45th) **727/365-0544**

La Veranda B&B [GS] 111 5th Ave N **727/224-1057** *1 block from the beach*

The Pier Hotel [GS,NS,WI,GO] 253 2nd Ave N (at 2nd St) **727/822-7500, 800/735-6607**

Postcard Inn on the Beach [GF,F,SW,WI] 6300 Gulf Blvd **727/367-2711, 800/237-8918**

Villa Da Costa [GS,GO] 7555 46th Ave N **727/546-1477** *motel*

Florida • USA

Bars

Detour [M,NH,D,K,WI,WC] 2612 Central Ave (at 26th) **727/327-8204** 2pm-2am, patio

Haymarket Pub [M,NH,WC] 8308 4th St N (at 83rd) **727/577-9621** 5pm-2am

Oar House [MW,NH,F,K] 4807 22nd Ave S **727/327-1691** 9am-2am, from 11am Sun

Pepperz [★MW,D,K,WC] 4918 Gulfport Blvd S (at 49th), Gulfport **727/623-4837** 2pm-2am

Sporters Bar [M,NH,B,CW,L,WC,GO] 187 Dr Martin Luther King St N **727/821-1920** 2pm-2am

Nightclubs

Georgie's Alibi [MW,NH,D,F,DS,S,V, WI,WC,GO] 3100 3rd Ave N (at 31st St N) **727/321-2112** 11am-3am, patio

Glass [MW,D,DS,TG] 16 2nd St N (at Vintage Ultra Lounge) **727/898-2222** Sat only

Restaurants

Central Avenue Oyster Bar 249 Central Ave **727/897-9728** 11am-midnight

Sea Porch Cafe 3400 Gulf Blvd (at Don Cesar Beach Resort) **727/360-1884**

Skyway Jack's 2795 34th St S **727/867-1907** 5am-3pm, Southern cooking (diner-style)

Entertainment & Recreation

Bedrocks Beach/ Sunset Beach W Gulf Blvd (at S end of Treasure Island, Sunset Beach) popular park

Dali Museum 1 Dali Blvd **727/823-3767, 800/442-3254**

Fort DeSoto Park Pinellas Bayway S

Men's Services

➤**MegaMates** **727/490-0800** Call to hook up with HOT local men. FREE to listen & respond to ads. Use FREE code DAMRON. MegaMates.com.

Erotica

XTC Adult Supercenter 4800 34th St S **727/865-6977** arcade

Cruisy Areas

Fort DeSoto Park [AYOR] Pinellas Bayway S days, beautiful beach, after leave North Beach parking lot & cross rainbow bridge

North Shore Park [AYOR]

Tallahassee

Info Lines & Services

The Family Tree 5126C Woodlane Cir **850/222-8555** LGBT community center, call for hours

Accommodations

Hampton Inn Quincy [GF,SW,WI,WC] 165 Spooner Rd (Pat Thomas Pkwy), Quincy **850/627-7555**

Men's Services

➤**MegaMates** **850/385-9900** Call to hook up with HOT local men. FREE to listen & respond to ads. Use FREE code DAMRON. MegaMates.com.

Erotica

Rick's Toy Box 618 W Tennessee St **850/577-9000**

X-Mart Adult Supercenter [AYOR] 5021 W Tennessee (US 90) (Capital Circle W) **850/575-2169** 24hrs, arcade

Tampa

see also St Petersburg

Accommodations

Don Vicente de Ybor Inn [GS] 1915 Republica de Cuba **813/241-4545, 866/206-4545** historic boutique hotel

Gram's Place Hostel [GS,N,NS,WI] 3109 N Ola Ave **813/221-0596**

Hampton Inn & Suites [GS,SW,WI,WC] 1301 East 7th Ave **813/247-6700**

Hyatt Regency [GS,F,SW,WI,WC] 211 N Tampa St **813/225-1234**

Sawmill Camping Resort [M,D,E,K,SW,N,GO] 21710 US Hwy 98, Dade City **352/583-0664** RV hookups, cabins, tent spots

Bars

2606 [★M,L,S,WC,GO] 2606 N Armenia Ave (at St Conrad) **813/875-6993** 3pm-3am, also leather shop from 9pm

Baxter's [M,NH,K,S,WC] 1519 S Dale Mabry (at W Neptune) **813/258-8830** *noon-3am*

Body Shop Bar [M,NH,K,S,GO] 14905 N Nebraska **813/971-3576** *3pm-3am*

Bradley's on 7th [M,D,DS] 1510 E 7th Ave, Ybor City **831/241-2723** *4pm-3am*

Chelsea Lounge [★MW,NH,D,K,DS] 1502 N Florida Ave (at Hwy 275) **813/228-0139** *3pm-3am*

City Side [MW,D,NH,K,WI] 3703 Henderson Blvd (at Dale Mabry) **813/350-0600** *11am-3am, patio*

Collage Ybor [GS,E,K] 1701 8th Ave, Ybor City

Hamburger Mary's [MW,F,K,DS,WC] 1600 E 7th Ave (at N 16th St) **813/241-6279** *11am-11pm, till 3am wknds*

Reservoir Bar [GS,NH,WC] 1518 E 7th Ave **813/248-1442** *7pm-3am*

◼NIGHTCLUBS

The Castle [GS,D] 2004 N 16th St **813/247-7547** *10:30pm-3am, clsd Tue-Wed, theme nights*

Crowbar [GS,D,E,K] 1812 N 17th St **813/241-8600** *10pm-3am*

G Bar [★MW,D,DS,V,18+,GO] 1401 E 7th Ave **813/247-1016** *4pm-3am, clsd Sun-Mon*

Metro Tampa [M,D] 2606 N Armenia Ave (at St Conrad) **813/876-4650** *3pm-3am, from 1pm Sun*

Steam Fridays [★M,D,DS,18+] 1507 E 7th Ave (at the Honey Pot) **813/247-4663** *10pm Fri only, 3 flrs*

Valentines Nightclub [M,D,K,DS,S] 7522 N Armenia Ave (btwn Sligh & Waters) **813/936-1999** *3pm-3am*

Ybor City Social Club/ Eagle Club [M,D,B,L] 1909 N 15th St (btwn 8th & 9th), Ybor City *10pm-3am, Eagle downstairs*

◼CAFES

Joffrey's Coffee [F,WI] 1600 E 8th Ave **813/247-4600** *7am-10pm, till midnight wknds*

Sacred Grounds Cafe [MW,E,WI] 4819 E Busch Blvd (at Hyaleah Rd) **813/983-0837** *6pm-midnight, till 2am Fri-Sat, open mic Mon*

Tre Amici [BW] 1907 19th St N **813/247-6964** *8am-5pm, till 11pm Th, clsd Sun, cafe & wine bar*

◼RESTAURANTS

Bernini 1702 E 7th Ave **813/248-0099** *lunch Mon-Fri, dinner nightly, Italian*

Centro Cantina 1600 E 8th Ave **813/241-8588** *Tex Mex, great balcony*

Columbia 2117 E 7th Ave **813/248-4961** *11am-close, from noon Sun, Cuban & Spanish*

Crabby Bill's 401 Gulf Blvd, Indian Rocks Beach **727/595-4825** *inexpensive seafood joint*

Fresh Mouth 1600 E 8th Ave (plaza level) **813/241-8845** *11am-9pm, till 2am wknds*

Gaspar's Grotto [E,K,WI] 1805 E 7th Ave **813/248-5900** *11am-3am, patio*

JJ's Cafe & Bar 1601 E 7th Ave (at N 16th St) **813/247-4125** *11am-10pm, till 2:30am wknds*

The Laughing Cat [WC] 1820 N 15th St **813/241-2998** *Italian*

The Metro Restaurant & Lounge [DS] 511 N Franklin St **813/225-1111** *4:30pm-11pm, till 1am Fri-Sat, clsd Mon, drag shows wknds*

The Queen's Head 2501 Central Ave, St Petersburg **727/498-8584** *4:30pm-2am, from noon wknds, clsd Mon, full bar*

◼ENTERTAINMENT & RECREATION

Picnic Island Picnic Island Blvd (across from the military base, on E side) *gay beach at end of park*

◼RETAIL SHOPS

King Corona Cigars 1523 E 7th Ave **888/248-3812** *local, handmade cigars.also cafe & bar*

The MC Film Festival 1901 N 15th St (at 8th Ave) **813/247-6233** *LGBT pride gift store*

Urban Body 715 S Howard Ave #1301 813/251-5522 *11am-7pm, noon-5pm Sun*

■ PUBLICATIONS

Watermark 813/655-9890, 877/926-8118 *bi-weekly LGBT newspaper for Central FL*

What's Happening Magazine 407/690-0809 *statewide LGBT entertainment & lifestyle magazine*

■ MEN'S CLUBS

Rainbow Cabaret [AYOR,WI] 4421 N Hubert Ave (behind Playhouse Theatre) 813/877-7585 *24hrs*

Tampa Men's Club 4061 W Crest Ave 813/876-6367 *24hrs*

Ybor Resort & Spa [MO,WI,PC] 1512 E 8th Ave 813/242-0900 *full accommodations*

■ MEN'S SERVICES

► **MegaMates** 813/251-4744 *Call to hook up with HOT local men. FREE to listen & respond to ads. Use FREE code DAMRON. MegaMates.com.*

■ EROTICA

Buddies Video 4322 W Crest Ave (at Hillsborough) 813/876-8083

Planet X 9921 Adamo Dr 813/740-8484 *24hrs*

Playhouse Theatre [AYOR] 4421 N Hubert Ave (at Alva) 813/873-9235 *24hrs*

Tres Equis [★] 6220 Adamo Dr (behind Goldrush topless bar) 813/740-8664 *24hrs*

■ CRUISY AREAS

Al Lopez Park [AYOR] N Himes Ave (1 blk S of Hillsborough), West Tampa *take I-275 N toward Ocala, take Hillsborough exit, then go W on Hillsborough Ave for 2 1/2 miles, turn left on Himes Ave*

Picnic Island [AYOR] Picnic Island Blvd (across from the military base, on E side) *gay beach at end of park, past the last parking lot & beyond the mangroves*

Venus

■ ACCOMMODATIONS

Camp Mars [M,SW,N,GO] 326 Goff Rd 863/699-6277 *campground w/ cabins, tents, RV hookups, 2 hours from Fort Lauderdale & Miami*

West Palm Beach

■ ACCOMMODATIONS

Grandview Gardens B&B [GF,SW,NS,WI,WC,GO] 1608 Lake Ave (at Palm) 561/833-9023

Hibiscus House B&B [GS,SW,NS,WI,GO] 501 30th St 561/863-5633, 800/203-4927

Hotel Biba [GF] 320 Belvedere Rd 561/832-0094 *mid-century chic motor lodge*

Scandia Lodge [GS,SW,NS] 625 S Federal Hwy (at 6th Ave), Lake Worth 561/586-3155

■ BARS

Fort Dix [★M,D,NH,WC] 6205 Georgia Ave (at Colonial) 561/533-5355 *noon-3am, till 4am Fri-Sat, patio*

HG Rooster's [★M,NH,F,K,DS,S,WC] 823 Belvedere Rd (btwn Parker & Lake) 561/832-9119 *3pm-3am, till 4am Fri-Sat*

■ NIGHTCLUBS

Monarchy [GF,D] 221 Clematis St 561/835-6661 *10pm-3am, till 4am Fri-Sat, clsd Sun, Tue & Th*

Respectable Street [GF,D,A,E,18+] 518 Clematis St 561/832-9999 *9pm-3am, till 4am Fri-Sat, clsd Sun-Tue, retro & new wave nights*

■ RESTAURANTS

Rhythm Cafe [BW] 3800-A S Dixie Hwy 561/833-3406 *6pm-10pm, clsd Sun-Mon*

Thai Bay 1900 Okeechobee Blvd (in Palm Beach Market Pl) 561/640-0131 *lunch & dinner, clsd Sun*

■ ENTERTAINMENT & RECREATION

MacArthur Beach Singer Island, N Palm Beach

■ BOOKSTORES

Changing Times Bookstore 911 Village Blvd #806 (at Palm Beach Lakes) **561/640-0496** *10am-7pm, till 5pm Sat-Sun*

■ RETAIL SHOPS

Eurotique 814 Northlake Blvd, North Palm Beach **561/684-2302** *10am-8pm, till 6pm Sat, noon-5pm Sun*

■ MEN'S SERVICES

▶**MegaMates** 561/909-1100 *Call to hook up with HOT local men. FREE to listen & respond to ads. Use FREE code DAMRON. MegaMates.com.*

■ EROTICA

Redlight Adult Video Outlet 3900 Byron Dr **561/629-7331**

■ CRUISY AREAS

Jupiter Beach [AYOR] Jupiter *going S on A1A, it's the 3rd catwalk past Jupiter Key on the left*

Wilton Manors

see Fort Lauderdale

GEORGIA

Athens

■ ACCOMMODATIONS

Ashford Manor B&B [GF,SW,NS,WI,GO] 5 Harden Hill Rd (at Main St), Watkinsville **706/769-2633**

■ BARS

The Globe [GF,F] 199 N Lumpkin St (at Clayton) **706/353-4721** *11am-2am, till midnight Sun, 40 single-malt scotches*

■ NIGHTCLUBS

Forty Watt Club [GF,E,WC] 285 W Washington St (at Pulaski) **706/549-7871** *call for hours, live music venue*

■ CAFES

Jittery Joe's Coffee [WI,WC] 297 E Broad St (at Jackson) **706/613-7449** *7am-11pm, from 8am wknds*

■ RESTAURANTS

The Grit [WC] 199 Prince Ave **706/543-6592** *11am-10pm, great wknd brunch 10am-3pm*

■ CRUISY AREAS

Ben Burton Park [AYOR] Mitchell Bridge Rd (just before Oconee River Bridge)

Kangaroo Truck Stop [AYOR] Hwy 29 N

Atlanta

■ INFO LINES & SERVICES

Galano Club 585 Dutch Valley Rd (at Monroe) **404/881-9188** *meetings throughout the day, LGBT recovery club*

■ ACCOMMODATIONS

Atlanta Perimeter Hotel & Suites [GF,SW,NS,WI,WC] 111 Perimeter Center W (at Ashford Dunwoody Rd) **770/396-6800** *also restaurant*

The Georgian Terrace Hotel [GF,SW,NS,WI,WC] 659 Peachtree St NE (at Ponce de Leon) **404/897-1991, 800/651-2316** *hosted Gone w/ the Wind world-premier reception in 1939*

Glenn Hotel [GS,WI] 110 Marietta St NW (at Spring) **404/521-2250, 888/717-8851** *boutique hotel, also restaurant & rooftop lounge*

Hello B&B [MW,NS,WI,GO] 1865 Windemere Dr **404/892-8111** *hot tub*

Hotel Indigo [WI] 683 Peachtree St NE (at 3rd) **404/874-9200, 800/863-7818** *cozy, stylish no-frills hotel, workout room, also restaurant*

In the Woods Campground & Resort [M,N,SW,GO] 142 Casey Ct (at Hwy 327 & Hwy 51), Canon **706/246-0152** *campground w/ 36+ campsites & 20+ RV hookups*

Microtel Inn & Suites Buckhead [GF,WI,WC] 1840 Corporate Blvd (off Buford Hwy) **404/325-4446, 800/337-0044**

Renaissance Midtown Atlanta [GF] 866 W Peachtree St NW (at 7th St NE) **678/412-2400, 800/716-6009** *hip boutique hotel in midtown*

Georgia • USA

Sheraton Atlanta Hotel
[GF,F,WI,NS,SW,WC] 165 Courtland St (at International Blvd) 404/659-6500, 800/325-3535 *3 restaurants, full bar, gym*

The St Charles Inn [GS,NS,WI,GO] 1001 St Charles Ave NE 404/875-1001 *1913 craftsman-style B&B*

Stonehurst Place B&B [GS,NS,WI,GO] 923 Piedmont Ave NE (at 8th St) 404/881-0722, 877/285-2246

W Atlanta Midtown [GS,WI,SW] 188 14th St NE (at Juniper St NE) 404/892-6000 *stylish hotel, convenient location*

■ BARS

Amsterdam [★M,D,F,V] 502 Amsterdam Ave NE 404/892-2227 *11:30am-close, video & sports bar*

Atlanta Eagle [★M,D,B,L,GO] 306 Ponce de Leon Ave NE (at Argonne) 404/873-2453 *7pm-3am, from 5pm Sat, clsd Sun, also leather store*

BJ Roosters [M,NH,K,S,WC,GO] 2345 Cheshire Bridge Rd NE (La Vista) 404/634-5895 *7pm-3am*

Blake's on the Park [★MW,NH,F,P,S,V] 227 10th St (at Piedmont) 404/892-5786 *11am-3am, till midnight Sun*

Bulldogs [★M,NH,D,L,MR-AF,V] 893 Peachtree St NE (btwn 7th & 8th) 404/872-3025 *2pm-4am Sun-Fri, till 3am Sat, cruise bar*

Burkhart's Pub [MW,NH,F,K,S,WC] 1492-F Piedmont Ave NE (at Monroe, in Ansley Square) 404/872-4403 *4pm-2:30am, from 2pm wknds, till midnight Sun, patio*

The Cockpit [M,NH,F] 465 Boulevard SE (off I-20) *5pm-close*

The Daiquiri Factory [MW] 889 W Peachtree St (at 7th) 404/881-8188 *11am-2:30am, the name says it all*

Eastside Lounge [GS,D,MR,V,E,K] 485-A Flat Shoals Ave (at Glenwood) 404/521-9666 *9pm-2:30am, from 8pm Fri-Sat, clsd Sun*

Eddie's Attic [GS,E] 515-B N McDonough St (at Trinity Place), Decatur 404/377-4976 *5pm-close Mon-Th, till 2am Fri-Sat, open 1 hr before showtime Sun, live music, comedy, also restaurant, rooftop deck*

Felix's on the Square [M,F,WC] 1510-G Piedmont Ave NE (Ansley Square) 404/249-7899 *2pm-3am, from 1pm Sat, 1pm-midnight Sun*

Friends on Ponce [MW,NH,V,WC] 736 Ponce de Leon NE (at Ponce de Leon Pl) 404/817-3820 *2pm-3am, from noon Sat, till midnight Sun, rooftop patio*

Halo Lounge [GS,F] 817 W Peachtree St (6th St, btwn W Peachtree & Peachtree) 404/962-7333 *9pm-3am, from 6pm Sat, clsd Sun*

The Hideaway [M,NH,OC,WC] 1544 Piedmont Ave NE (at Monroe, in Ansley Mall) 404/874-8247 *2pm-2am Mon-Th, till 3am Fri-Sat, till midnight Sun*

Le Buzz [MW,NH,D,F,K,DS,S,WC] 585 Franklin Rd A-10 (at S Marietta Pkwy, in Longhorn Plaza), Marietta 770/424-1337 *5pm-3am, clsd Sun, DJ Fri, patio*

Mary's [MW,NH,D,K,V,WC] 1287B Glenwood Ave (at Flat Shoals) 404/624-4411 *5pm-3am, clsd Sun*

Mixx [M,NH,D,K,P,B,F] 1492-B Piedmont Ave NE (at Monroe, in Ansley Square) 404/228-4372 *4pm-2am, till 3am Fri-Sat, clsd Sun*

Model T [M,NH,F,K,DS,OC,WC] 699 Ponce de Leon NE #11 (at Barnett) 404/872-2209 *9am-3am, till midnight Sun, cruisy*

Opus I [M,NH,WC] 1086 Alco St NE (at Cheshire Bridge) 404/634-6478 *11am-3am, 12:30pm-midnight Sun*

Oscar's Video Bar [M,V] 1510-C Piedmont Ave NE (in Ansley Mall) 404/815-8841 *3pm-2:30am, clsd Sun*

Tripps [M,NH,F] 1931 Piedmont Circle (at Cheshire Bridge) 404/724-0067 *2pm-3am, 12:30pm-midnight Sun*

Woofs on Piedmont [★M,NH,F,GO] 2425 Piedmont Rd NE (at Lindbergh) 404/869-9422 *11:30am-2am, sports bar*

◼ NIGHTCLUBS

The Heretic [★M,D,L,F,S,WC] 2069 Cheshire Bridge Rd (at Piedmont) **404/325-3061** *9am-3am, clsd Sun, till 11pm Mon-Tue, patio, theme nights, also Heretic Leathers store*

Masquerade [GF,D,F,E,18+,$] 695 North Ave NE **404/577-8178** *hours vary*

Opera [GS,D] 1150 Crescent Ave (at 14th St NE) **404/874-3006**

Phase One [GS,D,MR-AF,S] 4933 Memorial Dr (at Delano), Decatur **404/296-4895** *hrs vary, call for theme nights*

Rush [M,D,MR] 2715 Buford Hwy (at Lenox Rd) **678/568-9657** *10pm-4am, more gay Tue & Sun*

Sutra Lounge [GF,D] 1136 Crescent Ave NE (at 13th) **404/607-1160** *10pm-3am Wed-Sat*

Swinging Richard's [M,S,$] 1400 Northside Dr NW (btwn I-75 & Northside Dr) **404/352-0532** *6:30pm-close, clsd Sun-Mon, gay strip club, nude dancers*

Traxx [M,D,MR-AF,E] 866/602-5553 *dance parties & events around Atlanta*

Wild Mustang/ Jungle [★MW,D,DS,$] 2115 Faulkner Rd NE (off Cheshire Bridge Rd NE) **404/844-8800** *10pm-3am, clsd Sun, also 11pm Mon for Stars of the Century [DS]*

XS Ultra Lounge [M,D,MR-AF] 708 Spring St (at 3rd) **678/705-5537, 866/602-5553**

◼ CAFES

Apache Cafe [MR,F,E] 64 3rd St NW **404/876-5436** *food served, poetry readings, events, gallery*

Aurora Coffee 468 Moreland Ave **404/523-6856** *6:30am-9pm, from 7am wknds*

Australian Bakery Cafe 48 S Park Square, Marietta **678/797-6222** *7am-5:30pm, 9am-4pm wknds*

Intermezzo [WI] 1845 Peachtree Rd NE **404/355-0411** *10am-2am, 10am-3am wknds, classy, full bar, great desserts, [WI] till 7pm*

Urban Grounds 38 N Avondale Rd, Avondale Estates **404/499-2136** *6:30am-9pm, till 10pm Fri, 7:30am-10pm Sat, 8am-4pm Sun*

◼ RESTAURANTS

Amuse 560 Dutch Valley Rd **404/888-1890** *dinner only, wknd brunch, clsd Mon, full bar, int'l bistro*

Apres Diem 931 Monroe Dr #C-103 **404/872-3333** *11:30am-midnight, till 2am Fri-Sat, from 11am wknds, brunch Sat-Sun, French bistro, live jazz Wed, full bar*

Aria 490 E Paces Ferry **404/233-7673** *dinner only, clsd Sun*

Aurum [GS] 915 Peachtree St (at 8th St) **404/815-9426** *9pm-2am, till 3am wknds, lounge*

Bacchanalia/ Star Provisions/ Quinones 1198 Howell Mill Rd NW **404/365-0410** *dinner only, clsd Sun, upscale*

Buckhead Diner 3073 Piedmont Rd NE **404/262-3336** *lunch Mon-Sun, dinner nightly, Sun brunch, upscale diner fare*

Cafe Sunflower 2140 Peachtree Rd NW (at Bennett St) **404/352-8859** *lunch & dinner, clsd Sun, vegetarian*

The Colonnade 1879 Cheshire Bridge Rd NE **404/874-5642** *dinner nightly, lunch wknds, traditional Southern*

Cowtippers [TG,WC] 1600 Piedmont Ave NE (at Monroe) **404/874-3751** *11am-11pm, till midnight Fri-Sat, steak house*

Ecco [R,WC] 40 7th St NE **404/347-9555** *5:30pm-10pm, till 11pm Fri-Sat, till 10pm Sun, Italian*

Einstein's [★WC] 1077 Juniper St (at 12th) **404/876-7925** *11am-11pm, till midnight Fri-Sat, from 10am Sun, wknd brunch, full bar, patio*

The Flying Biscuit Cafe [★BW,WC] 1655 McLendon Ave (at Clifton) **404/687-8888** *7am-10pm, healthy brkfst all day; multiple locations*

Fresh To Order 860 Peachtree St NE (at 7th St NE) **404/593-2333** *11am-10pm, patio brunch Sun from 10am, healthy fast food, patio*

Georgia • USA

Frogs 931 Monroe Dr NE **404/607-9967** *11am-10pm, till 11pm wknds, Mexican*

Gilbert's Cafe & Bar 219 10th St NE (at Piedmont) **404/872-8012** *dinner Tue-Sat, wknd brunch, food till 2am, bar till 3am, till midnight Sun*

Hobnob [WC] 1551 Piedmont Ave NE (at Monroe) **404/968-2288** *11am-11pm, till 3pm Sun*

Joe's On Juniper 1049 Juniper St NE **404/875-6634** *11am-2am, till midnight Sun, American*

Las Margaritas [E,WC] 1842 Cheshire Bridge Rd **404/873-4464** *lunch & dinner, Latin fusion*

The Lobby at Twelve [R] 361 17th St **404/961-7370** *brkfst, lunch & dinner, upscale American*

Majestic Diner [★AYOR,WC] 1031 Ponce de Leon Ave (at Highland) **404/875-0276** *24hrs, diner right from the '50s, cantankerous waitresses included*

Mi Barrio Restaurante Mexicano [WC] 571 Memorial Dr SE **404/223-9279** *lunch Tue-Sat, dinner nightly, clsd Sun*

Murphy's [★WC] 997 Virginia Ave NE (at N Highland Ave) **404/872-0904** *11am-10pm, till midnight Fri-Sat, from 8am wknds*

No Más! Cantina [GO] 180 Walker St **404/574-5678** *lunch & dinner daily, wknd brunch, Mexican, also huge furniture & gift store*

Pastries A Go Go [WC] 235 Ponce De Leon Place (at Commerce), Decatur **404/373-3423** *7:30am-4pm, clsd Tue, delicious baked goods*

R Thomas Deluxe Grill [BW,WC] 1812 Peachtree Rd NW (btwn 26th & 27th) **404/872-2942, 404/881-0246** *24hrs, healthy Californian/ juice bar, popular late night*

Ria's Bluebird Cafe [★BW,TG,WC] 421 Memorial Dr (at Cherokee) **404/521-3737** *8am-3pm, gourmet brunch in quaint old diner in Grant Park*

Roxx Tavern & Diner [WC] 1824 Cheshire Bridge Rd NE (at Manchester) **404/892-4541** *lunch & dinner, Sun brunch, patio*

Sauced [WC] 753 Edgewood Ave (at Waddell St NE) **404/688-6554** *dinner nightly till 1am, clsd Mon-Tue, retro kitsch decor, Southern, plenty veggie, full bar*

Sawicki's 250 W Ponce De Leon Ave, Decatur **404/377-0992** *11am-7pm, till 8pm Fri-Sat, noon-5pm Sun, deli, great sandwiches*

The Shed at Glenwood 475 Bill Kennedy Way **404/835-4363** *dinner nightly, Sun brunch, also bar*

Swan Coach House 3130 Slaton Dr NW **404/261-0636** *11am-2:30pm, clsd Sun, also gift shop & art gallery*

Table 1280 1280 Peachtree St NE (at Woodruff Arts Center) **404/897-1280** *lunch & dinner, wknd brunch, clsd Mon, also lounge, upscale American & tapas*

Thumbs Up Diner 573 Edgewood Ave SE (at Randolph) **404/223-0690** *7am-3pm, 8am-4pm wknds, brkfst all day*

TWO urban licks [E,R] 820 Ralph McGill Blvd **404/522-4622** *dinner nightly, brunch Sun, great grill, full bar, live blues*

Veni Vidi Vici [WI,WC] 41 14th St **404/875-8424** *lunch Mon-Fri, dinner nightly, upscale Italian*

The Vortex [18+] 438 Moreland Ave NE (at Euclid) **404/688-1828** *11am-midnight, till 3am wknds, biker ambiance, great burgers*

Watershed [WC] 1820 Peachtree St **404/809-3561** *11am-10pm, Sun brunch, wine bar, also gift shop, owned by Emily Saliers of the Indigo Girls*

■ ENTERTAINMENT & RECREATION

AIDS Memorial Quilt/ NAMES Project 204 14th St **404/688-5500** *visit The Quilt at the foundation offices*

Ansley Park Playhouse 1545 Peachtree St **404/875-1193** *some LGBT-themed productions*

Georgia • USA

Atlanta Gay Men's Chorus 781 Peachtree St NE 30308 **404/320-1030**

Joining Hearts, Inc Piedmont Park Pool **678/318-1446** *great dance/ pool party in July, 100% of every dollar raised is donated*

Lambda Radio Report WRFG 89.3 FM **404/523-8989, 404/523-3471** *6pm Tue, LGBT radio program*

Little 5 Points, Moreland & Euclid Ave S of Ponce de Leon Ave *hip & funky area w/ too many restaurants & shops to list*

Martin Luther King, Jr Center for Non-Violent Social Change 449 Auburn Ave NE **404/526-8900** *includes King's birth home, the church where he preached in the '60s & his gravesite*

Piedmont Park [AYOR] NE of Piedmont at 10th *hilltop sunbathing*

▪BOOKSTORES

Brushstrokes/ Capulets [GO] 1510 Piedmont Ave NE (near Monroe) **404/876-6567** *10am-10pm, till 11pm Fri-Sat, LGBT variety store*

▪RETAIL SHOPS

The Boy Next Door 1447 Piedmont Ave NE (btwn 14th & Monroe) **404/873-2664** *10am-8pm, noon-6pm Sun, clothing*

The Junkman's Daughter [WC] 464 Moreland Ave NE (at Euclid) **404/577-3188** *11am-7pm, till 8pm Fri, till 9pm Sat, from noon Sun, hip stuff*

Piercing Experience 1654 McLendon Ave NE (at Clifton) **404/378-9100** *call for appt*

▪PUBLICATIONS

▶**David Atlanta** **404/418-8901** *gay entertainment magazine w/ extensive nightlife calendar, maps & directory*

Fenuxe **404/835-2016**

Georgia Voice **404/815-6941** *bi-weekly LGBT publication*

▪GYMS & HEALTH CLUBS

Gravity Fitness 2201 Faulkner Rd (off Cheshire Bridge Rd) **404/486-0506** *day passes available*

Urban Body Fitness 500 Amsterdam Ave **404/885-1499**

▪MEN'S CLUBS

Bliss [M,D] 2284 Cheshire Bridge Rd **404/320-1924** *8pm-3am Wed-Sat, nude dancers*

The Den [MO,MR-AF,PC] 2135 Liddell Dr (at Cheshire Bridge) **404/292-7746**

Flex [SW,WI] 76 4th St NW (at Spring St) **404/815-0456** *24hrs*

Manifest4u 2103 Faulkner Rd NE (off Cheshire Bridge Rd) **404/549-2815** *10pm-3am Th, till 6am Fri-Sat, from 9pm Sun, theme nights, also yoga classes*

▪MEN'S SERVICES

▶**MegaMates** **404/244-7000** *Call to hook up with HOT local men. FREE to listen & respond to ads. Use FREE code DAMRON. MegaMates.com.*

▪EROTICA

Insecretion 1739 Cheshire Bridge Rd **404/262-9113**

Lollipop Adult Treats 3165 Roswell Rd (at Peachtree St) **404/816-8299** *24hrs*

Southern Nights Videos 2205 Cheshire Br Rd (at Woodland Ave NE) **404/728-0701** *24hrs*

Starship 2275 Cheshire Bridge Rd **404/320-9101, 800/215-1053** *24hrs, many locations in Atlanta*

▪CRUISY AREAS

Piedmont Park [AYOR] 10th St (at Monroe)

Augusta

see also Aiken, South Carolina

▪ACCOMMODATIONS

▶**Parliament Resort** [MO,L,V,18+,BYOB,SW,N,WI,PC,GO] 1250 Gordon Hwy **706/722-1155** *24hrs, motel complex w/ hot tub, pride shop, cafe, video lounge, maze, novice dungeon*

▪BARS

Club Rehab [GS,D] 913 Broad St **706/826-4431** *4pm-3am, from 6pm Sat, clsd Sun*

The Filling Station [M] 1258 Gordon Hwy **706/828-7400** *8pm-close Th-Sat only*

◼NIGHTCLUBS

Club Argos [NH,D,TG,K,DS,V,GO] 1923 Walton Way (at Heckle) **706/481-8829** *8pm-2am, clsd Sun*

Carrollton

◼CRUISY AREAS

Lake Carroll Park [AYOR]

Cartersville

◼EROTICA

The Lion's Den Adult Superstore 33 Kent Dr (exit 296, off I-75) **770/607-5113** *24hrs*

Columbus

◼EROTICA

Foxes Cinema 3009 Victory Dr **706/689-2211**

MACA Bookstore 3016 Victory Dr **706/689-2212** *9am-midnight, booths*

◼CRUISY AREAS

Cooper Creek Park [AYOR] 4816 Milgen Rd

Flat Rock Park [AYOR] 6250 Warm Springs Road

Dahlonega

◼ACCOMMODATIONS

Mountain Laurel Creek Inn [GS,NS,GO] 202 Talmer Grizzle Rd (at Hwy 19 & McDonald Rd) **706/867-8134** *spa & pub*

◼RESTAURANTS

Smith House 84 S Chestatee St **706/867-7000, 800/852-9577** *lunch daily, dinner Fri-Sun, clsd Mon, family-style Southern*

Georgia • USA

Dalton

■RESTAURANTS

Dalton Depot [E,K] 110 Depot St
706/867-7000, 800/852-9577 7am-9pm, till 7pm Sun, also bar

Decatur

see Atlanta

Dewy Rose

■ACCOMMODATIONS

The River's Edge [M,F,E,SW,N,NS,WC]
2311 Pulliam Mill Rd **706/213-8081**
cabins, camping, RV

Lake Lanier

■ENTERTAINMENT &
RECREATION

Gay Cove btwn Athens Park Rd & Frank Boyd Rd (Channel Marker 21) a rainbow rendezvous for the pleasure-boating crowd—look for the rainbow flag

Macon

■CRUISY AREAS

Central City Park [AYOR] Walnut St (at 7th)

Rest Area [AYOR] I-475 bypass (off I-75, after Mercer University Dr)

Marietta

see Atlanta

Savannah

■INFO LINES & SERVICES

First City Network 307 E Harris St
912/236-2489 info & events line, social group, newsletter

■ACCOMMODATIONS

The Azalea Inn & Gardens
[GF,SW,NS,WI] 217 E Huntingdon St (at Abercorn St) **912/236-6080,
800/582-3823** 19th-c Italianate, vintage gardens, full Southern brkfst

Catherine Ward House Inn [GS,WI,NS]
118 E Waldburg St (at Abercorn)
912/234-8564, 800/327-4270 full brkfst

The Galloway House [GS] 107 E 35th St **912/658-4419** furnished apts, cont'l brkfst

Kehoe House [GF,WI] 123 Habersham St **912/232-1020, 800/820-1020** full brkfst

Mansion on Forsyth Park
[GF,SW,NS,WI,WC] 700 Drayton St
912/238-5158, 888/213-3671

Park Avenue Manor [GF,NS,WI]
107-109 W Park Ave **912/233-0352** full brkfst

Statesboro Inn [GF,WI] 106 S Main, Statesboro **912/489-8628,
800/846-9466** full brkfst

Thunderbird Inn [GF,NS,WI,GO] 611 W Oglethorpe Ave (at MLK Blvd)
912/232-2661, 866/324-2661

Tybee Vacation Rentals [GF,SW,NS,WI]
1010 Hwy 80 E, Tybee Island
866/935-3861, 877/214-7353
rental homes, cottages & condos, some gay-owned

■BARS

Chuck's Bar [GS,NH,YC] 305 W River St
912/232-1005 hrs vary, clsd Sun

■NIGHTCLUBS

Club One [MW,D,F,K,C,DS,S,V] 1 Jefferson St (at Bay) **912/232-0200**
5pm-3am, till 2am Sun, "home of the Lady Chablis"

■CAFES

Cafe Gelatohhh 202 W St Julian St
912/234-2344 artisanal gelato; also coffee, sandwiches

The Sentient Bean 13 E Park Ave
912/232-4447 7am-10pm, food served, vegetarian/ vegan, shows at night

■RESTAURANTS

B Matthews [WC] 325 E Bay St
912/233-1319 8am-9pm, till 10pm Fri-Sat, till 3pm Sun, casual bistro

Bar Food [WC,GO] 4523 Habersham St **912/355-5956** 4pm-1am, clsd Sun

Casbah 118 East Broughton St
912/234-6168 dinner nightly, Moroccan, also entertainment

Churchill's Pub 13 W Bay St
912/232-8501 *5pm-1am*

Clary's Cafe 404 Abercorn (at Jones)
912/233-0402 *7am-4pm, from 8am
Sat-Sun, country cookin*

The Distillery [WC] 416 W Liberty St
912/236-1772 *11am-1am, till 3am
Fri-Sat, noon-9pm Sun*

Fannie's on the Beach [D,E] 1613
Strand Ave (at Silver Ave), Tybee Island
912/786-6109 *noon-11pm, till 2am
wknds*

Firefly Cafe [WC] 321 Habersham St
912/234-1971

Green Truck Neighborhood Pub
[BW,WC,GO] 2430 Habersham St
912/234-5885 *11am-11pm, clsd Sun-
Mon*

Local 11 Ten 1110 Bull St
912/790-9000 *dinner nightly, upscale
dining in a restored 1950s bank; also
Perch rooftop bar*

Mellow Mushroom [WC] 11 W Liberty
St 912/495-0705 *11am-10pm, pizza &
beer*

Olde Pink House/ Planters Tavern [E]
23 Abercorn St 912/232-4286
*upscale Southern dining upstairs, cozy
bar downstairs, live jazz*

Rocks on the Roof 102 W Bay St (on
the roof of The Bohemian Hotel)
912/721-3900 *7am-10pm, till 11pm
wknds, fantastic views*

Soho South Cafe 12 W Liberty St
912/233-1633 *11am-4pm daily,
eclectic*

Wright Square Cafe [★GO] 21 W York
St 912/238-1150 *7:30am-5pm, from
9am Sat, clsd Sun, patio*

▦ ENTERTAINMENT & RECREATION

Savannah Walks, Inc [GF]
912/238-9255, 888/728-9255
walking tours of downtown Savannah

▦ MEN'S SERVICES

▶**MegaMates** 912/344-9494 *Call to
hook up with HOT local men. FREE to
listen & respond to ads. Use FREE code
DAMRON. MegaMates.com.*

▦ EROTICA

Home Run Video & News [GO] 4 E
Liberty St (at Bull St) 912/236-5192
large LGBT section

Unadilla

▦ EROTICA

Lion's Den 790 Pine St (Exit 121, off I-
75) 478/627-2782 *24hrs*

Valdosta

▦ CRUISY AREAS

Langdale Park [AYOR] N Valdosta Rd
days

Washington

▦ CAFES

Talk of the Town [GO] 1 East Public Sq
(at Robert Toombs Ave) 706/678-7661
10am-5pm, clsd Sun

HAWAII

Please note that cities are grouped
by islands:
Hawaii (Big Island)
Kauai
Maui
Molokai
Oahu (includes Honolulu)

HAWAII (BIG ISLAND)

▦ MEN'S SERVICES

▶**MegaMates** 808/930-3300 *Call to
hook up with HOT local men. FREE to
listen & respond to ads. Use FREE code
DAMRON. MegaMates.com.*

Captain Cook

▦ ACCOMMODATIONS

Aloha Guest House
[GS,N,NS,WI,WC,GO] 84-4780
Mamalahoa Hwy 808/328-8955,
800/897-3188

Areca Palms Estate B&B [GF,NS]
808/323-2276, 800/545-4390

Horizon Guest House
[GS,SW,NS,WI,WC,GO] 808/328-2540,
888/328-8301

Hawaii • USA

Ka'awa Loa Plantation [GS,SW,WI,GO]
82-5990 Napoopoo Rd 96704
808/323-2686 *plantation-style B&B on 5-acre start-up coffee farm*

Kealakekua Bay B&B [GS,NS]
808/328-8150, 800/328-8150

Hilo

■RESTAURANTS

Cafe Pesto [E] 308 Kamehameha Ave
808/969-6640 *pizzas, salads, pastas*

■ENTERTAINMENT & RECREATION

Best of Hilo Adventures Tours [GO]
1477 Kalanianaole Ave 808/987-3905

Richardson Beach at end of
Kalanianaole Ave (Keaukaha)

■CRUISY AREAS

Reeds "Gay" Bay Tearooms [AYOR]
Banyan Dr *1st beach S of the hotels*

Honaunau-Kona

■ACCOMMODATIONS

Dragonfly Ranch Healing Arts Center [GS,NS,WI] 1 1/2 miles down
City of Refuge Rd 808/328-2159 *eco-spa; luxuriously rustic upscale treehouse*

Kailua-Kona

■INFO LINES & SERVICES

Gay AA 808/329-1212

■ACCOMMODATIONS

1st Class B&B Kona Hawaii
[GF,NS,WI] 77-6504 Kilohana St
808/329-8778, 888/769-1110

KonaLani Hawaiian Inn & Coffee Plantation [MW,NS,WI,GO] 76-5917H
Mamalahoa Hwy 808/324-0793

Puako B&B [GS,NS,GO] 25 Puako Beach
Dr 808/882-1331, 800/910-1331
on Kohala coast

Royal Kona Resort
[GF,F,E,SW,NS,WI,WC] 75-5852 Ali'i Dr
808/329-3111, 800/222-5642

■BARS

The Mask-querade
[★MW,NH,D,B,E,K,GO] 75-5660 Kopiko
St 808/329-8558 *10am-2am*

My Bar [GF] 74-5601 Luhia St (btwn
Kaiwi & Eho St) 808/331-8789 *10am-2am, from 11am wknds*

■RESTAURANTS

Agnes' Portuguese Bake Shop 46
Hoolai St 808/262-5367 *6am-6pm, till 2pm Sun, clsd Mon*

Buzz's Original Steak House [WC] 413
Kawailoa Rd 808/261-4661 *across from beach, great Mai Tais*

Huggo's [E,K] 75-5828 Kahakai Rd (on
Kailua Bay) 808/329-1493 *dinner only, also bar, patio*

Moke's Bread & Breakfast 27 Ho'olai
St 808/261-5565 *6:30am-3pm, clsd Tue, great brkfst*

■BOOKSTORES

Kona Stories 78-6831 Ali'i Dr #142
(in the Keauhou Shopping Ctr)
808/324-0350 *bookstore that hosts PFLAG meetings & other LGBT groups*

■CRUISY AREAS

67 Beach Old Puako Rd *take Rte 19 N to Puako Beach Rd, take 1st right onto Old Puako Rd, look for telephone pole #67, then go north for about 0.5 miles. You drive to the shore on an unpaved lane & walk to the water*

Honokohau Beach [AYOR] 5 miles S of
airport, Kailua-Kona *far N end of beach*

Kahaluu Beach Park [AYOR]

Old Airport Park *the beach area just north of the end of the parking area, which is the old airport runway*

Pahoa

■ACCOMMODATIONS

Absolute Paradise B&B
[MO,SW,N,NS,WI,GO] 808/965-1828,
888/285-1540 *B&B, outdoor hot tub, some shared baths*

Coconut Cottage B&B [GS,GO]
808/965-0973, 866/204-7444

Isle of You Naturally Farm & Retreat [M,NS,GO] 808/965-1639
cabin & yurts on naturist farm retreat

Kalani [GS,F,SW,N,NS,WI,WC,GO]
808/965-7828, 800/800-6886

Plantation Hale
Suites
In the heart of Kauai!

Our one bedroom suite accommodations feature full kitchens, daily maid service, Blu-Ray DVD players, and much more!

Plantation Hale Suites invites you to experience an unforgettable Hawaiian vacation. Located on the scenic Royal Coconut Coast, and just steps from scenic Waipouli Beach, you couldn't picture a more beautiful and central location.

Our on-site concierge can book any island activity from snorkeling cruises to adventurous helicopter tours.

525 Aleka Loop Kapaa, HI 96746
808 822-4941 • 800 775-4253
E-mail: phale@plantation-hale.com

 plantation-hale.com

Enter DAMRON promo code for private offer.

Hawaii • USA

Pamalu—Hawaiian Country House
[GS,SW,NS,WI,GO] 808/965-0830
secluded country retreat

Rainbow Retreat Center
[GS,SW,NS,WI,WC,GO] 808/965-9011

■ENTERTAINMENT & RECREATION

Kehena Beach off Hwy 137 (trailhead at 19-mile marker phone booth) *lava rock trail to clothing-optional black-sand beach*

■CRUISY AREAS

Steam Vents [AYOR] 3 miles S of Pahoa on Keaau-Pahoa Rd *early evenings*

Volcano Village

■ACCOMMODATIONS

The Artist Cottage at Volcano Garden Arts [GF,WI] 19-3834 Old Volcano Rd (at Wright Rd) 808/985-8979

The Chalet Kilauea Collection [GF,NS,WI] 19-4178 Wright Rd (at Laukapu) 808/967-7786, 800/937-7786

Hale Ohia Cottages [GS,NS,WI,GO] 808/967-7986, 800/455-3803

■CAFES

Ono Cafe 19-3834 Old Volcano Rd (at Volcano Garden Arts) 808/985-8979 *10am-4pm*

KAUAI

■MEN'S SERVICES

➤**MegaMates** 808/240-3300 *Call to hook up with HOT local men. FREE to listen & respond to ads. Use FREE code DAMRON. MegaMates.com.*

Anahola

■ACCOMMODATIONS

Mahina Kai Ocean Villa [GS,SW,N,NS,WI,GO] 4933 Aliomanu Rd 808/822-9451, 800/337-1134

Hanalei

■NIGHTCLUBS

Tahiti Nui [GF,D,F,E,K,WC] 5-5134 Kuhio Hwy (near Hanalei Center) 808/826-6277 *11am-2am, 4pm-11pm Sun, also restaurant*

Kapaa

■ACCOMMODATIONS

17 Palms Kauai [GS,NS,WI,WC,GO] 808/822-5659, 888/725-6799 *2 secluded cottages 200 steps from beach*

Anuenue Plantation B&B [M,NS,WI,GO] 808/823-8335, 888/371-7716

Fern Grotto Inn [GS,WI,NS] 4561 Kuamoo Rd (at Kuhio Hwy) 808/821-9836, 808/822-4845

➤**Plantation Hale Suites** [GF,SW,WI,WC] 525 Aleka Loop 808/822-4941, 800 /775-4253 *enter the code DAMRON for a 10% discount off our best available rate*

■RESTAURANTS

Eggbert's [WC] 4-484 Kuhio Hwy (in Coconut Plantation Marketplace) 808/822-3787 *7am-1pm, light fare until 6pm Mon-Sat*

Mema [BYOB,WC] 4-369 Kuhio Hwy (in shopping center) 808/823-0899 *lunch Mon-Fri, dinner nightly, Thai & Chinese*

■CRUISY AREAS

Coconut Marketplace 484 Kuhio Hwy (NW corner)

Donkey Beach [AYOR] off Hwy 56, N of Kapaa (btwn 11 & 12-mile markers) *walk along cane field, down through ironwood trees & then to the right on the dirt road to the beach*

Kilauea

■CRUISY AREAS

Secret Beach [AYOR] *inquire locally*

Lihue

■ACCOMMODATIONS

Kauai Beach Resort [GF,SW,NS,WI] 4331 Kauai Beach Dr 808/245-1955, 866/971-2782 *also restaurant/ bar*

■ENTERTAINMENT & RECREATION

Lydgate State Park Beach off Hwy 56 btwn Lihue & Kapaa (S of Wailua River) *gay beach btwn the condos & the golf course*

Poipu Beach

■ACCOMMODATIONS

Poipu Plantation B&B Inn & Vacation Rental Suites [GS,NS,WI,GO] 1792 Pe'e Rd 808/742-6757, 800/634-0263

Princeville

■ACCOMMODATIONS

Kauai Oceanfront Condo [GS,SW,WI,NS] 5300 Ka Haku Rd 610/793-7539

Puunene

■RESTAURANTS

Roy's Poipu Bar & Grill 2360 Kiahuna Plantation Dr (in Poipu Shopping Ctr) **808/742-5000** *5:30pm-10pm*

Wailua

■RESTAURANTS

Caffe Coco [E,BYOB,WC] 4-369 Kuhio Hwy **808/822-7990** *lunch Tue-Fri, dinner nightly, clsd Mon*

Waimea

■ACCOMMODATIONS

Aston Waimea Plantation Cottages [GF,SW,WI] **808/338-1625**, 877/997-6667

MAUI

■INFO LINES & SERVICES

Both Sides Now *LGBT community resources & events*

■MEN'S SERVICES

➤MegaMates 808/270-3300 *Call to hook up with HOT local men. FREE to listen & respond to ads. Use FREE code DAMRON. MegaMates.com.*

Hana

■ACCOMMODATIONS

Hana Accommodations [GS,NS,GO] 808/248-7868, 800/228-4262 *studios & tropical cottages, hot tub*

Huelo

■ACCOMMODATIONS

Cliff's Edge [GF,SW,NS,WI] 808/268-4530, 866/262-6284

Kaanapali

■ACCOMMODATIONS

The Royal Lahaina Resort [GF,F,SW,WC] 2780 Kekaa Dr 808/661-3611, 800/222-5642

Kihei

■ACCOMMODATIONS

Anfora's Dreams [GS,SW,GO] 323/467-2991, 800/788-5046 *rental condo near ocean*

Eva Villa [GF,SW,WI,WC] 815 Kumulani Dr **808/874-6407**, 800/884-1845 *near Wailea beaches*

Koa Lagoon [GF,SW,WI,WC] 800 S Kihei Rd **808/879-3002**, 800/367-8030

➤Maui Sunseeker LGBT Resort [MW,SW,N,NS,WI,GO] 551 S Kihei Rd (at Wailana Place) **808/879-1261**, 800/532-6284 *beachfront island hideaway*

Tutu Mermaids on Maui B&B [GS,SW,NS,WI,GO] 2840 Umalu Pl **808/874-8687**, 800/598-9550

■BARS

Diamond's Ice Bar & Grill [GF,F,E] 1279 S Kihei Rd **808/879-9299** *11am-2am, from 7am Sun*

■CAFES

Cafe at La Plage [WI,WC] 2395 S Kihei Rd (at Kam Beach I) **808/875-7668** *7am-5pm, till 3pm Sun*

■RESTAURANTS

Jawz Tacos [WC] 1279 S Kihei Rd **808/874-8226** *11am-9pm*

Stella Blues Cafe [E,WC] 1279 S Kihei Rd (in Azeka II Shopping Center) **808/874-3779** *7:30am-11pm*

ENTERTAINMENT & RECREATION

➤**Maui Massage for Men** [GO]
808/280-7175

EROTICA

The Love Shack 1913 S Kihei Rd (in
Kalama Vlg) **808/875-0303**

CRUISY AREAS

Kalama Park [AYOR]

Kula

ACCOMMODATIONS

The Upcountry B&B [GF,NS,WI,WC]
4925 Lower Kula Rd (at Copp St)
808/878-8083

Lahaina

RESTAURANTS

Betty's Beach Cafe 505 Front St
808/662-0300 *8am-10pm, full bar till
midnight*

Lahaina Coolers [WC] 180 Dickenson
St **808/661-7082** *8am-1am, patio*

RETAIL SHOPS

Skin Deep Tattoo 626 Front St (across
from the Banyan Tree) **808/661-8531**
10am-10pm, till 8pm Sun-Mon

CRUISY AREAS

Front St [AYOR] along Beach Walk

Makawao

ACCOMMODATIONS

Aloha Cottage [GS,WI,GO]
808/573-8555, 888/328-3330
*designed for comfort, style, charm &
seclusion, outdoor soaking tub*

Hale Ho'okipa Inn B&B [GF,NS,WI,WC]
32 Pakani Pl **808/572-6698,
877/572-6698** *gracious old Hawaiian
plantation home*

RESTAURANTS

Casanova Restaurant & Deli [D,E]
1188 Makawao Ave **808/572-0220**
*lunch & dinner, Italian, full bar till 2am,
live music*

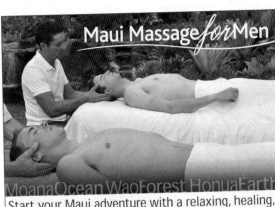

Hawaii • *USA*

Makena

■ENTERTAINMENT & RECREATION

Little Beach at Makena [MW] *Pilani Hwy S to Wailea, right at Wailea Ike Dr, left on Wailea Alanui Dr to public beach, then take trail up hill at right end of beach*

Wailea

■ACCOMMODATIONS

Ho'olei at Grand Wailea [GF,SW,WI,WC] 146 Ho'olei Cir (at Wailea Alanui Dr) 877/346-6534

Wailuku

■INFO LINES & SERVICES

AA Gay/ Lesbian 70 Central Ave #1 808/244-9673 *7:30am Sun*

■ACCOMMODATIONS

Maalaea Kai Condo [GF] 70 Hauoli St (Maalaea Village) 562/212-3312

MOLOKAI

Kaunakakai

■RESTAURANTS

Kanemitsu Bakery & Coffee Shop 79 Ala Malama St 808/553-5855 *5:30am-5pm, clsd Tue, great sweet bread*

OAHU

■PUBLICATIONS

Odyssey Magazine Hawaii 808/955-5959 *everything you need to know about gay Hawaii*

Aiea

■CAFES

Cloud Nine Internet Cafe 99-115 Aiea Heights Dr (Aiea Shopping Center) 808/487-2944

■EROTICA

Video Warehouse 98-019 Kamehameha Hwy (at Hekaha St) 808/487-1750 *24hrs, booths*

Honolulu

■INFO LINES & SERVICES

Gay/ Lesbian AA 310 Pa'okalani Ave, Room 203A 808/946-1438 *7pm & 8pm Sat*

■ACCOMMODATIONS

Aqua Palms Waikiki [GF,SW,NS,WI,WC] 1850 Ala Moana Blvd (at Kalia & Ena) 808/947-7256, 866/406-2782

Aston Waikiki Circle Hotel [GF,NS,WI] 2464 Kalakaua Ave (at Uluniu St, Waikiki) 808/923-1571, 877/997-6667

Hotel Renew [GF,NS,WI] 129 Paoakalani Ave (at Lemon Rd, Waikiki) 808/687-7700, 888/485-7639

Waikiki Grand Hotel [M,NS,SW] 134 Kapahulu Ave 808/923-1814, 808/923-1511 *rentals above Hula's Bar, near gay beach*

■BARS

Bacchus Waikiki [MW,NH,] 408 Lewers St 808/926-4167 *noon-2am*

In Between [M,NH,K] 2155 Lau'ula St (off Lewers, across from Planet Hollywood, Waikiki) 808/926-7060 *noon-2am*

Lo Jax [MW,NH,F,V,WI] 2256 Kuhio Ave, 2nd flr (at Seaside, Waikiki) 808/922-1422 *noon-2am*

Tapa's Restaurant & Lanai Bar [GS,E,F,K,GO] 407 Seaside, 2nd flr (at Kuhio Ave) 808/921-2288 *9am-2am, lanai bar, also restaurant for dinner & Sun brunch*

Wang Chung's [MW,K,WC] 2410 Koa Ave (at Kaiulani) 808/921-9176 *5pm-2am*

■NIGHTCLUBS

Bar 7 [GS,D,MR-A,S,YC,WC] 1344 Kona St (at Piikoi Rd) 808/955-2640 *9pm-4am, [DS] Sat*

Fusion Waikiki [M,D,TG,K,DS,S,V] 2260 Kuhio Ave, 2nd flr (at Seaside) 808/924-2422 *10pm-4am, from 8pm Fri-Sat*

Hawaii • *USA*

➤**Hula's Bar & Lei Stand**
[★M,D,TG,F,S,V,YC,WI] 134 Kapahulu Ave
(2nd flr of Waikiki Grand Hotel)
808/923-0669 *10am-2am, near gay beach, go-go boys Th-Sun, weekly catamaran cruise*

■CAFES

Leonard's Bakery 933 Kapahulu Ave
808/737-5591 *5:30am-9pm, till 10pm Fri-Sat, irresistible malasadas & doughnuts*

Mocha Java Cafe [WI,WC] 1200 Ala Moana Blvd (in Ward Center)
808/591-9023 *8am-9pm, till 6pm Sun, outdoor seating*

■RESTAURANTS

Alan Wong's 1857 S King St (at Pumehana St) 808/949-2526 *dinner only, upscale*

Arancino di Mare 2552 Kalakaua Ave (in Waikiki Beach Marriott)
808/931-6273 *brkfst, lunch & dinner, Italian*

Cafe Che Pasta [MW,D,E] 1001 Bishop St, Ste 108 (enter off Alakea St)
808/524-0004 *lunch & dinner, clsd Sun, full bar*

Cafe Sistina [WC] 1314 S King St
808/596-0061 *lunch Mon-Fri, dinner nightly, northern Italian, full bar*

Cha Cha Cha 342 Seaside Ave
808/923-7797 *lunch & dinner, Mexican, happy hour, full bar*

Cheeseburger in Paradise 2500 Kalakaua Blvd 808/923-3731 *7am-11pm, full bar*

Eggs 'n' Things 343 Saratoga Rd (at Kalakaua Ave) 808/923-3447 *6am-2pm, 5pm-10pm; also at 2464 Kalakaua Ave, 808/ 926-3447*

House Without A Key 2199 Kalia Rd (at Lewers St, at Halekulani Hotel)
808/923-2311 *7am-9pm, stunning sunset views, Hawaiian music nightly*

Hula Grill [E] 2335 Kalakaua Ave (in Outrigger Hotel) 808/923-4852

Indigo [E,WC] 1121 Nu'uanu Ave
808/521-2900 *lunch Tue-Fri, dinner Tue-Sat, Eurasian*

Keo's in Waikiki [R,WC] 2028 Kuhio Ave 808/951-9355 *5pm-10pm, Thai*

La Cucaracha 2446 Koa Ave
808/924-3366 *noon-11pm, Mexican, full bar*

Liliha Bakery [WC] 515 N Kuakini St (at Liliha St) 808/531-1651 *open 24hrs, till 8m Sun, clsd Mon, diner fare & baked goods*

Lulu's [E] 2586 Kalakaua Ave
808/926-5222 *7am-2am, full bar*

Rock Island Cafe 131 Kaiulani Ave (off Kalakaua, in King's Village Waikiki)
808/923-8033 *old-fashioned soda fountain*

Singha Thai [E] 1910 Ala Moana Blvd
808/941-2898 *4pm-10pm*

Tiki's Grill & Bar [E] 2570 Kalakaua Ave (in ResortQuest Hotel)
808/923-8454

■ENTERTAINMENT & RECREATION

Diamond Head Beach [GS] *take road from lighthouse to beach; some nude sunbathing*

Hawaii Gay Tours [GO] 1947 Alaeloa St 218/234-2310

Honolulu Gay/ Lesbian Cultural Foundation 1670 Makaloa St #204
808/675-8428 *last wknd of May Honolulu Rainbow Film Festival*

Queen's Surf Beach Kapiolani Park (off Kalakaua) *popular gay beach at far end of Waikiki Beach*

Rainbow Sailing Charters [MW,GO]
808/347-0235 *day & overnight sailing adventures*

■RETAIL SHOPS

Eighty Percent Straight 134 Kapahulu Ave, Ste B (in Waikiki Grand Hotel)
808/923-9996 *10am-11pm, till midnight Fri-Sat, noon-11pm Sun, LGBT*

Over Easy Down Under 2301 Kuhio Ave, Ste 220 (Level 2, Waikiki Town Center) 808/926-4994 *10am-8pm, 11am-4pm Sun, men's swimwear*

■PUBLICATIONS

Expression Magazine 808/393-7994 *monthly glossy LGBT magazine*

Odyssey Magazine Hawaii
808/955-5959 *everything you need to know about gay Hawaii*

MEN'S CLUBS

Max's Gym [V,18+,PC] 438 Hobron Ln, 4th flr (at Ala Moana Blvd, in Eaton Square) **808/951-8232** *noon-4am, 24hrs wknds*

MEN'S SERVICES

➤**MegaMates 808/599-6999** *Call to hook up with HOT local men. FREE to listen & respond to ads. Use FREE code DAMRON. MegaMates.com.*

EROTICA

Suzie's Secrets 1370 Kapiolani Blvd **808/949-4383** *24hrs*

Velvet Video 2155 Lau'ula St, 2nd flr (above In Between, Waikiki) **808/924-0868** *24hrs, booths, toys*

CRUISY AREAS

Ala Moana Beach Park [AYOR] *near Waikiki Yacht Club*

Alan Davis Beach Rte 27 *turn past Sandy Beach but before Makapuu Point Lighthouse*

Diamond Head Road [AYOR] *on trails across the street from the lighthouse*

Windward Coast

ACCOMMODATIONS

Ali'i Bluffs Windward B&B [GS,SW,NS,WI,GO] 46-251 Ikiiki St, Kane'ohe **808/235-1124, 800/235-1151**

IDAHO

Statewide

PUBLICATIONS

Diversity Newsmagazine 208/336-3870 *statewide LGBT newspaper, monthly*

Boise

INFO LINES & SERVICES

The Community Center 305 E 37th St, Garden City **208/336-3870** *volunteer staff*

ACCOMMODATIONS

Bed & Buns [MO,N,NS,WI,GO] **208/866-2759, 208/362-1802** *B&B, hot tub*

Hotel 43 [GS,F,WI] 981 Grove St **800/243-4622**

The Modern Hotel & Bar [GF,WI] 1314 W Grove St **208/424-8244, 866/780-6012**

BARS

The Lucky Dog [M,NH,B,L,WI] 2223 W Fairview Ave (at 23rd) **208/333-0074** *2pm-2am, from noon wknds, patio*

Neurolux [GF,D,E] 111 N 11th St (at W Idaho) **208/343-0886** *1pm-2am, live music*

Pitchers & Pints [GS,NH,GO] 1108 W Front St. *3pm-2am, scruffy outside but nice inside & nice patio*

NIGHTCLUBS

The Balcony Club [★MW,D,K,WC,GO] 150 N 8th St #226 (at Idaho) **208/336-1313** *4pm-2am, theme nights*

CAFES

Flying M Coffeehouse [WI] 500 W Idaho St (at 5th St) **208/345-4320** *6:30am-11pm, from 7:30am wknds, till 6pm Sun*

River City Coffee 5517 W State St **208/853-9161** *6am-5pm, till 4pm Sun*

Tully's [WI] 794 Broad St **208/472-1308** *7am-8pm, till 6pm Sat, 8am-5pm Sun*

RESTAURANTS

Lucky 13 Pizza 3662 S Eckert Rd **208/344-6967** *11am-9pm, till 10pm wknds*

ENTERTAINMENT & RECREATION

The Flicks [F,E,BW,WC] 646 Fulton St **208/342-4222** *opens 4pm, from noon Fri-Sun, 4 movie theaters, patio*

RETAIL SHOPS

The Record Exchange [E] 1105 W Idaho St (at 11th) **208/344-8010** *9am-9pm, till 7pm Sun, also cafe*

MEN'S SERVICES

➤**MegaMates 208/343-8500** *Call to hook up with HOT local men. FREE to listen & respond to ads. Use FREE code DAMRON. MegaMates.com.*

Idaho • *USA*

■EROTICA

The O!Zone 1615 Broadway Ave
208/395-1977, 888/326-3713

Pleasure Boutique 5022 Fairview Ave
(at Orchard) **208/433-1161**

Vixen Video [GO] 5777 W Overland Rd
208/672-1844

■CRUISY AREAS

Ann Morrison Park [AYOR] near baseball fields

Coeur d'Alene

see also Spokane, Washington

■ACCOMMODATIONS

The Clark House on Hayden Lake
[GF,NS,WI,GO] 5250 E Hayden Lake Rd,
Hayden Lake **208/772-3470,**
800/765-4593

Lava Hot Springs

see also Pocatello

■ACCOMMODATIONS

Aura Soma Lava [GS,SW] 196 E Main
St **208/776-5800, 800/757-1233**
also retail store

Moscow

■INFO LINES & SERVICES

Inland Oasis LGBTA Center 1320 S
Mountain View Ave **208/596-4449** *HIV
testing, youth group & more*

■BOOKSTORES

Bookpeople 521 S Main (btwn 5th &
6th) **208/882-2669** *9am-8pm*

Nampa

■CAFES

Flying M Coffee Garage [E] 1314 2nd
St S **208/467-5533** *7am-11pm, till
6pm wknds*

Pocatello

■NIGHTCLUBS

Club Charleys [MW,D,E,DS,K,WC] 331 E
Center St **208/232-9606** *5pm-2am,
clsd Sun*

■CAFES

Main St Coffee & News 234 N Main
St (btwn Lander & Clark)
208/234-9834 *6:30am-4pm, from
8am Sat, from 9am Sun*

■EROTICA

Main Street Video 657 N Main St
208/235-9457

Pegasus Book Store 246 W Center St
208/232-6493

The Silver Fox 143 S 2nd St (at Center)
208/234-2477

■CRUISY AREAS

Ross Park [AYOR] *upper level*

Powell

■CRUISY AREAS

Jerry Johnson Hot Springs [AYOR] US
12 *days*

Twin Falls

■CAFES

Annie's Lavender & Coffee Cafe
[F,WC] 591 Addison Ave W (at 8th St)
208/736-2003 *6am-5pm, seasonal
wknd hrs*

■RESTAURANTS

Pizza Planet 720 Main St (at 8th St),
Buhl **208/543-8560** *11am-8pm, till
9pm Fri-Sat*

■CRUISY AREAS

City Park [AYOR] Shoshone & 4th Ave E

Rock Creek Park [AYOR] W on Hwy 30
days

ILLINOIS

Alton

see also St Louis, Missouri

■NIGHTCLUBS

Bubby & Sissy's [MW,D,DS,K,F,WC] 602
Belle St (at 6th) **618/465-4773** *3pm-
2am, till 3am Fri-Sat, clsd Mon*

■CRUISY AREAS

Rock Springs Park [AYOR] College Ave
(at Rock Springs Dr)

Arlington Heights
see Chicago

Bloomington

■CAFES

Coffee Hound [WI] 407 N Main St **309/827-7575** *6:30am-6pm, 8am-5pm Sun*

Kelly's Bakery & Cafe [WC] 113 N Center St **309/820-1200** *7am-6pm, till 2pm Sat, clsd Sun*

Blue Island
see also Chicago

■NIGHTCLUBS

Club Krave [MW,NH,TG,F,K,C,DS,S,WC] 13126 S Western Ave (at Grove) **708/597-8379** *8pm-2am, till 3am Fri-Sat, from 6pm Mon*

Bradley

■RESTAURANTS

La Villetta 801 W Broadway St **815/939-4960** *11am-9pm, till 8pm Sun, Italian*

■EROTICA

Slightly Sinful 101 N Kinzie Ave (at Broadway) **815/937-5744**

Calumet City

■CRUISY AREAS

Clayhole Woods, Shabonna Woods & Sandridge Forest Preserves [AYOR]

Carbondale

■INFO LINES & SERVICES

AA Lesbian/ Gay 618/549-4633

■NIGHTCLUBS

Club Traz [GF,NH,D,E,S,V,GO] 213 E Main St **618/218-3829** *9pm-2am, clsd Mon-Tue & Th*

Flirt [MW,D,DS] 1215 E Walnut (at Sky Bar) **618/529-5511** *bi-monthly party, check local listings*

■CRUISY AREAS

Crab Orchard Lake [AYOR] Cambria Neck Ln *exit off Rte 13 onto Cambria Rd, drive 1 mile N, on right side of Cambria Rd is side road called Cambria Neck Ln, turn right onto it*

Centreville
see also St Louis, Missouri

■NIGHTCLUBS

Boxers 'n' Briefs [M,D,F,DS,18+,WC,$] 55 Four Corners Ln (next to PT's Show Club) **618/332-6141** *7pm-4am, till 6am Fri-Sat, till 3am Sun, clsd Mon, nude dancers*

Champaign/ Urbana

■ACCOMMODATIONS

Sylvia's Irish Inn [GF,NS,WI] 312 W Green St, Urbana **217/384-4800**

■BARS

Emerald City Lounge [MW,F,E,WC,GO] 118 N First St (at University Ave), Champaign **217/398-8661** *5pm-2am Th-Sat, from 10am Sun*

Mike 'N Molly's [GF,E,D] 105 N Market St (at University), Champaign **217/355-1236** *4pm-2am, live music, beer garden*

■NIGHTCLUBS

Chester Street [MW,D,DS,GO] 63 Chester St (at Water St), Champaign **217/356-5607** *5pm-2am*

■CAFES

Aroma Cafe 118 N Neil St, Champaign **217/356-3200** *7am-10pm, from 8am wknds*

Cafe Kopi [F,NS,WI] 109 N Walnut, Champaign **217/359-4266** *7am-midnight, full bar*

Espresso Royale 602 E Daniel St (at 6th St), Champaign **217/328-1112** *7am-midnight*

Pekara Bakery & Bistro 116 N Neil St, Champaign **217/359-4500** *7am-8pm, from 8am Sun*

■RESTAURANTS

Boltini Lounge 211 N Neil St, Champaign **217/378-8001** *4pm-2am, from 6pm Sat, clsd Sun, also full bar*

Illinois • *USA*

The Courier Cafe 111 N Race St, Urbana **217/328-1811** *7am-11pm*

Dos Reales [WC] 1407 N Prospect Ave, Champaign **217/351-6879** *11am-10pm, Mexican*

Farren's Pub & Eatery [WC] 308 N Randolph St, Champaign **217/359-6977** *11am-9pm, till 10pm Fri, from noon wknds, full bar*

Fiesta Cafe [GO] 216 S 1st St (at E Clark), Champaign **217/352-5902** *11am-11pm, bar till 1am, Mexican*

The Great Impasta [E,WC] 156-C Lincoln Sq, Urbana **217/359-7377** *11am-9pm, till 10pm Fri, 5pm-10pm Sat*

Radio Maria 119 N Walnut St, Champaign **217/398-7729** *4pm-2am, wknd brunch, eclectic Mexican cuisine*

Silvercreek [E] 402 N Race St, Urbana **217/328-3402** *lunch & dinner, brunch Sun*

■**RETAIL SHOPS**

Dandelion 9 Taylor St, Champaign **217/355-9333** *11am-6pm, noon-5pm Sun, vintage clothing*

■**GYMS & HEALTH CLUBS**

Refinery [GF] 2302 W John St, Champaign **217/355-4444**

■**EROTICA**

Fantasy's 3604 N Cunningham Ave (Cunningham exit off I-74 E), Urbana **217/328-1199** *24hrs, video booths*

Illini Video Arcade 33 E Springfield Ave (S Neil exit, off I-74), Champaign **217/359-8529** *24hrs*

■**CRUISY AREAS**

Crystal Lake Park [AYOR] at Park & University Sts, Urbana

CHICAGO

Chicago is divided into 5 geographical areas:
    Chicago—Overview
    Chicago—North Side
    Chicago—Boystown/ Lakeview
    Chicago—Near North
    Chicago—South Side

Chicago—Overview

includes some listings for Greater Chicagoland; please check individual cities like Oak Park as well

■**INFO LINES & SERVICES**

AA/ New Town Alano Club [WC] 909 W Belmont Ave, 2nd flr (btwn Clark & Sheffield) **773/529-0321** *5pm-11pm, from 8:30am wknds*

The Center on Halsted 3656 N Halsted St (at Waveland) **773/472-6469, 773/472-1277** (TTY) *8am-10pm, LGBT center, organic grocery store, cafe, theater, gym, technology center*

■**ENTERTAINMENT & RECREATION**

Chicago Neighborhood Tours [GF] 77 E Randolph St (at Michigan Ave, at Chicago Cultural Center) **312/742-1190** *the best way to make the Windy City your kind of town*

Heartland Cafe 7000 N Glenwood Ave (in Rogers Park) **773/465-8005** *cafe w/ full bar, theater, lots of live music*

John Hancock Observatory 875 N Michigan Ave (in John Hancock Center) **312/751-3681, 888/875-8439** *9am-11pm, also check out the "Signature Lounge at the 96th"*

Leather Archives & Museum 6418 N Greenview Ave **773/761-9200** *11am-7pm Th-Fri, till 5pm Sat-Sun, membership required (purchase at door)*

Second City [GF,E] 1616 N Wells St (at North) **312/337-3992, 312/337-3992** *legendary comedy club, call for reservations*

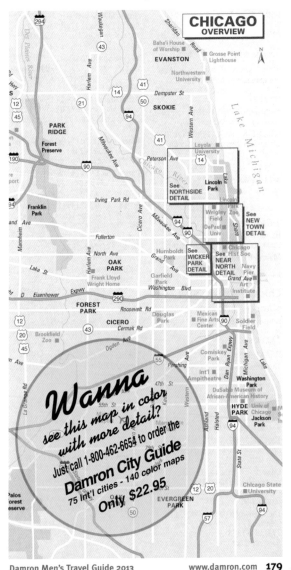

Illinois • USA

Willis/ Sears Tower Skydeck 233 S Wacker Dr (enter at Jackson Blvd) **312/875-9447, 312/875-9696** *see the city from the 99th & 103rd floors of North America's tallest building*

▪PUBLICATIONS

boi magazine **773/975-0264** *slick glossy w/ bar listings, articles, photos & circuit dish*

Nightspots **773/871-7610** *weekly LGBT nightlife magazine*

Windy City Times **773/871-7610** *weekly LGBT newspaper & calendar guide*

▪MEN'S SERVICES

▶**MegaMates** **312/377-6533** *Call to hook up with HOT local men. FREE to listen & respond to ads. Use FREE code DAMRON. MegaMates.com.*

▪CRUISY AREAS

Humboldt Park [AYOR] North Ave & Sacramento *near pavilion & bushes*

Marquette Park [AYOR] 7100 S Kedzie Avenue (at 71st Street W) *use S entrance*

Chicago—North Side

▪ACCOMMODATIONS

House 5863 B&B [GS,NS,WI,GO] 5863 N Glenwood (at Admore) **773/682-5217**

▪BARS

The Anvil [M,NH,V] 1137 W Granville (E of Broadway) **773/973-0006** *9am-2am*

Big Chicks [MW,NH,D,F,V,WI,WC] 5024 N Sheridan (btwn Foster & Argyle) **773/728-5511** *4pm-2am, from 3pm wknds, patio, Sun BBQ*

The Call [MW,D,CW,DS,V,WC] 1547 W Bryn Mawr (at Clark) **773/334-2525** *4pm-2am*

Crew [MW,F,V] 4804 N Broadway St (at Lawrence) **773/784-2739** *11:30am-midnight, 11am-2am Fri-Sun, sports bar & grill, patio*

The Glenwood [MW,NH,WC] 6962 N Glenwood Ave (at Morse) **773/764-7363** *3pm-2am, from noon Sun, sports bar*

Green Mill [★GS,E] 4802 N Broadway Ave (at Lawrence) **773/878-5552** *noon-4am, noted jazz venue, hosts the Uptown Poetry Slam*

In Fine Spirits [GS,F] 5420 N Clark St (at Rascher Ave) **773/334-9463** *4pm-midnight, 3pm-2am Fri-Sat, wine bar, patio, also wine store*

Jackhammer [★M,NH,D,K,L,S,V] 6406 N Clark St (at Devon) **773/743-5772** *5pm-4am, till 5am Sat, from 2pm Sun, patio*

Marty's [GF,F] 1511 W Balmoral Ave (at Clark) **773/321-7481** *5pm-2am, upscale wine & martini bar*

Parlour on Clark [★MW,D,C,DS] 6341 N Clark St **773/564-9274** *7pm-2am, from noon Sun, clsd Mon-Tue*

Scot's [M,NH] 1829 W Montrose Ave (at Damen) **773/528-3253** *3pm-2am, 1pm-3am Sat, from 11am Sun*

Sidecar [GS] 6920 N Glenwood Ave (at Morse) **773/764-2826** *5pm-close, martini lounge*

Sofo [M,NH,V,WC] 4923 N Clark St (at Argyle) **773/784-7636** *5pm-2am, from 2pm wknds, backyard beer garden*

Spyner's Pub [W,NH,K] 4623 N Western Ave (at W Eastwood) **773/784-8719**

T's [W,NH,F,K,WC] 5025 N Clark St (at Winnemac) **773/784-6000** *5pm-2am, 11am-3am, till 2am Sun*

Touché [★M,L] 6412 N Clark St (at Devon) **773/465-7400** *5pm-4am, 3pm-5am Sat, noon-4am Sun*

▪NIGHTCLUBS

Atmosphere [MW,D,DS,CS,WI,GO] 5355 N Clark St (at W Balmoral Ave) **773/784-1100** *6pm-2am, till 3am Sat, from 3pm Sat-Sun, clsd Mon*

▪CAFES

Charmer's Cafe [MW,WI,WC] 1500 W Jarvis (at Greenview) **773/743-2233** *6am-6pm, from 7am wknds*

Coffee Chicago [F,WI,WC] 5256 N Broadway St (btwn Berwyn & Foster) **773/784-1305** *7am-9pm, from 8am wknds*

KOPI: A Traveler's Cafe [E,F,WC] 5317 N Clark St (at Summerdale) 773/989-5674 *8am-11pm*

Metropolis Coffee [★WI] 1039 W Granville Ave (at Kenmore) 773/764-0400

■ **RESTAURANTS**

Andie's [WC] 5253 N Clark (btwn Berwyn & Farragut) 773/784-8616 *11am-11pm, eastern Mediterranean, full bar*

Anteprima [WC] 5316 N Clark St (at Summerdale) 773/506-9990 *dinner nightly, Italian*

Deluxe Diner [K] 6349 N Clark St (at Devon) 773/743-8244 *24hr diner*

Fat Cat [WC] 4840 N Broadway (at Lawrence Ave) 773/506-3100 *4pm-2am, from 11am wknds, full bar*

Fireside [WI,WC] 5739 N Ravenswood (at Rosehill) 773/561-7433 *11am-4am, Cajun & pizza, patio, full bar*

Hamburger Mary's/ Rec Room/ Attic [MW,E,K,DS,WC] 5400 N Clark St (at Balmoral) 773/784-6969 *11:30am-11pm, from 10:30am wknds, also full bar*

Hot Woks Cool Sushi 30 S Michigan Ave (at Madison) 312/345-1234 *11am-9pm, sushi/ Thai*

Jin Ju [WC] 5203 N Clark St (at Summersdale) 773/334-6377 *dinner only, clsd Mon, Korean, also bar*

Pauline's [WC] 1754 W Balmoral (at Ravenswood) 773/561-8573 *7am-3pm, hearty brkfsts*

Reza's Restaurant [WC] 5255 N Clark (btwn Berwyn & Farragut) 773/561-1898 *lunch & dinner Mediterranean/ Persian, full bar*

Svea Restaurant [WC] 5236 N Clark (btwn Berwyn & Farragut) 773/275-7738 *7am-2pm, till 3pm wknds, Swedish/ American comfort food*

Tedino's [★WC] 5335 N Sheridan Rd (at Broadway) 773/275-8100 *11am-midnight, from 3pm Mon, pizza, full bar*

Thai Pastry & Restaurant [WC] 4925 N Broadway St, Unit E (at Argyle) 773/784-5399 *11am-10pm, till 11pm Fri-Sat*

Tweet [WI] 5020 N Sheridan Rd (at Argyle) 773/728-5576 *9am-3pm, clsd Tue, brkfst & brunch, cash only*

■ **ENTERTAINMENT & RECREATION**

Hollywood /Osterman Beach [★] at Hollywood & Sheridan Sts *"the" gay beach*

■ **RETAIL SHOPS**

Enjoy, An Urban General Store 4727 N Lincoln Ave (Lincoln Square) 773/334-8626 *10am-7pm, till 6pm Sun, pride items*

Gaymart 3457 N Halsted St (at Cornelius) 773/929-4272 *11am-8pm, till 6pm Sun*

Leather 6410 [GO] 6410 N Clark St (at Devon, btwn Jackhammer & Touché) 773/508-0900 *noon-midnight, till 4am Th, till 5am Fri, till 6am Sat, from 4pm Sun-Mon*

■ **GYMS & HEALTH CLUBS**

Cheetah Gym 5248 N Clark St (at Foster) 773/728-7777, 866/961-6840

Sir Spa [GS,GO] 773/271-7000

■ **MEN'S CLUBS**

Man's Country [PC,S] 5015 N Clark St (at Argyle) 773/878-2069 *24hrs, nude strippers Fri-Sat*

■ **EROTICA**

Admiral Theater 3940 W Lawrence Ave (at Pulaski) 773/478-8111, 773/478-8263

Banana Video 4923 N Clark St (at Argyle, 2nd flr) 773/561-8322 *arcade*

■ **CRUISY AREAS**

Hollywood Beach [AYOR] along lake (at 5700 N)

Lincoln Park [AYOR] E of Lake Shore Dr (btwn Foster & Montrose)

Illinois • *USA*

Chicago—Boystown/Lakeview

■ACCOMMODATIONS

Best Western Hawthorne Terrace [GF,WI,WC] 3434 N Broadway St (at Hawthorne Pl) 773/244-3435, 888/860-3400 *in heart of Chicago's gay community, gym*

City Suites Hotel [GF,WI] 933 W Belmont Ave (btwn Clark & Sheffield) 773/404-3400, 800/248-9108 *European style*

Majestic Hotel [GF,NS,WI] 528 W Brompton Ave (at Addison) 773/404-3499, 800/727-5108

The Willows [GS,NS,WI] 555 W Surf St (at Broadway) 773/528-8400, 800/787-3108

■BARS

3160 [MW,NH,E,P,C,WC] 3160 N Clark St (at Belmont) 773/327-5969 *3pm-2am, noon-3am Sat, 11am-3am Sun*

Beat Kitchen [GF,F,E] 2100 W Belmont (btwn Hoyne & Damen) 773/281-4444 *4pm-2am, from 11:30am Sat-Sun, till 3am Sat, live bands, also grill*

Blues [★GF,E] 2519 N Halsted St (at Lill Ave) 773/528-1012 *8pm-2am, till 3am Sat, classic Chicago blues spot*

Bobby Love's [MW,NH,K,WC] 3729 N Halsted St (at Waveland) 773/525-1200 *3pm-2am, from noon wknds, till 3am Sat*

Buck's Saloon [M,NH] 3439 N Halsted St (btwn Cornelia & Newport) 773/525-1125 *noon-2am, till 3am Sat, from 11am Sun, great beer garden*

Cell Block [M,D,B,L,WC] 3702 N Halsted St (at Waveland) 773/665-8064 *2pm-3am, back bar wknds from 10pm*

Charlie's Chicago [M,D,CW,K] 3726 N Broadway St (btwn Waveland & Grace) 773/871-8887 *3pm-4am, till 5am Sat, club music after 1am*

The Closet [★MW,NH,K,V] 3325 N Broadway St (at Buckingham) 773/477-8533 *4pm-4am, noon-5am Sat, till 4am Sun*

Cocktail [MW,NH,F,D,S,V,WC] 3359 N Halsted St (at Roscoe) 773/477-1420 *5pm-2am, from 2pm Sun, from 8pm Th, go-go dancers*

DS Tequila Company [GS,F] 3352 N Halsted St (at Roscoe) 773/697-9127 *5pm-2am, noon-3am wknds*

Elixir [M] 3452 N Halsted St (at Cornelia) 773/975-9244 *6pm-close, from 4pm Sun, swank cocktails*

Little Jim's [★M,NH] 3501 N Halsted St (at Cornelia) 773/871-6116 *noon-4am, till 5am Sat*

The Lucky Horseshoe Lounge [M,NH,S] 3169 N Halsted St (at Briar) 773/404-3169 *3pm-2am, 1pm-3am Sat*

Manhandler Saloon [★M,NH,V] 1948 N Halsted St (at Armitage) 773/871-3339 *noon-4am, till 5am Sat, patio*

Minibar [★MW,F,WC] 3341 N Halsted St (at Roscoe) 773/871-6227 *5pm-2am, from 11am wknds*

The North End [M,NH,WC] 3733 N Halsted St (at Grace) 773/477-7999 *2pm-2am, from 11am wknds, sports bar*

Roscoe's [★MW,NH,D,F,K,DS,S,V] 3354-56 N Halsted St (at W Roscoe) 773/281-3355 *4pm-2am, from 3pm Fri, from 2pm Sat, patio*

Scarlet [M,E,C,P] 3320 N Halsted St (at Aldine) 773/348-1053 *6pm-2am, from 2pm wknds, piano bar*

Sidetrack [★MW,NH,V,WC] 3349 N Halsted St (at Roscoe) 773/477-9189 *3pm-2am, till 3am Sat*

Winebar [MW,F] 3341 N Halsted St (at Roscoe) 773/871-6227 *dinner 5pm-11pm, bar till 3am, Sun brunch 11am-3pm*

■NIGHTCLUBS

Berlin [★MW,D,TG,S,V,WC] 954 W Belmont (at Sheffield) 773/348-4975 *5pm-4am, from 8pm Sun-Mon*

Circuit/Rehab [M,D,MR,S] 3641 N Halsted St (at Addison) 773/325-2233 *9pm-4am, till 5am Sat, clsd Mon-Wed, Latin nights Th & Sun (T-dance)*

Hydrate [★GS,D,E,DS,S] 3458 N Halsted St (at Cornelia) 773/975-9244 *8pm-4am, till 5am Sat, opens earlier in summer*

Planet Earth [GS,D] 3534 W Belmont (at Late Bar) 773/267-5283 *10pm-5am Sat, New Wave*

Smart Bar [★GF,D,A,E] 3730 N Clark St (downstairs at the Metro) 773/549-0203 *10pm-4am, till 5am Sat, clsd Mon-Tue, theme nights*

Spin [MW,D,K,DS,S,V,YC] 800 W Belmont (enter on Halsted) 773/327-7711 *4pm-2am, from 2pm wknds*

Stardust Thursdays [W,D,F] 954 W Belmont (at Berlin) 773/348-4975

Urbano [M,D,MR-AF,MR-L] 3641 N Halsted St (at Addison) 773/325-2233

CAFES

Caribou Coffee [WI] 3300 N Broadway St (at Aldine) 773/477-3695 *from 5:30am, from 6:30am Sat, till midnight Fri-Sat*

The Coffee & Tea Exchange 3311 N Broadway St (at Roscoe) 773/528-2241 *8am-8pm, 10am-6pm Sun*

RESTAURANTS

Angelina Ristorante [WC] 3561 N Broadway St (at Addison) 773/935-5933 *5:30pm-11pm, wknd brunch, Italian, full bar*

Ann Sather's [★] 909 W Belmont Ave (at Sheffield) 773/348-2378 *7am-3pm, till 4pm Sat-Sun, Swedish diner & Boystown fixture*

Cesar's [WI] 2924 N Broadway (at Oakdale) 773/296-9097 *"home of the killer margaritas"*

Chicago Diner [BW] 3411 N Halsted St (at Roscoe) 773/935-5696 *11am-10pm, from 10am wknds, till 11pm Fri-Sat, hip & vegan*

Halsted's Bar & Grill [★MW,GO] 3441 N Halsted St (btwn Newport & Cornelia) 773/348-9696 *dinner nightly, brunch wknds, neighborhood sports bar*

Home Bistro [★BYOB,WC] 3404 N Halsted St (at Roscoe, btwn Addison & Belmont) 773/661-0299 *dinner only, clsd Mon*

Horizon Cafe [WC] 3805 N Broadway St (corner w/ Halsted & Grace) 773/883-1565 *7am-9pm, till 10pm Fri-Sat, brkfst anytime*

Joy's Noodles & Rice [WC] 3257 N Broadway St (at Melrose) 773/327-8330 *11am-10pm, till 11pm Fri-Sat, Thai, patio*

Kanok [BYOB,WC] 3422 N Broadway St (at W Hawthorne Pl) 773/529-2525 *4pm-10:30pm, sushi/ Asian*

Kit Kat Lounge & Supper Club [C,DS,GO] 3700 N Halsted St (at W Waveland Ave) 773/525-1111 *5:30pm-1am, brunch Sun (seasonal)*

Kitsch'n On Roscoe 2005 W Roscoe (at Damen) 773/248-7372 *8:30am-3pm, dinner served in summer, full bar*

Las Mananitas [★WC] 3523 N Halsted St (at Cornelia) 773/528-2109 *11am-11pm, till midnight Fri-Sat, strong margaritas*

Mon Ami Gabi 2300 N Lincoln Park W (at Belden) 773/348-8886 *dinner only, French bistro*

Nookie's Tree [★BYOB,WC] 3334 N Halsted St (at Roscoe) 773/248-9888 *7am-midnight, 24hrs wknds*

Orange 2413 N Clark St 773/549-7833 *8am-3pm, popular brunch spot*

Panino's Pizzeria [WC] 3702 N Broadway (at Waveland) 773/472-6200 *11:30am-11pm, till 10pm Sun, full bar*

Pick Me Up Cafe 3408 N Clark St (at Roscoe) 773/248-6613 *11am-3am, 24hrs Fri-Sat, brkfst all day*

Pie Hole Pizza 3477 N Broadway 773/525-8888 *5pm-3am, noon-5am wknds*

Pingpong [WC] 3322 N Broadway St 773/281-7575 *5pm-midnight, noon-10pm Sun, Asian fusion, patio*

The Raw Bar & Grill [E,WC] 3720 N Clark St (at Waveland) 773/348-7291, 773/348-7961 *11am-2am, till 3am Sat, seafood*

Illinois • USA

Sushisamba Rio [WC] 504 N Wells St (at W Illinois) 312/595-2300 *lunch & dinner, popular brunch, glitzy lounge atmosphere*

Tapas Gitana [MW] 3445 N Halsted St (btwn Newport & Cornelia) 773/296-6046 *5pm-11pm, clsd Mon, full bar, patio*

Taverna 750 [WC] 750 W Cornelia Ave (at Halsted) 773/904-7466 *5:30-late, Sun brunch, upscale Italian, full bar*

Yoshi's Cafe [★WC] 3257 N Halsted St (at Melrose) 773/248-6160 *dinner Tue-Sun, also Sun brunch, Asian-inspired French*

■ BOOKSTORES

Unabridged Books [★] 3251 N Broadway St (at Aldine) 773/883-9119 *10am-9pm, till 7pm wknds, LGBT section*

■ RETAIL SHOPS

Uncle Fun 1338 W Belmont (at Racine) 773/477-8223 *heaven for kitsch lovers*

■ MEN'S CLUBS

Steamworks Men's Gym/ Sauna [WI] 3246 N Halsted St (N of Belmont) 773/929-6080 *24hrs*

■ EROTICA

Batteries Not Included 3420 N Halsted St (at Newport) 773/935-9900 *11am-midnight, till 1am Fri, 10am-2am Sat*

Cupid's Treasures 3519 N Halsted St (at Cornelia) 773/348-3884 *11am-midnight*

The Pleasure Chest 3436 N Lincoln Ave (btwn Roscoe & Addison) 773/525-7152, 800/525-7152 *clsd Sun*

➤ **The Ram Bookstore** 3511 N Halsted St (at Addison) 773/525-9528

■ CRUISY AREAS

Belmont Rocks [AYOR]

Chicago—Near North

ACCOMMODATIONS

Allegro Chicago [GF,F,E,WI,WC] 171 W Randolph St (at LaSalle) 312/236-0123, 866/672-6143

Comfort Inn & Suites Downtown [GF,WI,WC] 15 E Ohio St (at State St) 312/894-0900, 888/775-9223

Dana Hotel & Spa [GF,F,NS,WC] 660 N State St (at Erie) 312/202-6000, 888/301-7946

Flemish House of Chicago [GS,NS,WI,GO] 68 E Cedar St (btwn Rush & Lake Shore Dr) 312/664-9981 *B&B, studios & apts*

Gold Coast Guest House B&B [GF,NS,WI] 113 W Elm St (btwn Clark & LaSalle) 312/337-0361

The Hotel Burnham [GF,NS,WI] One W Washington St (at State) 312/782-1111, 866/690-1986

Hotel Indigo Chicago Gold Coast [GF,WI,WC] 1244 N Dearborn Pkwy (btwn Goethe & Division) 312/787-4980, 866/521-6950

Hotel Monaco [GF,WI,NS] 225 N Wabash (at S Water & Wacker Pl) 312/960-8500, 800/397-7661

Millennium Knickerbocker Hotel [GF,F,WC] 163 E Walton Pl (Michigan Ave) 312/751-8100, 800/621-8140

Old Town Chicago Guest House [GS,NS,WI] 1442 N North Park Ave (near Wells & North) 312/440-9268

Palmer House Hilton [GF,SW] 17 E Monroe St (at State St) 312/726-7500

W Chicago—City Center [GF,NS,WI,WC] 172 W Adams St (at LaSalle) 312/332-1200, 877/WHOTELS (reservations only) *in the Loop, also restaurant & bar*

W Chicago—Lakeshore [GF,SW,NS,WI,WC] 644 N Lake Shore Dr (at Ontario) 312/943-9200, 877/WHOTELS (reservations only)

BARS

Club Foot [GF,NH,D,WC] 1824 W Augusta Blvd (in Wicker Park) 773/489-0379 *8pm-2am, till 3am Sat, kitschy*

Davenport's [GS,C,P] 1383 N Milwaukee (in Wicker Park) 773/278-1830 *7pm-midnight, till 2am Fri-Sat, till 11pm Sun, clsd Tue*

Downtown [★M,E,C,P,V] 440 N State (at Illinois) 312/464-1400 *3pm-2am, till 3am Sat*

Second Story Bar [M,NH] 157 E Ohio St (at Michigan Ave) 312/923-9536 *1pm-2am, 2pm-3am Sat*

Wang's [GS] 3317 N Broadway St 773/296-6800 *4pm-11pm, till 2am Fri-Sat, noon-10pm Sun, more gay men late night*

NIGHTCLUBS

Baton Show Lounge [MW,DS,WC] 436 N Clark St (btwn Illinois & Hubbard) 312/644-5269 *showtimes at 8:30pm, 10:30pm, 12:30am, clsd Mon-Tue, reservations advised, since 1969!*

Chances Dances [MW,D] 2011 W North Ave (at Damen, at Subterranean) *10pm-2am 3rd Mon; also 2nd Tue at Danny's,1959 W Dickens Ave*

Sound Bar/ Y Bar [GS,D] 226 W Ontario (btwn Franklin & Wells) 312/787-4480 *10pm-4am, till 5am Sat, clsd Sun-Wed*

Underground Wonder Bar [GF,E,MR,P] 710 N Clark St 312/266-7761 *5pm-close*

CAFES

Earwax Cafe & Film [F,WC] 1561 N Milwaukee Ave (in Wicker Park) 773/772-4019 *11am-5pm, till 8pm wknds, food served, some vegan*

RESTAURANTS

Blackbird 619 W Randolph St (at Des Plaines) 312/715-0708 *lunch Mon-Fri, dinner nightly, clsd Sun*

Catch 35 35 W Wacker Dr (at Dearborn) 312/346-3500, 312/346-3535 *lunch Mon-Fri, dinner nightly, steak & seafood*

Illinois • USA

Fireplace Inn 1448 N Wells St (at North Ave) **312/664-5264, 312/664-5264** lunch & dinner, BBQ, full bar open late

Hot Chocolate [WC] 1747 N Damen Ave (in Wicker Park) **773/489-1747** lunch, dinner & dessert, wknd brunch, clsd Mon

Ina's 1235 W Randolph St (at Racine) **312/226-8227** brkfst & lunch, full bar

Kiki's Bistro [WC] 900 N Franklin St (at Locust) **312/335-5454** lunch Mon-Fri, dinner nightly, clsd Sun, French, full bar

Lou Mitchell's 565 W Jackson Blvd (at Jefferson) **312/939-3111** great brkfst

Manny's [WC] 1141 S Jefferson St (at Roosevelt) **312/939-2855** 6am-8pm, clsd Sun, killer corned beef

Moonshine 1824 W Division St (at Honore, in Wicker Park) **773/862-8686** dinner nightly, lunch Wed-Fri, wknd brunch, American, also bar

Nacional 27 325 W Huron (at N Orleans) **312/664-2727** dinner nightly, clsd Sun, Nuevo Latino, also lounge open late

Park Grill 11 N Michigan Ave (in Millennium Park) **312/521-7275** 11am-10pm

Parthenon Restaurant [WC] 314 S Halsted St (near W Jackson) **312/726-2407** 11am-midnight, full bar, "best gyros in Chicago"

Shaw's Crab House [E,WC] 21 E Hubbard St (at State St) **312/527-2722** lunch & dinner, full bar

Topolobampo/ Frontera Grill 445 N Clark St (btwn Illinois & Hubbard) **312/661-1434** lunch & dinner, Sat brunch (Frontera only), clsd Sun-Mon

Vermilion [★WC] 10 W Hubbard St (at State) **312/527-4060** lunch Mon-Fri, dinner nightly, Latin-Indian fusion, full bar, patio

■BOOKSTORES

After-Words New & Used Books [WI] 23 E Illinois St (btwn State & Wabash) **312/464-1110** 10:30am-10pm, till 11pm Fri-Sat, noon-7pm Sun

Quimby's Bookstore [WC] 1854 W North Ave (at Wolcott, in Wicker Park) **773/342-0910** noon-9pm, 11am-10pm Sat, noon-6pm Sun

■RETAIL SHOPS

Flight 001 1133 N State St (at Elm) **312/944-1001** 11am-6pm, till 7pm Sat, way cool travel gear

■GYMS & HEALTH CLUBS

Cheetah Gym 1934 W North Ave (at Damen, in Wicker Park) **773/394-5900**

■EROTICA

Bijou Theatre 1349 N Wells St (at North Ave) **312/943-5397** 24hrs

Frenchy's 872 N State St (at Delaware) **312/337-9190** 24hrs

Lover's Playground 109 W Hubbard (at Clark) **312/828-0953** 24hrs

Lover's Warehouse [WC] 1246 W Randolph (at Elizabeth) **312/226-5222** 24hrs

Wells Books 178 N Wells (at Lake) **312/263-9266**

Chicago—South Side

■BARS

Club Escape [MW,D,DS,MR-AF,F] 1530 E 75th St (at Stoney Island Ave) **773/667-6454** 4pm-2am, till 3am Sat

Inn Exile [M,D,V,WI,WC] 5758 W 65th St (at Menard, near Midway Airport; 1 mile W of Midway hotel center at 65th & Cicero) **773/582-3510** 8pm-2am, till 3am Sat

Jeffery Pub [★MW,D,MR-AF,DS,WC] 7041 S Jeffery Blvd (at 71st) **773/363-8555** noon-4am, till 5am Sat, clsd Mon

■NIGHTCLUBS

Escapades [M,D,V] 6301 S Harlem Ave (at 63rd) **773/229-0886** 9pm-4am, till 5am Sat

■BOOKSTORES

57th St Books 1301 E 57th St, Hyde Park (at Kimbark St) **773/684-1300** 10am-8pm

Powell's Bookstore [★WC] 1218 S Halsted St (at W Roosevelt) **312/243-9070** 9am-9pm, 10am-6pm Sun; also 1501 E 57th St, 773/ 955-7780

De Kalb

■ NIGHTCLUBS

Otto's [GF,E] 118 E Lincoln Hwy
815/758-2715 *6:30pm-close, live music venue*

■ EROTICA

Paperback Grotto 157 E Lincoln Hwy (at 2nd) 815/758-8061

Decatur

■ BARS

The Flashback Lounge [MW,NH,D] 2239 E Wood St (at 22nd) 217/422-3530 *9am-2am*

■ RESTAURANTS

Robbie's Grill 122 N Merchant St 217/423-0448 *11am-10pm, till 3am Sat, clsd Sun, full bar*

■ EROTICA

Romantix Adult Superstore 2015 N 22nd St 217/362-0105 *booths*

■ CRUISY AREAS

Fairview Park [AYOR] *in the back*

Elk Grove Village

see also Chicago

■ NIGHTCLUBS

Hunter's Night Club [★M,D,E,K,S,V,WC,GO] 1932 E Higgins Rd (at Busse) 847/439-8840 *4pm-2am, till 4am Th-Sat, patio*

■ CRUISY AREAS

Busse Woods Forest Preserve [AYOR]

Elkhart

■ CAFES

Bluestem Bake Shop 107 Governor Oglesby St 217/947-2222 *9am-4pm, clsd Mon, Wed & Sat*

Forest Park

■ NIGHTCLUBS

Hideaway [M,D,K,DS,V] 7301 W Roosevelt Rd (at Marengo) 708/771-4459 *3pm-2am, till 3am Fri-Sat, male dancers*

Forest View

■ BARS

Forest View Lounge [W,F,E] 4519 S Harlem Ave 208/484-9778 *11am-midnight, till 2am wknds, clsd Sun*

Galesburg

■ MEN'S CLUBS

Hole in the Wall [MO,B,L,MR, F,V,18+,N,PC,WC,GO] 1438 Knox Hwy 9 (off I-74 at Exit 51) 309/289-2375 *10am-11pm, 24hrs Th-Sun, clsd Mon-Tue, steam room*

■ EROTICA

Romantix Adult Superstore 595 N Henderson St (at Losey) 309/342-7019

Hoffman Estates

■ CRUISY AREAS

Beverly Lake Forest Preserve [AYOR] Rte 72 (btwn 25 & 59)

Ina

■ CRUISY AREAS

Rend Lake [AYOR] off I-57 (S of Mt Vernon, N of Carbondale) *near boat ramp, beware of cops*

Joliet

■ INFO LINES & SERVICES

Community Alliance & Action Network [WI] 68 N Chicago St #401 (at Jefferson) 815/726-7906 *by appointment, LGBT community center*

■ NIGHTCLUBS

Maneuvers & Co [MW,D,TG,DS] 118 E Jefferson (at Chicago) 815/727-7069 *8pm-2am, till 3am Fri-Sat, patio, frequent events*

■ CRUISY AREAS

Hammill Woods [AYOR] Rte 59 (2 miles N of Hwy 52) *beware of cops*

Illinois • *USA*

Kankakee

■CRUISY AREAS

Kankakee River State Park [AYOR]
Rte 102 *across from main entrance,
Dan Uze Area*

LaGrange

■CRUISY AREAS

Possum Hollow Woods [AYOR] 31st St
(W of LaGrange Rd)

Leroy

■CRUISY AREAS

Moraine View State Park [AYOR]
around Dawson Lake & Timber Point

Monticello

■RESTAURANTS

The Brown Bag 212 W Washington St
217/762-9221 *9am-7pm, till 8pm Tue
& Fri, till 4pm Sat, clsd Sun*

Morris

■EROTICA

Forty-Seven Video 50 Gore Rd (N of
exit 112, off I-80) 815/942-8309
24hrs

Normal

■CAFES

Coffeehouse & Deli [E,WI] 114 E
Beaufort St 309/452-6774 *7am-
10pm, vegetarian/ vegan*

O'Fallon

■RESTAURANTS

Paulo's at the Mansion [WC,GO] 1680
Mansion Wy (at Lakepointe Center Dr)
618/624-0629 *5pm-9pm Tue-Th, till
10pm Fri-Sat, steakhouse*

Oak Park

see also Berwyn & Chicago

Oakwood

■EROTICA

Oasis Books & Video 504 N Oakwood
St (off I-74) 217/354-4820 *24hrs,
arcade*

Ottawa

■EROTICA

Brown Bag Video 3042 N State Rte 71
(at I-80, exit 93) 815/313-4125 *24hrs*

■CRUISY AREAS

Matthiessen State Park [AYOR] 1 mile
E of I-39 (at Exit 54) *river area*

Peoria

■ACCOMMODATIONS

Hotel Pere Marquette [GF,WI] 501
Main St 309/637-6500,
800/447-1676 *buffet brkfst*

■BARS

Buddies On Adams [MW,NH,K,WI] 807
SW Adams St (at Oak St)
309/676-7438 *6pm-1am, till 4am Fri-
Sat, clsd Mon*

■CAFES

One World [WI,WC] 1245 W Main St
(at University) 309/672-1522 *7am-
11pm, from 8am wknds*

■RESTAURANTS

Two 25 225 NE Adams St (at Mark
Twain Hotel) 309/282-7777 *lunch
Mon-Fri, dinner nightly, clsd Sun*

■EROTICA

The Green Door 2610 W Farmington
Rd (near Sterling Ave) 309/674-4337

Swingers World 335 SW Adams (at
Harrison) 309/676-9275

Quincy

■NIGHTCLUBS

Irene's Cabaret [★MW,D,B,L,MR,
TG,E,K,DS,WC,GO] 124 N 5th St (at
Washington Park, enter rear)
217/222-6292 *9pm-2:30am, from
7pm Fri-Sat, till 3:30am Sat, clsd Sun-
Tue*

■EROTICA

Chelsea Entertainment 4804 Gardner
Expwy 217/224-7000

■CRUISY AREAS

Parker Heights Park [AYOR] *parking
lot by archery range*

Rockford

■NIGHTCLUBS

The Office Niteclub
[★MW,D,E,K,DS,S,V] 513 E State St (btwn 2nd & 3rd) **815/965-0344** *5pm-2am, from noon Sun*

■RESTAURANTS

Lucerne's Fondue & Spirits [R,WC] 845 N Church St (at Whitman) **815/968-2665** *5pm-11pm, clsd Mon*

Maria's 828 Cunningham St (at Corbin) **815/968-6781** *4:30pm-9pm, clsd Sun-Mon, full bar*

Schiller Park

■CRUISY AREAS

Schiller Woods [AYOR] Irving Park Rd (btwn N Cumberland Ave & River Rd)

Springfield

■INFO LINES & SERVICES

The Phoenix Center 109 E Lawrence Ave **217/528-5253** *8:30am-4:30pm, clsd wknds*

■ACCOMMODATIONS

The State House Inn [GF,WI,WC] 101 E Adams St (at First St) **217/528-5100**

■BARS

The Station House [MW,NH,D,WC] 304-306 E Washington (btwn 3rd & 4th Sts) **217/525-0438** *5pm-1am, till 3am Th-Sat*

■RETAIL SHOPS

New Age Tattoos & Body Piercings 2915 S MacArthur Blvd **217/546-5006** *11am-8pm, till 6pm Sun*

■MEN'S SERVICES

➤**MegaMates** **217/801-9220** *Call to hook up with HOT local men. FREE to listen & respond to ads. Use FREE code DAMRON. MegaMates.com.*

■CRUISY AREAS

Douglas Park [AYOR] MacArthur & Mason

Riverside Park [AYOR] Peoria Rd N, past river

Waukegan

■CRUISY AREAS

Green Belt Forest Preserve Hwy 120 E, right on Green Bay Rd

INDIANA

Anderson

■EROTICA

After Dark 2012 Mounds Rd **765/649-7597** *10am-11pm, till midnight Fri-Sat, noon-10pm Sun*

Bloomington

■BARS

Uncle Elizabeth's [MW,NH,D,K,DS] 1614 W 3rd St **812/331-0060** *4pm-3am, 7pm-midnight Sun, patio*

■CAFES

Rachael's Cafe [E] 300 E 3rd St **812/330-1882** *8am-9pm, till 7pm Sun*

Soma Coffee House [WI] 322 E Kirkwood Ave (below Laughing Planet) **812/331-2770** *7am-11pm, from 8am Sun*

■RESTAURANTS

Laughing Planet Cafe 322 E Kirkwood Ave (enter on Grant) **812/323-2233** *11am-9pm, outdoor seating*

Village Deli 409 E Kirkwood **812/336-2303** *7am-8pm, 8am-8pm wknds*

■ENTERTAINMENT & RECREATION

BloomingOut WFHB 91.3 & 98.1 & 100.7 & 106.3FM **812/325-7870 & 323-1200** *6pm Th, "your midwest queer connection"*

■RETAIL SHOPS

Athena Gallery [WC] 116 N Walnut **812/339-0734** *10:30am-7pm, till 8:30pm Fri, noon-5pm Sun, clothing, drums, incense, gifts, etc*

■EROTICA

College Adult Bookstore 1013 N College Ave (at 14th) **812/332-5160** *24hrs*

Indiana • USA

CRUISY AREAS
Cascades Park [AYOR] *beware of cops late evenings!*

Columbus

CRUISY AREAS
Nobblitt Park [AYOR] 17th St (1 1/2 blocks W of Washington) *walk to train bridge*

Elkhart

see also South Bend

Evansville

NIGHTCLUBS
Someplace Else [MW,D,K,DS] 930 Main St (at Sycamore) **812/424-3202** *4pm-3am*

EROTICA
Bookmart of Evansville 519 N Main (by Lucky Lady) **812/423-2011** *24hrs*

Exotica 4605 Washington Ave **812/401-7399**

Fulton Ave Adult Books 201 S Fulton Ave (at 2nd) **812/421-0222**

CRUISY AREAS
Mesker Park [AYOR] *police patrols are heavy*

Fort Wayne

INFO LINES & SERVICES
Gay/ Lesbian AA 501 W Berry St (at Plymouth church) **260/423-9424** *2nd Tue at 6:30pm, 1pm every Sun*

NIGHTCLUBS
After Dark [M,D,K,DS,S,WC,GO] 1601 S Harrison St (at Grand St) **260/456-6235** *noon-3am, 6pm-12:30am Sun*

Babylon [M,D,K] 112 E Masterson Ave **260/247-5092** *8pm-3am Fri-Sat only*

CAFES
Firefly [E,WI] 3523 N Anthony Blvd **260/373-0505** *6:30am-8pm, from 8am wknds*

RESTAURANTS
The Loving Cafe [WC] 7605 Coldwater Rd **260/489-8686** *10am-8pm, clsd Sun, vegetarian/ vegan*

RETAIL SHOPS
Boudoir Noir 512 W Superior St **260/420-0557** *10am-midnight, noon-8pm Sun, gifts, toys, leather*

CRUISY AREAS
Swinney Park [AYOR] *be alert—major crackdown on cruising in Fort Wayne*

Gary

see also Chicago, Illinois

EROTICA
Romantix Adult Superstore 8801 W Melton Rd/ US 20 (at Ripley Rd) **219/938-2194** *24hrs*

Trucker's World [AYOR] 5480 W 25th Ave (off I-80/ 94, at Burr St) **219/844-3123**

Goshen

see also South Bend

CAFES
The Electric Brew [E] 136 S Main St **574/533-5990** *6am-10pm, noon-7pm Sun*

Hammond

ACCOMMODATIONS
Sibley Courtyard Inn [MO,NS,WI,PC,GO] 629 Sibley Blvd (at Calumet Ave) **219/933-9604** *gay men's guesthouse w/ bathhouse facilities: steam room, sauna, hot tub, private courtyard*

BARS
Dick's R U Crazee? [M,NH,K,DS] 1221 E 150th St **219/852-0222** *8pm-3am, from 7pm wknds*

Hebron

EROTICA
The Lion's Den Adult Superstore 18010 Colorado St (exit 240, off I-65) **219/696-1276** *24hrs*

Indiana Dunes

ACCOMMODATIONS
The Gray Goose Inn B&B [GS,WI] 350 Indian Boundary Rd (at I-95), Chesterton **219/926-5781, 800/521-5127** *full brkfst*

Indianapolis

■ INFO LINES & SERVICES

AA Gay/ Lesbian 317/632–7864 *various LGBT meeting, check web (www.indyaa.org) for meeting times & locations*

■ ACCOMMODATIONS

The Fort Harrison State Park Inn [GF,NS,WC] 5830 N Post Rd 317/638–6000 *luxury inn in historic Fort Harrison in NE Indianapolis*

Sycamore Knoll B&B [GS,NS,WI,GO] 10777 Riverwood Ave, Noblesville 317/776–0570 *1886 estate near the White River, full brkfst, lesbian-owned*

Wyndham Indianapolis West [GF,SW] 2544 Executive Dr (off Airport Expy) 317/248–2481, 800/444–2326 *WI) in lobby, restaurant & lounge*

■ BARS

501 Eagle [★M,D,B,L] 501 N College (at Michigan St) 317/632–2100 *5:30pm-3am, from 7:30pm Sat, 4pm-12:30am Sun*

Downtown Olly's [M,NH,K,V,WC] 822 N Illinois St (at St Clair) 317/636–5597 *open 24hrs, sports & video bar, brkfst, lunch, dinner*

The Metro Nightclub & Restaurant [★MW,F,K,P,WC] 707 Massachusetts Ave (at College) 317/639–6022 *3pm-3am, noon-midnight Sun, patio, also restaurant, giftshop*

Noah Grant's Grill House & Raw Bar [GF,NH,F] 65 S 1st St (at W Oak St), Zionsville 317/732–2233 *4pm-close, clsd Mon, wine bar & bistro, full serving lunch & dinner, Sun brunch, patio*

Varsity Lounge [M,NH,F,K,WI] 1517 N Pennsylvania Ave (S of 16th) 317/635–9998 *10am-3am, till midnight Sun*

Zonie's Closet [GS,K,DS] 1446 E Washington St (at Arsenal) 317/266–0535 *8am-3am, noon-midnight Sun*

■ NIGHTCLUBS

Greg's [★M,D,DS,CW,V,WC] 231 E 16th St (at Alabama) 317/638–8138 *4pm-3am, patio*

Talbott Street [★GS,D,DS,GO] 2145 N Talbott St (at 22nd St) 317/931–1343 *9pm-2am Fri-Sat*

The Ten [★MW,D,DS,S,WC] 1218 N Pennsylvania St (at 12th, enter rear) 317/638–5802 *6pm-3am, till 1am Wed, till midnight Sun, clsd Mon-Tue*

The Unicorn Club [★M,D,S,PC] 122 W 13th St (at Illinois) 317/262–9195 *8pm-3am, male strippers nightly*

■ CAFES

Bjava 5510 Lafayette Rd (at 56th St) 317/280–1236 *6am-5pm, 7am-3pm Sat, clsd Sun*

Cornerstone Coffeehouse [F,WI] 651 E 54th St (at N College Ave, Broad Ripple) 317/726–1360 *6am-10pm, from 7am Sat, till 9pm Sun, also full bar*

Earth House Collective [WI] 237 N East St 317/636–4060 *11am-9pm, clsd Sun, coffeehouse, also art, music & classes*

Henry's on East Street [★F,WI,GO] 627 N East St 317/951–0335 *7am-7pm, till 9pm Fri, from 8am wknds*

Hubbard & Cravens [F,WI] 4930 N Pennsylvania St (in Broad Ripple) 317/251–5161 *6am-7pm, 7am-8pm Sun*

Monon Coffee Company 920 E Westfield Blvd (at Guilford) 317/255–0510 *6:30am-8pm, till 10pm Fri, from 7am Sat, 8am-8pm Sun*

■ RESTAURANTS

14 West 14 W Maryland St 317/636–1414 *lunch & dinner, seafood & steaks, patio*

Adobo Grill [WC] 110 E Washington 317/822–9990 *lunch Fri-Sun, dinner nightly, Mexican, full bar*

Aesop's Tables [BW,WC] 600 E Massachusetts Ave 317/631–0055 *lunch & dinner, clsd Sun, authentic Mediterranean*

BARcelona 201 N Delaware St 317/638–8272 *11am-11pm, also full bar, tapas*

Bazbeaux Pizza 329 Massachusetts Ave 317/636–7662 *lunch & dinner*

Indiana • *USA*

Cafe Zuppa 320 N Meridian St (at New York St) 317/634-9877 *7am-2:30pm, Sun brunch buffet*

Creation Cafe & Euphoria 337 W 11th St (in Buggs' Temple) 317/955-2389 *8am-9pm, clsd Sun, outdoor seating*

English Ivy's [WI,WC] 944 S Alabama (at 10th) 317/822-5070 *11am-3am from 10am wknds, also full bar*

India Garden [WC] 830 Broad Ripple Ave (btwn Carrollton & Guilford) 317/253-6060 *lunch & dinner, Indian; also 207 N Delaware St, 317/634-6060*

King David Dogs 15 N Pennsylvania St *great hot dogs*

La Piedad 6524 Cornell Ave 317/475-0988 *lunch & dinner, Mexican*

Mama Carolla's [★WC] 1031 E 54th St (at Winthrop) 317/259-9412 *dinner only, clsd Sun-Mon, traditional Italian*

Naked Tchopstix [★BW] 6253 N College Ave (in Broad Ripple) 317/252-5555 *lunch & dinner, Korean, Japanese, Chinese cuisine, also sushi bar*

Oakley's Bistro [★WC] 1464 W 86th St (at Ditch Rd) 317/824-1231 *lunch & dinner, clsd Sun-Mon, gourmet cont'l, reservations suggested*

Pancho's Taqueria [★WC] 7023 Michigan Rd (at Westlane) 317/202-9015 *11am-9pm, authentic Mexican*

Sawasdee [WC] 1222 W 86th St (at Ditch Rd) 317/844-9451 *lunch Mon-Sat, dinner nightly, Thai, some veggie*

Three Sisters Cafe 6360 N Guilford Ave (at Main St) 317/257-5556 *8am-9pm, till 3pm Sun, plenty veggie & vegan, popular Sun brunch*

Usual Suspects 6319 Guilford Ave (at Broad Ripple) 317/251-3138 *5pm-10pm, till 11pm Fri-Sat, till 9pm Sun, clsd Mon, eclectic, full bar, patio*

Yats [★WC] 659 Massachusetts Ave (at Walnut) **317/686-6380** *11am-9pm, till 10pm Fri-Sat, till 7pm Sun, Cajun; also also 5363 N College Ave & 8352 E 96th St*

▉ENTERTAINMENT & RECREATION

Indy Indie Artist Colony 26 E 14th St **317/295-9302** *noon-5pm Th-Sat, largest artist community in the city w/ 72 artist live/work spaces*

Theatre on the Square 627 Massachusetts Ave (at East) **317/685-8687**

▉BOOKSTORES

Big Hat Books 6510 Cornell Ave **317/202-0203** *10am-6pm, noon-5pm Sun, general independent*

Bookmamas 9 S Johnson Ave (at E Washington St, in Irvington) **317/375-3715** *open Wed-Sat, call for hours, used bookstore*

▉RETAIL SHOPS

All My Relations 7218 Rockville Rd **317/227-3925** *noon-6pm, till 7pm Wed-Th, 10am-6pm Sat, New Age/meta-physical store, also classes*

Metamorphosis [18+] 828 Broad Ripple Ave (at Carrollton) **317/466-1666** *1pm-9pm, till 5pm Sun, tattoo & piercing parlor*

▉PUBLICATIONS

Nuvo **317/254-2400** *Indy's alterna-tive weekly*

▶**The Word** **317/632-8840** *LGBT newspaper*

▉MEN'S CLUBS

Club Indianapolis [18+,SW,PC] 620 N Capitol Ave (at North & Walnut) **317/635-5796** *24hrs, steam, sauna, gym, outdoor patio*

The Works [WI,PC,GO] 4120 N Keystone Ave (at 38th) **317/547-9210** *24hrs*

▉MEN'S SERVICES

▶**MegaMates** **317/322-9000** *Call to hook up with HOT local men. FREE to listen & respond to ads. Use FREE code DAMRON. MegaMates.com.*

▉EROTICA

Annex Bookstore 6767 E 38th St (at Massachusetts) **317/549-3522** *9am-3am*

Southern Nights Videos 3760 Commercial Dr (at 38th St) **317/329-5505** *10am-10pm*

▉CRUISY AREAS

Damron does not list here as there are 9 cops to every 1 cruiser [AYOR]

Kokomo

▉BARS

Bar Blue [★MW,D,F,K,DS,S] 1400 W Markland Ave (at Park) **765/456-1400** *open Sat only, patio*

▉CRUISY AREAS

Highland Park [AYOR] *near "Old Ben"*

Lafayette

▉INFO LINES & SERVICES

Pride Lafayette, Inc 640 Main St #218 **765/423-7579** *community center 6pm-8pm, 5pm-9pm wknds, support/ social activities*

▉EROTICA

Fantasy East 2315 Concord Rd (at Teal) **765/474-2417** *10am-1am*

Logansport

▉CRUISY AREAS

Spencer Park [AYOR] *near tennis courts & trails along Eel River*

Madison

▉CRUISY AREAS

Clifty St Park [AYOR] *btwn poplar & oak groves*

Vaughn Dr [AYOR] *along river*

Marion

▉EROTICA

After Dark 1311 W Johnson St **765/662-3688** *10am-11pm, till midnight Fri-Sat, noon-10pm Sun*

Indiana • USA

Michigan City

■ACCOMMODATIONS

Duneland Beach Inn & Restaurant
[GF] 3311 Pottawattomie Trail (at
Duneland Beach Dr) 219/874-7729,
800/423-7729 *also restaurant/ bar, 1
block away from Lake Michigan, private
beach, 60 miles from Chicago*

Tryon Farm Guest House [GF,NS,WI]
1400 Tryon Rd (at Hwy 212)
219/879-3618 *full brkfst, hot tub*

Mishawaka

see also South Bend

■ACCOMMODATIONS

The Beiger Mansion [GF,SW,NS,WI,GO]
317 Lincolnway E 574/255-6300,
800/437-0131 *B&B in 4-level neo-
classical limestone mansion*

Morgantown

■ACCOMMODATIONS

Camp Buckwood [MO,SW,GO] 8670
Spearsville Rd 812/597-2450 *lodge
w/ tents & RV sites, cabins, play areas*

Muncie

■CRUISY AREAS

McCulloch Park [AYOR] on Broadway
(past the Muncie Mall)

New Albany

see Louisville, KY

Noblesville

see Indianapolis

Richmond

■EROTICA

Exotic Fantasies 12 S 11th St
765/935-5827

South Bend

■ACCOMMODATIONS

Council Oak Inn [MO,N,NS,GO] near
airport 574/273-6416,
574/315-7098 *B&B in private home*

Innisfree B&B [GF,NS] 702 W Colfax
574/283-0740 *1892 Queen Anne
minutes from Notre Dame, full brkfst*

■BARS

Jeannie's Tavern [GF,NH,TG,GO] 621 S
Bendix (at Ford St) 574/288-2962
2pm-2am

Vickies Inc [GS,NH,TG,F,GO] 112 W
Monroe St (at S Michigan St)
574/232-4090 *2pm-2am, football
party every Sat in season*

■ENTERTAINMENT &
RECREATION

GLBT Resource Center of Michiana
574/254-1411 *5pm-8pm Mon &
11am-2pm Sat*

■EROTICA

Romantix Adult Superstore 2715 S
Main St (at Eckman St) 574/291-1899

■CRUISY AREAS

Rum Village Park [AYOR] W Ewing Ave

Terre Haute

■NIGHTCLUBS

Zim Marss Nightclub [MW,D,TG,DS,S]
1500 Locust St (at 15th St)
812/232-3026 *8pm-3am, 7pm-
12:30am Sun, clsd Mon-Tue*

■CRUISY AREAS

Deming Park [AYOR]

Fairbanks Park [AYOR] S 1st Ave

Valparaiso

■ACCOMMODATIONS

Inn at Aberdeen [GF,NS,WI,WC] 3158 S
State Rd 2 219/465-3753,
866/761-3753 *1880s Queen Anne, full
brkfst*

Vevay

■CAFES

Java Bean Cafe & Confectionery
[GO] 117 W Main St 812/427-2888
7am-7pm, clsd Sun

Vincennes

■CRUISY AREAS

**George Rodgers Clark Memorial
Park** [AYOR]

Iowa

Statewide

■PUBLICATIONS
Accessline 712/560-1807 *LGBT newspaper*

Ames

■RESTAURANTS
Lucullan's Italian Grill 400 Main St (at Burnett) 515/232-8484 *dinner Tue-Sun, Italian, full bar*

■EROTICA
Romantix Adult Superstore 117 Kellogg St (at Lincoln Wy) 515/232-7717 *9am-4am*

Boone

■CRUISY AREAS
Roadside Park [AYOR] 1 mile W on US-30

Burlington

■ACCOMMODATIONS
Arrowhead Motel, Inc [GF,WI,WC,GO] 2520 Mt Pleasant St 319/752-6353

■BARS
Steve's Place [GS,F,WC,GO] 852 Washington St (at Central Ave) 319/754-5868 *9am-2am, clsd Sun, full menu*

■EROTICA
Risque IV 421 Dry Creek Ave, West Burlington 319/753-5455 *8am-midnight, 24hrs Th-Sat*

■CRUISY AREAS
Hunt Woods [AYOR] 1 mile S of town *days*

Cedar Rapids

■INFO LINES & SERVICES
Cedar Rapids Unity 319/415-15 *support groups, referrals*

■BARS
The Piano Lounge [GS,E] 208 2nd Ave SE 319/363-0606 *4pm-2am, clsd Sun*

■NIGHTCLUBS
Club Basix [MW,D,L,TG,DS,GO] 3916 1st Ave NE (btwn 39th & 40th) 319/363-3194 *5pm-2am, from noon wknds*

■CAFES
Blue Strawberry [NS] 118 2nd St SE 319/247-2583 *7am-8pm, 8am-5pm Sun*

■ENTERTAINMENT & RECREATION
CSPS Arts Center 1103 3rd St SE 319/364-1580 *many LGBT events*

■EROTICA
Adult Shop 630 66th Ave SW (at 6th St) 319/362-4939 *24hrs*

Adult Shop North 5539 Crane Ln NE 319/294-5360 *24hrs*

Clinton

■EROTICA
ABC Books 135 5th Ave S 563/242-7687

Council Bluffs

see also Omaha, Nebraska

■RESTAURANTS
Dixie Quick's [R] 157 W Broadway 712/256-4140 *lunch & dinner, brunch wkds, clsd Mon, Southern*

■EROTICA
Romantix Adult Superstore 3216 1st Ave (at Broadway) 712/328-2673 *24hrs*

Romantix Adult Superstore 50662 189th St 712/366-1764 *24hrs*

Davenport

■ACCOMMODATIONS
Hotel Blackhawk [GF] 200 East 3rd St 563/322 5000, 888/525-4455

■BARS
Mary's on 2nd [MW,NH,D,E,V,WC] 832 W 2nd St (btwn Warren & Brown) 563/884-8014 *4pm-2am, patio*

■NIGHTCLUBS

Connections [MW,D,DS,K] 822 W 2nd St (at Brown) 563/322-1121 *5pm-2am*

■EROTICA

TR Video 3727 Hickory Grove Rd (at Fairmont & Hickory Grove) **563/386-7914**

Venus News 902 W 3rd St (at Warren) **563/322-7576**

■CRUISY AREAS

Credit Island Park [AYOR] W River Dr (W end) *daytime*

Davenport Levee [AYOR] under the Centennial Bridge *dusk*

Le Clair Park [AYOR] on riverfront from Main to Ripley *late*

Des Moines

■INFO LINES & SERVICES

The Center/ Equality Iowa **515/243-0313**

■ACCOMMODATIONS

Hotel Fort Des Moines [GF,SW,NS,WI,WC] 1000 Walnut St (at 10th St) **515/243-1161, 800/532-1466**

The Renaissance Savery Hotel [GF,F,SW,WI,WC] 401 Locust St (at 4th) **515/244-2151, 800/514**

■BARS

The Blazing Saddle [★M,D,L,DS,S,WI,WC] 416 E 5th St (btwn Grand & Locust) **515/246-1299** *2pm-2am, from noon wknds*

Buddy's Corral [GF,K] 418 E 5th St (btwn Grand & Locust) **515/244-7140** *noon-2am, from 10am Sat*

■NIGHTCLUBS

The Garden [MW,D,K,S,V,YC,WC] 112 SE 4th St **515/243-3965** *8pm-2am, 5pm-midnight Sun, clsd Mon-Tue, patio*

Le Boi Bar [MW,D,DS] 508 Indianola Ave (at 7th) **515/284-1074** *8pm-2am, 3pm-midnight Sun, clsd Mon-Tue*

■CAFES

Baby Boomer's Cafe [F,GO,WC] 303 5th St (at Walnut) **515/244-9107** *6am-4pm, from 7am Sat, 8am-3pm Sun, great brkfst*

Drake Diner [F,WC] 1111 25th St (btwn University & Cottage Grove) **515/277-1111** *7am-11pm, try the cake shake, patio, also full bar*

Java Joe's [E,NS,WI,WC] 214 4th St (at Court Ave) **515/288-5282** *7am-11pm, till midnight Th-Sat, till 10pm Sun*

Ritual Cafe [E] 1301 E Locust St **515/288-4872** *7am-7pm, till 11pm Fri-Sat, clsd Sun*

Zanzibar's Coffee Adventure [WC] 2723 Ingersoll Ave (at 28th St) **515/244-7694** *6:30am-8pm, till 9pm Fri-Sat, 8am-6pm Sun*

■RESTAURANTS

Cafe di Scala [E,WC] 644 18th St (at Woodland) **515/244-1353** *dinner Th-Sat only*

■ENTERTAINMENT & RECREATION

First Friday Breakfast Club, Inc [MO,R] 1501 Woodland (at 15th) **515/288-2500, 515/284-0880** *7am-8:15am 1st Fri, gay & bisexual men, cont'l brkfst, guest speakers, call to reserve*

■RETAIL SHOPS

Liberty Gifts 333 E Grand Ave, Ste 105 (entrance on E 4th St) **515/508-0825** *10am-8pm, 11am-7pm Sun pride store*

■MEN'S SERVICES

➤**MegaMates** **515/267-0900** *Call to hook up with HOT local men. FREE to listen & respond to ads. Use FREE code DAMRON. MegaMates.com.*

■EROTICA

Gallery Book Store 1000 Cherry St (at 10th) **515/244-2916**

Minx Love Boutique 1510 NE Broadway **515/266-2744** *also Minx Show Palace*

Romantix Adult Superstore 2020 E Euclid Ave (at Delaware) **515/266-7992** *24hrs*

■CRUISY AREAS

West River Dr [AYOR] N of downtown, by the river (off 2nd Ave N)

Dubuque

CAFES
Cafe Manna Java [WI,GO] 700 Locust St (Roshek Building) 563/588-3105 *7am-9pm, 8pm-2am Sun, full bar*

CRUISY AREAS
Julien Dubuque Monument Park [AYOR]

Fort Dodge

EROTICA
Romantix Adult Superstore 15 N 5th St (on the square) 515/955-9756

Iowa City

INFO LINES & SERVICES
AA Gay/ Lesbian 500 N Clinton (at church) 319/338-9111 (AA#) *5pm Sun*

BARS
Deadwood Tavern [★GF,NH,WC] 6 S Dubuque St 319/351-9417 *11am-2am, mostly straight, college crowd*

Studio 13 [MW,D,DS,S,19+,GO] 13 S Linn St (in the alley btwn Linn & Dubuque Sts) 319/338-7185 *7pm-2am, clsd Mon*

RESTAURANTS
The Mill [E] 120 E Burlington St 319/351-9529 *lunch & dinner, wknd brunch, live music*

BOOKSTORES
Prairie Lights Bookstore [WC] 15 S Dubuque St (at Washington) 319/337-2681, 800/295-2665 *9am-9pm, till 6pm Sun, also cafe & wine bar*

RETAIL SHOPS
New Pioneer Co-op & Bakehouse [GF,WC] 22 S Van Buren (at Washington) 319/338-9441 *7am-11pm, health food store & deli; also Coralville location at 1101 2nd St*

EROTICA
Romantix Adult Superstore 315 Kirkwood Ave (at Gilbert) 319/351-9444 *8am-4am*

Marshalltown

EROTICA
Adult Odyssey 907 Iowa Ave E 641/752-6550 *10am-11pm, till 3am Fri-Sat*

Newton

EROTICA
The Lion's Den Adult Superstore 7717 Hwy F 48 West (Exit 159, off I-80) 641/792-9301 *24hrs*

Ottumwa

EROTICA
Cinema X 317 E Main St (downtown exit, off Rte 34) 641/683-1481 *clsd Mon*

CRUISY AREAS
Greater Ottumwa Park [AYOR]

Sioux City

NIGHTCLUBS
Jones Street Station [GS,D,MR,TG,K,DS,V,WC,GO] 412 Jones St (at 5th St) 712/258-6338 *8pm-2am, clsd Sun-Mon*

EROTICA
Romantix Adult Superstore 511 Pearl St 712/277-8566 *8am-4am, noon-2am Sun*

Waterloo

ACCOMMODATIONS
Stella's Guesthouse & Gardens [MW,N,NS,GO] 324 Summit Ave (at Chicago) 319/232-2122 *B&B in 107-year-old home, full brkfst, hot tub, shared baths*

NIGHTCLUBS
Kings & Queens Knight Club [GF,D,TG,DS,V,YC,WC] 304 W 4th St (at Jefferson) 319/232-3001 *6:30pm-2am, clsd Sun-Mon*

EROTICA
Adult Cinema 16 315 E 4th St (at Mulberry) 319/234-7459 *9am-2am, till midnight Sun*

Romantix Adult Superstore 1507 La Porte Rd (at Lock) 319/234-9340 *24hrs*

KANSAS

Statewide

PUBLICATIONS

The Liberty Press 316/652-7737
Kansas statewide LGBT newspaper

Abilene

EROTICA

The Lion's Den Adult Superstore
2349 Fair Rd (exit 272 off I-70)
785/263-9898

Great Bend

CRUISY AREAS

Fort Zarah Rest Area [AYOR] on Santa
Fe Trail (on Hwy 56) *2 miles E of Great
Bend*

Hutchinson

CRUISY AREAS

Carey Park [AYOR] Main St (at the very
S end)

Junction City

NIGHTCLUBS

Xcalibur Club [MW,D,E,DS,18+,GO] 384
Grant Ave **785/762-2050** *6pm-2am,
clsd Mon-Tue*

EROTICA

After Dark Video 785/762-4747
9am-2am, cruisy

Kansas City

see also Kansas City, Missouri

ENTERTAINMENT &
RECREATION

2nd Friday Art Walk downtown
913/371-0024 *5pm-8pm 2nd Fri, art
galleries & food*

MEN'S SERVICES

▶**MegaMates** 913/904-9974 *Call to
hook up with HOT local men. FREE to
listen & respond to ads. Use FREE code
DAMRON. MegaMates.com.*

CRUISY AREAS

Pierson Park [AYOR] Wyandotte County
(off Nieman Rd) *Mon-Fri*

Lawrence

NIGHTCLUBS

Granada [GS,D,E,NS,WC] 1020
Massachusetts (at 11th)
785/842-1390 *hours vary, live bands*

Jazzhaus [GF,E,K,WI] 926-1/2
Massachusetts St **785/749-3320,**
785/749-1387 *8pm-2am*

Wilde's Chateau [GS,D] 2412 Iowa St
785/856-1514 *9pm-2am Wed, Fri-Sat
only*

CAFES

Henry's [★WI] 11 E 8th St (btwn
Massachusetts St & New Hampshire St)
785/331-3511 *7am-2am, cafe downstairs, bar from 5pm upstairs*

Java Break [GO] 17 E 7th St (at New
Hampshire) **785/749-5282** *24hrs,
sandwiches, desserts*

RESTAURANTS

Teller's Restaurant & Bar [WC] 746
Massachusetts St (at 8th)
785/843-4111 *11am-10pm, till 11pm
Fri-Sat, from 10am Sun, Italian*

BOOKSTORES

The Dusty Bookshelf [GO] 708
Massachusetts St **785/749-4643**
*10am-8pm, till 10pm Fri-Sat, noon-6pm
Sun, LGBT section*

CRUISY AREAS

Memorial Drive [AYOR] E of Jayhawk
Blvd

Riverfront Park [AYOR] Hwy 24/40 (at
N 2nd St)

Manhattan

BOOKSTORES

The Dusty Bookshelf [GO] 700 N
Manhattan Ave **785/539-2839** *10am-
8pm, till 6pm Sat, noon-5pm Sun*

CRUISY AREAS

Tuttle Creek Park [AYOR]

Olathe

CRUISY AREAS

Cedar Lake [AYOR] on Lone Elm Rd

Overland Park

ACCOMMODATIONS

Hawthorn Suites [GF,SW,NS,WI,WC] 11400 College Blvd **913/826-6167**

BARS

The Fox [M,NH,D,TG,K,V] 7520 Shawnee Mission Pkwy (at Metcalf) **913/384-0369** 2pm-2am, from 6pm Sat & Mon, from noon Sun

Salina

CRUISY AREAS

Thomas Park [AYOR] 1/2 mile S of I-70 (at 9th St exit)

Topeka

INFO LINES & SERVICES

Freedom Group AA 3916 SW 17th St (at Gage, at St David's church) **785/272-9483** 8pm Fri

BARS

Skivies [M,NH,D,DS,CW,B,L,GO] 921 S Kansas Ave (near 10th St) **785/234-0482** 3pm-2am

CRUISY AREAS

Gage Park [AYOR] beware of cops!

Shunga Park [AYOR] 29th St & Fairlawn Rd

Wichita

INFO LINES & SERVICES

One Day at a Time Gay AA 156 S Kansas Ave (at MCC, enter on English) **316/684-3661** 8pm Tue & Th

ACCOMMODATIONS

Hawthorn Suites [GF,WI,WC] 2405 N Ridge Rd **316/729-5700** brkfst buffet

BARS

J's Lounge [MW,E,K,C,WC] 513 E Central Ave (at N Emporia St) **316/262-1363** 4pm-2am, cabaret, patio, "an upscale dive"

Rain Cafe & Lounge [MW,D,F,K,GO] 518 E Douglas Ave **316/261-9000** 11am-2am

Side Street Retro Lounge [M,D,CW,WC] 1106 S Pattie St (near Lincoln & Hydraulic) **316/267-0324** 2pm-2am, patio

The Store [W,NH] 3210 E Osie **316/683-9781** 2pm-2am, men welcome

NIGHTCLUBS

Fantasy Complex [MW,D,CW,K,DS,S,18+,WC] 3201 S Hillside (at 31st) **316/682-5494** 8pm-2am Th-Sun, also South Forty [CW]

CAFES

Riverside Perk [E,WI,WC] 1144 N Bitting Ave (at 11th) **316/264-6464** 7am-10pm, till midnight Fri-Sat, from 10am Sun; also Lava Lounge juice bar next door

The Vagabond [WI] 614 W Douglas Ave **316/303-1110** 7am-2am, also art gallery & bar, theme nights

RESTAURANTS

Moe's Sub Shop 2815 S Hydraulic St (at Wassall) **316/524-5511** 11am-8pm, clsd Sun

Oh Yeah! China Bistro [WC] 3101 N Rock Rd **316/425-7700** lunch & dinner

Old Mill Tasty Shop 604 E Douglas Ave (at St Francis) **316/264-6500** 11am-3pm, from 8am Sat, clsd Sun, old-fashioned soda fountain

Rain Cafe & Lounge [★D] 518 E Douglas (btwn St Francis & Emporia) **316/261-9000** 11am-2am, from 1pm Sun, full menu till 9pm, full bar, DJ on wknds

River City Brewing Company 150 N Mosley St **316/263-2739** 11am-10pm, till 2am wknds, also live music

Riverside Cafe 739 W 13th St (at Bitting) **316/262-6703** 6am-8pm, till 2pm Sun

ENTERTAINMENT & RECREATION

Cabaret Oldtown Theatre 412 1/2 E Douglas Ave (at Topeka) **316/265-4400** edgy, kitschy productions

Mosley Street Melodrama [F,$] 234 N Mosley St (btwn 1st & 2nd St) **316/263-0222** melodrama, homestyle buffet & full bar!

Kansas • USA

Wichita Arts 334 N Mead
316/462-2787 *promotes visual & performing arts; ArtScene publication has extensive cultural calendar*

◼PUBLICATIONS

The Liberty Press 316/652-7737
statewide LGBT newspaper

◼MEN'S SERVICES

➤**MegaMates** 316/267-8500 *Call to hook up with HOT local men. FREE to listen & respond to ads. Use FREE code DAMRON. MegaMates.com.*

◼EROTICA

Adult Superstore 5858 S Broadway
316/522-9040 *24hrs*

After Dark 7805 W Kellogg (at Tyler exit) 316/721-3160

Circle Cinema/ Video 2570 S Seneca St (at Crawford St) 316/264-2245
24hrs

Fetish Lingerie 2150 S Broadway St (btwn E Clark & E Kinkaid Sts)
316/264-7800 *11:30-7pm, clsd Sun-Mon*

Patricia's 6143 W Kellogg (at Dugan)
316/942-1244 *9am-1am, from noon-10pm Sun*

Xcitement Video 3909 W Pawnee St
316/942-0200 *24hrs*

◼CRUISY AREAS

Chisholm Trail Park [AYOR] Oliver & 29th St *days*

KENTUCKY

Ashland

◼CRUISY AREAS

Central Park [AYOR] *beware of cops on bikes!*

Campbellsville

◼CRUISY AREAS

Green River Dam [AYOR] Hwy 55 (below dam)

Covington

see also Cincinnati, Ohio

◼BARS

701 Bar & Lounge [GF,NH,D,F,E,K] 701 Bakewell St (at 7th St) 859/431-7011
3pm-1am, from 1pm Sun

Bar Monet [MW,D,F,S] 837 Willard St
859/491-2403 *4pm-1am*

Rosie's Tavern [GS,NH,GO] 643 Bakewell St (at 7th St) 859/291-9707
3pm-2:30am

Yadda Club [MW,NH,MR,F,E,K,WC] 404 Pike St (at Main St) 859/491-5600
8pm-2:30am Wed-Sun, patio

◼CAFES

Pike Street Lounge [K] 266 Pike St
859/916-5430 *8am-1am, from 11am wknds, coffee & cocktails, local art*

◼CRUISY AREAS

Devou Park [AYOR] Covington exit, off Rte 75

Jamestown

◼CRUISY AREAS

Kendall Recreation Area [AYOR] below Wolf Creek Dam (10 miles S on Hwy 127) *also pull-off areas & overlook above dam*

Lexington

◼INFO LINES & SERVICES

Gay/ Lesbian AA 530 E High St (at Woodland Church) 859/225-1212
(AA#) *8pm Wed, also 7:30pm Fri at 205 E Short St*

GLSO Pride Center of the Bluegrass
389 Waller Ave #100 859/253-3233
10am-3pm Mon-Fri

◼ACCOMMODATIONS

The Bear & Boar B&B Resort
[MO,SW,WI,GO] Wood Creek Lake, London 606/862-6557 *also camping, theme parties*

Hyatt Regency Lexington
[GF,F,SW,WC] 401 W High St
859/253-1234

Ramada Limited [GF,SW,NS,WI,WC]
2261 Elkhorn Rd (off I-75)
859/294-7375, 800/272-6232

BARS

The Bar Complex [★MW,D,DS,S,WI,WC] 224 E Main St (at Esplanade) **859/255-1551** *4pm-midnight, till 2am wknds*

Crossings [M,NH,K,L,S,WC] 117 N Limestone St **859/233-7266** *4pm-2am*

Soundbar [GS,D,K] 208 S Limestone **859/255-6338** *4:30pm-close*

CAFES

Third Street Stuff [F] 257 N Limestone **859/255-5301** *6:30am-11pm, from 8am Sun, salads & sandwiches, also funky boutique*

RESTAURANTS

Alfalfa Restaurant [E] 141 E Main St **859/253-0014** *lunch & dinner, brunch wknds, healthy multi-ethnic, folk music wknds*

Natasha's Bistro & Bar [E] 112 Esplanade (at Main St) **859/259-2754** *lunch & dinner, clsd Sun, eclectic dining, plenty veggie, also live theater & music*

BOOKSTORES

Joseph-Beth [WI,WC] 161 Lexington Green Circle (at Nicholasville Rd) **859/273-2911, 800/248-6849** *9am-10pm, till 11pm Fri-Sat, 11am-9pm Sun, also cafe*

Sqecial Media 371 S Limestone St (btwn Pine & Winslow) **859/255-4316** *10am-8pm, noon-6pm Sun, also pride items*

PUBLICATIONS

GLSO (Gay/ Lesbian) News **859/253-3233** *local news & calendar*

EROTICA

Hook Novelty 940 Winchester Rd **859/252-2093**

Romantix Adult Superstore 933 Winchester Rd (at Liberty Rd) **859/252-0357** *24hrs*

CRUISY AREAS

Jacobson Park [AYOR] Richmond Rd (3 miles W of Lexington) *take 3 rights inside park to sunbathing area*

Woodland Park [AYOR] E High St

Louisville

INFO LINES & SERVICES

Gay AA 1722 Bardstown Rd (Bardstown Rd Pres Church) **502/587-6225** *6:30pm Wed, 7pm Fri; also 4:30pm Sun & 6pm Mon at MCC 1432 Highland Ave*

ACCOMMODATIONS

21c Museum Hotel [★GF] 700 W Main **502/217-6300, 877/217-6400** *boutique hotel w/ museum*

The Brown Hotel [GF,WI,NS] 335 W Broadway (at 4th) **502/583-1234, 888/387-0498** *also restaurant & bar*

Columbine B&B [GF,NS,WI,GO] 1707 S 3rd St (near Lee St) **502/635-5000, 800/635-5010** *1896 Greek Revivial mansion, full brkfst*

Galt House Hotel & Suites [GF] 140 N 4th St (at W Main) **502/589-5200, 800/843-4258** *waterfront hotel*

Inn at the Park [GF,NS,WI] 1332 S 4th St (at Park Ave) **502/638-0045** *restored mansion, full brkfst*

BARS

Magnolia Bar [GF,NH,YC] 1398 S 2nd St (at Magnolia) **502/637-9052** *2pm-4am*

Teddy Bears Bar & Grill [M,NH,WC] 1148 Garvin Pl (at St Catherine) **502/589-2619** *11am-4am, from 1pm Sun*

Tryangles [M,K,S,WC] 209 S Preston St (at Market) **502/583-6395** *4pm-4am, from 1pm Sun*

NIGHTCLUBS

Boots [★M,L] 120 S Floyd St (in Connections Complex) **502/585-5752** *9pm-2am, till 4am Fri-Sat, clsd Sun-Tue, dress code, fireplace, patio*

The Connection Complex [★MW,D,C,P,V,WC] 120 S Floyd St (at Market) **502/585-5752** *8pm-4am, till 2am Mon-Tue, 5 bars*

Lisa'a Oak Street Lounge [GS,E,K] 1004 E Oak St **502/637-9315** *9pm-1am, 7pm-3am Fri-Sat*

Kentucky • USA

■RESTAURANTS

The Bodega at Felice [WI,GO] 829 E Market St **502/569-4100** *7am-7pm, till 11pm Fri, 9am-4pm Sat, clsd Sun, gourmet market & deli, coffee bar*

Cafe Mimosa 1543 Bardstown Rd (at Stevens Ave) **502/458-2233** *lunch & dinner, Vietnamese, Chinese & sushi*

El Mundo [★WC] 2345 Frankfort Ave **502/899-9930** *11:30am-10pm, full bar till 2am Th-Sat, clsd Sun-Mon, Mexican*

Havana Rumba 4115 Oechsli Ave (off State Hwy 1447) **502/897-1959** *lunch & dinner, Cuban*

Jack Fry's [WC] 1007 Bardstown Rd **502/452-9244** *lunch & dinner, steak/ Southern, live jazz*

Lynn's Paradise Cafe [★MW,WI,GO] 984 Barret Ave (at Baxter) **502/583-3447** *7am-10pm, from 8am wknds, also bar*

Mayan Cafe 813 E Market St **502/566-0651** *lunch Mon-Fri, dinner nightly, clsd Sun, Mayan/ Mexican*

Porcini 2730 Frankfort Ave (at Bayly) **502/894-8686** *dinner nightly, clsd Sun, Italian*

Proof on Main 702 W Main St (at 7th, at 21c Hotel) **502/217-6360** *brkfst & lunch Mon-Fri, dinner nightly, upscale, American w/ Tuscan influence*

Ramsi's Cafe on the World [WC] 1293 Bardstown Rd **502/451-0700** *11am-1am, till 2am Fri-Sat, Sun brunch, eclectic menu*

Third Avenue Cafe [WC] 1164 S 3rd St (at W Oak) **502/585-2233** *11am-9pm, till 10pm Fri-Sat, clsd Sun, vegan/ vegetarian, patio*

Vietnam Kitchen [WC] 5339 Mitscher Ave **502/363-5154** *clsd Wed, plenty veggie*

Zen Garden [WC] 2240 Frankfort Ave **502/895-9114** *lunch & dinner, clsd Sun, Asian, vegetarian*

■ENTERTAINMENT & RECREATION

Pandora Productions PO Box 4185 40204 **502/216-5502** *LGBT-themed productions*

Rudyard Kipling [E] 422 W Oak St (btwn 4th & Garvin) **502/636-1311** *live music & theater, also restaurant, open wknds*

■BOOKSTORES

Carmichael's 1295 Bardstown Rd (at Longest Ave) **502/456-6950** *8am-10pm, till 11pm Fri-Sat,*

■PUBLICATIONS

The Community Letter *LGBT newspaper*

■MEN'S SERVICES

▶**MegaMates** **502/561-6666** *Call to hook up with HOT local men. FREE to listen & respond to ads. Use FREE code DAMRON. MegaMates.com.*

■EROTICA

Arcade Adult Bookstore 2822 7th St (at Arcade) **502/637-8388**

Blue Movies 140 W Jefferson St (at 2nd) **502/585-4627** *9am-1am*

Louisville Manor 4600 Dixie Hwy (at San Jose Ave) **502/449-1443** *24hrs*

Metro Station 4948 Poplar Level Rd **502/968-2353**

Showboat Adult Bookstore 3524 S 7th St (at Berry Blvd) **502/361-0007** *hustlers*

Theatair X 4505 Hwy 31 E (1/2 mile N of I-65), Clarksville, IN **812/282-6976** *24hrs*

Madisonville

■CRUISY AREAS

Grapevine Lake [AYOR]

Madisonville City Park [AYOR] Park Ave (off Pennyrile Pkwy) *go W thru 3 traffic lights, go left & drive 1 mile*

Midway

■CAFES

Tavern 815 [WI] 131 E Main St (inside Le Marché boutique mall) **859/846-4688** *11am-3pm, till 4pm Sat*

Morehead

■CRUISY AREAS

Cave Run State Park [AYOR]

Daniel Boone Campground [AYOR]

Newport

see also Cincinnati, Ohio

■ BARS

The Crazy Fox Saloon [GS,NH,E] 901 Washington Ave (at 9th)
859/261-2143 *3pm-2:30am, patio*

■ CRUISY AREAS

James Taylor Park [AYOR] on Newport Levee

Paducah

■ EROTICA

Romantix Adult Superstore 243 Brown (at Irvin Cobb Dr)
270/442-5584

Somerset

■ CRUISY AREAS

Alpine Rest Area [AYOR] S Hwy 27 Daniel Boone Nat'l Forest

Upton

■ EROTICA

The Lion's Den Adult Superstore 2833 Weldon Loop (exit 76 off I-65)
270/369-8171

Whitesburg

■ CRUISY AREAS

Carr Creek Dam [AYOR] Hazard

LOUISIANA

Statewide

■ PUBLICATIONS

▶**Ambush Mag** 504/522-8049 *oldest LGBT newspaper for the Gulf South (Texas through Florida)*

Alexandria

■ EROTICA

Alexandria Adult Emporium 3117 Masonic Dr (across from Bringhurst Park) 318/561-0306 *24hrs*

Capri Video #3 1820 N MacArthur Dr (off Hwy 1) 318/767-1669 *arcade*

■ CRUISY AREAS

Bringhurst Park [AYOR] 3016 Masonic Dr

Baton Rouge

■ INFO LINES & SERVICES

Freedom of Choice/ Gay AA 7747 Tom Dr (at MCC) 225/930-0026 **(AA#)** *8pm Th & Sat*

■ BARS

George's Place [★MW,NH,K,S,V,WC] 860 St Louis 225/387-9798 *3pm-2am, from 5pm Sat, clsd Sun, [S] Fri*

Hound Dogs [MW,NH,WC] 668 Main St (at 7th) 225/344-0807 *2pm-2am, from 4pm Mon-Tue, clsd Sun*

■ NIGHTCLUBS

Splash [★MW,D,DS,18+,WC] 2183 Highland Rd 225/242-9491 *9pm-2am, clsd Sun-Wed*

■ RESTAURANTS

Drusilla Seafood 3482 Drusilla Ln (at Jefferson Hwy) 225/923-0896, 800/364-8844 *11am-10pm*

Mestizo 2323 Acadian Thruway (just off I-10) 225/387-2699 *lunch & dinner, Louisiana-Mexican fusion*

Ralph & Kacoo's [WC] 6110 Bluebonnet Blvd (off I-10 & Perkins) 225/766-2113 *11am-9:30pm, till 10:30pm Fri-Sat, Cajun, full bar*

■ PUBLICATIONS

▶**Ambush Mag** 504/522-8049 *LGBT newspaper for the Gulf South (TX through FL)*

■ EROTICA

Grand Cinema Station 10732 Florida Blvd 225/272-2010

■ CRUISY AREAS

Capitol Lakes Park [AYOR] New Orleans *also adjacent area*

Manchac Park [AYOR] Hwy 73 (N of Bayou Manchac)

Breaux Bridge

■ ACCOMMODATIONS

Maison des Amis [GF,WI] 111 Washington St (at Bridge St)
337/507-3399

Louisiana • *USA*

Egan

■ EROTICA

The Lion's Den Adult Superstore 191 Bocage Rd (exit 72 off I-10) **337/783-5000** *24hrs*

Lafayette

■ INFO LINES & SERVICES

AA Gay/ Lesbian 115 Leonie St **337/991-0830 (AA#)** *call for times & locations*

■ NIGHTCLUBS

Jules Downtown [MW,D] 533 Jefferson St **337/264-8000** *7pm-2am Th-Fri, from 8pm Sat*

Tonic [M,D,K,DS,YC,GO] 2013 Pinhook Rd **337/269-6011** *5pm-2am, noon-midnight Sun*

■ CRUISY AREAS

Acadiana Park, Beaver Park & Moore Park [AYOR]

Lake Charles

■ ACCOMMODATIONS

Aunt Ruby's B&B [GS,WI] 504 Pujo St (at Hodges) **337/430-0603** *full brkfst*

■ NIGHTCLUBS

Crystal's [MW,D,CW,F,DS,WC,GO] 112 W Broad St **337/433-5457** *9pm-2am, till 4am Fri*

■ RESTAURANTS

Pujo St Cafe [GO] 901 Ryan St (at Pujo) **337/439-2054** *11am-9pm, till 10pm Fri-Sat, clsd Sun, full bar*

■ CRUISY AREAS

Pindarosa Park [AYOR] Sampson St, Westlake

Prien Lake Park & Tuten Park [AYOR]

Metairie

see New Orleans

Monroe

■ BARS

The Corner Bar [MW,NH,MR,E,K,DS,18+,GO] 512 N 3rd St (at Pine) **318/329-0046** *8pm-2am, 3pm-midnight Sun, clsd Mon & Wed, seasonal hrs*

■ NIGHTCLUBS

Club Pink [M,NH,D,K,18+,WC,GO] 1914 Roselawn Ave **318/654-7030** *7pm-2am*

■ CRUISY AREAS

Forsythe Park [AYOR] Forsythe Ave (at Riverside Dr)

Natchitoches

■ ACCOMMODATIONS

Chez des Amis B&B [GS,NS,WI,GO] 910 Washington St (btwn Texas & Pavie) **318/352-2647** *full brkfst*

Judge Porter House B&B [GS,WI,GO] 321 Second St **318/527-1555, 800/441-8343**

New Iberia

■ EROTICA

Leisure Time Entertainment 7600 Hwy 90 W **337/364-1883** *24hrs, arcade*

New Orleans

■ INFO LINES & SERVICES

AA Lambda Center 1024 Elysian Fields Ave **504/838-3399 (general AA office #)** *daily meetings, call for schedule*

LGBT Community Center of New Orleans [WC] 2114 Decatur St (btwn Elysian Fields & Frenchmen) **504/945-1103** *2pm-8pm, noon-6pm Fri-Sat, clsd Sun, call first*

■ ACCOMMODATIONS

1896 O'Malley House B&B [GS,NS,WI,GO] 120 S Pierce St (at Canal St) **504/488-5896, 866/226-1896**

5 Continents B&B [GS,WI,GO] 1731 Esplanade Ave (at Claiborne) **504/324-8594, 800/997-4652** *full brkfst*

Aaron Ingram Haus [GS,WI,GO] 1012 Elysian Fields Ave (btwn N Rampart & St Claude) **504/949-3110** *guesthouse, apts, courtyard*

Andrew Jackson Hotel [GF,WI,NS] 919 Royal St (btwn St Philip & Dumaine) **504/561-5881, 800/654-0224** *historic inn*

Antebellum Guest House [GS,N,NS,WI,GO] 1333 Esplanade Ave (at Marais St) 504/943-1900 *full brkfst*

Ashton's B&B [GF,NS,WI] 2023 Esplanade Ave (at Galvez) 504/942-7048, 800/725-4131

Auld Sweet Olive B&B [★GS,NS,WI] 2460 N Rampart St (at Spain) 504/947-4332, 877/470-5323

B&W Courtyards B&B [GF,NS,WI,GO] 2425 Chartres St (btwn Mandeville & Spain) 504/324-3396, 800/585-5731

Biscuit Palace Guest House [GF,WI,WC] 730 Dumaine (btwn Royal & Bourbon) 504/525-9949 *1820s Creole mansion in the French Quarter*

Bon Maison Guest House [GS,NS,GO] 835 Bourbon St (btwn Lafitte's & Bourbon Pub) 504/561-8498

Bourbon Orleans Hotel [GF,F,SW,WI,NS] 717 Orleans (at Bourbon St) 504/523-2222, 866/513-9744

➤**Bourgoyne Guest House** [★MW] 839 Bourbon St (at Dumaine St) 504/524-3621, 504/525-3983 *1830s Creole mansion furnished w/ antiques, courtyard*

The Burgundy B&B [GS,NS,WI,GO] 2513 Burgundy St (at St Roch) 504/942-1463, 800/970-2153 *1890s "double shotgun" in Faubourg Marigny, near French Quarter, hot tub* [N]

Canal Street Inn [GS,NS,WI] 3620 Canal St (at Telemachus) 504/483-3033

Chez Palmiers B&B [GS,SW,NS,WI,GO] 1744 N Rampart St 877/233-9449

The Chimes B&B [GF,NS,WI] 1146 Constantinople St (in Garden District) 504/899-2621, 504/453-2183

The Cornstalk Hotel [GF,WI] 915 Royal St 504/523-1515, 800/759-6112

Louisiana • *USA*

Crescent City Guest House
[GS,N,NS,WI,GO] 612 Marigny St (at Chartres) 504/944-8722, 877/281-2680 *near French Quarter, hot tub*

Elysian Guest House [GF,NS,WI,GO] 1008 Elysian Fields Ave (at Rampart St) 504/324-4311

The Frenchmen Hotel
[GS,SW,NS,WI,WC] 417 Frenchmen St (where Esplanade, Decatur & Frenchmen intersect) 504/948-2166, 800/831-1781

The Green House Inn
[MW,SW,NS,WI,GO] 1212 Magazine St (at Erato) 504/525-1333, 800/966-1303 *gym, hot tub*

Harrah's Casino [GF,F,WC] 228 Poydras St 504/533-6000, 800/847-5299

Historic Rentals [GS,WI,NS,GO] 800/537-5408 *1- & 2-bdrm apts in French Quarter*

Hotel Monteleone [GF,SW,WI,SW] 214 Royal St (at Iberville) 504/523-3341, 800/535-9595

Kerlerec House [GS,NS,WI,GO] 928 Kerlerec St (at Dauphine St) 504/944-8544 *1 block from the French Quarter, gardens*

La Dauphine, Residence des Artistes [GS,NS,WI,GO] 2316 Dauphine St (btwn Elysian Fields & Marigny) 504/948-2217 *B&B, no unregistered overnight guests*

La Maison Marigny B&B on Bourbon [GS,NS,WI,GO] 1421 Bourbon St (at Esplanade) 504/948-3638, 800/570-2014 *on the quiet end of Bourbon St*

Lafitte Guest House [GS,NS,WI] 1003 Bourbon St (at St Philip) 504/581-2678, 800/331-7971 *elegant French manor house*

Lamothe House Hotel [GS,SW,NS,WI,GO] 621 Esplanade Ave (btwn Royal & Chartres) 504/947-1161, 800/367-5858

Maison Dupuy Hotel [GF,SW,WI] 1001 Toulouse St 504/586-8000, 800/535-9177

The Olivier House [GF,SW,WI,WC] 828 Toulouse (at Bourbon) 504/525-8456, 866/525-9748

Pierre Coulon Guest House [GS,NS,WI,GO] 504/943-6692, 877/943-6692 *quiet apt*

Royal Street Courtyard [GS,WI,GO] 2438 Royal St (at Spain) 504/943-6818, 888/846-4004 *historic 1850s guesthouse, hot tub*

W New Orleans—French Quarter [GF,SW,WI,WC] 316 Chartres St 504/581-1200, 877/WHOTELS (reservations only) *also Bacco restaurant*

■ BARS

700 Club [MW,V,F,WC] 700 Burgundy (at St Peter) 504/561-1095 *noon-4am, kitchen clsd Mon-Tue*

Big Daddy's [MW,NH,WC] 2513 Royal St (at Franklin) 504/948-6288 *24hrs*

Bourbon Pub & Parade [★MW,D,DS,S,V,18+,YC,WI] 801 Bourbon St (at St Ann) 504/529-2107 *24hrs, theme nights, Sun T-dance*

Cafe Lafitte in Exile/ The Balcony Bar [★M,D,S,V] 901 Bourbon St (at Dumaine) 504/522-8397 *24hrs*

The Corner Pocket [★M,NH,DS,S] 940 St Louis (at Burgundy) 504/568-9829 *noon-2am, 24hrs Fri-Sat, male dancers nightly*

Country Club [★GS,F,V,K,S,SW,N,WI] 634 Louisa St (at Royal) 504/945-0742 *11am-1am, not your father's country club!*

Cutter's [MW,NH,E,WI,WC] 706 Franklin Ave (at Royal) 504/948-4200 *3pm-3am, from 11am wknds*

The Double Play [M,NH,TG] 439 Dauphine (at St Louis) 504/523-4517 *24hrs*

The Four Seasons [M,NH,E,DS,GO] 3229 N Causeway Blvd (at 18th), Metairie 504/832-0659 *3pm-close, also the Out Back Bar summers, patio*

The Friendly Bar [★M,NH,WC] 2301 Chartres St (at Marigny) 504/943-8929 *11am-close*

Good Friends Bar [M,NH,K,WC] 740 Dauphine (at St Ann) **504/566-7191** *also Queens Head Pub upstairs Fri-Sun, popular piano sing-along 4pm-8pm*

JohnPaul [M,D,E,DS] 940 Elysian Fields Ave (at N Rampart) **504/948-1888** *3pm-2am, from noon wknds*

Le Roundup [M,NH,TG] 819 St Louis St (at Dauphine) **504/561-8340** *24hrs, very MTF-friendly crowd*

Michael's in the Park [MW,NH,DS,WC] 834 N Rampart (at Dumaine) **504/267-3615** *noon-2am, 24hrs Fri-Sun, patio*

Napoleon's Itch [★MW,E] 734 Bourbon (at St Ann) **504/237-4144** *noon-2am, till 4am Fri-Sat, wine & martini bar*

Orlando's Society Page Lounge [M,NH,TG] 542 N Rampart (at Toulouse) *6pm-2am, from 3pm wknds*

Phoenix [★M,NH,B,L,F,GO] 941 Elysian Fields Ave (at N Rampart) **504/945-9264** *24hrs, cruise room, beer busts, also The Eagle* [D] *9pm-5am*

Rawhide 2010 [M,NH,D,A,B,L,V] 740 Burgundy St (at St Ann) **504/525-8106** *1pm-5am*

Rubyfruit Jungle/ 1135 [GS,D,TG,V,18+] 1135 Decatur St (at Governor Nicholls) **504/571-1863** *goth theme nights & electronica*

Spotted Cat [GF,E,D,WC] 623 Frenchmen St **206/337-3273** *4pm-2am, excellent live jazz in the Faubourg Marigny*

Tubby's Golden Lantern [M,NH,DS,S] 1239 Royal St (at Barracks) **504/529-2860** *8am-2am*

▪ NIGHTCLUBS

All Ways Lounge & Theater [M,NH,D,CW,E,WI] 2240 St Claude Ave (at Marigny) **504/218-5778** *open 6pm, clsd Mon,*

Club Fusions [M,D,MR-AF] 2004 AP Tureaud Ave (at N Galvez St) **504/301-5121** *10pm-4am Sat & Mon only, hip hop club*

Oz [★M,D,E,DS,S,V,YC,WC] 800 Bourbon St (at St Ann) **504/593-9491, 850/433-7499** *24hrs*

▪ CAFES

Cafe Rose Nicaud [WI] 632 Frenchmen St (btwn Royal & Chartres) **504/949-3300** *7am-7pm*

CC's Coffee House [WI] 941 Royal St **504/581-6996** *7am-9pm*

Croissants d'Or [WC] 617 Ursulines St **504/524-4663** *6am-3pm, clsd Tue, delicious pastries*

The Orange Couch [F,E,WI,WC] 2339 Royal St **504/267-7327** *7am-10pm, ultra mod cafe*

Royal Blend Coffee & Tea House 621 Royal St **504/523-2716** *6am-8pm, till midnight wknds, on a quiet, hidden courtyard, also salads & sandwiches*

Z'otz [E] 8210 Oak St **504/861-2224** *7am-1am, coffee shop & art space*

▪ RESTAURANTS

13 Monaghan's [WC] 517 Frenchmen St **504/942-1345** *11am-4am, brkfst, lunch & dinner all the time, full bar*

Acme Oyster House 724 Iberville St (at Royal) **504/522-5973** *11am-10pm, till 11pm wknds, long line moves quickly, worth the wait!*

Angeli on Decatur [WI,WC] 1141 Decatur St (at Gov Nicholls) **504/566-0077** *11am-2am, till 4am Fri-Sat, pizza*

Brennan's [R] 417 Royal St (at Conti) **504/525-9711** *brkfst, lunch & dinner, upscale*

Cafe Amelie 912 Royal St (in Princess of Monaco Courtyard) **504/412-8965** *lunch & dinner, Sun brunch, clsd Mon-Tue, Creole*

Cafe Negril [E,D,WC] 606 Frenchman St (at Chartres St) **504/944-4744** *dinner, clsd Sun-Mon, Caribbean*

Casamento's [WC] 4330 Magazine St (at Napoleon Ave) **504/895-9761** *lunch, dinner Th-Sat, clsd Sun-Mon (also clsd June-Aug), best oyster loaf in city*

Clover Grill [★] 900 Bourbon St (at Dumaine) **504/598-1010** *24hrs, diner fare*

Louisiana • USA

Commander's Palace [★R,WC] 1403 Washington Ave (at Coliseum St, in Garden District) **504/899-8221** *lunch Mon-Fri, dinner nightly, jazz brunch wknds, upscale Creole, dress code*

Coquette [WC] 2800 Magazine St (at Washington Ave) **504/265-0421** *lunch Wed-Sat, dinner Mon-Sat*

The Court of Two Sisters 613 Royal St **504/522-7261** *daily jazz brunch buffet 9am-3pm, dinner nightly, Creole*

Dante's Kitchen [WC] 736 Dante St (at River Rd) **504/861-3121** *dinner nightly, wknd brunch, clsd Tue, Cajun*

EAT New Orleans 900 Dumaine St (at Dauphine) **504/522-7222** *lunch & dinner, Sun brunch, clsd Mon, Cajun/ Creole, some veggie, cute waiters*

Elizabeth's 601 Gallier St **504/944-9272** *7am-10pm, from 8am wknds, clsd Mon, Cajun*

Feelings Cafe [P,WC] 2600 Chartres St (at Franklin Ave) **504/945-2222** *dinner Th-Sun, also Sun brunch, Creole, also piano bar*

Fiorella's Cafe 45 French Market Pl (at Gov Nicholls & Ursulines) **504/553-2155** *noon-midnight, till 2am Fri-Sat, awesome Fried Chicken*

Gott Gourmet Cafe 3100 Magazine St (at 8th St) **504/373-6579** *11am-9pm, 8am-5pm wknds*

Gumbo Shop 630 St Peter St (at Chartres) **504/525-1486** *award-winning gumbo*

Herbsaint 701 St Charles Ave **504/524-4114** *lunch & dinner, bistro menu afternoons, clsd Sun, French/ Southern*

La Peniche 1940 Dauphine St (at Touro St) **504/943-1460** *24hrs, clsd Tue-Wed, Southern comfort foods, popular for brkfst*

Marigny Brasserie 640 Frenchmen St **504/945-4472** *lunch Mon-Fri, dinner nightly, wknd brunch, French*

Meauxbar Bistro 942 N Rampart St (at St Philip) **504/569-9979** *6pm-10pm, clsd Sun-Mon*

Mike's On The Avenue [WC] 628 St Charles Ave (in the Lafayette Hotel) **504/523-7600** *lunch & dinner, great views of St Charles Ave*

Mona Lisa [BW,GO,WC] 1212 Royal St (at Barracks) **504/522-6746** *11am-10pm, from 5pm Mon-Th, Italian*

Mona's 504 Frenchmen St **504/949-4115** *11am-10pm, till 11pm Fri-Sat, noon-9pm Sun, cheap Middle Eastern eats*

Moon Wok 800 Dauphine St **504/523-6910** *11am-9pm, till 10pm Fri-Sat, Chinese*

Napoleon House [WC] 500 Chartres St **504/524-9752** *lunch daily, dinner only Mon, clsd Sun, po' boys & mufflettas*

Olivier's [WC] 204 Decatur St **504/525-7734** *5pm-10pm, Creole*

Orleans Grapevine [WC] 718-720 Orleans Ave **504/523-1930** *4pm-10:30pm, till 11:30pm Fri-Sat, wine bar & bistro*

Phillips [WC,GO] 733 Cherokee St (at Maple) **504/865-1155** *4pm-2am, upscale*

Praline Connection [E] 542 Frenchmen St (at Chartres) **504/943-3934** *11am-10pm, soul food*

Restaurant August [WC] 301 Tchoupitoulas St (at Gravier St) **504/299-9777** *lunch Mon-Fri, dinner nightly, upscale French/ Mediterranean*

Sammy's Seafood 627 Bourbon St (across from Pat O' Brien's) **504/525-8442** *11am-11pm, Cajun/ Creole*

Stanley 547 St Ann St (at Chartres) **504/587-0093** *7am-10pm, upscale diner fare*

Stella [WC] 1032 Chartres St (at Ursulines Ave) **504/587-0091** *dinner nightly, upscale global fusion cuisine*

The Upperline Restaurant [WC] 1413 Upperline St **504/891-9822** *dinner Wed-Sun, Creole, fine dining, full bar*

Louisiana • USA

■ENTERTAINMENT & RECREATION

Cafe du Monde [WC] 800 Decatur St (at St Ann, corner of Jackson Square) **504/525-4544, 800/772-2927** *till you've had a beignet—fried dough, powdered w/ sugar, that melts in your mouth—you haven't been to New Orleans & this is the "the" place to have them 24hrs a day*

Haunted History Tour **504/861-2727, 888/644-6787** *guided 2-1/2-hour tours of New Orleans' most famous haunts, including Anne Rice's former home*

Mardi Gras World 1380 Port of New Orleans Pl **504/361-7821** *tour this year-round Mardi Gras float workshop*

Pat O'Brien's [GF,F,WC] 718 St Peter St (btwn Bourbon & Royal) **504/525-4823, 800/597-4823** *more than just a bar—come for the Hurricane, stay for the kitsch*

Preservation Hall [NS,$] 726 St Peter St (btwn Bourbon & Royal) **504/522-2841, 888/946-5299** *8pm-midnight, set begins at 8:30pm, come & hear the music that started jazz: New Orleans-style jazz!*

St Charles Streetcar St Charles St (at Canal St) **504/248-3900** *it's not named Desire, but you should still ride it, Blanche, if you want to see the Garden District*

■BOOKSTORES

FAB -Faubourg Marigny Art & Books 600 Frenchmen St (at Chartres) **504/947-3700** *1pm-11pm, LGBT books & art*

Garden District Book Shop 2727 Prytania Pl (at Washington) **504/895-2266** *10am-6pm, till 4pm Sun*

Kitchen Witch Cook Books [GF] 631 Toulouse St (at Royal St) **504/528-8382** *10am-7pm, clsd Tue, cookbooks from rare to campy*

■RETAIL SHOPS

Angela King Gallery [GO] 241 Royal St **504/524-8211**

Bourbon Pride 909 Bourbon St (at Dumaine) **504/566-1570** *10am-8pm, till 11pm wknds, LGBT cards, gifts*

NOLA Tattoo 1820 Hampson St (Uptown, at Riverbend) **504/524-6147** *tattoos & piercing*

Rab-Dab 918 Royal St (at Dumaine) **504/525-6662** *noon-6pm, men's clothing/ clubwear & gifts*

Second Skin Leather 521 St Philip St (btwn Decatur & Chartres) **504/561-8167** *noon-8pm, till 10pm wknds*

■PUBLICATIONS

➤**Ambush Mag** **504/522-8049** *LGBT newspaper for the Gulf South (TX through FL)*

■MEN'S CLUBS

The Club New Orleans [18+,PC,V,WI] 515 Toulouse St (at Decatur) **504/581-2402** *24hrs*

■MEN'S SERVICES

➤**MegaMates** **504/733-3939** *Call to hook up with HOT local men. FREE to listen & respond to ads. Use FREE code DAMRON. MegaMates.com.*

■EROTICA

Airline Adult Books 1404 26th St (off Bainbridge), Kenner **504/468-2931**

Mr Binky's 107 Chartres St (off Canal St) **504/302-2095** *24hrs*

Paradise Adult Video [WC] 41 W 24th St (at Crestview), Kenner **504/461-0000** *arcade*

Shreveport

■ACCOMMODATIONS

Twenty-Four Thirty-Nine Fairfield [GF,WI] 2439 Fairfield Ave **318/424-2424, 877/251-2439** *1905 Victorian*

■BARS

Korner Lounge II [M,NH,K] 800 Louisiana Ave (near Cotton) **318/222-9796** *3pm-2am*

■ NIGHTCLUBS

Central Station [★MW,D,CW,DS,TG,WC] 1025 Marshall St (btwn Fairfield & Creswell) **318/222-2216** *5pm-close, till 4am Fri-Sat*

■ EROTICA

Capri Video 2010 Nelson St **318/221-5427** *10am-midnight, includes 2 theaters*

Fun Shop Too 9434 Mansfield Rd **318/688-2482** *clsd Sun, adult, novelty & gag gifts & toys*

Slidell

■ BARS

Anything Geauxs [MW,D,DS,TG,E,K] 1540 W Lindberg Dr (at Gause Blvd) **504/722-2101** *6pm-2am, clsd Mon-Wed*

Billy's [MW,NH,K,DS,WI] 2600 Hwy 190 W **985/847-1921** *6pm-1am*

MAINE

Albion

■ ACCOMMODATIONS

Twin Ponds Lodge [MO,SW,N,WI] 96 York Town Rd (at Libby Hill Rd) **207/437-2200**

Aroostook County

■ ACCOMMODATIONS

Magic Pond Wildlife Sanctuary & Guest House [MW,NS,GO] Blaine **215/287-4174**

Augusta

includes Hallowell

■ ACCOMMODATIONS

Annabessacook Farm [★GS,SW,NS,WI,GO] 192 Annabessacook Rd, Winthrop **207/377-3276** *restored 1810 farmhouse, full brkfst*

Maple Hill Farm B&B Inn [GS,NS,WI,WC,GO] Hallowell **207/622-2708, 800/622-2708** *historic Victorian farmhouse, full brkfst*

■ RESTAURANTS

Slates [E] 167 Water St (Franklin), Hallowell **207/622-9575, 207/622-4104** *lunch Tue-Fri, dinner Mon-Sat, brunch wknds, also bakery*

Bangor

■ BARS

Therapy Lounge [MW,K,DS] 336 Odlin Rd (in Howard Johnson) **207/942-5251** *4pm-1am, till 11pm Sun-Mon*

■ BOOKSTORES

Pro Libris Bookshop 10 3rd St (at Union) **207/942-3019** *10am-6pm, clsd Sun-Mon, new & used*

■ CRUISY AREAS

Valley Avenue Park [AYOR] along river bank

Bar Harbor

■ ACCOMMODATIONS

Aysgarth Station [GF,NS,WI] 20 Roberts Ave (at Cottage St) **207/288-9655** *10-minute drive from Acadia, cats on premises*

The Colonial Inn [GF,SW,WI] 321 High St (at US1), Ellsworth **207/667-5548, 888/667-5548**

Manor House Inn [GF,NS,WI] 106 West St (near Bridge St) **207/288-3759, 800/437-0088** *open April-Oct, 1887 Victorian mansion, full brkfst, some rooms w/ whirlpools*

■ RESTAURANTS

Mama DiMatteo's [GO] 34 Kennebec Pl (at Firefly Ln) **207/288-3666** *4:30pm-10pm, full bar*

■ ENTERTAINMENT & RECREATION

ImprovAcadia 15 Cottage St (2nd flr) **207/288-2503** *live improvised theater*

■ CRUISY AREAS

Lake Wood [AYOR] off Crooked Rd (1 mile from Hulls Cove) *follow trail to the "Ledges"*

Thompson Island [AYOR] Mt Desert Island *beware of cops!*

Maine • *USA*

Bath

ACCOMMODATIONS

The Galen C Moses House [GS,NS,WI,GO] 1009 Washington St 207/442-8771, 888/442-8771 *full brkfst*

The Inn at Bath [GS,NS,WC] 969 Washington St (at North St) 207/443-4294, 800/423-0964 *1810 Greek Revival B&B, full brkfst*

Bingham

EROTICA

Bingham Village Video 10 Murray St (at Rte 201) 207/672-4900

Boothbay Harbor

ACCOMMODATIONS

Hodgdon Island Inn [GS,SW,NS,WI] PO Box 603, Boothbay 04571 207/633-7474, 800/314-5160 *1810 sea captain's home, full brkfst*

Sur La Mer Inn [GF,NS,GO] 18 Eames Rd, PO Box 663, 04538 207/633-7400, 207/380-6400 *seasonal luxury oceanfront B&B, May-Oct*

Brunswick

BOOKSTORES

Gulf of Maine Books 134 Maine St (at Pleasant) 207/729-5083 *9:30am-5:30pm, clsd Sun*

Bucksport

ACCOMMODATIONS

Williams Pond Lodge B&B [GS,WI,GO] 207/460-6064

Corea

ACCOMMODATIONS

The Black Duck Inn on Corea Harbor [GS,NS,WI,GO] 207/963-2689 *full brkfst, restored farmhouse on harbor, also cottages*

Deer Isle

RESTAURANTS

Fisherman's Friend 5 Atlantic Ave, Stonington 207/367-2442 *seasonal, 11am-9pm, till 10pm Fri-Sat*

Dexter

ACCOMMODATIONS

Brewster Inn [GF,NS,WI,WC] 37 Zion's Hill Rd (at Dexter St) 207/924-3130 *historic mansion, full brkfst*

Farmington

BOOKSTORES

Devany, Doak & Garrett Booksellers 193 Broadway (at High St) 207/778-3454 *10am-5pm, till 5:30pm Th, till 6:30pm Fri, 9am-5pm Sat, noon-3pm Sun, LGBT section*

Freeport

ACCOMMODATIONS

The Royalsborough Inn [GF,NS,WI] 1290 Royalsborough Rd, Durham 207/353-6372, 800/765-1772 *full brkfst, spa services, massage, also alpaca farm*

RESTAURANTS

Harraseeket Lunch & Lobster Co 36 Main St (at Harraseeket Rd), S Freeport 207/865-4888, 207/865-3535 *open May-Oct*

Hancock

RESTAURANTS

Le Domaine Restaurant & Inn 207/422-3395, 800/554-8498 *open June-Oct, 6pm-9pm, Sun brunch, clsd Mon*

Kennebec Valley

ACCOMMODATIONS

The Sterling Inn [GF,WI,GO] 1041 US Route 201, Caratunk 207/672-3333 *mention Damron for special rates*

Kennebunkport

ACCOMMODATIONS

The Colony Hotel [GF,F,SW,NS,WI] 140 Ocean Ave (at Kings Hwy) 207/967-3331, 800/552-2363 *May-Oct, oceanfront property w/ private beach, also rental cottages*

White Barn Inn & Spa [GF,SW,F,NS,WI] 37 Beach Ave 207/967-2321 *also restaurant*

RESTAURANTS

Bartley's Dockside [WI] 4 Western Ave 207/967-6244, 207/233-6037 *lunch & dinner, full bar*

Kittery

see also Portsmouth, New Hampshire

EROTICA

Amazing 92 Rte 236 N (1 mile from traffic circle), Eliot 207/439-6285

Lewiston

ACCOMMODATIONS

Ware Street Inn B&B [GF,NS,WI] 52 Ware St (at College St) 207/783-8171, 877/783-8171

EROTICA

Paris Adult Book Store 297 Lisbon St (at Chestnut) 207/783-6677, 800/581-6901

Naples

ACCOMMODATIONS

Lambs Mill Inn [GS,NS,WI,GO] 207/693-6253 *1860s farmhouse, full brkfst, lesbian-owned*

Newcastle

ACCOMMODATIONS

The Tipsy Butler B&B [GF,NS,WI] 11 High St 207/563-3394 *on the Damariscotta River*

Ogunquit

ACCOMMODATIONS

2 Village Square Inn Ogunquit [★M,SW,NS,WI,GO] 14 Village Square Ln (at Main St) 207/646-5779 *open May-Oct, Victorian w/ ocean views, hot tub*

Abalonia Inn [GS,SW,WI,GO] 268 Main St (at Shore Rd) 207/646-7001 *pets ok*

Beaver Dam Campground [GF,SW] 551 School St, Rte 9, Berwick 207/698-2267 *campground on 20-acre spring-fed pond*

Belm House Vacation Units [MW,WI,GO] 207/641-2637 *rental units w/ kitchens*

Black Boar Inn [MW,NS,GO] 277 Main St (at Ogunquit Rd) 207/646-2112 *weekly rentals only*

Distant Sands B&B [GS,NS,WI,GO] 207/646-8686 *18th-c farmhouse, full brkfst*

Leisure Inn [GF,NS,WI] 73 School St (at Main St) 207/646-2737 *seasonal*

Meadowmere Resort [GF,SW,NS,WI,WC] 74 S Main St (at Rte 1) 207/646-9661, 800/633-8718 *health club & spa*

Moon Over Maine B&B [MW,NS,WI,GO] Berwick Rd 207/646-6666 *hot tub*

Ogunquit Beach Inn [MW,WI,GO] 67 School St 207/646-1112 *5 minutes walk to beach*

The Ogunquit Inn [MW,NS,WI,GO] 17 Glen Ave 207/646-3633, 866/999-3633 *clsd Nov-March, Victorian B&B*

OgunquitCottages.com [MW,NS,GO] 25 Mill St, N Reading, MA 01864 207/646-3840, 978/664-5813 *weekly rentals, seasonal (June-Sept), near bars & beach*

Rockmere Lodge B&B [GS,NS,GO] 150 Stearns Rd 207/646-2985, 800/646-2985 *Maine shingle cottage, near beach*

Yellow Monkey Guest Houses & Motel [GS,WC,GO] 280 Main St 207/646-9056 *seasonal, jacuzzi, ocean view, gym*

BARS

Front Porch Cafe [GS,F,P] 9 Shore Rd (at Beach St) 207/646-4005 *seasonal, lunch & dinner*

Vine Cafe [F] 478 Main St 207/646-0288, 877/646-0288 *seasonal, 4pm-close, also restaurant, good wine selection*

NIGHTCLUBS

Maine Street [★MW,D,F,K,C,GO] 195 Main St/ US Rte 1 207/646-5101 *5pm-1am, T-dance from 3pm wknds, seasonal*

CAFES

Bread & Roses 246 Main St 207/646-4227 *7am-7pm, seasonal*

Maine • USA

Fancy That Cafe Main St (at Beach St & Rte 1) 207/646-4118 *April-Oct, 6:30am-11pm*

■RESTAURANTS

Amore Breakfast 309 Shore Rd 207/646-6661, 866/641-6661 *brkfst only, seasonal*

Angelina's Ristorante 655 Main St 207/646-0445 *dinner, Italian*

Arrows [★R] 41 Berwick Rd (2 miles W of Rte 1), Cape Neddick 207/361-1100 *open April-Dec, 6pm-9pm Th-Sun, eclectic*

Beachfire Bar & Grill 658 Main St 207/646-8998 *dinner nightly, wknd brunch, outdoor fire pit*

Bessie's 8 Shore Rd (Rte 1) 207/646-0888 *brkfst, lunch & dinner, also bar*

Clay Hill Farm [P] 220 Clay Hill Rd (off Logging Rd), Cape Neddick (York) 207/361-2272 *dinner only, seafood, also piano bar*

Five-0 [★] 50 Shore Rd 207/646-5001 *5pm-midnight, martini bar & restaurant, full bar*

Jonathan's [E,WC] 92 Bourne Ln 207/646-4777 *dinner nightly, steak/ seafood, full bar*

La Pizzeria [BW,GO] 239 Main St 207/646-1143 *open April-Dec, lunch & dinner*

Wild Blueberry Cafe & Bistro [E] 82 Shore Rd 207/646-0990 *brkfst, lunch & dinner, jazz brunch 10am-1pm Sun*

■ENTERTAINMENT & RECREATION

Ogunquit Playhouse 10 Main St 207/646-5511 (box office), 207/646-2402 *summer theater, some LGBT-themed productions*

■CRUISY AREAS

Ogunquit Beach [AYOR] off Rte 1 *200 yds N of beach entrance*

Portland

■ACCOMMODATIONS

Auberge by the Sea B&B [GF,NS,WI] 103 East Grand Ave (at Old Orchard St), Old Orchard Beach 207/934-2355

The Chadwick B&B [GS,WI,GO] 140 Chadwick St 207/774--5141, 800/774-2137

The Inn at St John [GS,NS,WI,GO] 939 Congress St 207/773-6481, 800/636-9127

The Inn by the Sea [GF,SW,NS,WC] 40 Bowery Beach Rd, Cape Elizabeth 207/799-3134, 800/888-4287

The Percy Inn [GF,WI,NS] 15 Pine St (at Longfellow Square) 207/871-7638, 888/417-3729

The Pomegranate Inn [GF,NS,WI] 49 Neal St (at Carroll St) 207/772-1006, 800/356-0408

Sea View Inn [GS,SW,NS,WI,WC] 65 W Grand Ave (at Atlantic Ave), Old Orchard Beach 207/934-4180, 800/541-8439 *motel*

West End Inn [GF,NS,WI] 146 Pine St (at Neal St) 207/772-1377, 800/338-1377

Wild Iris Inn [GF,NS,WI] 273 State St (at Grant St) 207/775-0224, 800/600-1557

■BARS

Blackstones [M,NH,WC] 6 Pine St (off Longfellow Square) 207/775-2885 *4pm-1am, from 3pm wknds, [L] 3rd Sat, theme nights*

The Wine Bar [GS,F] 38 Wharf St 207/772-6976 *5pm-close*

■NIGHTCLUBS

Styxx [★MW,D,E,DS,GO] 3 Spring St (at Center St) 207/828-0822 *7pm-1am, from 4pm Th-Sat*

■CAFES

Coffee by Design 43 Washington Ave (at Oxford St) 207/879-2233 *8am-5pm, clsd wknds*

■RESTAURANTS

Becky's [WC] 390 Commercial St (at High St) 207/773-7070 *4am-10pm, great brkfst & chowdah*

Grace 15 Chestnut St 207/828-4422 *fine dining in renovated old church*

Katahdin 27 Forest Ave 207/774-1740 *5pm-11pm, clsd Sun-Mon, American menu, bar*

Street & Co [★BW,WC] 33 Wharf St (btwn Dana & Union) 207/775-0887 *5:30pm-9:30pm, till 10pm Fri-Sat, seafood*

Walter's Cafe [WC] 2 Portland Sq (at Union) 207/871-9258 *lunch & dinner, dinner nightly, seafood/ pasta*

▇ BOOKSTORES

Longfellow Books 1 Monument Way 207/772-4045 *9am-7pm, till 6pm Sat, 9:30am-5pm Sun, LGBT section*

▇ RETAIL SHOPS

The Corner General Store 154 Middle St (at Market) 207/253-5280 *8am-1am, great wine selection*

Emerald City [GO] 564 Congress St 207/774-8800 *10am-6pm, First Friday Art Walk; gifts, pride items & more*

▇ MEN'S SERVICES

▶**MegaMates** 207/828-0000 *Call to hook up with HOT local men. FREE to listen & respond to ads. Use FREE code DAMRON. MegaMates.com.*

▇ EROTICA

Condom Sense 424 Fore St (at Union) 207/871-0356, 877/871-0356 *10am-8pm, till 9pm Th, till 10pm Fri-Sat, till 6pm Sun*

Video Expo 666 Congress St (at State) 207/774-1377

▇ CRUISY AREAS

Cutter Street [AYOR] *at the foot of the street on the Eastern Promenade*

Rockland

▇ ACCOMMODATIONS

Captain Lindsey House Inn [GF,NS,WI,WC] 5 Lindsey St 207/596-7950, 800/523-2145

The Old Granite Inn [GF,NS,WI] 546 Main St 207/594-9036, 800/386-9036 *1880s stone guesthouse, full brkfst*

Rockport

▇ RESTAURANTS

Chez Michel 2530 Atlantic Hwy (at Rte 1), Lincolnville 207/789-5600 *dinner Wed-Sun, full bar, some veggie*

Lobster Pound [WC] Rte 1, Lincolnville Beach 207/789-5550 *11:30am-8pm May-Oct, full bar, patio*

Tenants Harbor

▇ ACCOMMODATIONS

Eastwind Inn [GF,F] 207/372-6366, 800/241-8439 *clsd Dec-April, full brkfst, rooms & apts*

Waterville

▇ EROTICA

Treasure Chest II [★GO] 5 Sanger Ave (at Main) 207/873-7411

Video 54 [★GO] 18 Water St (at Sherwin St) 207/873-4201

White Mtns

▇ ACCOMMODATIONS

Mountain Village Farm B&B [GF,NS,WI] 164 Main St, Kingfield 04947 207/265-2030, 866/577-0741 *rural & sophisticated B&B, full brkfst*

York Harbor

▇ RESTAURANTS

York Harbor Inn 480 York St 207/363-5119, 800/343-3869 *lunch Mon-Sat, dinner nightly, Sun brunch, also the Cellar Pub, also lodging*

MARYLAND

Annapolis

▇ INFO LINES & SERVICES

AA Gay/ Lesbian 199 Duke of Gloucester St (at St Anne's Parish) 410/268-5441 *8pm Tue*

▇ ACCOMMODATIONS

Two-O-One B&B [GS,NS,WI,GO] 201 Prince George St (at Maryland Ave) 410/268-8053 *full brkfst*

Maryland • *USA*

■RESTAURANTS

Cafe Sado 205 Tackle Cir (at Castle Marina Rd), Chester **410/604-1688** *lunch & dinner, sushi/ Asian fusion*

Baltimore

■INFO LINES & SERVICES

AA Gay/ Lesbian 410/663-1922 *6:30pm Sat, call for other mtg times*

Gay, Lesbian, Bisexual & Transgender Community Center of Baltimore 241 W Chase St (at Read) 410/837-5445

■ACCOMMODATIONS

Abacrombie Fine Food & Accommodations [GS,NS] 58 W Biddle St (at Cathedral) **410/244-7227, 888/922-3437**

Biltmore Suites [GF,NS,WI] 205 W Madison St (at Park) **410/728-6550, 800/868-5064** *Victorian hotel*

Pier 5 Hotel [GS,F,WI,WC] 711 Eastern Ave (at President) **410/539-2000, 866/583-4162**

Scarborough Fair B&B [GF,GO] 801 S Charles St **410/837-0010, 877/954-2747**

■BARS

Baltimore Eagle [★M,L,WC] 2022 N Charles St (enter on 21st) **443/524-3333** *6pm-2am, leather & video store, patio*

Club Bunns [MW,D,MR-AF,S] 608 W Lexington St (at Greene St) **410/234-2866** *5pm-2am, 7pm-1am Sun*

The Drinkery [M,NH,K] 205 W Read St (at Park) **410/225-3100** *11am-2am*

The Gallery Bar & Studio Restaurant [MW,WC] 1735 Maryland Ave (at Lafayette) **410/539-6965** *6pm-1am, dinner Mon-Fri*

Grand Central [★MW,D,F,K,DS,V,18+] 1001 N Charles St (at Eager) **410/752-7133** *4pm-close, 3 bars*

Hippo [★MW,D,TG,E,K,DS,P,V,WC] 1 W Eager St (at Charles) **410/547-0069** *4pm-2am, 3 bars*

Jay's on Read [M,P] 225 W Read St **410/225-0188** *4pm-1am*

Leon's [MW,NH,B,F,WI,WC] 870 Park Ave (at Chase) **410/539-4993, 410/539-4850** *4pm-2am, also Singer's restaurant*

Mixers [MW,NH,D,E,K] 6037 Belair Rd (at Glenarm Ave) **410/483-6011** *5pm-2am*

The Quest [M,NH] 3607 Fleet St (at Conkling) **410/563-2617** *4pm-2am*

The Rowan Tree [GS,K] 1633 S Charles St (at E Heath) **410/468-0550** *noon-2am, "where diversity is our name"*

Ziascoz [GS,NH,K,MR-AF] 1313 E Pratt St (at Eden) **410/276-5790** *7pm-2am*

■NIGHTCLUBS

Club 1722 [GS,D,MR,18+,PC] 1722 N Charles St (at Lafayette) **410/547-8423** *afterhours club, Fri-Sat only, 2am-close, BYOB*

Club Orpheus [GS,D] 1003 E Pratt St **410/276-5599**

The Paradox [★GS,D,MR,F,E,V,WC] 1310 Russell St (at Ostend) **410/837-9110** *11pm-5am, midnight-6am Sat, more gay Sat*

Peer Pressure [MW,D] 701 S Bond St (at The Get Down) **443/708-3564** *1st Wed, monthly queer dance party*

■CAFES

Station North Arts Cafe 1816 N Charles St **410/625-6440** *8am-3pm, from 11am Sat, clsd Sun, also art gallery, events*

■RESTAURANTS

Aldos [★WC] 306 S High St **410/727-0700** *dinner nightly, Italian*

Alonso's [NS,WC] 415 W Cold Spring Ln (at Keswick Rd) **410/235-3433** *4pm-10:30pm, from 11:30am Fri-Sat, full bar*

Cafe Hon [WC] 1002 W 36th St (at Roland) **410/243-1230** *7am-9pm, 9am-close wknds*

The Dizz 300 W 30th St **443/869-5864** *10am-2am, full bar*

Golden West Cafe 1105 W 36th St **410/889-8891** *brkfst, lunch & dinner, New Mexican, also bar, live bands*

Jerry D's Seafood 7804 Harford Rd, Parkville **410/668-1299**

Loco Hombre 413 W Cold Spring Ln (at Roland) **410/889-2233** *11:30am-10:30pm, till 11:30pm Fri-Sat, Tex-Mex, burgers*

Mari Luna 1225 Cathedral St **410/637-8013** *modern Mexican, also lounge*

Mount Vernon Stable & Saloon 909 N Charles St (btwn Eager & Read) **410/685-7427** *11:30am-midnight, till 1am Fri-Sat, Sun brunch, also bar*

Trinidad Gourmet 418 E 31st St **410/243-0072** *7am-8:30pm, clsd Sun, Caribbean, delicious & inexpensive*

Viccino 1317 N Charles St **410/347-0349** *11am-11pm, till 9pm Sun, New American, full bar*

Woodberry Kichen [WC] 2010 Clipper Park Rd #126 **410/464-8000** *dinner nightly, wknd brunch, organic & sustainable, full bar*

XS Baltimore 1307 N Charles St **410/468-0002** *7am-midnight, till 2am Fri-Sat, sushi restaurant, cafe & lounge*

▇PUBLICATIONS

Baltimore OUTloud 410/244-6780

Gay Life 410/837-7748 *LGBT newspaper*

▇MEN'S SERVICES

▶**MegaMates** 410/468-4000 *Call to hook up with HOT local men. FREE to listen & respond to ads. Use FREE code DAMRON. MegaMates.com.*

▇EROTICA

Big Top Video & News 429 E Baltimore **410/547-2495**

Chained Desires 136 W Read St **410/528-8441, 888/886-8442** *11am-8pm, till 9pm Fri-Sat, clsd Mon*

Greenmount Books 3222 Greenmount Ave (at 33rd St) **410/467-0403**

Sugar [TG,GO] 927 W 36th St (at Roland) **410/467-2632**

▇CRUISY AREAS

Druid Hill Park [MR-AF,YC,AYOR] W side of town (near Park Cir)

Lake Montebello Park [AYOR] Lake Montebello Terr (at Harford Rd) *in the woods*

Wyman Dell Park [AYOR] Charles St (btwn 29th & 33rd) *hustlers on the sidewalk, cruising on the Wyman Park Dr side*

Beltsville

see Washington, District of Columbia

College Park

see Washington, District of Columbia

Cumberland

▇RESTAURANTS

Acropolis 45 E Main St, Frostburg **301/689-8277** *4pm-10pm, clsd Sun-Mon, full bar*

Edgewood

▇EROTICA

Bush River Books & Video 3909 Pulaski Hwy (Rte 40), Abingdon **410/676-9051**

Frederick

▇CRUISY AREAS

Gambrill State Park [AYOR] W of Frederick (off I-70) *go to the summit, turn left*

Greenbelt

see also Washington, District of Columbia

▇CRUISY AREAS

Greenbelt Park [AYOR]

Hagerstown

▇NIGHTCLUBS

The Lodge [M,D,DS,MR,K,TG,GO] 21614 National Pike, Boonsboro **301/591-4434** *9pm-2am, till midnight Sun, clsd Mon-Th*

Spin [MW,D] 43 S Potomac St **301/302-7202** *4pm-midnight, theme nights, also restaurant*

Hyattsville

see Washington, District of Columbia

Maryland • USA

Laurel

see also Washington, District of Columbia

■BARS

PW's Sports Bar & Grill
[MW,NH,F,DS,K,WI,GO] 9855 N Washington Blvd (at Whiskey Bottom Rd) **301/498-4840, 301/498-4841** *5am-2am, sports bar*

■EROTICA

Route 1 News Agency 106 Washington Blvd (at Main) **410/880-4253**

Potomac

see Washington, District of Columbia

Princess Anne

■ACCOMMODATIONS

The Alexander House Booklovers B&B [GF,NS] 30535 Linden Ave (at corner of Beckford) **410/651-5195** *literary-themed B&B, full brkfst*

Rock Hall

■ACCOMMODATIONS

Tallulah's on Main [GS,NS,WC,GO] 5750 Main St (at Sharp St) **410/639-2596** *small suite hotel*

Rockville

see also Washington, District of Columbia

■RESTAURANTS

The Vegetable Garden 11618 Rockville Pk **301/468-9301** *lunch Mon-Fri, dinner nightly, vegetarian/ vegan*

■CRUISY AREAS

Lake Needwood [AYOR] N of Rte 28 (off Avery Rd)

Salisbury

■EROTICA

Salisbury News Agency 616 S Salisbury Blvd (near Vine) **410/543-4469**

Silver Spring

see Washington, District of Columbia

Snow Hill

■ACCOMMODATIONS

River House Inn [GF,SW,WI,GO] 201 E Market St (at Green St) **410/632-2722**

MASSACHUSETTS

Amherst

see also Northampton

■BOOKSTORES

Amherst Books 8 Main St **413/256-1547, 800/503-5865** *6:30am-9pm, till 5pm Sun, independent, LGBT section*

Food For Thought [WC] 106 N Pleasant St (at Main) **413/253-5432** *10am-6pm, progressive bookstore*

Attleboro

■EROTICA

State Line Video 1124 Washington St (off I-95, Broadway exit), South Attleboro **508/761-4900** *arcade*

Barre

■ACCOMMODATIONS

Jenkins Inn & Restaurant [GF,F,NS,WI,GO] **978/355-6444, 800/378-7373** *also restaurant & full bar*

Berkshires

■ACCOMMODATIONS

The B&B at Howden Farm [GS,NS,GO] 303 Rannapo Rd, Sheffield **413/229-8481** *on 250-acre working farm, full brkfst*

Broken Hill Manor [GF,NS,WI,GO] 771 West Rd (at Rte 23), Sheffield **413/528-6159, 877/535-6159** *B&B, full brkfst*

Gateways Inn [GF,NS,WI] 51 Walker St (at Church St), Lenox **413/637-2532, 888/492-9466** *also bar & restaurant*

Guest House at Field Farm [GF,TG,NS,SW,WI] 554 Sloan Rd, Williamstown 413/458-3135

Mount Greylock Inn [GS,GO] 6 East St, Adams 413/743-2665 *views of Mt Greylock*

River Bend Farm B&B [GF,NS] 643 Simonds Rd, Williamstown 413/458-3121

The Rookwood Inn [GS,NS,WI] 11 Old Stockbridge Rd (at Walker St/ Rte 183), Lenox 413/637-9750, 800/223-9750 *Victorian inn near Tanglewood & skiing*

The Thaddeus Clapp House [GF,NS] 74 Wendell Ave, Pittsfield 413/499-6840, 888/499-6840

Topia Inn [GS,NS,WI,WC,GO] 10 Pleasant St (at Rte 8), Adams 413/743-9600, 888/868-6742

Windflower Inn [GF,SW,WI,NS] 684 S Egremont Rd, Great Barrington 413/528-2720, 800/992-1993 *country inn in the Berkshires, full brkfst*

■RESTAURANTS

Allium Restaurant + Bar 42 Railroad St (at Main), Great Barrington 413/528-2118 *5pm-9pm, till 10pm Fri-Sat, bar open late*

Cafe Lucia 80 Church St (at Tucker), Lenox 413/637-2640 *dinner only, clsd Mon, seasonal*

Church Street Cafe 65 Church St (at Franklin), Lenox 413/637-2745 *lunch & dinner, seasonal, American bistro*

Mezze Bistro + Bar 777 Cold Spring Rd, Williamstown 413/458-0123 *5pm-9pm, till 10pm Fri-Sat, seasonal hrs*

■ENTERTAINMENT & RECREATION

Tanglewood [E] 197 Rte 183, Lenox 888/266-1200 *summer home of the Boston Symphony/ Pops*

Williamstown Theatre Festival just E of Rte 2 & Rte 7 junction, Williamstown 413/597-3400, 413/458-3200 *call for season calendar*

■EROTICA

Amazing.net Video Store 1021 South St/ Rte 20, Pittsfield 413/496-8055

■CRUISY AREAS

Onota Lake [AYOR] parking lot near woods, Pittsfield

Boston

■INFO LINES & SERVICES

Fenway Health 1340 Boylston St (at Jersey St) 617/267-0900, 888/242-0900 *medical & HIV services, LGBT health resources*

Gay AA 12 Channel St #604 617/426-9444 (AA#)

GLBT Helpline 617/267-9001, 888/340-4528 *6pm-11pm*

■ACCOMMODATIONS

463 Beacon St Guest House [GS,NS,WI,GO] 463 Beacon St 617/536-1302

Beacon Hill Hotel & Bistro [GS,F,WI] 25 Charles St (at Chestnut St) 617/723-7575

Chandler Inn [GF,NS,WI] 26 Chandler St (at Berkeley) 617/482-3450, 800/842-3450 *European-style hotel*

The Charles Hotel [GF] 1 Bennett St (at Eliot), Cambridge 617/864-1200, 800/882-1818

The Charles Street Inn [GS,NS,WC,GO] 94 Charles St (at Mount Vernon, Beacon Hill) 617/314-8900, 877/772-8900

Clarendon Square Inn [GS,NS,WI,GO] 198 W Brookline St (btwn Tremont & Columbus) 617/536-2229

Encore B&B [GF,NS,GO] 116 W Newton St (at Tremont) 617/247-3425 *19th-c town house in Boston's South End*

Fifteen Beacon Hotel [GF,F,WI] 15 Beacon St (at Somerset) 617/670-1500, 877/982-3226

Holiday Inn Express & Suites Boston Garden [GF,WI,NS,WC] 280 Friend St (at Causeway) 617/720-5544

Hotel 140 [GS,NS,WC] 140 Clarendon St (at Stuart St) 617/585-5600, 800/714-0140

Hotel Onyx [GF,WI,NS] 155 Portland St (at Causeway) 617/557-9955, 866/660-6699

Massachusetts • USA

The Liberty Hotel [GF,NS,WI,WC] 215 Charles St (at Cambridge St) **617/224-4000, 866/507-5245** *in the former Charles St Jail*

Nine Zero Hotel [GF,WI,NS,WC] 90 Tremont St (at Bosworth) **617/772-5800, 866/646-3937** *luxury hotel, full brkfst, jacuzzi*

➤**Oasis Guest House** [★GS,NS,WI,WC,GO] 22 Edgerly Rd (at Westland) **617/267-2262, 800/230-0105** *in Back Bay*

Whitman House Inn [GS,NS,WI,GO] 17 Worcester St (at Norfolk St), Cambridge **617/945-5350, 617/913-6189**

■**BARS**

The Alley [★M,NH,D,B,K,WC,GO] 14 Pi Alley (at 275 Washington St) **617/263-1449** *10pm-2am, from noon wknds*

Boston Eagle [M,NH,WC] 520 Tremont St (near Berkeley) **617/542-4494** *3pm-2am, from noon Sun*

Boston Ramrod [★M,D,B,L,WC] 1254 Boylston St (at Ipswich, 1 block from Fenway Park) **617/266-2986** *noon-2am*

➤**Club Cafe Restaurant, Nightclub & Cabaret** [★MW,D,F,E,K,P,V,WC] 209 Columbus (at Berkeley) **617/536-0966** *4pm-2am, from noon Fri-Sat, Sun brunch from 11am*

Encore Lounge [GS,E,WC] 275 Tremont St (at Stuart St, in hotel) **617/728-2162** *5pm-2am, lounge & cabaret*

Fritz [★MW,NH,WC] 26 Chandler St (in the Chandler Inn) **617/482-4428** *noon-2am, brunch Sat-Sun, sports bar*

Jacque's [★M,TG,C,DS,$] 79 Broadway (at Stuart) **617/426-8902** *11am-midnight, from noon Sun*

Milky Way Lounge & Lanes [GS,F,E,K] 284 Amory St, Jamaica Plain **617/524-3740** *6pm-1am, live music, poetry, bowling, also restaurant*

Club Café

DINE DRINK DANCE

209 COLUMBUS AVE. IN BOSTON, MA USA
617 536 0966 CLUBCAFE.COM

Massachusetts • *USA*

Paradise [M,D,S,K,V] 180 Massachusetts Ave, Cambridge **617/868-3000** *9pm-1am, 7pm-2am Fri-Sat*

Ryles [GS,F,E] 212 Hampshire St (at Cambridge St, in Inman Square), Cambridge **617/876-9330** *great wknd jazz brunch*

Sister Sorel/ Tremont 647 [MW,NH,WC] 647 Tremont (at W Brookline) **617/266-4600** *dinner only, wknd brunch*

■NIGHTCLUBS

dbar [GS,D,WC] 1236 Dorchester Ave (at Hancock St), Dorchester **617/265-4490** *5pm-midnight, till 2am wknds, also restaurant, dinner nightly*

Epic Saturday [M,D] 15 Lansdowne St (House of Blues) **888/693-2583** *10:30pm Sat only*

The Estate [GS,D,19+,$] 1 Boylston Pl (at The Alley) **617/351-7000** *gay Th only for Glam Life*

Foxy [M,D] 474 Massachusetts Ave (at Zuzu), Cambridge **617/864-3278** *1st & 3rd Sun only, foxy boys*

The Glam Life [MW,D,19+,$] 1 Boylston Pl (at Estate) **617/351-7000** *Th only, hip-hop*

Hot Mess Sundays [M,D] 275 Tremont St (at Stuart St, at Underbar) **617/292-0080** *Sun only*

Machine [★M,D,V,S,YC,WC] 1254 Boylston St (at Park, below Boston Ramrod) **617/536-1950** *10pm-2am*

The Middle East [GF,A,F,E,YC,$] 472 Massachusetts Ave (in Central Square), Cambridge **617/864-3278** *11am-1am, till 2am wknds, live music*

►Napoleon Cabaret [★E,F,P,OC,WC] 209 Columbus (at Club Cafe) **617/536-0966** *nightly piano & vocals*

Rise [GS,D,PC] 306 Stuart St (btwn Berkeley & Arlington) **617/423-7473** *1am-6am 2nd Sat of the month only*

■CAFES

1369 Cafe 757 Massachusetts Ave (in Central Square), Cambridge **617/576-4600** *7am-11pm*

Berkeley Perk [F,WC,GO] 69 Berkeley St (at Chandler) **617/426-7375** *6:30am-5pm, from 7:30am Sat, clsd Sun*

Diesel Cafe [WC,GO] 257 Elm St (in Davis Square), Somerville **617/629-8717** *6am-11pm, from 7am wknds*

Fiore's Bakery [GO] 55 South St (at Bardwell), Jamaica Plain **617/524-9200** *7am-7pm, from 8am wknds, some vegan*

Francesca's [WC] 564 Tremont St (at Clarendon) **617/482-9026** *8am-11pm*

South End Buttery [WC] 314 Shawmut Ave (at Union Park St) **617/482-1015** *cupcakes! also brkfst, lunch & dinner, full bar*

■RESTAURANTS

28 Degrees 1 Appleton St (at Tremont St) **617/728-0728** *upscale restaurant & lounge*

BarLola [E] 160 Commonwealth Ave (at Dartmouth) **617/266-1122** *4pm-midnight*

Boston Pita Pit [WC] 479 Harvard St (at Commonwealth), Brookline **617/738-7482** *10am-midnight, till 2am wknds*

Casa Romero 30 Gloucester St (at Commonwealth) **617/536-4341** *dinner, Mexican, also bar*

Charlie's Sandwich Shoppe [WC] 429 Columbus Ave (at Pembroke St) **617/536-7669** *great brkfst, clsd Sun*

City Girl Cafe [BW,GO] 204 Hampshire St (at Inman), Cambridge **617/864-2809** *noon-10pm, from 10am Sat-Sun, clsd Mon, Italian, great sandwiches*

►Club Cafe [★E,P,V,WC] 209 Columbus (adjacent to Club Cafe) **617/536-0966** *dinner & Sun brunch, also 3 bars*

Geoffrey's Cafe 142 Berkeley St (at Columbus Ave) **617/424-6711** *11am-midnight, from 10am wknds, popular disco brunch*

Johnny D's Restaurant & Music Club [E,WC] 17 Holland St (in Davis Square), Somerville **617/776-2004** *dinner nightly, lunch Tb-Sun*

My Thai Cafe 3 Beach St, 2nd flr (at Washington) **617/451-2395** *11am-10pm, till 11pm Fri-Sat, Asian, vegetarian/ vegan*

Rabia's [WC] 73 Salem St (at Cross St) **617/227-6637** *11am-10:30pm, fine Italian*

Ristorante Lucia [WC] 415 Hanover St (at Harris) **617/367-2353** *great North End pasta*

Stella [WI,WC] 1525 Washington St (at W Brookline) **617/247-7747** *dinner & Sun brunch, full bar till 2am, also cafe 7am-3pm*

Trattoria Pulcinella 147 Huron Ave (at Concord), Cambridge **617/491-6336** *5pm-10pm, fine Italian*

Veggie Planet 47 Palmer St (at Club Passim), Cambridge **617/661-1513** *11:30am-10:30pm*

ENTERTAINMENT & RECREATION

Freedom Trail **617/357-8300** *start at the Visitor Information Center in Boston Common (at Tremont & West Sts), the most famous cow pasture & oldest public park in the US, then follow the red line to some of Boston's most famous sites*

New Repertory Theatre 321 Arsenal St, Watertown **617/923-8487 (box office), 617/923-7060**

Urban AdvenTours 103 Atlantic Ave (at Richmond St) **617/670-0637, 800/979-3370** *guided bike tours & bike rentals*

BOOKSTORES

Calamus Bookstore [★] 92-B South St **617/338-1931, 888/800-7300** *9am-7pm, noon-6pm, complete LGBT bookstore*

Trident Booksellers & Cafe [F,BW,WI,WC] 338 Newbury St (off Mass Ave) **617/267-8688** *8am-midnight*

PUBLICATIONS

Bay Windows **617/464-7280** *LGBT newspaper*

The Rainbow Times **413/282-8881, 617/444-9618** *bi-weekly LGBT news magazine for MA, northern CT & southern VT*

MEN'S SERVICES

➤**MegaMates** **617/423-6666** *Call to hook up with HOT local men. FREE to listen & respond to ads. Use FREE code DAMRON. MegaMates.com.*

EROTICA

Amazing Express 57 Stuart St **617/338-1252**

Good Vibrations [★WC] 308 Harvard St, Brookline **617/264-4400** *10am-9pm, till 10pm Th-Sat*

Hubba Hubba 534 Massachusetts Ave (at Brookline, in Central Square), Cambridge **617/492-9082** *fetish & drag gear*

CRUISY AREAS

Carson Beach [AYOR] William J Day Blvd

Charles River Esplanade [AYOR] *across foot bridge at end of Dartmouth St, near lagoon go to the right*

The Fens (FenwayVictory Gardens) [AYOR] *near the Ramrod bar*

Brookline

see Boston

Cambridge

see Boston

Cape Ann

RETAIL SHOPS

Bearskin Neck Leathers 7 Old Harbor Rd **978/546-2258** *10am-5pm, from noon Sun*

Cape Cod

see also Provincetown listings

INFO LINES & SERVICES

Gay/ Lesbian AA **508/775-7060** *call for info*

ACCOMMODATIONS

The Colonial House Inn & Restaurant [GF,SW,WI,GO] 277 Main St, Rte 6A (at Strawberry Ln), Yarmouthport **508/362-4348, 800/999-3416** *dinner & light brkfst included, jacuzzi, also restaurant & lounge*

Massachusetts • USA

Lamb & Lion Inn [GF,NS,SW,WI] 2504 Main St (Rte 6A), Barnstable **508/362-6823, 800/909-6923**

White Swan B&B [GF,NS,WI] 146 Manomet Point Rd, Plymouth **508/224-3759** *in 200-year-old farmhouse, open year-round, at mouth of Cape Cod*

Woods Hole Passage [GF,NS,WI] 186 Woods Hole Rd, Falmouth **508/548-9575, 800/790-8976** *full brkfst, near beaches*

■CRUISY AREAS

Boardwalk [AYOR] Jarvis St (off 6-A, exit 1), Sandwich *nights*

Crow's Pasture [AYOR] N on 6-A to South St, past cemetery, Dennis *in dunes*

Kalmus Park Beach [AYOR] end of Ocean St, Hyannis *behind parking lot*

Ryder Woods Conservation Area [AYOR] Rte 130 to Cotuit Rd (toward Mashpee for 3.5 miles), Sandwich *trails along the lake*

Skaket Beach [AYOR] Dennis *off to the right*

Chelsea

see Boston

Greenfield

■ACCOMMODATIONS

Brandt House [GF,NS,WI] 29 Highland Ave **413/774-3329, 800/235-3329** *16-rm estate on hill, full brkfst, formal garden*

■RESTAURANTS

Hope & Olive 44 Hope St **413/774-3150** *lunch & dinner, clsd Mon*

■BOOKSTORES

World Eye Bookshop 156 Main St (at Miles St) **413/772-2186** *9:30am-6:30pm, 9am-5pm Sat, 11am-4pm Sun, LGBT section*

Haverhill

■CAFES

Wicked Big Cafe [WI,WC,GO] 19 Essex St (at Wingate) **978/556-5656** *7am-4pm, 8am-1pm Sat, clsd Sun*

Ipswich

■CRUISY AREAS

Crane's Beach [AYOR] 1/2 mile to the right

Lenox

see Berkshires

Lowell

■EROTICA

Tower News 101 Gorham St **978/452-8693**

Lynn

■BARS

The Cirque [MW,NH,D,L,K,DS,V,GO] 47 Central Ave **781/586-0551** *11am-1am, DJ wknds*

Fran's Place [MW,D,WC] 776 Washington St (at Sagamore) **781/598-5618** *3pm-1am, also sports bar*

Martha's Vineyard

■ACCOMMODATIONS

Arbor Inn [GF,NS] 222 Upper Main St, Edgartown **508/627-8137, 888/748-4383** *some shared baths*

Martha's Vineyard Surfside Motel [GF,NS,WI,WC] 7 Oak Bluffs Ave, Oak Bluffs **508/693-2500, 800/537-3007**

The Shiverick Inn [GS,NS,WI,GO] 5 Pease's Pt Wy, Edgartown (at Pent Ln) **508/627-3797, 800/723-4292**

■RESTAURANTS

The Black Dog Tavern [WC] Beach St Extension #21 (at Water St) **508/693-9223** *brkfst, lunch & dinner, seasonal*

Le Grenier [BW] 96 Main St (at Drummer Ln), Vineyard Haven **508/693-4906** *dinner, French*

■BOOKSTORES

Bunch of Grapes 44 Main St (at Center St), Vineyard Haven **508/693-2291, 800/693-0221** *9am-6pm, 11am-5pm Sun, some LGBT titles*

Medford

■EROTICA

Amazing.net Video Store 423 Mystic Ave/ Rte 38 781/391-7438

New Bedford

■BARS

Le Place [★MW,D,K] 20 Kenyon St (at Belleville Ave) 508/990-1248 *2pm-2am*

■EROTICA

Amazing.net Video Store 10 Sconticut Neck Rd/Rte 6, Fairhaven 508/991-8191

Newton

see Boston

North Adams

see Berkshires

Northampton

see also Amherst

■ACCOMMODATIONS

Clarion Hotel & Conference Center [GF,SW,NS,WI,WC] 1 Atwood Dr 413/586-1211, 800/582-2929 *also restaurants & bar*

Corner Porches [GS,NS] 82 Baptist Corner Rd (at Main), Ashfield 413/628-4592 *30 minutes from Northampton*

The Hotel Northampton [GF,NS,WI,WC] 36 King St (near Bridge St) 413/584-3100, 800/547-3529 *cafe & historic tavern*

■NIGHTCLUBS

Diva's [★MW,D,E,K,DS,S,YC] 492 Pleasant St (at Conz St) 413/586-8161 *9pm-2am, clsd Sun-Mon, theme nights, [18+] Tue-Fri*

Pearl Street [GS,D,E,YC] 10 Pearl St (at Main) 413/586-8686 *7pm-1am, live music*

■CAFES

Haymarket Cafe [★F,WC] 185 Main St 413/586-9969 *7am-10pm, till 11pm Fri-Sat, also restaurant*

■RESTAURANTS

Bela [WC,GO] 68 Masonic St 413/586-8011 *noon-8:30pm, clsd Sun-Mon, vegetarian*

Bueno Y Sano 134 Main St (at Center St) 413/586-7311 *11am-10pm, till 9pm Sun, Mexican*

Paul & Elizabeth's [BW,WC] 150 Main St (in Thorne's Marketplace) 413/584-4832 *lunch & dinner, Sun brunch, seafood*

■ENTERTAINMENT & RECREATION

The Iron Horse 20 Center St (at Main) 413/586-8686 *5:30pm-close, live music, all ages*

■RETAIL SHOPS

Oh My A Sensuality Shop 122 Main St (at Center) 413/584-9669 *noon-7pm, till 8pm Fri-Sat, noon-5pm Sun*

Pride & Joy [WC,GO] 20A Crafts Ave (at Main) 413/727-3758 *open 7 days, LGBT books & gifts*

■PUBLICATIONS

▶**Metroline** 860/233-8334 *covers CT, RI & MA*

■CRUISY AREAS

Northampton Meadows [AYOR] next to the Connecticut River (dirt roads) *not far from I-91 rest areas*

Pulaski Park [AYOR] Main St *summer nights*

Provincetown

see also Cape Cod listings

■INFO LINES & SERVICES

Provincetown Business Guild 508/487-2313

■ACCOMMODATIONS

Admiral's Landing Guest House [M,NS,WI] 158 Bradford St (btwn Conwell & Pearl) 508/487-9665, 800/934-0925 *1860s Greek Revival home & studio efficiencies*

Aerie House & Beach Club [MW,WI,GO] 184 Bradford St (at Miller Hill) 508/487-1197, 800/487-1197

Massachusetts • USA

Ampersand Guesthouse [M,NS,WI,GO]
6 Cottage St (at Commercial)
508/487-0959, 800/574-9645

Anchor Inn Beach House [GS,NS,WC]
175 Commercial St (at Winthrop)
508/487-0432, 800/858-2657
private beach

Bayberry Accommodations
[MW,NS,WI,GO] 16 Winthrop St (at
Commercial) 508/487-4605,
800/422-4605

Beachfront Realty 139 Commercial St
508/487-1397 *vacation rentals*

Beaconlight Guest House
[M,NS,WI,GO] 12 Winthrop St (at
Bradford) 508/487-9603,
800/696-9603

Benchmark Inn [MW,SW,NS,WI,WC,GO]
6-8 Dyer St 508/487-7440,
888/487-7440

The Black Pearl Inn [MW,NS,WI,GO]
11 & 18 Pearl St (at Bradford)
508/487-0302, 800/761-1016
"friends of Bill welcome"

Boatslip Resort [★M,SW,GO] 161
Commercial St 508/487-1669,
877/786-9662 *seasonal, also several
bars & popular T-dance*

The Bradford Carver House
[MW,NS,WI,GO] 70 Bradford St
508/487-0728, 800/826-9083
*restored mid-19th-c home, centrally
located*

Brass Key Guesthouse
[★M,SW,NS,WI,WC,GO] 67 Bradford St
(at Carver) 508/487-9005,
800/842-9858

Captain's House B&B [M,B,NS,WI,GO]
350-A Commercial St (at Center)
508/487-9353, 800/457-8885

Carl's Guest House [MO,NS,NS,WI,GO]
68 Bradford St (at Court St)
508/487-1650 *sundeck*

Carpe Diem Guesthouse & Spa
[MW,NS,WI,GO] 12 Johnson St
508/487-4242, 800/487-0132

The Carriage House Guesthouse
[GS,GO] 7 Central St (at Commercial)
508/487-8855, 800/309-0248

Chicago House [MW,NS,WI,GO]
6 Winslow St (at Bradford)
508/487-0537, 800/733-7869
rooms & apts

Christopher's by the Bay
[MW,NS,WI,GO] 8 Johnson St (at
Commercial) 508/487-9263,
877/487-9263 *some shared baths,
patio*

The Clarendon House [GS,NS] 118
Bradford St (btwn Ryder & Alden)
508/487-1645, 800/669-8229

Crown & Anchor [MW,SW,NS,WI,GO]
247 Commercial St 508/487-1430
also cabaret & poolside bars

**Crowne Pointe Historic Inn & Shui
Spa** [MW,SW,NS,WI,WC,GO] 82 Bradford
St 508/487-6767, 877/276-9631
also restaurant

Designer's Dock [GS,WI,GO] 349
Commercial St 508/776-5746,
800/724-9888 *weekly condos in town
& on beach, seasonal*

Dexter's Inn [MW,NS,WI,GO] 6 Conwell
St (at Railroad) 508/487-1911,
888/521-1999 *sundeck*

Enzo [GS,WI] 186 Commercial St (at
Court) 508/487-7555,
888/873-5001 *Italian restaurant &
piano bar on premises*

Fairbanks Inn [★MW,NS,WI,GO] 90
Bradford St 508/487-0386,
800/324-7265 *parking*

Four Gables [GS,GO] 15 Race Rd
508/487-2427, 866/487-2427

Gabriel's at The Ashbrooke Inn
[★MW,NS,WI,GO] 102 Bradford St
508/487-3232 *full brkfst, hot tub*

The Gallery Inn [MW] 3 Johnson St (at
Commercial) 508/487-3010,
800/676-3010

Gifford House Inn [MW,WI,GO]
11 Carver St 508/487-0688,
800/434-0130 *seasonal, also several
bars & restaurant*

Grand View Inn [MW,NS,GO] 4 Conant
St (at Commercial) 508/487-9193,
888/268-9169

Harbor Hill at Provincetown [GF,GO]
4 Harbor Hill Rd 508/487-0541

Heritage House [MW,WI,GO] 7 Center St **508/487-3692** *shared baths, lesbian-owned*

The Inn at Cook Street [GF,NS,GO] 7 Cook St (at Bradford) **508/487-3894, 888/266-5655**

Inn at the Moors [GF,SW,NS,WI,GO] 59 Provincelands Rd **508/487-1342, 800/842-6379** *motel, across from Nat'l Seashore Province Lands, seasonal*

John Randall House [MW,NS,WI,GO] 140 Bradford St (at Center) **508/487-3533, 800/573-6700**

Land's End Inn [GS,NS,WI,GO] 22 Commercial St **508/487-0706, 800/276-7088**

Lotus Guest House [MW,WI,GO] 296 Commercial St (at Standish) **508/487-4644, 888/508-4644** *seasonal, decks, garden*

Moffett House [MW,GO] 296-A Commercial St (at Ryder) **508/487-6615, 800/990-8865**

Prince Albert Guest House [M,NS,WI,GO] 164-166 Commercial St (at Central) **508/487-1850**

Ravenwood Guest House [MW,NS,WC,GO] 462 Commercial St (at Cook) **508/487-3203** *private beach*

The Red Inn [GF,NS,WC,GO] 15 Commercial St (at Point) **508/487-7334, 866/473-3466**

Revere Guesthouse [MW,NS,GO] 14 Court St (btwn Commercial & Bradford) **508/487-2292, 800/487-2292**

Romeo's Holiday [MW,N,WI,GO] 97 Bradford St (btwn Gosnold & Masonic) **508/487-6636, 877/697-6636** *hot tub*

Rose & Crown Guest House [GS,GO] 158 Commercial St (at Central) **508/487-3332**

Sage Inn & Lounge [GS,NS,WC] 336 Commercial St **508/487-6424**

Sandbars [GS] 570 Shore Rd, Beach Pt, North Truro **508/487-8700**

Sandcastle Resort and Club [GS,SW,WI] 929 Commercial St **508/487-9300**

Seasons, An Inn for All [MW,NS,WI,GO] 160 Bradford St (at Pearl) **508/487-2283, 800/563-0113** *Victorian B&B, full brkfst*

The Secret Garden Inn [MW,NS] 300-A Commercial St **508/487-9027, 866/786-9646**

Snug Cottage [GS,NS,WI,GO] 178 Bradford St **508/487-1616, 800/432-2334**

Somerset House [MW,NS,WI,GO] 378 Commercial St (at Pearl) **508/487-0383, 800/575-1850**

Sunset Inn [MW,N,NS,WI,GO] 142 Bradford St (at Center) **508/487-9810, 800/965-1801** *seasonal, some shared baths*

Surfside Hotel & Suites [GS,SW,NS,WI] 543 Commercial (at Kendall Ln) **508/487-1726, 800/421-1726** *seasonal, waterfront hotel w/ lots of amenities, private beach*

The Tucker Inn [MW,NS,WI,GO] 12 Center St (at Bradford) **508/487-0381, 800/477-1867**

Victoria House [MW,WI,NS,GO] 5 Standish St **508/487-4455, 877/867-8696**

The Waterford [GS,WI] 386 Commercial St (at Pearl) **508/487-6400, 800/487-0784** *deck w/ full bar, also restaurant*

Watership Inn [M,WI,GO] 7 Winthrop St (at Commercial St) **508/487-0094, 800/330-9413**

West End Inn [GF,WI,NS,GO] 44 Commercial St **508/487-9555, 800/559-1220** *seasonal*

White Porch Inn [M,WI] 7 Johnson St **508/364-2549, 866/922-0333**

White Wind Inn [MW,WI,GO] 174 Commercial St (at Winthrop) **508/487-1526, 888/449-9463**

■BARS

The Boatslip Resort [★MW,D,F,YC] 161 Commercial St **508/487-1669, 877/786-9662** *seasonal, popular T-dance 4pm daily, special events, outdoor/ waterfront grill*

Massachusetts • USA

Governor Bradford [GF,F,E,K,DS] 312 Commercial St (at Standish) 508/487-2781 *11am-1am, from noon Sun, also restaurant in summer*

PiedBar [★MW,D,F,E,P,S,WC] 193-A Commercial St (at Court St) 508/487-1527 *seasonal May-Oct, noon-1am, mostly men 6:30pm-9:30pm at After Tea T-Dance*

Porchside Lounge [M,NH,P] 11 Carver St (in the Gifford House) 508/487-0688 *5pm-1am, Lobby Bar from 10pm, also restaurant*

Shipwreck Lounge [MW] 10 Carver St (at Bradford) 508/487-1472 *upscale lounge, outdoor seating w/ fire pit*

Vault [MO,B,L] 247 Commercial St (downstairs in the Crown & Anchor) 508/487-1430 *9pm-1am Th-Sun only*

Wave Video Bar [MW,NH,K] 247 Commercial St (in the Crown & Anchor) 508/487-1430 *6pm-1am, from noon in season, T-dance Sun*

■ NIGHTCLUBS

Atlantic House (The "A-House") [★M,D] 6 Masonic Pl 508/487-3169 *10pm-1am, 3 bars, weekly theme parties, also The Little Bar [M,NH] & the Macho Bar [M,L]*

Club Purgatory [MW,D,L] 9-11 Carver St (at Bradford St, in the Gifford House) 508/487-8442 *opens 7pm, from 9pm Sun (in season)*

Paramount [★MW,D,E,C,DS,$] in the Crown & Anchor 508/487-1430 *10pm-1am wknds, seasonal*

■ CAFES

Post Office Cafe Cabaret [MW,E] 303 Commercial St (upstairs) 508/487-3892 *8am-11pm, seasonal hours*

■ RESTAURANTS

Bayside Betsy's [WC] 177 Commercial St 508/487-6566 *lunch & dinner, brkfst wknds, bar till 10pm, on waterfront*

Big Daddy's Burritos 205 Commercial St 508/487-4432 *11am-10pm (May-Oct)*

Bubala's by the Bay [★] 183-185 Commercial 508/487-0773 *lunch & dinner, bar till 1am, patio*

Ciro & Sal's [R] 4 Kiley Ct (btwn Bangs St & Lovett's Ct) 508/487-6444 *dinner from 5:30pm, Northern Italian*

Fanizzi's [★WC] 539 Commercial St (at Kendall Lane) 508/487-1964

Front Street Restaurant [BW] 230 Commercial St 508/487-9715 *seasonal, bistro 6pm-10:30pm, bar till 1am*

Lobster Pot [WC] harborside (at 321 Commercial St) 508/487-0842 *11:30am-10pm (April-Nov)*

Lorraine's [★MW,BW,GO] 133 Commercial St (at Pleasant) 508/487-6074 *dinner, clsd Mon-Th off-season, Mexican*

The Mews Restaurant & Cafe [★E,WC] 429 Commercial St (at Bangs St) 508/487-1500 *dinner, seasonal Sun brunch, waterfront dining*

Napi's Restaurant [WC] 7 Freeman St 508/487-1145, 800/571-6274 *dinner (lunch Oct-April), int'l/ seafood*

The Red Inn [★GF,NS,WC,GO] 15 Commercial St (at Point) 508/487-7334, 866/473-3466 *dinner nightly, brunch Th-Sun, clsd Jan-April, reservations a must, full bar*

Relish 93 Commercial St 508/487-8077 *yummy baked goods, pick up a sandwich on the way to the beach!*

Spiritus Pizza [★] 190 Commercial St 508/487-2808 *noon-2am, great espresso shakes & late-night hangout for a slice*

■ ENTERTAINMENT & RECREATION

Art House Theatre & Cafe 214 Commercial St 508/487-9222

Art's Dune Tours [GO] 4 Standish St 508/487-1950, 800/894-1951 *day trips, sunset tours & charters through historic sand dunes & Nat'l Seashore Park*

Dolphin Fleet Whale Watch [GF,WC] 305 Commercial St 508/240-3636, 800/826-9300 *3-hr day & evening cruises*

Herring Cove Beach

Ptown Bikes [GO] 42 Bradford 508/487-8735 *9am-6pm, rentals*

Spaghetti Strip *nude beach, 1.5 miles S of Race Point Beach*

■ RETAIL SHOPS

HRC Action Center & Store 209-211 Commercial St 508/487-7736, 888/932-7472 *Human Rights Campaign merchandise & info*

Piercings by the Bearded Lady [GO] 336 Commercial St #4 508/487-7979 *noon-8pm, seasonal*

■ PUBLICATIONS

Provincetown Banner 167 Commercial St 508/487-7400 *newspaper*

Provincetown Magazine 508/487-1000 *seasonal, Provincetown's oldest weekly magazine*

■ GYMS & HEALTH CLUBS

Mussel Beach Health Club [MW] 35 Bradford St (btwn Montello & Conant) 508/487-0001 *6am-9pm, till 8pm in winter*

Provincetown Gym [MW] 82 Shank Painter Rd (at Winthrop) 508/487-2776

■ EROTICA

MG Leather Inc [GO] 338 Commercial St (at Standish St) 508/487-4036 *leather, fetish*

■ CRUISY AREAS

Dick Dock [AYOR] behind Boatslip Beach Club *late*

Herring Cove Beach [AYOR]

Quincy

see also Boston

■ NIGHTCLUBS

My House [MW,D,F,K] 609 Washington St (at Cleverly Ct) 617/302-4285 *6pm-1am, clsd Mon*

Randolph

■ BARS

Randolph Country Club/ RCC [★MW,D,F,K,C,S,V,SW,WC] 44 Mazzeo Dr 781/961-2414 *2pm-2am, from 10am summer, 2 dance clubs, cabaret, poolside grill, volleyball*

Raynham

■ EROTICA

Video Xtra 508/821-7800

Salisbury

■ BARS

Hobo's Club & Cafe [MW,NH,F,K,GO] 5 Broadway 978/465-4626

Somerville

see Boston

Springfield

■ BARS

Pure [M,NH,F,WC] 234 Chestnut St (E of Main) 413/205-1483 *noon-2am*

■ NIGHTCLUBS

Oz Nightclub [M,NH,D,K] 397 Dwight St (at Taylor) 413/732-4562 *7pm-2am, clsd Sun-Mon*

Xstatic [M,D,S] 240 Chestnut St (at Liberty) 413/736-2618, 800/710-2618 *7pm-2am, from 1pm wknds, nude dancers*

■ MEN'S SERVICES

➤**MegaMates** 413/271-3700 *Call to hook up with HOT local men. FREE to listen & respond to ads. Use FREE code DAMRON. MegaMates.com.*

Stoneham

■ CRUISY AREAS

Sheep's Fold Conservation Area [AYOR] Rte I-93 exit 33 (off Rte 28) *top of the hills*

Taunton

■ BARS

Bobby's Place [MW,D,F,K,DS] 62 Weir St (at Route 44, 138 & 140, at Taunton Green) 508/824-9997 *5pm-1am, till 2am Fri-Sat, from 2pm Sun*

Massachusetts • USA

Weymouth

▆EROTICA
Amazing.net Video Store 138 Bridge St (Rte 3A), North Weymouth 781/335-0446

Williamstown

see Berkshires

Worcester

▆BARS
MB Lounge [MW,NH,WI,WC,GO] 40 Grafton St (at Franklin) 508/799-4521 5pm-2am, from 3pm wknds

Mixers Cocktail Lounge [MW,D] 105 Water St 508/756-2227 6pm-2am, clsd Mon

▆NIGHTCLUBS
Club Remix [M,D,K] 105 Water St (at Harrison) 508/756-2227 9pm-2am, from 8pm Wed, clsd Mon-Tue

▆RETAIL SHOPS
Glamour Boutique 850 Southbridge St, Auburn 508/721-7800 large-size dresses, wigs, etc

▆PUBLICATIONS
Central Mass Pride Magazine centralmasspridemag.com

MICHIGAN

Statewide

▆PUBLICATIONS
Out Post 313/702-0272 bi-weekly nightlife guide for SE Michigan

Albion

▆EROTICA
The Lion's Den 2101 N Concord Rd (exit 127, off I-94) 517/531-5051 24hrs

Ann Arbor

▆INFO LINES & SERVICES
The Jim Toy Community Center 319 Braun Ct 734/995-9867 LGBT resource center, HIV testing 5pm-7pm Sun

Lesbian/ Gay AA 734/482-5700

▆BARS
\'aut\ Bar [★MW,NH,F,WC] 315 Braun Ct (at Catherine) 734/994-3677 4pm-2am, from 11am Sat, 10am Sun, patio

▆NIGHTCLUBS
The Necto [GS,D,V,18+,YC] 516 E Liberty (at Maynard) 734/994-5436 9pm-2am, theme nights, gay night Tue & Fri

▆CAFES
Cafe Verde [★F] 214 N Fourth Ave (at Catherine St) 734/994-9174 7am-9:30pm, 9am-8pm Sun, fair trade & organic coffee & tea

▆RESTAURANTS
Dominick's [BW,WC] 812 Monroe St (at Tappan Ave) 734/662-5414 10am-10pm, clsd Sun, Italian, full bar

The Earle [BW,WC] 121 W Washington (at Ashley) 734/994-0211 5:30pm-9pm, till 11pm Fri-Sat, 5pm-8pm Sun

Seva 314 E Liberty (at 5th Ave) 734/662-1111 11am-9pm, from 10am wknds, vegetarian, also cafe & wine bar

Zingerman's Delicatessen [GO] 422 Detroit St (at Kingsley) 734/663-3354, 888/636-8162 7am-10pm, also ship food worldwide

▆ENTERTAINMENT & RECREATION
The Ark [GF,E] 316 S Main St (btwn William & Liberty) 734/761-1818, 734/761-1800 concert house

▆BOOKSTORES
Common Language [WC] 317 Braun Ct (at 4th) 734/663-0036 11am-10pm, till midnight Fri-Sat, till 7pm Sun, LGBT

Crazy Wisdom Books & Tea Room 114 S Main St (btwn Huron & Washington) 734/665-2757 11am-9pm, till 11pm Fri-Sat, 11am-8pm Sun

Battle Creek

▆NIGHTCLUBS
Partners [MW,D,K,S,V,WC] 910 North Ave (at Morgan) 269/964-7276 7pm-2am, clsd Mon

▆EROTICA
Romantix Adult Superstore 690 W Michigan Ave (at Grand) 269/964-3070

Bay City

■BARS

Malickey's Pub [GS,DS] 501 S Madison 989/414-6667 *11:30am-1:30am*

Bellaire

■ACCOMMODATIONS

Applesauce Inn B&B [GF,WI,NS] 7296 S M-88 231/533-6448 *B&B in 100-year-old farmhouse*

Bellaire B&B [GS,WI,GO] 212 Park St (at Antrim) 231/533-6077, 800/545-0780 *stately 1879 home, full brkfst*

Big Bay

■ACCOMMODATIONS

Big Bay Depot Motel [GF,WI,GO] 906/345-9350

Big Rapids

■EROTICA

Fantasies Unlimited 13480 Northland Dr (at Arthur Rd) 231/792-8052

Cheboygan

■EROTICA

Fantasies Unlimited 1116 E State St 231/627-4665

Copemish

■ACCOMMODATIONS

Jeralan's Farm B&B [GF,NS] 18361 Viaduct Rd (at Simpson Rd) 231/378-2926, 866/250-8444 *1872 farmhouse on 80 acres of woods & ponds*

Detroit

■INFO LINES & SERVICES

Affirmations Helpline 290 W 9 Mile Rd (at Planavon), Ferndale 800/398-4297 *4pm-9pm, clsd Sun, support & resources line*

Helpline 800/398-4297 *4pm-9pm Tue-Sat, support & resources line*

■ACCOMMODATIONS

The Atheneum Suite Hotel [GF,WI,WC] 1000 Brush Ave (at Lafayette) 313/962-2323, 800/772-2323

Detroit Marriott at the Renaissance Center [GF,WC] 400 Renaissance Center Dr 313/568-8000, 800/228-9290

Honor & Folly [GS,WI] 2138 Michigan Ave (above Slows BBQ) *design-focused B&B; cooking classes, bike rentals & goods made by local designers & artisans*

Milner Hotel [GF] 1538 Centre St (at Grand River Ave) 313/963-3950, 877/645-6377

■BARS

Adam's Apple [M,NH,K,GO] 18931 W Warren Ave (at Artesian) 313/240-8482 *3pm-2am, from noon wknds*

Centaur Bar [GS,F] 2233 Park Ave (at W Montcalm St) 313/963-4040 *4pm-2am*

Club Gold Coast [★M,D,DS,S,WI,WC] 2971 E 7 Mile Rd (at Conant) 313/366-6135 *7pm-2am, male dancers nightly*

Gigi's [M,D,TG,K,DS,S,GO] 16920 W Warren (at Clayburn, enter rear) 313/584-6525 *noon-2am, from 2pm wknds*

Hayloft Saloon [M,NH,B,L,OC,WI,WC] 8070 Greenfield Rd (S of Joy Rd) 313/581-8913 *3pm-2am*

Male Box Bar [M,NH,D,K,DS,18+,GO] 23365 Hoover Rd (N of 9 Mile), Warren 313/893-7696 *2pm-2am*

Menjo's [★M,D,K,V,YC] 928 W McNichols Rd (at Hamilton) 313/863-3934 *1pm-2am, popular happy hour*

Other Side Lounge [M,NH,D,K,DS,WI,GO] 4933 E 7 Mile Rd 313/305-7793 *4pm-2am*

Otherside Lounge [M,K,S,WI] 4933 E 7 Mile Rd 313/305-7793 *4pm-2am*

Pronto [★MW,F,V] 608 S Washington (at 6th St), Royal Oak 248/544-7900 *11am-2am, patio*

R&R Saloon [M,NH,D,L,F,WI] 7330 Michigan Ave (at Central) 313/849-2751 *2pm-2am, till 5am Wed & wknds*

Michigan • *USA*

Soho [MW,K] 205 W 9 Mile (at Woodward), Ferndale **248/542-7646** *4pm-close, from 6pm wknds*

The Woodward Video Bar & Grill [★M,D,MR,F,K,V] 6426 Woodward Ave (at Milwaukee, rear entrance) **313/872-0166** *2pm-2am*

The Works Detroit [GS,D,V] 1846 Michigan Ave (at Rosa Parks) **313/961-1742** *10pm-3am Th, till 5am Fri-Sat, mostly gay Sat*

■ NIGHTCLUBS

Escape [MW,NH,F,DS,GO] 19404 Sherwood (at 7 Mile) **313/892-1765** *10pm-5am*

Hellbound **248/541-3979** *this party is held at various nightclubs & venues in the Detroit area every 2 to 3 months; check www.noirleather.com*

Leland City Club [GF,D,A,18+] 400 Bagley St (at Leland Hotel) **313/962-2300** *10pm-4:30am Fri-Sat, goth/ alternative crowd*

Luna [GF,D,A] 1815 N Main St (at 12 Mile), Royal Oak **248/589-3344** *from 9pm, clsd Sun-Tue, theme nights*

The Rainbow Room [MW,D,K,DS,18+] 6640 E 8 Mile Rd (at Sherwood) **313/891-1020** *7pm-2am Wed-Sun*

Stiletto's [MW,D,DS,E,K] 1641 Middlebelt Rd (btwn Michigan Ave & Cherry Hill Rd), Inkster **734/729-8980** *8pm-2am Th-Sun*

Temple [GS,D,MR-AF,TG,WC] 2906 Cass Ave (btwn Charlotte & Temple) **313/832-2822** *1pm-2am, popular wknds*

■ CAFES

Avalon International Breads [GO] 422 W Willis (at Cass) **313/832-0008** *6am-6pm, clsd Sun-Mon*

Coffee Beanery Cafe [WI] 28557 S Woodward Ave (S of 12 Mile), Berkley **248/336-9930** *7am-11pm*

Five 15 [E,WI,GO] 515 S Washington St, Royal Oak **248/515-2551** *11am-5pm, till 5pm Sun, clsd Mon, Drag Bingo Fri-Sat, performances, art shows*

Trixie's Cafe [E] 25925 Gratiot Ave, Roseville *noon-1am, from 6pm Sun, hosts open mics*

■ RESTAURANTS

Amici's 3249 12 Mile Rd (at Gardner Ave), Berkley **248/544-4100** *gourmet pizza & martinis*

Atlas Global Bistro 3111 Woodward Ave (at Charlotte) **313/831-2241** *lunch & dinner, Sun brunch, American/ int'l, upscale*

Cacao Tree Cafe 204 W 4th St, Royal Oak **248/336-9043** *9am-9pm, gourmet raw food/ vegan*

Cass Cafe [WI] 4620 Cass Ave (at Forest) **313/831-1400** *11am-2am, 5pm-1am Sun, full bar*

Coach Insignia 200 Renaissance Ctr, 71st Fl **313/567-2622** *dinner, clsd Sun, steakhouse*

Como's [WC] 22812 Woodward (at 9 Mile), Ferndale **248/548-5005** *11am-2am, till 4am Fri-Sat, Italian, full bar, patio*

Elwood Bar & Grill 300 Adams (at Brush, by Comerica Park) **313/962-2337** *11am-8pm, till 2pm Mon, clsd Sun (unless there's a Tiger's game); Art Deco diner*

Inn Season 500 E 4th St (at Knowles), Royal Oak **248/547-7916** *lunch & dinner, Sun brunch, clsd Mon, organic vegetarian/ vegan*

La Dolce Vita [MW,WC] 17546 Woodward Ave (at McNichols) **313/865-0331** *lunch & dinner, Sun brunch, clsd Mon, Italian, patio*

Mercury Burger & Bar 2163 Michigan Ave **313/964-5000** *11am-11pm*

One-Eyed Betty's [GO] 175 W Troy, Ferndale **248/808-6633** *4pm-2am, from 9am wknds*

Pete's Place Broadway Cafe [BYOB,WI,WC] 1225 Woodward Hts (at Hilton Rd), Ferndale **248/544-4215** *3pm-10pm, brunch wknds*

Red Star 13944 Michigan Ave, Dearborn **313/581-1451** *Chinese, plenty veggie/ vegan*

Roast 1128 Washington Ave (at State St) **313/961-2500** *dinner nightly, steakhouse*

Seva 66 E Forest **313/974-6661** *11am-9pm, till 11pm Fri-Sat, vegetarian*

Sweet Lorraine's Cafe & Bar [★WC] 29101 Greenfield Rd (at 12 Mile), Southfield 248/559-5985 *11am-10pm, till 11pm Fri-Sat, till 9:30pm Sun*

Traffic Jam & Snug [WC] 511 W Canfield St (at SE corner of 2nd Ave) 313/831-9470 *11am-10:30pm, till midnight Fri-Sat, till 9pm Sun, also full bar, bakery, dairy & brewery*

Vivio's [WC] 2460 Market St (at Napoleon St) 313/393-1711 *lunch & dinner, clsd Sun, full bar*

Wolfgang Puck Grille 1777 3rd St (at the MGM Grand Hotel) 313/465-1648 *5pm-10pm, 9am-2pm Sat-Sun, clsd Mon-Tue*

■ ENTERTAINMENT & RECREATION

Charles H Wright Museum of African American History 315 E Warren Ave (at Cass) 313/494-5800

Motown Historical Museum 2648 W Grand Blvd 313/875-2264

■ BOOKSTORES

Just 4 Us [GO] 211 W 9 Mile Rd (at Woodward), Ferndale 248/547-5878 *11am-8pm, till 10pm Th-Fri, till 5pm Sun, also cafe*

■ RETAIL SHOPS

Royal Oak Tattoo 820 S Washington Ave (at Lincoln), Royal Oak 248/398-0052 *tattoo & piercing studio*

■ PUBLICATIONS

Between the Lines 734/293-7200 *statewide LGBT weekly*

Metra Magazine PO Box 71844, Madison Heights 48071 248/543-3500 *covers IN, IL, MI, OH, PA, WI & Ontario, Canada*

■ MEN'S CLUBS

Body Zone Health Club [MO,V,18+,PC,GO] 1617 E McNichols (at I-75) 313/366-9663 *24hrs*

TNT Health Club [MO,V,18+,PC,GO,$] 13333 W 8 Mile Rd (at Schaefer, enter rear) 313/341-7250 *11am-8pm*

■ MEN'S SERVICES

➤**MegaMates** 313/962-5000 *Call to hook up with HOT local men. FREE to listen & respond to ads. Use FREE code DAMRON. MegaMates.com.*

■ EROTICA

Blue Moon Video 7041 W 8 Mile Rd (2 blocks W of Livernois) 313/340-1730 *11am-1am, till 10pm Sun*

Escape Adult Bookstore 18728 W Warren Ave (8 blocks W of Southfield) 313/336-6558 *10am-midnight, from noon Sun*

Noir Leather [WC] 124 W 4th St (at S Center St), Royal Oak 248/541-3979 *11am-9pm, till 10pm Fri-Sat, noon-7pm Sun*

Uptown Book Store 16541 Woodward Ave (at 6 Mile Rd), Highland Park 313/869-9477

Douglas

see Saugatuck

Escanaba

■ EROTICA

Sensual Arts Adult Bookstore [GO] 615 N Lincoln Rd (at 6th Ave N) 906/786-9020

Flint

■ BARS

MI [★MW,D,MR,WI] 2406 N Franklin Ave (at Belle Ave) 810/234-9481 *5pm-2am*

Pachyderm Pub [MW,NH,D,MR,TG,K,F,WI,GO] G-1408 E Hemphill Rd (btwn I-475 & Saginaw St), Burton 810/744-4960 *3pm-2am, from 5pm wknds, patio*

State Bar [★MW,D,K,WC] 2512 S Dort Hwy (at Lippincott) 810/767-7050 *2pm-2am*

■ NIGHTCLUBS

Club Triangle [★MW,D,S,18+] 2101 S Dort (at Lippincott) 810/767-7550 *9pm-close Wed-Sun*

Pride Night at Purple Moon [MW,D] 2525 S Dort Hwy 810/424-9579 *9pm-2am 1st Mon only*

Michigan • *USA*

◼CAFES

The Good Beans Cafe [E,WI,WC,GO]
328 N Grand Traverse (at 1st Ave)
810/237-4663 *7:30am-4pm, till 9pm
Th-Fri, open some wknds*

◼MEN'S SERVICES

▶**MegaMates** 810/597-0597 *Call to
hook up with HOT local men. FREE to
listen & respond to ads. Use FREE code
DAMRON. MegaMates.com.*

Frankfort

◼ACCOMMODATIONS

Wayfarer Lodgings [GF,NS,WI] 1912 S
Scenic Hwy (M-22) 231/352-9264,
800/735-8564

Grand Rapids

◼INFO LINES & SERVICES

**Lesbian/ Gay Network of W
Michigan** 343 Atlas Ave SE (behind
Spirit Dreams in Eastown)
616/458-3511 *11am-5:30pm, clsd
wknds*

◼ACCOMMODATIONS

Radisson Riverfront Hotel
[GF,NS,SW,WI,WC] 270 Ann St NW (at
Turner Ave) 616/363-9001,
800/395-7046

◼BARS

Apartment Lounge [M,NH,WC] 33
Sheldon NE (at Library) 616/451-0815
1pm-2am, from noon wknds

Diversions [★MW,D,K,V,18+,WC] 10
Fountain St NW (at Division)
616/451-3800 *8pm-2am*

Pub 43 [MW,NH,F] 43 S Division St (at
Weston) 616/458-2205 *3pm-2am*

◼NIGHTCLUBS

Rumors Nightclub
[MW,D,DS,K,S,V,WC,GO] 69 S Division Ave
(at Oakes St) 616/454-8720 *4pm-
2am*

◼RESTAURANTS

Brandywine 1345 Lake Dr SE (in East
Town) 616/774-8641 *7am-8pm, from
7:30am Sat, 8am-2:30pm Sun*

Cherie Inn [WC] 969 Cherry St SE (at
Lake Dr) 616/458-0588 *7am-3pm,
from8am wknds, clsd Mon*

Gaia Cafe 209 Diamond Ave SE (at
Cherry St) 616/454-6233 *8am-8pm,
till 3pm wknds, clsd Mon, vegetarian*

◼MEN'S CLUBS

Diplomat Health Club [PC] 2324
Division Ave (at Whithey)
616/452-3754 *24hrs*

◼EROTICA

Cina-Mini I 415 Bridge St NW
616/454-7531 *also at 1358 Plainfield
NE, Th-Sat only*

Grayling

◼EROTICA

Fantasies Unlimited 6131 M-72 West
989/348-4665

Houghton

◼EROTICA

Backroom Multi Entertainment [GO]
109 Sheldon Ave (at Bridge)
906/482-0637

Kalamazoo

◼INFO LINES & SERVICES

**Kalamazoo Gay/ Lesbian Resource
Center** 629 Pioneer St 269/349-4234
9am,-5pm, clsd wknds

Lansing

◼BARS

Esquire [MW,NH,K] 1250 Turner St (at
Clinton) 517/487-5338 *3pm-2am*

◼NIGHTCLUBS

Spiral [M,D,S,DS,18+,WC] 1247 Center St
(at Clinton) 517/371-3221 *8pm-2am,
clsd Mon-Tue, theme nights*

X-cel [★GF,D,K,S,YC,$] 224 S
Washington Square (at Washtenaw St)
517/484-2399, 517/281-9502 *9pm-
2am, clsd Mon*

◼BOOKSTORES

Everybody Reads 2019 E Michigan Ave
517/346-9900 *11am-7pm, 10am-
4pm Sun, cool general bookstore, also
coffeehouse*

Saugatuck • Michigan

■RETAIL SHOPS

Splash of Color 515 E Grand River Ave, Ste F (at Division), East Lansing **517/333-0990** *tattoo & piercing studio*

■MEN'S SERVICES

▶**MegaMates 517/318-0333** *Call to hook up with HOT local men. FREE to listen & respond to ads. Use FREE code DAMRON. MegaMates.com.*

■EROTICA

Fantasies Unlimited 3208 S MLK Blvd (at Southland Ave) **517/393-1159**

Marquette

■ACCOMMODATIONS

The Landmark Inn [GF,NS,WI] 230 N Front St (at Ridge St) **906/228-2580, 888/752-6362** *historic boutique hotel overlooking Lake Superior, restaurant & bar*

■CRUISY AREAS

Presque Isle Point [AYOR]

Mount Pleasant

■CRUISY AREAS

Mission Creek Park [AYOR] Harris St *summers*

Petoskey

■ACCOMMODATIONS

Coach House Inn [GF,WI,NS,GO] 1011 N US 31 (at Mitchell) **231/347-8281, 877/347-8088** *basic amenities*

Pontiac

■BARS

Liberty Bar [MW,D,F] 85 N Saginaw **248/758-0771** *11:30am-2am, from 2pm wknds*

■NIGHTCLUBS

Manductive [M,D] 40 W Pike St (at Reunion nightclub) *check www.maductive.com for upcoming parties*

■EROTICA

Fantasies Unlimited 974 Joslyn Ave **248/338-2442**

■CRUISY AREAS

Hawthorne Park [AYOR] N Telegraph Rd (at Dixie Hwy)

Port Huron

■NIGHTCLUBS

Seekers [MW,D,DS] 3301 24th St (btwn Oak & Little) **810/985-9349** *7pm-2am*

■CRUISY AREAS

Pine Grove Park [AYOR]

Saginaw

■NIGHTCLUBS

The Mixx Nightclub [MW,D,F,K,V,18+,WC] 115 N Hamilton St (at Court St) **989/498-4022** *5pm-close Th-Sun*

Saugatuck

■ACCOMMODATIONS

Beechwood Manor Inn & Cottage [GS,NS,WI,GO] 736 Pleasant St (at Allegan) **269/857-1587, 877/857-1583**

Bella Vita Spa & Suites [GF,WI] 119 Butler St **269/857-8482** *upscale, modern suites overlooking downtown Saugatuck; also day spa*

The Belvedere Inn & Restaurant [GF,NS,WI] 3656 63rd St **269/857-5777, 877/858-5777** *full brkfst*

Bird Center Resort [GF,WI] 584-586 Lake St **269/857-1750** *cottages across from Sautatuck Harbo*

The Bunkhouse B&B at Campit [MW,SW,NS,WI,GO] **269/543-4335, 877/226-7481**

Campit Outdoor Resort [MW,SW,WI,GO] 6635 118th Ave, Fennville **269/543-4335, 877/226-7481** *seasonal, campsites & RV hookups, membership required*

Douglas House B&B [GS,NS,GO] 41 Spring St (at Wall St), Douglas **269/857-1119** *near gay beach*

The Dunes Resort [MW,D,TG,F,E,DS,SW,WC,GO] 333 Blue Star Hwy, Douglas **269/857-1401**

Michigan • USA

Hidden Garden Cottages & Suites
[GF,NS,WI] 247 Butler St
269/857-8109, 888/857-8109

Hillby Thatch Cottages [GS,NS] 1438-1440 71st St, Glenn **847/864-3553**

The Hunter's Lodge [GS,NS,WI,GO] 2790 68th St (at US 31), Fennville **269/857-5402** *vintage rustic log cabin*

J Paules Fenn Inn [GF,NS] 2254 S 58th St, Fennville **269/561-2836, 877/561-2836** *full brkfst*

The Kingsley House B&B
[GF,NS,WI,GO] 626 West Main St, Fennville **269/561-6425, 866/561-6425** *full brkfst*

Kirby House [GS,SW,NS,WI,GO] 294 Center St (at Blue Star Hwy) **269/857-2904, 800/521-6473** *full brkfst*

Maple Ridge Cottages [GS,NS,GO] 713-719 Maple **269/857-5211 (Pines #)** *quaint cottages, hot tubs*

The Newnham SunCatcher Inn
[GF,SW,NS,WI] 131 Griffith (at Mason) **269/857-4249, 800/587-4249**

The Park House Inn B&B [GF,NS,WI] 888 Holland St **269/857-4535, 866/321-4535** *B&B in one of Saugatuck's oldest residences*

The Pines Motor Lodge & Cottages
[GS,NS,WI,GO] 56 Blue Star Hwy (at Center St), Douglas **269/857-5211** *boutique retro motel, also retro gift gallery*

The Spruce Cutter's Cottage [GS,GO] 6670 126th Ave (at Blue Star Hwy & M-89), Fennville **269/543-4285, 800/493-5888**

◼BARS

Dunes Disco [MW,D,TG,E,C,DS,GO] 333 Blue Star Hwy (at the Dunes Resort) **269/857-1401** *9am-2am*

◼CAFES

Uncommon Grounds [WI] 127 Hoffman (at Water) **269/857-3333** *6:30am-10pm, coffee & juice bar*

◼RESTAURANTS

Back Alley Pizza Joint 22 Main St (at Center), Douglas **269/857-7277** *11am-10pm, till 11pm Fri-Sat*

Chequers 220 Culver St **269/857-1868** *11:30am-9pm, seasonal, great fish & chips*

Everyday People Cafe [E,WC] 11 Center St (at Main), Douglas **269/857-4240** *call for hours*

Kalico Kitchen [WC] 312 Ferry St, Douglas **269/857-2678** *7am-9pm winter, clsd summer*

Marro's Italian [D] 147 Water St (at Mason St) **269/857-4248** *dinner only, clsd Mon-Tue, nightclub till 2am Fri-Sat*

Monroe's Cafe-Grille 302 Culver St (at Griffith) **269/857-1242** *8am-9pm, clsd Nov-March*

Phil's Bar & Grille 215 Butler St (at Mason) **269/857-1555** *11:30am-10pm, till 11pm Fri-Sat, patio*

Pumpernickel's [WI] 202 Butler St (at Mason) **269/857-1196** *8am-4pm*

Restaurant Toulouse [R,E,WC] 248 Culver **269/857-1561** *dinner nightly, lunch wknds (seasonal), full bar*

Scooters 322 Culver St (at Griffith) **269/857-1041** *noon-9pm, till 10pm wknds, clsd Tue, great pizza*

The White House Bistro [E] 149 Griffith (at Mason) **269/857-3240** *4pm-10pm, 9am-midnight Sat, 9am-9pm Sun, live music*

Wicks Park [E,WC] 449 Water St **269/857-2888** *dinner nightly, live music wknds*

Wild Dog Grill 24 W Center St (at Spring), Douglas **269/857-2519** *dinner nightly, from noon wknds, clsd Mon-Tue*

◼ENTERTAINMENT & RECREATION

Earl's Farm Market [GO] 1630 Blue Star Hwy, Fennville **269/227-2074** *8am-9pm May-Oct only, pick your own berries!*

Oval Beach consult local map for driving directions, Douglas *popular beach on Lake Michigan*

Tulip Time Festival Holland **800/822-2770**

■RETAIL SHOPS

Amaru Leather 322 Griffith St (at Hoffman St) **269/857-3745** *"original & custom creations in leather by two resident designers"*

Groovy! Groovy! Retro Gift Gallery [GO] 56 Blue Star Hwy (at Center St), Douglas **269/857-5211** *seasonal hours, antiques, funky gifts & goods*

Hoopdee Scootee 133 Mason (at Butler) **269/857-4141** *seasonal, clothing, gifts*

Saugatuck Drug Store 201 Butler St (at Mason) **269/857-2300** *seasonal, old-fashioned corner drug store, including actual soda fountain!*

■GYMS & HEALTH CLUBS

Pump House Gym 6492 Blue Star Hwy (at 135th) **269/857-7867** *day passes*

■CRUISY AREAS

Oval Beach [AYOR] *walk north*

South Haven

■ACCOMMODATIONS

Yelton Manor B&B [GS,NS,WI,WC] 140 North Shore Dr (at Dyckman) **269/637-5220** *full brkfst*

St Ignace

■ACCOMMODATIONS

Budget Host Inn & Suites [GF,SW,WI,WC] 700 N State St **906/643-9666, 800/872-7057**

Traverse City

■ACCOMMODATIONS

Neahtawanta Inn [GF,SW,NS,WI,WC] 1308 Neahtawanta Rd (at Peninsula Dr) **231/223-7315, 800/220-1415** *sauna*

■NIGHTCLUBS

Side Traxx [MW,D,V,GO] 520 Franklin St (at E 8th) **231/935-1666** *5pm-2am, cruise bar*

■BOOKSTORES

The Bookie Joint 124 S Union St (btwn State & Front) **231/946-8862** *noon-6pm, clsd Sun, pride gifts, used books*

■CRUISY AREAS

Westend Beach Hwy 31 (N of Munson Hospital)

Union Pier

■ACCOMMODATIONS

Blue Fish Guest House & Cottage [GS,NS,GO] 10234 Community Hall Rd **269/469-0468 x112** *cottages & guesthouses*

Fire Fly Resort [GS,NS,GO] 15657 Lakeshore Rd **269/469-0245** *1- & 2-bdrm units*

Ypsilanti

see Ann Arbor

MINNESOTA

Bemidji

■CRUISY AREAS

Diamond Point Park [AYOR] *summers*

The Indian Trail [AYOR] below Lake Blvd (btwn 10th & 12th St)

Duluth

see also Superior, Wisconsin

■ACCOMMODATIONS

The Olcott House B&B Inn [GF,NS,WI,GO] 2316 E 1st St (at 23rd Ave) **218/728-1339, 800/715-1339**

■CAFES

Jitters [WI] 102 W Superior St **218/720-6015** *7am-7pm, 9am-1pm Sun*

■BOOKSTORES

At Sara's Table Chester Creek Cafe [E,WI,WC] 1902 E 8th St (at 19th) **218/724-6811** *7am-8pm*

■MEN'S CLUBS

Duluth Family Sauna 18 N 1st Ave E **218/726-1388** *noon-10:30pm*

■EROTICA

Wabasha Books 114 E 1st St **218/723-1980**

Minnesota • *USA*

Lanesboro

■ACCOMMODATIONS
Stone Mill Hotel & Suites
[GS,NS,WI,WC,GO] 100 E Beacon St (at
Parkway Ave) 507/467-8663,
866/897-8663

Mankato

■CAFES
The Coffee Hag [E,WC] 329 N
Riverfront Dr 507/387-5533 *7am-
10pm, till 11pm Fri-Sat*

■EROTICA
Pure Pleasure 2102 N Riverfront Dr
507/388-6871 *24hrs*

Minneapolis/ St Paul

■INFO LINES & SERVICES
AA Intergroup 952/922-0880

OutFront Minnesota 310 E 38th St
#204, Minneapolis 612/822-0127,
800/800-0350 *info line w/ 24hr pre-
recorded visitor info*

Quatrefoil Library 1619 Dayton Ave
#105, St Paul 651/641-0969 *7pm-
9pm, 10am-5pm Sat, 1pm-5pm Sun,
LGBT resource center*

■ACCOMMODATIONS
The Depot Renaissance Minneapolis
[GF,F] 225 3rd Ave S, Minneapolis
612/375-1700, 866/211-4611

Graves 601 Hotel [GF,NS,WI] 601 1st
Ave N (at 6th St N), Minneapolis
612/677-1100, 866/523-1100

Hotel 340 [GF,SW,WI] 340 Cedar St
651/280-4120

Water Street Inn [GF,WI,WC] 101 S
Water St, Stillwater 651/439-6000
also restaurant & pub]

■BARS
19 Bar [M,NH,WC] 19 W 15th St (at
Nicollet Ave), Minneapolis
612/871-5553 *3pm-2am, from 1pm
wknds*

Bev's Wine Bar [GF,F,WC] 250 3rd Ave
N #100 (at Washington Ave),
Minneapolis 612/337-0102 *4:30pm-
1am, patio*

Brass Rail [★M,K,P,S,V,WC] 422
Hennepin Ave (at 4th), Minneapolis
612/332-7245 *noon-2am*

Bryant Lake Bowl [GF,F,E,WC] 810 W
Lake St (near Bryant), Minneapolis
612/825-3737 *8am-2am, bar, theater
& bowling alley*

Camp Bar [★M,D,F,K,S,V,WC] 490 N
Robert St (at 9th St), St Paul
651/292-1844 *4pm-2am, bear party
4th Fri*

Eagle Bolt Bar [M,B,L,F] 515
Washington Ave S (btwn Portland & 5th
Ave), Minneapolis 612/338-4214
*4pm-2am, from 10am Sat-Sun, beer
bust Sun, also Bolt underground dance
bar*

Jetset [MW,D,K] 115 N First St (at 1st
Ave N), Minneapolis 612/339-3933
5pm-close, from 6pm Sat, clsd Sun-Mon

Lush Food Bar [MW,D,C,DS,F] 990
Central Ave (at Spring St), Minneapolis
*8am-2am, clsd Mon, brunch served
everyday till 2pm*

Lush Food Bar [MW,D,F] 990 Central
Avenue NE, Minneapolis
612/612-0000 *8am-2am, clsd Mon*

The Town House
[★MW,D,E,F,K,C,DS,P,GO] 1415 University
Ave W (at Elbert), St Paul
651/646-7087 *2pm-2am, from noon
wknds*

■NIGHTCLUBS
The Boys Present [M,D] Minneapolis
*seasonal monthly party,check
www.theboyspresent.com*

Gay 90s [★MW,D,MR,F,E,K,DS,18+,WC]
408 Hennepin Ave (at 4th St S),
Minneapolis 612/333-7755 *8am-2am
(dinner Wed-Sun), also Men's Room
[MO,L]*

Ground Zero [★GS,D,S,WC] 15 NE 4th
St (at Hennepin), Minneapolis
612/378-5115 *10pm-2am Th-Sat
only, more gay Sat for Bondage-A-Go-
Go*

Kitty Cat Klub [GF,F,E] 315 14th Ave SE
(at SE University Ave) 612/331-9800
lounge w/ eclectic decor, live bands

The Saloon [★M,D,F,S,YC,WC,GO] 830 Hennepin Ave (at 9th), Minneapolis 612/332-0835 *noon-2am, from 11am Sun*

▪CAFES

Anodyne at 43rd [F,E,WC] 4301 Nicollet Ave S (at 43rd), Minneapolis 612/824-4300 *7am-10pm, till 8pm Fri-Sun*

Black Dog Coffee & Wine Bar [F] 308 Prince St (at Broadway), St Paul 651/228-9274 *7am-10pm, till 9pm Sat, 8am-8pm Sun*

Blue Moon [WI,GO] 3822 E Lake St, Minneapolis 612/721-9230 *7am-10pm, from 8am wknds*

Cahoots [WI,WC] 1562 Selby Ave (at Snelling), St Paul 651/644-6778 *6:30am-10:30pm, from 7am wknds*

Cuppa Java [BW,WI] 400 Penn Ave S, Minneapolis 612/374-4806 *7am-10pm, deliver 9am-3pm*

Moose & Sadie's [WI,WC] 212 3rd Ave N (at 2nd St), Minneapolis 612/371-0464 *7am-8pm, 9am-2pm wknds*

Quixotic Coffee [WI] 769 Cleveland, St Paul 651/699-5448 *7am-9pm, till 6pm Sun*

Uncommon Grounds 2809 Hennepin Ave (at W 28th St), Minneapolis 612/872-4811 *noon-midnight, till 1am Fri-Sat, patio*

The Urban Bean [WI,WC] 3255 Bryant Ave S (at 33rd), Minneapolis 612/824-6611 *6:30am-11pm*

Wilde Roast Cafe [BW,WC,GO] 65 Main St SE (at Hennepin Ave), Minneapolis 612/331-4544 *7am-10pm*

▪RESTAURANTS

Al's Breakfast [★] 413 14th Ave SE (at 4th), Minneapolis 612/331-9991 *6am-1pm, from 9am Sun, great hash*

Barbette 1600 W Lake St (at Irving), Minneapolis 612/827-5710 *8am-1am, till 2am Fri-Sat*

Birchwood Cafe [WI,WC] 3311 E 25th St, Minneapolis 612/722-4474 *7am-9pm, from 8am Sat, 9am-8pm Sun, veggie/ vegan*

Brasa Premium Rotisserie [BW,WC] 600 E Hennepin, Minneapolis 612/379-3030

French Meadow [BW] 2610 Lyndale Ave S, Minneapolis 612/870-7855 *6:30am-9pm, till 10pm Fri-Sat organic & local, plenty veggie/ vegan*

Hard Times Cafe [WI] 1821 Riverside Ave, Minneapolis 612/341-9261 *6am-4am, vegan/ vegetarian, punk rock ambiance*

Hell's Kitchen 80 9th St S, Minneapolis 612/332-4700 *7am-9pm, till 2am Fri-Sat, great brkfst & gospel brunch Sun*

Joe's Garage 1610 Harmon Pl, Minneapolis 612/904-1163 *lunch & dinner, full bar till 1am, rooftop seating*

Loring Kitchen & Bar [GO] 1359 Willow St, Minneapolis 612/843-0400 *11am-11pm, till 1am Fri-Sat, from 9am Sat-Sun*

Lucia's Restaurant & Wine Bar [WC] 1432 W 31st St, Minneapolis 612/825-1572 *lunch & dinner, clsd Mon*

Monte Carlo [WC] 219 3rd Ave N, Minneapolis 612/333-5900 *lunch & dinner, bar till 1am*

Murray's 26 S 6th St (at Hennepin), Minneapolis 612/339-0909 *lunch Mon-Fri, dinner nightly*

Nye's Polonaise [E,P] 112 E Hennepin Ave, Minneapolis 612/379-2021 *4pm-2am, from 11am Fri-Sat*

Psycho Suzi's Motor Lounge [E,WC] 2519 Marshall St NE, Minneapolis 612/788-9069 *11am-2am, pu-pu's & pizza*

Punch Neapolitan Pizza [WC] 704 Cleveland Ave S, St Paul 651/696-1066 *11am-9:30pm; also at 210 E Hennepin Ave*

Red Stag Supperclub [E,WC] 509 1st Ave NE (at 5th St), Minneapolis 612/767-7766 *11am-2am, from 9am Sat-Sun*

Restaurant Alma 528 University Ave SE, Minneapolis 612/379-4909 *dinner nightly, organic New American*

Minnesota • *USA*

Seward Cafe [WC] 2129 E Franklin Ave, Minneapolis 612/332-1011 *7am-3pm, 8am-4pm wknds, vegetarian/ vegan*

Toast Wine Bar & Cafe 415 N 1st St (in the Heritage Landing Bldg) 612/333-4305 *5pm-11pm, till midnight Fri-Sat*

Trattoria da Vinci [E,WC] 400 Sibley St, St Paul 651/222-4050 *11am-9pm, 5pm-10pm Sat, clsd Sun-Mon*

■ENTERTAINMENT & RECREATION

Calhoun 32nd Beach 3300 E Calhoun Pkwy (33rd & Calhoun Blvd), Minneapolis 612/230-6400

Twin Lake Beach [N] in Wirth Park (33rd & Calhoun Blvd), Minneapolis *aka Hidden Lake, hard to find, inquire locally*

■RETAIL SHOPS

The Rainbow Road [WC] 109 W Grant St (at LaSalle), Minneapolis 612/872-8448 *10am-10pm, LGBT*

■PUBLICATIONS

Lavender Magazine 612/436-4660, 877/515-9969 *LGBT newsmagazine for IA, MN, ND, SD, WI*

My Scene City 612/886-3151 *LGBTQA Twin Cities publication*

■MEN'S SERVICES

▶**MegaMates** 952/938-8700 *Call to hook up with HOT local men. FREE to listen & respond to ads. Use FREE code DAMRON. MegaMates.com.*

■EROTICA

Cockpit 2321 Hennepin Ave S *11am-8pm, till 6pm Sat, noon-5pm Sun*

Fantasy Gifts 1437 University Ave, St Paul 651/256-7484 *noon-8pm, clsd Sun-Tue*

Lickety Split 251 3rd Ave S, Minneapolis 612/333-0599

SexWorld 241 2nd Ave N (at Washington), Minneapolis 612/672-0556 *24hrs*

The Smitten Kitten [TG,GO] 3010 Lyndale Ave S, Minneapolis 612/721-6088, 888/751-0523

■CRUISY AREAS

"Bare Ass" Beach [AYOR] E bank of the Mississippi (btwn the Franklin Ave & I-94 bridges), Minneapolis *especially summer afternoons*

Loring Park [AYOR] 15th St (near 35 W & I-94 exchange), Minneapolis

Moorhead

see also Fargo, North Dakota

■INFO LINES & SERVICES

Pride Collective & Community Center 810 4th Ave S #220 218/287-8034 *6pm-7:30pm Tue & 1pm-3pm Sat*

■CAFES

Atomic Coffee [E,GO] 16 4th St S (at Main) 218/299-6161 *6:30am-9pm, from 8am Sun, also gallery*

Owatonna

■EROTICA

The Lion's Den Adult Superstore 1178 W Frontage Rd (exit 42B, off I-35) 507/214-3900 *24hrs*

MISSISSIPPI

Biloxi

■BARS

Club Veaux [M,D,F] 834 Howard Ave 228/207-3271

Just Us Lounge [MW,NH,D,E,K,DS,S] 906 Division St (at Caillavet) 228/374-1007 *24hrs*

■CRUISY AREAS

Hiller Park [AYOR] off Pass Rd

Gulfport

■BARS

Knuckle Heads [GF,NH,D,K] 1105 Broad Ave (at Railroad) 228/864-0463

The Other Bar [MW,D,DS,WC] 2218 25th Ave 228/284-1674 *4pm-close*

Jackson

■INFO LINES & SERVICES

Lambda AA 4866 N State St (at Unitarian Church) 601/856-5337 *6:30pm Mon*

■BARS

Bottoms Up [MW,D] 3911 Northview Dr
601/981-2188 *9pm Fri-Sat only*

Jack's Construction Site (JC's)
[MW,NH,BYOB,WI] 425 N Mart Plaza
601/362-3108 *5pm-2am, from 7pm
Th-Sat, clsd Mon*

■CRUISY AREAS

Battlefield Park [AYOR] Terry Rd (at
Hwy 80) *afternoons*

Natchez

■ACCOMMODATIONS

Historic Oak Hill Inn B&B [NS,WI,GO]
409 S Rankin St (at Orleans St)
601/446-2500, 601/446-8641
antebellum mansion near the Mississippi

Mark Twain Guesthouse [GF] 25 Silver
St 601/446-8023 *above Under the Hill
Saloon*

■BARS

Under the Hill Saloon [GF,NH,E,WI] 25
Silver St 601/446-8023 *10am-close*

Oxford

■CRUISY AREAS

Pat Lamar Park [AYOR]

Tupelo

■CRUISY AREAS

**Chickasaw Village & Old Town Site
Scenic Overlooks** [AYOR] Natchez Trace
Pkwy *closes at sunset*

Confederate Grave Site [AYOR] Hwy
78-Natchez Trace Pkwy interchange (5
miles N)

Vicksburg

■CRUISY AREAS

Rest Stop I-20 E (2nd rest stop)

MISSOURI

Ava

■ACCOMMODATIONS

Cactus Canyon Campground
[MO,N,GO] 16 miles E of Ava on Hwy 14
(N 1 mile on County 223)
417/683-9199

Boonville

■MEN'S CLUBS

Megaplex Health Club & Spa [MO,V]
11674 Old Hwy 40 (off I-70 exit 98)
660/882-0008

■EROTICA

Passions Video 17701 Old Five Dr (off
I-70 exit 103) 660/882-9426

Branson

see also Springfield & Eureka
Springs, Arkansas

■ACCOMMODATIONS

Branson Stagecoach RV Park
[GF,SW,WI,GO] 5751 State Hwy 165
417/335-8185, 800/446-7110 *pull-
thru & back-in RV sites, cabins*

■CRUISY AREAS

Table Rock Lake Dam [AYOR] Fish
Hatchery area

Bridgeton

■EROTICA

Spanky's Video 3419 N Lindbergh Blvd
(at Morrow Dr) 314/209-7779

Cape Girardeau

■ACCOMMODATIONS

Rose Bed Inn [GS,F,NS,WI,WC,GO] 611 S
Sprigg St 573/332-7673, 866/767-
3233 *full brkfst, hot tub, gourmet dining*

■NIGHTCLUBS

Independence Place [MW,D,TG,DS] 5 S
Henderson St (at Independence, at
Holiday Happenings) 573/334-2939
*8:30pm-1:30am, from 7pm Fri-Sat, clsd
Sun*

■CRUISY AREAS

Capaha Park [AYOR]

Clinton

■CRUISY AREAS

Sparrowfoot Park [AYOR] 4 miles S off
Hwy 13 Lithuania *swimming & boat
launch area at Truman Lake*

Missouri • *USA*

Columbia

BARS

The Arch & Column Pub
[M,NH,K,WC,GO] 1301 Business Loop 70
E (at College) 573/441-8088 *5:30pm-
1:30am, clsd Sun*

SoCo Club [MW,D,F,K,DS,V,WC] 119 S
7th St 573/499-9483 *5pm-1:30am,
clsd Mon, patio*

CAFES

Ernie's Cafe 1005 E Walnut St (at
10th) 573/874-7804 *6:30am-3pm*

Uprise Baker/ RagTag Cinema [F,BW]
10 Hitt St (Broadway) 573/443-4359,
573/441-8504 *5pm-close, from 2pm
wknds, independent & alternative
cinema, also theater, music & dance*

RESTAURANTS

Main Squeeze [WI,WC] 28 S 9th St (at
Cherry St) 573/817-5616 *10am-8pm,
till 9pm Sun, local organic ingredients,
vegetarian*

BOOKSTORES

The Peace Nook 804 C East Broadway
(btwn 8th & 9th) 573/875-0539
*10am-9pm, noon-6pm Sun, LGBT
section, books, pride products*

EROTICA

Bocomo Bay [★] 1122-A Wilkes Blvd
573/443-0873 *smoke shop too*

**Olde Un Theatre/ Midwest Adult
Book Store** 101 E Walnut St (at 1st)
573/442-6622 *7am-midnight*

Venus [GO] 1010 Old Hwy 63 N
573/442-4319 *24hrs Tue-Sat, till 1pm
Sun, from 9am-1am Mon*

CRUISY AREAS

Cosmopolitan Park [AYOR] W side of
town (off Business Loop 70)

Hannibal

ACCOMMODATIONS

Garden House B&B [GF,MW,NS,GO] 301
N 5th St (at Bird) 573/221-7800,
866/423-7800

Rockcliffe Mansion [GF,NS,WI,GO]
1000 Bird St (at 10th)
573/221-4140, 877/423-4140

RESTAURANTS

LaBinnah Bistro [BW,GO] 207 N 5th St
(at Center) 573/221-7800 *dinner only,
in a Victorian home*

Joplin

INFO LINES & SERVICES

**Gay Lesbian Family & Corporate
Center** 417/434-1149

BARS

Pla Mor Lounge [MW,NH,D,K] 532 S
Joplin Ave 417/624-2722 *5pm-1am,
clsd Sun-Mon*

Kansas City

see also Kansas City & Overland
Park, Kansas

INFO LINES & SERVICES

**Lesbian & Gay Community Center
of Greater Kansas City** 4008 Oak St
#10 816/931-4420 *call for events*

Live & Let Live AA 3901 Main St #211
(at 39th) 816/531-9668 *6pm daily,
noon Sun*

ACCOMMODATIONS

Hotel Phillips [GF,WI] 816/221-7000,
800/433-1426 *art deco landmark in
downtown KC*

Ken's Place [MW,SW,WI,GO] 18 W 38th
St (at Baltimore) 816/753-0533 *some
shared baths, near gay bars*

Q Hotel & Spa [★GF,WI,WC] 560
Westport Rd (at Mill St)
816/931-0001, 800/942-4233

The Raphael [GF,F,WI] 325 Ward Pkwy
(at Wornall Rd) 816/756-3800,
800/821-5343

Su Casa B&B [GF,SW,NS,WI] 9004 E
92nd St (off James A Reed Rd)
816/965-5647, 816/916-3444 (cell)
Southwest-style home

BARS

Buddies [M,NH] 3715 Main St (at 37th)
816/561-2600 *9am-3am, clsd Sun*

Hamburger Mary's KC [MW,K,F,E] 101
Southwest Blvd (at Baltimore Ave)
816/842-1919 *11am-1:30am, juicy
burgers w/ a side of camp*

Missie B's/ Bootleggers [MW,NH,D,L,TG,K,DS,S] 805 W 39th St (at SW Trafficway) **816/561-0625** *noon-3am*

Outa Bounds [M,NH,F,WC] 3601 Broadway St (W 36th) **816/214-8732** *noon-1:30am, till midnight Sun, gay sports bar*

Sidekicks [MW,D,CW,DS,WC] 3707 Main St (at 37th) **816/931-1430** *2pm-3am, from 4pm Sun, clsd Mon*

Sidestreet Bar [M,NH,GO] 413 E 33rd St (at Gillham Rd) **816/531-1775** *10am-1:30am, clsd Sun*

Social [MW,D,F,K,WC,GO] 1118 McGee **816/472-4900** *3pm-3am, from 5pm Sat, clsd Sun-Mon*

The View [M,NH,GO] 204 Orchard St (at Tenny Ave), KS **913/281-0833** *4pm-2am, from noon Sun, clsd Mon*

CAFES

Broadway Cafe [F,NS] 4106 Broadway (at Westport) **816/531-2432** *7am-9pm; also 412 Washington*

RESTAURANTS

Beer Kitchen [E] 435 Westport Rd (at Pennsylvania) **816/389-4180** *11am-3am, from 10am wknds, gastro pub, live music*

Bistro 303 [★WC,GO] 303 Westport Rd **816/753-2303** *open 3pm, from 11am Sat-Sun, patio*

Blue Bird Bistro [WC] 1700 Summit St (at W 17th St) **816/221-7559** *7am-10pm, 10am-2pm Sun, organic fare*

Cafe Trio/ Starlet Lounge [P,GO] 4558 Main St **816/756-3227** *5pm-11pm, clsd Sun, live jazz*

Chubby's [WC] 3756 Broadway St (at 38th) **816/931-2482** *open 24hrs, popular late nights, diner fare*

Classic Cup Cafe [WC] 301 W 47th St (at Central) **816/753-1840** *brkfst, lunch, dinner, Sun brunch*

Grand Street Cafe [NS,WC] 4740 Grand St (at 47th St) **816/561-8000** *lunch & dinner, Sun brunch, patio seating*

Jardine's 4536 Main St **816/561-6480** *dinner nightly, steak/ sea food, live jazz*

Le Fou Frog 400 E 5th St (at Oak St) **816/474-6060** *dinner only, French bistro*

McCoy's Public House 4057 Pennsylvania Ave **816/960-0866** *11am-3am, till midnight Sun, huge patio*

The Mixx [WC] 4855 Main St (at W 48th) **816/756-2300** *lunch & dinner, fast & healthy, huge selection of salads*

Tannin Wine Bar **816/842-2660** *11:30am-1:30am, from 4pm wknds, wine & cheese flights, patio seating*

YJ's Snack Bar [WC] 128 W 18th St (at W Baltimore Ave) **816/472-5533** *8am-10pm, 24hrs Th-Sat*

ENTERTAINMENT & RECREATION

First Fridays Art Walk Crossroads District (Baltimore & 20th) **816/994-9325** *5pm-10pm 1st Fri, art gallery walk, also live music & vendors*

Nelson-Atkins Museum 4525 Oak St **816/751-1278** *American Indian galleries*

MEN'S SERVICES

▶**MegaMates** **816/326-9926** *Call to hook up with HOT local men. FREE to listen & respond to ads. Use FREE code DAMRON. MegaMates.com.*

EROTICA

Erotic City 8401 E Truman Rd (off I-435, at Alice Ave) **816/252-3370**

Hollywood at Home 9063 Metcalf Ave (at 91st), Overland Park, KS **913/649-9666** *10am-11pm*

Video Mania [GO] 208 Westport Rd **816/561-6397**

Moberly

CRUISY AREAS

Rothwell Park [AYOR]

Missouri • *USA*

Osage Beach

■ACCOMMODATIONS

Utopian Inn [MW,NS,GO] 1962 Alcorn Hollow Rd, Roach 573/347-3605 *3-bdrm rental on a lake*

Overland

■EROTICA

Patricia's 10210 Page Ave (E of Ashby) 314/423-8422

Springfield

■INFO LINES & SERVICES

AA Gay/ Lesbian [NS] 518 E Commercial St 417/823-7125 (AA #) *6pm Sat*

Gay & Lesbian Community Center of the Ozarks [WC] 518 E Commercial St 417/869-3978 *many groups, newsletter*

■BARS

The Edge [MW,D,K,DS,WC,GO] 424 N Boonville 417/831-4700 *4:30pm-1:30am, clsd Sun*

Martha's Vineyard [MW,NH,D,DS,18+,WC,$] 219 W Olive St (at S Patton) 417/864-4572 *5pm-1:30am, from 2pm Sun, clsd Mon, patio*

Mud Lounge [GF,F] 321 E Walnut 417/865-6964 *4pm-1:30am, clsd Sun*

■NIGHTCLUBS

Club Vibe [M,D,DS] 2526 S Campbell Ave 417/501-1041

■CAFES

Mudhouse [F] 323 South Ave 417/832-1720 *7am-midnight, 9am-8pm Sun*

■EROTICA

Patricia's 1918 S Glenstone (at E Cherokee) 417/881-8444

■CRUISY AREAS

Lake Springfield Park [AYOR] *NW side, north of power plant, days*

Phelps Grove Park [AYOR]

St Joseph

■CRUISY AREAS

Riverfront Park [AYOR] *downtown*

St Louis

■ACCOMMODATIONS

➤A St Louis Guesthouse [M,N,NS,WI,GO] 1032 Allen Ave (at Menard) 314/773-1016 *in historic Soulard district, hot tub, cash discount*

Brewers House B&B [MW,NS,WI,GO] 1829 Lami St (at Lemp) 314/771-1542, 888/767-4665 *1860s home, jacuzzi*

The Cheshire [GS,SW,WI] 6300 Clayton Rd 314/647-7300

Dwell 912 B&B [GF,NS,WI,GO] 912 Hickory St (at S 9th St) 314/599-3100

Grand Center Inn [GS,WI,NS,GO] 3716 Grandel Sq (at N Grand Blvd) 314/533-0771

Napoleon's Retreat B&B [GS,NS,WI,GO] 1815 Lafayette Ave (at Mississippi) 314/772-6979, 800/700-9980 *restored 1880s town house, full brkfst*

■BARS

Absolutli Goosed Martini Bar, Etc [MW,NH,WC,GO] 3196 S Grand (at Wyoming) 314/771-9300 *4pm-midnight, till 1am Fri-Sat, clsd Sun, also desserts, appetizers, patio*

Bad Dog Bar & Grill [M,NH,B,L,F,GO] 3960 Chouteau Ave (at S Vandeventer Ave) 314/652-0011 *4pm-1:30am, 2pm-midnight Sun*

Cicero's [GS,E,F] 6691 Delmar Blvd (at Kingsland Ave), University City 314/862-0009 *11am-12:30am, till 11pm Sun, Italian restaurant*

Clementine's [★M,NH,L,F,WC] 2001 Menard St (at Allen) 314/664-7869 *10am-midnight, from 11am Sun, patio*

Club Escapades [MW,D,DS,F,K,S,WI] 133 W Main St (at 2nd), Belleville, IL 618/222-9597 *6pm-2am, clsd Sun-Mon*

St Louis • Missouri

Erney's 32 Degree [M,D] 4200 Manchester Ave (at Boyle) **314/652-7195** 8pm-3am, clsd Mon

Grey Fox Pub [MW,NH,TG,DS,S] 3503 S Spring (at Potomac) **314/772-2150** 2pm-1:30am, noon-midnight Sun, patio

Hummel's Pub [MW,NH,F,K,GO] 7101 S Broadway (at Blow St) **314/353-5080** 11am-1am, from 2pm Mon

JJ's Clubhouse & Bar [M,NH,B,L,WC] 3858 Market St (at Vandeventer) **314/535-4100** 3pm-3am

Just John [MW,NH,D,K,V] 4112 Manchester Ave **314/371-1333** 3pm-3am, from noon-1am Sun

Keypers Piano Bar [MW,NH,P,F] 2280 S Jefferson (at Shenandoah) **314/664-6496** 1pm-1:30am, 2pm-midnight Sun, patio

Korners Bar [MW,D,DS] 7109 S Broadway (at Blow St) **314/352-3088** 4pm-1:30am, clsd Sun-Mon

Meyer's Grove [MW,DS] 4510 Manchester Ave **314/932-7003** 4pm-1:30pm, clsd Sun

Novak's Bar & Grill [W,D,F,E,K,S,WC] 4121 Manchester (at Sarah) **314/531-3699** 4pm-3am, patio

Premium Lounge [GS,F] 4199 Manchester Rd (at Boyle) **314/652-8585** opens 4pm, clsd Sun

Rehab Lounge [GS,NH,F] 4052 Chouteau Ave (at Boyle) **314/652-3700** 11am-1:30am, also restaurant

Rosie's Place [GS,NH] 4573 Laclede Ave **314/361-6423** 11am-1:30am

Soulard Bastille [M,NH] 1027 Russell Blvd (at Menard) **314/664-4408** 11am-1:30am

■**NIGHTCLUBS**

Atomic Cowboy [GS,F,E,WI] 4140 Manchester Ave (btwn Kentucky & Talmadge) **314/775-0775** 11am-3am, from 5pm Sat-Sun, also Fresh-Mex Mayan grill

A St. Louis Guesthouse

Located in Historic Soulard
next door to Clementines

Accommodations with:
- Private Bath
- Phone
- Hot Tub in Courtyard

1032-38 Allen Ave., St. Louis, MO 63104
www.stlouisguesthouse.com
(314) 773-1016

Missouri • *USA*

Attitudes [MW,D,DS,K] 4100 Manchester Ave (at S Sarah) 314/534-0044 *7pm-3am, clsd Mon*

Bubby & Sissy's [MW,D,E,F,K,DS,V,WC] 602 Belle St (at 6th St), Alton, IL 618/465-4773 *3pm-2am, till 3am Fri-Sat*

Magnolia's [MW,D,MR-AF] 5 S Vandeventer Ave (at Laclede) 314/652-6500 *hip hop/ R&B club*

■CAFES

Coffee Cartel [★F,WI,WC] 2 Maryland Plaza (at Euclid) 314/454-0000 *24hrs*

MoKaBe's [★E,WC] 3606 Arsenal (at S Grand) 314/865-2009 *8am-midnight, from 9am Sun*

Soulard Coffee Garden Cafe [F,WI,WC] 910 Geyer Ave (btwn 9th & 10th) 314/241-1464 *6:30am-4pm, from 8am wknds*

■RESTAURANTS

Billie's Diner [WC] 1802 S Broadway 314/621-0848 *5am-2:30pm, midnight-1:30pm wknds*

Cafe Osage 4605 Olive St 314/454-6868 *7am-2pm, till 5pm Th-Sat, from 9am Sun*

City Diner [★WC] 3139 S Grand Blvd 314/772-6100 *7am-11pm, 24hrs Fri-Sat, till 10pm Sun*

Dressel's [E,WC] 419 N Euclid (at McPherson) 314/361-1060 *11am-1am, till midnight Sun, great Welsh pub food, full bar*

Eleven Eleven Mississippi 1111 Mississippi 314/241-9999 *lunch Mon-Fri, dinner nightly, clsd Sun, wine country bistro*

Hamburger Mary's [E,K] 3037 Olive St 314/533-6279 *11am-midnight, till 1am Th-Sat*

Joanie's Pizza 2101 Menard St 314/865-1994 *11am-11pm, till midnight wknds*

Majestic Cafe [WC] 4900 Laclede Ave (at Euclid) 314/361-2011 *6am-10pm, bar till 1:30am, Greek-American diner fare*

Mango 1101 Lucas Ave 314/621-9993 *11am-10pm, bar till 1:30am Fri-Sat, 4pm-9pm Sun, Latin American/ Peruvian*

Meskerem 3210 S Grand Blvd 314/772-4442 *lunch & dinner, Ethiopian, plenty veggie*

Pappy's Smokehouse 3106 Olive St 314/535-4340 *11am-8pm, till 4pm Sun, excellent BBQ*

Rue 13 [D,C] 1311 Washington 314/588-7070 *5pm-3am, clsd Sun-Mon, sushi, full bar*

Spaghetteria Mamma Mia 904 S Vandeventer Ave 314/531-9100 *lunch & dinner, clsd Sun-Mon*

Ted Drewes Frozen Custard [★WC] 6726 Chippewa (at Jameson) 314/481-2652, 314/481-2124 *11am-10pm, seasonal, a St Louis landmark; also 4224 S Grand Blvd, 314/352-7376*

Three Monkey's 153 Morgan Ford Rd 314/772-9800 *11am-1:30am*

Tony's [R,WC] 410 Market St (at Broadway) 314/231-7007 *dinner only, clsd Sun-Mon, Italian fine dining*

Van Goghz [WI,WC] 3200 Shenandoah (at Compton) 314/865-3345 *11am-11pm, till 1:30am Fri-Sat, 9:30am-3pm Sun, also martini bar*

Vin de Set [WC] 2017 Chouteau Ave (at S 21st St) 314/241-8989 *lunch & dinner, dinner only wknds, clsd Mon, rooftop bar & bistro*

The Wild Flower Restaurant & Bar [WC] 4590 Laclede Ave (at Euclid) 314/367-9888 *lunch & dinner, bar till 1:30am, clsd Tue, Sun brunch*

■BOOKSTORES

Left Bank Books [★] 399 N Euclid Ave (at McPherson) 314/367-6731 *10am-10pm, 11am-6pm Sun, feminist & LGBT titles; also at 321 N 10th St*

■RETAIL SHOPS

CheapTRX [WC] 3211 S Grand Blvd (at Wyoming St) 314/664-4011 *alternative shopping, body piercing, tattoos*

■PUBLICATIONS

Vital Voice 314/256–1196 *bi-weekly news & features publication*

■GYMS & HEALTH CLUBS

Marbles Yoga Studio [GO] 1908 Cherokee **314/225–7701**

■MEN'S CLUBS

Club St Louis [PC,SW,18+] 2625 Samuel Shepard Dr (at Jefferson) **314/533–3666** *24hrs*

■MEN'S SERVICES

►**MegaMates** 314/209–0300 *Call to hook up with HOT local men. FREE to listen & respond to ads. Use FREE code DAMRON. MegaMates.com.*

■EROTICA

Patricia's 3552 Gravois Ave (at Grand) **314/664–4040**

■CRUISY AREAS

Creve Coeur Park [AYOR] Dorset Rd W (off Hwy 2-70)

Steele

■EROTICA

The Lion's Den Adult Superstore 36 E Outer Rd (exit 8, off I-55) **573/695–7294**

MONTANA

Billings

■BARS

The Loft [MW,D,E,K,WC] 1123 1st Ave N (at 12th) **406/259–9074** *10am-2am*

■EROTICA

Big Sky Books 1203 1st Ave N (at 12th St) **406/259–0051**

The Victorian [P] 2019 Minnesota Ave (at 21st) **406/245–4293** *noon-midnight, clsd Sun-Mon, also HIV & Hep B/C testing*

Bozeman

■ACCOMMODATIONS

Gallatin Gateway Inn [GF,F,SW,WC] 76405 Gallatin Rd/ Hwy 191 **406/763–4672, 800/676–3522**

Lehrkind Mansion Inn [GS,NS,WI,GO] 719 N Wallace Ave **406/585–6932**

■CAFES

The Leaf & Bean [E,WC] 35 W Main St **406/587–1580** *6am-9pm, till 10pm Fri-Sat; also 1500 N 19th Ave*

The Nova Cafe 312 E Main St (at Rouse Ave) **406/587–3973** *7am-2pm*

■EROTICA

Erotique 12 N Willson Ave (at Main) **406/586–7825**

Butte

■RESTAURANTS

Matt's Place 2339 Placer St (btwn Montana & Rowe) **406/782–8049** *11:30am-7pm, clsd Sun-Mon, classic soda-fountain diner*

Pekin Noodle Parlor 117 S Main St, 2nd flr **406/782–2217** *5pm-11pm, till midnight Fri-Sat, clsd Tue*

Pork Chop John's 2400 Harrison Ave **406/782–1783** *10:30am-10:30pm, clsd Sun; also 8 W Mercury, 406/782-0812*

Uptown Cafe [WC] 47 E Broadway **406/723–4735** *lunch weekdays & dinner nightly, bistro, full bar*

Kalispell

■INFO LINES & SERVICES

Flathead Valley Alliance **406/758–6707** *LGBT referral service*

Missoula

■INFO LINES & SERVICES

KISMIF Gay/ Lesbian AA 405 University Ave (at church) **406/543–0011** *7pm Mon*

Western Montana Gay/ Lesbian Community Center 127 N Higgins Ave #202 **406/543–2224** *LGBT resource center*

■BARS

The Oxford [★GF] 337 N Higgins Ave (at Pine) **406/549–0117** *8am-2am, 24hr cafe & casino*

■CAFES

The Catalyst 111 N Higgins **406/542–1337** *7am-3pm*

Montana • USA

RESTAURANTS

Montana Club [WC] 2620 Brooks
406/543-3100 *6am-10pm, till 11pm Fri-Sat, casino open till 2am*

BOOKSTORES

Fact & Fiction [WC] 220 N Higgins
406/721-2881 *9am-6pm, 10am-5pm Sat, noon-4pm Sun*

RETAIL SHOPS

Jeannette Rankin Peace Center 519 S Higgins Ave, Bozeman
406/543-3955 *10am-6pm, clsd Sun, fair trade gift store; also peace resource center*

PUBLICATIONS

Out Words 127 N Higgins Ave #202
406/543-2224 *Montana's LGBT publication*

CRUISY AREAS

McCormick Park [AYOR] W side of Orange St Bridge

Swan Valley

ACCOMMODATIONS

Holland Lake Lodge [GF,WI,WC,GO] 1947 Holland Lake Rd (at Hwy 83)
406/754-2282, 877/925-6343 *resort w/ lakefront cabins, restaurant & bar*

NEBRASKA

Columbus

CRUISY AREAS

Pawnee Park [AYOR]

Lincoln

INFO LINES & SERVICES

Rainbow Group Gay/ Lesbian AA 2325 S 24 St (at Sewell, at St Matthew's) **402/438-5214** *7:30pm Mon & 7pm Fri*

BARS

Panic [MW,E,WI,WC,GO] 200 S 18th St (at N St) **402/435-8764** *4pm-1am, from 1pm wknds, patio*

NIGHTCLUBS

The Q [MW,D,E,DS,S] 226 S 9th St (btwn M & N Sts) **402/475-2269** *8pm-1am, clsd Mon*

CRUISY AREAS

15th St [AYOR] from A St to State Capitol

Pioneers & Van Dorn Parks [AYOR]

Norfolk

CRUISY AREAS

Tahazooka Park [AYOR]

Omaha

INFO LINES & SERVICES

AA Gay/ Lesbian 851 N 74th St (at Presbyterian Church) **402/556-1880** *8:15pm Fri*

Rainbow Outreach Center 1719 Leavenworth St **402/341-0330** *call for hrs*

ACCOMMODATIONS

Castle Unicorn [GS,NS,WI,GO] 57034 Deacon Rd (at Hwy 34 & I-29), Pacific Jct, IA **712/527-5930** *medieval-style B&B*

The Cornerstone Mansion Inn [GF,NS,WI] 140 N 39th St (at Dodge) **402/558-7600, 888/883-7745**

BARS

Connections [W,D,K,WC,GO] 1901 Leavenworth St (at 19th)
402/933-3033 *6pm-1:30am, from 4pm Fri-Sun, clsd Mon, guys night Wed*

DC's Saloon [MW,D,CW,S,WC] 610 S 14th St (at Jackson) **402/344-3103** *4pm-2am, from 2pm wknds*

Myth [GS,E] 1105 Howard St (Old Market) **402/884-6985** *7pm-1am, from 5pm Th-Sat, clsd Sun-Mon*

The Omaha Mining Company [M,D,S,18+,WC] 1715 Leavenworth St (btwn 17th & 18th) **402/449-8703** *2pm-1am, till 4am Fri-Sat, very cruisy*

■NIGHTCLUBS

Flixx Lounge [M,D,C,DS] 1019 S 10th St 402/408–1020 *5pm–1am*

The Max [★M,D,DS,S,V,WC,$] 1417 Jackson St (at 15th St) 402/346–4110 *4pm–1am, till 2am Th-Sat, patio*

■RESTAURANTS

The Boiler Room [WC] 1110 Jones St 402/916–9274 *dinner only, clsd Sun, full bar*

California Tacos & More [BW,WC] 3235 California St 402/342–0212 *11am–9pm, clsd Sun*

The Flatiron Cafe [WC] 1722 St Marys Ave 402/345–7477 *dinner only, clsd Sun, full bar*

M's Pub [WC] 422 S 11th St 402/342–2550 *11am–1am, from 5pm Sun, full bar*

McFoster's Natural Kind Cafe [WC] 302 S 38th St 402/345–7477 *lunch & dinner, vegetarian, full bar*

■MEN'S SERVICES

➤**MegaMates** 402/341–4000 *Call to hook up with HOT local men. FREE to listen & respond to ads. Use FREE code DAMRON. MegaMates.com.*

■CRUISY AREAS

Glen Cunningham Lake [AYOR] *along W side*

Scottsbluff

■CRUISY AREAS

Riverside Zoo Park [AYOR]

NEVADA

Carson City

■ACCOMMODATIONS

West Walker Motel [GF,WI] 106833 Hwy 395, Walker, CA 530/495–2263 *in Toiyabe Nat'l Forest near West Walker River*

■MEN'S SERVICES

➤**MegaMates** 775/888–9995 *Call to hook up with HOT local men. FREE to listen & respond to ads. Use FREE code DAMRON. MegaMates.com.*

Elko

■CRUISY AREAS

Elko City Park [AYOR]

Lake Tahoe

see Lake Tahoe, California

Las Vegas

■INFO LINES & SERVICES

Alcoholics Together 900 E Karen, 2nd flr #A-202 (at Sahara, in Commercial Center) 702/598–1888 *12:15pm & 8pm daily, call for other mtgs*

The Gay/ Lesbian Community Center of Southern Nevada 953 E Sahara Ave #B-31 702/733–9800 *11am–7pm, clsd wknds*

■ACCOMMODATIONS

➤**Blue Moon Resort** [MO,SW,N,WI,NS,WC,GO] 2651 Westwood Dr 702/784–4500, 866/798–9194 *private resort, coffeehouse, sundeck, steam room & jacuzzi grotto*

El Cortez Cabana [GF] 651 E Ogden Ave (at 7th St) 702/385–5200, 800/634–6703 *recently renovated, bringing Miami-style glamour to Fremont St*

Lucky You B&B [M,SW,N,GO] 702/384–1129 *hot tub, sauna, shared baths*

➤**Paris, Las Vegas Resort & Casino** [GF] 3655 Las Vegas Blvd S 702/946–7000, 800/630–7933 *see ad in front color section*

Vdara Hotel & Spa [GF,SW,NS] 2600 W Harmon Ave 702/590–2767, 866/745–7767

■BARS

Backdoor Lounge [MW,NH,D,MR-L,WC] 1415 E Charleston (near Maryland Pkwy) 702/385–2018 *24hrs, patio*

Badlands Saloon [M,NH,D,CW,WC,GO] 953 E Sahara Ave #22 (in Commercial Center) 702/792–9262 *24hrs*

The Buffalo [★M,B,LV,WC] 4640 Paradise Rd #11 (at Naples) 702/733–8355 *24hrs*

Las Vegas • Nevada

Charlie's Las Vegas [★M,D,DS,CW,WC] 5012 S Arville St (at Tropicana) 702/876-1844 *24hrs, dance lessons 7pm-9pm Mon, Th-Sat*

Crews'n [M,NH,DS,K,P,WI] 1000 E Sahara Ave #105 702/731-0951 *24hrs*

Escape Lounge [MW,NH,V,WC] 4213 W Sahara Ave 702/364-1167 *24hrs*

Flex [MW,D,DS,S,WC] 4347 W Charleston (at Arville) 702/385-3539, 702/878-3355 *24hrs*

Freezone [MW,NH,D,TG,F,K,DS,S,YC,GO] 610 E Naples 702/794-2300 *24hrs, also restaurant*

Fun Hog Ranch [M,D,B,L] 495 E Twain (off Paradise) 702/791-7001 *24hrs*

The Garage [M,NH,B,L,WC] 1487 E Flamingo Rd #C (at Maryland) 702/440-6333 *24hrs*

Goodtimes [M,NH,D,WC] 1775 E Tropicana Ave (at Spencer, in Liberace Plaza) 702/736-9494 *24hrs, DJ Mon, [K] Wed, after-hours Fri-Sat*

The Las Vegas Eagle [M,L] 3430 E Tropicana (at Pecos) 702/458-8662 *24hrs, DJ Wed & Fri*

Las Vegas Lounge [GF,NH,TG,DS,S] 900 E Karen Ave (at Maryland Pkwy) 702/737-9350 *24hrs*

Snick's Place [M,NH] 1402 S 3rd St (at Imperial) 702/385-9298 *24hrs*

■NIGHTCLUBS

Drink & Drag [GS,DS] 450 Fremont St #250 (at Neonopolis) 702/489-3724 *4pm-4am*

The Gipsy [M,D,S,V,YC] 4605 S Paradise Rd (at Naples) 702/666-8661 *open Wed-Sun*

House of Blues [GF,D,F,S,$] 3950 Las Vegas Blvd S (at Hacienda Ave, in Mandalay Bay) 702/632-7600

Krave [M,D] 3663 S Las Vegas Blvd (at Harmon St, next to Planet Hollywood) 702/836-0830 *11pm-close, clsd Mon*

Mix [$] 3950 Las Vegas Blvd S (at Mandalay Bay) 702/632-9500

for when "gay friendly" doesn't cut it!

BOYS & BURGERS
EVERY SUNDAY POOLSIDE AT BLUE MOON

Blue Moon
HOTEL FOR MEN · LAS VEGAS

2651 Westwood Drive, Las Vegas NV 89109 BlueMoonLasVegas.com 866-798-9194

Nevada • USA

Piranha [MW,D,WC] 4633 Paradise Rd (at Naples) **702/791-0100** *opens 10pm nightly*

Revolution Lounge [GF] 3400 Las Vegas Blvd S (at the Mirage) **702/791-7111** *10am-4am, clsd Tue, psychedelic Beatles-influenced decor, gay night Sun*

Share Nightclub & Ultra Lounge [M,D] 4636 Wynn Rd **702/258-2681**

▪RESTAURANTS

Bootlegger Bistro [GF] 7700 S Las Vegas Blvd (btwn Windmill & Robindale) **702/736-4939** *24hrs, a Vegas classic, Italian*

Border Grill 3950 Las Vegas Blvd S (at the Mandalay Bay Resort & Casino) **702/632-7403** *11:30am-close, Mexican, full bar, patio*

Carluccio's Tivoli Gardens 1775 E Tropicana (at Spencer St) **702/795-3236** *4:30pm-10pm, clsd Mon, Italian, formerly owned by Liberace; check out the mirrored, auto-graphed grand piano!*

Chicago Joe's 820 S 4th St (at Gass Ave) **702/382-5637** *11am-10pm, from 5pm Sat, clsd Sun-Mon, old-school Italian, in downtown arts district*

Cupcakery 7175 W Lake Mead **702/835-0060**

The Egg & I [★WC] 4533 W Sahara Ave (near Arville) **702/364-9686** *6am-3pm*

Firefly [WC] 3900 Paradise Rd #A **702/369-3971** *11am-2am, tapas, also bar*

Go Raw 2381 E Windmill Ln **702/450-9007** *8am-8pm, till 5pm Sun, organic vegan, also juice bar; also at 2910 Lake East Dr, 702/254-5382*

Grand Lux Cafe 3355 Las Vegas Blvd S (at the Venetian) **702/414-3888** *open 24hrs, generous portions*

Lindo Michoacan [★] 2655 E Desert Inn Rd (near Eastern) **702/735-6828** *11am-11pm, till midnight wknds, Mexican*

Lotus of Siam [★WC] 953 E Sahara Ave #A-5 (in Commercial Center) **702/735-3033** *lunch Mon-Fri, dinner nightly, Thai*

Mon Ami Gabi [WC] 3655 Las Vegas Blvd S (at Paris Las Vegas) **702/944-4224** *7am-11pm, outdoor seating*

Mr Lucky's [WC] 4455 Paradise Rd (at Hard Rock Hotel) **702/693-5000** *24hrs*

Paymon's Mediterranean Cafe & Lounge [WC] 4147 S Maryland Pkwy (at E Flamingo Rd) **702/731-6030** *11am-1am, plenty veggie; also at 8380 W Sahara Ave, 702/731-6030*

Society Cafe Encore 3121 Las Vegas Blvd S (at Encore) **702/248-3463** *7am-11pm, till 1am wknds, upscale American*

Wichcraft at MGM Grand **702/891-1111** *10am-5pm, creative sandwiches, eat-in or take-out*

▪ENTERTAINMENT & RECREATION

Cupid's Wedding Chapel [GS] 827 Las Vegas Blvd S (1 block N of Charleston) **702/598-4444, 800/543-2933** *commitment ceremonies*

Erotic Heritage Museum 3275 Industrial Rd **702/369-6442** *6pm-10pm Wed-Th, 3pm-midnight Fri, from noon wknds, clsd Mon-Tue*

Frank Marino's Divas Las Vegas [DS] 3535 Las Vegas Blvd S (at the Imperial Palace) **702/794-3261, 888/777-7664** *show at 7:30pm, Frank Marino & friends impersonate the divas, from Joan Rivers to Tina Turner*

Kà by Cirque du Soleil at MGM Grand **702/796-9999, 877/264-1844** *6:30pm & 9:30pm Tue-Sat*

Mystère by Cirque du Soleil at Treasure Island **800/963-9634**

Onyx Theatre 953 E Sahara Ave # 16A (at Maryland Pkwy) **702/732-7225** *alternative films & performances*

Red Rock Lanes 11011 W Charleston Blvd (at Red Rock Casino) **702/797-7777** *72 lanes, Cosmic Bowling wknds*

Thanks Babs, the Day Tripper [GO] 702/370-6961

Viva Las Vegas Wedding Chapel [GO] 1205 Las Vegas Blvd 800/574-4450

Zumanity [18+] at New York–New York Hotel & Casino 702/740-6815, 866/606-7111 *explores human sexuality in an intimate, cabaret-style setting*

BOOKSTORES

Get Booked 4640 S Paradise Rd #15 (at Naples) 702/737-7780 *10am-midnight, till 2am Fri-Sat, LGBT*

RETAIL SHOPS

Glamour Boutique II 714 E Sahara Ave #104 (at S 6th St) 702/697-1800, 866/692-1800 *clsd Sun, large-size dresses, wigs, etc*

The Rack [WC] 953 E Sahara Ave, Ste 101, Bldg 16 (in Commercial Center) 702/732-7225 *leather, fetish*

PUBLICATIONS

Las Vegas Night Beat 702/369-8441

QVegas 702/650-0636 *monthly LGBT news & entertainment magazine*

GYMS & HEALTH CLUBS

The Las Vegas Athletic Club [GF] 2655 S Maryland Pkwy 702/734-5822 *day passes*

MEN'S CLUBS

Entourage Vegas [MO,SW] 953 E Sahara Ave #A19 (near Paradise & Maryland, at Commercial Center entrance) 702/650-9191 *24hrs*

Hawks Gym [MO,PC,AYOR,GO,$] 953 E Sahara (at SE corner of Commercial Center) 702/731-4295 *24hrs wknds*

Power Exchange [TG,18+,$] 3610 S Highland Dr 702/255-4739 *play space open to hetero, gay, bi, trans, men & women; cover charge for men*

MEN'S SERVICES

▶**MegaMates** 702/932-7373 *Call to hook up with HOT local men. FREE to listen & respond to ads. Use FREE code DAMRON. MegaMates.com.*

EROTICA

Adult World/ Mini Theaters [V] 3781 Meade Ave (at Valley View) 702/579-9735 *24hrs*

Bare Essentials Fantasy Fashions [GO] 4029 W Sahara Ave (near Valley View Blvd) 702/247-4711 *exotic/ intimate apparel, toys*

Desert Adult Books 4350 N Las Vegas Blvd (at Craig Rd) 702/643-7982 *24hrs*

Fantasy World Arcade/ Theaters 6760 Boulder Hwy (btwn Sunset & Russell) 702/433-6311 *24hrs*

Industrial Road Adult Books 3427 Industrial Rd (at Spring Mtn) 702/734-7667 *24hrs*

Price Video 700 E Naples Dr #102 (at Swenson) 702/734-1342

Rancho Adult Entertainment Center 4820 N Rancho Dr (at Lone Mtn) 702/645-6104 *24hrs*

Tropicana Book & Video/ Adult Super Store 3850 W Tropicana (at Valley View) 702/798-0144 *24hrs, cruisy theaters*

Wild J's 2923 S Industrial Rd (behind Circus Circus) 702/892-0699 *24hrs*

CRUISY AREAS

Jaycee Park [AYOR] Eastern & St Louis (N of Sahara)

Sunset Park [AYOR]

Laughlin

see Bullhead City, Arizona

Reno

ACCOMMODATIONS

Silver Legacy Resort & Casino [GF,F,SW] 407 N Virginia St 775/325-7401, 800/687-8733

Terrible's Sands Regency Casino Hotel Downtown Reno [GF,SW,E] 345 N Arlington Ave 775/348-2200, 800/233-4939

BARS

Cadillac Lounge [MW,NH] 1114 E 4th St (at Sutro) 775/324-7827 *noon-2am*

Carl's Pub [M,NH,D,L] 3310 S Virginia St (at Moana) 775/829-8886 *2pm-2am, till midnight Sun, patio, theme nights*

Nevada • USA

Five Star Saloon [GS,NH,D,TG,WI,WC]
132 West St (at 1st) **775/329-2878**
24hrs

The Patio [MW,NH,E,K] 600 W 5th St
(btwn Washington & Ralston)
775/323-6565 *11am-2am*

■NIGHTCLUBS

Neutron [★GS,D,MR-L, DS] 340 Kietzke
Ln (btwn Glendale & Mill)
775/786-2121 *2pm-close, clsd Sun-
Tue*

Tronix [★GS,D,MR,TG,V,YC,WI,WC,GO]
303 Kietzke Ln (at E 2nd St)
775/333-9696 *noon-2am, till 5am
Fri-Sat*

■RESTAURANTS

4th Street Bistro 3065 W 4th St
775/323-3200 *dinner nightly, clsd
Sun-Mon, upscale, extensive wine list*

The Daily Bagel 495 Morill Ave # 102
775/786-1611 *6:30am-2pm, till 3pm
Wed-Fri, 8am-2pm, Sat, clsd Sun*

Pneumatic Diner 501 W 1st St (in
Truckee River Apts, 2nd flr)
775/786-8888 x106 *11am-10pm,
from 8am Sun, vegetarian*

■ENTERTAINMENT &
RECREATION

Brüka Theatre 99 N Virginia St
775/323-3221 *alternative theater &
performance space*

■BOOKSTORES

Sundance Books 1155 W 4th St #106
(at Keystone) **775/786-1188** *9am-
9pm, 9am-5pm wknds, independent*

■PUBLICATIONS

Reno Gay Page **775/453-4058**
*monthly, bar & resource listings,
community events, arts & entertainment*

■MEN'S CLUBS

Steve's [PC] 1030 W 2nd St (at
Keystone) **775/323-8770** *24hrs, spa*

■MEN'S SERVICES

➤**MegaMates** **775/334-6666** *Call to
hook up with HOT local men. FREE to
listen & respond to ads. Use FREE code
DAMRON. MegaMates.com.*

■EROTICA

Suzie's 195 Kietzke Ln (at E 2nd St)
775/786-8557 *24hrs*

■CRUISY AREAS

Crissie Caughlin Park [AYOR] W end of
the park *days*

Winnemuca

■BARS

Cheers [GF,NH] 320 S Bridge St
775/623-2660 *9am-close*

■CRUISY AREAS

Button Point [AYOR] I-80, exit 187 (3
miles E of Winnemuca)

NEW HAMPSHIRE

Concord

■CRUISY AREAS

Rollings Park [AYOR] S end of town

Franklin

■ACCOMMODATIONS

Gile House Inn [M,SW,WI,GO] 40 Giile
Rd **603/491-8584**

Keene

■ACCOMMODATIONS

The Lane Hotel [GS,F,NS,WI,WC]
30 Main St **603/357-7070,
888/300-5056**

Manchester

■ACCOMMODATIONS

Radisson Hotel Manchester
[GF,F,SW,WI,WC] 700 Elm St
603/625-1000, 800/395-7046

■BARS

The Breezeway [MW,NH,D,C,DS,GO] 14
Pearl St **603/621-9111** *4pm-1am,
theme nights*

Club 313 [★MW,D,F,E,K,DS,NS,WI,WC]
93 S Maple St (at S Willow)
603/628-6813 *7pm-1am, clsd Sun-
Mon & Wed*

Doogie's Bar & Grill [M,NH,F,D,WC,GO]
37 Manchester St **603/232-0732**
4pm-1am, patio

Element Lounge [MW,D,F,K,DS] 1055 Elm St **603/627-2922** *3pm-1:30am, clsd Mon*

Nashua

■ACCOMMODATIONS

Radisson Hotel [GF,SW,WI,WC] 11 Tara Blvd **603/888-9970**

■NIGHTCLUBS

The Amber Room [GS] 53 High St **603/881-9060** *9:30pm Fri-Sat, more gay Fri*

Newfound Lake

■ACCOMMODATIONS

The Inn on Newfound Lake [GS,SW,NS,WI,GO] 1030 Mayhew Tpke Rte 3-A, Bridgewater **603/744-9111, 800/745-7990** *private beach on cleanest lake in NH, also restaurant, full bar*

Portsmouth

■ACCOMMODATIONS

Ale House Inn [GF,WI,GO] 121 Bow St (at Market St) **603/431-7760**

■CAFES

Breaking New Grounds [WI] 14 Market Square **603/436-9555** *6:30am-11pm*

■RESTAURANTS

The Mombo [WC] 66 Marcy St (at State St) **603/433-2340** *dinner only, clsd Sun-Mon*

■EROTICA

Moonlight Reader 940 Rte 1 Bypass N **603/436-9622**

White Mtns

■ACCOMMODATIONS

Beal House [GF,WI] 2 W Main St, Littleton **603/444-2661** *also restaurant*

The Horse & Hound Inn [GF,F,NS,WI,GO] 205 Wells Rd, Franconia **603/823-5501, 800/450-5501** *also restaurant*

The Inn at Bowman [GS,SW,NS,WC,GO] 1174 Rte 2 (Presidential Hwy), Randolph **603/466-5006**

Inn at Crystal Lake [GS,NS,WI,GO] 2356 Eaton Rd (at Rte 16), Eaton **603/447-2120, 800/343-7336**

The Notchland Inn [GS,F,NS,GO] 2 Morey Rd, Hart's Location **603/374-6131, 800/866-6131**

Riverbend Inn B&B [GS,NS,WI,GO] 273 Chocorua Mtn Hwy (at Rte 113), Chocorua **603/323-7440, 800/628-6944** *full brkfst*

Wyatt House Country Inn [GS,WI,GO] 3046 White Mountain Hwy, N Conway **603/356-7977, 800/527-7978**

■RESTAURANTS

Polly's Pancake Parlor 672 Rte Sugar Hill Rd (exit 38 off 93 N), Sugar Hill **603/823-5575** *7am-2pm, till 3pm wknds, clsd winters*

The Red Parka Steakhouse & Pub Rte 302, Glen **603/383-4344** *open from 3pm, also bar*

■ENTERTAINMENT & RECREATION

Reel North Fly Fishing [GO] **603/858-4103** *casting lessons, half & full day river trips*

■CRUISY AREAS

Scenic Rest Area [AYOR] on left of Rte 16 N, Chocorua

NEW JERSEY

Please note: this book went to print shortly after Hurricane Sandy damaged much of New Jersey's coastline. Please call ahead before visiting.

Statewide

■PUBLICATIONS

Out in Jersey 743 Hamilton Ave, Trenton 08629 **609/213-9310** *bimonthly glossy magazine for all of New Jersey's LGBT community*

Asbury Park

■ACCOMMODATIONS

Empress Hotel [GF,SW,WI] 101 Asbury Ave **732/774-0100** *also Empress Lobby Lounge on wknds*

New Jersey • USA

■BARS
Georgie's [MW,NH,F,K,DS] 812 5th Ave (at Main) **732/988-1220** *2pm-2am*

■NIGHTCLUBS
Paradise [MW,D,E,P,SW] 101 Asbury Ave (at Ocean Ave) **732/988-6663** *4pm-2am, from 2pm Sat, from noon Sun, 2 dance flrs, also piano bar & tiki/ pool bar in summer*

■RESTAURANTS
Bistro Olé [★BYOB, GO] 230 Main St **732/897-0048** *dinner nightly, clsd Mon-Tue, Spanish-Portuguese*

Moonstruck [E] 517 Lake Ave (at Grand) **732/988-0123** *dinner only, clsd Mon-Tue, also bar, live music wknds*

Atlantic City

■ACCOMMODATIONS
The Carisbrooke Inn [GF,NS,WI] 105 S Little Rock Ave, Ventnor **609/822-6392** *on a beach block*

Ocean House [MO,V,N,GO] 127 S Ocean Ave **609/345-8203**

Tropicana Casino & Resort [GF,SW] 2831 Boardwalk (at Brighton) **609/340-4000, 800/345-8767**

■NIGHTCLUBS
Pro Bar [MW,D,DS] 1133 Boardwalk (at Resorts Casino) **800/334-6378** *8pm-3am, clsd Mon-Wed*

■RESTAURANTS
Dock's Oyster House [WC] 2405 Atlantic Ave **609/345-0092** *5pm-10pm, till 11pm Fri-Sat*

White House Sub Shop 2301 Arctic Ave (at Mississippi) **609/345-1564** *10am-10pm, till 11pm Fri-Sat, from 11am Sun*

■EROTICA
Atlantic City News 101 S Martin Luther King Jr Blvd (at Pacific) **609/344-9444** *24hrs*

Belmar

■CRUISY AREAS
Belmar Beach [AYOR] *under fishing pier*

Boonton

■NIGHTCLUBS
Switch [MW,D,CW,F,S] 202 Myrtle Ave (off Washington) **973/263-4000** *3pm-2am*

Camden

■ENTERTAINMENT & RECREATION
The Walt Whitman House 30 Mickle Blvd (btwn S 3rd & S 4th Sts) **856/964-5383** *the last home of America's great & controversial poet*

Cape May

■ACCOMMODATIONS
Congress Hall [GF,SW,WI] 251 Beach Ave **609/884-8421, 888/944-1816**

Cottage Beside the Point [NS,GO] **609/204-0549, 609/898-0658** *studio*

Highland House [GF,NS] 131 N Broadway (at York) **609/898-1198**

The Virginia Hotel [GF,WI] 25 Jackson St (btwn Beach Dr & Carpenter's Ln) **609/884-5700, 800/732-4236** *also The Ebbitt Room restaurant*

■BARS
The King Edward Room [M] 301 Howard St (at The Chalfonte Hotel) **609/884-8409** *3pm-1am summer only*

■CAFES
Higher Grounds [E,WI] 479B W Perry St **609/884-1131** *8:30am-4:30pm, clsd Sun*

■CRUISY AREAS
Cape May Promenade [AYOR] Beach Ave (btwn Broadway & 2nd)

Higbee Beach [AYOR]

Cherry Hill

■CRUISY AREAS
Cooper River Park [AYOR] Cuthbert Blvd S (off Rte 70)

Cliffwood

■CRUISY AREAS
Cliffwood Beach [AYOR]

Hammonton

■NIGHTCLUBS
Club In Or Out [MW,D,DS,TG,E,K] 19 N Egg Harbor Rd (at Orchard Ave) 609/561-2525 *6pm-3am Fri-Sat, 5pm-1am Sun*

Highland Park

■INFO LINES & SERVICES
Pride Center of New Jersey 85 Raritan Ave (at S 1st Ave) 732/846-2232 *info line & meeting space for various groups*

Hoboken

■NIGHTCLUBS
Maxwell's [★GF,A,F] 1039 Washington St 201/653-1703 *live music venue*

Jamesburg

■RESTAURANTS
Fiddleheads [BYOB,GO] 27 E Railroad Ave 732/521-0878 *lunch & dinner, Sun brunch, clsd Mon-Tue, upscale bistro*

Jersey City

■INFO LINES & SERVICES
Hudson Pride Connections 32 Jones St 201/963-4779 *"serving the LGBT communities & all people living w/ HIV, since 1993"*

■ACCOMMODATIONS
Hyatt Regency Jersey City [GF,SW,NS,WC] 2 Exchange Pl (on the Hudson) 201/645-4712, 201/469-1234 *luxury waterfront hotel, short ride to NYC*

■BARS
Lamp Post [GS,F] 382 2nd St 201/222-1331 *11:30am-2am, till 3am Fri-Sat, live bands*

LITM [GS] 140 Newark Ave (at Grove) 201/536-5557 *5pm-1am, till 2am Fri-Sat, 11am-midnight Sun, also restaurant & gallery*

RESTAURANTS

Baja 117 Montgomery St 201/915-0062 *lunch & dinner, Mexican, DJ wknds*

Lodi

■RESTAURANTS
Penang Malaysian & Thai Cuisine [WC,GO] 334 N Main St (at Garibaldi Ave) 973/779-1128 *11am-11pm, full bar*

Morristown

■INFO LINES & SERVICES
GAAMC (Gay Activist Alliance in Morris County) 21 Normandy Hts Rd (at Columbia Rd, Unitarian Fellowship) 973/285-1595 *info line 7:30pm-9pm*

New Brunswick

■BARS
The Den [M,D,MR,DS,V,WC] 700 Hamilton St (at Douglas), Somerset 732/545-7354 *8pm-2am Wed-Sat only*

■RESTAURANTS
The Frog & the Peach [WC] 29 Dennis St (at Hiram Square) 732/846-3216 *lunch Mon-Fri, dinner nightly, full bar, upscale*

Sofie's Bistro 700 Hamilton St (at Douglas), Somerset 732/545-7778 *dinner only, clsd Mon, patio*

Stage Left [★WC,GO] 5 Livingston Ave (at George) 732/828-4444 *full bar, expensive*

Newark

■NIGHTCLUBS
Rainbow Tuesday [M,D,DS] 70 Jabez St (at XL Lounge) 973/207-4261 *Tue only*

■MEN'S SERVICES
▶**MegaMates** 973/679-2020 *Call to hook up with HOT local men. FREE to listen & respond to ads. Use FREE code DAMRON. MegaMates.com.*

New Jersey • USA

■EROTICA
Little Theatre 562 Broad St
973/623-5177

Ocean City

■CRUISY AREAS
58th St Pavilion [AYOR] *late*

Princeton

■CRUISY AREAS
Herrontown Woods Park [AYOR] off
Snowden Ln, btwn mailbox 586 & 603
(no sign, entrance looks like private
driveway) *beware of cops!*

River Edge

■NIGHTCLUBS
Feathers [★M,D,K,S,V,YC,WC] 77
Kinderkamack Rd (at Grand)
201/342-6410 *9pm-2am, till 3am Sat,
clsd Mon-Tue*

■CRUISY AREAS
Park & Ride [AYOR] off Rte 4 (across
the street from Feathers nightclub)

Sandy Hook

■ENTERTAINMENT &
RECREATION
Gunnison Nude Beach Beach G parking lot (near Gunnison Park, S end) *at
the beach go right (all the way) to the
gay section, cruisy area year-round*

Sayreville

■NIGHTCLUBS
Deko Lounge [M,D] 1979 Hwy 35
South 732/727-4141, 732/727-6410
9pm-2am, gay Fri only

Toms River

■CRUISY AREAS
Winding River [AYOR] Rte 37 (near
Garden State Pkwy)

NEW MEXICO

Alamogordo

■ACCOMMODATIONS
Best Western Desert Aire Motor Inn
[GF,SW,WI,WC] 1021 S White Sands Blvd
505/437-2110, 800/637-5956

■CRUISY AREAS
Alameda Park [AYOR] off White Sands
Blvd *nights*
Foothills Park [AYOR] 1st St E (past
Scenic Dr) *days*

Albuquerque

*includes Bernalillo, Corrales,
Placitas & Rio Rancho*

■INFO LINES & SERVICES
AA Gay/ Lesbian [NS,WC]
505/266-1900 (AA#)

Common Bond Info Line
505/891-3647 *24hrs, covers LGBT
community*

■ACCOMMODATIONS
Adobe Nido [GF,NS,WI] 1124 Major Ave
NW (at 12th St & Candilaria NW)
505/344-1310, 866/435-6436 *B&B,
also aviary*

Bottger Mansion of Old Town
[GF,TG,WI] 110 San Felipe (at Central
Ave) 505/243-3639, 800/758-3639
B&B

**Brittania & W E Mauger Estate
B&B** [GF,NS,WI] 701 Roma Ave NW (at
7th) 505/242-8755, 800/719-9189

Casa Manzano B&B [GS,GO] 103
Forest Rd 321 (at State Rte 55), Tajique
505/384-9767

Casas de Suenos [GS] 310 Rio Grande
Blvd SW (btwn York & Alhambra)
505/247-4560, 800/665-7002

La Casita B&B [GF,NS,WI] 317 16th St
NW (at Lomas Blvd) 505/242-0173
adobe guesthouse

Casitas at Old Town [GS,NS,GO] 1604
Old Town Rd NW (at Mountain Rd)
505/843-7479 *classic adobe bldg,
private patios*

Golden Guesthouses [MW,NS,GO] 2645 Decker NW (at Glenwood) 505/344-9205, 888/513-GOLD

The Nativo Lodge [GF] 6000 Pan American Fwy NE 505/798-4300, 888/628-4861

Sandia Courtyard Hotel [GF,SW,F,WI] 10300 Hotel Ave (at Eubank) 505/296-4853, 800/877-4852

Sheraton Albuquerque Airport Hotel [GF,F,SW] 2910 Yale Blvd SE (at Gibson) 505/843-7000, 800/325-3535

■BARS

Albuquerque Social Club [★MW,D,PC] 4021 Central Ave NE (at Morningside, enter rear) 505/262-1088 2pm-2am, noon-midnight Sun

Sidewinders Ranch [M,D,CW,B,K,WC] 8900 Central SE (at Wyoming) 505/554-2078 4pm-2am, till midnight Sun, clsd Mon

■NIGHTCLUBS

Effex [MW,D] 420 Central SW (at 5th) 505/842-8870 9pm-2am Th-Sat

■CAFES

Java Joe's 906 Park Ave SW 505/765-1514 6:30am-3:30pm, coffee & pastries, monthly art shows

■RESTAURANTS

Artichoke Cafe [WC] 424 Central Ave SE (at Arno St) 505/243-0200 lunch Mon-Fri, dinner nightly, bistro

Cafe Cubano at Laru Ni Hati [GO] 3413 Central Ave NE (btwn Tulane & Amherst) 505/255-1575 10am-9pm, till 8pm Sat, noon-5pm Sun, clsd Mon, cigars & cheap Cuban food, also unisex hair salon

Copper Lounge [WC] 1504 Central Ave SE (at Maple) 505/242-7490 11am-2am, clsd Sun, pizza, burgers, full bar

Desert Fish 4214 Central Ave NE 505/266-5544 dinner nightly, wknd brunch, clsd Mon, seafood

El Patio [★YC,BW,WC] 142 Harvard St SE (at Central) 505/268-4245 11am-9pm, plenty veggie

El Pinto 10500 4th St NW (at Roy Ave) 505/898-1771 lunch & dinner, Sun brunch, Mexican

Flying Star Cafe [WI,WC] 3416 Central Ave SE (2 blocks W of Carlisle) 505/255-6633 6am-11pm, till midnight Fri-Sat

Frontier 2400 Central Ave SE (at Cornell) 505/266-0550 5am-1am, good breakfast burritos

The Original Garcia's Kitchen [WC] 1113 4th St NW (at Mountain) 505/247-9149 7am-9pm, awesome little down home place

The Range Cafe 2200 Menaul NE (at University Blvd) 505/888-1660 7:30am-9pm, Southwestern

Romano's Macaroni Grill [WC] 2100 Louisiana NE (at Winrock Mall) 505/881-3400 11am-10pm, Italian

Sadie's Cocinita [★WC] 6230 4th St NW (near Osuna) 505/345-5339 11am-10pm, 10am-9pm Sun, New Mexican

Zinc Wine Bar & Bistro [E,R] 3009 Central Ave NE (at Dartmouth) 505/254-9462 lunch & dinner, brunch wknds, also Blues Cellar till 1am Mon-Sat, live music

■ENTERTAINMENT & RECREATION

Bio Park Botanic Garden 2601 Central Ave NW (at New York Ave) 505/768-2000 an oasis in the desert: native & exotic plants, butterflies

■BOOKSTORES

Page One 11018 Montgomery NE (at Juan Tabo Blvd) 505/294-2026, 800/521-4122 9am-9pm, till 6pm Sun, "New Mexico's Largest Independent Bookstore"

■MEN'S SERVICES

▶**MegaMates** 505/268-1111 Call to hook up with HOT local men. FREE to listen & respond to ads. Use FREE code DAMRON. MegaMates.com.

■EROTICA

Castle Megastore 5110 Central Ave SE (at San Mateo) 505/262-2266

Self Serve [GO] 3904-B Central Ave SE (at Morningside) 505/265-5815 noon-7pm, till 8pm Fri, till 6pm Sun

New Mexico • USA

Video Maxxx 810 Comanche NE (at I-25) 505/341-4000 *leather, novelties, books, etc*

Viewpoint [★] 6406 Central Ave SE (at San Pedro) 505/268-6373 *24hrs*

Chimayo

▦ACCOMMODATIONS

Casa Escondida B&B [GF,NS,WI] 505/351-4805, 800/643-7201 *full brkfst, hot tub*

Clovis

▦CRUISY AREAS

Main St [AYOR] btwn 2nd & 7th

Farmington

▦ACCOMMODATIONS

Quality Inn [GF,WI,WC] 1901 E Broadway 505/325-3700, 877/424-6423

Hobbs

▦EROTICA

Oasis Video & Bookstore 515 Hwy 132 (at Hwy 83), Lovington 575/392-2310

Stateline Video 6100 W Carlsbad Hwy 62 (across from airport) 575/393-3616

Las Cruces

▦ACCOMMODATIONS

Hotel Encanto de Las Cruces [GF] 705 S Telshor Blvd 575/522-4300, 866/383-0443

▦RETAIL SHOPS

Spirit Winds Gifts & Cafe [E,F,WI,WC] 2260 S Locust St (at Thomas Dr) 575/521-0222 *7:30am-7pm, 8am-6pm Sun, patio*

▦CRUISY AREAS

Burn Lake [AYOR] btwn W Amador & Westgate

Madrid

▦BARS

Mineshaft Tavern [GF,F,E] 2846 State Hwy 14 505/473-0743 *11:30am-close, also restaurant*

▦CAFES

Java Junction [WI] 2855 State Hwy 14 505/438-2772 *7am-4pm, till 5pm wknds, also giftshop & B&B*

Ramah

▦ACCOMMODATIONS

El Morro RV Park, Cabins & Cafe [GS,NS,WI,GO] 4018 Hwy 53 505/783-4612 *in Zuni Mtns, full brkfst, lesbian-owned*

Ruidoso

▦ENTERTAINMENT & RECREATION

Mountain Annie's Center for the Arts [E,NS,WC] 2710 Sudderth Dr (at Grindstone Canyon Rd) 575/257-7982

▦CRUISY AREAS

Cedar Creek [AYOR] off Mechem Dr

Santa Fe

▦INFO LINES & SERVICES

AA Gay/ Lesbian 1601 S St Francis Dr 505/982-8932 *6pm Mon; also 6pm Tue at Friendship Club, 1915 Rosina St*

▦ACCOMMODATIONS

Bishop's Lodge Resort & Spa [GF,SW,NS,WC] 1297 Bishops Lodge Rd 505/983-6377, 800/419-0492 *on 450 acres*

El Farolito B&B [GS,NS,WI,GO] 514 Galisteo St (at Paseo de Peralta) 505/988-1631, 888/634-8782 *adobe compound w/ casitas*

Four Kachinas Inn [GS,NS,WI,WC,GO] 512 Webber St 505/982-2550, 800/397-2564 *courtyard, near the Plaza*

Hacienda Nicholas [GS,NS,WI,WC] 320 E Marcy St 505/986-1431, 888/284-3170 *full brkfst*

▶**Inn of the Turquoise Bear B&B** [MW,NS,WI,GO] 342 E Buena Vista St (at Old Santa Fe Tr) 505/983-0798, 800/396-4104 *Out & About Editors' Choice Award 1999-03 & Santa Fe Heritage Preservation Award 1999, New Mexico Preservation Award 2000*

Inn on the Alameda [GF,WI,WC] 303 E Alameda (at Canyon Rd) **505/984-2121, 888/984-2121** *afternoon wine reception, hot tubs*

Las Palomas [GF,NS,WI,WC] 460 W San Francisco St **505/982-5560, 877/982-5560** *luxury hotel 3 blocks from historic Plaza*

The Madeleine Inn [GS,NS,WI] 106 Faithway St **505/982-3465, 888/877-7622** *Queen Anne Victorian, full brkfst, hot tub, also spa*

Marriott Residence Inn [GF,SW,NS,WI,WC] 1698 Galisteo St (at St Michaels) **505/988-7300, 800/331-3131** *suites, hot tub*

Rosewood Inn of the Anasazi [GF,WI,WC] 113 Washington Ave **505/988-3030, 888/767-3966** *luxury hotel 1/2 block from historic Plaza, also restaurant*

The Triangle Inn—Santa Fe [MW,WI,WC,GO] 14 Arroyo Cuyamungue (12 miles N of Santa Fe) **505/455-3375, 877/733-7689** *adobe casitas, nonsmoking available, hot tub, lesbian-owned*

Vanessie Santa Fe [GF,NS,WI,WC] 427 W Water St **505/984-1193, 800/646-6752** *historic adobe inn, also restaurant & live music club*

◾BARS

The Matador [GF,NH] 116 W San Francisco St (at Galisteo) **505/984-5050** *friendly neighborhood dive bar*

SilverStarlight Lounge [MW,E,DS] 500 Rodeo Rd **505/428-7777** *5pm-midnight Wed-Sun*

◾RESTAURANTS

Anasazi Restaurant [WC] 113 Washington Ave (at Inn of the Anasazi) **505/988-3030** *brkfst, lunch, dinner & wknd brunch*

Inn of the Turquoise Bear

gay headquarters for visitors to santa fe, new mexico
an historic bed and breakfast on the Witter Bynner Estate

- ◆ Walk to Plaza, museums, galleries, restaurants & gay nightlife
- ◆ Close to opera, theater, skiing, hiking, biking, tours of pueblos & archaeological sites
- ◆ 11 rooms, private baths & entrances
- ◆ Secluded gardens & patios
- ◆ TV/VCRs
- ◆ Southwest Decor
- ◆ Expanded continental breakfasts & sunset refreshments

www.turquoisebear.net
342 E. Buena Vista Street • Santa Fe, NM 87505-2623 • 800.396.4104
505.983.0798 • FAX 505.988.4225 • IGLTA • email: bluebear@newmexico.com

New Mexico • *USA*

Bobcat Bite 420 Old Las Vegas Hwy **505/983-5319** *11am-7:50pm Wed-Sat, award-winning burgers & steaks*

Cafe Pasqual's [★BW,WC] 121 Don Gaspar Ave (at Water St) **505/983-9340, 800/722-7672** *brkfst, lunch, dinner & Sun brunch, Southwestern*

The Compound Restaurant [★GS,NS,R,WC] 653 Canyon Rd (at Delgado) **505/982-4353** *lunch Mon-Sat & dinner nightly, upscale, Southwestern, patio*

Cowgirl BBQ 319 S Guadalupe St (at Aztec) **505/982-2565** *11am-11pm, till midnight Fri-Sat, great margaritas*

El Farol 808 Canyon Rd **505/983-9912** *Spanish/ tapas, live music*

Garbo's at RainbowVision [WC] 500 Rodeo Rd (ar S St Francis) **505/428-2925** *lunch & dinner, clsd Sun-Tue, full bar*

Geronimo's [WC] 724 Canyon Rd (at Camino del Monte Sol) **505/982-1500** *dinner nightly, eclectic gourmet, full bar from 11am-11pm*

Harry's Roadhouse 96 Old Las Vegas Hwy **505/989-4629** *7am-9:30pm, patio, popular brunch*

Pink Adobe 406 Old Santa Fe Trl **505/983-7712** *steak & seafood, also Dragon Room bar*

Santacafe [WC] 231 Washington Ave **505/984-1788** *lunch & dinner, Southwestern/ Asian*

Tune Up Cafe [BW,WC] 1115 Hickox St (at Cortez) **505/983-7060** *7am-10pm, from 8am wknds, New Mexican*

Vanessie of Santa Fe [★MW,P] 434 W San Francisco St (at Guadalupe) **505/982-9966** *5pm-9pm (bar 4:30pm-midnight), steak house, piano bar*

▓ENTERTAINMENT & RECREATION

Ten Thousand Waves [N] 3451 Hyde Park Rd (4 miles out of town) **505/982-9304** *Japanese health spa & lodging, clothing-optional*

▓BOOKSTORES

Downtown Subscription [WC] 376 Garcia St (at Acequia Madre) **505/983-3085** *7am-6pm, newsstand & coffee shop*

▓RETAIL SHOPS

The Ark 133 Romero St (at Agua Fria) **505/988-3709** *10am-6pm, 11am-5pm Sun, spiritual*

▓MEN'S SERVICES

➤**MegaMates** 505/216-3000 *Call to hook up with HOT local men. FREE to listen & respond to ads. Use FREE code DAMRON. MegaMates.com.*

Silver City

▓ACCOMMODATIONS

Gila House Hotel & Gallery [GF] 400 N Arizona **575/313-7015** *also Gallery 400*

West Street Inn 575/534-2302

▓BARS

Isaac's Bar & Grill [GF,D,E] 200 N Bullard St **575/388-4090** *4pm-close, clsd Tue*

▓CAFES

Shevek & Co [BW,GO] 602 N Bullard St (at 6th St) **575/534-9168** *dinner nightly, clsd Wed, Mediterranean cuisine, espresso, "the best service in town"*

▓RESTAURANTS

Diane's Restaurant & Bakery [BW] 510 N Bullard **575/538-8722**

Taos

▓ACCOMMODATIONS

Adobe & Stars B&B [GS,NS,WI,WC] 584 State Hwy 150 (at Valdez Rim Rd) **575/776-2776, 800/211-7076**

Casa Benavides B&B [GF,NS,WI,WC] 137 Kit Carson Rd (at Paseo del Pueblo Sur) **575/758-1772, 800/552-1772** *fireplaces, hot tubs, mtn views, full brkfst*

Casa Europa Inn & Gallery [GS,NS,WI] 840 Upper Ranchitos Rd (at Ranchitos Rd) **575/758-9798, 888/758-9798** *full brkfst*

Casa Gallina [GS,NS,WC,GO] **575/758-2306** *3 adobe casitas in pastoral setting*

Dobson House [GF,NS] 484 Tune Dr 575/776-5738 *luxury suites, full brkfst, solar-powered eco-resort*

Dreamcatcher B&B [GF,NS,WI,WC] 416 La Lomita Rd (at Valverde) 575/758-0613, 888/758-0613 *full brkfst, hot tub*

The Historic Taos Inn [GF] 125 Paseo del Pueblo Norte (at Bent St) 575/751-2233, 888/518-8267 *several adobe houses date from the 1800s, pueblo-style fireplaces, also restaurant & bar*

San Geronimo Lodge [★GS,SW,NS,WI,WC] 1101 Witt Rd (off Kit Carson) 575/751-3776, 800/894-4119 *full brkfst, hot tub & massage available*

RESTAURANTS

Sabroso [★E,WC] 470 State Hwy 150, Arroyo Seco 575/776-3333 *5pm-10pm, American & Mediterranean, also full bar, patio*

ENTERTAINMENT & RECREATION

Llama Trekking Adventures 800/758-5262 *day hikes & multiday llama treks in Sangre de Cristo Mtns & Rio Grande Gorge*

Truth or Consequences

ACCOMMODATIONS

The Belair Inn [GS,NS,WI] 705 N Date St (at 7th Ave) 575/894-8977 *"retro 1950s motel w/ 21st-century amenities"*

NEW YORK

Adirondack Mtns

ACCOMMODATIONS

The Cornerstone Victorian [GF] 3921 Main St (Rte 9), Warrensburg 518/623-3308 *gourmet brkfst*

The Doctor's Inn [GF,NS] 304 Trudeau Rd (at Bloomingdale Ave), Saranac Lake 518/891-3464, 518/418-9479 *Adirondack guesthouse*

Falls Brook Yurts in Adirondacks [GF] John Brannon Rd, Minerva 518/761-6187 *access to hiking, fishing & boating*

King Hendrick Motel [GF,SW,NS,WI,WC] 1602 State Rte 9, Lake George 518/792-0418, 866/521-6883 *cabins available*

Rainbow Woods Campgrounds [MO] 134 Rte 74 (at Rte 9), Schroon Lake 518/351-0002 *summer campground*

Secluded Retreat Cabin [MW,NS] Lake Luzerne 518/361-2375 *secluded, rustic cabin*

Tea Island Resort [GF] 3020 Lake Shore Dr, Lake George 518/668-2776

Albany

see Capital District

Angelica

ACCOMMODATIONS

Jones Pond Campground [MO,SW,N,WI,GO] 9835 Old State Rd 585/567-8100 *May-Oct 15, theme wknds, campsites & RV, guesthouse & log cabins*

Binghamton

see also Scranton, Pennsylvania

INFO LINES & SERVICES

AA Gay/ Lesbian 607/722-5983

BARS

Merlin's [MW,NH,D,E,K] 201 State St 607/722-1022 *8pm-close, till 3am Fri-Sat, [18+] Wed-Fri & Sun*

Squiggy's [MW,NH,D,K,DS] 34 Chenango St (at Court) 607/722-2299 *6pm-midnight, till 2am Fri-Sat, from 8pm Sat, clsd Sun*

CAFES

Lost Dog Cafe [★E,BW,WC] 222 Water St (at Henry) 607/771-6063 *11:30am-10pm, till 11pm Fri-Sat, clsd Sun*

RESTAURANTS

The Whole in the Wall 43 S Washington St 607/722-5138 *11:30am-9pm, clsd Sun-Mon, plenty veggie/ vegan*

EROTICA

North Street Bookshop 17 Washington Ave (at North), Endicott 607/785-1588

New York • *USA*

Buffalo

■INFO LINES & SERVICES

Lesbian/ Gay AA 18 Trinity Pl (at AIDS Community Svc) 716/852-7743 *8pm Mon & Wed*

Pride Center of Western NY 206 S Elmwood Ave 716/852-7743 *meetings, resources & more*

■ACCOMMODATIONS

Beau Fleuve B&B [GF] 242 Linwood Ave 716/882-6116, 800/278-0245

The Mansion on Delaware [GS,WI,WC] 414 Delaware Ave 716/886-3300

■BARS

Cathode Ray [M,NH,V,WC] 26 Allen St (at N Pearl) 716/884-3615 *1pm-4am*

Fugazi [GS,V] 503 Franklin St (near Allen St) 716/881-3588 *5pm-2am, cocktail lounge*

K Gallagher's [GF,NH,MR,F,WC] 73 Allen St 716/886-6676 *lunch & dinner, till 3pm Sun*

Q [MW,NH] 44 Allen St 716/332-2223 *3pm-4am, from noon wknds*

The Underground [M,NH,D,K] 274 Delaware Ave (at Johnson) 716/853-0092 *noon-4am*

■NIGHTCLUBS

Club Marcella [MW,D,DS,WC,18+] 622 Main St 716/847-6850 *10pm-4am, clsd Mon-Wed*

■CAFES

Cafe 59 [WI,GO] 59 Allen St (at Franklin) 716/883-1880 *7am-4pm, 10am-4pm Sat, clsd Sun*

■RESTAURANTS

Allen Street Hardware Cafe [E] 245 Allen St (at College) 716/882-8843 *from 5pm daily, full bar, live music, art*

Anchor Bar 1047 Main St 716/886-8920, 716/884-4083 *11am-10pm, till midnight Fri-Sat, home of the original Buffalo Chicken Wing*

Atmosphere 62 62 Allen St (at Franklin) 716/881-0062 *from 4pm Wed-Sat, full bar*

Mothers 33 Virginia Pl (at Virginia St) 716/882-2989 *4pm-11pm, till 2am Sat*

Rue Franklin 341 Franklin St (at W Tupper) 716/852-4416 *5:30pm-10pm, clsd Sun-Mon, upscale, contemporary French*

Tempo 581 Delaware Ave (at Allen St) 716/885-1594 *dinner only, clsd Sun, upscale Italian/ American*

Towne Restaurant 186 Allen St 716/884-5128 *7am-5am, clsd Sun, Greek*

■ENTERTAINMENT & RECREATION

Babeville 341 Delaware Ave (at W Tupper) 716/852-3835 *Ani Di Franco's rehabbed church performance space, also Hallwalls Arts Center*

Buffalo United Artists 119 Chippewa (btwn Delaware & Elmwood) 716/886-9239 *gay-themed theater company*

■BOOKSTORES

Talking Leaves 3158 Main St (btwn Winspear & Hertel Aves) 716/837-8554 *10am-6pm, till 8pm Wed-Th, clsd Sun; also 951 Elmwood Ave*

■PUBLICATIONS

Outcome Buffalo 495 Linwood Ave 716/228-8828 *monthly*

■MEN'S SERVICES

▶**MegaMates** 716/852-4800 *Call to hook up with HOT local men. FREE to listen & respond to ads. Use FREE code DAMRON. MegaMates.com.*

■EROTICA

Elmwood Books Adult Mart 3102 Delaware Ave (at Sheridan), Kenmore 716/874-1045 *24hrs*

Video Liquidators 1770 Elmwood Ave 716/874-7223 *24hrs*

■CRUISY AREAS

South Park Lake [AYOR] 15 minutes from downtown *best btwn 5pm & midnight*

Canandaigua

■ACCOMMODATIONS

Chalet of Canandaigua Bed & Breakfast [GF,WI,GO] 3770 State Rte 21 (at Nott Rd) 585/394-9080

Canton

■ RESTAURANTS

Spicy Iguana 21 Miner St
315/714-2155 *4pm-9pm, till 2am Fri-Sat, clsd Sun-Mon, Mexican*

Capital District

includes Albany, Cohoes, Salem, Schenectady & Troy

■ INFO LINES & SERVICES

Capital District Lesbian/ Gay Community Center 332 Hudson Ave, Albany 518/462-6138 *social & human service programs; also Rainbow Cafe 6pm-9pm, clsd Sat*

Gay AA 332 Hudson Ave (at L/G Community Center), Albany 518/462-6138 *7pm Sun, men only 7:30pm Mon*

■ ACCOMMODATIONS

The Morgan State House [GF,NS,WI] 393 State St, Albany 518/427-6063, 888/427-6063 *1800s town house*

■ BARS

Oh Bar [MW,NH,MR,K,V,WC] 304 Lark St (at Madison), Albany 518/463-9004 *2pm-4am*

Clinton Street Pub [MW,NH,D,E,K] 159 Clinton St, Schenectady 518/377-8555 *11am-close, from 8am Sat, from noon Sun*

Rocks [MW,NH,K,GO] 77 Central Ave (at Elk), Albany 518/472-3588 *2pm-4am*

Waterworks Pub [M,NH,D,F,E,K,18+,WC] 76 Central Ave (btwn Lexington & Northern), Albany 518/465-9079 *1pm-4am, garden bar, DJ wknds*

■ NIGHTCLUBS

Fuze Box [GS,D,E,GO] 12 Central Ave, Albany 518/703-8937 *8pm-4am Th-Sat, swing dancing*

■ RESTAURANTS

Bomber's Burrito Bar [GO] 258 Lark St, Albany 518/463-9636 *11am-2am, till 3am wknds, plenty veggie*

Debbie's Kitchen 456 Madison Ave (btwn Lark St & Washington Park), Albany 518/463-3829 *10am-7pm, 11am-6pm Sat, clsd Sun*

El Loco Mexican Cafe 465 Madison Ave (btwn Lark & Willett), Albany 518/436-1855 *lunch Wed-Sat, dinner nightly, clsd Mon, full bar*

Midtown Tap & Tea Room [WC,GO] 289 New Scotland Ave, Albany 518/435-0202 *11am-10pm, from 4pm Sat, clsd Mon*

Yono's [E,WC] 25 Chapel St (at Sheridan), Albany 518/436-7747 *5:30pm-10pm, clsd Sun-Mon*

■ RETAIL SHOPS

Romeo's Gifts 299 Lark St (at Madison), Albany 518/434-4014 *noon-9pm, till 5pm Sun*

■ MEN'S CLUBS

River Street Club [MO,V,N,NS,PC,WC,GO] 540 River St (at corner of River & Hoosick St), Troy 518/272-0340 *7am-11pm, from noon wknds*

■ MEN'S SERVICES

▶**MegaMates** Albany 518/207-0707 *Call to hook up with HOT local men. FREE to listen & respond to ads. Use FREE code DAMRON. MegaMates.com.*

■ CRUISY AREAS

Empire State Plaza [AYOR] Albany

Catskill Mtns

■ ACCOMMODATIONS

Beds on Clouds [GS] 5320 Main St/ Rte 23 (at CR21), Windham 518/734-4692

Bradstan Country Hotel [GF,C,P] 1561 Rte 17-B, White Lake 845/583-4114 *also piano bar & cabaret from 9pm-1am Fri-Sat*

Country Suite [GF,NS,GO] Rte 23, Windham 518/734-4079 *B&B, Victorian-style farmhouse, full brkfst, antique shop*

Cuomo's Cove [GF,NS] 33 Cumo's Cove Rd (at South St), Windham 518/734-5903, 800/734-5903

ECCE B&B [GS,NS,WI,GO] 19 Silverfish Rd, Barryville 845/557-8562, 888/557-8562 *above Upper Delaware River, full brkfst*

Fairlawn Inn [GF,WI,GO] 7872 Main St, Hunter 518/263-4183

New York • *USA*

Kate's Lazy Meadow Motel [GF,NS,WI]
5191 Rte 28, Mt Tremper
845/688-7200 *love shack owned by
Kate Pierson of the B-52s*

Point Lookout Mountain Inn
[GF,NS,WC] The Mohican Trail, Rte 23,
East Windham **518/734-3381**

**The Roxbury, Contemporary Catskill
Lodging** [GS,NS,WI,WC,GO] 2258 County
Hwy 41 (at Bridge St), Roxbury
607/326-7200 *hip country motel, kids
ok*

Village Green [GO] **845/679-0313**

■BARS

Public Restaurant & Lounge [GF,GO]
2318 City Hwy 41 (Bridge St), Roxbury
607/326-4026, 607/326-7056 *5pm-
9pm, till midnight Fri-Sat, clsd Mon-Tue*

■RESTAURANTS

Catskill Rose 5355 Rte 212, Mt
Tremper **845/688-7100** *5pm-close Th-
Sun, full bar, patio, also lodging*

■ENTERTAINMENT &
RECREATION

Frog Hollow Farm 570 Old Post Rd,
Esopus **845/384-6424** *riding school*

■BOOKSTORES

Golden Notebook [WC] 29 Tinker St,
Woodstock **845/679-8000** *11am-
6pm, till 7pm Fri-Sat*

■EROTICA

Exotic Gifts & Videos Old Rte 52 (at
Rte 52), Liberty **845/292-1140**

Cherry Creek

■ACCOMMODATIONS

The Cherry Creek Inn [GF] 1022 West
Rd (CR68) (at Center Rd)
716/296-5105 *B&B, full brkfst*

Cooperstown

■ACCOMMODATIONS

Cobblescote on the Lake [GF,NS,W,F,GO]
6515 State Hwy 80 **607/437-1146**
*spectacular views at refurbished water-
front resort*

Corning

■ACCOMMODATIONS

Black Sheep Inn [GS,WI] 8329 Pleasant
Valley Rd (Rte 54), Hammondsport
607/569-3767, 877/274-6286

Hillcrest Manor B&B [GF,NS,WI,GO]
227 Cedar St (at Fourth St)
607/936-4548, 607/654-9136 *1890
mansion*

Rufus Tanner House B&B
[GS,NS,WI,WC] 60 Sagetown Rd, Pine
City **607/732-0213, 800/360-9259**
full brkfst, hot tub

Croton-on-Hudson

■ACCOMMODATIONS

Alexander Hamilton House
[GS,SW,NS,WI] 49 Van Wyck St
914/271-6737 *full brkfst, 1889
Victorian*

Elmira

■BARS

Chill [MW,NH,D,F,K,DS,GO] 200 W 5th
607/738-9343 *6pm-1am, clsd Sun-
Tue*

■EROTICA

Deluxe Books 123 Lake St
607/734-9656

Findley Lake

■ACCOMMODATIONS

Blue Heron Inn [GF,NS] 10412 Main St
(at Shadyside Rd) **716/769-7852** *B&B,
full brkfst*

Fire Island

see also Long Island

■INFO LINES & SERVICES

AA 631/654-1150 *call for meeting
times*

■ACCOMMODATIONS

➤**Belvedere Guest House for Men**
[MO,SW,WC,GO] **631/597-6448**
*Venetian-style palace, hot tub, jacuzzi,
gym*

Dune Point Guesthouse [GF,NS,WC]
631/597-6261, 631/560-2200 (cell)
hot tub

Belvedere

GUEST HOUSE FOR MEN
FIRE ISLAND'S FINEST

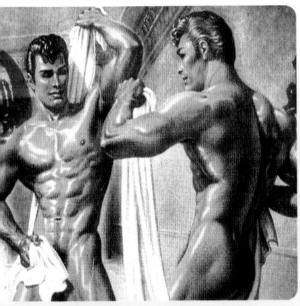

www.belvederefireisland.com
(631) 597-6448

New York • *USA*

Grove Hotel [M,SW,N,WC,GO] Dock Walk, Cherry Grove **631/597-6600** *nonsmoking room available, also 4 bars*

Hotel Ciel [M,F,SW,WC] Harbor Walk **631/597-6500** *also restaurant*

The Madison Fire Island Pines [M,SW,NS,WI,GO] 22 Atlantic Walk **631/597-6061** *near beach, roof deck, hot tub*

Pines Bluff Overlook [M] **631/597-3064**

■BARS

Blue Whale [★MW,D,F,WC] Harbor Walk, The Pines **631/597-6600** *seasonal, popular Low Tea dance*

Cherry's On the Bay [★MW,D,F,E,DS,P] 158 Bayview Walk, Cherry Grove **631/597-7859** *seasonal, noon-4am, patio, also restaurant*

Pines Bistro & Martini Bar [M,D,E,P] 36 Fire Island Blvd, The Pines **631/597-6862** *seasonal, opens 6pm*

Sip n' Twirl [M,D,E,P] 36 Fire Island Blvd, The Pines **631/597-3599** *seasonal, noon-4am, also piano bar*

■NIGHTCLUBS

Ice Palace [MW,D,DS,WC] Bayview Walk, Cherry Grove **631/597-6600** *hours vary*

■CAFES

Canteen [★M,F,WC] Harbor Walk, The Pines **631/597-6500** *coffee, smoothies, cocktails & food*

■RESTAURANTS

Cherry Grove Pizza Dock Walk (under the GroveHotel), Cherry Grove **631/597-6629** *11am-10pm*

Marina Meat Market Harbor Walk, The Pines **631/597-6588** *great sandwiches*

Pines Pizza 36 Fire Island Blvd, The Pines **631/597-3597** *seasonal, 11am-11pm*

Sand Castle 140 Lewis Walk, Cherry Grove **631/597-4174** *seasonal, lunch & dinner, also bar*

■ENTERTAINMENT & RECREATION

Cherry Grove Beach [MW] *nude beach; head left for gay section*

Invasion of the Pines The Pines dock (July 4th wknd) *come & enjoy the annual fun as boatloads of drag queens from Cherry Grove arrive to terrorize the posh Pines*

The Pines Beach [M] *nude beach*

■GYMS & HEALTH CLUBS

Deck Pool & Gym Harbor Walk, The Pines *7am-6pm, day passes available*

■CRUISY AREAS

Meat Rack [AYOR] *trail btwn Cherry Grove & W end of Pines where the boys of Fire Island really work out*

Geneva

■ACCOMMODATIONS

Belhurst [GF,F] 4069 Rte 14 S (near Snell Rd) **315/781-0201** *fireplaces, also restaurant*

Glens Falls

■ACCOMMODATIONS

Glens Falls Inn [GF,WI] 25 Sherman Ave **646/743-9365** *Victorian B&B, full brkfst*

Hamptons

see Long Island—Suffolk/ Hamptons

Hudson Valley

Hudson Valley includes Catskill, High Falls, Highland, Hudson, Hyde Park, Kinderhook, Kingston, New Paltz, Poughkeepsie, Rhinebeck & Saugerties

■ACCOMMODATIONS

Barclay Heights B&B [GF,NS] 158 Burt St (at Trinity Place), Saugerties **845/246-3788** *full brkfst*

The Country Squire B&B [GS,NS,WI,GO] 251 Allen St (at 3rd), Hudson **518/822-9229**

Harmony House B&B [GS,WI,GO] 1659 Route 212, Saugertie **845/679-1277**

Van Schaack House [GF,NS,GO] 20 Broad St (at Albany Rd), Kinderhook **518/758-6118** *B&B, full brkfst*

◼RESTAURANTS

215 Hugenot St (behind conference center), New Paltz **845/255-7888** *5pm-close, Sun brunch 11am-3pm, clsd Mon-Tue*

Armadillo Bar & Grill 97 Abeel St, Kingston **845/339-1550** *lunch wknds, dinner nightly, clsd Mon*

Northern Spy Cafe [WC] Rte 213, High Falls **845/687-7298** *dinner only, clsd Mon*

Rock & Rye Tavern 215 Hugenot St (behind conference center), New Paltz **845/255-7888** *5pm-close, Sun brunch 11am-3pm, clsd Mon-Tue*

Terrapin 6426 Montgomery St, Rhinebeck **845/876-3330** *lunch & dinner, bistro, also bar, patio*

The Would Restaurant [GO] 120 North Rd (off Rte 9 W), Highland **845/691-9883** *dinner nightly, clsd Sun, full bar, patio*

◼ENTERTAINMENT & RECREATION

Dia:Beacon Riggio Galleries 3 Beekman St (at Rte 9D), Beacon **845/440-0100** *modern art museum*

◼EROTICA

Hamilton Book & Video 216 N Hamilton St (at Parker), Poughkeepsie **845/473-1776**

Ulster Video & Gifts 584 Ulster Ave, Kingston **845/331-6023**

Ithaca

◼INFO LINES & SERVICES

AA Gay/ Lesbian 607/273-1541

◼ACCOMMODATIONS

Juniper Hill B&B [GF,NS,WI,GO] 16 Elm St (at Main St), Trumansburg **607/387-3044, 888/809-1367** *full brkfst*

Noble House Farm [GF,NS,WC,GO] 215 Connecticut Hill Rd, Newfield **607/277-4798** *near gorges & wine tours*

William Henry Miller Inn [GF,WI] 303 N Aurora St (at E Buffalo St) **607/256-4553, 877/256-4553**

◼BARS

Felicia's Atomic Lounge [GF,F,E,P,GO] 508 W State St (Meadow St) **607/273-2219** *4pm-1am, clsd Mon*

Oasis [★MW,D,MR,E,WC] 1230 Danby Rd/ Rte 96-B (at Comfort) **607/273-1505** *4pm-1am, clsd Mon, also restaurant*

◼CAFES

Sarah's Patisserie [GO] 200 Pleasant Grove Rd (at Hanshaw Rd) **607/257-4257** *10am-6pm, clsd Sun-Mon*

◼ENTERTAINMENT & RECREATION

Out Loud Chorus 607/280-0374

◼CRUISY AREAS

Stewart Park [AYOR]

Jamestown

◼ACCOMMODATIONS

Fairmount Motel [GF,WI,GO] 138 W Fairmount (Rte 394) **716/763-9550** *near Lake Chautauqua*

◼BARS

Sneakers [MW,WC] 100 Harrison (at Institute) **716/484-8816** *2pm-2am, clsd Mon*

◼ENTERTAINMENT & RECREATION

The Lucille Ball/ Desi Arnaz Center 2 W 3rd St (at Main) **716/484-0800, 877/582-9326** *for those who love Lucy*

Little Falls

◼CAFES

Piccolo Cafe 365 S Ann St **315/823-9856** *lunch Tue-Fri, dinner Wed-Sun, clsd Mon*

LONG ISLAND

Long Island is divided into 2 geographical areas:
Long Island—Nassau
Long Island—Suffolk/ Hamptons

see also Fire Island

Long Island—Nassau

■INFO LINES & SERVICES

The Center at Garden City 400 Garden City Plaza #110, Garden City **516/323-0011** *Long Island GLBT services network*

Gay/ Lesbian Switchboard of Long Island (GLSB of LI) 631/665-3700 *7pm-10pm weekdays only*

■BARS

Blanche [M,NH,K,E,S] 47 Boundary Ave, South Farmingdale **516/694-6906** *5pm-4am, from 3pm Sun*

Bullitt's Saloon [GF,NH,E] 2955 Merrick Rd, Bellmore **516/765-3892** *5pm-4am, from noon Sun*

■RESTAURANTS

RS Jones 153 Merrick Ave (off Sunrise), Merrick **516/378-7177** *dinner, clsd Mon, Tex-Mex*

■ENTERTAINMENT & RECREATION

Jones Beach walk E from Field #6, Wantagh

Pride for Youth Coffeehouse [MW] 2050 Bellmore Ave, Bellmore **516/679-9000** *7:30pm-11:30pm Fri, ages 13-20, live music*

■PUBLICATIONS

PM Entertainment Magazine 516/845-0759 *covers Long Island, NJ & NYC*

■EROTICA

Sugar Bush 102 Marine St (off Rte 110), Farmingdale **631/753-3931**

Long Island—Suffolk/ Hamptons

■ACCOMMODATIONS

The Atlantic - Hampton Resorts & Hospitality [GF,SW,WC] 1655 Country Rd 39, Southampton **631/283-6100**

Comfort Inn [GF,SW,WI,WC] 2695 Rte 112 (exit 64 off LI Expwy), Medford **631/654-3000, 877/424-6423** *also Gateway Lounge*

East Hampton Village B&B [GS,NS,WI] 172 Newtown Ln (at McGuirk St), East Hampton **631/324-1858** *lovely turn-of-the-century home*

Mill House Inn [GF,NS,WI,WC] 31 N Main St (at Newtown Lane), East Hampton **631/324-9766** *full brkfst, kids/ dogs ok*

Stirling House B&B [GF,NS,WI,GO] 104 Bay Ave, Greenport **631/477-0654, 800/551-0654** *full brkfst, jacuzzi*

Sunset Beach [GF,F] 35 Shore Rd, Shelter Island **631/749-2001** *seasonal*

■BARS

The Long Island Eagle [M,NH,L] 94 N Clinton St (at Union Blvd), Bay Shore **631/968-2750** *5pm-4am, from 9pm Sun*

For more resources and the latest updates

DAMR⊕N
Online
www.damron.com

the first name and the last word in gay travel guides

■NIGHTCLUBS

Bunkhouse [M,D,K,S,WC,GO,$] 620 Waverly Ave, Patchouge *theme nights*

Da Bunk [MW,D] 620 Waverly Ave (at Bunkhouse), Patchouge **631/506-6600** *Sat only*

■RESTAURANTS

Babette's 66 Newtown Ln, East Hampton **631/329-5377** *seasonal, brkfst, lunch & dinner, healthy*

Club Mojo [E,K] 191 Higbie Ln, W Islip **631/661-2233** *11:30am-close, karaoke, entertainment*

■EROTICA

Sugar Bush 290A Knickerbocker Ave (btwn Sunrise & Vets Hwy), Bohemia **631/567-9779**

■CRUISY AREAS

Fowler Beach [AYOR] Southampton *go right*

Smith Point Park [AYOR] Fire Island Nat'l Seashore (at end of William Floyd Pkwy), Shirley

Middletown

■ACCOMMODATIONS

Best Western Inn at Hunt's Landing [GF,SW,WI] 120 Rtes 6 & 209, Matamoras, PA **570/491-2400, 800/528-1234** *restaurant & bar*

Montgomery

■ACCOMMODATIONS

The Borland House B&B [GF,WI] 130 Clinton St **845/457-1513**

NEW YORK CITY

New York City is divided into 9 geographical areas:
NYC—Overview
NYC—Soho, Greenwich & Chelsea
NYC—Downtown
NYC—Midtown
NYC—Uptown
NYC—Brooklyn
NYC—Queens
NYC—Bronx
NYC—Staten Island

NYC—Overview

■INFO LINES & SERVICES

AA Gay/ Lesbian Intergroup at Lesbian/ Gay Community Center **212/647-1680**

LGBT Community Center [WC] 208 W 13th (at 7th Ave) **212/620-7310** *tons of groups & resources, museum*

■NIGHTCLUBS

Sholay Productions/ Desilicious [MW,D,MR] **212/713-5111** *monthly party, Bollywood, bhangra & house music, call for dates*

■ENTERTAINMENT & RECREATION

Before Stonewall: A Lesbian & Gay History Tour meet: Washington Square Arch (at Big Onion Walking Tours) **212/439-1090**

■PUBLICATIONS

Gay City News **646/229-1890** *LGBT newspaper, weekly*

MetroSource **212/691-5127** *LGBT lifestyle magazine & resource directory*

Next **212/627-0165** *entertainment & nightlife paper*

▶**Odyssey Magazine** **323/874-8788** *dish on NYC's club scene*

PM Entertainment Magazine **516/845-0759** *events, listings, classifieds & more for Long Island, NJ & NYC*

■MEN'S SERVICES

Escort Guys **44-(0) 7722/062 077, 571/527-1022**

The source to gay nightlife, music, photos and beauty.

ODYSSEY NY

odysseymagazine.net

New York • USA

➤**MegaMates** 212/971-7272 *Call to hook up with HOT local men. FREE to listen & respond to ads. Use FREE code DAMRON. MegaMates.com.*

NYC—Soho, Greenwich & Chelsea

■ INFO LINES & SERVICES

Audre Lorde Project [TG] 147 W 24th St 212/463-0342 *1pm-7pm Tue-Th only, LGBT center for people of color, events, resources, HIV services*

■ ACCOMMODATIONS

Ace Hotel [GF] 20 W 29th St (at Broadway) 212/679-2222 *hip hotel near Flatiron District*

Chelsea Mews Guest House [MO,NS,GO] 344 W 15th St (btwn 8th & 9th Aves) 212/255-9174 *some shared baths*

➤**Chelsea Pines Inn** [MW,WI,GO] 317 W 14th St (btwn 8th & 9th Aves) 212/929-1023, 888/546-2700 *"Chelsea Pines is the premier LGBT choice in the heart of the community," featured in the NY Times*

The Chelsea Savoy Hotel [GS,WI,WC] 204 W 23rd St (at 7th Ave) 212/929-9353, 866/929-9353

Chelsea Star Hotel [GS,WI] 300 W 30th St (at 8th Ave) 212/ 244-7827, 877/ 827-6969

➤**Colonial House Inn** [MW,N,NS,GO] 318 W 22nd St (btwn 8th & 9th Aves) 212/243-9669, 800/689-3779 *1850 brownstone in Chelsea, rooftop patio*

Crosby Street Hotel [GF,WI] 79 Crosby St (at Spring) 212/226-6400 *chic boutique hotel in Soho*

Eventi [GF] 851 6th Ave (at 30th St) 212/564-4567, 866/996-8396

➤**The GEM Hotel Chelsea** [GF,WI,WC] 300 W 22nd St (at 8th Ave) 212/675-1911

➤**The GEM Hotel SoHo** [GF,WI,WC] 135 E Houston St (btwn 1st & 2nd Aves) 212/358-8844

Gershwin Hotel [GF,WI] 7 E 27th St (at 5th Ave) 212/545-8000 *artsy hotel w/ model's floor dorms & rooms*

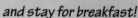

Hotel 17 [GF] 225 E 17th St 212/475-2845 *"East Village chic" budget hotel, shared baths*

➤**The Jade Hotel** [GF] 13th St (at 6th Ave) 212/375-1300

The Jane [GS,WI] 113 Jane St (at Hudson River Pk) 212/924-6700 *inspired by luxury train cabins, some shared baths*

Soho Grand Hotel [GF,WI,WC] 310 W Broadway (at Canal St) 212/965-3000, 800/965-3000 *big, glossy, over-the-top hotel*

The Standard Hotel [GF] 848 Washington St (at W 13th) 212/645-4646, 877/550-4646 *ultra-modern, luxe hotel straddling the High Line*

Tribeca Grand [GS,WI] 2 Ave of the Americas 212/519-6600

Washington Square Hotel [GF,F,WI] 103 Waverly Pl (at MacDougal St) 212/777-9515, 800/222-0418 *on historic Washington Square Park*

➤**Wyndham Garden Hotel Chelsea** [GF,WI,WC] 37 W 24th St 212/243-0800

■**BARS**

Arrow Bar [GS,D] 85 Ave A (btwn 5th & 6th) 212/673-1775 *4pm-close, theme nights*

Barracuda [★M,S] 275 W 22nd St (at 8th Ave) 212/645-8613 *4pm-4am, live DJs*

Beauty Bar [GS,D,E] 231 E 14th St (at 3rd Ave) 212/539-1389 *5pm-4am, from 7pm wknds*

The Boiler Room [M,NH,WI] 86 E 4th St (at 2nd Ave) 212/254-7536 *4pm-4am*

Boots & Saddle [M,NH,B,L,MR,S,18+,YC] 76 Christopher St (at 7th Ave S) 212/633-1986 *noon-4am, go-go dancers*

Boxers NYC [M,NH,F,V,WC] 37 W 20th St (at 6th Ave) 212/255-5082 *4pm-2am, from 1pm wknds*

New York • USA

Cake Shop [GF] 152 Ludlow St (btwn Stanton & Rivington) 212/253-0036 9am-2am, till 4am wknds, cafe/ bakery by day, punk bands at night

The Cock [M,K,S,$] 29 2nd Ave (1 blk above Houston) 212/473-9406 11pm-4am, a "sleazy rock 'n' roll bar," live DJs

Cubbyhole [MW,NH] 281 W 12th St (at 4th St) 212/243-9041

Desire [MW,NH,F] 45 W 8th St (btwn 5th & 6th Aves) 646/454-9950 3pm-close

Duplex [GF,C,P,$] 61 Christopher St (at 7th Ave) 212/255-5438 4pm-4am, piano bar from 9pm

The Eagle [★M,L] 554 W 28th St (btwn 10th & 11th) 646/473-1866 10pm-4am

Eastern Bloc [★MW,D,S,WC] 505 E 6th St (at Ave A) 212/777-2555 7pm-4am, trendy lounge

G Lounge [★M,GO] 225 W 19th St (at 7th Ave) 212/929-1085 4pm-4am, lounge, live DJs

Gym Sports Bar [M,NH] 167 8th Ave (btwn 18th & 19th) 212/337-2439 4pm-close, from 1pm wknds

The Hangar [M,DS,S] 115 Christopher St (at Bleecker) 212/627-2044 3pm-4am

Marie's Crisis [MW,P] 59 Grove St (at 7th Ave) 4pm-4am, piano bar from 9:30pm

►The Monster [★M,D,C,P,WC] 80 Grove St (at W 4th St, Sheridan Square) 212/924-3558 4pm-4am, from 2pm wknds, piano bar, T-dance Sun

Nowhere [MW,NH,TG] 322 E 14th St (btwn 1st & 2nd) 212/477-4744 3pm-4am

Phoenix [MW,NH] 447 E 13th (at Ave A) 212/477-9979 4pm-4am, patio

Pieces [M,NH,D,K,C] 8 Christopher St (btwn 6th & 7th) 212/929-9291 2pm-4am

Rawhide NYC [M,L,S] 212 8th Ave (at 21st) 212/242-9332 noon-4am

Rockbar [M,NH,E,WC] 185 Christopher St (at Weehawken St) 212/242-9113 noon-close

Secret Lounge [M,MR-A,S] 525 W 29th St (at 10th Ave) 212/268-5580 10pm-4am, clsd Sun-Wed

►Splash [★M,D,S,V,YC] 50 W 17th St (at 6th Ave) 212/691-0073 4pm-5am

Stonewall Inn [M,NH,D,DS,B,E] 53 Christopher St (at 7th Ave) 212/488-2705 2pm-4am

Twist'd Saturdays [M,D,YC] 225 W 19th St (at 7th Ave, at G Lounge) Sat only

Ty's [M,NH,L,B,GO] 114 Christopher St (btwn Bleecker & Hudson) 212/741-9641 3pm-4am

UC Lounge [M,NH,K,DS] 87 Ludlow St (btwn Broome & Delancey) 212/677-1100 4pm-2am, till 4am wknds

Urge [M,NH,F,S] 33 2nd Ave (at 2nd St) 212/533-5757 4pm-4am, cruisy lounge, go-go boys

■NIGHTCLUBS

Alegria [★M,D] 8 parties a year, during holiday wknds & Black Party in March

Bar 13 [GS,D,YC] 35 E 35th St (btwn Broadway & 5th Ave) 212/979-6677 check local listings for gay events

Beige [GS] 848 Washington St (at the Standard Hotel) 11pm Tue only

Big Apple Ranch [M,D,CW,BW,$] 39 W 19th St, 5th flr (btwn 5th & 6th, at Dance Manhattan) 8pm-1am Sat only, two-step lessons

The F Word [M,D] 50 W 17th St (at Splash) 646/374-4977 popular Fri party

Happy Ending [GS,D,E] 302 Broome St (at Forsyth) 212/334-9676 7pm-4am, from 10pm Tue, clsd Sun-Mon, theme nights

Hot Mess [M,C,DS] 512 W 42nd St (at XL Nightclub) 212/244-3636 Wed only

Invasion Thursdays [M,D,YC] 35 E 35th St (btwn Broadway & 5th Ave, at Bar 13) 212/979-6677 Th only

Pyramid [GS,D] 101 Ave A (at 7th St) 212/228-4888 theme nights

Rasputin: Russian Love Machine NYC [M,D] 579 6th Ave (off 16th St) 213/621-4051 10pm-6am Sat only

Rockit [M,D] 512 W 42nd St (at XL Nightclub) 212/244-3636 *Fri only*

Saint-At-Large [★M,D] 212/674-8541 *producers of the Black Party in March*

Sea Tea [M,D,MR,F,P,S,GO,$] leaves from Pier 40 (West Side Hwy at Houston St) 212/675-2971 *6pm-10pm Sun (June-Sept)*

Sunday Situation [M,D] 80 Grove St (at W 4th St, Sheridan Square, at the Monster) 212/924-3558 *Sun T-dance*

Vandam [M,D] 150 Varick St (btwn Spring & Vandam, at Greenhouse) 212/807-7000 *gay Sun only, spectacular lighting*

Westgay [M,D,YC] 75 Clarkson St, at Westway (btwn Washington & West) *Tue only, freaky dance party*

XES Lounge [★M,D,K,C,V,GO] 157 W 24th St (at 7th Ave) 212/604-0212 *4pm-4am, smoking patio*

■ CAFES

Brown Cup Cafe 334 8th Ave (at 27th St) 212/675-7765 *7am-8pm, 8am-6pm Sat, clsd Sun*

■ RESTAURANTS

7A [★] 109 Ave A (at 7th St) 212/673-6583 *24hrs*

Agave 140 Seventh Ave (btwn 10th St & Charles) 212/989-2100 *noon-close, Southwestern, popular brunch*

Angelica Kitchen 300 E 12th St (at 1st Ave) 212/228-2909 *11:30am-10:30pm, vegetarian/ vegan*

Antica Venezia 396 West St (at W 10th St) 212/229-0606 *dinner nightly, Italian*

Awash 338 E 6th (btwn 1st & 2nd Aves) 212/982-9589 *11am-11pm, Ethiopian*

Benny's Burritos 93 Ave A (at 6th St) 212/254-2054 *11am-midnight, till 1am Fri-Sat, cheap & huge; also 113 Greenwich (at Jane), 212/727-0584*

Big Gay Ice Cream Shop 125 E 7th St (at 1st Ave) **212/533-9333** *1pm-midnight; also Big Gay Ice Cream Truck from May-Oct*

Blue Ribbon [WC] 97 Sullivan St (at Spring St) **212/274-0404** *4pm-4am, cont'l/ American, chef hangout*

Bone Lick Park [WC] 75 Greenwich Ave (at 7th Ave) **212/647-9600** *BBQ, full bar*

Budhu Lounge 531 Hudson St (at Charles St) **917/262-0836** *5:30pm-2am, till 4am Fri-Sat, 11am-midnight Sun*

Cola's [★] 148 8th Ave (at 17th St) **212/633-8020** *lunch & dinner, Italian*

Cowgirl Hall of Fame 519 Hudson St (at W 10th) **212/633-1133** *lunch, dinner, wknd brunch*

Crispo 240 W14th St (at 7th) **212/229-1818** *dinner only, great caramelized cauliflower & carbonara*

The Dish 201 8th Ave (btwn 20th & 21st) **212/352-9800, 212/352-3003** *brkfst, lunch & dinner, also bar*

East of Eighth 254 W 23rd St (at 8th) **212/352-0075** *lunch & dinner, bar open late*

Elmo 156 7th Ave (at 20th St) **212/337-8000** *lunch & dinner, also lounge*

Les Enfants Terribles 37 Canal St (at Ludlow) **212/777-7518** *8am-4am, African/Moroccan, Brazilian, French, full bar & DJ*

Garage [E] 99 7th Ave S (at Grove St) **212/645-0600** *noon-3am, contemporary American, live jazz*

Gobo 401 Ave of the Americas (at W 8th) **212/255-3242** *11:30am-11pm, vegetarian/ vegan*

Intermezzo 202 8th Ave (at 21st St) **212/929-3433** *noon-midnight, Italian, great wknd brunch*

LaVagna 545 E 5th St (btwn Aves A & B) **212/979-1005** *dinner only, affordable Italian*

Lucky Cheng's [★K,DS] 24 1st Ave (at 2nd St) 212/995-5500, 212/473-0516 5:30pm-midnight, Asian/fusion, full bar, drag shows

The Noho Star 330 Lafayette St (at Bleecker) 212/925-0070 8am-midnight, from 10:30am wknds, eclectic European & Chinese

Omai 158 9th Ave (at 19th St) 212/633-0550 dinner nightly, Vietnamese

Philip Marie 569 Hudson St (at 11th St) 212/242-6200 noon-11pm, clsd Mon

Red Bamboo 140 W 4th St (at MacDougal) 212/260-1212 noon-midnight, vegetarian/ vegan

Sacred Chow [WC] 227 Sullivan St (btwn W 3rd St & Bleecker) 212/337-0863 11am-10pm, till 11pm Fri-Sat, gourmet vegan

Sigiri 91 1st Ave (btwn 5th & 6th Sts) 212/614-9333 lunch & dinner, Sri Lankan

Trattoria Pesce Pasta 262 Bleecker St (at 6th Ave) 212/645-2993 noon-midnight

Veselka 144 2nd Ave (at 9th St) 212/228-9682 24hrs, Ukrainian, great pierogi

■ ENTERTAINMENT & RECREATION

Chelsea Classics 260 W 23rd St (btwn 7th & 8th, at Clearview Cinema) 212/691-5519 Th night only, drag diva Hedda Lettuce hosts camp movies

Dixon Place 161 Chrystie St (at Delancey) 212/219-0736 many gay-themed productions; also HOT Festival of queer performance in July

High Line Gansevoort & W 30th St (btwn 10th & 11th Ave) 212/500-6035 elevated train track converted to beautiful urban park

La Mama 74 E 4th St 212/475-7710 experimental theater

Leslie/ Lohman Gay Art Foundation & Gallery 26 Wooster St (btwn Grand & Canal) 212/431-2609 noon-6pm, clsd Sun-Mon

PS 122 150 1st Ave (at E 9th St) 212/477-5829, 212/352-3101 (tickets) it's rough, it's raw, it's real New York performance art

The Will Clark Show 8 Christopher St (at 6th Ave, at Pieces) 8pm Wed, Porno Bingo, cheap drinks, cheap men!

■ RETAIL SHOPS

DeMask 144 Orchard St 212/466-0814 European fetish fashion

Flight 001 96 Greenwich Ave (btwn Jane & 12th) 212/989-0001, 877/354-4481 11am-8pm, noon-6pm Sun, way cool travel gear

Nasty Pig 265 West 19th St (at 8th Ave) 212/691-6067 noon-8pm, 1pm-6am Sun

Rainbows & Triangles 192 8th Ave (at 19th St) 212/627-2166 11am-10pm, noon-9pm Sun, LGBT cards, books, gifts & more

■ MEN'S CLUBS

Hard Drive [MO,BYOB] 250 W 26th St (btwn 7th & 8th, at Paddles) 212/366-9339 8pm Wed only, dungeon party

►**West Side Club** [★M,PC] 27 W 20th St, 2nd flr (at 6th Ave) 212/691-2700 24hrs

■ EROTICA

Blue Door Video 87 1st Ave (at 6th St) 212/995-2248 24hrs, gay movie theater

Leather Man 111 Christopher St (at Bleecker) 212/243-5339

Pleasure Chest 156 7th Ave S (at Charles) 212/242-2158

Purple Passion [GO] 211 W 20th St (at 7th Ave) 212/807-0486 fetishwear

Unicorn 277-C W 22nd St (btwn 7th & 8th Ave) 212/924-2921

NYC—Downtown

■ ACCOMMODATIONS

Gild Hall Wall Street [GS,WC] 15 Gold St (at Platt) 212/232-7700, 212/232-7800 (reservations) high-tech boutique hotel, also restaurant & lounge

New York • *USA*

Millenium Hilton [SW,WC] 55 Church St 212/693-2001, 877/692-4458

■RESTAURANTS

La Flaca [WC] 384 Grand St 646/692-9259 *noon-4am, Mexican, full bar*

NYC—Midtown

■ACCOMMODATIONS

Chambers Hotel [GF] 15 W 56th St (at 5th Ave) 212/974-5656, 866/204-5656 *upscale boutique hotel; fabulous art collection*

Comfort Inn - Midtown West [GF,WI,WC] 442 W 36th St (btwn 9th & 10th) 212/714-6699

Distrikt Hotel [GF,WI] 342 W 40th St (at 9th Ave) 646/831-6780 , 888/444-5610 *upscale boutique hotel*

➤**The GEM Hotel Midtown West** [GF,WI,WC] 449 W 36th St (at 10th Ave) 212/967-7206

Hotel 57 [GF,NS,WI,WC] 130 E 57th St (at Lexington) 212/753-8841, 800/497-6028

Hotel Grace [GF,SW,NS,WI,WC] 125 W 45th St (near Sixth Ave) 212/354-2323

The Hotel Metro [GF,WI,WC] 45 W 35th St (at 5th Ave) 212/947-2500, 800/356-3870

Hudson Hotel [GF,WI,WC] 356 W 58th St (at 9th) 512/554-6000, 800/697-1791 *magical hotel w/ trendy bars*

Ink48 [GF,WI] 653 11th Ave (at 48th St) 212/757-0088, 877/843-8869 *luxe hotel in former printing house*

The MAve [GF,WI] 61 Madison Ave (at 27th St) 212/532-7373

The Out NYC [MW] 510 W 42nd S 212/947-2999, 855/568-8692 *NYC's first straight-friendly urban resort; restaurant & club on site*

The Pod Hotel [NS,WI,WC] 230 E 51st Street (near 2nd Ave) 212/355-0300, 800/742-5945 *compact rooms, rooftop lounge*

The Strand [GF,WI] 33 W 37th St 212/448-1024

➤**Travel Inn** [GF,SW,WC] 515 W 42nd St (at 10th Ave) 212/695-7171, 800/869-4630 *fitness center*

The Tuscany [GS,WI,WC] 120 E 39th St (at Park Ave) 212/686-1600, 877/WHOTELS (reservations only) *also Parisian-style cafe-bar*

■BARS

9th Avenue Saloon [M,NH,K] 656 9th Ave (at 46th St) 212/307-1503 *noon-4am*

Adonis [M,S,$] 221 E 58th St (at Evolve) 845/536-3323 *7pm-1am Wed, M4M Weekly Strip Show*

Bar Centrale [GS] 324 W 46th St (at 8th Ave) 212/581-3130 *5pm-close, celebs a-plenty*

Bar Tini Ultra Lounge [M] 642 10th Ave (at 45th) 917/388-2897 *4pm-4am, theme nights*

Barrage [M] 401 W 47th St (at 9th Ave) 212/586-9390 *5pm-2am*

Don't Tell Mama [★GF,C,P,YC,$] 343 W 46th St (at 9th Ave) 212/757-0788 *4pm-4am, cover + 2-drink minimum for [C]*

Evolve [M,E,DS,S,V,GO] 221 E 58th St (at 2nd Ave) 212/355-3395 *4pm-4am, theme nights*

Fairytail Lounge [M,NH] 500 W 48th St 646/684-3897 *5pm-2am, tiny, trippy lounge*

Flaming Saddle's Saloon [MW,D,CW] 793 9th Ave 212/713-0481 *4pm-2am, from 2pm Sat-Sun*

Hardware [M] 697 10th Ave (at 48th) 212/924-9885 *4pm-2am*

HK Hell's Kitchen [MW] 523 9th Ave (at 39th St) 212/913-9092 *swank lounge, theme nights, also restaurant*

Industry [M] 355 W 52nd St (at 9th Ave) 646/476-2747 *4pm-4am*

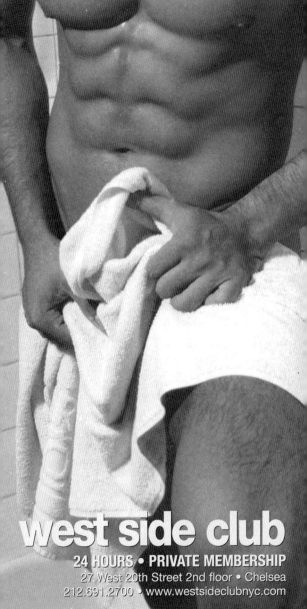

west side club

New York • USA

Posh Bar & Lounge [M,NH] 405 W 51st St (at 9th Ave) **212/957-2222** *4pm-4am, popular happy hour, DJ nightly*

The Ritz [M,D] 369 W 46th St (btwn 8th & 9th Aves) **212/333-2554** *great place for a drink pre- or post- theater*

Therapy [MW,F,E,C] 348 W 52nd St (at 9th) **212/397-1700** *5pm-4am*

Townhouse Bar [M,E,C,P] 236 E 58th St (btwn 2nd Ave & 3rd Ave) **212/754-4649** *4pm-3am, till 4am Fri-Sat, upscale, dress code*

Vlada [M] 331 W 51st St (btwn 8th & 9th) **212/974-8030** *4pm-4am, slick gay lounge*

The Web [M,D,MR-A,K,S] 40 E 58th St (at Madison) **212/308-1546** *4pm-close, from 8pm wknds, theme nights, go-go boys*

■ NIGHTCLUBS

Escuelita [M,D,MR-L,TG,DS,S,18+,$] 301 W 39th St (at 8th Ave) **212/631-0588** *10pm-5am, clsd Mon & Wed*

Jim Caruso's Cast Party [★GS,E,C] 315 W 44th St (btwn 8th & 9th Aves, at Birdland) **212/581-3080** *9:30pm-1am Mon only*

The XL [M,D,E,C,DS] 512 W 42nd S **917/239-2999** *4pm-4am*

■ RESTAURANTS

44 1/2 [WC,GO] 626 10th Ave (btwn 44 & 45) **212/399-4450** *5:30pm-close, brunch wknds*

44 & X Hell's Kitchen [WC,GO] 622 10th Ave (at 44th St) **212/977-1170** *lunch & dinner*

A Voce [R] 41 Madison Ave (at 26th) **212/545-8555** *lunch Mon-Fri, dinner nightly, Italian*

Arriba Arriba [★] 762 9th Ave (at 51st) **212/489-0810** *noon-midnight, till 1am wknds, Mexican, great margaritas*

Bamboo 52 344 W 52nd St (btwn 8th & 9th Aves) **212/315-2777** *noon-4am, from 4pm Sun, sushi, also sake bar, garden*

Bann 350 W 50th St (btwn 8th & 9th Aves) **212/582-4446** *lunch Mon-Fri, dinner nightly, Korean*

Beacon 25 W 56th St (btwn 5th & 6th) **212/332-0500** *lunch & dinner, wknd brunch, open-fire cooking, also bar*

Lips [DS] 227 E 56th St (at 3rd Ave) **212/675-7710** *6pm-midnight, till 1:30am Fri-Sat, gospel brunch Sun, clsd Mon, full bar, "the ultimate in drag dining"*

Market Cafe [GO] 496 9th Ave (at 38th St) **212/967-3892** *lunch & dinner, wknd brunch*

Vynl 754 9th Ave (at 51st St) **212/974-2003** *11am-11pm, also bar; also at 102 8th Ave*

■ ENTERTAINMENT & RECREATION

Ars Nova 511 W 54th St (at 10th Ave) **212/489-9800** *many gay-themed productions*

Empire State Building 350 5th Ave (btwn 33rd & 34th) *spectacular views of the city; visit day or night*

Naked Boys Singing [WC] 340 W 50th St (btwn 8th & 9th) **212/302-4848** *Off-Broadway smash hit*

Sex & the City Hotspots Tour [R] 5th Ave, in front of the Pulitzer Fountain (at 58th St) **212/209-3370** *3 hours, reservations a must!*

■ MEN'S CLUBS

➤**East Side Club** [★PC] 227 E 56th St, 6th flr (btwn 2nd & 3rd) **212/753-2222, 212/888-1884** *24hrs*

NYC—Uptown

■ ACCOMMODATIONS

710 Guest Suites [GF] 710 St Nicholas Ave (at 145th) **212/491-5622** *modern, chic apt suites*

BB Lodges [GS,NS,WI,GO] 1598 Lexington Ave (btwn 101st & 102nd) **917/345-7914** *private rooms w/ private kitchens*

Country Inn the City [GF,NS] W 77th St (at Broadway) **212/580-4183** *studio apts in restored 1891 town house*

Harlem Renaissance House [GS,NS,WI,GO] **212/226-1590**

"Still one of the most reliable
GOOD TIME
places in the United States."

east side club

New York • USA

Hotel Newton [GS,NS,WC] 2528 Broadway (btwn 94th & 95th) **212/678-6500, 800/643-5553** *nearest hotel to Columbia University*

Mount Morris House B&B [GS,WI,GO] 12 Mount Morris Park W (at 121st St) **917/478-6214**

▮BARS

Brandy's Piano Bar [MW,P] 235 E 84th St (at 2nd Ave) **212/650-1944** *4pm-4am, piano from 9:30pm*

Candle Bar [M,NH] 309 Amsterdam Ave (at 74th) *4pm-4am, from 3pm wknds*

Cava Wine Bar [GF] 185 W 80th St (at Amsterdam) **212/724-2282** *5:30pm-2am, from 3:30pm Sun, also tapas*

Suite [M,NH,K,DS] 992 Amsterdam (at 109th St) **212/222-4600** *5pm-4am*

Tool Box [M,NH,V] 1742 2nd Ave (at 91st St) **212/348-1288** *8pm-4am, cruisy*

▮RESTAURANTS

Billie's Black [E,K,GO] 271 W 119th St (at St Nicholas Ave) **212/280-2248** *noon-midnight, till 4am Fri-Sat, soul food, also full bar, live music Th-Fri*

Joanne Trattoria 70 W 68th St (btw Columbus & Central Park W), New York **212/721-0068**

▮EROTICA

Les Hommes 217-B W 80th St, 2nd flr (btwn Broadway & Amsterdam) **212/580-2445** *10am-2am, till 3am Fri Sat*

▮CRUISY AREAS

The Rambles [AYOR] in Central Park

NYC—Brooklyn

▮INFO LINES & SERVICES

Audre Lorde Project [TG] 85 S Oxford St **718/596-0342** *1pm-7pm Tue-Th only, LGBT center for people of color*

▮ACCOMMODATIONS

Hotel Le Bleu [GF,WI] 370 4th Ave **718/625-1500, 866/427-6073**

Hotel Le Jolie [GF] 235 Meeker Ave **718/625-2100, 866/526-4097**

The Loralei B&B [GS,NS,WI,GO] 667 Argyle Rd (at Foster Ave) **646/228-4656** *1904 Victorian*

▮BARS

The Abbey [GS,NH] 536 Driggs Ave (btwn N 7th & 8th), Williamsburg **718/599-4400** *3pm-4am*

Alligator Lounge [GS,F,K] 600 Metropolitan Ave (at Lorimer) **718/599-4440** *3pm-4am, free pizza from 6pm*

Bar 4 [GS,NH,E] 444 7th Ave (at 15th St, in Park Slope) **718/832-9800** *6pm-4am, DJ Fri-Sat*

Branded Saloon [GS,NH,E,K,GO] 603 Vanderbilt Ave (at Bergen) **718/484-8704**

Excelsior [MW] 390 5th Ave (btwn 6th & 7th) **718/832-1599** *6pm-4am, from 2pm wknds, patio*

Ginger's Bar [MW,NH,E] 363 5th Ave (btwn 5th & 6th Sts, in Park Slope) **718/788-0924** *5pm-4am, from 2pm wknds, patio*

Metropolitan [MW,NH,D,WI] 559 Lorimer St (at Metropolitan Ave), Williamsburg **718/599-4444** *3pm-4am, comfy bar w/ fireplaces & patio*

Sugarland [MW,D,E,K] 221 N 9th St (at Driggs Ave) **718/599-4044** *9pm-4am*

▮NIGHTCLUBS

Club Langston [M,D,MR-AF] 1073 Atlantic Ave (btwn Franklin & Classon) **718/622-5183** *10pm-4am Th-Sun*

Glasslands Gallery [GS,D] 289 Kent Ave, Williamsburg (btwn S 1st & S 2nd) **718/599-1450** *performance, art & dance space*

Gumbo [MW,D] 16 Main St (at Water St, at Galapagos Art Space) **718/222-8500** *rotating events, gay DUMBO party, www.gumbonyc.com for details*

Public Assembly [GF] 70 N 6th St **718/384-4586**

▮CAFES

Outpost [MW,YC,BW,GO] 1014 Fulton St (at Downing) **718/636-1260** *7:30am-midnight, 9am-11pm wknds, also lounge, art gallery*

■RESTAURANTS

Alma 187 Columbia St (at Degraw) 718/643-5400 *dinner nightly, wknd brunch, upscale Mexican, outdoor rooftop seating w/ view of Manhattan, also B61 Bar downstairs*

Beast 638 Bergen St (at Vanderbilt Ave) 718/399-6855 *dinner nightly, wknd brunch, also bar from 5pm*

Belleville Bistro & Lounge [GO] 330 5th St (at 5th Ave) 718/832-9777 *theme nights, also bar*

Bogota Latin Bistro [E,GO] 141 5th Ave (at St John's Pl) 718/230-3805 *dinner nightly, wknd brunch, clsd Tue*

ChipShop [★] 383 5th Ave (at 6th St) 718/244-7746 *noon-10pm, till 11pm Th-Sat, from 11am wknds, home of the famous fried Twinkie!*

home made [GO] 293 Van Brunt St (btwn Pioneer & King) 347/223-4135

Johnny Mack's [E] 1114 8th Ave (btwn 11th & 12th) 718/832-7961 *4pm-2am, from noon wknds*

Krescendo 364 Atlantic Ave *famed chef Elizabeth Falkner makes pizza*

Life Cafe NINE83 983 Flushing Ave (at Central Ave) 718/386-1133 *10am-midnight, till 1am Fri-Sat, full bar, new bohemian hangout*

Nita Nita 146 Wythe Ave (at N 8th) 718/388-5328 *4pm-2am, brunch wknds, also full bar, tapas*

Santa Fe Grill [WC] 62 7th Ave (at Lincoln) 718/636-0279 *5pm-close, from noon wknds, also bar*

Superfine [E,GO] 126 Front St (at Pearl St) 718/243-9005 *11:30am-3am, 2pm-11pm Sat, 11am-10pm Sun, clsd Mon, also bar*

Tandem 236 Troutman St (btwn Wilson & Knickerbocker, in Bushwick) 718/386-2369 *6pm-4am, also full bar, occasional gay parties*

■ENTERTAINMENT & RECREATION

Galapagos Art Space 16 Main St (at Water St) 718/222-8500 *performance & art space; occasional gay parties*

The Spectrum [MW,TG,E] 59 Montrose Ave *queer performance space*

■EROTICA

Babeland 462 Bergen St (at 5th Ave) 718/638-3820 *noon-9pm, till 7pm Sun*

NYC—Queens

■BARS

Albatross [GS,NH,GO] 36-19 24th Ave (at 37th), Astoria 718/204-9045 *6pm-4am, more gay wknds*

Bungalo Astoria [GS,F] 32-03 Broadway (at 32nd St) 718/204-7010 *5pm-4am, from 3pm Fri-Sat, dress code*

Friend's Tavern [M,NH,MR-L] 78-11 Roosevelt Ave, Jackson Hts 718/397-7256 *4pm-4am, DJ Wed-Sun*

Hell Gate Social [GS,D] 12-21 Astoria Blvd (at 14th St) 718/204-8313 *7pm-4am*

Hombres Lounge [M,NH,K] 85-25 37th Ave #206, Jackson Heights 718/930-0886 *5pm-4pm*

True Colors [M,NH,D,MR-L] 79-15 Roosevelt Ave (btwn 79th & 80th Sts, Jackson Hts) 718/672-7505 *4pm-4am*

■NIGHTCLUBS

Evolution [MW,D,MR-L,DS] 76-19 Roosevelt Ave (at 77th St), Jackson Hts 718/457-3939 *4pm-4am*

Lucho's Place [M,NH,D,TG,C,DS,18+,YC] 38-19 69th St, Woodside 718/424-9181 *10pm-4am Wed-Sun*

■RESTAURANTS

Monika's Cafe Bar 3290 36th St, Astoria 718/204-5273 *10am-2am, till 4am Fri-Sat, Th gay night*

Mundo Cafe 31-18E Broadway (at 32nd St), Astoria 718/777-2829 *5pm-11:30pm, clsd Wed, Mediterranean/Turkish*

■MEN'S CLUBS

Northern Men's Sauna [PC] 3365 Farrington St, Flushing 718/445-9775 *11am-10pm, run-down*

New York • USA

NYC—Bronx

■BARS

Le Boy [M,D,MR-L] 104 Dyckman St (at Nagle) **646/692-4630** *6pm-4am Wed-Sun*

No Parking [M,D,K,MR-L] 4168 Broadway (at 177th St) **212/923-8700** *6pm-3am, go-go boys*

■NIGHTCLUBS

Boyz Nightz/ Escandalo [M,D] 3534 Broadway (at 145th St, at El Morocco) **212/939-0909** *Sun only, gay Latin night*

Nyack

■NIGHTCLUBS

Barz [MW,D,A,K] 327 Rte 9 W **845/353-4444** *8pm-4am, from 3pm Sun, clsd Sun-Mon*

Orange County

■EROTICA

Exotic Gifts & Videos 658 Rte 211 E (exit 120, off Rte 17), Middletown **845/692-6664**

Rochester

■INFO LINES & SERVICES

AA Gay/ Lesbian 17 Fitzhugh St (St Lukes & Simon Church) **585/232-6720** (AA#) *8pm Sun*

Gay Alliance of the Genesee Valley (GAGV) 875 E Main St, 5th flr **585/244-8640** *events, education, SAGE & youth services*

■ACCOMMODATIONS

Silver Waters Bed & Breakfast [GS,GO] 8420 Bay St (at Lummis), Sodus Point **315/483-8098**

■BARS

140 Alex Bar & Grill [MW,D,E,K,DS,V,GO] 140 Alexander St (at Broadway) **585/256-1000** *4pm-2am, from 2pm Sun, also restaurant*

Avenue Pub [★M,NH,D] 522 Monroe Ave (at Goodman) **585/244-4960** *4pm-2am, patio*

The Bachelor Forum [M,B,L] 670 University Ave (at Atlantic) **585/271-6930** *2pm-2am*

■NIGHTCLUBS

Tilt Nightclub [GS,D,DS] 444 Central Ave **585/232-8440** *10pm-2:30am Th-Sat*

Vertex [GS,D] 169 N Chestnut St **585/232-5498** *10pm-2am Wed-Sat, goth club*

■CAFES

Little Theatre Cafe [★E,BW,WC] 240 East Ave **585/258-0400** *5pm-10pm, till 11pm Fri-Sat, till 8pm Sun*

■RETAIL SHOPS

Equal Grounds 750 South Ave (at Caroline) **585/256-2362** *7am-midnight, from 10am wknds, LGBT gifts & books, also coffeehouse*

Outlandish [GO] 274 N Goodman St (in the Village Gate) **585/760-8383** *11am-9pm, noon-5pm Sun*

■PUBLICATIONS

Empty Closet **585/244-8640** *LGBT newspaper, resource listings*

■MEN'S CLUBS

➤**Rochester Spa & Body Club** [PC] 109 Liberty Pole Way **585/454-1074** *24hrs*

■MEN'S SERVICES

➤**MegaMates** **585/563-2820** *Call to hook up with HOT local men. FREE to listen & respond to ads. Use FREE code DAMRON. MegaMates.com.*

New York • USA

Saratoga Springs

ACCOMMODATIONS

The Inn at Round Lake [GF,SW,NS,WI,GO] 14 Covel Ave (at Burlington), Round Lake **518/899-4914** *Victorian B&B*

The Mansion [GF,NS,WC,GO] 801 Rte 29, Rock City Falls **518/885-1607, 888/996-9977** *1860 Victorian mansion, full brkfst*

BARS

Desperate Annie's [GF,NH] 12 Caroline St (off Broadway) **518/587-2455** *4pm-close*

RESTAURANTS

Esperanto [★YC] 6 1/2 Caroline St (off Broadway) **518/587-4236** *11am-close, doughboys!*

Little India [BW] 60 Court St **518/583-4151** *lunch & dinner*

Sharon Springs

ACCOMMODATIONS

American Hotel [GS,F,NS,WI,WC,GO] 192 Main St **518/284-2105** *1847 Nat'l Register hotel, restaurant & bar*

Edgefield [GS,NS,GO] 153 Washington St **518/284-3339** *well-appointed English Country house*

The TurnAround Spa Lodge [MW,F,NS,GO] 105 Washington St **518/284-9708, 212/628-9008** *small hotel & health spa, full brkfst, hot tub*

RETAIL SHOPS

The Finishing Touch 197 Main St (Rte 10) **518/284-2884** *call for hours, gallery & gift shop*

Syracuse

INFO LINES & SERVICES

AA Gay/ Lesbian 315/463-5011 (AA#) *call for meeting schedule*

ACCOMMODATIONS

B&B Wellington [GF,NS,WI] 707 Danforth St (at Carbon) **315/474-3641, 800/724-5006** *full brkfst wknds, kids ok*

Yellow Lantern Kampground [GF,SW] 1770 Rte 13 N, Cortland **607/756-2959** *campsites & RV hookups*

BARS

Rain Lounge [M,NH,MR,TG,E,K,GO] 103 N Geddes St **315/218-5951** *4pm-2:30am*

NIGHTCLUBS

Trexx [M,D,DS,S,V,18+WC] 319 N Clinton St (exit 18, off Rte 81) **315/474-6408** *8pm-2am, till 4am Fri-Sat, clsd Sun-Wed, go-go dancers*

Twist Ultralounge [MW,D,DS,P,18+] 252 W Genesee (at Franklin) **315/725-4314** *4pm-2am, clsd Mon, theme nights, piano bar Wed*

RESTAURANTS

Cafe Mira [WC,GO] 14 Main St, Adams **315/232-4470** *open 5pm Wed-Sat only*

EROTICA

Boulevard Books 2576 Erie Blvd E (at Seeley) **315/446-1595** *24hrs*

Salt City Book & Video 2807 Brewerton Rd **315/454-0629** *24hrs*

CRUISY AREAS

Thornden Park [AYOR] pink triangle rock

Utica

NIGHTCLUBS

That Place [M,D,YC,WC] 216 Bleecker St (at Genesee) *9pm-2am Th & Sat*

RESTAURANTS

The Hadley [E,WC,GO] 2008 Genesee St (at Arnold Ave) **315/507-4264** *5pm-10pm, clsd Sun, also bar*

Westchester

BARS

B Lounge [MW,D,K] 4 Broadway, Valhalla **914/437-5093** *5pm-1am, till 4am Wed-Fri, 8pm-4am Sat, 6pm-1am Sun*

White Plains

INFO LINES & SERVICES

The LOFT 252 Bryant Ave **914/948-2932, 914/948-4922** (helpline) *LGBT community center, call for hours, also newsletter*

NORTH CAROLINA

Statewide

▪PUBLICATIONS

Q Notes 704/531-9988 *bi-weekly LGBT newspaper for the Carolinas*

Asheville

▪INFO LINES & SERVICES

Lambda AA 9 Swan St (at Cathedral of All Souls Episcopal Church) **828/254-8539 (AA#), 800/524-0465** *7pm Mon & Wed, 8pm Fri*

▪ACCOMMODATIONS

1889 WhiteGate Inn & Cottage [GS,NS,WI,GO] 173 E Chestnut St **828/253-2553, 800/485-3045**

The 1900 Inn on Montford [GF,NS,WI] 296 Montford Ave **828/254-9569, 800/254-9569**

Biltmore Village Inn [GF,NS,WI,GO] 119 Dodge St (at Irwin) **828/274-8707, 866/274-8779**

Cedar Crest Inn [GS,GO] 674 Biltmore Ave **828/252-1389 , 877/251-1389**

Mountain Laurel B&B [MW,NS,WI,GO] 139 Lee Dotson Rd, Fairview **828/628-9903, 828/712-6289 (cell)**

North Lodge on Oakland B&B [GS,WI,GO] 84 Oakland Rd (at Victoria Rd) **828/252-6433, 800/252-3602**

The Tree House [W,TG,NS,GO] 190 Tessie Ln, Black Mountain **828/669-3889**

▪BARS

O Henry's/ Underground [M,NH,D,B,L,DS,WC] 237 Haywood St **828/254-1891** *2pm-2am, from noon wknds; Underground from 8pm Fri-Sat only*

Smokey's After Dark [M,NH] 18 Broadway **828/253-2155** *4pm-2am*

Tressa's [GS,D,E] 28 Broadway **828/254-7072** *4pm-2:30am, from 6pm Sat, clsd Sun, jazz/ cigar bar*

▪NIGHTCLUBS

Club Hairspray [MW,NH,D,E,K,C,DS] 38 N French Broad Ave (at Patton Ave) **828/258-2027** *8pm-2am, patio*

Scandals [MW,D,DS,V,18+,PC,WC] 11 Grove St (at Patton) **828/252-2838** *10pm-3am Th-Sun*

▪CAFES

Laurey's [★WC,GO] 67 Biltmore Ave **828/252-1500** *9am-6pm, till 4pm Sat, clsd Sun*

▪RESTAURANTS

Avenue M 791 Merrimon Ave **828/350-8181** *5pm-late, 10am-2:30pm Sun, clsd Mon, full bar*

Barley's Taproom & Pizzeria [E] 42 Biltmore **828/255-0504** *11:30am-2am, till midnight Sun*

Charlotte Street Grill & Pub [WI,GO] 157 Charlotte St **828/252-2948** *noon-2am*

Early Girl Eatery 8 Wall St **828/259-9292** *brkfst & lunch daily, dinner Tue-Sat, wknd brunch*

Firestorm Cafe & Books [E,WI] 48 Commerce St **828/255-8115** *10am-11pm, clsd Sun, vegetarian*

Laughing Seed Cafe [BW,WC] 40 Wall St (at Haywood) **828/252-3445** *11:30am-9pm, till 10pm Fri-Sat, Sun brunch from 10am, clsd Tue, vegetarian/ vegan, patio*

Table 48 College St **828/254-8980** *11am-2:30pm & 5:30pm-11pm, Sun brunch, clsd Tue*

Tupelo Honey Cafe 12 College St **828/255-4404** *9am-10pm*

▪ENTERTAINMENT & RECREATION

LaZoom Tours [BYOB] 90 Biltmore Ave **828/225-6932** *city-wide comedy tours of Asheville, afternoons & evenings*

▪BOOKSTORES

Malaprop's Bookstore/ Cafe [E] 55 Haywood St (at Walnut) **828/254-6734, 800/441-9829** *9am-9pm, till 7pm Sun*

Montford's Books [WI] 31 Montford Ave **828/285-8805** *11am-6pm, clsd Mon*

North Carolina • USA

■EROTICA

BedTyme Stories 2334 Hendersonville Rd, Arden **828/684-8250**

■CRUISY AREAS

The Blue Ridge Parkway [AYOR] Sleepy Gap & Chestnut Cove overlooks (at mile marker 397 & 398)

Blowing Rock

■ACCOMMODATIONS

Blowing Rock Victorian Inn [GF,NS,WI,GO] 242 Ransom St (at US 321) **828/295-0034**

Brevard

■ACCOMMODATIONS

Ash Grove Mountain Cabins & Camping [GS,NS,WI,GO] 749 E Fork Rd **828/885-7216** *camping & cabins, hot tub*

Charlotte

■INFO LINES & SERVICES

Acceptance Group Gay/ Lesbian AA 2830 Dorcester Pl (at St Paul United Methodist Church) **704/377-0244, 877/233-6853** *8pm Fri*

The Lesbian/ Gay Community Center 820 Hamilton St #B11 (at Seaboard St) **704/333-0144** *5pm-8pm Tue-Th, 10am-1pm Fri-Sat, clsd Sun-Mon*

■ACCOMMODATIONS

VanLandingham Estate [GF,NS,WI,GO] 2010 The Plaza (at Belvedere) **704/334-8909, 888/524-2020**

■BARS

The Bar At 316 [★MW,NH,V,PC] 316 Rensselaer Ave (at South Blvd) **704/910-1478** *5pm-2am, from 3pm Sun*

Hartigan's Irish Pub [★GS,NH,D,F,E,K,WI,GO] 601 S Cedar St (at W Hill St) **704/347-1841** *11am-10pm, till 2am wknds, clsd Sun*

Petra's Piano Bar [GS,E,K,WI] 1917 Commonwealth Ave (at Thomas) **704/332-6608** *5pm-2am, clsd Mon*

Sidelines Sports Bar & Billiards [GF,NH,F,WI,PC,WC,GO] **704/525-2608** *4pm-2am, from noon wknds*

Wine Up [GS,NH,E,MR] 3306 N Davidson St **704/372-2633** *poetry readings, open mic & live music, frequent LGBT events*

The Woodshed [M,NH,B,L,F,PC,WC] 4000 Queen City Dr (at Little Rock) **704/394-1712** *5pm-2am, from 3pm Sun, also patio bar*

■NIGHTCLUBS

Chasers [M,D,S,V,PC,WC] 3217 The Plaza (at 36th) **704/339-0500** *6pm-2am*

Halo [GF,D] 820 Hamilton St (at Seaboard St) **704/332-4256** *10pm-2am Th-Sat*

Marigny Dance Club [★M,D,S,18+] 1440 S Tryon St #110 **704/910-4444** *10pm-2am, from 7pm Tue, clsd Sun-Mon*

The Nickel Bar [MW,D,MR-AF] **704/916-9389** *9pm-2am, from 5pm Sun, clsd Mon-Wed*

Scorpio's [MW,D,MR,DS,V,18+,PC,WC] 2301 Freedom Dr (at Berryhill Rd) **704/373-9124** *9pm-3am Wed & Fri-Sun*

■CAFES

Amelie's French Bakery 2424 N Davidson St **704/376-1781** *open 24hrs*

Caribou Coffee [WI] 1531 East Blvd (near Scott) **704/334-3570** *6am-11pm*

Smelly Cat Coffee 514 E 36th St **704/374-9656** *7am-10pm, till 1am Fri-Sat*

■RESTAURANTS

300 East [WC] 300 East Blvd (at Cleveland) **704/332-6507** *11am-10pm, Sun brunch, full bar*

Alexander Michael's 401 W 9th St (at Pine) **704/332-6789** *lunch & dinner, clsd Sun, full bar*

Cosmos Cafe 300 N College (at 6th) **704/372-3553** *11am-2am, clsd Sun, also martini lounge*

Dish 1220 Thomas Ave (at Central) **704/344-0343** *11am-10pm, till 11pm Fri-Sat, clsd Sun, patio*

Foskoskies Neighborhood Cafe
[E,WC,GO] 2121 Shamrock Dr
704/535-2220 *lunch & dinner, clsd Mon, full bar*

Lupie's Cafe [★] 2718 Monroe Rd
(near 5th St) **704/374-1232** *11am-10pm, from noon Sat, clsd Sun*

Penguin Drive-In 1921
Commonwealth Ave (at Thomas)
704/375-1925 *11am-1am, till 2am wknds, full bar*

The Pewter Rose Bistro [E] 1820
South Blvd (near East Blvd)
704/332-8149 *lunch & dinner, outdoor dining*

◼ENTERTAINMENT & RECREATION

One Voice Chorus [GO] PO Box 9241 28299

◼BOOKSTORES

Paper Skyscraper [WC] 330 East Blvd
(at Euclid Ave) **704/333-7130** *10am-7pm, till 6pm Sat, noon-5pm Sun, books & funky gifts*

◼PUBLICATIONS

Q Notes **704/531-9988** *bi-weekly LGBT newspaper for the Carolinas*

◼MEN'S SERVICES

▶**MegaMates** **704/556-0006** *Call to hook up with HOT local men. FREE to listen & respond to ads. Use FREE code DAMRON. MegaMates.com.*

◼EROTICA

Carolina Video Source 8829 E Harris
Blvd (at Albemarle Rd) **704/566-9993**

Hwy 74 Video & News 3514 Barry Dr
(at Wilkinson Blvd) **704/399-7907**

◼CRUISY AREAS

Freedom Park [AYOR]

Fayetteville

◼NIGHTCLUBS

Alias [MW,D,MR,TG,E,S,V,18+,PC,GO] 984
Old McPherson Church Rd (at Raeford
Rd) **910/484-7994** *9pm-2:30am Fri-Sat only*

◼EROTICA

Cupid's Boutique 137 N Reilly Rd (at
Morganton) **910/860-7716**

Fort Video & News 4431 Bragg Blvd
(near 401 overpass) **910/868-9905**
24hrs

Priscilla McCall's 3800 Sycamore Dairy
Rd (at Bragg Blvd) **910/860-1776**

Greensboro

◼INFO LINES & SERVICES

Live & Let Live AA 617 N Elm St (at
Presbyterian Church) **336/854-4278**
(AA#) *8pm Tue; also Free Spirit, 8pm
Sat, 2105 W Market St (at Episcopal
Church)*

◼ACCOMMODATIONS

Biltmore Greensboro Hotel
[GS,NS,WI,GO] 111 W Washington St (at
Elm St) **336/272-3474,**
800/332-0303

O Henry Hotel [GF,SW,WC] 624 Green
Valley Rd (at Benjamin Pkwy)
336/854-2000, 800/965-8259 *bar/
restaurant popular w/ local gay community*

◼BARS

The Q [MW,NH,D,18+,WI] 708 W Market
St **336/272-2587** *4pm-close, from
9pm Sat, from 7pm Sun, patio*

◼NIGHTCLUBS

Warehouse 29 [M,D,DS,S,V,18+,PC] 1011
Arnold St **336/333-9333** *9:30pm-
2:30am Th-Sun, T-dance Sun (summers),
also patio bar*

◼MEN'S SERVICES

▶**MegaMates** **336/617-2032** *Call to
hook up with HOT local men. FREE to
listen & respond to ads. Use FREE code
DAMRON. MegaMates.com.*

◼EROTICA

The Lion's Den Adult Superstore
4018 W Wensover Ave (exit 214, off
I-40) **336/851** *10am-3am*

New Vision Video & News [PC,$] 507
Mobile St (off Randleman Rd)
336/274-6443

Greenville

◼CRUISY AREAS

Green Springs Park [AYOR] 5th St
(behind Pizza Hut)

North Carolina • *USA*

Havelock

■NIGHTCLUBS

Club Above & Beyond [MW,D,DS,PC] 114 Crocker Rd **252/266-0114** *open 8pm, from 10pm Sat, clsd Wed*

Hickory

■NIGHTCLUBS

Club Cabaret [MW,D,S,WI,PC,WC] 101 N Center St (at 1st Ave) **828/322-8103** *8pm-2am, from 9pm Fri-Sat, clsd Mon-Wed*

■CAFES

Taste Full Beans [GO] 29 2nd St NW **828/325-0108** *7am-5:30pm, till 2:30pm Sat, clsd Sun, art exhibits*

Jacksonville

■EROTICA

Gruntz Adult Store 303 Henderson Dr (at Rte17) **910/ 381-1030** *10am-midnight, friendly adult store near military bases, all welcome*

Priscilla McCall's 113-A Western Blvd **910/355-0765**

Little Switzerland

■ACCOMMODATIONS

La Petite Chalet [GS,GO] 38 Orchard Ln (at Hwy 226A) **888/828-1654**

Madison

■ACCOMMODATIONS

Hunter House B&B [GS,SW,NS,WI,GO] 216 W Hunter St **336/445-4730** *patio, gardens, pets on premises*

Mooresville

■RESTAURANTS

Pomodoro's Italian American Cafe [BW,WC,GO] 168 Norman Station Blvd **704/663-6686** *11am-10pm, till 11pm Fri-Sat*

Raleigh/Durham/Chapel Hill

■INFO LINES & SERVICES

Common Solutions Gay/ Lesbian AA Crownwell Bldg, East Campus (at Duke University), Durham **919/286-9499** (AA#) *6:30pm Mon*

LGBT Center of Raleigh 411 Hillsborough St, Raleigh **919/832-4484**

■ACCOMMODATIONS

Heartfriends Inn B&B [GS,WI,WC,GO] 4389 Siler City/Snow Camp Rd (at Ed Clapp Rd), Siler City **919/663-1707, 877/679-0980**

The King's Daughters Inn [GF] 204 N Buchanan Blvd, Durham **919/354-7000, 877/534-8534**

■BARS

Flex [★M,B,E,K,DS,PC] 2 S West St (at Hillsborough), Raleigh **919/832-8855** *5pm-close, from 2pm Sun*

Hibernian Restaurant & Pub [GF,F,E] 311 Glenwood Ave (at W Lane St), Raleigh **919/833-2258** *11am-2am*

■NIGHTCLUBS

313 [M,D,MR,P,DS,18+,WI,PC,WC] 313 W Hargett St (at Harrington), Raleigh **919/755-9599** *8pm-close*

The Bar [MW,D,E,K,PC,GO] 711 Rigsbee Ave, Durham **919/956-2929** *4pm-2am*

Icon Nightclub [MW,D,DS,K,MR-AF,18+,PC,WC] 320 E Durham Rd, Cary **919/460-4343** *8pm-2am Tue & 9pm-3:30am Fri-Sat*

Legends/ View [MW,D,DS,S,YC,PC,WC] 330 W Hargett St (at S Harrington St), Raleigh **919/831-8888** *5pm-2:30am*

The Pinhook [GS,E] 117 W Main St, Durham **991/667-1100** *5pm-2am, 6pm-midnight Sun, patio*

Stir [M,D] 201 E Franklin St (at East End Martini Bar), Chapel Hill **919/929-0024** *9pm Sun only*

The T [MW] 423 W Franklin St (at the Lantern), Chapel Hill **919/969-8846** *10pm Tue only, chic, eclectic crowd*

■CAFES

Bean Traders 105-249 W NC Hwy 54, Durham **919/484-2499** *6am-8pm, from 8am wknds*

Cafe Helios [F,BW] 413 Glenwood Ave (at North St), Raleigh **919/838-5177** *7am-10pm, 8am-6pm Sun*

Raleigh/Durham/Chapel Hill • North Carolina

Caffe Driade [E,BW] 1215 E Franklin St #A (at Elizabeth St), Chapel Hill **919/942-2333** 7am-11pm

Third Place [F] 1811 Glenwood Ave (at W Whitaker Mill Rd), Raleigh **919/834-6566** 6am-7pm

RESTAURANTS

Blu Seafood & Bar 2002 Hillsborough Rd (at 9th St), Durham **919/286-9777** lunch & dinner, clsd Sun

The Borough [WI] 317 W Morgan St, Raleigh **919/832-8433** 4pm-2am, also bar

Crooks Corner [WC] 610 Franklin St (at Merritt Mill Rd), Chapel Hill **919/929-7643** dinner nightly, Sun brunch, clsd Mon, Southern cooking, full bar

Dain's Place [WI] 754 9th St (at Markham), Durham 11am-2am, from 5pm Mon, 9am Sat, great burgers & pub food, also bar

Elmo's Diner 776 9th St (in the Carr Mill Mall), Durham **919/416-3823** 6:30am-10pm

Five Star 511 W Hargett St (at West St), Raleigh **919/833-3311** 5:30pm-2am, Asian-fusion

Humble Pie 317 S Harrington St (at Martin), Raleigh **919/829-9222** 5pm-11pm, bar open late, brunch only Sun, small plates

Irregardless Cafe [E] 901 W Morgan St (at Hillsborough), Raleigh **919/833-8898** lunch Tue-Fri, dinner Tue-Sat, Sun brunch, clsd Mon

Lantern 423 W Franklin St, Chapel Hill **919/969-8846** dinner nightly, clsd Sun, Asian, also cocktail lounge till 2am

The Mad Hatter's Bakeshop & Cafe [WI] 1802 W Main St (at Broad), Durham **919/286-1987** 7am-9pm, 8am-3pm Sun

The Pit 328 W Davie St (at S Dawson), Raleigh **919/890-4500** 11am-10pm, till 11pm wknds, upscale BBQ

Rue Cler 401 E Chapel Hill St (at Mangum St), Durham **919/682-8844** lunch & dinner, wknd brunch, French

Solas 919/755-0755 dinner, Sun brunch, upscale dining, dress code, also rooftop lounge & nightclub

Spotted Dog 111 E Main St (at N Greensboro St), Carrboro **919/933-1117** 11:30am-midnight, clsd Mon, plenty veggie

Sunrise Biscuit Kitchen 1305 E Franklin St, Chapel Hill **919/933-1324** great brkfst, drive-thru only

Vivace 4209 Lassiter Mill Rd #115 (at Pamlico Dr), Raleigh **919/787-7747** lunch & dinner, Sun brunch, Italian, patio seating, full bar

BOOKSTORES

Internationalist Books & Community Center 405 W Franklin St (at Kenan St), Chapel Hill **919/942-1740** 11am-8pm, noon-6pm Sun, progressive/ alternative, cooperatively run, nonprofit; readings & events

Quail Ridge Books 3522 Wade Ave (at Ridgewood Center), Raleigh **919/828-1588, 800/672-6789** 9am-9pm, LGBT section

The Regulator Bookshop 720 9th St (btwn Hillsborough & Perry), Durham **919/286-2700** 10am-9pm, noon-6pm Sun

MEN'S SERVICES

►**MegaMates** 919/829-7300 Call to hook up with HOT local men. FREE to listen & respond to ads. Use FREE code DAMRON. MegaMates.com.

EROTICA

Capitol Blvd News 2236 Capitol Blvd, Raleigh **919/831-1400**

Castle Video & News 1210 Capitol Blvd, Raleigh **919/836-9189** 24hrs

Cherry Pie [18+] 1819 Fordham Blvd, Chapel Hill **919/928-0499** 10am-midnight

Eagles/ Videos for the Mature 9016 Glenwood Ave, Raleigh **919/787-0016** 24hrs

Frisky Business 1720 New Raleigh Hwy, Durham **919/957-4441**

Our Place 327 W Hargett (at Harrington), Raleigh **919/833-8968** 24hrs

North Carolina • *USA*

Rocky Mount

▥NIGHTCLUBS
Liquid Nightclub [M,D,A,S,MR-AF,AYOR] 313 Falls Rd **252/266-6464** *8pm-3am Sat only*

Washington

▥CAFES
Back Water Jack's Tiki Bar [WC] 1052 E Main St (at Havens St) **252/975-1090** *lunch & dinner, clsd Mon, also bar*

Wilmington

▥ACCOMMODATIONS
Best Western Coastline Inn [GS,NS,WC,WI,GO] 503 Nutt St **910/763-2800**

Rosehill Inn B&B [GF,NS,WI] 114 S 3rd St (at Dock St) **910/815-0250, 800/815-0250**

The Taylor House Inn [GS,NS] 14 N 7th St **910/763-7581, 800/382-9982**

▥BARS
Costello's [M,E,P,V,PC,WC,GO] 211 Princess St (btwn 2nd & 3rd) **910/470-9666** *7pm-2am, from 5pm Fri*

Tool Box [M,NH,D,K,WI,GO] 2325 Burnett Blvd **910/343-6988** *5pm-2am, from 7pm Tue -Sat*

▥NIGHTCLUBS
Ibiza [M,D,K,DS,S,YC,PC,WC,GO] 118 Market St (rear) **910/251-1301** *8pm-3am Wed-Sun only*

▥RESTAURANTS
Caffe Phoenix [GO] 9 S Front St **910/343-1395** *11:30am-10pm, Sun brunch, Mediterranean, some veggie*

▥ENTERTAINMENT & RECREATION
Cinematique 310 Chestnut St (at Thalian Hall) **910/343-1640** *classic, foreign & notable films*

Winston-Salem

▥NIGHTCLUBS
CO2 [★MW,D,B,MR,TG,C,DS,18+,PC,WC,GO,$] 4019 Country Club Rd (at Hedgecock Ave) **336/602-2720** *9pm-3am, clsd Mon*

▥MEN'S SERVICES
▶**MegaMates 336/201-5553** *Call to hook up with HOT local men. FREE to listen & respond to ads. Use FREE code DAMRON. MegaMates.com.*

▥EROTICA
New Vision Video & News 1045 N Cherry St (at N Huff) **336/725-8034** *also 3061 Kennersville Rd, 336/788-0020*

NORTH DAKOTA

Fargo

▥INFO LINES & SERVICES
Pride Collective & Community Center 116 12th St S (at Main Ave), Moorhead, MN **218/287-8034** *6pm-7:30pm Tue, referrals, support/ social groups, check www.pridecollective.com for events*

▥ACCOMMODATIONS
The Hotel Donaldson [GS,F,WI] 101 Broadway **701/478-1000 , 888/478-8768**

▥CAFES
Atomic Coffee [F,WI] **701/478-6160** *7am-11pm, 8pm-10pm Sun*

▥RESTAURANTS
Fargo's Fryn' Pan [★WC] 300 Main St (at 4th) **701/293-9952** *24hrs*

Mom's Kitchen 1322 Main St **701/235-4460** *6am-10pm, full bar*

▥RETAIL SHOPS
One World Imports [GO] 614 Main Ave (at Broadway) **701/297-8882** *10am-7:30pm, noon-4pm Sun*

Zandbroz Variety 420 N Broadway **701/239-4729** *9am-8pm, noon-5pm Sun, books & gifts*

■EROTICA

Romantix Adult Superstore 417 N Pacific Ave **701/235-2640** *9am-3am*

■CRUISY AREAS

Island Park [AYOR] *near pool*

Grand Forks

■EROTICA

Romantix Adult Superstore 102 S 3rd St (at Kittson) **701/772-9021**

Mandan

■EROTICA

Risque's II 2113 Memorial Hwy **701/663-9013**

Minot

■EROTICA

Risque's 1514 S Broadway **701/838-2837**

■CRUISY AREAS

Rest Area [AYOR] Hwy 2 (10 miles E of town)

OHIO

Statewide

■PUBLICATIONS

Gay People's Chronicle **216/916-9338** *Ohio's largest bi-weekly LGBT newspaper w/ extensive listings*

Outlook 614/268-8525 *statewide LGBT newsweekly*

Akron

■INFO LINES & SERVICES

AA Intergroup 330/253-8181 (AA#)

Akron Pride Center 895 N Main St **330/252-1559** *call for meeting schedule*

■BARS

Adams Street Bar [★M,D,F,P,S,WI] 77 N Adams St (at Upson) **330/434-9794** *4pm-2am, from 9pm Sun, [P] Wed*

Cocktails [M,D,DS,V] 1009 S Main St (at Crosier) **330/376-2625** *4pm-2:30am, clsd Sun, Daddy's [L] upstairs wknds*

Inferno [M,D,K,E] 1348 S Arlington St (in Arlington Plaza) **330/773-7733** *4pm-2am, from noon wknds*

The Office Bistro & Lounge [GF,NH,MR,P,WI,WC] 778 N Main St (at Cuyahoga Falls Ave) **330/376-9550** *11am-2:30am, bistro & lounge, bi-sexual friendly*

Tear-Ez [MW,NH,DS,WI,WC] 360 S Main St (near Exchange St) **330/376-0011** *11am-2:30am, from noon Sun*

■NIGHTCLUBS

Interbelt [MW,D,DS,S,V] 70 N Howard St (near Perkins & Main) **330/253-5700** *9pm-2:30am, patio*

Square [M,D,E,K,WC,GO] 820 W Market St (near Portage Path) **330/374-9661** *5pm-2:30am, from 8pm Sat, from 7pm Sun*

■CAFES

Angel Falls Coffee Company [WC,WI,GO] 792 W Market St (btwn S Highland & Grand) **330/376-5282** *7am-10pm, patio*

■RESTAURANTS

Aladdin's Eatery 782 W Market St (at Grand) **330/535-0110** *11am-10pm, Middle Eastern*

Bricco [GO] 1 W Exchange St (at S Main St) **330/475-1600** *11am-midnight, till 1am Fri-Sat, 4pm-9pm Sun, Italian, also bar*

Bruegger's Bagels 1821 Merriman Rd **330/867-8394** *6am-4pm*

■MEN'S CLUBS

Akron Steam & Sauna [PC] 41 S Case Ave (near River Rd) **330/252-2791** *noon-midnight, 24hrs wknds*

■MEN'S SERVICES

▶**MegaMates 330/315-3000** *Call to hook up with HOT local men. FREE to listen & respond to ads. Use FREE code DAMRON. MegaMates.com.*

Brunswick

see also Akron & Cleveland

■RESTAURANTS

Pizza Marcello 67-A Pearl Rd (near Boston Rd) **330/225-1211** *3pm-close, from noon wknds, Italian*

Ohio • *USA*

Canton

▦NIGHTCLUBS

Crew [MW,D,K,C] 304 Cherry Ave NE (at 3rd) **330/452-2739** *6pm-2:30am, from 9pm Sat-Sun*

Cincinnati

▦INFO LINES & SERVICES

AA Gay/ Lesbian 328 W McMillan St (enter at 445 Herman St), Corryville **513/351-0422 (AA#)** *8pm Wed, call for locations of wknd meetings*

Gay/ Lesbian Community Center of Greater Cincinnati 4119 Hamilton Ave (near Blue Rock) **513/591-0200** *6pm-9pm, noon-9pm Sat, clsd Sun*

▦ACCOMMODATIONS

Cincinnatian Hotel [GF,NS,WI,WC] 601 Vine St (at 6th St) **513/381-3000, 800/942-9000** *restaurant & lounge*

Crowne Plaza [GF,SW,WI,WC] 5901 Pfeiffer Rd (at I-71) **513/793-4500, 800/468-3597**

First Farm Inn [GF,NS,WI,WC] 2510 Stevens Rd, Petersburg, KY **859/586-0199** *20 minutes from Cincinnati*

Millennium Hotel Cincinnati [GF,SW,WI,WC] 150 W 5th St **513/352-2100, 800/876-2100** *outdoor rooftop pool & sundeck*

Weller Haus B&B [GF,NS,WI] 319 Poplar St, Bellevue, KY **859/391-8315, 800/431-4287**

▦BARS

Below Zero Lounge [GS,D,F,E,K,WI] 1120 Walnut St (at E Central Pkwy) **513/421-9376** *4pm-2:30am, clsd Mon-Tue*

Junkers Tavern [GF,NH,K,E] 4158 Langland St (at Chase) **513/541-5470** *9am-1am, live bands*

The Main Event [GS,NH] 835 Main St (at 9th) **513/421-1294** *6am-2:30am, from 1pm Sun*

Milton's [GF,NH] 301 Milton St (at Sycamore) **513/784-9938** *4pm-2:30am*

On Broadway [M,NH,CW,B,L,K,DS,V,GO] 817 Broadway (at 9th) **513/421-2555** *4pm-2:30am*

The Serpent [M,L] 4042 Hamilton Ave (at Blue Rock) **513/681-6969** *9pm-2:30am,clsd Mon*

Shooters [M,D,CW,K,S] 927 Race St (at Court) **513/381-9900** *4pm-2:30am, [K] Wed*

Simon Says [★M,NH,P,WC] 428 Walnut St (at 5th) **513/381-7577** *11am-2:30am, from 1pm Sun*

▦NIGHTCLUBS

Adonis [MW,D,TG,DS] 4601 Kellogg Ave (at Stites Rd) **513/871-1542** *9pm-3am Sat only*

The Cabaret [M,DS] 1122 Walnut St (at E Central Pkwy) **513/284-2050** *10pm-2am Th-Sun*

The Dock [★MW,D,DS,MR-AF,19+,WC] 603 W Pete Rose Wy (near Central) **513/241-5623** *10pm-3am, till 4am Fri-Sat, clsd Mon-Wed*

▦CAFES

College Hill Coffee Co [E,WI,WC] 6128 Hamilton Ave (at North Bend Rd) **513/542-2739** *6:30am-6:30pm, till 10pm Fri, 8:30am-10pm Sat, till 4pm Sun, clsd Mon*

Zen & Now [WI] 4453 Bridgetown Rd **513/598-8999** *7am-7pm, till 10pm Fri-Sat, clsd Sun*

▦RESTAURANTS

Boca [WC] 3200 Madison Rd (at Brazee St), Oakley **513/542-2022** *dinner Tue-Sat, clsd Sun-Mon, full bar*

Honey [WC] 4034 Hamilton Ave (at Blue Rock) **513/541-4300** *dinner & Sun brunch, clsd Mon, casual fine dining*

The Loving Hut 6227 Montgomery Rd (at Woodmont) **513/731-2233** *11am-7pm, clsd Sun-Mon, vegetarian/ vegan*

Melt Eclectic Deli 4165 Hamilton Ave (at Lingo St) **513/681-6358** *11am-9pm, 10am-3pm Sun*

Myra's Dionysus 121 Calhoun St (at Dennis St) **513/961-1578** *11am-10pm, till 11pm Fri-Sat, from 5pm Sun, diverse menu, plenty veggie*

Cleveland • Ohio

Tucker's [WC] 1637 Vine St (at Green) **513/721-7123** *great brkfst hole in wall, vegan too*

ENTERTAINMENT & RECREATION

Ensemble Theatre of Cincinnati 1127 Vine St (at 12th) **513/421-3555**

Know Theatre 1120 Jackson St (at Central Pkwy) **513/300-5669** *contemporary multicultural theater*

RETAIL SHOPS

Park & Vine 1202 Main St **513/721-7275** *eco-friendly merchandise*

Pink Pyramid 907 Race St (btwn 9th & Court) **513/621-7465** *noon-9pm, till 11pm Fri-Sat, 1pm-7pm Sun, pride items, also leather*

PUBLICATIONS

CNKY Scene 513/309-9729 *LGBT publication*

Gay People's Chronicle 440/986-0051

MEN'S SERVICES

▶**MegaMates** 513/821-4500 *Call to hook up with HOT local men. FREE to listen & respond to ads. Use FREE code DAMRON. MegaMates.com.*

Cleveland

INFO LINES & SERVICES

AA Gay/ Lesbian 6600 Detroit Ave (at LGBT Center) **216/241-7387, 800/835-1935**

LGBT Community Center [WC] 6600 Detroit Ave **216/651-5428** *1pm-8pm, clsd wknds*

ACCOMMODATIONS

Clifford House [GS,NS,WI,GO] 1810 W 28th St (at Jay) **216/589-0121** *near downtown*

Radisson Hotel Cleveland–Gateway [GF,WI,WC] 651 Huron Rd (at Prospect) **216/377-9000, 800/967-9033** *also restaurant*

Stone Gables B&B [GS,WI,WC,GO] 3806 Franklin Blvd (at W 38th) **216/961-4654, 877/215-4326** *full brkfst, sauna*

BARS

A Man's World [M,D,K,WI] 2909 Detroit Ave (at 29th St) **216/589-9322** *7am-2:30am, from noon Sun-Mon, DJ Sat, Sun eve [CW], patio*

ABC The Tavern [GF,NH,F] 1872 W 25th St **216/861-3857** *4pm-2:30am, from noon wknds, dive bar w/ great food*

The Church Bar [MW,NH,K] 13751 Madison Ave, Lakewood **216/226-1770** *5pm-2am*

Cocktails Cleveland [★M,D,L,B,K,S,V,WI] 9208 Detroit Ave (at W 93rd St) **216/961-3115** *4pm-2:30am, patio*

The Hawk [MW,NH,WC] 11217 Detroit Ave (at 112th St) **216/521-5443** *noon-2:30am, from 1pm Sun*

Leather Stallion Saloon [★M,NH,B,L,F] 2205 St Clair Ave (near E 21st St) **216/589-8588** *3pm-2am, DJ Sun, patio*

Now That's Class [GF,NH,E,WC] 11213 Detroit Ave (at 112th St) **216/221-8576** *4pm-close, punk & metal bands; food served, plenty veggie/ vegan*

Twist [★MW,NH,D,P] 11633 Clifton (at 117th St) **216/221-2333** *11:30am-2:30am, from noon Sun*

Union [★MW,F,V,GO] 2814 Detroit Ave (at W 28th) **216/357-2997** *5pm-2:30am; also Bounce [D,DS] Fri-Sat*

NIGHTCLUBS

Bottoms Up [MW,D] 1572 W 117th (at Franklin), Lakewood **216/712-7750** *4pm-close*

Mean Bull 1313 E 26th St (at St Clair) **216/812-3304** *11:30pm-2:30am Fri-Sat only*

CAFES

Gypsy Beans & Baking Co [★WI,WC] 6425 Detroit Ave (at W 65th St, next to Cleveland Public Theatre) **216/939-9009** *7am-9pm, till 11pm Fri-Sat, fresh-baked gourmet pastries, soups, sandwiches*

Lucky's Cafe [WI,WC] 777 Starkweather Ave (at Professor Ave) **216/622-7773** *7am-5pm, 8am-3pm wknds, popular wknd brunch, cafe & bakery, outdoor seating*

Ohio • USA

Phoenix Coffee [★E,WI,WC] 2287 Lee Rd (at Essex), Cleveland Heights **216/932-8227** 6am-10pm, till 11pm Fri, from 7am Sat, 7am-7pm Sun, great sandwiches, patio

■RESTAURANTS

Ali Baba [★BYOB] 12021 Lorain Ave (at W 120th St) **216/251-2040** 5pm-10pm Th-Sat, the best Middle Eastern food you'll have outside the Middle East, plenty veggie

Bar Cento [BW,WC] 1948 W 25th St (at Lorain Ave) **216/274-1010** 4:30pm-2am, from noon Sat, great pizza

Battiste & Dupree Cajun Grill & Bar [WC] 1992 Warrensville Ctr Rd (at Wyncote) **216/381-3341** lunch & dinner, clsd Sun-Mon

Cafe Tandoor [WC] 2096 S Taylor Rd (at Cedar), Cleveland Heights **216/371-8500** lunch & dinner, 3pm-9pm Sun, Indian

The Coffee Pot 12415 Madison Ave (at Robin), Lakewood **216/226-6443** 6am-4pm, till 3pm Sat, till 2pm Sun, clsd Mon, diner

Crop Bistro 2537 Lorain Ave (at 25th) **216/696-2767** lunch Tue-Fri, dinner nightly, clsd Mon, innovative American

Diner on Clifton [M] 11637 Clifton Blvd (at W 117th St) **216/521-5003** 7am-11pm

Flying Fig 2523 Market Ave (at W 25th St) **216/241-4243** lunch & dinner, wknd brunch

Happy Dog [E,WC] 5801 Detroit Ave (at 58th St) **216/651-9474** 4pm-2am, from 11am Fri, hot dogs w/ 50 toppings, veggie/ vegan choices; live bands, full bar

Hecks [★WC] 2927 Bridge Ave (at W 30th) **216/861-5464, 800/677-8592** lunch & dinner, brunch Sun, gourmet burgers

The Inn on Coventry [WC] 2785 Euclid Heights Blvd (at Coventry), Cleveland Heights **216/371-1811** 7am-8:30pm, from 8:30am-3pm wknds, homestyle, popular Bloody Marys

Johnny Mango World Cafe & Bar [NS] 3120 Bridge Ave (btwn Fulton & W 32nd, in Ohio City) **216/575-1919** 11am-10pm, till 11pm Fri-Sat, healthy world food & juice bar, also full bar till 1am

Latitude 41N [WI,WC,GO] 5712 Detroit Ave (at W 58th St, Detroit Shoreway) **216/961-0000** 8am-9pm, till 10pm Fri, till 3pm Sun, restaurant & cafe

Lolita [★] 900 Literary Rd (at Professor Ave, in Tremont) **216/771-5652** 5pm-11pm, till 1am Fri-Sat, 4pm-9pm Sun, clsd Mon, upscale cont'l, full bar

Luchita's [★] 3456 W 117th St (at Governor) **216/252-1169** lunch & dinner, clsd Mon, Mexican, full bar

Luxe [E,WC] 6605 Detroit Ave (at W 65th St) **216/920-0600** 5pm-midnight, lounge till 2am, gourmet comfort food, also lounge

Momocho [WC] 1835 Fulton Rd (at Woodbine Ave) **216/694-2122** 5pm-close, from 4pm Sun, modern Mexican, also bar

My Friend's Deli & Restaurant [WI,BW] 11616 Detroit Ave (at W 117th) **216/221-2575** 24hrs

Pearl of the Orient [WC] 19300 Detroit Rd (in Beachcliff Market Sq), Rocky River **440/333-9902** lunch & dinner, pan-Asian, some veggie, also restaurant on East Side

Tommy's [WI,WC] **216/321-7757** 9am-9pm, till 10pm Fri, 7:30am-10pm Sat, plenty veggie, great milkshakes

■ENTERTAINMENT & RECREATION

Rock & Roll Hall of Fame 1100 Rock & Roll Blvd (at E 9th & Lake Erie) **216/781-ROCK** even if you don't like rock, stop by & check out IM Pei's architectural gift to Cleveland

■BOOKSTORES

Loganberry Books 13015 Larchmere Blvd, Shaker Heights **216/795-9800** 10am-6pm, till 8pm Th, clsd Sun, used & rare books

Mac's Backs 1820 Coventry Rd (next to Tommy's), Cleveland Heights **216/321-2665** 10am-9pm, till 10pm Fri-Sat, 11am-8pm Sun, great new & used, 3 floors, reading series, some LGBT titles

■RETAIL SHOPS

Big Fun 1814 Coventry Rd (at Hampshire), Cleveland Heights **216/371-4386** 11am-8pm, till 10pm Fri-Sat, till 6pm Sun, kitschy variety store

Dean Rufus House of Fun 1422 W 29th St (at Detroit) **216/348-1386** 1pm-midnight, till 2:30am Fri-Sat, clsd Mon, clothing, DVDs

Goddess Blessed 15729 Madison Ave (at Hilliard), Lakewood **216/221-8755** 11am-7pm, clsd Sun-Mon, goddess-focused & occult gifts & supplies, tarot readings, events & classes

Torso [GO] 11520 Clifton Blvd (at Warren), Lakewood **216/862-3987** 11am-9pm, till 5pm Sun, clsd Mon, clothing

■PUBLICATIONS

Gay People's Chronicle **216/916-9338** Ohio's largest bi-weekly LGBT newspaper w/ extensive listings

■MEN'S CLUBS

Flex [★MR,SW,V,PC] 2600 Hamilton Ave **216/812-3304** 24hrs

■MEN'S SERVICES

➤**MegaMates** **216/912-6000** Call to hook up with HOT local men. FREE to listen & respond to ads. Use FREE code DAMRON. MegaMates.com.

■EROTICA

Adult Mart [AYOR] 16700 Brookpark Rd (at W 150th) **216/267-9019**

Adult Mart 19121 Neff Rd **216/738-0133**

Bank News 4025 Clark Ave (at W 41st St) **216/281-8777** general magazine store w/ section for adult videos, magazines, toys

Body Language 11424 Lorain Ave (at W 115th St) **216/251-3330, 888/429-7733** 11am-10pm, noon-5pm Sun, "one stop GLBT shop"

Rocky's Entertainment & Emporium [AYOR] 13330 Brookpark Rd (at W 130th) **216/267-4659**

Columbus

■INFO LINES & SERVICES

AA Gay/ Lesbian 614/253-8501, 800/870-3795 (in OH)

Stonewall Columbus Community Center/ Hotline [WC] 1160 N High St (at E 4th Ave) **614/299-7764** 9am-5pm, clsd wknds

■ACCOMMODATIONS

The Blackwell [GF,F,WI] 2110 Tuttle Park Pl (at Lane Ave) **614/247-4000, 866/247-4000** on OSU campus

Harrison House B&B [GF,NS,WI] 313 W 5th Ave (at Neil Ave) **614/421-2202, 800/827-4203**

The Lofts [GF,WI] 55 E Nationwide Blvd (at High St) **614/461-2663, 800/735-6387**

The Westin Columbus [GF] 310 S High St (at Main) **614/223-3800, 800/937-8461**

■BARS

Arch City Tavern [★MW,NH,D,F,K,E] 862 N High (at 1st Ave) **614/421-9697** 6pm-2am, clsd Mon, karaoke, live bands

AWOL [M,NH,K,WC] 49 Parsons Ave (at Oak) **614/621-8779** 2pm-2:30am, from noon wknds

The Bow Wow [M,NH] 1602 S 4th St **614/444-4088**

Cavan Irish Pub [GF,E,K] 1409 S High St (at Jenkins) **614/725-5502** 2pm-2:30am, from noon wknds

Club 20 [M,NH,K] 20 E Duncan (at N Pearl) **614/261-9111** noon-2:30am, from 1pm Sun, patio

Club Diversity [MW,E,P,WI] 863 S High St (at Whittier) **614/224-4050** 4pm-midnight, till 2:30am Fri, noon-2:30am Sat

Exile [★M,NH,L,S,WC] 893 N 4th St (at 2nd Ave) **614/299-0069** 4pm-2:30am

Ohio • *USA*

Inn Rehab [M,D,F,K,DS] 627 Greenlawn Ave (at Harmon) 614/754-7326 11am-2:30am

Level Dining Lounge [GS,F,D,K,WC] 614/754-7111 11am-2:30am

Slammers [W,D,F,E,WI,WC] 202 E Long St (at N 5th St) 614/221-8880 11am-12:30am, till 2:30am Fri-Sat, from 4pm wknds, clsd Mon-Tue

The South Bend Tavern [MW,NH,DS,WC] 126 E Moler St (at 4th St) 614/444-3386 noon-2:30am

Tremont [M,NH,OC] 708 S High St (at Frankfort) 614/445-9365 1pm-2:30am

Union Cafe [★MW,F,V,WI,WC] 782 N High St (at Hubbard) 614/421-2233 11am-2:30am

NIGHTCLUBS
Axis [★M,D,C,DS,S,18+,WC,GO] 775 N High St (at Hubbard) 614/291-4008 10pm-2:30am Fri-Sat only, also Pump lounge

Wall Street [★MW,D,CW,DS,P,YC,WC] 144 N Wall St (at Spring St) 614/464-2800 9pm-2:30am, from 10pm Wed, 8pm-midnight Th, clsd Mon-Tue

CAFES
Cup O Joe Cafe [F,WI,WC] 627 S 3rd St (at Sycamore) 614/221-1563 6am-10pm, till 11pm Fri-Sat, from 7am wknds, till 10pm Sun

RESTAURANTS
Alana's Food & Wine 2333 N High St (at Patterson) 614/294-6783 from 5pm, clsd Sun-Tue

Banana Leaf [WC] 816 Bethel Rd (at Olentangy River Rd) 614/459-4101 11:30am-9:30pm, vegetarian/ vegan Indian

Betty's [E] 680 N High St 614/228-6191 11am-2am, plenty veggie, also bar

Blue Nile 2361 N High St (at W Patterson) 614/421-2323 lunch & dinner, clsd Mon, Ethopian

Cap City Diner 1299 Olentangy River Rd (at W 5th) 614/291-3663 11am-10pm, till 11pm Fri-Sat, till 9pm Sun

L'Antibes [WC,GO] 772 N High St #106 (at Warren) 614/291-1666 dinner from 5pm, clsd Sun-Mon

Lemongrass [★R] 641 N High (at Russell) 614/224-1414 lunch & dinner, clsd Sun-Mon, Asian

Northstar Cafe [★] 951 N High St (at W 2nd Ave) 614/298-9999 9am-10pm, plenty veggie

Surly Girl Saloon [E] 1126 N High St (at W 4th Ave) 614/294-4900 11am-2am, plenty veggie, also bar

Till 247 King Ave 614/298-9986 lunch & dinner, wknd brunch, patio

Tip Top Kitchen & Cocktails [★] 73 E Gay St (at 3rd St) 614/221-8300 11am-2am

Whole World Bakery & Restaurant [WC] 3269 N High St (at W Como Ave) 614/268-5751 11am-8pm, Sun brunch, clsd Mon, vegetarian/ vegan

BOOKSTORES
The Book Loft of German Village 631 S 3rd St (at Sycamore) 614/464-1774 10am-11pm, till midnight Fri-Sat, LGBT section

RETAIL SHOPS
Hausfrau Haven 769 S 3rd St (at Columbus) 614/443-3680 10am-7pm, noon-5pm Sun, cards, wine & gifts

Piercology [GO,WC] 190 W 2nd Ave (at Hunter Ave) 614/297-4743 noon-8pm

Schmidt's Fudge Haus 220 E Kossuth St (in Historic German Village) 614/444-2222 noon-close, old fashioned fudge & candy, gifts

Torso [GO] 772 N High St (at Warren) 614/421-7663 11am-10pm, till 5pm Sun-Mon, clothing

PUBLICATIONS
Gay People's Chronicle 216/916-9338

Outlook Weekly 614/268-8525 statewide LGBT weekly

■MEN'S CLUBS

The Club Columbus [SW] 795 W 5th Ave (at Olentangy River Rd) 614/291-0049 *gym, steam, sauna*

■MEN'S SERVICES

➤**MegaMates** 614/888-7777 *Call to hook up with HOT local men. FREE to listen & respond to ads. Use FREE code DAMRON. MegaMates.com.*

■EROTICA

The Garden 1174 N High St (btwn 4th & 5th Ave) 614/294-2869 *11am-3am, noon-midnight Sun*

The Lion's Den Adult Superstore 4315 Kimberly Pkwy (off Hamilton Rd) 614/861-6770 *6am-midnight*

Dayton

■INFO LINES & SERVICES

AA Gay/ Lesbian 20 W 1st St (off Main, at Christ Episcopal Church) 937/222-2211 *8pm Sat*

Greater Dayton Lesbian/ Gay Center 117 E 3rd St 937/274-1776

■ACCOMMODATIONS

Dayton Marriott [GF] 1414 S Patterson Blvd 937/223-1000, 800/450-8625

■BARS

MJ's Cafe [M,D,F,K,S] 119 E 3rd St (at S Jefferson) 937/223-3259 *3pm-2:30am, deck*

Stage Door [M,L,WC] 44 N Jefferson St (at 2nd) 937/223-7418 *3pm-2:30am*

■NIGHTCLUBS

Aquarius [MW,D,DS,WC] 135 E 2nd (at St Clair) 937/223-1723 *9pm-3am Wed-Sun*

Masque [★M,D,DS,S,18+] 34 N Jefferson St (btwn 2nd & 3rd) 937/228-2582 *8pm-2:30am, till 5am wknds*

■CAFES

Expressions Coffee House 937/308-8345 *7am-9pm, 9am-2pm Sat, clsd Sun, live music*

■RESTAURANTS

Cold Beer & Cheeseburgers [WC] 33 S Jefferson St (at 4th St) 937/222-2337 *11am-close, clsd Sun, grill, full bar*

The Spaghetti Warehouse 36 W 5th St (at Ludlow) 937/461-3913 *11am-10pm, till 11pm wknds, more gay Tue w/ Friends of the Italian Opera*

■BOOKSTORES

Books & Co 4453 Walnut St (in Greene Shopping Ctr) 937/429-2169 *9am-11pm, till 8pm Sun*

■PUBLICATIONS

Gay Dayton 937/623-1590 *monthly LGBT publication*

■MEN'S SERVICES

➤**MegaMates** 937/395-9001 *Call to hook up with HOT local men. FREE to listen & respond to ads. Use FREE code DAMRON. MegaMates.com.*

■EROTICA

Adult Total X [V] 6388 N Dixie Dr (at Needmore Ave) 937/454-9999

Findlay

■EROTICA

Findlay Adult Books & Video 623 Trenton Ave (at I-75, exit 159) 419/422-1301

Kent

■BARS

The Zephyr Pub [GF,E] 106 W Main St (at Water St) 330/678-4848 *3pm-close*

Lima

■NIGHTCLUBS

Somewhere in Time [MW,D,DS,S] 804 W North St (at Baxter) 419/227-7288 *5pm-2:30am, from 8pm wknds*

Logan

■ACCOMMODATIONS

Glenlaurel—A Scottish Country Inn [GS,NS,WC] 14940 Mt Olive Rd (off State Rte I-80), Rockbridge 740/385-4070, 800/809-7378 *full brkfst, hot tub*

Inn & Spa at Cedar Falls [GS,NS,WI,WC] 21190 State Rte 374 740/385-7489, 800/653-2557

Ohio • USA

Lazy Lane Cabins [GF,NS]
740/385-3475, 877/225-6572
secluded cabins sleep 2-8, hot tubs, fireplaces

Lorain

▓BARS

Tim's Place [MW,NH,D,DS,WC] 2223
Broadway (btwn 22nd & 23rd)
440/218-2223 *8pm-2:30am, clsd
Mon, patio*

Monroe

▓BARS

Old Street Saloon [MW,NH,D,K,DS] 13
Old St (at Elm St) **513/539-9183**
*8pm-2am Th-Sat, till 1am Wed, clsd
Sun-Tue*

Niles

▓EROTICA

Niles Books 5970 Youngstown Warren
Rd (off Rte 46) **330/544-3755**

Oberlin

▓ACCOMMODATIONS

Hallauer House B&B [GF,SW,WI] 14945
Hallauer Rd **440/774-3400,
877/774-3406** *eco-friendly historic
inn 3 miles S of Oberlin*

▓RESTAURANTS

The Feve [★NS] 30 S Main St (at
College St) **440/774-1978** *11am-
midnight, popular weekend brunch,
plenty veggie, full bar from 5pm*

Weia Teia [WC] 9 S Main St (at College
St) **440/774-8880** *lunch & dinner,
Thai/ Asian fusion, upscale, some veggie*

▓BOOKSTORES

MindFair Books 13 W College St
(shares storefront w/ Ben Franklin)
440/774-6463 *10am-6pm, till 8pm
Fri, noon-5pm Sun*

Oxford

▓CRUISY AREAS

Hueston Woods State Park [AYOR]
mornings & at dusk

Perrysville

▓ACCOMMODATIONS

Circle JJ Ranch [M,21+] 1104
Amsterdam Rd SE, Scio **330/627-3101**
*open April-Oct, special events, theme
wknds*

Quaker City

▓EROTICA

The Lion's Den Adult Superstore
65799 Batesville Rd (exit 193, off I-70)
740/758-5210 *24hrs*

Sandusky

▓NIGHTCLUBS

Crowbar [MW,NH,D,K,GO] 206 W Market
St (at Jackson St) **419/624-0109**
6pm-2:30am, clsd Tue

▓RESTAURANTS

Mona Pizza Gourmet [MR,TG,GO] 135
Columbus Ave (at Market St)
419/626-8166 *11am-10pm, till 3am
wknds*

▓CRUISY AREAS

Boeckling Boat Dock [AYOR]

Springfield

▓NIGHTCLUBS

Diesel [GF,D,E,K] 1912-14 Edwards Ave
(at N Belmont Ave) **937/324-0383**
8:30pm-2:30am, clsd Mon-Tue, patio

▓CRUISY AREAS

Clarence J Brown Reservoir Beach
[AYOR]

Steubenville

▓EROTICA

Past Time Adult Bookstore & Arcade
118 N 6th St **740/282-1907**

Toledo

▓INFO LINES & SERVICES

AA Gay/ Lesbian 3535 Executive Pkwy
(at Unity) **419/380-9862** *8pm Wed*

▓ACCOMMODATIONS

Mansion View Inn [GF,NS,WI] 2035
Collingwood Blvd (at Irving)
419/244-5676 *1887 Victorian near
downtown*

■Bars

Blush [M,DS] 119 N Erie St **419/255-4010** *9pm-2:30am Fri-Sat only*

Outskirts [W,D,K] 5038 Lewis Ave **419/476-1577** *3pm-2:30am, till 3:30am Fri-Sat, clsd Sun-Tue*

R House [M,D] 5534 Secor Rd (btwn Laskey & Alexis) **419/474-2929** *4pm-2:30am, patio*

Rip Cord [M,NH,K,S,DS,F] 115 N Erie St (btwn Jefferson & Monroe) **419/243-3412** *9am-2:30am, Sun brunch*

■Nightclubs

Bretz [MW,D,K,DS,S,18+,WC] 2012 Adams St **419/243-1900** *9pm-2:30am, till 4:30am Fri-Sat, clsd Mon-Tue, patio*

■Men's Clubs

Diplomat Health Club [PC] 1313 N Summit St (along Maumee River) **419/255-3700** *24hrs*

■Men's Services

➤**MegaMates** 419/873-3000 *Call to hook up with HOT local men. FREE to listen & respond to ads. Use FREE code DAMRON. MegaMates.com.*

Warren

■Nightclubs

Club 441 [MW,D,S,WC] 441 E Market St (at Vine, enter rear) **330/394-9483** *4pm-2:30am, from 2pm wknds*

The Funky Skunk [M,D,DS,K] 143 E Market St (at Park Ave) *9pm-close*

West Lafayette

■Restaurants

Lava Rock Grill at Unusual Junction [WC,GO] 56310 US Hwy 36 **740/545-9772** *'50s-style diner in restored railroad station*

Yellow Springs

■Restaurants

Winds Cafe & Bakery [WC] 215 Xenia Ave (at Cory St) **937/767-1144** *lunch & dinner, Sun brunch, clsd Mon, full bar*

Youngstown

■Bars

Mineshaft [M,NH] 1105 Poland Ave 330/207-6437

■Nightclubs

Liquid Niteclub [MW,D,K] 1281 Salt Springs Rd 234/855-0351 *4pm-2:30am, from 8pm Sat-Sun*

Split Level/ Pulse [MW,D,DS,K] 169 S Four Mile Run Rd (at S Mahoning Ave) 330/318-9830

Utopia Video Nightclub [MW,D,DS] 876 E Midlothian Blvd (at Zedaker St) 330/781-9000 *5pm-close, clsd Mon*

■Cafes

The Lemon Grove Cafe [F,BW,E] 122 W Federal Plaza W (at Hazel St) 330/744-7683 *7am-2am, from 11am wknds, events, movies, art, food served, also bar*

OKLAHOMA

Bartlesville

■Cruisy Areas

Johnstone Park [AYOR]

Grand Lake

■Accommodations

Southern Oaks Resort & Spa [GF,SW,NS,GO] 2 miles S of Hwy 28/ 82 Junction, Langley 918/782-9346, 866/452-5307 *19 cabins on 30 acres*

■Restaurants

The Artichoke Restaurant & Bar 35896 S Hwy 82, Langley 918/782-9855 *5pm-10pm, clsd Sun-Mon*

Frosty & Edna's Cafe Highway 28, Langley 918/782-9123 *6am-9:30pm*

Lighthouse Supper Club Highway 85 & Main, Ketchum 918/782-3316 *5pm-9pm, clsd Sun-Tue*

Lawton

■Cruisy Areas

The Strip [AYOR] Fort Sill Blvd, near Cache Rd *by car*

Oklahoma • USA

Oklahoma City

▓INFO LINES & SERVICES

AA Live & Let Live 3405 N Villa
405/947-3834 *8pm Mon*

▓ACCOMMODATIONS

➤**Habana Inn** [★MW,SW,NS,WC] 2200
NW 39th St (at Youngs)
405/528-2221, 800/988-2221
(reservations only) *gay resort, also 3
bars, restaurant, gift shop*

Hawthorn Suites [GF,SW,WI] 1600 NW
Expy (Richmond Square)
405/840-1440, 800/527-1133

Waterford Marriott [GF,SW,NS,WI]
6300 Waterford Blvd (at Pennsylvania)
405/848-4782 *also restaurant & bar*

▓BARS

Alibi's [GS,NH,TG,GO] 1200 N
Pennsylvania (at NW 11th)
405/605-3795 *noon -2am*

The Boom [MW,NH,F,K,DS,WI,WC] 2218
NW 39th St (at Pennsylvania)
405/601-7200 *4pm-2am, from noon
Fri-Sun, clsd Mon*

Edna's [GF,NH,F] 5137 N Classen Blvd
(at NW 51st) 405/840-3339 *noon-
2am, dive bar*

➤**The Finishline** [MW,NH,D,CW,WC] at
Habana Inn 405/525-2900 *noon-
2am, poolside bar*

Hi-Lo Club [MW,NH,D,E,DS] 1221 NW
50th St (btwn Western & Classen)
405/843-1722 *noon-2am, live bands*

➤**The Ledo** [MW,F,K,NS,WC] at Habana
Inn 405/525-0730 *4pm-10:30pm, till
2am Fri-Sat, martini lounge*

Partners 4 Club [W,NH,D,E,K,WC] 2805
NW 36th St (at May Ave)
405/942-2199

Partners Too [MW,D,WC] 2807 NW
36th St (at May Ave) 405/602-2030
open Wed-Sat

Phoenix Rising [M,NH,D,CW,B,L,GO]
2120 NW 39th St (at Pennsylvania Ave)
405/601-3711 *4pm-2am, from 2pm
Sun, patio*

Tramps [M,D,S,WI,WC] 2201 NW 39th St
(at Barnes) 405/521-9888 *noon-2am,
from 10am wknds*

▓NIGHTCLUBS

➤**The Copa** [★MW,D,E,DS,K,S,WC] at
Habana Inn 405/525-0730 *9pm-2am,
clsd Mon, male dancers Fri-Sat*

The Park [★M,D,S,V,WC] 2125 NW 39th
St (at Pennsylvania) 405/528-4690
*5pm-2am, from 3pm Sun (free buffet),
patio, cruisy*

Wreck Room [★MW,D,DS,S,YC] 2127
NW 39th St (at Pennsylvania)
405/525-7610 *10pm-close Fri-Sat
only, [18+] after 1am*

▓CAFES

The Red Cup [F,E,NS,WI] 3122 N
Classen Blvd (at NW 30th St)
405/525-3430 *7am-5pm, till 8pm Th-
Fri, from 9am wknds, vegetarian*

▓RESTAURANTS

Bricktown Brewery Restaurant 1 N
Oklahoma Ave (at Sheridan)
405/232-2739 *11am-10pm, till
midnight Sat, from noon Sun, full bar*

Cheever's Cafe [R] 2409 N Hudson Ave
(at NW 23rd) 405/525-7007 *11am-
9:30pm, 5pm-10:30pm Sat*

Earl's Rib Palace 216 Johnny Bench
Dr, Ste BBQ (in Bricktown)
405/272-9898 *11am-9pm, till 10pm
Fri-Sat, noon-8pm Sun*

➤**Gusher's** [WC] at Habana Inn
405/525-0730 *11am-10:30pm, from
9am wknds, till 3:30am Fri-Sat (after-
hours brkfst)*

Iguana Bar & Grill 9 NW 9th St (at N
Santa Fe Ave) 405/606-7172 *lunch &
dinner, Mexican*

Ingrid's Kitchen 3701 N Youngs (btwn
Penn & May, on NW 36th)
405/946-8444 *7am-8pm, 10am-2pm
Sun, German/ American bakery & deli*

Pops 660 W Hwy 66, Arcadia
405/928-7677 *brkfst, lunch & dinner,
diner fare, look for the 66-foot tall soda
bottle*

Rococo Restaurant & Fine Wine
2824 N Pennsylvania (at NW 27th St)
405/528-2824 *lunch Mon-Fri, dinner
nightly, Sun jazz brunch, full bar*

Someplace Else Deli & Bakery [★]
2310 N Western Ave 405/524-0887
7am-6:30pm, 9:30am-4pm Sat, clsd Sun

Sushi Neko 4318 N Western (btwn
42nd & 43rd) 405/528-8862 *11am-
11pm, clsd Sun*

Ted's Cafe Escondido 8324 S Western
Ave (at 84th St) 405/635-8337 *lunch
& dinner, Tex-Mex*

■ENTERTAINMENT & RECREATION

First Friday Gallery Walk from 28th
at N Walker to 30th at N Dewey
405/525-2688 *open tour of Paseo
Arts District galleries, first Fri-Sat*

■BOOKSTORES

Full Circle Bookstore [F] 50 Penn Pl,
1900 NW Expwy (in NE corner of 1st
level) 405/842-2900, 800/683-7323
*10am-9pm, noon-5pm Sun, also cafe &
coffee bar*

■RETAIL SHOPS

23rd St Body Piercing 411 NW 23rd
St (btwn Hudson & Walker)
405/524-6824 *noon-9pm, 1pm-6pm
Sun*

➤**Jungle Red** [WC] at Habana Inn
405/524-5733 *novelties, leather, gifts*

■PUBLICATIONS

Oklahoma Gazette 405/528-6000
"Metro OKC's independent weekly"

■MEN'S SERVICES

➤**MegaMates** 405/524-3838 *Call to
hook up with HOT local men. FREE to
listen & respond to ads. Use FREE code
DAMRON. MegaMates.com.*

■EROTICA

Christie's Toy Box 7914 N MacArthur
405/720-2453 *multiple locations in
OKC*

Naughty & Nice 3121 SW 29th St (at
I-44) 405/681-5044 *24hrs*

■CRUISY AREAS

Trosper Park [AYOR] *beware cops (!)*

Tulsa

■INFO LINES & SERVICES

Dennis R Neill Equality Center [WC]
621 E 4th St (at Kenosha)
918/743-4297 *3pm-9pm, clsd Sun,
also Pride store*

Gay/ Lesbian AA 2545 S Yale Ave (at
Community of Hope) 918/627-2224
5:30pm Sat

■ACCOMMODATIONS

The Mayo Hotel [GF,F,WI,WC] 115 W
5th St 918/582-6296

Tulsa Hyatt [GF,F,SW,WI,WC] 100 E
Second St (at 2nd St) 918/582-9000,
800/980-6429

■BARS

Bamboo Lounge [M,NH,D,K,DS,WC]
7204 E Pine 918/836-8700 *noon-
2am*

Club 209 [GS,E,K] 209 N Boulder Ave
(at Brady) 918/584-9944 *7pm-2am,
clsd Mon-Wed*

End Up [M,S] 5336 E Admiral Pl
918/836-0915 *4pm-2am, from noon
Tue*

New Age Renegade [MW,NH,K,C,S]
1649 S Main St (at 17th)
918/585-3405 *4pm-2am, patio*

Tulsa Eagle [★M,NH,K,L,WI,WC] 1338 E
3rd (at Peoria) 918/592-1188 *2pm-
2am*

The Yellow Brick Road
[MW,NH,WC,GO] 2630 E 15th St (at
Harvard) 918/293-0304 *1pm-2am*

■NIGHTCLUBS

Club Majestic [MW,D,DS,TG,YC,WC,GO]
124 N Boston (at Brady)
918/584-9494 *9pm-2am Th-Sun*

Club Maverick [MW,D,CW,K] 822 S
Sheridan (at 9th) 918/835-3301
4pm-2am

■CAFES

Gypsy's Coffee House [E,WI] 303 N
Cincinnati Ave 918/295-2181 *7am-
10pm, till 2am Fri-Sat, from 11am Sat-
Sun*

RESTAURANTS

The Brasserie [WC] 3509 S Peoria
918/779-7070 *4pm-10pm, till 11pm
Fri-Sat, 10am-9pm Sun*

Cancun International [BW,WC] 705 S
Lewis Ave (at 11th) **918/583-8089**
*11am-9pm, from 10am Sat-Sun, clsd
Wed*

Eloté [WC] 514 S Boston Ave
918/582-1403 *11am-10pm, till 2pm
Mon, clsd Sun, fresh Mexican & full bar*

James E McNellie's Public House
[WC] 409 E 1st St **918/382-7468**
11am-2am, great burgers & full bar

White Lion Pub 6927 S Canton Ave
(off 71st) **918/491-6533** *4pm-10pm,
clsd Sun-Mon, British-style pub*

Wild Fork [WC] 1820 Utica Square
918/742-0712 *7am-10pm, clsd Sun*

ENTERTAINMENT & RECREATION

Gilcrease Museum 1400 N Gilcrease
Museum Rd **918/596-2700,
888/655-2278** *one of the best collections of Native American & cowboy art
in the US*

Philbrook Museum of Art 2727 S
Rockford Rd (1 block E of Peoria, at end
of 27th St) **918/324-7941** *clsd Mon,
Italian villa built in the '20s oil boom
complete w/ kitschy lighted dance flr, the
gardens are a must in spring & summer*

RETAIL SHOPS

Brookside Piercing & Tattoo 3314 S
Peoria Ave **918/712-1122** *noon-
10pm, till midnight Fri-Sat*

The Pride Store [WC] 621 E 4th St
918/743-4297 *3pm-9pm, 3pm-6pm
Sun*

PUBLICATIONS

Urban Tulsa Weekly 918/592-5550
*"Tulsa Metro's only independent
newsweekly"*

MEN'S SERVICES

➤**MegaMates** 918/663-2700 *Call to
hook up with HOT local men. FREE to
listen & respond to ads. Use FREE code
DAMRON. MegaMates.com.*

EROTICA

Midtown Superstore 319 E 3rd St (at
Elgin) **918/584-3112** *24hrs*

OREGON

Ashland

INFO LINES & SERVICES

Gay/ Lesbian AA 541/732-1850

ACCOMMODATIONS

The Arden Forest Inn
[GS,NS,SW,WI,WC,GO] 261 W Hersey St
(at N Main) **541/488-1496,
800/460-3912** *full brkfst*

Ashland Creek Inn [GF,NS,GO] 70
Water St **541/482-3315** *gourmet
brkfst*

Country Willows B&B Inn
[GF,SW,NS,WI,WC] 1313 Clay St (at
Siskiyou Blvd) **541/488-1590,
800/945-5697** *full brkfst*

Lithia Springs Resort [GS,NS,WI] 2165
W Jackson Rd (at N Main)
541/482-7128, 800/482-7128

Romeo Inn B&B [GF,SW,NS,WI] 295
Idaho St **541/488-0884,
800/915-8899** *full brkfst, jacuzzi*

RESTAURANTS

The Black Sheep Pub & Restaurant
[E,WI] 51 N Main St (on the Plaza)
541/482-6414 *11:30am-1am*

Greenleaf Restaurant [BW] 49 N Main
St (on The Plaza) **541/482-2808** *8am-
8pm, creekside dining*

BOOKSTORES

Bloomsbury Books 290 E Main St
(btwn 1st & 2nd) **541/488-0029**
8:30am-9pm, 10am-6pm Sun

RETAIL SHOPS

Travel Essentials 252 E Main St
541/482-7383, 800/258-0758
*10am-5:30pm, 11am-5pm Sun, luggage,
books, accessories*

CRUISY AREAS

Keno Rock Quarry *take Dead Indian
Memorial Rd past Howard Prairie Lake to
mile marker 18, turn right at Keno Rd,
when you see pile of gravel on your left,
turn right into quarry*

Oregon • USA

Bend

ACCOMMODATIONS

Dawson House Lodge [GF,NS,WI]
109455 Hwy 97 N, Chemult
541/365-2232, 888/281-8375
*rustic inn w/ modern amenities, near
Crater Lake*

CRUISY AREAS

Drake Park [AYOR] Riverside Dr *clsd
winter*

Sawyer Park [AYOR] *evenings*

Eugene

INFO LINES & SERVICES

Gay/ Lesbian AA 1166 Oak St (at First
Christian Church) **541/342-4113** *7pm
Th, Fri & Sat & 5pm Sun*

ACCOMMODATIONS

C'est La Vie Inn [GF,NS,WI] 1006 Taylor
St (at W 10th) **541/302-3014,
866/302-3014** *full brkfst*

Valley River Inn [GF,SW,NS,WI,WC]
1000 Valley River Wy **541/743-1000,
800/543-8266**

NIGHTCLUBS

Diablo's Downtown Lounge [GF,D,E,K]
959 Pearl St **541/343-2346** *1pm-
2:30am, from 3pm wknds*

CAFES

Eugene Coffee Company [GO] 1840
Chambers St (at 18th) **541/344-0002**
7am-6pm

RESTAURANTS

Glenwood Restaurant 1340 Alder St
(at 13th Ave) **541/687-0355** *7am-
9pm*

Keystone Cafe 395 W 5th Ave (at
Lawrence) **541/342-2075** *7am-3pm,
popular brkfst*

ENTERTAINMENT &
RECREATION

**Glassbar Island Nude Beach/
Willamette River Beach** [GS] on the
Coast Fork (Franklin Blvd and I-5) *nude
beach, also hiking & biking, www.glass-
barisland.org for details*

EROTICA

Exclusively Adult 1166 South A St (at
10th St), Springfield **541/726-6969**
8pm-midnight, 24hrs Th-Sun

CRUISY AREAS

Skinner Butte Park [AYOR]

Idleyld Park

ACCOMMODATIONS

**Umpqua's Last Resort Wilderness
RV Park & Campground** [GS,WI,GO]
115 Elk Ridge Ln **541/498-2500**

Jacksonville

ACCOMMODATIONS

The TouVelle House [GF,SW,NS,WI] 455
N Oregon St (at E St) **541/899-8938,
800/846-8422** *1916 Craftsman*

Klamath Falls

ACCOMMODATIONS

Crystal Wood Lodge [GF,SW,WI,GO]
38625 Westside Road (at Hwy 140)
541/381-2322, 866/381-2322

CRUISY AREAS

Haglestein Park [AYOR] Hwy 97 (about
10 miles N of town, past Klamath Lake)

Moore Park [AYOR] *summers*

Lincoln City

RESTAURANTS

Dory Cove Restaurant [BW,WC] 2981
SW Hwy 101 (at 29th) **541/557-4000**
7am-9pm, try the chowder

Mist Restaurant 2945 NW Jetty Ave
(at Surftides Inn) **541/994-3877**
8am-9pm, full bar open later

Medford

EROTICA

Castle Megastore 1601 Riverside
541/608-9540

CRUISY AREAS

Jackson County Sports Park [AYOR]

Touvelle Park [AYOR] along Rogue
River

Ontario

▪CRUISY AREAS
Ontario State Park [AYOR] on the Snake River

Portland

see also Vancouver, Washington

▪INFO LINES & SERVICES
Live & Let Live Club 1210 SE 7th Ave **503/238-6091** *12-step meetings*

Q Center [WI] 4115 N Mississippi Ave (at N Mason St) **503/234-7837** *LGBTQ community center*

▪ACCOMMODATIONS
The Ace Hotel [GS,NS,WI,WC] 1022 SW Stark St (at 11th) **503/228-2277** *hip hotel for "cultural influencers on a budget"*

Hotel deLuxe [GF,NS,WI] 729 SW 15th Ave (at SW Morrison) **503/219-2094, 866/895-2094**

Hotel Monaco Portland [GF,WI] 506 SW Washington (at 5th Ave) **503/222-0001, 866/861-9514** *also restaurant, gym*

Hotel Vintage Plaza [★GF,WI,WC] 422 SW Broadway (at SW Washington) **503/228-1212, 800/263-2305** *upscale, also restaurant*

Inn at Northrup Station [GF] 2025 NW Northrup St (at NW 21st) **503/224-0543, 800/224-1180** *cute, colorful boutique hotel*

Jupiter Hotel [GF,NS,WI,WC] 800 E Burnside **503/230-9200, 877/800-0004**

The Lion & the Rose [GS,NS,WI,GO] 1810 NE 15th Ave (at NE Schuyler) **503/287-9245, 800/955-1647** *in 1906 Queen Anne mansion*

McMenamins Crystal Hotel [GS,SW,WI] 303 SW 12th Ave (at Stark) **503/972-2670, 855/205-3930** *former bathouse, also restaurant & bar*

Portland's White House B&B [GS,NS,WI,GO] 1914 NE 22nd Ave (at NE Hancock St) **503/287-7131, 800/272-7131** *in 1911 Greek Revival mansion*

Riverplace Hotel [GF] 1510 SW Harbor Way **503/228-3233** *restaurant & bar*

▪BARS
Boxxes [★M,D,K,V,WI,WC] 1035 SW 11th Ave (at SW 11th) **503/226-4171** *5pm-close, also Brig [MW,D], also Red Cap Garage*

CC Slaughter's [★M,D,CW,K,V,WI,WC] 219 NW Davis St (at 3rd) **503/248-9135, 888/348-9135** *3pm-2am, also martini lounge, Bear Night 4th Fri*

Chopsticks Express II [GS,F,K,YC,WC] 2651 E Burnside St (at NE 26th Ave) **503/234-6171** *noon-2am*

Crush [GS,F,WI,WC] 1400 SE Morrison (at SE 14th) **503/235-8150** *4pm-2am, clsd Mon, wine & martini bar*

Darcelle XV [GS,F,C,DS,S,WC] 208 NW 3rd Ave (at NW Davis St) **503/222-5338** *6pm-11pm, till 2am Fri-Sat, clsd Sun-Tue*

Eagle Portland [M,B,L,N,WC] 835 N Lombard St (at N Albina Ave) **503/283-9734** *2pm-2:30am*

Fox & Hounds [★M,WC] 217 NW 2nd Ave (btwn Everett & Davis) **503/243-5530** *11am-2am, also restaurant, brunch wknds*

JOQ's Tavern [M,NH,F,WC] 2512 NE Broadway (at NE 25th Ave) **503/287-4210** *1pm-2am*

Moonstar [GS] 7410 NE Martin Luther King Jr Blvd (at NE Lombard St) **503/285-1230** *11am-1:30am*

Rotture [GF,E] 315 SE 3rd Ave (at SE Pine) **503/234-5683** *9pm-2:30am, live music venue*

Scandals [M,NH,K,E,F,WC,GO] 1125 SW Stark St (at SW 12th) **503/227-5887** *noon-2am, friendly bar*

Silverado [★M,D,F,K,S,WC,GO] 318 SW 3rd Ave (at SW Oak St) **503/224-4493** *9am-2:30am, strippers*

Starky's [★MW,NH,F,WC] 2913 SE Stark St (at SE 29th Ave) **503/230-7980** *11am-2am, also restaurant, Sun brunch, patio*

Oregon • USA

Vault Martini Bar [GS,F,WC] 226 NW 12th Ave (btwn 12th & Davis Sts) **503/224-4909** *4pm-1am, till 2am Th-Sat, 1pm-10pm Sun, full menu*

Vino Vixens [GS,NS] 2929 SE Powell Blvd (at SE 29th) **503/231-8466** *1pm-9pm, till 11pm wknds, clsd Mon, "Portland's first rock 'n' roll wine shop," retail & lounge*

◼NIGHTCLUBS

Casey's [MW,D,K] 610 NW Couch St (at 6th) **503/505-9468** *11am-2:30am*

Embers [★,MW,D,F,DS,WC] 110 NW Broadway (at NW Couch St) **503/222-3082** *11am-3am, also restaurant*

Escape [MW,D,DS,V] 333 SW Park (btwn SW Oak & SW Stark) **503/227-0830** *10:30pm-close Fri-Sat only, Portland's only all-ages gay club*

Holocene [GS,D,E,DS] 1001 SE Morrison (at SE 10th) **503/239-7639** *many gay theme nights*

Under Wonder Lounge [GS,F,TG,DS,NS,GO] 128 NE Russell **503/284-8686** *5pm-midnight, open show nights only*

◼CAFES

Blend [WI,WC] 2710 N Killingsworth (at Greeley) **503/473-8616** *7am-6pm, 8am-5pm Sun*

Cup & Saucer Cafe [★,F,NS,BW,WC] 3566 SE Hawthorne Blvd (at SE 36th) **503/236-6001** *7am-9pm, full menu, some veggie*

Elephant's Delicatessen [WC] 115 NW 22nd Ave (at NW Davis)
503/299-6304 *7am-7:30pm, 9:30am-6:30pm Sun*

Marco's Cafe & Espresso Bar [F,BW,WC] 7910 SW 35th (at Multnomah Blvd), Multnomah **503/245-0199** *7am-9pm, from 8am Sat, 8am-2pm Sun*

The Pied Cow [WC] 3244 SE Belmont St (at 33rd Ave) **503/230-4866** *4pm-midnight, till 1am Fri, noon-1am Sat, till midnight Sun, funky Victorian, great desserts, patio*

Pix Pâtisserie [BW,WC] 3402 SE Division St (at SE 34th) **503/232-4407** *2pm-midnight, noon-2am Fri-Sat, dessert*

Three Friends Coffeehouse [WI,WC] 201 SE 12th Ave (at Ash)
503/236-6411 *7am-10pm, from 9am Sun*

Voodoo Doughnut 22 SW 3rd Ave **503/241-4704** *24hrs*

◼RESTAURANTS

Andina 1314 NW Glisan St (at 13th Ave) **503/228-9535** *lunch, dinner & tapas, Peruvian, full bar*

Aura Restaurant & Lounge [D,WC] 1022 W Burnside St (btwn SW 10th & 11th) **503/597-2872** *5pm-midnight, till 2:30am Fri-Sat, clsd Sun-Tue, also bar*

Bastas Trattoria [WC] 410 NW 21st (at Flanders) **503/274-1572** *dinner nightly, northern Italian, full bar till late*

Berbati's Pan [WC] 19 SW 2nd Ave (btwn Burnside & Ankeny)
503/226-2122 *11am-2am, from 3pm Sun-Mon, Greek, full bar*

Besaw's [WC] 2301 NW Savier (at NW 23rd) **503/228-2619** *7am-10pm Tue-Fri, from 8am Sat, 8am-3pm Sun-Mon, American*

Bijou Cafe [★,WI,WC] 132 SW 3rd Ave (at Pine St) **503/222-3187** *7am-2pm, from 8am wknds*

Bluehour [WC] 250 NW 13th Ave (at NW Everett St) **503/226-3394** *lunch Sun-Fri, dinner nightly, Sun brunch, extensive wine list*

Bread & Ink Cafe [★,WI,WC] 3610 SE Hawthorne Blvd (at 36th)
503/239-4756 *brkfst, lunch & dinner, packed for brunch on Sun, full bar*

Dingo's Mexican Grill [★,GO,WC] 4612 SE Hawthorne Blvd (at SE 46th) **503/233-3996** *noon-10pm, till 11pm Th, till 9pm Sun*

Dot's Cafe [★,WC] 2521 SE Clinton (at 26th) **503/235-0203** *noon-2am, full bar*

Equinox [WC] 830 N Shaver St (at Mississippi) **503/460-3333** *dinner, brunch wknds, clsd Mon, int'l, patio*

Esparza's Tex-Mex Cafe [★WC] 2725 SE Ankeny St (at 28th) **503/234-7909** *11:30am-10pm, funky*

Farm Cafe [WC] **503/736-3276** *5pm-11pm, Northwest cuisine*

Fish Grotto [★WC] 1035 SW Stark (at SW 11th Ave, at Boxxes) **503/226-4171** *5pm-10pm, till 9pm Sun-Mon, full bar*

Genie's Cafe [WC] 1101 SE Division St (at 12th) **503/445-9777** *8am-3pm, brunch, house-infused vodkas*

Gypsy Restaurant & Lounge [K,WC] 625 NW 21st (btwn Hoyt & Irving) **503/796-1859** *4pm-2:30am, clsd Sun-Mon, full bar, inexpensive*

Hamburger Mary's [DS,K] 19 NW 5th Ave **503/688-1200** *11am-midnight, 10am-3pm Sun*

Hobo's [P,WC] 120 NW 3rd Ave (btwn Davis & Couch) **503/224-3285** *4pm-2:30am*

Masu [WI,WC] 406 SW 13th Ave (at Burnside) **503/221-6278** *lunch Mon-Th, dinner nightly, sushi*

Mayas Taqueria [WC] 1000 SW Morrison (at SW 10th) **503/226-1946** *11am-10pm, till 9pm Sun*

Melt Bistro & Bar 716 NW 21st Ave (at Johnson) **503/295-4944** *11am-10pm, clsd Sun, sandwiches & more*

Mint [GO,WC] 816 N Russell St **503/284-5518** *5pm-10pm, till 11pm Fri-Sat, clsd Sun-Mon, fusion food, also 820 Lounge*

Montage [★WC] 301 SE Morrison (at 3rd) **503/234-1324** *lunch Tue-Fri, dinner till 2am, till 4am Fri-Sat, Louisiana-style cookin', full bar*

Nicholas' [WC] 318 SE Grand (btwn Oak & Pine) **503/235-5123** *11am-9pm, from noon Sun, Middle Eastern*

Nostrana [WC] 1401 SE Morrison **503/234-2427** *lunch Mon-Fri, dinner nightly; fresh, local, wood-fired Italian*

Old Town Pizza [WC] 226 NW Davis (at NW 3rd) **503/222-9999** *11:30am-11pm, above Shanghai Tunnels, supposedly home to 100-year-old ghost*

Old Wives Tales [★BW,E,WC] 1300 E Burnside St (at 13th) **503/238-0470** *8am-9pm, till 10pm Fri-Sat, multi-ethnic vegetarian*

Paley's Place 1204 NW 21st Ave (at NW Northrup St) **503/243-2403** *dinner nightly, Northwest cuisine*

Paradox Cafe [★WC] 3439 SE Belmont St (at SE 35th) **503/232-7508** *brkfst, lunch & dinner, vegetarian diner, killer Reuben*

Pour [WC] 2755 NE Broadway (at NE 28th) **503/288-7687** *4:30pm-11pm, till close Fri-Sat, clsd Sun, wine bar & bistro*

The Roxy [★WI,WC] 1121 SW Stark St (btwn 11th & 12th) **503/223-9160** *24hrs, clsd Mon, retro American diner*

Santa Fe Taqueria [★E,WC] 831 NW 23rd (at Kearney) **503/220-0406** *11am-midnight*

Saucebox [D,WC,GO] 214 SW Broadway (at Burnside) **503/241-3393** *5pm-close, pan-Asian, full bar*

Vita Cafe [WC] 3023 NE Alberta St (btwn 30th & 31st) **503/335-8233** *brkfst, lunch & dinner, mostly vegetarian/vegan*

West Cafe [E,WI,WC] 1201 SW Jefferson St (12th Ave) **503/227-8189** *lunch Mon-Fri, dinner nightly, Sun brunch, "comfort food w/ a twist"*

Yakuza Lounge [WC] 5411 NE 30th Ave (at Killingsworth) **503/450-0893** *5pm-close, clsd Mon-Tue, Japanese, full bar*

■ ENTERTAINMENT & RECREATION

Gay Skate 1 SE Spokane St (at Oaks Park Way, at Oaks Rink) **503/233-5777** *7pm-9pm 3rd Mon only*

Out Dancing [MW] 975 SE Sandy Blvd (at SE Ankeny St & SE 9th Ave) **503/236-5129** *LGBT dance lessons*

Sauvie's Island Beach 25 miles NW (off US 30) *follow Reeder Rd to the Collins beach area, park at the farthest end of the road, then follow path to beach; also "Rooster Rock," 22 miles E on Columbia River*

Oregon • USA

■ BOOKSTORES

CounterMedia 927 SW Oak (btwn 9th & 10th) **503/226-8141** *11am-7pm, noon-6pm Sun, alternative comics, vintage gay books/ periodicals/ erotica*

Laughing Horse Bookstore [WC] 12 NE 10th Ave (near Burnside) **503/236-2893** *11am-7pm, clsd Sun, alternative/ progressive*

Powell's Books [★WC] 1005 W Burnside St (at 10th) **503/228-4651, 800/878-7323** *9am-11pm, huge new & used bookstore, cafe, readings*

Reading Frenzy [WC] 921 SW Oak St (at 9th) **503/274-1449** *noon-6pm, zines, comics, LGBT selection*

■ RETAIL SHOPS

Hip Chicks Do Wine 4510 SE 23rd Ave (SE Holgate & 26th) **503/234-3790** *11am-6pm*

Under U4 Men 800 SW Broadway St (at Washington) **503/274-2555** *10am-7pm, till 9pm Fri, 11am-6pm Sun, designer underwear & in-store underwear models*

■ GYMS & HEALTH CLUBS

Common Ground Wellness Center [GF,R] 5010 NE 33rd Ave (at Alberta St) **503/238-1065** *10am-11pm, wellness center, public hot tubs, call for men's & trans nights*

■ MEN'S CLUBS

Hawks PDX 234 SE Grand Ave **503/946-8659**

Steam Portland [MO,PC,GO] 2885 NE Sandy Blvd **503/736-9999** *24hrs*

■ MEN'S SERVICES

►MegaMates **503/299-9911** *Call to hook up with HOT local men. FREE to listen & respond to ads. Use FREE code DAMRON. MegaMates.com.*

■ EROTICA

Fantasy for Adults 1512 W Burnside (near 15th) **503/295-6969**

Fat Cobra Video 5940 N Interstate Ave **503/247-3425**

Spartacus Leathers 300 SW 12th Ave (at Burnside) **503/224-2604**

Taboo Video 237 SE MLK, Jr Blvd (at Pine) **503/239-1678** *24hrs*

■ CRUISY AREAS

Kelly Point [AYOR] on Marine Dr *follow trail to left of parking lot*

Salem

■ NIGHTCLUBS

Southside Speakeasy [GS,NH,D,F,K,DS,WI,GO] 3529 Fairview Industrial Dr SE (at Madrona) **503/362-1139** *11am-2am, from 3:30pm wknds*

■ RESTAURANTS

Davinci's 180 High St SE **504/399-1413** *dinner only, clsd Sun, full bar*

Word Of Mouth **503/930-4285** *7am-3pm*

■ EROTICA

Bob's Adult Bookstore 3815 State St (at Lancaster) **503/363-3846**

■ CRUISY AREAS

Bush Park [AYOR] 12th & State Sts *days only*

Sauvie Island

■ ENTERTAINMENT & RECREATION

Collins Beach [GS,N,AYOR] take Hwy 30 N from Portland, turn onto "Sauvie Island Bridge" (then take Gillihan Rd to Reeder Rd) *get a parking permit before you go (available at general store at base of Sauvie Island Bridge)*

Silverton

■ ACCOMMODATIONS

The Oregon Garden Resort [GF,F,SW,WI] 895 W Main St **800/966-6490** *boutique-style resort*

Yachats

■ ACCOMMODATIONS

See Vue Motel [GS,NS,WI,GO] 95590 Hwy 101 **541/547-3227, 866/547-3237** *ocean view*

PENNSYLVANIA

Abington

■BARS

Kitchen Bar [GF,D,F,E] 1482 Old York Rd 215/576-9766 *noon-2am, from 8am wknds*

■RESTAURANTS

Vintage Bar & Restaurant [WC] 1116 Old York Rd 215/887-8500 *11am-2am*

Allentown

see also Bethlehem

■ACCOMMODATIONS

Grim's Manor B&B [MW,NS,GO] 10 Kern Rd, Kutztown 610/683-7089

■BARS

Candida's [MW,NH,D,F,K] 247 N 12th St (at Chew) 610/434-3071 *4pm-2am, from 2pm Fri-Sun*

Stonewall, Moose Lounge Bar & Grille [★M,D,F,E,K,DS,S,V] 28 N 10th St (at Hamilton) 610/432-0215 *7pm-2am, clsd Mon*

■MEN'S SERVICES

➤**MegaMates** 484/244-0144 *Call to hook up with HOT local men. FREE to listen & respond to ads. Use FREE code DAMRON. MegaMates.com.*

■EROTICA

Adult World 880 S West End Blvd/ Rte 309, Quakerstown 215/538-1522

■CRUISY AREAS

Union Terrace Park [AYOR] Union & St Elmo's Sts

Upper Macungie Park [AYOR] Rte 100 (1 mile N of the I-78 exit)

Altoona

■NIGHTCLUBS

Escapade [MW,D,GO] 2523 Union Ave, Rte 36 814/946-8195 *8pm-2am*

■EROTICA

Adult World Old Rte 220 (Bellwood exit, off I-99) 814/742-7781

Beaver Falls

■EROTICA

Video Hobby Land 7211 Big Beaver Blvd (on Rte 18) 724/847-3777

Berwick

■CRUISY AREAS

Test Track Park [AYOR] S Eaton St (off Rte 11)

Bethlehem

■NIGHTCLUBS

Diamonz [W,D,F,E,K,WC] 1913 W Broad St (at Pennsylvania Ave) 610/865-1028 *7pm-2am, from 5pm Fri-Sat*

■EROTICA

Green Door Video 1162 Pembroke Rd 610/865-5855 *24hrs; also Cupid's Treasures 861 Stefko Blvd, 610/868-6616*

Bristol

■EROTICA

Bristol News World 576 Bristol Pike/ Rte 13 N 215/785-4770

■CRUISY AREAS

Silver Lake Park [AYOR]

Bryn Mawr

■RETAIL SHOPS

TLA Video 761 Lancaster Ave 610/520-1222 *10am-11pm, extensive LGBT titles*

Butler

■NIGHTCLUBS

M&J's Lounge [MW,NH,18+,PC,BYOB] 124 Mercer St 724/496-8955 *9pm-midnight Th, 9:30pm-3am Fri-Sat*

Vertigo [MW,D,BYOB] 564 W Cunningham St *6pm Wed & Sun, from 9pm Fri-Sat*

■CRUISY AREAS

Moraine State Park [AYOR] Bear Run area (south shore)

Pennsylvania • *USA*

Edinboro

■CRUISY AREAS
Lakeside Commons [AYOR] Rte 6 N (behind the mall overlooking the lake), Waterford *days*

Elizabeth

■EROTICA
51 Video & Books - Adult Mart 931 Hayden (Rte 51) 412/384-6383 *24hrs*

Erie

■NIGHTCLUBS
Craze Nightclub [GS,D,K,DS] 1607 Raspberry St (at 16th) 814/456-3027 *9pm-2am, from 5pm Wed, clsd Tue & Th, [18+] Mon*

The Zone [MW,D,B,F,DS] 133 W 18th St (at Peach) 814/452-0125 *8pm-2am, from 4pm Wed*

■RESTAURANTS
La Bella [BYOB,GO] 802 W 18th St 814/456-2244 *5pm-9pm, clsd Sun-Tue*

Pie in the Sky Cafe [BYOB,R,WC] 463 W 8th St (at Walnut) 814/459-8638 *lunch & dinner, clsd Sun-Mon*

■RETAIL SHOPS
Ink Assassins Tattoos & Piercings 2601 Peach St 814/455-6752 *noon-10pm, till 6pm Sun*

■PUBLICATIONS
Erie Gay News 814/456-9833 *covers news & events in the Erie, Cleveland, Pittsburgh, Buffalo & Chautauqua County (NY) region*

Gay People's Chronicle 216/916-9338 *Ohio's largest bi-weekly LGBT newspaper w/ extensive listings*

■EROTICA
Eastern Adult Books - Adult Mart 1313 State St (btwn 13th & 14th) 814/459-7014

Modern News 1113 State St (at 12th) 814/453-6932

■CRUISY AREAS
Glenwood Park [AYOR] park on the hill (overlooking the zoo)

Gettysburg

■ACCOMMODATIONS
Battlefield B&B [GS,WI,WC,GO] 2264 Emmitsburg Rd (at Ridge Rd) 717/334-8804, 888/766-3897 *full brkfst, Civil War home*

The Beechmont Inn B&B [GF,NS,WI,WC] 315 Broadway, Hanover 717/632-3013, 800/553-7009

Sheppard Mansion B&B [GS,NS,WI] 117 Frederick St (at High St), Hanover 717/633-8075, 877/762-6746 *also restaurant & bar*

Gibson

■ACCOMMODATIONS
Hillside Campgrounds [★MO,D,SW,N,WI,21+GO] Creek Rd, 3 miles off I-81, at exit 219 570/756-2007 *seasonal, campground, cabins, disco Fri-Sat*

Greensburg

■NIGHTCLUBS
Longbada Lounge [MW,D,K,DS,WC] 108 W Pittsburgh St (at Pennsylvania Ave) 724/837-6614 *9pm-2am, clsd Sun-Mon, patio*

■CRUISY AREAS
Harrison Ave [AYOR] off Otterman St

Harrisburg

■INFO LINES & SERVICES
LGBT Community Center Coalition of Central PA 221 N Front St, 3rd flr 717/920-9534

■BARS
Bar 704 [M,NH,OC,WC] 704 N 3rd St 717/234-4226 *4pm-2am*

The Brownstone Lounge [MW,NH,F,WC] 412 Forster St (btwn 3rd & 6th) 717/234-7009 *11am-2am, from 5pm wknds*

L Bar & Lounge [MW,NH,F] 881 Eisenhower Blvd 717/939-5573 *11am-2am*

The Liquid 891 [MW,D,TG,F,E,DS,V] 891 Eisenhower Blvd (near exit 19) 717/939-3590 *8pm-2am, till 11pm Th, clsd Mon-Wed*

■NIGHTCLUBS

Stallions [★M,D,E,K,DS,S,V,WC] 706 N 3rd St (enter rear) **717/232-3060** *7pm-2am*

■CRUISY AREAS

Riverfront Park [AYOR] Front & State Sts

Johnstown

■NIGHTCLUBS

Lucille's [MW,D,K,DS,S] 520 Washington St (near Central Park) **814/539-4448** *6pm-2am, clsd Sun-Mon*

■CRUISY AREAS

Central Park [AYOR]

Lancaster

■ACCOMMODATIONS

Cameron Estate Inn [GS,F,NS,WC,GO] 1855 Mansion Ln, Mount Joy **717/492-0111, 888/422-6376**

Lancaster Arts Hotel [GF,F,WC] 300 Harrisburg Ave **717/299-3000, 866/720-2787**

■BARS

Dad's Bar & Grill [GS,NH,F,K] 168 S Main St, Manheim **717/665-1960** *4pm-2am, from 11am Fri*

Tally Ho [MW,D,K,DS,YC] 201 W Orange St (at Water) **717/299-0661** *8pm-2am*

■RESTAURANTS

The Loft above Tally Ho bar **717/299-0661** *lunch & dinner, clsd Sun, contemporary American/ French*

■EROTICA

The Den 53 N Prince St **717/299-1779**

■CRUISY AREAS

Lancaster County Park [AYOR]

Long's Park [AYOR] Rte 30 at Harrisburg Pike

Lebanon

■EROTICA

Hobbeze Lebanon Adult Gifts 1604 E Cumberland St/ Rte 422 (at 15th Ave) **717/273-6398**

■CRUISY AREAS

Union Canal Tunnel Park [AYOR]

Liverpool

■EROTICA

Adult Depot [GO] 64 Old Trail Rd (near Rte 11 & 104 Jct) **717/444-3894** *all-male theater*

Milford

■ACCOMMODATIONS

Hotel Fauchere [GF,NS,WI,WC] 401 Broad St (at Catharine St) **570/409-1212** *historic boutique hotel, also restaurant & bar*

Montgomery

■EROTICA

Adult Playtime Boutique 737 Rte 15 (top of the mountain, near the rest area) **570/547-2663**

New Hope

see also Lambertville & Sergeantsville, New Jersey

■ACCOMMODATIONS

Ash Mill Farm B&B [GF,NS,WI] 5358 York Rd (at Rte 202), Holicong **215/794-5373**

The Lexington House [★GS,SW,NS,GO] 6171 Upper York Rd **215/794-0811** *1749 country home, full brkfst*

Silver Maple Organic Farm & B&B [GS,SW,NS,WI,WC,GO] 483 Sergeantsville Rd (Rte 523), Flemington, NJ **908/237-2192**

The Wishing Well Guesthouse [GS,NS,GO] 144 Old York Rd **215/862-8819**

■BARS

Bob Eagans [GS,C,F] 6426 Lower York Rd (at the Nevermore Hotel) **215/862-5225** *cabaret, dinner served, also hotel*

Havana [GS,FE,K] 105 S Main St **215/862-9897** *noon-2am*

■RESTAURANTS

Eagle Diner [WC] 6522 Lower York Rd **215/862-5575** *24hrs*

Pennsylvania • *USA*

Karla's 5 W Mechanic St (at Main) 215/862-2612 *noon-11pm, till midnight Fri-Sat, from 11am Sun, full bar till 2am*

Wildflowers 8 W Mechanic St 215/862-2241 *seasonal, noon-9pm, full bar*

▇EROTICA

Grownups [GO] 2 E Mechanic St (at Main) 215/862-9304

Le Chateau Exotique 27 W Mechanic St 215/862-3810 *fetishwear*

New Milford

▇ACCOMMODATIONS

Oneida Campground & Lodge [M,D,SW,N,WI,GO] 570/465-7011 *seasonal*

Norristown

▇BARS

Beagle Tavern [GS,F,K,C] 1003 E Main St 610/272-3133 *11am-2am, more gay Wed & Fri*

Philadelphia

▇INFO LINES & SERVICES

William Way LGBT Community Center 1315 Spruce St (at Juniper) 215/732-2220 *9am-10pm, from 11am Sat, till 7pm Sun*

▇ACCOMMODATIONS

Alexander Inn [GS,NS,WI,GO] Spruce (at 12th St) 215/923-3535, 877/253-9466

The Gables B&B [GS,NS,WI,GO] 4520 Chester Ave 215/662-1918

The Independent Hotel [GS,WI,WC] 1234 Locust St (at 13th) 215/772-1440

Latham Hotel [GF,WI,WC] 135 S 17th St (at Walnut) 215/563-7474, 877/528-4261

Lippincott House [GF,WI] 2023 Locust St 215/523-9251 *exquisite grand mansion*

Morris House Hotel [GF,NS,WI] 225 S 8th St 215/922-2446

Palomar Philadelphia [GF,WI,WC] 117 S 17th St 215/563-5006, 888/725-1778

Uncles Upstairs Inn [M,NS,GO] 1220 Locust St (at 12th) 215/546-6660

Wyndham Garden [GF,SW,WI] 815 N Pottstown Pike (Exit 312), Exton 610/363-1100, 888/253-6119

▇BARS

Bike Stop [M,D,B,L,K] 204-206 S Quince St (btwn 11th & 12th, Walnut & Locust) 215/627-1662 *4pm-2am, from 2pm wknds, cruisy*

ICandy [M,D] 254 S 12th St (btwn Locust & Spruce) 267/324-3500 *4pm-2am*

Khyber Pass Pub [GF,F,E,WC] 56 S 2nd St (btwn Market & Chestnut) 215/238-5888 *11am-2am*

L'Etage [GS,D,C] 624 S 6th St (at Bainbridge) 215/592-0656 *7:30pm-1am, till 2am Fri-Sat, clsd Mon, also crepe restaurant downstairs*

North Third [GS,F] 801 N 3rd (at Brown) 215/413-3666 *4pm-2am, from 10am wknd brunch*

Stir Lounge [MW,NH,D,V] 1705 Chancellor St (at Rittenhouse Sq btwn Walnut & Spruce) 215/732-2700 *4pm-2am*

Tabu Lounge & Sports Bar [GS,F,K] 200 S 12th St 215/964 -9675 *noon-2am*

Tavern on Camac [MW,D,C,P] 243 S Camac St (at Spruce) 215/545-0900 *4pm-2am, also restaurant*

U-Bar [M,NH] 1220 Locust St (at 12th) 215/546-6660 *11am-2am*

Venture Inn [MW,NH,F] 255 S Camac (at Spruce) 215/545-8731 *11am-2am*

The Westbury [MW,NH,F,WC,GO] 261 S 13th St (at Spruce) 215/546-5170 *4pm-2am*

Woody's [M,D,CW,F,K,S,WI,YC,WC] 202 S 13th St (at Walnut) 215/545-1893 *11am-2am, [18+] Wed, Latin Th*

▇NIGHTCLUBS

Bob & Barbara's Lounge [GS,E,DS] 1509 South St 215/545-4511 *3pm-2am, from 6pm Sun, [DS] Th, live jazz Fri-Sat*

Fluid [GF,D,E,S,$] 613 S 4th St (at Kater) 215/629-3686 9pm-2am, more gay wknds

Shampoo [GS,D,A] 417 N 8th St (at Willow) 215/922-7500 9pm-2am, clsd Mon-Tue & Th, more gay Fri

Sisters [W,D,F,E,K,DS,WC] 1320 Chancellor St (at Juniper) 215/735-0735 5pm-2am, from 4pm Sun, clsd Mon, also restaurant, dinner Wed-Sat, Sun brunch from noon

Voyeur [M,D,K,C,DS,PC] 1221 St James St (off 13th & Locust) 215/735-5772 1am-3am, from 9pm wknds

▇CAFES

10th Street Pour House [WC] 262 S 10th St (at Spruce) 215/922-5626 7:30am-3pm, from 8:30am wknds, popular brunch wknds

B2 Cafe [WI] 1500 E Passyunk Ave 215/271-5520 great vegan soft serve ice cream

Capogiro 119 S 13th St (at Sansom) 215/351-0900 7:30am-11:30pm, till 1am Fri-Sat, gelato

Capriccio 110 N 16th St (at Benjamin Franklin Pkwy) 215/735-9797 6:30am-7pm, 8am-8pm wknds

Cosi 1128 Walnut St 215/413-1608 7am-11pm

A Full Plate Cafe [MR,TG,BYOB,GO] 1009 N Bodine St (at George St) 215/627-4068 11am-9pm, till 10pm Fri-Sat, till 3pm Sun, patio

Green Line Cafe [F,E] 4239 Baltimore Ave (at 43rd) 215/222-3431 7am-11pm, 8am-8pm Sun

▇RESTAURANTS

13th Street Pizza 209 S 13th St (at Chancellor St) 215/546-4453 11am-4am, popular late night

Alfa 1709 Walnut St (at 17th) 215/751-0201 5pm-2am, also bar

Bar Ferdinand 1030 N 2nd St great tapas & wine

The Caboose Grille 2 W Broad St, Souderton 215/721-1001 lunch & dinner Tue-Sat, brkfst wknds, clsd Mon

Cantina Feliz [WC] 424 S Bethlehem Pike, Fort Washington 215/646-1320 11am-9pm, from 4pm Sat-Sun, till 10pm Fri-Sat

The Continental 138 Market St (at 2nd) 215/923-6069 lunch, dinner, wknd brunch, also bar until 2am

Hinge Cafe [BYOB,E,GO] 2652 E Somerset St (at Edgemont) 215/425-6614 8am-3pm Mon-Tue, till 10pm Th, till 11pm Fri-Sat, till 8pm Sun, cash only

Honey's 800 N 4th St 215/925-1150 7am-8pm, till 9pm Fri-Sat, till 5pm Sun

Knock 226 S 12th St 215/925-1166 lunch & dinner, Sun brunch, American, also bar

Liberties 705 N 2nd St (at Fairmount) 215/238-0660 lunch & dinner, full bar till 2am

Lolita [BYOB] 106 S 13th St (at Sansom) 215/546-7100 5pm-10pm, upscale Mexican

Mercato [BYOB] 1216 Spruce St 215/985-2962 dinner, Italian

Midtown II [TG] 122 S 11th St 215/627-6452 24hrs, diner, popular late night

Mixto 1141 Pine St 215/592-0363 lunch & dinner, brkfst wknds, Latin American

More Than Just Ice Cream 1119 Locust St (at 12th) 215/574-0586 11am-11pm

My Thai 2200 South St (at 22nd) 215/985-1878 5pm-10pm, till 11pm Fri-Sat, full bar

New Harmony 135 N 9th St (at Cherry) 215/627-4520 11am-11pm, vegan/Chinese

Paesano's 1017 S 9th St 215/440-0371 11am-7pm, great sandwiches

Sabrina's 910 Christian St 215/574-1599 8am-10pm, till 8pm Tue-Th, till 4pm Sun-Mon

El Vez 121 S 13th St (at Sansom) 215/928-9800 lunch Mon-Sat, dinner nightly, Sun brunch, full bar

Pennsylvania • *USA*

White Dog Cafe [E] 3420 Sansom St (at Walnut) **215/386-9224** *lunch & dinner, brunch Sun, full bar, cool Mon reading & Sun film series*

Zócalo [WI] 3600 Lancaster Ave (at 36th) **215/895-0139** *noon-9pm, clsd Sun*

■ENTERTAINMENT & RECREATION

The Walt Whitman House 328 Mickle Blvd, Camden, NJ **856/964-5383** *the last home of America's great & controversial poet, just across the Delaware River*

■BOOKSTORES

Giovanni's Room [★] 345 S 12th St (at Pine) **215/923-2960** *11:30am-7pm, from 1pm Sun, legendary LGBT bookstore*

Robin's Bookstore 108 S 13th St **215/735-9600** *11am-7pm, till 8pm Sat, clsd Sun*

■RETAIL SHOPS

Infinite Body Piercing 626 S 4th St (at South) **215/923-7335** *noon-10pm, till 8pm Sun*

■PUBLICATIONS

PGN (Philadelphia Gay News) **215/625-8501** *LGBT newspaper w/ extensive listings*

■GYMS & HEALTH CLUBS

12th St Gym [SW] 204 S 12th St (btwn Locust & Walnut) **215/985-4092**

■MEN'S CLUBS

Club Body Center [NS,WI,PC] 1220 Chancellor St (at 12th & Walnut) **215/735-7671** *24hrs, 5 flrs*

Philly Jacks [MO,18+,PC] 1318 Walnut St (btw 13th & Broad) **215/618-1519** *4 sex parties per month, club only open during parties; call for dates*

▶**Sansom Street Gym** [★MO,V,PC] 2020 Sansom St **267/330-0151** *24hrs*

■MEN'S SERVICES

➤**MegaMates** 215/877-3337 *Call to hook up with HOT local men. FREE to listen & respond to ads. Use FREE code DAMRON. MegaMates.com.*

■EROTICA

Adonis Cinema Complex [★] 2026 Sansom St (at 20th) 215/557-9319 *24hrs*

Condom Kingdom 437 South St (at 5th) 215/829-1668 *safer sex materials & toys*

Danny's 133 S 13th St (at Walnut) 215/925-5041 *24hrs*

Fantasy Island Adult Books 7363 State Rd 215/332-5454

Passional Boutique 704 S 5th St (at Bainbridge) 215/829-4986, 877/826-7738 *noon-10pm*

Sexploratorium 620 S 5th St 215/923-1398 *noon-10pm*

Pittsburgh

■INFO LINES & SERVICES

AA Gay/ Lesbian 412/471-7472 *call for times & location*

Gay/ Lesbian Community Center 210 Grant St 412/422-0114 *9am-9pm, noon-6pm Sun*

■ACCOMMODATIONS

Arbors B&B [MO,NS,WI,GO] 745 Maginn St 412/231-4643

Camp Davis [MW,D,SW] 311 Red Brush Rd, Boyers 724/637-2402 *1 hour from Pittsburgh, cabins & campsites, variety of events*

The Inn on Negley [GF,NS,WI,WC] 703 S Negley Ave (at Elmer St) 412/661-0631

The Inn on the Mexican War Streets [MW,F,NS,WI,GO] 604 W North Ave 412/231-6544

Morning Glory Inn B&B [GF,WI] 2119 Sarah St 412/431-1707

The Parador Inn [GF,WI,GO] 939 Western Ave 412/231-4800, 877/540-1443

The Priory [GF,NS,WI,WC] 614 Pressley St (near Cedar Ave) 412/231-3338, 866/377-4679

■BARS

5801 [★MW,V,WC] 5801 Ellsworth Ave (at Maryland) 412/661-5600 *4pm-2am, from 2pm Sun, also restaurant*

The Backdraft Bar & Grill [GS,F,E,K] 3049 Churchview Ave 412/885-1239 *11am-2am, till midnight Sun*

Blue Moon Bar & Lounge [M,NH,TG,S] 5115 Butler St (at Stanton) 412/781-1119 *4pm-2am, till midnight Mon*

Cattivo [W,D,DS,K,F] 146 44th St 412/687-2157 *4pm-2am Wed-Sun, clsd Mon-Tue*

Cruze Bar [MW,D,E,GO] 1600 Smallman St (at 16th St) 412/471-1400 *4pm-2am, clsd Mon*

Images [M,K,S,V] 965 Liberty Ave (at 10th St) 412/391-9990 *2pm-2am, go-go boys*

Leather Central [★M,D,L,F,V] 1226 Herron Ave (downstairs) 412/682-6839 *9pm-2am Fri-Sat, 6pm-11pm Sun*

PTown [MW,D,S,WI] 4740 Baum Blvd 412/621-0111 *6pm-2am*

Real Luck Cafe [MW,NH,F,S,WC] 1519 Penn Ave (at 16th) 412/471-7832 *4pm-2am*

Remedy [GS,NH,D,MR] 5121 Butler St, Lawrenceville 412/781-6771 *4pm-2am, from 12:30pm Sun, also restaurant upstairs*

Spin Bartini/Ultra Lounge [GS,E,WC] 5744 Ellsworth Ave, Shadyside 412/362-7746 *4pm-2am*

There Ultra Lounge [MW,K,WC] 931 Liberty Ave (at Smithfield) 412/642-4435 *3:30pm-2am, from 7:30pm Sat-Sun*

■NIGHTCLUBS

1226 on Herron [MW,D] 1226 Herron Ave (at Liberty) 412/682-6839 *6pm-2am, clsd Mon-Wed, leather bar Fri-Sat lower level*

941 Saloon [MW,D,K] 941 Liberty Ave (at Smithfield St, 2nd flr) 412/281-5222 *2pm-2am*

The Link [MW,D,F,E,DS,S] 91 Wendel Rd, Herminie 724/446-7717 *7pm-2am, clsd Mon, patio*

Pennsylvania • *USA*

Tilden [M,D,PC] 941 Liberty Ave (at Smithfield St, upstairs) *after-hours 1am-3am, from 11pm Fri-Sat, membership required*

◼CAFES

Square Cafe [E,GO] 1137 S Braddock Ave **412/244-8002** *7am-3pm, from 8am Sun*

Zeke's Coffee 6012 Penn Ave **724/201-1671** *9am-5pm, till 2pm Mon, till 8pm Th, clsd Sun*

◼RESTAURANTS

Abay 130 S Highland Ave (at Baum Blvd) **412/661-9736** *lunch & dinner, clsd Mon, Ethiopian, plenty veggie*

Capri 6001 Penn Ave (at Highland Ave) **412/363-1250** *11am-midnight, 6pm-2am Th-Sat*

Dinette 5996 Penn Cir S **412/362-0202** *dinner only, clsd Sun-Mon, plates to share, starters & thin-crust pizzas*

Dish 128 S 17th St (at Sarah) **412/390-2012** *5pm-2am, clsd Sun, Italian, also bar*

Double Wide Grill 2339 E Carson St (at S 24th St) **412/390-1111** *lunch & dinner, wknd brunch, BBQ, plenty veggie/vegan*

Eleven 1150 Smallman St (at 11th) **412/201-5656** *lunch & dinner, Sun brunch*

Harris Grill 5747 Ellsworth Ave **412/362-5273** *dinner nightly, wknd brunch, full bar*

Kaya 2000 Smallman St (at 20th) **412/261-6565** *lunch & dinner, Latin/Caribbean, plenty veggie*

NOLA On the Square [E] 24 Market Sq **412/471-9100** *11am-11pm, clsd Sun*

OTB Bicycle Cafe 2518 East Carson St (at S 26th) **412/381-3698** *11am-10pm, burgers, plenty veggie, also bar*

Pamela's Diner [★GO] 60 21st St **412/281-6366** *7am-3pm, from 8am Sun, also 5 other locations in Pittsburgh*

Point Brugge Cafe 401 Hastings (at Reynolds) **412/441-3334** *lunch & dinner, Sun brunch, clsd Mon, Belgian/ European*

Primanti Brothers [★] 46 18th St **412/263-2142** *Pittsburgh iconic sandwich shop with many locations*

Quiet Storm [WI,WC] 5430 Penn Ave (at Graham St) **412/661-9355** *9am-9pm, 10am-4pm Sat, clsd Sun & Tue, vegetarian/ vegan*

Red Oak Cafe 3610 Forbes Ave (at Lothrop) **412/621-2221** *7am-7pm, till 5pm Fri, clsd wknds*

Spoon 134 S Highland Ave **412/362-6001** *fresh farm-to-table menu & lounge*

Zenith [WC] 86 S 26th St **412/481-4833** *11am-9pm, Sun brunch, clsd Mon-Wed, vegetarian/ vegan, also antiques store*

▓ ENTERTAINMENT & RECREATION

Andy Warhol Museum 117 Sandusky St (at General Robinson) **412/237-8300** *10am-5pm, till 10pm Fri, clsd Mon, is it soup or is it art? see for yourself*

Burgh Bits & Bites Food Tour **412/209-3370, 800/979-3370** *exploring the vivid history and culinary delights of the Steel City*

Pittsburgh Public Market 2100 Smallman St **412/281-4505** *the goodness of locally grown produce, fresh-baked goods, handmade crafts*

▓ RETAIL SHOPS

Slacker [WC] 1321 E Carson St (btwn 13th & 14th) **412/381-3911** *noon-9pm, 11am-6pm Sun, magazines, clothing, leather*

Who New? [GO] 5156 Butler St **412/781-0588** *noon-6pm, clsd Mon-Tue, open Sun by chance, vintage modern design*

▓ PUBLICATIONS

Cue Pittsburgh 866/638-3822 *monthly LGBT glossy*

▶**Out** 724/733-0828 *Pittsburgh region's largest and most respected LGBTQ publication serving Pennsylvania, Ohio and West Virginia since 1973!*

▓ MEN'S CLUBS

Club Pittsburgh [★,PC] 1139 Penn Ave (enter side) **412/471-6790** *24hrs*

▓ MEN'S SERVICES

▶**MegaMates** 412/937-9999 *Call to hook up with HOT local men. FREE to listen & respond to ads. Use FREE code DAMRON. MegaMates.com.*

▓ EROTICA

Adult Mart 346 Blvd of the Allies **412/261-9119** *24hrs*

Monroeville News - Adult Mart 2735 Stroschein Rd (off Rte 22), Monroeville **412/372-5477** *24hrs, 13 miles from Pittsburgh*

▓ CRUISY AREAS

Schenley Park [AYOR]

Poconos

▓ ACCOMMODATIONS

Frog Hollow [MW,GO] 3535 High Crest Rd, Canadensis **570/595-2032** *secluded 1920s cottage*

Rainbow Mountain Resort [MW,D,TG,E,K,SW,WI,GO] **570/223-8484** *also restaurant & bar, DJ Fri-Sat*

The Woods Campground [MW,SW,18+] 845 Vaughn Acres Ln, Lehighton **610/377-9577**

Reading

▓ BARS

The Peanut Bar & Restaurant [GF,NS,WI] 332 Penn St **610/376-8500, 800/515-8500** *11am-11pm, till midnight Fri-Sat, clsd Sun, a Reading landmark!*

The Red Star [M,NH,D,L,MR,TG,DS,OC,GO] 11 S 10th St (at Penn St) **610/375-4116** *9pm-2am, clsd Sun-Tue*

▓ RESTAURANTS

Judy's On Cherry 332 Cherry St **610/374-8511** *lunch Tue-Fri, dinner Tue-Sat, clsd Sun-Mon, Mediterranean*

Pennsylvania • *USA*

The Ugly Oyster [E] 21 S 5th St (at Cherry) **610/373-6791** *11:30am-10pm, from noon Sat, clsd Sun, traditional Irish pub (bar open till 2am)*

■CRUISY AREAS
Mt Penn [AYOR] *btwn pagoda & fire tower & surrounding woodlands*

Scranton

■BARS
Twelve Penny Saloon [MW,NH,L,TG,F,K,DS,WC,GO] 3501 Birney Ave, Moosic **570/941-0444** *6pm-2pm, from 3pm wknds*

■CRUISY AREAS
Court House Square [AYOR]

Shippensburg

■EROTICA
The Lion's Den Adult Superstore 8071 Olde Scotland Rd (Penn exit 24, off I-81) **717/530-8032** *24hrs*

State College

■ACCOMMODATIONS
The Atherton Hotel [GF,WI,WC] 125 S Atherton St (at College Ave) **814/231-2100, 800/832-0132**

■BARS
Chumley's [★M,NH,WC] 100 W College **814/238-4446** *5pm-2am, from 6pm Sun*

■NIGHTCLUBS
Indigo [GS,D,V,YC] 112 W College Ave **814/234-1031** *9pm-2am, clsd Mon-Wed, "Alternative" night Sun*

■CRUISY AREAS
The Wall [AYOR] 100 blk of College Ave

Sunbury

■BARS
CC's [MW,D,K,DS] 555 Klinger Rd **570/286-6022** *7pm-2am Th-Sat, clsd Sun-Wed*

■CRUISY AREAS
Market St & Park [AYOR] *downtown*

Uniontown

■BARS
Eddie's Tavern [GF,F,K] 200 Francis St **724/438-9563** *11am-midnight, try the wings*

■NIGHTCLUBS
Club 231 [M,NH,D,TG,K,DS,GO] 231 Pittsburgh St/ Rte 51 (at Fulton) **724/430-1477** *9pm-close*

■CRUISY AREAS
Dunlap Creek Park [AYOR]

West Chester

■CRUISY AREAS
Court House Wall [AYOR] *late nights*

Wilkes-Barre

■INFO LINES & SERVICES
NEPA Rainbow Alliance Resource Center [WI] 67 Public Square, 5th flr, Edwardsville **570/763-9877**

■NIGHTCLUBS
Twist [M,D,MR,K,DS,WC] 1170 Hwy 315 (in Fox Ridge Plaza) **570/970-7503** *8pm-2am, from 6pm Sun, patio*

■EROTICA
Cinema 309 [AYOR] Rte 309 (Blackman St exit, off I-81) **570/822-2694** *about a half mile on Route 309*

■CRUISY AREAS
Nesbitt Park [AYOR] Susquehanna River (N of Pierce St bridge), Kingston

Williamsport

■CRUISY AREAS
Scenic Overlook [AYOR] 3 miles S, on Rte 15 N

York

■ACCOMMODATIONS
Yorktowne Hotel [GF,F,WI,WC] 48 E Market St **717/848-1111**

■NIGHTCLUBS

Altland's Ranch [MW,CW,D,K] 8505 Orchard Rd, Spring Grove **717/225-4479** *8pm-2am Fri-Sat only*

Club XS [MW,D,DS,C] 36 W 11th Ave (at Hwy 30 & N George St) **717/846-6969** *4pm-2am, also Underground Lounge*

■EROTICA

Cupid's Connection Adult Boutique 244 N George St (at North) **717/846-5029**

RHODE ISLAND

Newport

■INFO LINES & SERVICES

Sobriety First 135 Pelham St (at Channing Memorial Church) **401/438-8860** *8pm Fri*

■ACCOMMODATIONS

Architect's Inn [GF,NS,WI,GO] 2 Sunnyside Pl **401/845-2547, 877/466-2547** *fireplaces, near beach, shops & restaurants*

Francis Malbone House Inn [GF,NS,WI,WC] 392 Thames St (at Memorial Blvd) **401/846-0392, 800/846-0392**

Hilltop Inn [GF,NS,WI,GO] 2 Kay St **800/846-0392**

Hydrangea House Inn [★GS,NS,WI,GO] 16 Bellevue Ave **401/846-4435, 800/945-4667** *full brkfst, near beach*

The Spring Seasons Inn [GF,NS] 86 Spring St (btwn Mary St & Touro) **401/849-0004, 877/294-0004** *full brkfst*

■RESTAURANTS

Donick's Restaurant & Ice Cream Spa [BYOB,GO] 16 Broadway **401/835-5183** *6am-2am*

Whitehorse Tavern [NS] 26 Marlborough St (at Farewell) **401/849-3600** *lunch & dinner, Sun brunch, upscale dining, patio*

■EROTICA

Newport Video 228 JT Connell Hwy **401/847-4480** *arcade*

North Kingstown

■EROTICA

Amazing.net Video Store 6774 Post Rd/ Rte 1 **401/885-0209**

Providence

■INFO LINES & SERVICES

Brothers in Sobriety 372 Wayland Ave (at Community Church) **401/438-8860, 800/439-8860** *7:30pm Sat*

■ACCOMMODATIONS

Edgewood Manor [GF,NS,WI] 232 Norwood Ave (at Broad) **401/781-0099** *1905 Greek Revival mansion*

Hotel Dolce Villa [GS,NS] 63 De Pasquale Square (at Atwells) **401/383-7031**

The Hotel Providence [GS,F,WI,NS] 139 Mathewson **401/861-8000, 800/861-8990**

NYLO Hotel [GS,WI,WC] 400 Knight St, Warwick **401/734-4460** *also restaurant & bar*

Renaissance Providence Hotel [GS,F,NS,WI,WC] 5 Avenue of the Arts (at Francis) **401/919-5000, 800/468-3571**

■BARS

Alleycat [MW,NH,V,GO] 17 Snow St (at Washington) **401/272-6369** *3pm-1am, till 2am Fri-Sat*

Club Gallery [MW,NH,D,K,WC] 681 Valley St **401/751-7166** *1pm-1am, till 2am Fri-Sat, patio*

Deville's Cafe [MW,F,GO] 345 S Water St **401/383-8883** *4pm-midnight, till 1am Fri-Sat, clsd Mon*

The Providence Eagle [M,B,L,WC] 198 Union St (at Westminster) **401/421-1447** *3pm-1am, till 2am Fri, from noon wknds*

The Stable [MW,NH,V,WC] 125 Washington (at Mathewson) **401/272-6950** *2pm-1am, till 2am Fri-Sat, from noon Sat-Sun*

Union [M,B,L,K,P] 200 Union St (next to the Providence Eagle) **401/831-5366** *5pm-1am, till 2am Fri-Sat*

Rhode Island • *USA*

■NIGHTCLUBS

Hush RI [MO,S,18+] 257 Allens Ave (beside The Gay Mega-Plex) 401/862-4050 *8pm-1am, till 2am Fri-Sat, clsd Mon, nude male dancers*

Luna's Ladies Night [W,D,E,F] 276 Westminster St (at Roots Cultural Center) 401/499-9753

Mirabar [M,D,S,WC] 15 Elbow St (at Weybosset) 401/331-6761 *3pm-1am, till 2am Fri-Sat, male dancers*

Platforms Dance Club [GS,D,18+] 165 Poe St 401/781-3121 *gay night Sat, Salsa Sun*

■CAFES

Coffee Exchange 207 Wickenden St 401/273-1198 *6:30am-11pm, deck*

Nicks on Broadway 500 Broadway 401/421-0286 *lunch & dinner Wed-Sat, Sun brunch, clsd Mon-Tue*

Pastiche Fine Desserts 92 Spruce St 401/861-5190 *8:30am-11pm, 10am-10pm Sun*

White Electric Coffee 711 Westminster 401/453-3007 *7am-6:30pm*

■RESTAURANTS

Al Forno [★] 577 S Main St 401/273-9760 *dinner only, clsd Sun-Mon*

Blaze Restaurant [GO] 776 Hope St 401/277-2529 *lunch & dinner, clsd Mon*

Bravo Brasserie 123 Empire St 401/490-5112 *lunch Tue-Sat, dinner nightly, Sun brunch*

Caffe Dolce Vita 59 DePasquale Plaza (at Spruce St) 401/331-8240 *8am-1am, till 2am wknds, wknd brunch, authentic Italian cafe, patio*

Camille's 71 Bradford St (at Atwell's Ave) 401/751-4812 *lunch & dinner, clsd Sun, full bar*

CAV 14 Imperial Pl 401/751-9164 *11am-10pm, till 1am Fri, wknd brunch*

Fellini Pizzeria [★GO] 166 Wickenden St 401/751-6737

Julian's [BW] 318 Broadway (at Vinton) 401/861-1770 *lunch & dinner*

Local 121 121 Washington St (at Matthewson St) 401/274-2121 *lunch Tue-Sat, dinner nightly*

■ENTERTAINMENT & RECREATION

Cable Car Cinema & Cafe 204 S Main St 401/272-3970 *art-house flicks & free popcorn refills*

WaterFire Waterplace Park 401/272-3111 *May-Oct only, bonfire installations along the Providence River at sunset*

■BOOKSTORES

Books on the Square 471 Angell St (at Wayland) 401/331-9097, 888/669-9660 *9am-9pm, 10am-6pm Sun, some LGBT*

■PUBLICATIONS

Get RI Magazine 401/226-9033 *GLBT magazine*

➤**Metroline** 860/231-8445, 800/233-8334 *covers CT, RI & MA*

Options 401/724-5428 *LGBT community magazine*

■MEN'S CLUBS

Club Body Center [WI,PC] 257 Weybosset St, 2nd flr (at Richmond) 401/274-0298 *24hrs*

Gay Mega-Plex [PC,WC,GO] 257 Allens Ave (S of Public St) 401/780-8769 *24hrs*

■MEN'S SERVICES

➤**MegaMates** 401/738-7788 *Call to hook up with HOT local men. FREE to listen & respond to ads. Use FREE code DAMRON. MegaMates.com.*

■EROTICA

Adult Video News 255 Allens Ave (at Bay) 401/785-1324 *arcade*

Mister Sister 268 Wickenden St 401/421-6969 *fetishwear, sex toys, classes*

■CRUISY AREAS

State House Circle Road [AYOR] *nights*

Warwick

■CRUISY AREAS

Salter Grove Park [AYOR] Narragansett Pkwy (off Post Rd)

Westerly

■CRUISY AREAS

Misquamicut State Beach [AYOR] go left before the bridge (at Fenway Beach)

SOUTH CAROLINA

Statewide

■PUBLICATIONS

Q Notes 704/531-9988 *bi-weekly LGBT newspaper for the Carolinas*

Aiken

■NIGHTCLUBS

Marlboro Station [MW,D,S] 141 Marlboro St NE 803/644-6485 *10pm-close Fri-Sun*

Beaufort

■RESTAURANTS

Old House Restaurant [WC,GO] Hwy 462 (at Hwy 336), Ridgeland 843/258-4444 *5pm-9pm*

Blacksburg

■EROTICA

BedTyme Stories 145 Simper Rd (I-85, exit 100) 864/839-0007

Bowman

■EROTICA

The Lion's Den Adult Superstore 2269 Homestead Rd (exit 159, off I-26) 803/829-1781 *24hrs*

Charleston

■INFO LINES & SERVICES

Acceptance Group (Gay AA) 45 Moultrie St (at St Barnabus Lutheran Church) 843/723-9633 (AA#) *7pm Mon, Th & Sat*

■ACCOMMODATIONS

A B&B @ 4 Unity Alley [GS,NS] 4 Unity Alley 843/577-6660 *18th-c warehouse, full brkfst*

Aloft Charleston Airport & Convention Center [GF,SW,WI,WC] 4875 Tanger Outlet Blvd (at International Blvd), N Charleston 843/566-7300, 877/462-5638

Charleston Place [GF,F] 205 Meeting St 843/722-4900, 888/635-2350

■BARS

Dudley's on Ann [M,NH,K,18+,GO] 42 Ann St (at King St) 843/577-6779 *4pm-2am*

■NIGHTCLUBS

Club Pantheon [M,D,MR,E,C,DS,18+,GO] 28 Ann St (at King) 843/577-2582 *10pm-2am Fri-Sun only*

Club Patrick's [MW,D,TG,E,K,S,WC] 1377 Ashley River Rd/ Hwy 61 843/571-3435 *6pm-2am, patio bar*

Deja Vu II [W,D,F,E,DS,K,S,PC,WC,GO] 4628 Spruill Ave 843/554-5959 *5pm-close Th, from 10pm Fri-Sat*

■CAFES

Bear E Patch [WC] 1980-A Ashley River Rd 843/766-6490 *7am-9pm, 8am-8pm Sat, clsd Sun*

■RESTAURANTS

82 Queen 82 Queen St 843/723-7591, 800/849-0082 *lunch & dinner, Sun brunch, Lowcountry cuisine*

Fat Hen [★E,BW] 3140 Maybank Hwy, St Johns Island 843/559-9090 *dinner nightly, Sun brunch, French bistro, seafood*

Fig [WC] 232 Meeting St (near Hasell) 843/805-5900 *5:30pm-10:30pm, till 11pm Fri-Sat, clsd Sun, local ingredients*

High Cotton 199 E Bay St 843/724-3815 *dinner nightly, lunch Sat, Sun brunch, Southern cuisine, full bar*

Hominy Grill 843/937-0930 *brkfst, lunch & dinner, wknd brunch*

Joe Pasta 428 King St (at John) 843/965-5252 *11:30am-11pm, till midnight Fri-Sat, also full bar*

Mama Q's Kitchen [BW,WC,GO] 3157 Maybank Hwy #E, St Johns Island 843/559-0071 *11:30am-9pm, till 2pm Tue*

Melvin's Legendary Bar-B-Que 538 Folly Rd 843/762-0511 *10:45am-9:30pm, clsd Sun*

South Carolina • USA

▦ENTERTAINMENT & RECREATION

Historic Charleston Foundation 40 E Bay St **843/723-1623** *call for info on city walking tours (March-April only)*

▦PUBLICATIONS

Q Notes 704/531-9988 *bi-weekly LGBT newspaper for the Carolinas*

▦CRUISY AREAS

Folly Beach [AYOR] western tip of island (make a right at the island's only traffic light & drive all the way to county park)

West Ashley Park [AYOR]

Columbia

▦INFO LINES & SERVICES

The Harriet Hancock GLBT Community Center 1108 Woodrow St (at Millwood) **803/771-7713** *community info, resources, HIV programs & more*

Primary Purpose Gay/ Lesbian AA 5220 Clemson (in the house behind St Martin's Church) **803/254-5301**(AA#) *6:30 Tue, 7pm Fri & Sun*

▦ACCOMMODATIONS

Holiday Inn Express [GF,SW] 1011 Clemson Frontage Rd **803/419-3558**

▦BARS

Art Bar [GS,D,K] 1211 Park St **803/929-0198** *8pm-2am*

Capital Club [M,NH,P,PC,WC] 1002 Gervais St **803/256-6464** *5pm-2am*

▦NIGHTCLUBS

PTS 1109 [MW,D,MR,TG,S,WI,PC,GO] 1109 Assembly St (at Gervais St) **803/253-8900** *5pm-2am, till 6am Fri, till 3am Sat-Sun*

▦RESTAURANTS

Dianne's On Devine 2400 Devine St **803/254-3535** *dinner only, clsd Sun, upscale Italian*

Garibaldi's of Columbia 2013 Greene St **803/771-8888** *dinner nightly, full bar*

▦MEN'S SERVICES

➤**MegaMates** 803/939-0666 *Call to hook up with HOT local men. FREE to listen & respond to ads. Use FREE code DAMRON. MegaMates.com.*

▦EROTICA

Video Magic 5445 Two Notch Rd 803/786-8125

▦CRUISY AREAS

Senate Street [AYOR] near the university

Greenville

▦ACCOMMODATIONS

Walnut Lane Inn [GF,WI] 110 Ridge Rd (at Groce Rd), Lyman **864/949-7230** *full brkfst, mention Damron at booking for discount*

▦NIGHTCLUBS

The Castle [★MW,D,DS,S,V,YC,PC] 8-B Legrande Blvd **864/235-9949** *9:30pm-3am Wed-Sun*

▦BOOKSTORES

Out of Bounds 21 S Pleasantburg Dr **864/239-0106** *2pm- 8pm, till 6pm Sun, from 11am Fri-Sat*

▦MEN'S SERVICES

➤**MegaMates** 864/421-0400 *Call to hook up with HOT local men. FREE to listen & respond to ads. Use FREE code DAMRON. MegaMates.com.*

Hilton Head

▦ACCOMMODATIONS

Sonesta Resort Hilton Head Island [GF,F] 130 Shipyard Dr **843/842-2400, 800/334-1881**

▦BARS

Club Vibe [MW,NH,TG,F] 32 Palmetto Bay Rd #D-2 (at Sea Pines Cir) **843/341-6933** *5pm-3am, from 8pm Sat, clsd Sun*

▦CRUISY AREAS

Coligny Circle Beach [AYOR] S of the Holiday Inn (at the end of Pope Ave)

Pinckney State Park [AYOR] Hwy 278 *days*

Lake Wylie

■ NIGHTCLUBS

The Rainbow In [MW,D,K,DS,PC] 4376 Charlotte Hwy 803/831-0093 9pm-3am, clsd Sun

Leesville

■ EROTICA

The Lion's Den Adult Superstore 2662 Ben Franklin (exit 139, off I-20) 803/657-5921 24hrs

Myrtle Beach

■ ACCOMMODATIONS

Aquarius Motel [GS,SW,WI] 301 12th Ave N 843/448-7596, 800/244-4386

■ BARS

Club Pulse [MW,D,F,K,DS,WC,GO] 803 Main St 843/315-0019 5pm-4am

Time Out [★M,NH,D,K,DS,S,PC,WC] 520 8th Ave N (at Oak) 843/448-1180 5pm-close, till 2am Sat, patio bar

■ NIGHTCLUBS

Rainbow House [MW,D,DS,WC] 815 N Kings Hwy 843/626-7298 from 3pm Mon-Fri, 1pm wknds, patio

Rumors at Kono [MW,D] 1901 N Kings Hwy 855/878-6677 5pm-3am Th & Sun, from 9pm Fri-Sat, clsd Mon-Wed

■ RESTAURANTS

Carolina Roadhouse 4617 N Kings Hwy 843/497-9911 11am-10pm

Mr Fish 3401 N Kings Hwy 843/839-3474 11am-9:30pm, full bar

Sticky Fingers Smokehouse [WI,WC] 2461 Coastal Grand Cir 843/839-7427 a chain, but a good one

■ RETAIL SHOPS

Kilgor Trouts Music & More 512 8th Ave N 843/445-2800

■ EROTICA

X-citement Video 3106 Hwy 17 S 843/272-0744 24hrs

■ CRUISY AREAS

Huntington Beach State Park [AYOR] Hwy 17 S Mon-Fri

Hurl Rock Park [AYOR] at 21st Ave S (south end)

Rock Hill

■ BARS

Hideaway [MW,NH,K,DS,PC] 405 Baskins Rd 803/328-6630 9pm-2am Th-Sat

Spartanburg

■ NIGHTCLUBS

Club Chameleon [M,D,DS] 995 Asheville Hwy 864/699-9160 8pm-midnight, till 3am Fri-Sat, clsd Sun-Tue

Club South 29 [M,D] 9112 Greenville Hwy (off I-85 exit 66 or I-26 exit 21a) 864/574-6087 9pm-4am Fri-Sat only

■ MEN'S SERVICES

▶**MegaMates** 864/541-0522 Call to hook up with HOT local men. FREE to listen & respond to ads. Use FREE code DAMRON. MegaMates.com.

SOUTH DAKOTA

Murdo

■ ACCOMMODATIONS

Iversen Inn [GF,WI,GO] 108 E 5th St (on I-90 Business Loop) 605/669-2452

Pierre

■ CRUISY AREAS

LaFramboise Island [AYOR] off the causeway

Rapid City

■ INFO LINES & SERVICES

The Black Hills Center for Equality 1102 West Rapid St (at Omaha St) 605/348-3244 call for hours, clsd Sun, LGBT resource center

■ ACCOMMODATIONS

Camp Michael B&B [M,NS,GO] 1103 12th St 605/209-3503

Salem

■ ACCOMMODATIONS

Camp America [GF,SW,NS,WI,GO] 25495 US 81 605/425-9085 35 miles W of Sioux Falls

South Dakota • *USA*

Sioux Falls

▓INFO LINES & SERVICES
The Center for Equality   406 S 2nd Ave #102 **605/331-1153** *support groups, counseling, library & more*

▓BARS
Toppers [MW,K] 1213 N Cliff Ave **605/339-7686** *4pm-close, clsd Sun*

▓NIGHTCLUBS
Club David [GS,D,K,DS] 214 W 10th St (btwn Main & Dakota) **605/274-0700** *4:30pm-2am, also restaurant*

▓EROTICA
Romantix Adult Superstore 311 N Dakota Ave (btwn 6th & 7th) **605/332-9316**

▓CRUISY AREAS
Sherman Park [AYOR] Kiwanis (btwn 12th & 26th Sts)

Spearfish

▓CAFES
The Bay Leaf Cafe 126 W Hudson St **605/642-5462** *lunch & dinner, plenty veggie, espresso bar*

TENNESSEE

Bucksnort

▓EROTICA
Miranda's [GO] 4970 Hwy 230 **931/729-2006**

Chattanooga

▓BARS
Chuck's II [MW,NH,D] 27-1/2 W Main St (at Market) **423/265-5405** *6pm-1am, till 3am Fri-Sat, patio*

▓NIGHTCLUBS
Alan Gold's [★MW,D,F,DS,YC,WC] 1100 McCallie Ave (at National) **423/629-8080** *4:30pm-3am*

Images [MW,D,F,DS,WC] 6005 Lee Hwy **423/855-8210** *5pm-3am Th-Sun, also restaurant*

▓PUBLICATIONS
Out & About Newspaper **615/596-6210** *LGBT newspaper for Nashville, Knoxville, Chattanooga & Atlanta area, monthly*

▓MEN'S SERVICES
▶**MegaMates** **423/535-9900** *Call to hook up with HOT local men. FREE to listen & respond to ads. Use FREE code DAMRON. MegaMates.com.*

▓EROTICA
Miranda's [GO] 2025 Broadway **423/266-5956**

Clarksville

▓EROTICA
Miranda's [GO] 19 Crossland Ave **931/648-0365**

▓CRUISY AREAS
Fairground Park [AYOR]

Clifton

▓ACCOMMODATIONS
Bear Inn Resort [GS,WI,GO] 2250 Billy Nance Hwy **931/676-5552**

Gatlinburg

▓ACCOMMODATIONS
Big Creek Outdoors [GS,WC] 5019 Rag Mtn Rd, Hartford **423/487-5742, 423/487-3490** *cabins, camping, horseback riding*

Christopher Place, An Intimate Resort [GS,SW,NS,WC] 1500 Pinnacles Wy, Newport **423/623-6555, 800/595-9441** *full brkfst*

Mountain Vista Cabins [MW,NS,WI] 1805 Shady Grove Rd (at Old Birds Creek Rd), Sevierville **865/712-9897** *hot tub*

Stonecreek Cabins [GS,NS,GO] **865/429-0400** *private Smoky Mtn cabins*

Greeneville

▓ACCOMMODATIONS

Timberfell Lodge [MO,F,SW,N,NS,GO] 2240 Van Hill Rd (exit 36, off I-81) 423/234-0833, 800/437-0118 *also camping & RV hookups, full brkfst, hot tub*

Jackson

▓EROTICA

Miranda's 186 Providence Rd, Denmark 731/424-7226

▓CRUISY AREAS

Muse Park [AYOR]

Johnson City

▓ACCOMMODATIONS

Safe Haven Farm [GF,NS] 336 Stanley Hollow Rd, Roan Mountain 423/725-4262 *cabins, creekside privacy, fireplace, legally ordained minister*

▓NIGHTCLUBS

New Beginnings [★M,D,F,DS,WC] 2910 N Bristol Hwy 423/282-4446 *9pm-2am, from 8pm Fri-Sat, clsd Sun-Mon*

▓RETAIL SHOPS

My Secret Closet 2910 N Bristol Hwy (inside New Beginnings) 423/282-4446 *10pm-3am Fri-Sat only, pride gifts*

Kingsport

▓CRUISY AREAS

Sullivan St [AYOR] near library

Knoxville

▓INFO LINES & SERVICES

AA Gay/ Lesbian 2931 Kingston Pike (at Unitarian Church) 865/522-9667 (AA#) *7pm Th*

▓BARS

Club Exile [M,D,F,DS,WI,WC,GO] 4928 Homberg Dr (at Kingston Pike) 865/919-7490 *5pm-3am, from 11am Sun*

Hot Rods [MW,NH,F,DS,K,WC] 2909 Alcoa Hwy 865/766-5781 *7pm-3am, clsd Sun-Mon*

▓NIGHTCLUBS

Carousel II [MW,D,DS] 1501 White Ave *9pm-3am Wed-Sat*

Club XYZ [MW,D,DS,K] 1215 N Central 865/637-4999 *5:30pm-3am, from 9pm Sat, from 7pm Sun*

▓MEN'S SERVICES

▶**MegaMates** 865/291-0999 *Call to hook up with HOT local men. FREE to listen & respond to ads. Use FREE code DAMRON. MegaMates.com.*

▓EROTICA

Town & Country News 6927 Clinton Hwy 865/947-9153

West Knoxville News 5011 Kingston Pike 865/588-1972

▓CRUISY AREAS

The Block [AYOR] 100 Northview Dr (in Bearden area W of UT) *10pm-5am every night, hottest Fri-Sat after bars close*

Downtown [AYOR] btwn post office & library

IC King Park [AYOR] off Alcoa Hwy

Sharps Ridge [AYOR] off N Broadway

The Square [AYOR] intersection of Church, Market, Walnut & Union Sts

Memphis

▓INFO LINES & SERVICES

AA Intergroup 1835 Union Ave #302 (at McLean) 901/726-6750

Memphis Gay/ Lesbian Community Center 892 S Cooper (at Nelson) 901/278-6422 *2pm-9pm Mon-Fri*

▓ACCOMMODATIONS

Madison Hotel [GF,SW,NS] 79 Madison Ave (at Center Ln) 901/333-1200

Shellcrest Guesthouse [GS,NS,WI,GO] 671 Jefferson Ave (at N Orleans St) 901/277-0223 *suites in Victorian*

Talbot Heirs Guesthouse [GF,NS] 99 S 2nd St (btwn Union & Peabody Pl) 901/527-9772, 800/955-3956 *suites w/ kitchens, funky decor*

Tennessee • USA

■BARS

Dru's Place [W,NH,D,K,DS,BYOB] 1474 Madison (at McNeil) **901/275-8082** 11am-midnight, till 3am Fri-Sat, from noon Sun, beer & set-ups only

The Metro [MW,D,F,K,WC] 1349 Autumn St (at Cleveland) **901/725-1237** 4pm-3am

Mollie Fontaine Lounge [GS,F] 679 Adams Ave (at Orleans) **901/524-1886** 5pm-2am, clsd Sun-Tue

P&H Cafe [GS,F,E,K,BW,WC] 1532 Madison (at Adeline) **901/726-0906** 3pm-3am, from 5pm Sat, clsd Sun, dive bar

Pumping Station [M,D,WC] 1382 Poplar (at Cleveland) **901/272-7600** 4pm-3am, from 3pm wknds, courtyard

■NIGHTCLUBS

901 Complex [MW,D,MR-AF,DS, 18+,BYOB] 136 Webster Ave (at S 2nd St) **901/522-8455** from 10pm Fri-Sat only

Crossroads [MW,NH,K,DS] 1278 Jefferson Ave (at Claybrook) **901/272-8801** 3pm-midnight, till 3am Fri-Sat

Senses [GF,D,MR] 2866 Poplar Ave (at Walnut Grove Rd) **901/454-4081** theme nights

■CAFES

Java Cabana [E,WI,WC] 2170 Young Ave (at Cooper) **901/272-7210** 6:30am-10pm, 9am-midnight Fri-Sat, noon-10pm Sun, clsd Mon, also art gallery

Otherlands Coffee Bar [★F,E,WI,WC] 641 S Cooper (at Central) **901/278-4994** 7am-8pm, live music till 11pm Fri-Sat, also gift shop

■RESTAURANTS

Automatic Slim's Tonga Club [WC] 83 S 2nd St (at Union) **901/525-7948** lunch & dinner, Sun brunch, Caribbean & Southwestern, full bar

Cafe Eclectic 603 N McLean Blvd (at Faxon Ave) **901/725-1718** 6am-10pm, 9am-3pm Sun; also Harbortown location

Cafe Society [WC] 212 N Evergreen St (at Poplar) **901/722-2177** lunch Mon-Fri, dinner nightly, full bar

Circa [F] 6150 Poplar Ave **901/746-9130** lunch Mon-Fri, dinner nightly, clsd Sun, American

India Palace 1720 Poplar Ave (at Lemaster St) **901/278-1199** lunch & dinner

Leonard's Pit Barbecue 5465 Fox Plaza Dr (at Mt Moriah Rd) **901/360-1963** 11am-9pm, till 2:30pm Sun-Wed, Elvis ordered the pork sandwich at the original Leonard's (now closed), but the food is just as good here!

Molly's La Casita 2006 Madison Ave (at N Morrison St) **901/726-1873** lunch & dinner, Mexican

Restaurant Iris [WC] 2146 Monroe Ave (at Cooper) **901/590-2828** dinner Mon-Sat, French/ Creole, upscale

RP Tracks 3547 Walker Ave (at Brister) **901/327-1471** lunch & dinner, open till 3am, burgers, some veggie

Saigon Le 51 N Cleveland (at Jefferson) **901/276-5326** 11am-9pm, clsd Sun, pan-Asian

Tsunami [WC] 928 S Cooper (at Young) **901/274-2556** dinner only, Pacific Rim cuisine

■ENTERTAINMENT & RECREATION

Center for Southern Folklore [F] 119 S Main St (at Peabody Pl) **901/525-3655** 11am-5pm, clsd Sun, open later for shows, live music, gallery, also cybercafe

Graceland 3734 Elvis Presley Blvd **901/332-3322, 800/238-2000** no visit to Memphis would be complete w/out a trip to see The King

Memphis Rock 'N Roll Tours **901/359-3102** historical tour of Memphis music scene

■RETAIL SHOPS

Inz & Outz [WC] 553 S Cooper (at Peabody) **901/728-6535** 10am-8pm, noon-6pm Sun, pride items, books

MEN'S SERVICES

▶MegaMates 901/888-0888 *Call to hook up with HOT local men. FREE to listen & respond to ads. Use FREE code DAMRON. MegaMates.com.*

EROTICA

Cherokee Books 2947 Lamar 901/744-7494

Getwell Books 1275 Getwell (at Park) 901/454-7765

Paris Theater 2432 Summer Ave (at Hollywood) 901/323-2665

Romantix Adult Superstore 2220 E Brooks Rd 901/396-9050

Romantix Adult Superstore 5939 Summer Ave 901/373-5760

Romantix Airport Books 2214 Brooks Rd E (at Airways) 901/345-0657

Nashville

INFO LINES & SERVICES

AA Gay/ Lesbian 615/831-1050 *call for info*

ACCOMMODATIONS

The Big Bungalow B&B [GF,E,NS,WI] 618 Fatherland St (at 7th) 615/256-8375 *full brkfst, live music, massage available*

Doubletree Nashville [GF,WI] 315 4th Ave N (at Union St) 615/244-8200 *also restaurant & lounge, fitness center*

Hutton Hotel [GF,WI,WC] 1808 West End Ave (at 19th Ave) 615/340-9333

Top O' Woodland Historic B&B Inn [GF,NS] 1603 Woodland St (at 16th) 615/228-3868, 888/228-3868

Whispering Oaks Retreat Center [M,SW,N] 931/709-1192

BARS

Blue Gene's [M,B,K,WI] 1715 Church St (at 17th) 615/329-3508 *4pm-3am, from 3pm wknds, clsd Mon*

Canvas Lounge [M,D,K] 1707 Church St 615/320-8656 *4pm-3am*

Purple Heys [MW,NH,F,WC] 1401 4th Ave S (at Rains) 615/244-4433 *11am-3am*

Stirrup Nashville [M,NH,MR,F,WC] 1529 4th Ave S (at Mallory) 615/782-0043 *noon-3am, patio*

Trax [M,NH,K,WI] 1501 2nd Ave S (at Carney) 615/742-8856 *noon-3am*

Tribe/ Suzy Wong's House of Yum [★MW,F,E,V,WC,GO] 1517 Church St (at 15th Ave S) 615/329-2912 *4pm-midnight, till 2am wknds, upscale, full restaurant*

NIGHTCLUBS

508 [GS,D] 508 Lea Ave (at 6th) 615/669-4508 *midnight-7am Fri-Sat night only*

Bluebird Cafe [GF,E] 4104 Hillsboro Pike (nr Warfield Dr) 615/383-1461 *live country music venue*

Play Dance Bar [M,D,MR,TG,E,DS,18+,WC] 1519 Church St (at 16th Ave) 615/322-9627 *9pm-3am Wed-Sun*

Vibe [M,D,MR-L,DS,BYOB] 1713 Church St (at 17th & 18th) 615/329-3838 *afterhours bar, patio*

CAFES

Bongo Java [E] 2007 Belmont Blvd 615/385-5282 *7am-11pm, from 8am wknds, coffeehouse, deck, also serves brkfst, lunch & dinner*

Fido [F] 1812 21st Ave S 615/777-3436 *7am-11pm, till midnight Fri-Sat, from 8am wknds, also full menu*

Grins Vegetarian Cafe 2421 Vanderbilt Pl (at 25th Ave) 615/322-8571 *7am-9pm, till 3pm Fri, clsd wknds*

RESTAURANTS

Battered & Fried [WC] 1008 Woodland St (at S 10th) 615/226-9283 *lunch & dinner, seafood, full bar, also Wave sushi bar*

Beyond the Edge 112 S 11th St 615/226-3343 *11am-2am, pizza & sandwiches, full bar*

Cafe Coco [E,BW] 210 Louise Ave (at State) 615/321-2626 *24hrs, patio*

Couva Calypso Cafe 2424 Elliston Pl 615/321-3878 *11am-9pm, 11:30am-8:30pm wknds, Caribbean*

Tennessee • *USA*

International Market [BW,WC] 2010 Belmont Blvd (at International) **615/297-4453** *10:30am-9pm, Thai/Chinese, plenty veggie*

Mad Donna's 1313 Woodland St (at 14th) **615/226-1617** *11am-10pm, till 11pm Sat, clsd Mon, also lounge, drag bingo Tue*

The Mad Platter [R,WC] 1239 6th Ave N (at Monroe) **615/242-2563** *lunch Mon-Fri, dinner Wed-Sun, eclectic, local & fresh*

Nuvo Burrito 1000 Main St (at 10th) **615/866-9713** *11:30am-9pm, eclectic burrito menu, also bar, theme nights*

Pancake Pantry 1796 21st Ave S (at Wedgewood Ave) **615/383-9333** *6am-3pm, till 4pm wknds, popular for brkfst*

Rumba 3009 W End Ave (at 30th) **615/321-1350** *4pm-close, from 5pm Sun, Latin/ Asian*

Rumours Wine & Art Bar [WC] 2304 12th Ave S (at Linden) **615/292-9400** *5pm-midnight, till 9pm Sun*

Sky Blue Coffeehouse & Bistro 700 Fatherland St (at S 7th St) **615/770-7097** *brkfst & lunch*

Sole Mio [WC] 311 3rd Ave S **615/256-4013** *11am-10pm, till 11pm Fri-Sat, clsd Mon, Italian*

The Standard at the Smith House [R,WC] 167 Rosa Parks Ave (at Charlotte) **615/254-1277** *dinner Tue-Sat, clsd Sun-Mon*

Watermark [WC] 507 12th Ave S (at Division) **615/254-2000** *dinner nightly, clsd Sun, seafood & more, great wine list*

Yellow Porch [WC] 734 Thompson Ln (at Bransford Ave) **615/386-0260** *lunch & dinner, clsd Sun, fresh Southern cuisine*

▦ENTERTAINMENT & RECREATION

NashTrash Tours [R] tours leave from the Farmers Market (900 8th Ave N) **615/226-7300, 800/342-2132** *campy tours of Nashville w/ the Jugg Sisters*

Tennessee Repertory Theater 505 Deaderick St (at the Tennessee Performing Arts Center) **615/244-4878**

▦PUBLICATIONS

Inside Out Nashville 615/831-1806 *LGBT newspaper & bar guide*

Out & About Newspaper 615/596-6210

▦MEN'S SERVICES

➤**MegaMates** 615/777-0770 *Call to hook up with HOT local men. FREE to listen & respond to ads. Use FREE code DAMRON. MegaMates.com.*

▦EROTICA

The Lion's Den Adult Superstore 2807 Nolensville Pike **615/254-8891** *24hrs*

Miranda's [GO] 5329 Charlotte Ave **615/383-2160**

Miranda's [GO] 822 5th Ave S **615/256-1310**

▦CRUISY AREAS

J Percy Priest Dam [AYOR]

TEXAS

Abilene

▦CRUISY AREAS

Kirby Park [AYOR]

Amarillo

▦BARS

212 Club [MW,NH,D,DS,WC] 212 SW 6th Ave (at Harrison) **806/372-7997** *3pm-2am*

Kicked Back [MW,NH,K,GO] 521 SE 10th Ave (at Buchanan St) **806/371-3535** *3pm-2am, clsd Sun*

R&R [GF,NH,WC,GO] 701 S Georgia St **806/342-9000** *4pm-2am*

▦RESTAURANTS

Furrbie's [GO] 210 W 6th Ave **806/220-0841** *11am-7pm, till 3pm Sat & Mon*

▦EROTICA

Fantasy Gifts & Video 440 N Lakeside Dr **806/372-6500**

Arlington

see also Dallas & Fort Worth

■INFO LINES & SERVICES

Tarrant County Lesbian/ Gay Alliance 817/877-5544

■NIGHTCLUBS

The 1851 Club [MW,D,K,DS,V,WC] 1851 W Division (at Fielder) 817/801-9303 3pm-2am

Austin

■INFO LINES & SERVICES

Lambda AA (Live & Let Live) [NS,WC] 6809 Guadalupe St (at Galano Club) 512/444-0071, 512/832-6767 (en español) 6:30pm & 8pm daily, 10am Sat, 11am Sun

Q 3408 West Ave (2 blks W of Guadalupe & 34th) 512/420-8557 2pm-10pm Tue-Sat, support & information for GBTQI men 18-29

■ACCOMMODATIONS

Austin Folk House [GS,NS,WI,WC] 506 W 22nd St (at Nueces) 512/472-6700, 866/472-6700

Brava House [GF,NS,WI] 1108 Blanco St (at W 12th) 512/478-5034, 866/892-5726 close to downtown & 6th Street

Crowne Plaza Hotel Austin [GF] 6121 North IH 35 512/323-5466

Hilton Garden Inn Austin Downtown [GF] 500 North IH 35 512/480-8181

Hotel Saint Cecilia [GF,SW,WC] 112 Academy Dr 512/852-2400

Hotel San Jose [★GS,SW,NS,WC,GO] 1316 S Congress Ave 512/852-2350, 800/574-8897

Kimber Modern [GS,WI,WO] 110 The Circle 512/912-1046

Mt Gainor Inn B&B [GS,NS,WI] 2390 Prochnow Rd (at Mt Gainor Rd), Dripping Springs 512/858-0982, 888/644-0982

Omni Austin Hotel Downtown [GF,F,SW,WI,WC] 700 San Jacinto (at 8th) 512/476-3700, 800/843-6664

Park Lane Guest House [GS,SW,WC,GO] 221 Park Ln (at Drake) 512/447-7460, 800/492-8827 full brkfst, also cottage

Robin's Nest [GF,NS,WI] 1007 Stewart Cove 512/266-3413 on Lake Travis

■BARS

Bernadette's Bar [MW,D,E] 2039 Airport Blvd queer dive bar, live bands

'Bout Time [MW,NH,TG,K,WI,WC] 9601 N I H 35 (at Rundberg) 512/832-5339 2pm-2am, volleyball court

Casino El Camino [GF,NH,F,WI,WC] 517 E 6th St (at Red River) 512/469-9330 4pm-2am, psychedelic punk jazz lounge, great burgers

Chain Drive [M,D,L,WC] 504 Willow St (at Red River) 512/480-9017 6pm-2am, clsd Tue, cruisy

Cheer Up Charlie's [MW,NH,E,F] 1104 E 6th St 6pm-2am, clsd Mon, live bands, shows, also vegan restaurant

The Iron Bear [M,B] 121 W 8th St 512/482-8993 2pm-2am

Rusty's Austin [M,D,CW] 405 E 7th Street (E of Trinity) 512/482-9002 4pm-2am, from 7pm Mon, from 2pm Sun, patio

Town N Country [M,NH] 1502 W Ben White Blvd 512/445-9122 4pm-2am, from 2pm Sun

■NIGHTCLUBS

404 [MW,D,WC] 404 Colorado 512/522-4044 9pm-close Wed-Sat, from 5pm Sun

The Belmont [GF] 305 W 6th St 512/457-0300 live music venue

Oilcan Harry's [★M,D,K,S,DS,18+,WI,WC] 211 W 4th St (btwn Lavaca & Colorado) 512/320-8823 2pm-2am, patio

Rain [M,D,K,S,WC] 217-B W 4th St (at Colorado St) 512/494-1150 4pm-close, from 3pm Fri-Sun

■CAFES

Austin Java Cafe [F] 1608 Barton Springs Rd (at Kinney Ave) 512/482-9450 7am-11pm, from 8am Sat-Sun; also 1206 Parkway, 512/476-1829 & 300 W 2nd St, 512/481-9400

Texas • *USA*

Bouldin Creek Coffeehouse [F] 1900 S 1st St 512/416-1601 *7am-midnight, from 9am wknds, vegetarian; occasional live music*

Joe's Bakery & Coffee Shop [WC] 2305 E 7th St (at Morelos & Northwestern) 512/472-0017 *6am-3pm, clsd Mon, Tex-Mex*

Spider House Patio Bar & Cafe [E] 2908 Fruth St (at West Dr) 512/480-9562 *10am-2am, patio*

■RESTAURANTS

Changos 3023 Guadalupe 512/480-8226 *taqueria, open all day*

Chez Nous [WC] 510 Neches St 512/473-2413 *lunch Tue-Fri, dinner nightly, clsd Mon*

Chuy's [WC] 1728 Barton Springs Rd 512/474-4452 *11am-10pm, till 11pm Fri-Sat, Tex-Mex, full bar*

Corazon at Castle Hill [WC] 1101 W 5th St (at Baylor) 512/476-0728 *lunch weekdays & dinner nightly, clsd Sun*

Eastside Cafe [BW,WC] 2113 Manor Rd (at Breeze Terrace) 512/476-5858 *11:30am-9:30pm, 10am-10pm wknds*

El Sol y La Luna [★E,WC,GO] 600 E 6th St (at Red River) 512/444-7770 *11am-10pm, 9am-1pm Fri-Sat, 9am-4pm Sun*

Fonda San Miguel 2330 W North Loop (at Hancock Rd) 512/459-4121 *dinner only, popular Sun brunch, Mexican, full bar*

Galaxy 1000 W Lynn 512/478-3434 *7am-10pm, quick, stylish & tasty*

Guero's [E] 1412 S Congress (at Elizabeth) 512/447-7688 *11am-11pm, from 8am wknds, great Mexican & people-watching, outdoor seating, live music outdoors on wknds*

Imperia [WC] 310 Colorado St 512/472-6770 *dinner only, upscale Asian, full bar*

Jo's Hot Coffee & Good Food [WC,GO] 1300 S Congress Ave (at James) 512/444-3800 *7am-9pm, till 10pm Sat; also 242 W 2nd St, 512/469-9003*

Kenichi [WC] 419 Colorado St 512/320-8883 *dinner nightly, Asian/sushi*

Mother's Cafe & Garden [★BW,WC] 4215 Duval St (at 43rd) 512/451-3994 *11:15am-10pm, from 10am wknds, vegetarian*

Mr Natural 1901 E Cesar Chavez St 512/477-5228 *8am-8pm, vegetarian/vegan*

Polvos [WC] 2004 S 1st St (at Johanna) 512/441-5446 *7am-11pm, Mexican, outdoor seating*

Santa Rita Cantina 1206 W 38th St 512/419-7482 *lunch & dinner, wknd brunch*

Threadgill's [E] 6416 N Lamar 512/451-5440 *10am-10pm, till 9pm Sun, great chicken-fried steak; also 301 W Riverside Dr, 512/472-9304*

Wink [WC] 1014 N Lamar Blvd 512/482-8868 *dinner nightly, clsd Sun, upscale, also wine bar*

■ENTERTAINMENT & RECREATION

Barton Springs [N] Barton Springs Rd (in Zilker Park) 512/867-3080 *natural swimming hole*

Bat Colony Congress Ave Bridge (at Barton Springs Dr) *colony of bats that flies out from under this bridge every evening March-Oct*

Capital City Men's Chorus 512/477-7464 *call for events*

■BOOKSTORES

Bookpeople 603 N Lamar Blvd (at 6th) 512/472-5050, 800/853-9757 *9am-11pm*

MonkeyWrench Books 110 E North Loop 512/407-6925 *11am-8pm, from noon wknds, independent, radical bookstore*

■RETAIL SHOPS

Milk + Honey Spa 204 Colorado St (at 2nd) 512/236-1115 *9am-9pm*

Tapelenders [GO] 1114 W 5th St #501 (at Baylor) 512/472-0844 *10am-10pm, till midnight Fri-Sat, LGBT videos, novelties*

■PUBLICATIONS

➤**Ambush Mag** 504/522-8049
LGBT newspaper for the Gulf South (TX through FL)

Austin Chronicle 512/454-5766 *has extensive online gay guide (check out www.austinchronicle.com)*

■GYMS & HEALTH CLUBS

Hyde Park Gym 4125 Guadalupe (at 41st St) 512/459-9174 *5am-10pm, 7am-7pm Sat, 8am-7pm Sun*

■MEN'S CLUBS

Midtowne Spa—Austin [PC] 5815 Airport Blvd (at Koenig) 512/302-9696 *24hrs, outdoor hot tub, sundeck*

■MEN'S SERVICES

➤**MegaMates** 512/480-8400 *Call to hook up with HOT local men. FREE to listen & respond to ads. Use FREE code DAMRON. MegaMates.com.*

■EROTICA

Adult Video Megaplexxx 7111 S Ih 35 512/442-5430 *24hrs, arcade*

Forbidden Fruit 108 E North Loop 512/453-8090 *woman-owned & operated*

New Video 7901 S Ih 35 512/280-1142 *24hrs, arcade*

■CRUISY AREAS

Hippie Hollow–Lake Travis [AYOR]

Beaumont

■BARS

Orleans Street Pub & Patio [MW,NH,D,K,DS] 650 Orleans St (at Forsythe) 409/835-4243 *7pm-2am, clsd Mon-Tue*

■MEN'S SERVICES

➤**MegaMates** 409/812-0333 *Call to hook up with HOT local men. FREE to listen & respond to ads. Use FREE code DAMRON. MegaMates.com.*

Bryan

■BARS

Revolution Cafe & Bar [GF,NH,TG,F,E,WI,WC] 211 B S Main St (at 27th) 979/823-4044 *4pm-2am, from 8pm Sun-Mon, from 6pm Sat*

■NIGHTCLUBS

Halo Bar [MW,D,K,DS,V,18+,WC] 121 N Main St (at William J Bryan Pkwy) 979/823-6174 *9:30pm-2am Th-Sat*

Corpus Christi

■INFO LINES & SERVICES

Clean & Serene AA 3026 S Staples (at MCC church) 361/992-8911, 866/672-7029 *8pm Fri*

■ACCOMMODATIONS

Anthony's By The Sea [GS,SW,WI,NS,WC,GO] 732 S Pearl St, Rockport 361/729-6100, 800/460-2557

Port Aransas Inn [GS,SW,WI,WC] 1500 S 11th St (at Ave G), Port Aransas 361/749-5937

■BARS

The Hidden Door [M,NH,D,DS,WC] 802 S Staples St (at Coleman) 361/882-5002 *noon-2am, patio, also the Loft piano bar Fri-Sun*

■ENTERTAINMENT & RECREATION

Robert James Provisioners [TG,GO] 837 Redmond 361/937-4880 *8am-10pm, sailboat charters*

■MEN'S SERVICES

➤**MegaMates** 361/884-0884 *Call to hook up with HOT local men. FREE to listen & respond to ads. Use FREE code DAMRON. MegaMates.com.*

Dallas

see also Arlington, Fort Worth

■INFO LINES & SERVICES

John Thomas Gay/ Lesbian Community Center [WC] 2701 Reagan St (at Brown) 214/528-0144, 214/528-0022 *9am-9pm, till 5pm Sat, noon-5pm Sun*

Lambda AA 2438 Butler #106 214/267-0222, 214/887-6699 (Central Office #) *call for meeting details*

■ACCOMMODATIONS

Bailey's Uptown Inn [GF,NS,WI] 2505 Worthington St (at Hibernia) 214/720-2258

Texas • *USA*

Hotel ZaZa [GF,SW] 2332 Leonard St (at State) 214/468-8399, 888/880-3244

Lumen [GF,WI,WC] 6101 Hillcrest Ave 214/219-2400, 800/908-1140

MCM Eleganté Hotel & Suites [GF,SW,WI] 2330 W Northwest Hwy 214/358-7846, 877/351-4477

Palomar Dallas [GF] 5300 E Mockingbird Ln 214/520-7969, 888/253-9030

Warwick Melrose Hotel [GF,P,SW,WC] 3015 Oak Lawn Ave (at Cedar Springs) 214/521-5151

▆BARS

Alexandre's [GS,E,K,WC] 4026 Cedar Springs Rd (at Knight St) 214/559-0720 *9am-2pm, from 2pm Sun, live music*

Barbara's Pavillion [M,NH,K,WC] 325 Centre St 214/941-2145 *4pm-2am, from 2pm Sun, patio*

BJ's NXS [M,D,S,WC] 3215 N Fitzhugh (at Travis) 214/526-9510 *6pm-2am from 4pm Sun-Mon, patio*

Dallas Eagle [M,B,L] 5740 Maple Ave (at Inwood Rd) 214/357-4375 *5pm-2am, from 4pm wknds, clsd Mon*

Drama Room [M,E,V,S] 3851 Cedar Springs Rd 214/443-6020 *1pm-2am, from noon Sun*

Grapevine [GS,WI,WC] 3902 Maple Ave (at Shelby) 214/522-8466 *3pm-2am, from 1pm Sun, classic dive bar*

The Hidden Door [M,NH,L,WC] 5025 Bowser Ave (at Mahanna) 214/526-0620 *7am-2am, from noon Sun, patio*

JR's Bar & Grill [★MW,F,E,V,YC,WI,WC] 3923 Cedar Springs Rd (at Throckmorton) 214/528-1004 *11am-2am, from noon Sun-Mon*

The Mining Co [★M,D,L] 3903 Cedar Springs Rd (at Reagan) 214/521-4204 *5pm-4am, clsd Mon-Wed*

Pekers [MW,NH,E,K,C,DS,WC] 2615 Oak Lawn Ave, Ste 101 (btwn Fairmount & Brown) 214/528-3333 *10am-2am*

Pub Pegasus [M,NH,WI,WC] 3326 N Fitzhugh Ave (at Travis) 214/559-4663 *noon-2am, patio*

Sue Ellen's [★W,D,E,WC] 3014 Throckmorton (at Cedar Springs) 214/559-0707 *5pm-2am, 2pm-close wknds*

Tin Room [M,NH,WC] 2514 Hudnall St (at Maple Ave) 214/526-6365 *10am-2am, from noon Sun, patio*

Woody's [MW,K,V,WC] 4011 Cedar Springs Rd (btwn Douglas & Throckmorton) 214/520-6629 *2pm-2am, sports bar, patio*

Zippers [M,NH,S] 3333 N Fitzhugh (at Travis) 214/526-9519 *noon-2am*

▆NIGHTCLUBS

The Brick/Joe's Dallas [MW,D,MR,DS] 2525 Wycliff Ave (btwn Maple & Tollway) 214/521-3154 *4pm-2am, till 4am Fri-Sat, from noon Sat-Sun*

Club Los Rieles [M,D,DS,MR-L] 600 S Riverfront (Industrial) Blvd 214/741-2125 *Latin club, wknds only*

Elm & Pearl [MW,D,DS,MR-AF] 2204 Elm St (at S Pearl) 214/741-0000 *mostly men Fri, mostly women Sat*

Exklusive [MW,D,DS,MR-L] 4207 Maple Ave (at Knight St) 469/556-1395 *9pm-close Th-Sun*

Havana Bar & Grill [GS,D,MR-L,DS] 4006 Cedar Springs Rd (at Throckmorton) 214/526-9494 *grill 5pm-10pm, lounge from 10pm, clsd Mon*

Kaliente [M,D,MR-L,K,DS,WC] 4350 Maple Ave (at Hondo) 214/520-6676 *9pm-2am, clsd Tue, salsa & Tejano*

Panoptikon [GS,D] 3025 Main St (at Excuses) 214/741-1111 *monthly gothic/electro dance party*

Round-Up Saloon [★M,D,CW,K,WC] 3912 Cedar Springs Rd (at Throckmorton) 214/522-9611 *3pm-2am, from noon wknds*

Station 4 [★MW,D,C,DS,S,V,18+] 3911 Cedar Springs Rd (at Throckmorton) 214/526-7171 *9pm-4am Wed-Sun, also Rose Room cabaret, patio*

▆CAFES

Buli [WI,WC] 3908 Cedar Springs Rd 214/528-5410 *7am-close*

Opening Bell Coffee [E,BW,WI] 1409 S Lamar St, Ste 012 214/565-0383 *7am-10pm, from 9am wknds, till midnight wknds*

▮RESTAURANTS

3025 Main/ Excuses Cafe [WI] 3025 Main St (in Deep Ellum) 214/741-1111 11am-2am

Ali Baba Cafe 1901 Abrams Rd (near La Vista Dr) 214/823-8235 lunch & dinner

Bangkok Orchid [GO,BYOB,WC] 331 W Airport Fwy (at N Beltline), Irving 972/252-7770 lunch & dinner, clsd Mon, ask for Danny

Black-Eyed Pea [WC] 3857 Cedar Springs Rd (at Reagan) 214/521-4580 11am-10pm

Blue Mesa Grill 5100 Belt Line Rd (at Tollway), Addison 972/934-0165 11am-10pm

Bread Winners [WC] 3301 McKinney Ave 214/754-4940 4pm-2am, from 10am wknds

Cafe Brazil 3847 Cedar Springs Rd 214/461-8762 open 24hrs

Cosmic Cafe [E,BW,WC] 2912 Oak Lawn Ave 214/521-6157 11am-10:30pm, till 11pm Fri-Sat, noon-10pm Sun, veggie, also yoga & meditation

Cremona Bistro 2704 Worthington St (at Howell) 214/871-1115 lunch weekdays & dinner nightly, Italian, full bar, patio

Dish [E,WC] 4123 Cedar Springs Rd #110 214/522-3474 dinner & Sun brunch, full bar, patio

Dream Cafe [BW,WI,WC] 2800 Routh St (in the Quadrangle) 214/954-0486 7am-9pm, till 10pm Fri-Sat, brkfst served till 5pm

Hatties [WC] 418 N Bishop Ave 214/942-7400 lunch daily, dinner Tue-Sun, Southern

Hibiscus [WC] 2927 N Henderson Ave 214/827-2927 dinner only, clsd Sun, steak & seafood

Hunky's [★BW,WC,GO] 3940 Cedar Springs Rd (at Reagan) 214/522-1212 11am-10pm, till 11pm Sat, from noon Sun, burgers & salads, patio

Lucky's Cafe [WC] 3531 Oak Lawn 214/522-3500 7am-10pm, classic comfort food, great brkfst

Monica Aca y Alla [★TG,E,WC] 2914 Main St (at Malcolm X) 214/748-7140 lunch Mon-Fri, dinner Tue-Sun, brunch wknds, Mexican, full bar

Naga Kitchen & Bar 665 High Market St (Victory Park) 214/953-0023 lunch Mon-Sat, dinner nightly, authentic Thai

Patio Grill & Bar 3403 McKinney Ave 214/720-3838 4pm-2am, from 11am Sat-Sun

Stephan Pyles 1807 Ross Ave, Ste 200 214/580-7000 lunch Mon-Fri, dinner Mon-Sat, clsd Sun, Southwestern cuisine

Taco Joint [WC] 911 N Peak St 214/826-8226 6:30am-2pm, from 8am Sat, clsd Sun

Thai Soon [WC] 101 S Coit, Ste 401 (at Belt Line) 972/234-6111 lunch & dinner

Ziziki's [WC] 4514 Travis St, #122 (in Travis Walk) 214/521-2233 11am-10pm, Sun brunch, Greek & Italian, bar

▮RETAIL SHOPS

Obscurities 4008 Cedar Springs 214/559-3706 11am-9pm, 2pm-8pm Sun, clsd Mon, tattoo & piercing

Tapelenders [GO] 3926 Cedar Springs Rd (at Throckmorton) 214/528-6344 9am-midnight, LGBT

Union Jack 3920 Cedar Springs Rd 214/528-9600 men's clothing

▮PUBLICATIONS

Dallas Voice 214/754-8710 LGBT newspaper

▮MEN'S CLUBS

Club Dallas [SW,PC,WI] 2616 Swiss Ave (at Good Latimer) 214/821-1990 24hrs

Midtowne Spa–Dallas [PC] 2509 Pacific Ave (at Hawkins) 214/821-8989 24hrs, 3 flrs, rooftop sundeck

▮MEN'S SERVICES

▶**MegaMates** 214/615-0100 Call to hook up with HOT local men. FREE to listen & respond to ads. Use FREE code DAMRON. MegaMates.com.

▮EROTICA

Alternatives 1720 W Mockingbird Ln (at Hawes) 214/630-7071 24hrs

Texas • *USA*

Amazing Superstore 11311 Harry Hines Blvd #603 972/243-2707

Leather Masters 3000 Main St 214/528-3865 *noon-10pm, clsd Sun-Mon*

Lido Theatre 7035 John Carpenter Fwy (at Mockinbird Ln) 214/630-7127

Mockingbird Video 708 W Mockingbird Ln (at I-35 & Halifax) 214/631-3003 *24hrs, bookstore w/ arcade*

Odyssey Video 11505 Anaheim Dr (at Forest Ln) 972/484-4999 *24hrs*

Paris Adult Book & Video Store 11118 Harry Hines Blvd 972/263-0774 *24hrs, bookstore w/ arcade*

■CRUISY AREAS

Reverchon Park [AYOR]

Tom Braniff Park [AYOR] off SH 114 (at Tom Braniff exit) *beware cops (!)*

Denison

■BARS

Good Time Lounge [MW,E,K,DS,PC] 2520 Hwy 91 N 903/463-6086 *7pm-2am Wed-Sun*

Denton

■NIGHTCLUBS

Mable Peabody's Beauty Parlor & Chainsaw Repair [MW,D,E,K,DS,WC,GO] 1125 E University Dr 940/566-9910 *4pm-2am*

El Paso

see also Ciudad Juárez, Mexico

■INFO LINES & SERVICES

El Paso GLBT Community Center [F] 216 S Ochoa 206/600-4297 *24-hr hotline, events, pride store, De Ambiente Cafe*

■BARS

Briar Patch [MW,NH,K] 508 N Stanton St (at Missouri) 915/577-9555 *noon-2am, patio*

Chiquita's Bar [MW,NH,MR-L,WC] 310 E Missouri Ave (at Stanton) 915/351-0095 *2pm-2am*

Ms Lips Lounge [W,NH,E] 510 N Stanton St (at Missouri) 915/566-0378 *live bands*

The Tool Box [M,NH] 506 N Stanton St (at Missouri) 915/351-1896 *2pm-2am, patio*

The Whatever Lounge [MW,D,MR-L,K,DS,WC] 701 E Paisano Dr (at Ochoa) 915/533-0215 *2pm-2am*

■NIGHTCLUBS

San Antonio Mining Co [★MW,D,MR-L,DS,V,WC] 800 E San Antonio Ave (at Ochoa) 915/533-9516 *3pm-2am*

■RESTAURANTS

The Little Diner [BW,WC] 7209 7th St, Canutillo 915/877-2176 *11am-8pm, clsd Wed, true Texas fare*

■MEN'S SERVICES

▶**MegaMates** 915/541-8888 *Call to hook up with HOT local men. FREE to listen & respond to ads. Use FREE code DAMRON. MegaMates.com.*

■EROTICA

Venus Adult Theatre & Books 4812 Montana (near Reynolds) 915/566-8061

Eustace

■ACCOMMODATIONS

Captain's Quarters [GS] PO Box 577 75124 903/802-2771 *cabin rentals*

Circle J Ranch [M,18+,SW,N,WI,PC,GO] 903/479-4189 *campground (cabins, tents, RVs) 1 hour from Dallas*

Fort Worth

see also Arlington & Dallas

■INFO LINES & SERVICES

Tarrant County Lesbian/ Gay Alliance 817/877-5544 *info line & newsletter*

■ACCOMMODATIONS

Hotel Trinity InnSuites Hotel [GF,SW,NS,WI,WC] 2000 Beach St 817/534-4801, 800/989-3556

■BARS

Best Friends Club [MW,NH,D,F,K,DS] 2620 E Lancaster Ave 817/420-9220 *3pm-2am, clsd Mon*

Crossroads [M,NH] 515 S Jennings Ave (at Pennsylvania) **817/332-0071** *11am-2am, from noon Sun*

■NIGHTCLUBS

Rainbow Lounge [M,D,DS,WC] 651 S Jennings Ave (at Pennsylvania) **817/744-7723** *9am-2am*

■MEN'S SERVICES

▶**MegaMates** **817/282-2500** *Call to hook up with HOT local men. FREE to listen & respond to ads. Use FREE code DAMRON. MegaMates.com.*

■CRUISY AREAS

Benbrook Dam [AYOR] *parking lot & woods*

Trinity Park [AYOR] *parking lot & woods*

Galveston

■ACCOMMODATIONS

Hotel Galvez [GF,NS,WI] 2024 Seawall Blvd **409/765-7721, 877/999-3223**

Lost Bayou Guesthouse B&B [GS,NS,WI,GO] 1607 Ave L (at 16th) **409/770-0688** *1890 Victorian home survived hurricane of 1900*

Oasis Beach Cottage [GF,NS,GO] **713/256-3000** *on the Gulf of Mexico*

■BARS

3rd Coast Beach Bar [M,DS,S] 2416 Post Office St **409/765-6911** *4pm-2am, from 2pm wknds*

Pink Dolphin [M,K,BYOB] 1706 23rd St (at O Ave) **409/621-1808** *10am-midnight, strippers on wknds*

Robert's Lafitte [M,DS,WC] 2501 Q Ave (at 25th St) **409/765-9092** *7am-2am, from 10am Sun, [DS] wknds*

Stars Beach Club [MW,D,B,MR,K,DS] 3102 Seawall Blvd **409/497-4113** *noon-2am, theme nights*

■CAFES

Mod Coffee & Tea House [F,E,BW,WI] 2126 Post Office St (at 22nd) **409/765-5659** *7am-10pm*

■RESTAURANTS

Eat Cetera [BW,WC] 408 25th St **409/762-0803** *11am-7pm, clsd Sun*

Luigi's 2328 The Strand (at Tremont) **409/763-6500** *dinner only, clsd Sun*

Mosquito Cafe [WC] 628 14th St (at Winnie) **409/763-1010** *8am-9pm, 8am-9pm Sat, till 3pm Sun, clsd Mon*

The Spot [WC] 3204 Seawall Blvd (at 32nd St) **409/621-5237** *good burgers, great view, also Tiki Bar*

Star Drug Store [WC] 510 23rd St **409/766-7719** *9am-3pm, old-fashioned drug store & soda fountain*

■CRUISY AREAS

The Dunes [AYOR] at East Beach off Hwy 87

Groesbeck

■ACCOMMODATIONS

Rainbow Ranch Campground [MW,SW,NS,GO] 1662 LCR 800 **254/729-8484, 888/875-7596** *on Lake Limestone*

Gun Barrel City

■BARS

Garlow's [MW,D,DS] 308 E Main St **903/887-0853** *4pm-close*

Houston

■INFO LINES & SERVICES

Gay & Lesbian Switchboard Houston **713/529-3211, 888/843-4564** *24hr crisis hotline*

Houston GLBT Community Center 1900 Kane St (in Historic Dow School) **713/524-3818** *noon-9pm*

Lambda AA Center [WC] 1201 W Clay (btwn Montrose & Waugh) **713/521-1243**

■ACCOMMODATIONS

Alden Hotel [GF,F,WI] 1117 Prairie St (at Fannin) **832/200-8800, 877/813-1888**

Hotel Derek [GF] 2525 W Loop S (at Westheimer) **713/961-3000, 866/292-4100** *modern, chic hotel*

Hotel Sorella [GF] 800 W Sam Houston Pkwy N **713/973-1600, 866/842-0100**

The Houstonian [GF,WC] 111 N Post Oak Ln (near Woodway Dr) **713/680-2626, 800/231-2759**

Robin's Nest B&B Inn [GF,WI] 4104 Greeley St **713/528-5821, 800/622-8343**

Sycamore Heights B&B [GF,NS,WI,GO] 245 W 18th St **713/861-4117**

■BARS

13 The Heights Bar [MW] 1537 N Shepherd (at 16th St) **713/426-1313** *4pm-2am*

The 611 Club [★M,NH] 611 Hyde Park Blvd (at Stanford) **713/526-7070** *7am-2am, from noon Sun*

Bayou City Bar & Grill [MW,F] 2409 Grant St (at Hyde Park Blvd) **713/522-2867** *4pm-2am, clsd Mon*

Blur [MW,D,18+] 710 Pacific St (at Crocker) **713/529-3447** *10pm-2am, clsd Mon-Tue*

Boom Boom Room [GF] 2518 Yale St **713/868-3740** *4pm-2am, clsd Sun-Mon, wine & panini bar*

Brazos River Bottom (BRB) [★M,D,CW,DS,WI] 2400 Brazos (at McIlhenny) **713/528-9192** *noon-2am*

Club 2020 [MW,D,MR,18+] 2020 Leeland **713/227-9667** *10pm-4am Sat, mostly African American, hip hop*

Crocker [MW,NH,K,WI] 2312 Crocker St **713/529-3355** *11am-2am*

EJ's [M,D,E,S] 2517 Ralph (at Westheimer) **713/527-9071** *7am-2am, from 10am Sun, patio*

George Country Sports Bar [M,NH,CW,GO] 617 Fairview (at Stanford) **713/528-8102** *7am-2am, from 10am Sun, sports bar, patio*

Guava Lamp [MW,K,V,WI,WC] 570 Waugh Dr **713/524-3359** *4pm-2am, from 2pm Sun*

JR's [★M,K,DS,S,V,WC] 808 Pacific (at Grant) **713/521-2519** *noon-2am, patio*

Meteor [M,DS,S,WC,GO] 2306 Genesee St (at Fairview) **713/521-0123** *4pm-2am*

Michael's Outpost [M,NH,E,OC] 1419 Richmond (at Mandell) **713/520-8446** *3pm-2am, from noon wknds*

Montrose Mining Co [★M,CW,L,WC] 808 Pacific St (at Grant) **713/529-7488** *4pm-2am, till 3am Fri-Sat, patio*

Ripcord [M,L,WC] 715 Fairview (at Crocker) **713/521-2792** *noon-2am, till 4am Fri-Sat, popular after-hours*

TC's Show Bar [MW,NH,K,DS,TG] 817 Fairview (at Converse) **713/526-2625** *10am-2am*

Tony's Corner Pocket [MW,NH,K,S,WI] 817 W Dallas (btwn Arthur & Crosby) **713/571-7870** *noon-2am, large deck*

The Usual Pub [GS,NH,E,K,GO] 5519 Allen St **281/501-1478** *4pm-2am, from 2pm wknds, from 6pm Mon-Tue*

Whispers [MW,D,K] 226 1st St E (off I-59), Humble **281/359-2900** *4pm-2am, from 6pm Sat, clsd Mon*

■NIGHTCLUBS

Crystal [M,D,DS,MR-L] 6680 Southwest Fwy (at Colorado) **713/278-2582** *9pm-3am Wed-Sun, Latino club, theme nights*

F Bar Houston [MW,D,E,K] 202 Tuam St **713/522-3227** *5pm-2am, from 9pm Sat, 3pm Sun, clsd Mon*

Numbers [GF,D,E,V,YC] 300 Westheimer (at Taft) **713/526-6551**

Ranch Hill Saloon [MW,NH,D,CW,K,DS,WC,GO] 24704 I-45 N, Spring **281/298-9035** *1pm-2am*

Signature Lounge [MW,D] 5959 Richmond Ave **713/636-2087, 713/213-4560** *9pm-2am, till 3am Fri-Sun, till 5am Sat, clsd Mon-Wed*

South Beach Nightclub [M,D,S] 810 Pacific **713/521-0107, 713/529-7623** *9pm-4am Fri-Sat*

Viviana's Nite Club [M,D,MR-L,DS] 4624 Dacoma St **713/681-4101** *9pm-5am, till 6am Sat, clsd Mon-Th*

Vue [GS,D] 526 Waugh Dr **713/533-9333** *from 9pm Th-Sat*

Vue Saturday [W,D] 526 Waugh Dr (at Vue nightclub) **713/533-9333** *from 9pm Th-Sat*

■CAFES

Dirk's Coffee 4005 Montrose (btwn Richmond & W Alabama) **713/526-1319** *6am-11pm*

Empire Cafe [WI,WC] 1732 Westheimer Rd 713/528-5282 *7:30am-10pm, till 11pm Fri-Sat*

Java Java Cafe [WC] 911 W 11th (at Shepherd) 713/880-5282 *7:30am-3pm*

The Path of Tea [WC] 2340 W Alabama St 713/252-4473 *10am-9pm, till 11pm Fri-Sat, 1pm-6pm Sun*

▮RESTAURANTS

Aka 2390 W Alabama St 713/807-7875 *noon-11pm, sushi*

Argentina Cafe [WC] 3055 Sage Rd (at Hidalgo St) 713/622-8877 *9am-9pm, from 10am wknds*

Baba Yega's [WC] 2607 Grant (at Pacific) 713/522-0042 *11am-10pm, full bar, patio*

Barnaby's Cafe [★BW,WC] 604 Fairview (btwn Stanford & Hopkins St) 713/522-0106 *11am-10pm, multiple locations*

Beaver's 2310 Decatur (at Sawyer) 713/864-2328 *11am-10pm, till midnight Sat, clsd Mon, BBQ*

Block 7 Wine Company 720 Shepherd Dr 713 /572-2565 *dinner only, wine-inspired menu*

Bocado's [GS,D] 1312 W Alabama 713/523-5230 *lunch & dinner, clsd Sun-Mon, Mexican, full bar*

Brasil [BW,WC] 2604 Dunlavy (at Westheimer) 713/528-1993 *7:30am-midnight*

Chapultepec [WC] 813 Richmond (btwn Montrose & Main) 713/522-2365 *24hrs, Mexican*

El Tiempo Cantina [WC] 1308 Montrose Blvd 713/807-8996 *11am-9pm, till 10pm Wed-Th, till 11pm Fri-Sat, Mexican seafood*

House of Pies [★WC] 3112 Kirby Dr (btwn Richmond & Alabama) 713/528-3816 *24hrs*

Hugo's [WC] 1600 Westheimer Rd (at Mandell) 713/524-7744 *lunch & dinner, Mexican, popular brunch*

Julia's Bistro 3722 Main St (at W Alabama) 713/807-0090 *lunch Mon-Fri, dinner Mon-Sat, clsd Sun, Mexican*

Kelley's Country Cookin' [WC] 8015 Park Pl (at Gulf Fwy) 713/645-6428 *6am-10pm, great brkfst*

Mark's American Cuisine [WC] 1658 Westheimer Rd 713/523-3800 *lunch Mon-Fri, dinner nightly, located in renovated 1920s church*

Mo Mong 1201 Westheimer #B (at Montrose) 713/524-5664 *11am-10pm, clsd Sun, Vietnamese, full bar*

Ninfa's [★] 2704 Navigation Blvd (at N Delano St) 713/228-1175 *11am-11pm, Mexican, full bar*

Ruggles Green 2311 W Alabama 713/533-0777 *11am-10pm, organic & all-natural American*

Tafia [GO] 3701 Travis St 713/524-6922 *dinner Tue-Sat, Mediterranean, also bar*

▮ENTERTAINMENT & RECREATION

After Hours - Queer Radio With Attitude KPFT 90.1 FM (also 89.5 Galveston) 713/526-4000, 713/526-5738 (request line) *midnight-3am Sat/Sun, LGBT radio*

Beer Can House 222 Malone St 713/926-6368 *seasonal; 10am-2pm Wed-Fri; 50,000+ beer cans cover the building!*

DiverseWorks Art Space 1117 East Fwy (I-10 at N Main) 713/223-8346, 713/335-3443 *seasonal, some LGBT-themed art & performance*

Orange Show Center for Visionary Art 2402 Munger St 713/926-6368 *performance, music, public art*

▮RETAIL SHOPS

Black Hawk Leather 711 Fairview 713/532-8437 *noon-8pm, 2pm-7pm Sun*

The Chocolate Bar [WC] 1835 W Alabama St 713/520-8599 *chocolate gifts & yummy desserts*

Hollywood Super Center 2409 Grant St (at Crocker St) 713/527-8510 *10am-1am, till 3am Fri-Sat*

▮PUBLICATIONS

abOUT Magazine PO Box 130948, 713/396-2688

Texas • USA

OutSmart 713/520-7237 *monthly LGBT newsmagazine*

■GYMS & HEALTH CLUBS
Houston Gym [GF,GO] 1501 Durham Rd (at Washington & Eigel) 713/880-9191 *5am-10pm, 8am-8pm wknds*

YMCA Downtown [SW] 808 Pease 713/659-8501

■MEN'S CLUBS
The Club Houston [★SW,PC] 2205 Fannin St (at Webster) 713/659-4998 *24hrs*

Midtowne Spa–Houston [SW,PC] 3100 Fannin St (at Elgin) 713/522-2379 *24hrs*

■MEN'S SERVICES
►MegaMates 713/225-5500 *Call to hook up with HOT local men. FREE to listen & respond to ads. Use FREE code DAMRON. MegaMates.com.*

■EROTICA
Eros 1207 [GO] 1207 Spencer Hwy (at Allen Genoa) 713/910-0220

Loveworks 25170 I-45 N, Spring 281/292-0070

Kilgore

■EROTICA
Texas Adult Video [GO] 1907 Industrial Blvd 903/986-2090

Lockhart

■ACCOMMODATIONS
Lazy J Paradise Campground & Park [MW,SW,WI] 270 Hidden Path (CR 303 and FM 2001) 210/863-9314 *campground w/ RV area catering to the LGBT community*

Longview

■BARS
Decisions [MW,D,CW,K,DS,WC,GO] 2103 E Marshall (2 blocks E of Eastman Rd) 903/757-4884 *noon-2am*

■NIGHTCLUBS
Rainbow Members Club (RMC) [MW,D,PC,WC] 203 S High (at Cotton) 903/753-9393 *5pm-2am Wed-Sat, from 3pm Sun*

■CRUISY AREAS
Hinsley Park [AYOR]

Teague Park [AYOR]

Lubbock

■INFO LINES & SERVICES
AA Lambda 4501 University Ave (at MCC) 806/792-5562 *8pm Fri*

■ACCOMMODATIONS
LaQuinta Inns & Suites North [GF,NS,WI,WC,GO] 5006 Auburn St (at Winston) 806/749-1600

■NIGHTCLUBS
Club Luxor [GS,D,K,DS,WC] 2211 4th St 806/744-3744 *9pm-2am Fri-Sun, more gay Fri & Sun*

Heaven Nightclub [GF,D,MR,DS,18+,YC] 1928 Buddy Holly Ave (at I-27) 806/762-4466 *9pm-3am Th-Sun*

■CRUISY AREAS
McKenzie Park [AYOR]

Marfa

■ACCOMMODATIONS
El Cosmico [GS,WI,GO] 802 S. Highland Ave 432/729-1950, 877/822-1950 *vintage trailer, yurt & teepee hotel & campground*

McAllen

see Rio Grande Valley

Odessa/ Midland

■EROTICA
B&L Adult Bookstore 5890 W University Blvd (at Mercury), W Odessa 432/381-6855

County Line 6947 Commerce, Odessa 432/552-0055 *24hrs*

Rio Grande Valley

■BARS
PBD's [M,D,DS,S,WC] 2908 N Ware Rd (at Daffodil), McAllen 956/682-8019 *8pm-2am, clsd Mon*

■NIGHTCLUBS
Club 33 [MW,D,DS] 3300 N McColl Rd, McAllen 956/627-3312 *9pm-3am Fri-Sat only*

San Antonio

■INFO LINES & SERVICES

Lambda AA 319 Camden Rm #4
(Madison Square Presbyterian Church)
210/979-5939 *8:15pm daily*

■ACCOMMODATIONS

1908 Ayres Inn [GS,NS,WI,WC,GO] 124
W Woodlawn Ave (at N Main)
210/736-4232

Arbor House Suites B&B
[GS,NS,WC,GO] 109 Arciniega (btwn S
Alamo & S St Mary's) 210/472-2005,
888/272-6700

Brackenridge House [GF,SW,WI] 230
Madison (at Beauregard)
210/271-3442, 877/271-3442 *B&B
in historic King William district*

Emily Morgan Hotel [GF,F,SW,WI] 705
E Houston St (at Ave E)
210/225-5100, 800/824-6674

Fiesta B&B [M,NS,WI,GO] 1823
Saunders Ave (at Trinity)
210/226-5548, 210/887-0074

The Westin Riverwalk [GF,SW,WC] 420
W Market St 210/224-6500,
888/627-8396

■BARS

2015 Place [M,NH,K] 2015 San Pedro
(at Woodlawn) 210/733-3365 *4pm-
2am, patio, [K] Wed*

The Annex [M,NH,WC] 330 San Pedro
Ave (at Euclid) 210/223-6957 *2pm-
2am, cruise bar*

The Boss [M,NH] 1006 VFW Blvd
(Jeffersonville) 210/550-2322,
210/449-8506 *8pm-2am, dive bar*

Electric Company [MW,D,S,18+] 820
San Pedro Ave (at W Laurel)
210/212-6635

Essence [M,NH,K,S] 1010 N Main Ave (at
E Euclid) 210/223-5418 *2pm-2am*

The Flying Saucer [GF] 11255 Huebner
Rd #212 (at I-10) 210/696-5080
*11am-1am, till 2am Th-Sat, noon-
midnight Sun, large beer selection*

Mix [GF,E] 2423 N St Marys St
210/735-1313 *5pm-2am, from
7:30pm Sat-Sun, dive bar*

One-Oh-Six Off Broadway [M,NH,F]
106 Pershing St (at Broadway)
210/820-0906 *noon-2am*

Pegasus [M,K,L,S] 1402 N Main Ave
(btwn Laurel & Evergreen)
210/299-4222 *2pm-2am*

Silver Dollar Saloon [MW,D,CW,K]
1818 N Main Ave (at Dewey)
210/227-2623 *4pm-2am, clsd Mon*

Sparky's Pub [M,NH] 1416 N Main Ave
(at Evergreen) 210/320-5111 *3pm-
2am*

■NIGHTCLUBS

The Bonham Exchange
[★MW,D,YC,18+,GO] 411 Bonham St (at
3rd/ Houston) 210/271-3811 *4pm-
2am, from 8pm Sat*

Heat [M,D,S] 1500 N Main Ave (at
Evergreen) 210/227-2600 *9pm-2am,
clsd Mon-Tue*

The Industry [GS,D] 8021 Pinebrook Dr
(at Callaghan) 210/366-3229 *10pm-
2am Th, from 8pm Fri-Sat*

The Saint [M,D,DS,S,18+] 800 Lexington
Ave 210/225-7330 *4pm-3am*

■CAFES

**Candlelight Coffeehouse & Wine
Bar** [E,WI,WC] 3011 N St Mary's (at Rte
281) 210/738-0099 *2pm-midnight,
wknd brunch 10am-2pm, clsd Mon*

■RESTAURANTS

Chacho's [E,K,WC] 7870 Callaghan Rd
(at I-10) 210/366-2023 *24hrs,
Mexican*

Cool Cafe 12651 Vance Jackson
210/8775/5/20115001 *brkfst, lunch &
dinner, Mediterranean*

**Giovanni's Pizza & Italian
Restaurant** 913 S Brazos (at
Guadalupe) 210/212-6626 *11am-
7pm*

Guenther House 129 E Guenther (at S
Alamo St) 210/227-1061,
800/235-8186 *7am-3pm, located in
restored Pioneer Flour Mills founding
family home*

Lulu's Bakery & Cafe [WC] 918 N
Main (at W Elmira) 210/222-9422
24hrs, Tex-Mex

Texas • USA

Luther's Cafe [E,WC,GO] 1425 N Main Ave (at Evergreen) 210/223-7727 *11am-3am, great burgers, live music*

Madhatter's Tea House [BYOB,WI,WC] 320 Beauregard 210/212-4832 *8am-9pm, till 3pm Sun, patio*

El Mirador [BW,WC] 722 S St Mary's St (at Durango Blvd) 210/225-9444 *6:30am-9pm, till 2pm Sun, patio*

Taco Taco Cafe 145 E Hildebrand 210/822-9533 *7am-2pm*

WD Deli 3123 Broadway St 210/828-2322 *10:30am-5pm, till 4pm Sat, clsd Sun*

ENTERTAINMENT & RECREATION

First Friday Art Walk S Alamo St (at S St Mary's St) *6pm-10pm 1st Fri only, stroll the Southtown arts district*

RETAIL SHOPS

On Main/ Off Main 120 W Mistletoe Ave 210/737-2323 *10am-6pm, till 5pm Sat, clsd Sun*

ZEBRAZ.com 1608 N Main Ave (at E Park Ave) 210/472-2800, 800/788-4729 *9am-midnight, till 10pm Sun-Tue, LGBT dept store*

PUBLICATIONS

Ignite SA *LGBT publication for San Antonio*

MEN'S CLUBS

Alternative Club Inc [SW,PC] 827 E Elmira St (at St Mary's) 210/223-2177 *noon-9am, 24hrs wknds*

Executive Health Club [PC] 402 Austin St (at Lamar) 210/299-1400

MEN'S SERVICES

▶**MegaMates** 210/375-1155 *Call to hook up with HOT local men. FREE to listen & respond to ads. Use FREE code DAMRON. MegaMates.com.*

EROTICA

Broadway News 2202 Broadway (at Appler St) 210/223-2034

Dreamers 2376 Austin Hwy (at Walzem) 210/653-3538 *24hrs*

Encore Video 1031 NE Loop 410 210/821-5345

CRUISY AREAS

Please Note: All cruisy areas for San Antonio have been removed because the San Antonio Park Rangers aggressively police these areas.

Terrel

EROTICA

Dreamers 6086 W Hwy 80 (Frontage Rd exit) 972/524-1449 *24hrs*

Tyler

ACCOMMODATIONS

Cross Timber Ranch B&B [GS,SW,NS,WI,GO] 6271 FM 858 (at Hwy 64), Ben Wheeler 903/833-9000, 877/833-9002

CRUISY AREAS

Bergfeld Park [AYOR]

Waco

NIGHTCLUBS

Club Trix [MW,D,V,TG] 110 S 6th St 254/714-0767 *10pm-2am Th, 8pm-2am Fri-Sat*

CRUISY AREAS

Midway Park [AYOR]

Webster

BARS

Club Pride [MW,D] 229 E NASA Pkwy 281/557-4800 *9pm-2am Th-Sat*

Wichita Falls

BARS

Krank It Karaoke Kafe [GF,D,K, 18+,WC] 1400 N Scott Ave (at Old Iowa Park Rd) 940/761-9099 *8:30pm-2am, from 7pm Fri-Sat, clsd Mon-Tue*

Odds [MW,D,K,DS,18+,BW] 1205 Lamar St (at 12th) 940/322-2996 *4pm-2am, from 3pm Sun*

CRUISY AREAS

Lucy Park [AYOR]

Wimberley

ACCOMMODATIONS

Bella Vista [GS,SW,NS,GO] 2121 Hilltop 512/847-6425

UTAH

Bryce Canyon

■ACCOMMODATIONS

Hatch Station [GF,WI,WC] 177 S Main, Hatch **435/735-4015** *also restaurant, laundry & convenience store; safe oasis for LGBT travelers in S UT*

The Red Brick Inn of Panguitch B&B [GF,WI] 161 N 100 West (at 200 North), Panguitch **435/676-2141, 866/733-2745** *full brkfst*

■CAFES

Scoops from the Past [WI] 105 N Main St, Panguitch **435/676-8885** *noon-10pm, till 6pm Sun, retro ice cream parlor*

Logan

■CRUISY AREAS

Logan Canyon [AYOR] *Zanavoo loop*

Moab

■ACCOMMODATIONS

Mayor's House B&B [GF,GS,NS,WI,GO] 505 Rose Tree Ln (at 400 E) **435/259-6015, 888/791-2345** *hot tub, full brkfst*

Mt Peale Resort Inn, Lodge & Cabins [GS,NS,WI,GO] 1415 E Hwy 46 (at mile marker 14), Old La Sal **435/686-2284, 888/687-3253** *B&B & cabins, hot tub, lesbian-owned*

Red Cliffs Lodge [GF,SW,NS,WC] Hwy 128 (at mile marker 14) **435/259-2002, 866/812-2002** *resort, on Colorado River, hot tub*

Ogden

■MEN'S SERVICES

▶**MegaMates** **801/317-1111** *Call to hook up with HOT local men. FREE to listen & respond to ads. Use FREE code DAMRON. MegaMates.com.*

Park City

■RESTAURANTS

Loco Lizard Cantina [TG,WC] 1612 Ute Blvd (in Kimball Jct Shopping Ctr) **435/645-7000** *11am-10pm, till 11pm Fri-Sat, brunch wknds, Mexican, full bar*

■MEN'S SERVICES

▶**MegaMates** **435/608-0608** *Call to hook up with HOT local men. FREE to listen & respond to ads. Use FREE code DAMRON. MegaMates.com.*

Salt Lake City

■INFO LINES & SERVICES

Utah Pride Center 361 N 300 W, 1st flr **801/539-8800, 888/874-2743** *info, resource center, meetings, coffee shop, programs, youth activity center & much more*

■ACCOMMODATIONS

Anniversary Inn [GF] 460 S 1000 E (at 400) **801/363-4900, 800/324-4152** *elaborate, kitschy theme rms*

Hotel Monaco Salt Lake City [GF,F,WI,WC] 15 W 200 S (at S Main) **801/595-0000, 877/294-9710**

Parrish Place [GF,NS,WI] 720 E Ashton Ave (at 700 E) **801/832-0970, 855/832-0970** *Victorian mansion, hot tub*

Peery Hotel [GF,F,NS,WI,WC] 110 W 300 S **801/521-4300, 800/331-0073**

Under the Lindens [★M,NS,WI,GO] 128 S 1000 E (downtown) **801/355-9808** *mention Damron for discount*

■BARS

Club Try-Angles [M,NH,D,F,PC,GO] 251 W 900 S (at 300 W) **801/364-3203** *2pm-2am*

Jam [MW,NH,D,K,WI] 751 North 300 West (at Reed Ave) **801/891-1162** *5pm-2am, clsd Sun*

The Tavernacle Social Club [GF,F,K,P,NS,PC] 201 E 300 South (at 200 E) **801/519-8900** *5pm-close, from 8pm Sat-Mon, "Duelin' Pianos"*

The Trapp [MW,D,K,CW,WI,WC] 102 S 600 W (at 100 S) **801/531-8727** *11am-2am, patio*

W Lounge [GS,D,NS,PC] 358 SW Temple **801/359-0637** *9pm-2am, clsd Sun-Tue*

■NIGHTCLUBS

Area 51 [GS,D] 451 South 400 West (at 400 S) **801/534-0819** *'80s & goth theme nights Th-Sat only*

Utah • *USA*

Fusion [M,D] 540 W 200 South (at Metro Bar) *9pm-2am Sat only*

Mixx [M,D,K] 615 W 100 South **801/575-6499** *9pm-2am Fri-Sat*

Pachanga at Karamba [M,D,MR-L] 1051 East 2100 South **801/637-9197** *9pm Sun only, gay Latin night*

Pure [★,M,D] 579 W 200 S (at 600 W, at Club Sound) **801/328-0255** *9:30pm-2am Fri only*

■CAFES

Coffee Garden [WC] 878 E 900 S **801/355-3425** *6am-11pm*

■RESTAURANTS

Bambara 202 S Main St **801/363-5454** *lunch Mon-Fri, brkfst & dinner daily, upscale American*

Blue Plate Diner 2041 S 2100 E **801/463-1151** *7am-9pm, till 10pm Fri-Sat*

Cafe Trio Downtown 680 S 900 E **801/533-8746** *11am-10pm, Italian*

Cedars of Lebanon [WI,E] 152 E 200 South (at State St) **801/364-4096** *lunch & dinner, Lebanese, veggie/ vegan-friendly*

Citris Grill 2991 E 3300 South **801/466-1202**

Finn's 1624 S 1100 East (at Logan) **801/467-4000** *7:30am-2:30pm*

Fresco Italian Cafe 1513 S 1500 East **801/486-1300** *dinner nightly, patio*

Himalayan Kitchen 360 S State St (at 400 S) **801/328-2077** *lunch & dinner, dinner only Sun, Indian/Himalayan, plenty veggie*

Market St Grill [WC] 48 W Market St **801/322-4668** *11:30am-9pm, from 9am Sun, fresh seafood, full bar*

The Med 420 E 3300 South **801/493-0100** *lunch & dinner, Mediterranean*

The Metropolitan [R] 173 W Broadway **801/364-3472** *lunch Mon-Fri, dinner nightly, clsd Sun, New American*

The New Yorker [WC] 60 W Market St **801/363-0166** *lunch Mon-Fri, dinner nightly, clsd Sun, fine dining, steak*

Off Trax [MW,WI] 259 W 900 S **801/364-4307** *7am-7pm, till 3pm Fri, brunch Sun, also from 1am-3am Fri-Sat nights*

Omar's Rawtopia 2148 Highland Dr **801/486-0332** *noon-8pm, till 9pm Fri-Sat, clsd Sun, raw food*

Red Iguana [★] 736 W North Temple **801/322-1489** *lunch & dinner, Mexican*

Sage's Cafe 473 E 300 S **801/322-3790** *lunch & dinner, brkfst wknds, clsd Mon-Tue, vegan/ vegetarian*

Stoneground 249 E 400 South **801/364-1368** *11am-11pm, 5pm-9pm Sun, pizza & more*

Vertical Diner [WC] 2280 S West Temple **801/484-8378** *10am-9pm,vegetarian diner*

■ENTERTAINMENT & RECREATION

Lambda Hiking Club *hiking & other activities*

Plan B Theatre Company 138 West 300 South (at Rose Wagner Performing Arts Center, btwn W Temple & 200 West) **801/355-2787** *at least one LGBT-themed production each season*

Tower Theatre 876 E 900 South **801/321-0310** *alternative films, many LGBT movies*

■BOOKSTORES

Golden Braid Books [WI] 151 S 500 E **801/322-1162** *10am-9pm, till 6pm Sun, also Oasis Cafe, 8am-9pm, till 10pm wknds*

Sam Weller's 254 S Main St **801/328-2586, 800/333-7269** *10am-9pm, noon-5pm Sun*

■RETAIL SHOPS

Cahoots [WC,GO] 878 E 900 S (at 900 E) **801/538-0606** *10am-9pm, unique gift shop*

■PUBLICATIONS

Q Salt Lake **801/649-6663, 800/806-7357** *bi-weekly LGBT newspaper*

MEN'S SERVICES

▶**MegaMates** 801/595-0005 *Call to hook up with HOT local men. FREE to listen & respond to ads. Use FREE code DAMRON. MegaMates.com.*

EROTICA

All For Love [TG,WC] 3072 S Main St (at 33rd St S) 801/487-8358 *clsd Sun, lingerie & S/M boutique*

Blue Boutique 1383 E 2100 South 801/485-2072 *also piercing*

Mischievous 559 S 300 W (at 6th St S) 801/530-3100 *clsd Sun*

CRUISY AREAS

Memory Grove [AYOR] Canyon Rd (below the Capitol, on the E side)

Sugarhouse Park [AYOR] 21st S *also btwn 13th & 17th E*

Zion Nat'l Park

ACCOMMODATIONS

Canyon Vista Lodge B&B [GF,NS] 2175 Zion Park Blvd (at Hwy 9), Springdale 435/772-3801

Red Rock Inn [GS,NS,WC,GO] 998 Zion Park Blvd, Springdale 435/772-3139 *cottages w/ canyon views, full brkfst, hot tub*

CAFES

Cafe Soleil [BW,GO] 205 Zion Nat'l Park Blvd 435/772-0505 *6am-8pm seasonal*

VERMONT

Statewide

INFO LINES & SERVICES

Vermont Gay Tourism Association *Vermont's official office to promote gay & lesbian travel throughout the state, see www.vermontgaytourism.com*

Brattleboro

ACCOMMODATIONS

Frog Meadow Farm [M,NS,WI,GO] 34 Upper Spring Hill Rd, Newfane 802/365-7242, 877/365-7242

Nutmeg Inn [GS,WI,WC,GO] 153 Rte 9 W, Wilmington 802/464-3907, 855/868-8634

RESTAURANTS

Peter Havens [GO] 32 Elliot St (at Main) 802/257-3333 *6pm-10pm, clsd Sun-Tue, cont'l*

BOOKSTORES

Everyone's Books [WC] 25 Elliot St 802/254-8160 *9:30am-6pm, till 8pm Fri, till 7pm Sat, 11am-5pm Sun*

Burlington

INFO LINES & SERVICES

R.U.1.2? Community Center The Champlain Mill, 20 Winooski Falls Way #102, Winooski 802/860-RU12 (7812) *drop-in & cybercenter, support & advocacy, events*

ACCOMMODATIONS

The Black Bear Inn [GS,SW,NS,WI] 4010 Bolton Access Rd, Bolton Valley 802/434-2126, 800/395-6335 *mtn-top inn, full brkfst, hot tub*

The Inn at Essex [GF,SW,WI,WC] 70 Essex Way, Essex 802/878-1100, 800/727-4295 *culinary resort*

One of a Kind B&B [NS,WI] 53 Lakeview Terrace 802/862-5576

NIGHTCLUBS

Metronome/ Nectar's [GF,D,F,E] 188 Main St 802/658-4771, 802/865-4563

CAFES

Muddy Waters [BW] 184 Main St 802/658-0466 *9am-11pm*

Radio Bean Coffeehouse [E] 8 N Winooski Ave (at Pearl) 802/660-9346 *8am-midnight, till 2am Th-Sat, 10am-11pm Sun, cool bohemian coffeehouse*

RESTAURANTS

Bluebird Tavern [BW,GO] 86 St Paul St 802/540-1786 *4pm-10pm Th-Sat, 5pm-9pm Tue-Wed, clsd Sun-Mon, locally grown*

Daily Planet 15 Center St (at College) 802/862-9647 *4pm-close, also bar till 2am*

Leunig's Bistro & Cafe [GO] 115 Church St 802/863-3759

Vermont • *USA*

Loretta's [GO] 44 Park St (near 5 Corners), Essex Junction
802/879-7777 *lunch weekdays, dinner nightly, clsd Sun-Mon, Italian*

Shanty on the Shore 181 Battery St
802/864-0238 *11am-9pm, seafood, views of Lake Champlain*

Silver Palace 1216 Williston Rd
802/864-0125 *11:30am-9pm, 5pm-9pm Sun, Chinese, full bar*

▀RETAIL SHOPS

Peace & Justice Store 60 Lake St (at College St) **802/863-2345** *10am-6pm, limited hrs in winter, fair trade retail store*

▀CRUISY AREAS

The Loop [AYOR] downtown Bank, College & St Pauls Sts

Chester

▀ACCOMMODATIONS

Chester House Inn [GS,NS,WI,WC,GO] 266 Main St **888/875-2205** *inn circa 1780*

Dorset

▀CRUISY AREAS

Dorset Quarry [AYOR] on Rte 30 & Kelly Rd

Jay Peak

▀ACCOMMODATIONS

Phineas Swann B&B [GS,NS,WI,GO]
802/326-4306 *restored Victorian on Trout River, full brkfst*

Killington

▀ACCOMMODATIONS

Huntington House Inn [GF,WI,WC,GO] 19 Huntington Pl, Rochester
802/767-9140 *located on the park, restaurant & lounge*

The Inn of the Six Mountains
[GF,SW,WI,WC] 2617 Killington Rd
802/422-4302, 800/228-4676 *full brkfst, jacuzzi*

Salt Ash Inn [GF,F,WI,SW,WC] 4758 Rte 100A (at Rte 100), Plymouth
802/672-3224

Manchester

▀ACCOMMODATIONS

Hill Farm Inn [GF,NS,WI] 458 Hill Farm Rd (at Historic Rte 7-A), Arlington
802/375-2269, 800/882-2545 *full brkfst*

▀CAFES

Little Rooster Cafe Rte 7-A (at Hillvale Dr), Manchester Center
802/362-3496 *7am-2:30pm, clsd Wed (winters)*

▀RESTAURANTS

Bistro Henry [R] 1942 Depot St (.5 mile E of Rte 7), Manchester Center
802/362-4982 *dinner only, clsd Mon, Mediterranean, also bar*

Chantecleer Rte 7-A N, E Dorset
802/362-1616 *call for hours, seasonal*

▀BOOKSTORES

Northshire Bookstore 4869 Main St, Manchester Center **802/362-2200, 800/437-3700** *10am-7pm, till 9pm Fri-Sat*

Marshfield

▀ACCOMMODATIONS

Marshfield Inn & Motel [GF,WI,NS,GO] 5630 US Rte 2 **802/426-3383**

Montpelier

▀RESTAURANTS

Julio's [WI] 54 State **802/229-9348** *11:30am-10pm, till 11pm Fri-Sat, Mexican*

Sarducci's [WC] 3 Main St
802/223-0229 *11:30am-9:30pm, from 4:30pm Sun, Italian, full bar*

Wayside Restaurant [WC] 1873 Rte 302 **802/223-6611** *6:30am-9:30pm*

Plainfield

▀ACCOMMODATIONS

Comstock House [GF,WI,GO] 1620 Middle Rd **802/272-2693** *overlooks Winooski River Valley, full brkfst*

Richmond

■RESTAURANTS

The Kitchen Table Bistro 1840 W Main St **802/434-8686** *5pm-9pm, clsd Sun-Mon, seasonal menu, local food*

Rutland

■ACCOMMODATIONS

Lilac Inn [WC] 53 Park St, Brandon **802/247-5463, 800/221-0720** *full brkfst*

Saxtons River

■ACCOMMODATIONS

The Saxtons River Inn [GF,NS,WI,GO] 27 Main St (at Academy Ave) **802/869-2110** *historic Victorian inn w/ charming pub & restaurant, located in quaint New England village*

St Johnsbury

■ACCOMMODATIONS

Comfort Inn & Suites [GF,SW,WI,WC] 703 US Rte 5 S (at I-91) **802/748-1500, 800/424-6423**

Fairbanks Inn [GF,SW,WI,WC] 401 Western Ave **802/748-5666**

■RESTAURANTS

Elements 98 Mill St **802/748-8400** *dinner, clsd Sun-Mon, local food*

Stowe

■ACCOMMODATIONS

Arbor Inn [GS,SW,NS,WI] 3214 Mountain Rd **802/253-4772, 800/543-1293** *full brkfst, hot tub*

Fitch Hill Inn [GS,WI,NS] 258 Fitch Hill Rd, Hyde Park **802/888-3834, 800/639-2903** *full brkfst*

The Green Mountain Inn [GF,F,SW,NS,WI,WC] 18 Main St **802/253-7301, 800/253-7302**

Northern Lights Lodge [GF,SW,WI,GO] 4441 Mountain Rd **802/253-8541, 800/448-4554** *full brkfst, hot tub, sauna*

The Old Stagecoach Inn [GF,NS,WI] 18 N Main St (at Stowe St), Waterbury **802/244-5056, 800/262-2206** *historic village inn, full brkfst, also full bar*

Timberholm Inn [GS,NS,WI] 452 Cottage Club Rd **802/253-7603, 800/753-7603** *full brkfst, hot tub*

Waterbury

■ACCOMMODATIONS

Grünberg Haus B&B & Cabins [GS,NS,WI] 94 Pine St, Rte 100 S **802/244-7726, 800/800-7760** *full brkfst, also cabins*

Moose Meadow Lodge [GS,NS,WI,GO] 607 Crossett Hill **802/244-5378**

■RESTAURANTS

Cider House BBQ & Pub [GO] 1675 US Rte 2 **802/244-8400** *noon-9pm, clsd Mon-Wed, full bar, patio*

Wells River

■ACCOMMODATIONS

The Gargoyle House [M,N,NS,WI,GO] 3351 Wallace Hill Rd (at US 302 & I-91) **802/429-2341**

West Dover

■ACCOMMODATIONS

Deerhill Inn [GS,SW,NS,WI] 14 Valley View Rd **802/464-3100, 800/993-3379** *inn w/ restaurant*

Inn at Mount Snow [GF,NS,WI,GO] 401 Rte 100 **802/464-8388, 866/587-7669**

The Inn at Sawmill Farm [GS,NS,WC] 7 Crosstown Rd (at Rte 100) **802/464-8131, 800/493-1133**

Windham

■ACCOMMODATIONS

A Stone Wall Inn [GS,NS,WI,GO] 578 Hitchcock Hill Rd **802/875-4238**

Woodstock

■INFO LINES & SERVICES

The Woodstocker Inn B&B [GS,WI] 61 River St **802/457-3896, 866/662-1439**

Vermont • *USA*

■ACCOMMODATIONS

The Ardmore Inn [GF,NS,WI] 23 Pleasant St 802/457-3887 *1867 Greek Revival, full brkfst*

Deer Brook Inn [GF,NS,WI,GO] 4548 W Woodstock Rd 802/672-3713

VIRGINIA

Alexandria

see also Washington, District of Columbia

■ACCOMMODATIONS

Crowne Plaza Old Town Alexandria [GF,WI] 901 N Fairfax St 703/683-6000

Lorien Hotel & Spa [GF,F,WC] 1600 King St 703/894-3434, 877/956-7436

Morrison House [GF] 116 S Alfred St 703/838-8000, 866/834-6628

Arlington

see also Washington, District of Columbia

■INFO LINES & SERVICES

Arlington Gay/ Lesbian Alliance *monthly meetings & outreach events (see: www.agla.org)*

■BARS

Freddie's Beach Bar & Restaurant [MW,F,E,K,DS,WC] 555 S 23rd St (at Fern St) 703/685-0555 *4pm-2am, from 11am Fri, from 10am wknds for brunch, patio*

■CAFES

Java Shack [MW] 2507 N Franklin Rd (at Wilson Blvd & N Barton) 703/527-9556 *7am-8pm, 8am-6pm Sun*

■CRUISY AREAS

Seabee Memorial [AYOR] Memorial Dr

Bristol

■EROTICA

Exotic Illusions Adult Video 2003 W State St (at 20th St) 276/466-6909

Cape Charles

■ACCOMMODATIONS

Cape Charles House B&B [GF,NS] 645 Tazewell Ave (at Fig) 757/331-4920 *1912 colonial revival home w/ antiques*

Sea Gate B&B [GF,WI,GO] 9 Tazewell Ave 757/331-2206 *full brkfst*

Charlottesville

■ACCOMMODATIONS

The Inn at Court Square [GF,NS] 410 E Jefferson St 434/295-2800, 866/466-2877

■RESTAURANTS

Escafe [E,GO] 227 W Main St (next to the Omni Hotel) 434/295-8668 *5:30pm-11pm, 4:30pm-9:30pm Sun, clsd Mon, Asian/ American fusion, full bar*

■EROTICA

Sneak Reviews Video 2244 Ivy Rd 434/979-4420

■CRUISY AREAS

Chris Green Lake [AYOR] Rte 29 to Airport Rd

Danville

■CRUISY AREAS

Ballou Park [AYOR]

Hampton

■CAFES

The Java Junkies [F] 768 Settlers Landing Rd 757/722-6300 *7am-7pm, from 8am wknds, till 3pm Sun*

■CRUISY AREAS

Grandview Beach [AYOR] nude beach past rock mounds

Harrisonburg

■CAFES

Artful Dodger Coffeehouse [D,E,WC] 47 W Court Square 540/432-1179 *8:30am-2am, from 9am wknds, also bar*

Lynchburg

■CRUISY AREAS

Blackwater Creek area [AYOR]

Peaks View Park [AYOR]

Norfolk

■ACCOMMODATIONS

B&B at Historic Page House Inn
[GF,NS,WI] 323 Fairfax Ave
757/625-5033, 800/599-7659 *1899 mansion*

Tazewell Hotel & Suites [GF,WI,WC]
245 Granby St (at Tazewell St)
757/623-6200

■BARS

The Garage [M,NH,F,K,WC] 731 Granby St (at Brambleton) **757/623-0303** *4pm-2am*

Hershee Lounge & He Bar
[W,D,F,E,WC] 6117 Sewells Pt Rd (at Norview) **757/853-9842** *4pm-2am, boys bar in the back*

■NIGHTCLUBS

The Wave [M,D,S,WC] 4107 Colley Ave (at 41st St) **757/440-5911** *10pm-2am, from 5pm Sat, clsd Sun, Mon & Wed*

■CAFES

Oasis Cafe [GO] 142 W York St #101A (in York Center bldg) **757/627-6161** *7:30am-3pm Mon-Fri*

■RESTAURANTS

Charlie's Cafe [BW] 1800 Granby St (at 18th) **757/625-0824** *7am-2pm*

Tortilla West 508 Oropax St
757/440-3777 *dinner only, Sun brunch, open till 1am, Mexican, plenty veggie/ vegan*

■MEN'S SERVICES

►**MegaMates** **757/498-3555** *Call to hook up with HOT local men. FREE to listen & respond to ads. Use FREE code DAMRON. MegaMates.com.*

■EROTICA

Leather & Lace 149 E Little Creek Rd (at Granby) **757/583-4334**

Petersburg

■EROTICA

Thriller Books 1919 E Washington (on Rte 36) **804/733-0064**

Richmond

■ACCOMMODATIONS

Omni Richmond Hotel [GF,SW,WI,WC]
100 S 12th St (at Cary St)
804/344-7000, 800/843-6664
views of city & James River

■BARS

Babes of Carytown
[MW,D,CW,DS,F,E,K,WC] 3166 W Cary St (at Auburn) **804/355-9330** *11am-2am, from noon Sat, 10am-8pm Sun*

Barcode [M,NH,F,K,WI] 6 E Grace St (btwn 1st & Foushee Sts)
804/648-2040 *11am-2am, from 3pm wknds*

Godfrey's [MW,D,F,K,DS] 308 E Grace St (btwn 3rd & 4th) **804/648-3957**
10pm-close, clsd Mon-Tue, brunch Sun

■NIGHTCLUBS

Club Colours [MW,D,MR-AF,F,S,WC] 536 N Harrison St (at Broad)
804/353-9776 *9pm-3am Sat*

■RESTAURANTS

Galaxy Diner 3109 W Cary St
804/213-0510 *11am-midnight, till 2am wknds, some veggie, full bar*

The Village 1001 W Grace
804/353-8204 *8am-2am, bar till 2am, American*

■ENTERTAINMENT & RECREATION

Richmond Triangle Players 1300 Altamont Ave (at W Marshall St)
804/346-8113 *LGBT-themed plays, films & cabaret*

Venture Richmond 804/788-6466
tour the James River, lots of shops, restaurants, etc

■BOOKSTORES

Phoenix Rising [WC] 19 N Belmont Ave **804/355-7939** *11am-7pm, clsd Tue, LGBT*

■MEN'S SERVICES

►**MegaMates** **804/675-1100** *Call to hook up with HOT local men. FREE to listen & respond to ads. Use FREE code DAMRON. MegaMates.com.*

Virginia • *USA*

■ EROTICA

Quality Books 8 S Crenshaw Ave
804/257-7146

■ CRUISY AREAS

Deep Run Park [AYOR]

Forest Hill Park [AYOR] at 42nd St

Texas Beach/ North Bank Park
[AYOR] *also Great Shiplock Park*

Roanoke

■ BARS

Backstreet Cafe [MW,NH,F] 356 Salem
Ave (off Jefferson) **540/345-1542**
7pm-2am, clsd Sun-Mon

Cuba Pete's [GF,NH,F,K,WC] 120 Church
Ave SW (at First St SW, inside Macado's)
540/342-7231 *11am-2am, more gay
wknds, also Macado's restaurant*

■ NIGHTCLUBS

The Park [★MW,D,DS,V,YC,WC] 615
Salem Ave **540/342-0946** *9pm-close
Fri-Sun*

■ RESTAURANTS

Metro Restaurant & Nighclub [D] 14
Campbell Ave SE *11:30am-midnight, till
2:30am Fri-Sat*

Shenandoah Valley

■ ACCOMMODATIONS

Frog Hollow B&B [GS,GO] 492
Greenhouse Rd (at Rte 11), Lexington
540/463-5444 *full brkfst, hot tub*

The Olde Staunton Inn [GS,WI] 260 N
Lewis St, Staunton **540/886-0193,
866/653-3786** *B&B, hot tub*

Piney Hill B&B [GS,NS,GO] 1048 Piney
Hill Rd (at Mill Creek Crossroads), Luray
540/778-5261, 800/644-5261
country B&B, full brkfst, hot tub

Virginia Beach

■ ACCOMMODATIONS

Capes Ocean Resort Hotel
[GF,SW,NS,WI,WC] 2001 Atlantic Ave (at
20th St) **757/428-5421,
877/956-5421** *oceanfront rooms,
private balconies*

Ocean Beach Club [GF,F,WC] 3401
Atlantic Ave (at 34th St)
800/245-1003

■ BARS

Klub Ambush [MW,NH,D,F,K,DS,GO] 475
S Lynnhaven Rd (at Lynnhaven Pkwy)
757/498-4301 *5pm-2am*

Rainbow Cactus [M,D,CW,F,DS,WC]
3472 Holland Rd (at Diana Lee)
757/368-0441 *7pm-2am, clsd Mon-
Tue*

■ RESTAURANTS

Alexander's on the Bay 4536
Oceanview Ave **757/464-4999** *dinner
only, seafood, upscale, Chesapeake Bay
views*

■ MEN'S SERVICES

▶**MegaMates** **757/821-7373** *Call to
hook up with HOT local men. FREE to
listen & respond to ads. Use FREE code
DAMRON. MegaMates.com.*

■ EROTICA

Nancy's Nook 1301 Oceana Blvd
757/428-1498 *24hrs*

Washington

■ ACCOMMODATIONS

Gay Street Inn [GF,NS,WI,GO] 160 Gay
St **540/316-9220**

Waverly

■ EROTICA

Country Bookstore 111 S County Dr
(Rte 460) (at Rte 40) **804/834-1122**

WASHINGTON

Auburn

■ CRUISY AREAS

Isaac Evans Park [AYOR] Green River
Rd (off 104th Ave SE)

Bainbridge Island

■ BOOKSTORES

Eagle Harbor Book Co 157 Winslow
Wy E **206/842-5332** *9am-7pm, till
9pm Th, till 6pm Sat, 10am-6pm Sun*

Bellevue

see Seattle

Bellingham

■ BARS

Rumors [MW,D,WC] 1119 Railroad Ave (at Chestnut) **360/671-1846** *4pm-2am*

■ CAFES

Tony's Coffee House [WC] 1101 Harris Ave (at 11th), Fairhaven **360/738-4710** *7am-6pm*

■ RESTAURANTS

Bobby Lee's Pub & Eatery [GO,WC] 108 W Main St (Washington Ave), Everson **360/966-8838** *11am-2am, clsd Mon*

Skylark's Hidden Cafe [E] 1308 11th St (at McKenzie) **360/715-3642** *7am-midnight, outdoor seating, full bar, live jazz wknds*

■ BOOKSTORES

Village Books 1200 11th St (at Harris) **360/671-2626** *10am-7:30pm, till 7pm Sun, new & used*

■ EROTICA

Great Northern Bookstore 1308 Railroad Ave (at Holly) **360/733-1650**

■ CRUISY AREAS

Teddy Bear Cove [AYOR]

Bender Creek

■ ACCOMMODATIONS

Triangle Recreation Camp [MW,PC] PO Box 1226, Granite Falls 98252 *members-only camping on 80-acre nature conservancy; www.camptrc.org*

Bremerton

■ INFO LINES & SERVICES

AA Gay/ Lesbian 700 Callahan Dr (at St Paul's Episcopal) **360/475-0775, 800/562-7455** *7:30pm Tue*

Centralia

■ CRUISY AREAS

Fort Borst Park [AYOR] Harrison Ave

Edmonds

■ CRUISY AREAS

Edmonds City Park [AYOR] by ferry dock

Everett

■ INFO LINES & SERVICES

AA Gay/ Lesbian 2624 Rockefeller **425/252-2525** *7pm Sun*

■ MEN'S SERVICES

➤**MegaMates** **425/322-2200** *Call to hook up with HOT local men. FREE to listen & respond to ads. Use FREE code DAMRON. MegaMates.com.*

■ EROTICA

Airport Video 11732 Airport Rd (1 block W of Hwy 99, at 128th St) **425/290-7555** *24hrs*

■ CRUISY AREAS

Forest Park [AYOR] off 41st St

Glacier

■ ACCOMMODATIONS

Mt Baker B&B & Cabins [GS,NS,WI] 9434 Cornell Creek Rd **360/599-2299** *modern chalet, hot tub*

Issaquah

■ CRUISY AREAS

Sammamish State Park [AYOR] I-90 & SR 900

Kennewick

■ CRUISY AREAS

Columbia Park [AYOR] *days only, cops & bashers after dark*

Kent

■ BARS

Vibe [MW,D,K] 226 1st Ave S (btwn Meeker & Gowe) **253/852-0815** *noon-2am, till midnight Sun-Mon*

■ MEN'S SERVICES

➤**MegaMates** **253/234-0700** *Call to hook up with HOT local men. FREE to listen & respond to ads. Use FREE code DAMRON. MegaMates.com.*

■ EROTICA

The Voyeur 604 Central Ave S **253/850-8428** *videos, toys, clothing*

Washington • *USA*

La Conner

ACCOMMODATIONS

The Wild Iris [GF,NS,WI,WC,GO] 121 Maple Ave 360/466-1400, 800/477-1400

Long Beach Peninsula

ACCOMMODATIONS

Anthony's Home Court [GS,NS,WI,GO] 1310 Pacific Hwy N, Long Beach 360/642-2802, 888/787-2754 *cabins & RV hookups*

Bloomer Estates [GF,NS,WI,GO] 1004 41st Pl (at Oceanfront), Seaview 360/243-9510, 800/747-2096 *rental homes*

The Historic Sou'wester Lodge, Cabins & RV Park [GF,NS] Beach Access Rd (38th Pl), Seaview 360/642-2542 *inexpensive suites, cabins w/ kitchens & vintage trailers*

Mt Vernon

RESTAURANTS

Deli Next Door [WI,WC] 202 S 1st St (at Memorial Hwy) 360/336-3886 *8am-9pm, 9pm-8pm Sun*

CRUISY AREAS

Lions Park [AYOR] Freeway Dr (along the river)

Oak Harbor

CRUISY AREAS

Joseph Whidbey Park [AYOR] Swantown & Crosby

Olympia

INFO LINES & SERVICES

Free at Last AA 360/352-7344 *call for info*

ACCOMMODATIONS

Swantown Inn B&B [GF,NS,WI] 1431 11th Ave SE (at Central St) 360/753-9123, 877/753-9123

BARS

Hannah's [GS,NH,F] 123 5th Ave SW (at Columbia) 360/357-9890 *11am-2am, till midnight Sun-Mon*

NIGHTCLUBS

Jakes on 4th [MW,D,K] 311 E 4th 360/956-3247 *10am-2am*

CAFES

Darby's Cafe [GS,GO] 211 SE 5th Ave (at Washington) 360/357-6229 *7am-2pm, 8am-2pm wknds, clsd Mon-Tue*

RESTAURANTS

Saigon Rendez-Vous 117 5th Ave SW (btwn Columbia & Capitol Wy) 360/352-1989 *Vietnamese, plenty veggie*

Urban Onion [WC] 116 Legion Wy SE (at Capitol) 360/943-9242 *11am-9pm, 9am-2am wknds, plenty veggie, also lounge*

RETAIL SHOPS

Dumpster Values 302 4th (at Franklin) 360/705-3772 *10am-8pm, noon-6pm Sun, clothing, zines, records, toys*

CRUISY AREAS

Capitol Lake Marathon Park *take 5th Ave E to the parkway, follow signs to park*

Pasco

NIGHTCLUBS

Out & About Restaurant & Lounge [MW,D,F,K,C,DS,WC] 327 W Lewis 509/543-3796, 877/388-3796 *6pm-2am, clsd Sun-Mon, 18+ Fri, also restaurant*

Quinault

ACCOMMODATIONS

Lake Quinault Lodge [GF] 345 South Shore Rd (off US 101) 360/288-2900, 800/562-6672

Redmond

CRUISY AREAS

Marymoor Park [AYOR] *days (cops evenings)*

San Juan Islands

ACCOMMODATIONS

Inn on Orcas Island [GF,NS,GO] 360/376-5227, 888/886-1661 *waterfront, full brkfst*

Lopez Farm Cottages & Tent Camping [GS,NS] 555 Fisherman Bay Rd, Lopez Island 360/468-3555, 800/440-3556 *hot tub, also camping*

Spring Bay Cabin on Orcas Island [GS,NS,WI] Orcas Island 360/376-5531 *full brkfst, hot tub*

■ ENTERTAINMENT & RECREATION

Western Prince Whale & Wildlife Tours 2 Spring St (at Front), Friday Harbor 360/378-5315, 800/757-6722 *whale-watching & wildlife tours April-Oct*

Seattle

■ ACCOMMODATIONS

11th Avenue Inn [GF,NS,WI] 121 11th Ave E (at Boren) 206/720-7161, 800/720-7161

The Ace Hotel [GS,NS,WI,GO] 2423 1st Ave (at Wall St) 206/448-4721

Alexis Hotel [GF,WI,WC] 1007 1st Ave (at Madison) 206/624-4844, 866/356-8894 *luxury hotel w/ Aveda spa*

Bacon Mansion [GS,NS,WI,WC] 959 Broadway E (at E Prospect) 206/329-1864, 800/240-1864

Bed & Breakfast on Broadway [GS,NS,WI] 722 Broadway Ave E (at Aloha) 206/329-8933

Gaslight Inn [★GS,SW,NS,WI,GO] 1727 15th Ave (at E Howell St) 206/325-3654 *B&B in Arts & Crafts home*

Hotel 1000 [GF,WI] 1000 First Ave 206/957-1000, 877/315-1088

Inn at Queen Anne [GS,WI,NS] 505 1st Ave N (at Republican) 206/282-7357, 800/952-5043

MarQueen Hotel [GS] 600 Queen Anne Ave N (btwn Roy & Mercer) 206/282-7407, 888/445-3076 *in Theater District, kitchenettes*

Sleeping Bulldog Bed & Breakfast [GS,NS,WI,GO] 816 19th Ave S (at S Dearborn St) 206/325-0202

The Sorrento Hotel [GF,F,WI] 900 Madison St 206/622-6400, 800/426-1265

Wild Lily Cabins B&B [GS,SW,NS,GO] 25 miles W of Stevens Pass, Index 360/793-2103 *cabins on Skykomish River, 1 hour from Seattle, cedar sauna*

■ BARS

The Baltic Room [GS,E] 1207 Pine St (at Melrose) 206/625-4444 *9pm-2am, clsd Wed & Sun*

Bar Myx [GS,F,V] 2810 Western Ave (at Clay) 206/588-1834 *4pm-midnight, noon-2am wknds*

The Bottleneck Lounge [GS,GO] 2328 Madison St (at John St) 206/323-1098 *4pm-2am*

The Can Can [GS,F,C] 93 Pike St #307 (in the Pike Place Market) 206/652-0832 *6pm-2am*

Canterbury Ale & Eats [GF,NH] 534 15th Ave E (at Mercer) 206/322-3130 *11am-2am*

CC Attle's [★M,NH,F,V,WC] 1701 E Olive Way 206/323-4017 *noon-2am, patio, also Veranda Room & Men's Room*

Cha Cha Lounge & Bimbo's Cantina [GF,NH,GO] 1013 E Pike St (at 11th Ave) 206/322-0703 *5pm-2am, hipster lounge, big burritos*

Changes [M,NH,F,K,V,WC] 2103 N 45th St (at Meridian) 206/545-8363 *noon-2am*

Choice [MW,D] 1010 E Pike St (at Broadway, at Havana Social Club) 206/323-2822 *10pm Wed only, House music*

The Crescent Lounge [GS,NH,K,WC] 1413 E Olive Wy (at Bellevue) *noon-2am, karaoke nightly*

►The Cuff [★M,D,CW,B,WI,WC] 1533 13th Ave (at Pine) 206/323-1525 *2pm-2am, after-hours wknds, T-dance Sun, levi crowd, patio*

Diesel [M,NH,B,WC] 1413 14th Ave (at Madison) 206/322-1080 *2pm-2am, from noon wknds*

Double Header [GS,NH] 407 2nd Ave S Extension (at Washington) 206/464-9918 *10am-11pm, till 1am Fri-Sat*

Elite Tavern [MW,NH] 1520 E Olive Way (at Denny Way) 206/860-0999 *noon-2am*

Washington • USA

Hula Hula [GF,K] 106 1st Ave N (at Denny) **206/284-5003** *4pm-close, tiki bar*

The Lobby Bar [M,F,E] 916 E Pike St (at Broadway) **206/328-6703** *3pm-midnight, till 2am Th-Sat*

Madison Pub [★M,NH,WI,WC] 1315 E Madison St (at 13th) **206/325-6537** *noon-2am*

Poco Wine Room [GS,F] 1408 E Pine St (at 14th Ave) **206/322-9463** *5pm-close*

Pony [M] 1221 E Madison St (at 13th Ave) **206/324-2854** *5pm-2am*

R Place [M,NH,D,F,K,S,V,WI] 619 E Pine St (at Boylston Ave) **206/322-8828** *4pm-2am, from 2pm wknds*

Rendezvous [GF,C,E] 2322 2nd Ave (at Battery) **206/441-5823** *4pm-2am, live shows, also restaurant*

The Seattle Eagle [M,L,WC] 314 E Pike St (at Bellevue) **206/621-7591** *2pm-2am, patio, rock 'n' roll, theme nights*

The Social [MW,D,F,WC] 1725 E Olive Way **206/329-1423** *4pm-2am*

Sonya's Bar & Grill [M,NH,F] 1919 1st Ave (btwn Virginia & Stewart) **206/441-7996** *1pm-2am*

Temple Billiards [GF,F] 126 S Jackson **206/682-3242** *11am-2am, from 3pm wknds*

■NIGHTCLUBS

Contour [GF,D,F,E] 807 1st Ave (at Columbia) **206/447-7704** *3pm-2am, till 6am Fri-Sat, fire performances, also bar & restaurant*

Dimitriou's Jazz Alley [GF,F,E,NS,$] 2033 6th Ave (at Lenora) **206/441-9729** *call for events & reservations*

Neighbours Dance Club [★MW,D,YC,WC] 1509 Broadway (btwn Pike & Pine) **206/324-5358** *9pm-2am, till 3am Th, till 4am Fri-Sat, 2 flrs, also [18+] room Th-Sat*

Purr [M,F,K] 1518 11th Ave (at Pike St) **206/325-3112** *3pm-2am, till midnight Sun, cocktail lounge, Mexican-inspired food*

Re-bar [★GS,D,E,C] 1114 Howell (at Boren Ave) **206/233-9873** *10pm-2am, clsd Mon, DJ Wed-Sun*

Showbox [GF,E,$] 1426 1st Ave (at Pike) **206/628-3151** *live music venue*

■CAFES

The Allegro [WI] 4214 University Wy NE (at NE 42nd St) **206/633-3030** *7am-10:30pm*

Cafe Besalu 5909 24th Ave NW **206/789-1463** *7am-3pm, clsd Mon-Tue, great pastries*

Espresso Vivace [WI] 532 Broadway Ave **206/860-5869** *6am-11pm*

Fuel Coffee [WI] 610 19th Ave E **206/329-4700** *6am-9pm*

Insomniax Coffee & Juice [WI] 102 15th Ave E **206/322-6477** *7am-3pm, clsd Sun*

Kaladi Brothers Coffee [WI] 511 E Pike St (at Summit) **206/388-1700** *6am-9pm, from 8am wknds*

Louisa's 2379 Eastlake Ave E **206/325-0081** *7am-9pm, till 10pm Fri-Sat, 8am-3pm Sun*

■RESTAURANTS

Al Boccalino 1 Yesler Wy (at Alaskan) **206/622-7688** *lunch Tue-Fri, dinner nightly, classy southern Italian*

Bamboo Garden 364 Roy St (at Mercer St) **206/282-6616** *11am-10pm, Chinese vegetarian & kosher*

The Broadway Grill [★] 314 Broadway E (at E Harrison) **206/328-7000** *11am-11pm, from 8am wknds, full bar*

Cafe Flora [BW,NS,WC] 2901 E Madison St **206/325-9100** *lunch, dinner, wknd brunch*

Campagne [R] 86 Pine St (at 1st) **206/728-2800** *dinner only, clsd Mon*

Canlis 2576 Aurora Ave N **206/283-3313** *dinner only, fancy seafood*

Capitol Club [E] 414 E Pine St **206/325-2149** *tapas*

Dahlia Lounge 2001 4th Ave (at Virginia) **206/682-4142** *lunch Mon-Fri, dinner nightly, wknd brunch, full bar*

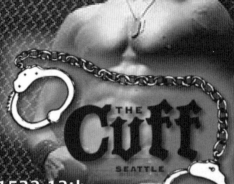

Washington • USA

Dick's Drive In 115 Broadway E (at Denny) 206/323-1300 *10:30am-2am, excellent fries & shakes*

Flying Fish 300 Westlake Ave N 206/728-8595 *lunch Mon-Fri, dinner nightly, full bar*

Fresh Bistro 4725 42nd Ave SW (btwn Alaska St & Edmunds) 206/935-3733 *dinner Mon-Sat, lunch Wed-Fri, wknd brunch*

Glo's [★] 1621 E Olive Wy (at Summit Ave E) 206/324-2577 *7am-3pm, till 4pm wknds, brkfst only*

Julia's [E] 300 Broadway E (at Thomas) 206/860-1818 *8am-11pm, till midnight Fri-Sat, full bar, [DS] Sat*

Kabul 2301 N 45th St 206/545-9000 *5pm-9:30pm, till 10pm Fri-Sat, Afghan*

Lola 2000 4th Ave (at Virginia) 206/441-1430 *6am-midnight, till 2am wknds, popular brunch*

Mae's Phinney Ridge Cafe [★WC] 6412 Phinney Ridge N (at 65th) 206/782-1222 *8am-2pm, till 3pm wknds, brkfst menu*

Mama's Mexican Kitchen 2234 2nd Ave (in Belltown) 206/728-6262 *lunch & dinner, cheap & funky*

Paseo 4225 Fremont Ave N (at N 43rd St) 206/545-7440 *11am-9pm, clsd Sun-Mon, Cuban*

Queen City Grill [★WC] 2201 1st Ave (at Blanchard) 206/443-0975 *dinner only, fresh seafood, full bar*

Restaurant Zoe 2137 2nd Ave (at Blanchard) 206/256-2060 *dinner only*

Snappy Dragon 8917 Roosevelt Wy NE 206/528-5575 *11am-9:30pm, 4pm-9pm Sun, Chinese*

Sunlight Cafe [BW,WC] 6403 Roosevelt Wy NE (at 64th) 206/522-9060 *8am-9pm, vegetarian*

Szmania's 3321 W McGraw St (in Magnolia Bluff) 206/284-7305 *dinner nightly, clsd Mon, full bar*

Tamarind Tree 1036 S Jackson St 206/860-1404 *11am-10pm, till midnight Fri-Sat, Vietnamese*

Teapot Vegetarian House 345 15th Ave E 206/325-1010 *11am-10pm, vegan*

Thaiger Room 206/632-9299 *11am-10pm, from noon wknds, Thai*

Wild Ginger Asian Restaurant & Triple Bar [★] 1401 3rd Ave (at Union) 206/623-4450 *lunch Mon-Sat, dinner nightly, bar till 1am*

Wild Mountain 1408 NW 85th St 206/297-9453 *8:30am-9pm, clsd Tue*

■ENTERTAINMENT & RECREATION

Alki Beach Park 1702 Alki Ave SW, West Seattle *popular on warm days*

Century Ballroom [MW,D,F] 915 E Pine, 2nd flr (at Broadway) 206/324-7263 *ballroom dancing; check schedule for gay nights*

Garage [★F,21+] 1130 Broadway 206/322-2296 *3pm-2am, way-cool pool hall, full bar, also bowling alley*

Northwest Lesbian & Gay History Museum Project 206/903-9517 *exhibits & publication*

The Vera Project [GF] corner of Warren Ave N & Republican St (in Seattle Center) 206/956-8372 *queer-friendly all-ages music arts center*

■BOOKSTORES

Elliott Bay Book Company 1521 10th Ave 206/624-6600, 800/962-5311 *10am-10pm, till 11pm Fri-Sat, till 9pm Sun*

Left Bank Books 92 Pike St (at 1st Ave) 206/622-0195 *10am-7pm*

■RETAIL SHOPS

Broadway Market [★] 401 Broadway E (at Harrison & Republican) *mall full of funky, hip stores*

Lifelong Thrift Store 1002 E Seneca 206/328-8979 *all proceeds to AIDS organization*

Metropolis 7321 Greenwood Ave N 206/782-7002 *10am-7pm, till 6pm Sat, noon-5pm Sun, cards & gifts*

Under U4 Men 709 Broadway E (at Roy) 206/324-6446 *11am-7pm, till 9pm Fri, designer underwear & swimwear & in-store models*

■PUBLICATIONS

SGN (Seattle Gay News)
206/324-4297 *weekly LGBT newspaper*

The Stranger 206/323-7101 *queer-positive alternative weekly*

■MEN'S CLUBS

Club Z [PC] 1117 Pike St (at Boren) 206/622-9958 *24hrs daily*

Steamworks [★WI,PC] 1520 Summit Ave (btwn Pike & Pine) 206/388-4818 *24hrs*

■MEN'S SERVICES

➤**MegaMates** 206/877-0877 *Call to listen & respond to ads. FREE to listen & respond to ads. Use FREE code DAMRON. MegaMates.com.*

■EROTICA

Castle Megastore 206 Broadway Ave E 206/204-0126

The Crypt Off Broadway 1516 11th Ave (at E Pine) 206/325-3882

Deja Vu Adult Superstore 1510 1st Ave (at Pike) 206/624-1784 *24hrs*

Fantasy Unlimited 2027 Westlake Ave (at 7th) 206/622-4669 *24hrs*

Hollywood Erotic Boutique 12706 Lake City Wy NE 206/363-0056 *24hrs, theater*

Taboo Video 1012 1st Ave 206/622-7399 *24hrs*

■CRUISY AREAS

Arboretum [AYOR] *days*

Green Lake Park [AYOR] 5500 blk of W Green Lake Wy (btwn putting course & aqua theater) *evenings*

Spokane

■INFO LINES & SERVICES

AA Gay/ Lesbian 1614 W Riverside 509/624-1442 *call for meeting times*

Inland Northwest LGBT Center 1522 N Washington #102 509/489-1914 *support groups, events, also art gallery*

■ACCOMMODATIONS

Montvale Hotel [GF,TG,F,NS,WI,GO] 1005 W First Ave (at Monroe) 509/747-1919, 866/668-8253 *luxury, boutique hotel*

■RESTAURANTS

Mizuna 214 N Howard 509/747-2004 *lunch Mon-Fri, dinner nightly, full bar*

■BOOKSTORES

Auntie's Bookstore [WC] 402 W Main Ave (at Washington) 509/838-0206 *9am-9pm, 11am-6pm Sun-Mon*

■MEN'S SERVICES

➤**MegaMates** 509/777-2100 *Call to hook up with HOT local men. FREE to listen & respond to ads. Use FREE code DAMRON. MegaMates.com.*

Suquamish

■INFO LINES & SERVICES

Kitsap Lesbian/ Gay AA 18732 Division Ave NE (at Congregational Church of Christ) 360/475-0775, 800/562-7455 *7pm Sun*

Tacoma

■INFO LINES & SERVICES

AA Gay/ Lesbian 759 S 45th St (at MCC) 253/474-8897 *7:30pm Fri*

Rainbow Center 741 St Helens Ave 253/383-2318 *1pm-5pm Mon-Fri, till 4pm Sat, community & resource center*

■ACCOMMODATIONS

Chinaberry Hill [GF,NS,WI] 302 Tacoma Ave N 253/272-1282 *full brkfst, jacuzzis, bay views, fireplaces*

Hotel Murano [GF,WI,WC] 1320 Broadway Plaza (at S 15th) 253/238-8000, 866/986-8083 *restaurants & bars*

■BARS

Airport Bar & Grill [MW,NH] 5406 S Tacoma Wy (at 54th) 253/475-9730 *2pm-2am*

■NIGHTCLUBS

➤**Club Silverstone** [MW,NH,D,F,K] 739 1/2 St Helens Ave (at 9th) 253/404-0273 *11am-2am*

■CAFES

Shakabrah Java Cafe [WC] 253/572-2787 *7am-4pm, clsd Sun*

Washington • *USA*

MEN'S SERVICES
➤MegaMates 253/882-0882 *Call to hook up with HOT local men. FREE to listen & respond to ads. Use FREE code DAMRON. MegaMates.com.*

EROTICA
Castle Megastore 6015 Tacoma Mall Blvd 253/471-0391

CRUISY AREAS
Wright Park [AYOR] 6th & G Sts

Vancouver
see also Portland, Oregon

MEN'S SERVICES
➤MegaMates 360/433-6100 *Call to hook up with HOT local men. FREE to listen & respond to ads. Use FREE code DAMRON. MegaMates.com.*

Walla Walla

ACCOMMODATIONS
The Boyer House [GS,SW,NS,GO] 741 Boyer Ave 888/526-8718

CRUISY AREAS
Fort Walla Walla Park [AYOR]

Pioneer Park [AYOR]

Wenatchee

CAFES
The Cellar Cafe [BW,GO] 249 N Mission St (at 5th) 509/662-1722 *9am-3pm Mon-Fri, patio*

CRUISY AREAS
River Walk [AYOR] at 19th St

Whidbey Island

ACCOMMODATIONS
Whidwood Inn [GS,NS,GO] 360/720-6228 *near historic Coupeville, hot tub*

Winthrop

ACCOMMODATIONS
Chewuch Inn [GF,NS,WI,WC] 223 White Ave 509/996-3107, 800/747-3107 *E of N Cascades Mtns*

Yakima

EROTICA
Yakima Magazine Center 1111 N 1st St 509/248-8598

WEST VIRGINIA

Statewide

PUBLICATIONS
➤Out 724/733-0828 *Pittsburgh's only LGBTQ newspaper since 1973! news, local events, classifieds & more for Western & Central PA, OH & WV*

Beckley

EROTICA
Blue Moon Video 3427 Robert C Byrd Dr (at New River Dr) 304/255-1200

Eccles Video 3517 Harper Rd, Harper 304/250-0068

Berkeley Springs

EROTICA
Action Books & Video [AYOR] US 522 (7 miles S of town) 304/258-2529 *24hrs Fri-Sat, arcade*

Bluefield

CRUISY AREAS
East River Mountain Overlook [AYOR] off Rte 460 (take lane nearest mtn & turn off, go all the way up mtn)

Charleston

ACCOMMODATIONS
Long Fork Campgrounds [M,SW,N,WI,GO] 114 Long Fork Camp Rd (at Charleston Rd), Walton 304/577-9347 *40 minutes from Charleston, also bar on wknds*

NIGHTCLUBS
Atmosphere Ultra Lounge [MW,D,DS] 706- 708 Lee St 304/343-3737 *5pm-2am, clsd Mon*

Broadway [M,D,DS] 210 Leon Sullivan Wy (at Lee) 304/343-2162 *12:30pm-3am*

■ENTERTAINMENT & RECREATION

Living AIDS Memorial Garden corner of Washington St E (at Sidney Ave) **304/346-0246**

■BOOKSTORES

Taylor Books [WI] 226 Capitol St **304/342-1461** *7:30am-8pm, till 10pm Fri, 9am-10pm Sat, till 3pm Sun, also cafe*

■EROTICA

Crazy Mitch's Adult Books 6721 Maccorkle Ave, St Albans **304/768-0947**

■CRUISY AREAS

Coonskin Park [AYOR] Greenbriar St (take Greenbriar St exit from I-77 heading from Beckley)

Daniel Boone Park [AYOR] Kanawha Blvd (just N of Capitol) *evenings*

Clarksburg

■EROTICA

Adult News 835 Philippi Pike (1/8 mile from Rte 58) **304/622-7909** *24hrs*

Fairmont

■CRUISY AREAS

Morris Park [AYOR] Pleasant Valley Rd

Follansbee

■BARS

Wild Coyote Saloon [MW,D,DS] 869 Main St **304/527-7191** *6pm-close*

Ghent

■EROTICA

The Lion's Den Adult Superstore 302 Odd Rd (exit 28 off I-77) **304/787-3333**

Harpers Ferry

■ACCOMMODATIONS

Laurel Lodge [GF,NS,WI,GO] 844 Ridge St **304/535-2886** *bungalow overlooking Potomac River gorge, full brkfst*

Huntington

■ACCOMMODATIONS

Pullman Plaza Hotel [GF,SW,NS,WI,WC] 1001 3rd Ave (at 10th St) **304/525-1001, 866/613-3611**

■BARS

Club Deception [M,D,B,K,DS,PC,WC] 1037 7th Ave (at 11th St) **304/522-3146** *5pm-2am, from 2pm wknds*

The Stonewall [★MW,D,K,DS,18+,WC,GO] 820 7th Ave (enter in alley) **304/523-2242** *8pm-3am, clsd Mon*

■RESTAURANTS

Sharkey's [E,K] 410 10th St **304/523-3200** *4pm-2:30am, clsd Sun, full bar*

■CRUISY AREAS

Rotary Park [AYOR] near 8th Ave & 29th St (off Rte 60 E, take 29th St exit)

Lewisburg

■CRUISY AREAS

Tuckwiller Park [AYOR] off Rte 60 (from I-64 take exit 161 & head E for 1 mile)

Logan

■CRUISY AREAS

Chief Logan State Park [AYOR] *daylight till 10pm*

Lost River

■ACCOMMODATIONS

Guest House at Lost River [MW,F,SW,NS,WI,GO] 288 Settlers Valley Wy (at Mill Gap Rd) **304/897-5707** *full brkfst, hot tub, restaurant & bar*

■RESTAURANTS

Lost River Grill & Motel [WI] St Rd 259 **304/897-6482** *11:45am-9pm, 8am-10pm Sat, 4pm-9pm Mon, full bar*

Martinsburg

■EROTICA

Variety Books & Video 255 N Queen St (at Race) **304/263-4334** *24hrs*

West Virginia • USA

■CRUISY AREAS

I-81 Rest Area 1/2 mile past exit 20 (in closed weigh station) *evenings*

Morgantown

■NIGHTCLUBS

Vice Versa [MW,D,K,DS,S,PC,18+,WC] 335 High St (enter rear) **304/292-2010** *8pm-3am Th-Sun*

Weezie's Pub & Club [MW,D,E] 3438 University Ave **304/292-3939** *8pm-close, clsd Sun*

■EROTICA

Adult Toy Boxxx Hartman Run Rd **304/296-3428** *bookstore w/ arcade*

■CRUISY AREAS

Cooper's Rock State Park [AYOR] 10 miles E of town (off I-68, take Cooper's State Park exit) *parking lot & woods*

Marilla Park [AYOR] E Brockway Ave (btwn Morgantown & Sabraton) *midday & evenings*

Parkersburg

■NIGHTCLUBS

The Otherside of the Nip n Cue [MW,D,K,DS] 1300 19th St **304/485-7752** *9pm Fri-Sat only*

Scruples [MW,D,K,DS] 322 5th St **304/916-1858** *clsd Sun-Tue*

■EROTICA

Pioneer Adult Books & Videos 6603 Emerson Ave **304/428-8604**

■CRUISY AREAS

Corning Boat Ramp [AYOR] Staunton Ave (off I-77)

Pliny

■EROTICA

Route 35 Adult Video & Books 1651 US Rte 35 N (near Buffalo) **304/937-4900** *24hrs*

Princeton

■EROTICA

Exotic Illusions Adult Bookstore 853 Frontage Rd/ Rte 460 (btwn Bluefield & Princeton) **304/487-2170** *24hrs*

Proctor

■ACCOMMODATIONS

Roseland Guest House & Campground [MO,F,SW,N,NS,GO] **304/455-3838** *222 secluded acres w/ campsites, theme wknds*

Summerville

■EROTICA

Fantasy Video 102 Lake Rd (off Rte 19), Mt Nebo **304/872-9030**

Wheeling

■EROTICA

Market St News 1437 Market St (at 14th St) **304/232-2414**

WISCONSIN

Algoma

■RETAIL SHOPS

The Flying Pig [GF,GO] N6975 Hwy 42 (at Tenth) **920/487-9902** *9am-6pm May-Oct, call for hrs off season, art gallery & coffee bar*

Appleton

■BARS

Rascals Bar & Grill [MW,F] 702 E Wisconsin Ave (at Lawe) **920/954-9262** *5pm-2am, from noon Sun, fish-fry Fri, patio*

Ravens [M,D,K,DS] 215 E College Ave **920/364-9599** *8pm-2am, clsd Sun-Mon*

■CAFES

Harmony Cafe [GS,E,YC] 233 E College Ave **920/734-2233** *7am-9pm, till 10pm Th-Sat, 8am-6pm Sun, also educational & support groups*

■MEN'S SERVICES

➤**MegaMates** **920/243-0043** *Call to hook up with HOT local men. FREE to listen & respond to ads. Use FREE code DAMRON. MegaMates.com.*

■EROTICA

Eldorado's 2545 S Memorial Dr (at Hwys 47 & 441) **920/830-0042**

■**CRUISY AREAS**

Lutz Park [AYOR]

Ashland

■**CRUISY AREAS**

Prentice Park [AYOR]

Beloit

■**BARS**

Club Impulse [MW,D,K,DS] 132 W Grand Ave **608/361-0000** *4pm-2am, till 2:30am Fri-Sat, from 7pm Sat*

Eau Claire

■**INFO LINES & SERVICES**

LGBT Community Center of the Chippewa Valley 1305 Woodland Ave **715/552-5428** *drop-in 7pm-10pm Fri, call for other hours, library & variety of events*

■**NIGHTCLUBS**

Scooters [MW,D,DS,WC] 411 Galloway (at Farwell) **715/835-9959** *3pm-2am*

■**EROTICA**

Adult Video Unlimited 1518 Bellinger St **715/834-3393**

Green Bay

■**INFO LINES & SERVICES**

Gay AA 920/432-2600 *call for times & locations*

■**BARS**

Napalese Lounge [M,NH,F,DS,WC] 1351 Cedar St **920/432-9646** *11am-close, DJ Fri-Sat*

■**NIGHTCLUBS**

Club XS [MW,D] 1106 Main St *7pm-2am*

The Shelter [MW,D,CW,B,L,TG,F,K, DS,V,GO] 730 N Quincy St (at 54302) **920/432-2662** *4pm-2am, theme nights*

■**CAFES**

Harmony Cafe [E] 1660 W Mason St **920/569-1593** *7am-9pm, 10am-6pm Sun, shows, support groups*

■**PUBLICATIONS**

Outbound/ Quest 920/655-0611, 800/578-3785 *news & arts reviews for WI's LGBT community*

■**EROTICA**

Lion's Den Adult Superstore 836 S Broadway (at 5th) **920/433-9640** *24hrs*

Hayward

■**ACCOMMODATIONS**

The Lake House [MW,SW,NS,WI,WC,GO] 5793 Division, Stone Lake **715/865-6803** *full brkfst, lesbian-owned*

Kenosha

see also Racine

■**BARS**

Club Icon [MW,D,K] 6305 120th Ave (on E Frontage road of I-94) **262/857-3240** *7pm-2am, from 3pm Sun, clsd Mon*

■**NIGHTCLUBS**

Fierté [MW,D,DS] 5722 3rd Ave **262/764-9713** *7pm-close, clsd Sun-Tue*

La Crosse

■**ACCOMMODATIONS**

Rainbow Ridge Farms B&B [GF,NS,WI] N 5732 Hauser Rd (at County S), Onalaska **608/783-8181, 888/347-2594**

■**BARS**

Chances R [MW,NH] 417 Jay St (at 4th) **608/782-5105** *3pm-close*

My Place [MW,NH,GO] 3201 South Ave (at East Ave) **608/788-9073** *3pm-close, from noon wknds*

Players [★MW,D,MR,TG,WC,GO] 300 S 4th St (at Jay St) **608/784-4200** *5pm-2am, from 3pm Fri-Sun, till 2:30am Fri-Sat*

■**EROTICA**

Pleasures [GS] 405 S 3rd **608/784-6350**

Wisconsin • USA

■CRUISY AREAS

Pettibone Park [AYOR] on the Mississippi River (off of North Beach, across from the Holiday Inn) *days only*

Madison

■INFO LINES & SERVICES

OutReach, Inc 600 Williamson St #P-1 **608/255-8582** *10am-7pm, noon-4pm Sat, clsd Sun*

■BARS

Five Nightclub [★MW,D,K,DS,V,TG] 5 Applegate Ct (btwn Fish Hatchery Rd & W Beltline Hwy) **608/277-9700, 877/648-9700** *5pm-2am, also Barracks leather bar, [18+] Tue*

Green Bush [GF,F] 914 Regent St (at Park) **608/257-2874** *4pm-midnight, clsd Sun*

Shamrock [★MW,F] 117 W Main St (at Fairchild) **608/255-5029** *11am-2am, from 4pm Mon-Tue*

Woof's [MW,NH,B,D,L,F] 114 King St (on Capitol Sq) **608/204-6222** *4pm-2am, from noon Sun*

■NIGHTCLUBS

Cardinal [GS,E,D] 418 E Wilson St (at S Franklin) **608/257-2473** *7pm-2am, from 4pm Fri*

IQ/ IndieQueer [MW,D] *weekly & monthly queer parties in Madison, check local listings for dates & info*

Plan B [MW,D,K] 924 Williamson St **608/257-5262** *4pm-2am, from 9pm Sun, clsd Mon*

Sotto [MW,D] 303 N Henry St **920/251-2753** *9pm-2am, clsd Sun-Mon*

■CAFES

Java Cat [F,WI] 3918 Monona Dr (at Cottage Grove Rd) **608/223-5553**

■RESTAURANTS

Fromagination 12 S Carroll (on Capital Sq) **608/255-2430** *9:30am-6pm, 9am-5pm Sat, clsd Sun*

La Hacienda [★] 515 S Park St **608/255-8227** *9am-3am, Mexican, popular & cruisy post-Club 5 spot*

Monty's Blue Plate Diner [BW,WC] 2089 Atwood Ave (at Winnebago) **608/244-8505** *7am-9pm, till 10pm wknds*

■PUBLICATIONS

Our Lives *LGBT publication,* *www.ourlivesmadison.com*

■EROTICA

Red Letter News 2528 E Washington (btwn North & Milwaukee) **608/241-9958**

■CRUISY AREAS

Burrows Park [AYOR]

Olin Park [AYOR] W shore of Lake Monona (parking lot near Sheraton) *afternoons*

Mazomanie

■CRUISY AREAS

Mazo Nude Beach [AYOR] *Madison 30 miles NW on Hwy 4, then 14 miles N to Laws Dr, turn left & go 1/2 mile to gravel rd*

Milwaukee

■INFO LINES & SERVICES

AA Galano Club 315 W Court #201 (in LGBT Community Center) **414/276-6936**

Milwaukee LGBT Community Center [WI] 1110 N Market St, 2nd flr **414/271-2656** *10am-10pm, from 6pm Sat, till 5pm Mon, clsd Sun*

■ACCOMMODATIONS

Ambassador Hotel [GS,WI,WC] 2308 W Wisconsin Ave (at N 24th) **414/345-5000, 888/322-3326**

The Brumder Mansion [GF,NS,WI] 3046 W Wisconsin Ave (at N 31st) **414/342-9767, 866/793-3676**

Comfort Inn & Suites [GF,WI,WC] 916 E State St (at Marshall) **414/276-8800, 800/328-7275**

Hotel of the Arts/ Days Inn [GF,NS,WI] 1840 N 6th St (at Reservoir Ave) **414/265-5629**

The Iron Horse Hotel [GF] 500 W Florida St (at S 5th St) **888/543-4766** *friendly hotel geared toward motorcycle enthusiasts*

The Milwaukee Hilton [GF,F,SW,WI,WC] 509 W Wisconsin Ave (at 5th St) **414/271-7250, 800/445-8667**

■BARS

Art Bar [GS,E,WI,GO] 722 E Burleigh St (at Fratney) **414/372-7880** 3pm-2am, from 10am wknds

Boom/ The Room [MW,NH,F,V,S] 625 S 2nd (at W Bruce) **414/277-5040** 5pm-2am, from 2pm wknds, patio, also martini bar

D.I.X. [M,V] 739 S 1st St (at National) **414/231-9085** 4pm-2am, from noon Sun

Fluid [M,NH,V] 819 S 2nd St (at W National) **414/643-5843** 5pm-close, from 3pm Fri, from 2pm wknds

Hamburger Mary's Milwaukee [MW,F,DS,K] 2130 Kinnickinnic **414/988-9324** 11am-10pm, 10am-midnight wknds

Harbor Room [M,L,F,V] 117 E Greenfield Ave (at S 1st St) **414/672-7988** 6am-2am

Hybrid Lounge [M] 707 E Brady (at Van Buren) **414/810-1809** 4pm-close, from 10am Sat-Sun

Kruz [M,L] 354 E National Ave (at S Water St) **414/272-5789** 3pm-close, patio, cruisy

The Nomad [GF] 1401 E Brady St (at Warren) **414/224-8111** 2pm-2am, from noon wknds, soccer pub

Taylor's [GS,NH,D,VC,GO] 795 N Jefferson St (at Wells) **414/271-2855** 4pm-close, patio

This Is It [M,OC] 418 E Wells St (at Jefferson) **414/278-9192** 3pm-2am

Two [GS] 718 E Burleigh St (at Fratney) 7pm-close Wed-Sat

Woody's [M,NH,WI] 1579 S 2nd St (at Lapham St) **414/672-0806** 4pm-close, from 2pm wknds, sports bar

■NIGHTCLUBS

La Cage/ Montage Lounge [★M,D,S,V,YC,WC] 801 S 2nd St (at National) **414/383-8330** 6pm-close, from 10pm Fri-Sat

■CAFES

Alterra Coffee Roasters [WI] 2211 N Prospect Ave (at North) **414/273-3753** 7am-6pm

Bella Caffe 189 N Milwaukee St **414/273-5620** 6am-9pm, till 11pm Fri-Sat, 8am-6pm Sun

Fuel Cafe [WI,WC] 818 E Center St **414/374-3835** 7am-10pm, from 8am wknds

■RESTAURANTS

Beans & Barley 1901 E North Ave (at Oakland Ave) **414/278-7878** 8am-9pm, vegetarian cafe & deli

Coquette Cafe [WC] 316 N Milwaukee St (btwn Buffalo & St Paul) **414/291-2655** 11am-10pm, till 11pm Fri, 5pm-11pm Sat, 11am-5pm Sun

Crisp Pizza Bar & Lounge 1323 E Brady St **414/727-4217** 4pm-2am, from 11:30am wknds

Harvey's [E] 1340 W Towne Sq Rd, Mequon **262/241-9589** dinner nightly, cont'l

Honeypie Cafe 2643 S Kinnickinnic Ave (at Potter) **414/489-7437** 10am-10pm, from 9am wknds, till 9pm Sun, homemade midwestern classics

The Knick [★WC] 1030 E Juneau Ave (at Waverly) **414/272-0011** 11am-midnight, from 9am wknds, full bar

La Perla 734 S 5th St (at National) **414/645-9888** 11am-10pm, till 11:30pm Fri-Sat, Mexican, also bar

Lulu [E] 2261 & 2265 S Howell Ave **414/294-5858** 11am-10pm, also bar till late, live music wknds

Meritage [WC] 5921 W Vliet St **414/479-0620** 5pm-10pm, till 11pm Fri-Sat, till 9pm Mon, clsd Sun

Range Line Inn [R] 2635 W Mequon Rd, Mequon **262/242-0530** 4:30pm-10pm, clsd Sun-Mon

Ryan Braun's Graffito 102 N Water St **414/727-2888** 5pm-9pm, from 11am Fri-Sun, clsd Mon

Sanford Restaurant 1547 N Jackson St **414/276-9608** dinner only, clsd Sun, Milwaukee fine dining Euro-style

Wisconsin • *USA*

■ENTERTAINMENT & RECREATION

Boerner Botanical Gardens 9400 Boerner Dr (in Whitnall Park), Hales Corners **414/525-5600, 414/525-5601** *8am-dusk, 40-acre garden & arboretum, garden clsd in winter*

Harley-Davidson Museum 400 Canal St (at N 6th St) **877/287-2789**

Milwaukee Gay Arts Center 703 S 2nd St (at National Ave) **414/383-3727** *art gallery, performance, theater, classes & more*

Mitchell Park Domes 524 S Layton Blvd (27th St, at Pierce) **414/257-5611** *botanical gardens*

Off the Wall Theatre 127 E Wells St **414/327-3552** *alternative theatre group*

■BOOKSTORES

OutWords Books, Gifts & Coffee [WC] 2710 N Murray Ave (at Park Pl) **414/963-9089** *11am-7pm, till 8pm Fri-Sat, noon-6pm Sun, LGBT, pride items*

Peoples' Books 2122 E Locust St (at Maryland) **414/962-0575** *10am-6pm, clsd Sun*

Woodland Pattern 720 E Locust St **414/263-5001** *11am-8pm, noon-5pm wknds, clsd Mon*

■PUBLICATIONS

Outbound/ Quest **920/655-0611, 800/578-3785** *news & arts reviews for WI's LGBT community*

■MEN'S CLUBS

Midtowne Spa–Milwaukee [PC,WC] 315 S Water (at Florida) **414/278-8989** *24hrs*

■MEN'S SERVICES

▶**MegaMates** **414/342-2222** *Call to hook up with HOT local men. FREE to listen & respond to ads. Use FREE code DAMRON. MegaMates.com.*

■EROTICA

Booked Solid 7035 W Greenfield Ave (at 70th), West Allis **414/774-7210**

■CRUISY AREAS

Juneau Park [AYOR] *beware after 10pm*

Oshkosh

■BARS

Deb's Spare Time [MW,NH,F,E,18+,GO] 1303 Harrison St (btwn Main & New York) **920/235-6577** *11am-2am, from 9am wknds*

PJ's [MW,NH,D] 1601 Oregon St **920/385-0442** *5pm-close Tue-Sat, clsd Sun-Mon*

■EROTICA

The Lion's Den Adult Superstore 1650 Plainview Dr (at Hwys 41 & 26) **920/235-9040** *24hrs*

Pure Pleasure 1212 Oshkosh Ave (off Hwy 21) **920/235-9727**

Supreme Lingerie & Gifts 1911 S Washburn St **920/235-2012**

Racine

■NIGHTCLUBS

JoDee's International [MW,D,E,K,DS,S] 2139 Racine St/ S Hwy 32 (at 22nd) **262/634-9804** *7pm-close, park in rear*

Sheboygan

■BARS

The Blue Lite [MW,NH,D] 1029 N 8th St (off Rte 143) **920/457-1636** *7pm-close, from 3pm Sun*

Stevens Point

■EROTICA

Eldorado's 3219 Church St (at Business 51 S) **715/343-9877**

Sturgeon Bay

■ACCOMMODATIONS

The Chadwick Inn [GF,NS,GO] 25 N 8th Ave **920/743-2771**

The Chanticleer Guest House [★GS,SW,NS,WI,WC,GO] 4072 Cherry Rd **920/746-0334, 866/682-0384** *on 70 acres*

Superior

■BARS

The Flame [MW,D,E,K,DS,WI] 1612 Tower Ave **715/395-0101** *3pm-2:30am*

The Main Club [M,D,L,E,WI,WC] 1217 Tower Ave (at 12th) **715/392-1756** *3pm-2am*

Wausau

■NIGHTCLUBS

Oz [M,D,K,DS,V] 320 Washington **715/842-3225** *7pm-close*

Wisconsin Dells

■BARS

Captain Dix [MW,K] 4124 River Rd (at Rainbow Valley Resort) **608/253-1818, 866/553-1818** *6pm-close, from 11am wknds, theme nights*

WYOMING

Casper

■EROTICA

Emporium Video Exchange 1210 East F St **307/265-9726**

■CRUISY AREAS

Morad Park [AYOR]

Cheyenne

see also Fort Collins, Colorado

■INFO LINES & SERVICES

Wyoming Equality/ United Gays & Lesbians of Wyoming 307/778-7645 *10am-2pm Mon-Fri, info, referrals & newsletter, social activities*

■BARS

Choice City Shots [MW,NH,D, K,S,WC,GO] 124 LaPorte Ave (at College), Fort Collins, CO **970/221-4333** *open 6:30pm*

■CRUISY AREAS

I-25 Rest Area Southbound [AYOR] *parking lot & woods, late nights*

Lions Park [AYOR] *near skating pond*

Etna

■RETAIL SHOPS

Blue Fox Studio & Gallery [GO] 107452 N US Hwy 89 **307/883-3310** *open 7 days, hours vary, pottery, jewelry & mask studio, local travel info*

Evanston

■EROTICA

Romantix Adult Superstore 1939 Harrison Dr **307/789-0800**

Gillette

■CRUISY AREAS

Camplex Park [AYOR] Garner Lake Rd (off I-90, Garner Lake Rd exit, go S 1 mile) *parking lot & woods*

Lander

■CRUISY AREAS

City Park 3rd St (at City Park Ave)

Laramie

■ACCOMMODATIONS

Cowgirl Horse Hotel [W] 32 Black Elk Trail **307/745-8794 or 399-2502** *specializing in women travelers & their horses, men welcome*

■BOOKSTORES

The Second Story 105 Ivinson Ave **307/745-4423** *10am-6pm, clsd Sun, independent*

■CRUISY AREAS

I-80 Rest Area [AYOR] Happy Jack Rd (13 miles E, take Happy Jack Rd exit off I-80) *afternoons, late evenings*

Rock Springs

■EROTICA

Exit 107 Video 1554 9th St (off I-80, exit 107) **307/362-0700** *arcade*

Sheridan

■CRUISY AREAS

Sheridan Information Center [AYOR] take 5th Ave exit off I-90 *parking lot & woods*

Canada

ALBERTA

Banff

■ACCOMMODATIONS

Simpson's Num-Ti-Jah Lodge [GF] 403/522-2167 *overlooks Bow Lake & Canadian Rockies, 40km N of Lake Louise*

Spruce Grove Inn [GF,SW,NS,WI,WC] 545 Banff Ave 403/762-3301, 800/879-1991

Calgary

■INFO LINES & SERVICES

Calgary Outlink: Centre for Gender & Sexual Diversity 223 12th Ave SW (at the Old Y Centre) 403/234-8973 *11am-2pm Tue, 4pm-7pm Wed, 3pm-6pm Fri, Community Cafe is the 2nd Fri of the month at 7pm*

Front Runners AA 1227 Kensington Close NW (at Hillhurst United Church) 403/777-1212 *8:30pm Wed & Sat*

■ACCOMMODATIONS

11th Street Lodging [GS,SW,WI,GO] 403/209-1800 *"no shoe" policy inside*

Calgary Westways Guest House [GS,NS,WI,GO] 216 25th Ave SW 403/229-1758, 866/846-7038 *full brkfst*

■BARS

The Back Lot [M,WC] 209 10th Ave SW (at 1st St SW) 403/265-5211 *2pm-2am, martini lounge, patio*

Ming [GF] 520 17th Ave SW 403/229-1986 *4pm-2am, martini lounge*

Texas Lounge [MO] 308 17th Ave SW (enter rear) 403/229-0911 *11am-2am*

■NIGHTCLUBS

Lolita's [GS,C] 1413 9th Ave SE 403/265-5739 *cabaret/ performance club, also restaurant*

Twisted Element [M,D,K,DS,S,WI] 1006 11th Ave SW 403/802-0230 *9pm-close, clsd Mon*

■CAFES

Caffe Beano [WC] 1613 9th St SW (at 17th Ave) 403/229-1232 *6am-midnight, from 7am wknds*

■RESTAURANTS

Halo 13226 Macleod Trail SE 403/271-4111 *lunch & dinner, steak, seafood & wine bar*

Melrose Cafe & Bar 730 17th Ave SW (at 7th St) 403/228-3566 *11am-2am, from 10am wknds, full bar till 2am, patio*

Thai Sa-On 351 10th Ave SW (at 4th) 403/264-3526 *lunch & dinner, clsd Sun*

■BOOKSTORES

Daily Globe News Shop 1004 17th Ave SW (at 10th St) 403/244-2060 *9am-10pm*

■RETAIL SHOPS

Priape 1322 17th Ave SW (enter on 16th) 403/215-1800, 800/461-6969 #25 *noon-8pm, till 6pm Sun, clubwear, leather & toys*

■PUBLICATIONS

Gay Calgary & Edmonton Magazine 888/543-6960 *monthly LGBT publication*

■MEN'S CLUBS

Goliath's Saunatel [F,PC] 308 17th Ave SW (enter rear) 403/229-0911 *24hrs, cocktails*

■CRUISY AREAS

North Glenmore Park [AYOR] S end of Crowchild *down the ravine*

Edmonton

■INFO LINES & SERVICES

AA Gay/ Lesbian 11355 Jasper Ave (at church) 780/424-5900 *7:30pm Mon; also 8pm Fri at 10804 119th St*

Pride Centre of Edmonton 10608 105 Ave 780/488-3234 *noon-9pm, 2pm-6:30pm Sat, clsd Sun-Mon*

■ACCOMMODATIONS

Labyrinth Lake Lodge [GS,NS,WI] 780/878-3301 *lodge on private lake, hot tubs*

Northern Lights B&B [MW,SW,NS,GO]
780/483-1572 *full brkfst*

■BARS

The Junction [MW,D,E,DS] 10242 106th
St **780/756-5667** *4pm-close, theme
nights, also restaurant*

Woody's Pub & Cafe [MW,NH,F,K]
11723 A Jasper (above Buddy's)
780/488-6557 *3pm-midnight, till
3am wknds*

■NIGHTCLUBS

Buddy's Nite Club [MW,D,DS] 11725-B
Jasper **780/488-6636** *9pm-3am, from
8pm Fri*

Flash [MW] 10018 105th St
780/969-9965 *9pm-3am Fri-Sat only*

■RESTAURANTS

Cafe de Ville [R] 10137 124th St
780/488-9188 *11:30am-10pm, till
midnight Fri-Sat, 10am-2pm & 5pm-
10pm Sun*

■BOOKSTORES

Audrey's Books [WC] 10702 Jasper Ave
(at 107th St) **780/423-3487** *9am-
9pm, 9:30am-5:30pm Sat, noon-5pm
Sun, large LGBT section*

Greenwood's Bookshoppe 10309 82
Ave **780/439-2005** *10am-6pm, till
8pm Th-Fri, 9:30am-5:30pm Sat, noon-
5pm Sun*

■RETAIL SHOPS

Divine Decadence 10441 82nd Ave (at
105th) **780/439-2977** *hip fashions,
accessories*

■PUBLICATIONS

Gay Calgary & Edmonton Magazine
Calgary **888/543-6960** *monthly LGBT
publication*

■MEN'S CLUBS

Steamworks [WI] 11745 Jasper Ave (at
118th St) **780/451-5554** *24hrs*

Westerose

■ACCOMMODATIONS

Pine Trails Getaway [MW] RR1
780/586-0002

Birken

■ACCOMMODATIONS

Birken Lakeside Resort [GF,SW,GO]
9179 Portage Rd **604/452-3255**
*cabins & campsites, hot tub, lesbian-
owned*

Chilliwack

■RESTAURANTS

Bravo Restaurant & Lounge [WC,GO]
46224 Yale Rd (at Nowell St)
604/792-7721 *5pm-close, clsd Sun-
Tue, Pacific NW cuisine, martinis*

Gulf Islands

■INFO LINES & SERVICES

**Gays & Lesbians of Salt Spring
Island (GLOSSI)** PO Box 644, Salt
Spring Island V8K 2W2 250/537-7773

■ACCOMMODATIONS

Bellhouse Inn [GS,NS,WI] 29 Farmhouse
Rd, Galiano Island 250/539-5667,
800/970-7464 *full brkfst*

Birdsong B&B [GS,WI] 153 Rourke Rd,
Salt Spring Island 250/537-4608
ocean & harbor views

Fulford Dunderry Guest House
[GF,NS,WI,GO] 2900 Fulford-Ganges Rd,
Salt Spring Island 250/653-4860

Hummingbird Lodge B&B [GF,NS]
1597 Starbuck Ln (at Whalebone Dr),
Gabriola **250/247-9300**,
877/551-9383

Island Farmhouse B&B [GS,NS,GO]
185 Horel Rd W, Salt Spring Island
250/653-9898, 877/537-5912 *kids/
pets ok, lesbian-owned*

Kamloops

■CRUISY AREAS

Mission Flats Beach [AYOR] off
Mission Flats Rd (15 miles W of town)
popular nude beach

Okanagan County

■INFO LINES & SERVICES

Okanagan Rainbow Coalition 1476 Water St, Kelowna **250/860-8555** *24-hr recorded info, support groups, social events & dances*

■ACCOMMODATIONS

Eagles Nest B&B [M,NS,WI,GO] 15620 Commonage Rd (at Carrs Landing Rd), Kelowna **250/766-9350, 866/766-9350** *full brkfst, hot tub, overlooking Lake Okanagan*

Grapeseed Guesthouse & Gardens [MW,GO,WI] 607 Munson Mountain Rd, Penticton **250/809-9998**

■CAFES

Bean Scene [WC] 274 Bernard Ave, Kelowna **250/763-1814** *6am-9pm, till 11pm Wed-Sat*

■RESTAURANTS

Greek House 3159 Woodsdale Rd, Kelowna **250/766-0090** *4pm-9pm, cont'l*

Prince George

■INFO LINES & SERVICES

GALA North **250/562-7124** *24-hr recorded info, call for drop-in hours & location*

■EROTICA

Doctor Love 1412 Patricia Blvd **250/614-1411**

Surrey

■CRUISY AREAS

Green Timbers Park [AYOR] 144th St & 100th Ave

Tofino

■ACCOMMODATIONS

Beachwood [GF,NS,GO] 1368 Chesterman Beach Rd **250/725-4250** *private apt, steps to the beach*

BriMar B&B [GS] 1375 Thornberg Crescent **250/725-3410, 800/714-9373** *on the beach, full brkfst*

Eagle Nook Wilderness Resort & Spa [GF] Ucluelet **800/760-2777** *private log cabins, gourmet meals, health spa*

■RESTAURANTS

Blue Heron [WC] 634 Campbell St **250/725-2043** *7am-10pm, full bar*

Vancouver

■INFO LINES & SERVICES

AA Gay/ Lesbian **604/434-3933**

The Greater Vancouver Pride Line **604/684-6869 x290, 800/566-1170** *7pm-10pm, info & support*

QMUNITY: BC's Resource Centre 1170 Bute St (btwn Davie & Pendrell Sts) **604/684-5307, 800/566-1170**

■ACCOMMODATIONS

Barclay House B&B [GS,NS,WI,GO] 1351 Barclay St (at Jervis) **604/605-1351, 800/971-1351** *full brkfst*

Granville B&B [GF,WI] 5050 Granville St (at 34th Ave) **604/739-9002, 866/739-9002**

L' Hermitage Hotel [GS,SW,WI] 788 Richards St (at Robson) **778/327-4100**

The Langtry [GS,NS,WI,GO] 968 Nicola St (at Barclay) **604/687-7892, 800/699-7892**

The Listel Hotel [★GS,F,SW,NS,WI] 1300 Robson Street (at Jervis) **604/684-8461, 800/663-5491** *boutique hotel, gym*

Moda Hotel [GS,WI] 900 Seymour St (at Smithe) **604/683-4251, 877/683-5522** *also 3 bars [M,S]*

Nelson House B&B [MW,WI,GO] 977 Broughton St (btwn Nelson & Barclay) **604/684-9793, 866/684-9793**

"O Canada" House B&B [GS,WI,GO] 1114 Barclay St (at Thurlow) **604/688-0555, 877/688-1114** *full brkfst*

Opus Hotel [GF,WC] 322 Davie St (at Hamilton, Yaletown) **604/642-6787, 866/642-6787** *also bar and restaurant*

The West End Guest House
[GS,NS,GO] 1362 Haro St (at Broughton)
604/681-2889, 888/546-3327

■ **BARS**

1181 [M] 1181 Davie St (at Bute)
604/687-3991 *4pm-close, upscale cocktail lounge*

The Fountainhead Pub [MW,NH,TG]
1025 Davie St (at Burrard)
604/687-2222 *11am-midnight, till 2am Fri-Sat, wknd brunch, patio*

The Oasis [MW,NH,F,E,P] 1240 Thurlow
(at Davie) **604/685-1724** *5pm-close, theme nights*

The PumpJack Pub [M,NH,L,WC] 1167
Davie St (off Bute) **604/685-3417**
1pm-1am, till 2am Fri-Sat

■ **NIGHTCLUBS**

816 Granville/ The World [M,D] 816
Granville St *midnight-6am Fri-Sun*

Club 23 West [GS,D] 23 W Cordova (at
Carrall) **604/200-2923** *10pm-4am Fri-Sat, call for events*

Five Sixty [GS,D,E] 560 Seymour St (at
Pender) **604/678-6322** *live bands, art gallery*

Junction Pub [M,D,F,DS] 1138 Davie St
604/669-2013 *1pm-3am Fri-Sat, from noon wknds*

Numbers [★M,D,K,V] 1042 Davie (btwn
Thurlow & Burrard) **604/685-4077**
9pm-2am, till 4am Fri-Sat, 8pm-2am Sun, cruisy

Shine [GF,D] 364 Water St (at Richards)
604/408-4321

Thickset [M,D,B] *monthly bear parties,
check thickset.ca*

■ **CAFES**

Coming Home [GO] 753 6th St (at 8th
Ave), New Westminster **604/288-9850**
9am-5pm, till 3pm wknds, clsd Mon, clsd Sun

Delaney's 1105 Denman St
604/662-3344 *6am-9pm, from 6:30am wknds, coffee shop*

Rhizome Cafe [F] 317 E Broadway
604/872-3166 *11am-10pm, till midnight Fri-Sat, till 3pm Sun, clsd Mon*

Sweet Revenge [GO] 4160 Main St (at
26th) **604/879-7933** *7pm-midnight, till 1am Fri-Sat, patisserie*

Turk's Coffee Exchange [WI] 1276
Commercial Dr **604/255-5805**
6:30am-11pm

■ **RESTAURANTS**

Bin 941 [★] 941 Davie St
604/683-1246 *5pm-2am, till midnight Sun, tiny tapas parlor*

Brioche 401 W Cordova (at Homer, in
Gastown) **604/682-4037** *7am-8:30pm, 8am-7:30pm wknds*

Cafe Deux Soleils [MW,E] 2096
Commercial Dr **604/254-1195** *8am-midnight, till 5pm Sun, vegetarian*

Cascade Room 2616 Main St (at 10th)
604/709-8650 *5pm-1am, from noon-2am wknds*

Chill Winston 3 Alexander St
604/288-9575 *11am-1am, in Gastown*

The Dish [GO] 1068 Davie St
604/689-0208 *7am-10pm, 9am-9pm Sun, veggie fast food*

Elbow Room Cafe 560 Davie St (at
Seymour) **604/685-3628** *8am-4pm, great brkfst*

Foundation Lounge 2301 Main St
604/708-0881 *noon-1am, till 2am wknds, vegetarian*

Glowbal Grill & Satay Bar 1079
Mainland St (Yaletown) **604/602-0835**
lunch, dinner, brunch wknds; also Afterglow Lounge

Hamburger Mary's 1202 Davie St (at
Bute) **604/687-1293** *8am-3am, till 4am Fri-Sat, till 2am Sun, full bar*

Havana [★] 1212 Commercial Dr
604/253-9119 *11am-11pm, Cuban fusion, full bar, patio*

Lickerish 903 Davie St (at Hornby)
604/696-0725 *5:30pm-midnight, till 1am Th-Sun, cocktail lounge*

Lift Bar & Grill 333 Menchions Mews
604/689-5438 *11:30am-midnight*

Lolita's 1326 Davie St (at Jervis)
604/696-9996 *4:30pm till late, wknd brunch, innovative Mexican, worth the wait*

British Columbia • CANADA

Maenam 1938 W 4th Ave 604/730-5579 *lunch Tue-Sat, dinner 5pm-midnight, Thai*

Martini's Whole Wheat Pizza 151 W Broadway (btwn Cambie & Main) 604/873-0021 *11am-2am, from 2pm Sat, till 1am Sun, great pizza & full bar*

Miura Waffle Milk Bar 829 Davie St 604/687-2909 *9am-7pm, from 10am Sat, clsd Sun*

Naam [E,WC] 2724 W 4th St (at MacDonald) 604/738-7151 *24hrs, vegetarian*

Score [MW,NH] 1262 Davie St (at Jervis St) 604/632-1646 *10am-late, sports bar*

Seasons in the Park Cambie St & W 33rd Ave 604/874-8008 *from 11:30am, 10:30am Sun*

Tanpopo Sushi 1122 Denman (at Pendrell) 604/681-7777 *lunch & dinner, excellent, affordable sushi*

■ ENTERTAINMENT & RECREATION

Capilano Suspension Bridge 3735 Capilano Rd, N Vancouver 604/985-7474

Cruisey T [MW,D,F,E,$] leaves from N foot of Denman St (at Harbor Cruises) 604/551-2628 *Sun (seasonal), 4-hour party cruise around Vancouver Harbour*

Rockwood Adventures 6578 Acom Rd, Sechelt 604/741-0802, 888/236-6606 *rain forest walks & city tours for all levels w/ free hotel pickup*

Sunset Beach Beach Ave, right in the West End (near Burrard St Bridge) *home of Vancouver AIDS memorial*

Vancouver Nature Adventures [$] 1251 Cardero St #2005 604/684-4922, 800/528-3531 *orca-watching safari, guided kayaking day trip & beach BBQ*

Wreck Beach below UBC

■ BOOKSTORES

Little Sister's [★WC] 1238 Davie St (btwn Bute & Jervis) 604/669-1753, 800/567-1662 (in Canada only) *10am-11pm, LGBT*

People's Co-op Bookstore 1391 Commercial Dr (btwn Kitchener & Charles) 604/253-6442, 888/511-5556 *LGBT section*

■ RETAIL SHOPS

Cupcakes 1116 Denman St (at Pendrell) 604/974-1300 *10am-9pm, till 10pm Fri-Sat; also at 2887 W Broadway*

Liquid Amber Tattoo 62 Powell St (at Columbia) 604/738-3667

Mintage 1714 Commercial Dr 604/646-8243 *vintage & future fashions*

Next Body Piercing 1068 Granville St (at Nelson) 604/684-6398 *noon-6pm, 11am-7pm Fri-Sat, also tattooing*

Priape 1148 Davie St (btwn Bute & Thurlow) 604/630-2330 *clubwear, leather, books, toys & more*

Top Drawers 1030 Denman St (at Comox) 604/684-4861 *men's underwear & swimwear*

■ PUBLICATIONS

Xtra! West 604/684-9696 *LGBT newspaper*

■ GYMS & HEALTH CLUBS

Fitness World 1214 Howe St (at Davie) 604/681-3232 *day passes*

Spartacus Gym 1522 Commercial Dr 604/254-6267

■ MEN'S CLUBS

Fahrenheit 212° [PC,WI] 1048 Davie St (at Burrard) 604/689-9719 *24hrs*

Steamworks 123 W Pender St (at Beatty St) 604/974-0602 *24hrs*

■ EROTICA

Love's Touch 1069 Davie St 604/681-7024

Tom's Video 2887 Grandview Hwy (at Renfew) 604/433-1722 *24hrs*

■ CRUISY AREAS

Central Park [AYOR] S side of the Boundary & Kingsway intersection *on the Vancouver/ Burnaby border*

Harbor Quay Promenade [AYOR] Port Alberni

Richmond Nature Park [AYOR] Richmond

Stanley Park [AYOR] Lee's Trail

Wreck Beach [AYOR] below UBC

Victoria

■ACCOMMODATIONS

Albion Manor B&B [GS,NS,WI,WC,GO] 224 Superior St 250/389-0012, 877/389-0012 *full brkfst*

Ambrosia Historic B&B [GS,NS] 522 Quadra (at Humboldt) 250/380-7705, 877/262-7672 *3 blocks from Victoria's inner harbor*

Inn at Laurel Point [GF,F,SW,WI,WC] 680 Montreal St (at Quebec St) 250/386-8721, 800/663-7667

Oak Bay Guest House [GF,NS] 1052 Newport Ave 250/598-3812, 800/575-3812 *1912 Tudor-style house, full brkfst, near beaches*

■BARS

The Castle [M,D,K] 1900 Douglas St 250/384-6969 *2pm-2am, till midnight Sun-Tue*

The Ledge [M,F] 1140 Government St (at Bedford Regency Hotel) 250/384-6835

Paparazzi [MW,D,K,DS,V,WC] 642 Johnson St (enter on Broad St) 250/388-0505 *1pm-2am, till midnight Sun*

■NIGHTCLUBS

Hush [GS,D] 1325 Government St (in basement) 250/385-0566 *9pm-2am, clsd Sun-Tue, more gay wknds*

■RESTAURANTS

Rosie's Diner [WC,GO] 253 Cook St 250/384-6090 *8am-9pm, '50s & '60s music & videos*

Santiago's Cafe [GO] 660 Oswego St 250/388-7376 *11am-9pm, tapas bar, patio*

■ENTERTAINMENT & RECREATION

Butchart Gardens [GF] 800 Benvenuto Ave, Brentwood Bay 250/652-5256, 866/652-4422

■BOOKSTORES

Bolen Books 1644 Hillside Ave #111 (in shopping center) 250/595-4232 *8:30am-10pm, LGBT section*

■RETAIL SHOPS

Oceanside Gifts [WC] 812 Wharf St, Ste 102 (across from Empress Hotel on the lower causeway) 250/380-1777 *10am-10pm, gifts from across Canada*

Out of the Closet 1736 Douglas St 250/590-2719 *high quality thrift store operated by Out of the Closet Queer Sustainability Society*

■MEN'S CLUBS

Steamworks [MO,V] 582 Johnson St (at Gov't St, look for red alley) 250/383-6623 *6pm-2am, till 8am wknds*

■CRUISY AREAS

Albert Head Beach [AYOR] Colwood

Beacon Hill Park [AYOR] Dallas Rd, near totem pole

Island View Beach [AYOR] Saanichton

Saxe Point Park [AYOR] take Esquimalt Rd to Fraser St, Esquimalt

Thetis Lake Park [AYOR] Highland Rd exit, toward Duncan (off Hwy 1) *look for parked cars & pathway to "Blowjob Hill"*

Whistler

■ACCOMMODATIONS

Best Western Listel Whistler Hotel [GF,SW,NS,WI,WC] 4121 Village Green (at Whistler Way) 604/932-1133, 800/663-5472 *hotel w/ pool, sauna & outdoor hot tub*

Coast Blackcomb Suites at Whistler [GF,SW,NS,WC] 4899 Painted Cliff Rd 604/905-3400, 800/716-6199 *bar & restaurant*

Four Seasons Resort Whistler [GF,SW,NS,WC] 4591 Blackcomb Wy 604/935-3400, 800/268-6282 *luxury resort & spa*

British Columbia • CANADA

Westin Whistler [GF,SW,NS,WI,WC]
4090 Whistler Wy **604/905-5000,
800/937-8461** *full-service resort
hotel, full bar & restaurant*

■RESTAURANTS

Araxi 4222 Village Square
604/932-4540 *lunch & dinner, local
ingredients, also seafood bar & lounge*

The Bearfoot Bistro [R] 4121 Village
Green **604/932-3433** *6pm-midnight,
excellent wine cellar*

La Rua 4557 Blackcomb Blvd
604/932-5011 *6pm-close, clsd Tue*

Quattro 4319 Main St **604/905-4844**
dinner nightly, Italian

Sachi Sushi 106-4359 Main St
604/935-5649 *lunch & dinner*

Southside Diner 2102 Lake Placid Rd
(off Hwy 99) **604/966-0668** *7am-
midnight, hosts occasional Gay Social*

Trattoria di Umberto [R] 4417 Sundial
Pl **604/932-5858** *lunch & dinner*

■ENTERTAINMENT & RECREATION

Ziptrek Ecotours PO Box 734 V0N 1B0
604/935-0001, 866/935-0001
*ziplines crisscross the Fitzsimmons Creek
btwn Whistler & Blackcomb*

■EROTICA

The Love Nest #102-4338 Main St
604/932-6906

■CRUISY AREAS

Lost Lake *from the parking lot, walk 1
km counter-clockwise around the lake to
Dick Dock*

White Rock

■CRUISY AREAS

Marine Dr/ White Rock Beach [AYOR]
walk E toward Crescent Beach

MANITOBA

Winnipeg

■INFO LINES & SERVICES

Rainbow Resource Centre 170 Scott
St (at Wardlaw) **204/474-0212,
204/284-5208** *call for hrs, clsd wknds,
also info line, many social/ support
groups*

■BARS

Club 200 [MW,K,DS,S,WC] 190 Garry St
(at St Mary Ave) **204/943-6045** *4pm-
2am, 6pm-midnight Sun*

Fame [MW,D] 279 Garry St
204/414-9433

■NIGHTCLUBS

Gio's Club & Bar [MW,D,E,DS,PC] 155
Smith St (at York Ave) **204/786-1236**
*4pm-11pm, till 2am Wed, Fri-Sat, till
midnight Sun, screened patio*

■RESTAURANTS

Buccacino's Cucina Italiana [E] 155
Osborne St **204/452-8251** *11am-
10pm, till 11pm Fri-Sat, from 10am Sun,
full bar, patio*

Step'N Out [WC] 157 Provencher Blvd
204/956-7837 *5pm-9pm, clsd Sun-
Mon*

■BOOKSTORES

McNally Robinson [WC] 1120 Grant
Ave #4000 (in the mall)
204/475-0483, 800/561-1833
*9am-10pm, till 11pm Fri-Sat, noon-6pm
Sun*

■PUBLICATIONS

Outwords **204/942-4599** *LGBT newspaper*

■MEN'S CLUBS

Adonis Spa [MO] 1060 Main St (at
Burrows) **204/589-6133** *24hrs*

■EROTICA

Dominion News 262 Portage Ave
(btwn Garry & Smith) **204/942-6563**
*8am-7pm, till 9pm Fri-Sat Sat, noon-
5pm Sun*

Love Nest 172 St Anne's Rd
204/254-0422 *also 1341 Main St,
204/589-4141; also Portage &
Westwood, 204/837-6475*

CRUISY AREAS

Assiniboine Ave [AYOR] parking lot (btwn Main & Smith Sts) *nights by car*

Assiniboine Park [AYOR] parking lot of central picnic area (1/4 km W of pavilion) *weekday afternoons*

Bonnycastle Park [AYOR]

Osborne St Village [AYOR]

NEW BRUNSWICK

Fredericton

NIGHTCLUBS

boom! [MW,D,K] 474 Queen St 506/463-2666 *8pm-2am, 4pm-7pm Sun, clsd Mon-Wed*

RESTAURANTS

Molly's Cafe 554 Queen St 506/457-9305 *9am-10pm, noon-midnight Fri-Sun, full bar, garden patio*

EROTICA

Pleasures N' Treasures 558 Queen St 506/458-2048 *11am-10pm, till 11pm Th-Sat*

CRUISY AREAS

The Green [AYOR]

Moncton

ACCOMMODATIONS

Auberge Au Bois Dormant Inn [GF,NS,WI,GO] 67 rue John (at Birch) 506/855-6767, 866/855-6767 *affordable luxury inn, full brkfst*

NIGHTCLUBS

Triangles [MW,NH,D,K] 234 St George St (at Archibald) 506/857-8779 *8pm-2am*

RESTAURANTS

Calactus Cafe 125 Church St (at St George) 506/388-4833 *11am-10pm, vegetarian*

EROTICA

X-Citement 651 Mountain Rd 506/388-2226

CRUISY AREAS

The Block [AYOR] Main St (btwn Highland & Fleet Sts)

Champlaine Place [AYOR]

St John

ACCOMMODATIONS

Mahogany Manor [GS,NS,WC,GO] 220 Germain St 506/636-8000, 800/796-7755 *full brkfst*

NIGHTCLUBS

Happinez Wine Bar [GF] 42 Princess St 506/634-7340 *4pm-midnight, till 2am Fri-Sat*

RESTAURANTS

Opera Bistro 60 Prince William St 506/642-2822 *lunch & dinner*

CRUISY AREAS

Rockwood Park [AYOR] at beach & on trails

NOVA SCOTIA

Annapolis Royal

ACCOMMODATIONS

Bailey House B&B [GF,WI] 150 St George St (at Drury Ln) 902/532-1285, 877/532-1285

King George Inn [MW,NS,WI,GO] 902/532-5286, 888/799-5464 *full brkfst*

Digby

ACCOMMODATIONS

Harbourview Inn [GF,SW,NS,WI,WC,GO] 25 Harbourview Rd (at Hwy 1), Smith's Cove 902/245-5686, 877/449-0705 *century-old country inn*

Seawinds Motel [GF,NS] 90 Montague Row 902/245-2573

Halifax

ACCOMMODATIONS

Fresh Start B&B [GF,NS,WI] 2720 Gottingen St (at Black) 902/453-6616, 888/453-6616 *Victorian mansion, women-owned*

BARS

Menz Bar & Mollyz Back Bar [MW,NH,DS,K,P] 2182 Gottingen St, Level 2 902/446-6969 *3pm-2am*

Reflections Cabaret [MW,D,E,C,DS,WC]
5184 Sackville St (at Barrington)
902/422-2957 *10pm-4am, clsd Tue*

CAFES

Coburg Coffee House [WI] 6085
Coburg Rd **902/429-2326** *7am-9pm*

The Daily Grind [F,WI] 5686 Spring
Garden Rd (near South Park)
902/429-6397 *8am-6pm, noon-5pm
Sun, also newsstand*

The Second Cup [F,WI] 5425 Spring
Garden Rd **902/429-0883** *7am-11pm,
till midnight Th-Sat, internet access*

Uncommon Grounds [WI] 1030 S Park
St **902/404-3124** *7am-10pm*

RESTAURANTS

Chez Tess Creperie [GO] 5687 Charles
St **902/406-3133** *lunch & dinner,
wknd brunch, clsd Mon*

Chives Canadian Bistro 1537
Barrington St **902/420-9626** *5pm-
9:30pm*

Heartwood 6250 Quinpool Rd
902/425-2808 *11am-9pm, 10am-
3pm Sun, vegetarian*

Jane's on the Common 2394 Robie St
902/431-5683 *lunch Tue-Sat, dinner
nightly, Sun brunch, clsd Mon*

ENTERTAINMENT &
RECREATION

The Khyber 1588 Barrington St
902/422-9668 *visual & performing
arts center*

BOOKSTORES

Atlantic News 5560 Morris St (at
Queen) **902/429-5468** *8am-10pm,
from 9am Sun*

Trident Booksellers & Cafe [WI] 1256
Hollis St (at Morris St) **902/423-7100**
*8am-5:30pm, 10am-5pm Sun, used,
popular cafe*

RETAIL SHOPS

Venus Envy 1598 Barrington St
902/422-0004, 877/370-9288

PUBLICATIONS

Wayves PO Box 34090 Scotia Square
B3J 3S1 **902/889-2229** *monthly
magazine "for the rainbow community
of Atlantic Canada"*

MEN'S CLUBS

SeaDog's Sauna & Spa
[MO,V,18+,PC,GO] 2199 Gottingen St (at
Cunard St) **902/444-3647,
888/837-1388** *24hrs wknds, steam,
darkroom, internet access*

EROTICA

Night Magic Fashions 5268 Sackville
St **902/420-9309** *clsd Sun*

X-Citement 6260 Quinpool Rd
902/492-0026

CRUISY AREAS

Citadel Hill [AYOR] *evenings*

Crystal Crescent Beach [N,AYOR] 45
minutes from Halifax *for nude beach,
head S from parking lot; 20-minute walk*

Scotsburn

ACCOMMODATIONS

The Mermaid & the Cow [MW,SW,GO]
West Branch **902/351-2714** *cabin &
campsites*

Tangier

ACCOMMODATIONS

Spry Bay Campground & Cabins
[GS,GO] 19867 Highway #7
902/772-2554, 866/229-8014 *also
restaurant & convenience store*

For more resources and the latest updates

DAMRON
Online
www.damron.com
the first name and the last word in gay travel guides

ONTARIO

Belleville

■CRUISY AREAS
Zwick's Park [AYOR]

Brighton

■BOOKSTORES
Lighthouse Books 65 Main St
613/475-1269 *9:30am-5:30pm, clsd
Sun-Mon*

Grand Valley

■ACCOMMODATIONS
Rainbow Ridge Resort [MW,F,SW,GO]
Country Rd 109 (at Hwy 25 S)
519/928-3262 *trailers & tents, located
on 72 acres on Grand River, restaurant,
dance hall, day visitors welcome,
seasonal*

Hamilton

■ACCOMMODATIONS
Cedars Campground [MW,D,SW,GO]
1039 5th Concession W Rd, Millgrove
905/659-3655, 905/659-7342
*private campground, also bar, restaurant
wknds*

■BARS
The Embassy Club [MW,D,TG,K,DS,V] 54
King St E (at Houston) 905/522-1100
noon-3am, nightclub from 10pm wknds

■MEN'S CLUBS
Central Spa [GO] 401 Main St W (at
Poulette) 905/523-7636 *10am-
midnight*

Karel's Steambaths [PC] 12 Holton
Ave N (at King St) 905/549-9666

■EROTICA
Stag Shop 58 Centennial Pkwy N
905/573-4242 *also 980 Upper James
St, 905/385-3300*

■CRUISY AREAS
Jackson St [AYOR] from Catherine to
City Hall

Kingston

■CRUISY AREAS
Little Cataraqui Conservation Area
[AYOR] King St W

MacDonald Park [AYOR]

Kitchener

■NIGHTCLUBS
Club Renaissance [MW,D,F,DS] 24
Charles St W 519/570-2406,
877/635-2352 *9pm-3am, clsd Sun-
Tue, also billiards lounge*

■EROTICA
Stag Shop 10 Manitou Dr
519/895-1228

London

■ACCOMMODATIONS
Hilton Hotel [GF,SW,WI,WC] 300 King St
800/210-9336

■BARS
Buck Wild Bar [M,D,DS,K,GO] 722 York
St (at Central Spa) 519/438-2625
8pm-close Th-Sat

■NIGHTCLUBS
Club Lavish [GS,D,K] 238 Dundas St
519/667-1222 *9pm-2am, clsd Sun-
Wed*

■RESTAURANTS
Blackfriars Bistro [★] 46 Blackfriars
(2 blocks S of Oxford) 519/667-4930
lunch & dinner, Sun brunch, full bar

■MEN'S CLUBS
Central Spa [F] 722 York St (at rear,
Complex 722) 519/438-2625 *10am-
2am, 24hrs Fri-Sat, also bar*

■EROTICA
Stag Shop 1548 Dundas St E
519/453-7676 *also 371 Wellington Rd
S, 519/668-3334*

Niagara Falls

■ACCOMMODATIONS
Absolute Elegance B&B [GS,NS,GO]
6023 Culp St (at Main & Ferry)
905/353-8522, 877/353-8522

Angels Hideaway [GS,NS] 4360 Simcoe
St (at River Rd) 905/354-1119

Britaly B&B [GF,WI,GO] 57 The Promenade (at Charlotte & John), Niagara-on-the-Lake **905/468-8778**

■CRUISY AREAS
Clifton Hill [AYOR]

Oshawa

■NIGHTCLUBS
Club 717 [MW,D,DS,K,WI] 717 Wilson Rd S #7 **905/434-4297** 7pm-midnight, 9pm-2am Fri-Sat, clsd Mon-Wed

■EROTICA
Forbidden Pleasures 1268 Simcoe St N **905/728-0834**

Ottawa

■INFO LINES & SERVICES
Pink Triangle Services 251 Bank St #301 **613/563-4818** many groups & services, library, call for times

■ACCOMMODATIONS
Ambiance B&B [GS,NS,WI,GO] 330 Nepean St **613/563-0421, 888/366-8772**

Brookstreet [GF,SW] 525 Legget Dr **613/271-1800, 888/826-2220**

Inn on Somerset [GS,NS,WI,GO] 282 Somerset St W (at Elgin) **613/236-9309, 800/658-3564**

Lord Elgin Hotel [GF,SW] 100 Elgin St **613/235-3333, 800/267-4298**

Rideau Inn [GS,NS,GO] 177 Frank St **613/688-2753, 877/580-5015**

■BARS
Centretown Pub [MW,D,V] 340 Somerset St W (at Bank) **613/594-0233** 2pm-2am; also Cell Block [L] & Silhouette Lounge [P] wknds

The Lookout [MW,F,WC,GO] 41 York, 2nd flr (in Byward Market) **613/789-1624** 2pm-2am, from noon wknds, men's night Th

Swizzles [MW,D,K,WI] 246 Queen St **613/232-4200** 11am-2am, from 7pm wknds, noon-10pm Tue, clsd Mon

■NIGHTCLUBS
Lotus Lounge [GS,D] 129 Bank St **613/216-9661** 10pm-2am Fri, till 7am Sat

Mercury Lounge [GS,D,E,F,WI] 56 Byward Market Sq (side door upstairs) **613/789-5324** 8pm-3am, clsd Sun-Tue, popular Wed Hump night party

Zaphod Beeblebrox [GS,NH,D,S] 27 York **613/562-1010** 4pm-2am, live music

■CAFES
Bridgehead Coffee [WI,GO] 366 Bank St (at Gilmour) **613/569-5600** 7am-9pm

Raw Sugar Cafe [E] 692 Somerset W **613/216-2850** vegan & gluten-free options

■RESTAURANTS
Ahora Mexican Cuisine [GO] 307 Dalhousie St (below Sweet Art) **613/562-2081** noon-10pm

The Buzz 374 Bank St **613/565-9595** dinner nightly, Sun brunch, also bar

Johnny Farina [WC] 216 Elgin St **613/565-5155** Italian

Kinki [DJ,E] 41 York St **613/789-7559** lunch & dinner, Asian fusion, full bar

La Dolce Vita 180 Preston Street **613/233-6239** gluten-free menu available

Shanghai Restaurant [K] 651 Somerset St W (at Bronson Ave) **613/233-4001** lunch Tue-Fri, dinner nightly, clsd Mon, also bar, DJ

■BOOKSTORES
Mags & Fags 254 Elgin St (btwn Somerset & Cooper) **613/233-9651** gay magazines

■RETAIL SHOPS
Venus Envy 320 Lisgar St (at Bank St) **613/789-4646**

■PUBLICATIONS
Capital Xtra! 416/925-6665 LGBT newspaper

■MEN'S CLUBS
Central Spa [PC] 1069 Wellington St **613/722-8978**

Steamworks 487 Lewis (at Bank St) **613/230-8431** 24hrs

◼EROTICA

One in Ten 256 Bank St (2nd Fl)
613/563-0110 *noon-10pm. clsd Sun*

Wicked Wanda's 382 Bank St
613/820-6032

Wilde's [WC] 367 Bank St (at Gilmour)
613/234-5512 *11am-7:30pm, till 9pm
Fri, noon-5pm Sun*

◼CRUISY AREAS

Elgin St [AYOR]

Remic Rapids Lookout [AYOR] *parking
spot along Ottawa river*

St Catharines

◼BARS

Envy [MW,D,GO] 127 Queenston St
905/682-7774 *theme nights*

Stratford

◼RESTAURANTS

Down the Street [★] 30 Ontario St
519/273-5886 *11am-midnight, clsd
Mon, bar till 1am*

Rundles [GO,WC] 9 Cobourg St
519/271-6442 *dinner Tue-Sun, lunch
wknds*

◼CRUISY AREAS

Shakespeare Memorial Gardens
[AYOR]

Toronto

◼INFO LINES & SERVICES

519 Church St Community Centre
[WC] 519 Church St (on Cawthra Park)
416/392-6874 *9am-10pm, till 5pm
wknds, LGBT info center & cafe*

AA Gay/ Lesbian 416/487-5591

Canadian Lesbian/ Gay Archives 34
Isabella **416/777-2755** *7:30pm-10pm
Tue-Th by appt*

◼ACCOMMODATIONS

**213 Carlton—Toronto Townhouse
B&B** [GS,NS,WI,GO] **416/323-8898,
877/500-0466**

312 Seaton [GS,NS,GO] 312 Seaton (at
Gerrard) **416/968-0775,
866/968-0775** *B&B, also rental apt,
dog on premises*

Bonnevue Manor B&B [GS,NS,WI] 33
Beaty Ave (at Queen St & Roncesvalles)
416/536-1455

Drake Hotel [GF,NS] 1150 Queen St W
(at Beaconsfield) **416/531-5042,
866/372-5386**

Dundonald House [M,NS,WI,GO] 35
Dundonald St (at Church)
416/961-9888, 800/260-7227

The Gladstone Hotel [★GS,NS,WI]
1214 Queen St W (at Gladstone Ave)
416/531-4635

Hazelton Hotel [GF,NS,WI] 118 Yorkville
Ave (at Avenue Rd) **416/963-6300,
866/473-6301**

Hotel Le Germain [GF,WI,WC] 30
Mercer St (at Peter St) **416/345-9500,
866/345-9501**

◼BARS

Andy Poolhall [GS,D] 489 College St (at
Markham) **416/923-5300** *7pm-2am,
clsd Sun-Mon*

Beaver Cafe [MW,D,F,GO] 1192 Queen
St W (at Northcote Ave)
416/537-2768 *11am-2am, patio*

Bistro 422 [GS,F] 422 College St (at
Bathurst St) **416/963-9416** *5pm-
2am, dive bar*

The Black Eagle [M,B,L,F] 457 Church
St (btwn Maitland & Alexander)
416/413-1219 *3pm-2am, heated
rooftop patio*

Boutique Bar [MW] 506 Church St
647/705-0006 *2:30pm-2am, patio*

The Cameron House [GS,E] 408 Queen
St W (at Cameron St) **416/703-0811**
4pm-close, also theater

The Churchmouse & Firkin [MW,NH]
475 Church St (at Maitland)
416/927-1735 *11am-2am, English
pub, leather brunch 3rd Sun*

Dakota Tavern [GF,CW,F] 249
Ossington Ave (at Dundas)
416/850-4579 *6pm-2am, bluegrass
brunch Sun*

Flash [MO,S,PC] 463 Church St *5pm-
2am*

The Hair of the Dog [GS,NH,F] 425
Church St (at Wood) **416/964-2708**
11am-2am, patio

Ontario • CANADA

The House on Parliament Pub
[GS,NH,F] 456 Parliament St (at Carlton)
416/925-4074 *11:30am-2am, patio*

LeVack Block [GS,D,F] 88 Ossington
Ave (at Humbert) **416/916-0571**
5pm-close, from 11am wknds, clsd Mon

Melody Bar [GS,E,K] 1214 Queen St W
(at Gladstone Hotel) **416/531-4635**
clsd Mon, more gay Wed

O'Grady's [GS,F] 518 Church St (at
Maitland) **416/323-2822** *11am-2am,
till 3am Fri-Sat, huge patio, bear night
Fri*

Pegasus [MW,NH] 489-B Church St (at
Wellesley, upstairs) **416/927-8832**
11am-2am

Pic Nic [GF,F] 747 Queen St E
647/435-5298 *wine bar*

The Raq [GS,D] 739 Queen St W, 2nd flr
(at Palmerston) **416/504-9120** *5pm-
1am, from 4pm Th-Sun, clsd Mon*

Remington's Men of Steel
[M,S,WC,GO] 379 Yonge St (at Gerrard)
416/977-2160 *5pm-2am, strip bar*

Slack's Restaurant & Bar
[★W,NH,D,F,E] 562 Church St (at
Wellesley) **416/928-2151** *4pm-2am,
clsd Mon*

Smiling Buddha [GS,C,YC] 961 College
St (at Dovercourt) **416/516-2531**
7:30pm-2am

Sneaky Dee's [GF,F,E] 431 College St (at
Bathurst) **416/603-3090** *11am-3am,
from 9am Sun*

Woody's/ Sailor
[★M,NH,E,DS,V,18+,WC] 465-467 Church
(at Maitland) **416/972-0887** *1pm-
2am*

The Zipperz/Cellblock [M,D,C,DS] 72
Carlton St (at Cross St) **416/921-0066**
*noon-2am, Cellblock 10pm-2am Wed-
Sun*

■NIGHTCLUBS

The Annex Wreck Room [GS,D,A,E]
794 Bathurst St (at Bloor)
416/536-0346 *10pm-close, bands*

AsianXpress (AX) [M,D,MR-A] *bi-
monthly, check out www.aznxp.com*

The Barn [M,D] 418 Church St (at
Carlton) **416/593-9696** *theme nights*

Big Primpin' [MW,D] 1279 Queen St W
(at Wrongbar) *10pm 1st Fri, monthly
hip-hop, dancehall, R&B club, check
local listings*

The Comfort Zone [GS,D] 480 Spadina
Ave (N of College) **416/763-9139**
after-hours wknds only

El Convento Rico [★GS,D,MR-L,TG,DS]
750 College St (at Crawford)
416/588-7800 *9pm-4am, clsd Mon-
Th*

Fly Nightclub [★M,D,$] 8 Gloucester St
(2 streets N of Yonge & Wellesley)
416/410-5426, 416/925-6222 *open
Fri-Sat only*

Goodhandy's [M,TG,S] 120 Church St,
2nd flr (at Richmond) *10pm-close, clsd
Sun-Mon, trans-themed club*

Guvernment [GF,D] 132 Queens Quay E
(at Lower Jarvis) **416/869-0045** *visiting big-name DJs*

Lee's Palace/ Dance Cave [GS,D,E] 529
Bloor St (at Albany) **416/532-1598**
dance cave Mon, Th-Sat

The Mod Club [GS,D] 722 College (at
Crawford) **416/588-4663** *10pm Fri-
Sat*

Pink Mafia *alternative queer &
straight events in hip locations, check
www.pinkmafia.ca*

Tattoo Rock Parlour [GS,D,E] 567
Queen St W (at Denison)
416/703-5488 *10am-3am Fri-Sun*

Wrongbar [GS,D] 1279 Queen St W (at
Brock) **415/516-8677** *Big Primpin 1st
Fri, check listing for other queer events*

■CAFES

Alternative Grounds 333 Roncesvalles
Ave **416/534-5543** *7am-7pm*

JetFuel [WI] 519 Parliament St
416/968-9982 *7am-8pm*

Timothy's [★WI] 500 Church St (at
Alexander) **416/925-8550** *7am-
midnight, till 3:30am wknds, cruisy steps
in summer*

■RESTAURANTS

Black Hoof 938 Dundas St W
416/551-8854 *6pm-midnight, clsd
Tue-Wed, charcuterie & cheese, not for
vegetarians!*

Byzantium [M,D,GO] 499 Church St (S of Wellesley) **416/922-3859** 5:30pm-11pm, Sun brunch 11am-3pm

C'est What Brew/Vin Pub [E] 67 Front St E (at Church) **416/867-9499**

Cafe 668 885 Dundas St W **416/703-0668** lunch & dinner, vegetarian

Cafe Diplomatico [★] 594 College (at Clinton, in Little Italy) **416/534-4637** 8am-2am, clsd Mon, Italian

Commensal 655 Bay St (enter on Elm St) **416/596-9364** brkfst, lunch & dinner, vegetarian

Corner Cafe [GF,NS] 1150 Queen St W (at Drake Hotel) **416/531-5042** 8am-11pm, till midnight wknds, popular brkfst spot

Easy Restaurant 1645 Queen St W **416/537-4893** 9am-5pm

Flo's Diner [GO] 70 Yorkville Ave (near Bay St) **416/961-4333** 7:30am-8pm, till 10pm Th-Sat, from 8am wknds

Fresh 147 Spadina (at Queen St W) **416/599-4442** lunch & dinner, vegetarian, patio; also at 894 Queen St W & 336 Bloor St W

Fressen 478 Queen St W (at Denison) **416/504-5127** dinner nightly, wknd brunch, upscale vegan

Golden Thai 105 Church St (at Richmond) **416/868-6668** 11:30am-9pm, from 5pm wknds

Il Fornello 1560 Yonge Street **416/920-7347** lunch Mon-Fri, dinner nightly, Sun brunch, Italian; also 214 King W **416/977-2855** & 576 Danforth Ave

Joy Bistro 884 Queen St E **416/465-8855** noon-1am

Kalendar 546 College St **416/923-4138** 10:30am-1am, patio

La Hacienda 640 Queen St W (near Bathurst) **416/703-3377** noon-1am, from 11am wknds

Mitzi's Sister [★E,GO] 1554 Queen St W **416/532-2570** 4pm-2am, popular wknd brunch from 10am

Nota Bene 180 Queen St W **416/977-6400** lunch Mon-Fri, dinner nightly, clsd Sun, Mediterranean

Saving Grace 907 Dundas St W (at Bellwoods) **416/703-7368** brkfst & lunch

Smith 553 Church St (at Dundonald) **416/926-2501**

Supermarket 268 Augusta Ave (at College) **416/840-0501** lunch Fri-Sun, dinner nightly, Asian, also bar w/ DJs

Urban Herbivore 64 Oxford St (at Augusta) **416/927-1231** 9am-7pm, vegetarian/vegan

Wine Bar 9 Church St **416/504-9463** noon-11pm, tapas

■ENTERTAINMENT & RECREATION

AIDS Memorial in Cawthra Square Park

The Bata Shoe Museum 327 Bloor St W **416/979-7799** 10,000 shoes from over 4,500 years—including the platforms of Elton John & the pumps of Marilyn Monroe

Buddies in Bad Times Theatre 12 Alexander St (at Yonge) **416/975-8555** LGBT theater; also Tallulah's cabaret

■BOOKSTORES

Glad Day Bookshop [★] 598-A Yonge St (at Wellesley) **416/961-4161, 877/783-3725** 10am-7pm, till 9pm Th-Sat, noon-6pm Sun, LGBT

■RETAIL SHOPS

Flatirons 469 Church St (at Alexander) **416/968-9274** wonderful kitsch & gay gifts

Out on the Street 551 Church St **416/967-2759, 800/263-5747** 10am-8pm, 11am-7pm Sun

Take a Walk on the Wild Side 161 Gerrard St E (at Jarvis) **416/921-6112, 800/260-0102** "hotel, boutique & club for crossdressers, transvestites, transexuals & other persons of gender"

■PUBLICATIONS

Xtra! **416/925-6665, 800/268-9872** LGBT newspaper

Ontario • CANADA

■MEN'S CLUBS

Central Spa 1610 Dundas St W (at Brock) 416/588-6191 *10am-midnight*

Spa Excess [★] 105 Carlton St (at Jarvis) 416/260-2363, 877/867-3301 *24hrs*

Steamworks [WI] 540 Church (at Wellesley, level 2) 416/925-1571 *24hrs*

■EROTICA

Come As You Are 701 Queen St W (at Bathurst) 416/504-7934 *co-op-owned sex store*

North Bound Leather [WC] 586 Yonge (W of Wellesley St) 416/972-1037 *toys & clothing*

Priape [★] 501 Church St 416/586-9914, 800/461-6969 *10am-9pm, till 10pm Fri-Sat, from noon Sun*

Seduction 577 Yonge St 416/966-6969

Stag Shop 239 Yonge St 416/368-3507 *also 449 Church St, 416/323-0772*

■CRUISY AREAS

Balfour Park [AYOR]

Cawthra Park [AYOR] Church St *summer sunbathing*

Hanlan's Pt Beach [AYOR] Toronto Islands *summers*

High Park [AYOR]

Yonge Street Walkway [★AYOR]

Turkey Point

■ACCOMMODATIONS

The Point Tent & Trailer Resort [MO,L,SW,N,GO] 906 Charlotteville Rd #2, RR 1, Vittoria 519/426-7275 *on 50 acres*

Waterloo

■ACCOMMODATIONS

Colonial Creekside [GS,SW,WI,GO] 485 Bridge St W (at Lexington) 519/886-2726

■RESTAURANTS

Ethel's Lounge 114 King St N (at Spring) 519/725-2361 *11:30am-2am, full bar, patio*

■EROTICA

Stag Shop 7 King St N 519/886-4500

Windsor

■ACCOMMODATIONS

Windsor Inn on the River [GF,NS,WI] 3857 Riverside Dr E (at George Ave) 519/945-2110, 866/635-0055 *full brkfst*

■BARS

Phog [GF,F,E] 157 University Ave W (at Church St) 519/253-1605 *5pm-2am, from 8pm Sun-Mon, art & events*

Vermouth [GF] 333 Ouellette 519/977-6102 *5pm-2am, from 6pm Sat, clsd Sun-Mon, popular martini lounge*

■NIGHTCLUBS

Club 2012 [MW,D,DS,S] 1056 Wyandotte St E (at Langlois Ave) 519/791-0816 *7pm-2am, till 4am Sat, clsd Sun-Mon*

The Loop [GF,D,E,YC] 156 Chatham St W (at Ferry St) 519/253-3474 *10pm-2am, clsd Mon & Wed*

■CAFES

The Coffee Exchange [WI] 266 Ouellette 519/971-7424 *7am-11pm, 8am-midnight wknds*

■EROTICA

Stag Shop 2950 Dougall Ave 519/967-8798

■CRUISY AREAS

Jackson Park [AYOR] area at Ouelette Overpass

River Front Park [AYOR] at foot of Ouellette St *evenings*

PRINCE EDWARD ISLAND

Charlottetown

■INFO LINES & SERVICES

Abegweit Rainbow Collective 375 University Avenue #2 (at Eden St, in AIDS PEI office) **902/894-5776, 877/380-5776** *24-hr info line, drop-in hrs 6:30pm-7:30pm Mon, monthly dances & other social activities*

■ACCOMMODATIONS

Evening Primrose [GF,NS,WI,GO] 114 Lord's Pond Rd, Albany **902/437-3134** *full brkfst, seasonal*

The Great George [GF,NS,WI,WC,GO] 58 Great George **902/892-0606, 800/361-1118**

The Hotel on Pownal [GF,WI] 146 Pownal St **902/892-1217, 800/268-6261**

Shipwright Inn Heritage B&B [GF,NS,WI] 51 Fitzroy St **902/368-1905, 888/306-9966** *full brkfst*

■BARS

Baba's Lounge [GF,F,E] 81 University Ave **902/892-7377** *noon-2am, 5pm-midnight Sun; also Cedars Lebanese restaurant*

■ENTERTAINMENT & RECREATION

Blooming Point Blooming Point *nude beach*

■BOOKSTORES

Book Mark 172 Queen St (in mall) **902/566-4888** *9am-8pm, till 9pm Th-Fri, till 5:30pm Sat, clsd Sun*

Hermanville

■ACCOMMODATIONS

Johnson Shore Inn [GS,WC,GO] 9984 Rte 16 **902/687-1340, 877/510-9669** *full brkfst, seasonal*

York

■ACCOMMODATIONS

Little York B&B [GF,WI,GO] 775 Rte 25 **902/569-0271, 800/953-6755** *full brkfst*

Stanhope Beach Resort [GF,SW,WI,WC,GO] 3445 Bayshore Rd **902/672-2701, 866/672-2701** *also restaurant & bar*

PROVINCE OF QUÉBEC

Hull

■RESTAURANTS

Le Twist 88 Montcalm St, Gatineau **819/777-8886** *opens 11am daily, full bar*

■CRUISY AREAS

Meech Lake Beach [AYOR]

Laurentides (Laurentian Mtns)

■ACCOMMODATIONS

Havre du Parc Auberge [GS,F,GO] 2788 Rte 125 N, St-Donat **819/424-7686** *quiet lakeside inn for nature lovers, full brkfst*

Le Septentrion B&B [MW,SW,NS,WI,GO] 901 chemin St-Adolphe, Morin-Heights/ St-Sauveur **450/226-2665**

Magog

■ACCOMMODATIONS

Au Gîte du Cerf Argenté B&B [GS,NS,GO] 2984 chemin Georgeville Rd (off Hwy 10) **819/847-4264** *renovated century-old farmhouse*

Auberge aux Deux Pères [GF,SW,WI,GO] 680 chemin des Pères **819/769-3115, 514/616-3114**

Montréal

Note: M°=Metro station

■INFO LINES & SERVICES

AA Gay/ Lesbian 514/376-9230

Gay/ Lesbian Community Centre of Montréal 2075 rue Plessis #110 (at Ontario) **514/528-8424** *10am-5:30pm, 1pm-8pm Wed & Fri, clsd wknds*

Gay Line/ Gai Ecoute 514/866-5090 (English) *7pm-11pm*

Province of Québec • CANADA

The Village Tourism Information Center/ Gay Chamber of Commerce 1307 rue Ste-Catherine Est 514/522-1885, 888/595-8110 *10am-6pm, clsd wknds*

■ACCOMMODATIONS

Alexandre Logan [GF,WI] 1631 rue Alexandre DeSève (at Logan) 514/598-0555, 866/895-0555

Alexandrie Hostel [GF,F,NS,WI,GO] 1750 Amherst (at Robin) 514/525-9420

Auberge le Pomerol [GF,F,NS,WI] 819 boul de Maisonneuve E (at St-Christophe) 800/361-6896

➤**Aubergell B&B** [MO,F,NS,WI,GO] 1641 Amherst (at de Maisonneuve) 514/597-0878, 514/525-7744 *also full bar, rooftop terrace*

Aux Studios Montcalm—Guesthouse [M,WI,GO] 1303 rue Montcalm (at Ste-Catherine St) 514/815-6195

B&B L'Escogriffe [MO,WI,GO] 1264 rue Wolfe (at rue Ste-Catherine E) 877/523-6105

B&B Le Cartier [GS,NS,WI,GO] 1219 rue Cartier (at Ste-Catherine Est) 514/917-1829, 877/524-0495 *private studio*

B&B Le Terra Nostra [GF,NS,WI] 277 rue Beatty (at Lasalle) 514/762-1223, 866/550-5235

BBV (B&B du Village) [M,WI] 1279 rue Montcalm (at Ste-Catherine) 514/522-4771, 888/228-8455

Les Bons Matins [MW,NS,WI] 1401 Argyle Ave 514/931-9167, 800/588-5280

Le Chasseur B&B [GS,GO] 1567 rue St-André (at Maisonneuve) 514/521-2238, 800/451-2238 *Victorian row house, summer terrace*

➤**La Conciergerie Guest House** [★M,M,NS,WI,GO] 1019 rue St-Hubert (at Viger) 514/289-9297 *hot tub, gym & sundeck*

Le Gîte Nuzone B&B [M,N,WI,GO] 1729 rue St-Hubert (at Ontario) 514/524-5292

Hôtel Dorion [GS,WI] 1477 rue Dorion (at Maisonneuve) 514/523-2427, 877/523-5908

Hotel du Fort [GS,WC] 1390 rue du Fort (at Ste-Catherine) 514/938-8333, 800/565-6333

Hôtel Gouverneur Montréal Place Dupuis [GF,SW,WI] 1415 rue St-Hubert (at Maisonneuve) 888/910-1111

Hotel Lord Berri [GF,WC] 1199 rue Berri (at Ste-Catherine) 514/845-9236, 888/363-0363 *also Italian resto-bar*

Jade Blue B&B [GS,NS,WI] 1225 de Bullion St (at Ste-Catherine) 514/878-9843, 800/878-5048 *theme rooms, full brkfst*

L Hotel Montreal [GF,WI] 262 rue St-Jacques W (at St Nicolas) 514/985-0019, 877/553-0019 *also bar & lounge*

Loews Hotel Vogue [GF,WC] 1425 rue de la Montagne (near Ste-Catherine) 514/285-5555, 800/465-6654

La Loggia Art & Breakfast [GS,NS,WI,GO] 1637 rue Amherst (at Maisonneuve) 514/524-2493, 866/520-2493 *in Gay Village, sundeck*

▶**Sir Montcalm B&B** [M,NS,WI,GO] 1453 Montcalm (at Ste Catherine St) 514/522-7747

Le St-Christophe [MO,N,NS,WI,GO] 1597 rue St-Christophe (at Maisonneuve) 514/527-7836, 888/521-7836 *full brkfst*

Turquoise B&B [M,GO] 1576 rue Alexandre DeSève (at Maisonneuve) 514/523-9943, 877/707-1576 *shared baths*

■BARS

Bar Le Cocktail [MW,NH,K] 1669 Ste-Catherine Est (at Champlain) 514/597-0814 *11am-3am*

Bar Rocky [M,DS,OC] 1673 rue Ste-Catherine Est (at Papineau) 514/521-7865 *8am-3am*

Province of Québec • CANADA

Black Eagle Bar (Aigle Noir) [M,L,PC] 1315 Ste-Catherine Est (at Visitation) 514/529-0040 *8am-3am, theme nights*

Cabaret Mado [★MW,D,K,C,DS,WC] 1115 rue Ste-Catherine Est (at Amherst, below Le Campus) 514/525-7566 *11am-3am, theme nights, owned by the fabulous Mado!*

Le Campus [M,S] 1111 rue Ste-Catherine Est, 2nd flr (at Amherst) 514/526-3616 *3pm-3am, from 1pm wknds, nude dancers, ladies night Sun*

Citibar [GS,NH,E,TG] 1603 Ontario Est (at Champlain) 514/525-4251 *11am-3am*

Club Bolo [MW,D,CW,$] 2093 rue de la Visitation (at Association Sportive) 514/849-4777 *9:30pm-12:30am Fri, special events Sat, T-dance from 3:30pm Sun, also lessons*

Club Date Piano Bar [MW,NH,K,P,S] 1218 rue Ste-Catherine Est (at Beaudry) 514/521-1242 *8am-3am*

Le Drugstore [MW,D,K,F,E,S] 1366 rue Ste-Catherine Est (at Panët) 514/524-1960 *10am-3am*

Foufounes Electriques [GF,D,E] 87 Ste-Catherine Est (at St-Laurent) 514/844-5539 *4pm-3am, patio*

Fun Spot [MW,NH,D,TG,K,DS,WI] 1151 rue Ontario Est (at Wolfe) 514/522-0416 *11am-3am, poker machines*

Le Gotha Lounge [M,NH,E] 1641 Amherst (at Maisonneuve) 514/526-1270 *4pm-3am*

Katakombes [M,YC] 1450 rue Ste-Catherine Est *4pm-3am*

Normandie [MW,NH,K] 1295 Amherst (at Ste-Catherine) 514/522-2766 *10am-3am, terrace, popular happy hour*

La Relaxe [M,NH] 1309 rue Ste-Catherine Est, 2nd flr (at Visitation) 514/523-0578 *noon-3am, open to the street—as the name implies, a good place to relax & people-watch*

St-Sulpice [GS,K,WI] 1680 rue St-Denis (at Ontario) 514/844-9458 *11am-3am, till midnight Sun, terrace*

Le Stud [MO,D,F,B,L] 1812 rue Ste-Catherine Est (at Papineau) 514/598-8243 *10am-3am*

◼NIGHTCLUBS

Apollon [M,D] 1450 rue Ste-Catherine Est *10pm-3am clsd Mon-Wed*

Circus After Hours [GS,D] 915 rue Ste-Catherine Est 514/844-3626 *2am-8am Th & Sun, 1am-10pm Fri-Sat*

Cirque du Boudoir [GS,D,E] 514/789-9068 *opulent quarterly theme parties*

Complexe Sky [★MW,D,SW,L,F,C,DS,S] 1474 rue Ste-Catherine Est 514/529-6969, 514/529-8989 *noon-3am*

Faggity Ass Fridays [MW,D,E] 5656 Ave du Parc (at The Playhouse) *last Fri only, benefits Head & Hands sex ed organization*

Red Lite (After Hours) [★GF,D,$] 1755 rue de Lierre, Laval 450/967-3057 *Fri-Sun only 2am-10am*

Stéréo [★GS,E,$] 858 rue Ste-Catherine Est (at St-Andre) 514/658-2646 *after-hours Fri-Sun only*

Stock Bar [★MO,S] 1171 Ste-Catherine (at Montcalm) 514/842-1336 *shows start at 8pm nightly, nude dancers*

Unity II [★MW,D,S,YC] 1171 rue Ste-Catherine Est (at Montcalm) 514/523-2777 *9pm-close Fri-Sat only, great rooftoop terrace*

◼CAFES

Cafe Santropol [WC] 3990 St-Urbain (at Duluth) 514/842-3110 *11:30am-10pm, from 9am during summer, unique sandwiches*

Cafe Titanic [★WI] 445 St-Pierre (in Old Montréal) 514/849-0894 *8am-4:30pm, clsd wknds, salads & soups*

Kilo 6744 rue Hutchison 514/270-3024, 877/270-3024 *9am-5pm, clsd wknds*

◼RESTAURANTS

L' Anecdote [GO] 801 rue Rachel Est (at St-Hubert) 514/526-7967 *7:30am-10pm, from 9am wknds*

Après le Jour [BYOB,WC] 901 rue Rachel Est (at St-Andre) **514/527-4141** *5pm-9pm, clsd Mon*

Au Pain Perdu 4489 rue de la Roche **514/527-2900** *7am-3pm, charming brunch spot in renovated garage*

Bangkok [WC] 1616 rue Ste-Catherine Ouest **514/935-2178** *9am-9pm*

Beauty's [★] 93 Mont-Royal Ouest **514/849-8883** *7am-3pm, 8am-4pm wknds, diner/ Jewish deli, worth the wait*

La Binerie 367 Mt-Royal **514/285-9078** *6am-8pm, 8am-3pm wknds*

Le Cagibi [E] 5490 boul St-Laurent **514/509-1199** *9am-1am, from 10:30am wknds, 6pm-midnight Mon, vegetarian*

La Colombe [BYOB] 554 Duluth Est **514/849-8844** *5:30pm-midnight, clsd Sun-Mon, French*

Commensal [BW,WC] 1720 rue St-Denis (at Ontario) **514/845-2627** *11am-10:30pm, till 11pm Fri-Sat, vegetarian*

Ella Grill [GO] 1237 Amherst **514/523-5553** *upscale Mediterranean/Greek*

L' Exception 1200 rue St-Hubert (at Réné-Lévèsque) **514/282-1282** *11am-8pm, fill 10pm Sat, terrace*

L' Express [★R,WC] 3927 rue St-Denis (at Duluth) **514/845-5333** *8am-2am, from 10am Sat-Sun, French bistro & bar, great pâté*

Fantasie [GO] 1355 rue Ste-Catherine Est **514/523-3466** *dinner only, sushi*

La Strega [WC] 1477 rue Ste-Catherine Est **514/523-6000** *11am-midnight, from 5pm wknds, inexpensive Italian*

Le Nouveau Palais 281 rue Bernard W **514/273-1180** *open till 3am wknds, clsd Mon, old school diner*

La Paryse [MW,GO] 302 rue Ontario Est (near Sanguinet) **514/842-2040** *11am-11pm, clsd Mon, '50s-style diner*

Le Planète [BW] 1451 rue Ste-Catherine Est (at Plessis) **514/528-6953** *5pm-10:30pm, brunch only Sun*

Resto du Village 1310 rue Wolfe **514/524-5404** *24hrs, "cuisine canadienne"*

Saloon Cafe [★] 1333 rue Ste-Catherine Est (at Panèt) **514/522-1333** *dinner nightly, lunch wknds only, big dishes & even bigger drinks*

Schwartz's Deli 3895 boul St-Laurent **514/842-4813** *8am-12:30am, till 1:30am Fri, till 2:30am Sat*

Thai Grill 5101 boul St-Laurent (at Laurier) **514/270-5566** *one of Montréal's best Thai eateries*

■ ENTERTAINMENT & RECREATION

Ça Roule 27 rue de la Commune Est **514/866-0633, 877/866-0633** *join the beautiful people skating up & & biking down Ste-Catherine*

Prince Arthur Est at boul St-Laurent, not far from Sherbrooke Métro station *closed-off street w/ tons of outdoor restaurants & cafés—it's touristy but oh-so-European*

■ RETAIL SHOPS

Cuir Mont-Royal 826-A Mont Royal Est (at St-Hubert) **514/527-0238, 888/333-8283** *leather, fetish*

Priape [★] 1311 Ste-Catherine Est (at Visitation) **514 /521-8451, 800/461-6969** *clubwear, leather, books, toys & more*

Screaming Eagle 1424 boul St-Laurent **514/849-2843** *leather shop*

■ PUBLICATIONS

2B **514/521-3873** *English-language LGBT publication covering Québec*

Fugues **514/848-1854, 888/848-1854** *glossy LGBT bar/ entertainment guide*

■ MEN'S CLUBS

Le 5018 Sauna [V] 5018 boul St-Laurent (at St-Joseph) **514/277-3555** *24hrs, hot tub*

Colonial Bath 3963 av Coloniale (at Napoléon) **514/285-0132** *noon-midnight, from 7am Sun*

Province of Québec • CANADA

GI Joe 1166 Ste-Catherine Est (at Montcalm) 514/528-3326 *24hrs*

L' Oasis [★V,PC] 1390 Ste-Catherine Est (at Plessis) 514/521-0785 *24hrs, hot tub*

Sauna 1286 [V] 1286 chemin de Chambly (at Breggs), Longueuil 450/677-1286 *24hrs*

Sauna 456 456 rue de la Gauchetière Ouest (at Metro Square) 514/871-8465 *will open again June 2013*

Sauna Centre-Ville [★V,WI] 1465 rue Ste-Catherine Est (at Plessis) 514/524-3486 *24hrs*

Sauna Pont-Viau [V] 1-A rue de Nevers (at boul de Prairies), Laval 450/663-3386 *24hrs*

Sauna St-Hubert [V] 6527 rue St-Hubert (at Beaubien) 514/277-0176 *24hrs Th-Sun*

■EROTICA

La Capoterie 2061 St-Denis 514/845-0027

Il Bolero 6846 St-Hubert (btwn St-Zotique & Bélanger) 514/270-6065 *fetish & clubwear emporium, ask about monthly fetish party*

■CRUISY AREAS

Angrignon Park [AYOR]

De Maisonneuve Park [AYOR]

Parc Mont-Royal [AYOR] Park Ave *summer nights*

Québec City

■ACCOMMODATIONS

ALT Hotel Québec [GF,NS,WI,WC] 1200 av Germain des Prés (at Laurier Blvd), Sainte-Foy 418/658-1224, 800/463-5253 *restaurant*

Asseline de Ronval [GS,WI,GO] 354 rue Richelieu 418/524-3588, 418/580-6694

Auberge Place D'Armes [GF,NS,WI] 24 rue Ste-Anne (at St-Louis) 418/694-9485, 866/333-9485

Le Château du Faubourg [GF,NS,GO] 429A rue St-Jean (at Claire Fontaine) 418/524-2902 *B&B in château, also beauty salon*

Dans les Bras de Morphée [GF,SW,WI,GO] 225 chemin Royal, St-Jean-De-L'Ile d'Orléans 418/829-3792, 866/220-4061 *full brkfst, near beach, shared baths*

Domaine de l' Arc-en-Ciel [MO,SW,18+] 1878 rang 5 Ouest (exit 266, off Rte 20), Joly 418/728-5522 *camping, full brkfst, also bar & restaurant*

Gite TerreCiel [GS,WI,GO] 113 rue Sainte Anne, Baie-Saint-Paul 418/435-0149

Hotel Le Clos Saint-Louis [GS,NS,WI] 69 St-Louis (at St-Ursule) 418/694-1311, 800/461-1311

Hôtel Le Germain Dominion 1912 [GF,WI,WC] 126 rue St-Pierre (at Marché Finlay) 418/692-2224, 888/833-5253 *boutique hotel in city's 1st skyscraper*

Hôtel-Motel Le Voyageur [GS,SW,WI] 2250 boul Ste-Anne (at Estimauville) 418/661-7701, 800/463-5568 *restaurant & bar*

Le Moulin de St-Laurent Chalets [GS,SW,NS] 754 chemin Royal, St Laurent, Ile d' Orleans 418/829-3888, 888/629-3888 *cottages, also restaurant*

■BARS

Bar Le Drague [★M,NH,D,F,K,C,DS,WC] 815 rue St-Augustin (at St-Jean) 418/649-7212 *10am-3am, terrace*

Bar St Matthew's [MW,NH] 889 côte Ste-Geneviève (at St-Gabriel) 418/524-5000 *11am-3am, patio*

ForHom [MO,OC,PC] 221 rue St-Jean (entrance at 225) 418/522-4918 *5pm-1am, till 3am Fri-Sat, good place for quiet conversation*

■RESTAURANTS

Le Commensal 860 rue St-Jean 418/647-3733 *11am-9pm, till 10pm Th-Sat, vegetarian/ vegan*

Le Hobbit 700 rue St-Jean (at Ste-Geneviève) 418/647-2677 *9am-10pm*

La Piazzetta 707 rue St-Jean 418/529-7489 *11am-10:30pm*

Le Poisson d'Avril 115 quai St-André (at St-Thomas) 418/692-1010, 877/692-1010 *5pm-close, name is French for "April Fools"*

Vertige 540 Ave Duluth E 514/842-4443 *5pm-10pm, till 11pm Fri-Sat, clsd Sun-Mon*

ENTERTAINMENT & RECREATION

Fairmont Le Château Frontenac 1 rue des Carrières 418/692-3861, 800/257-7544 *this hotel disguised as a castle remains the symbol of Québec, come & enjoy the view from outside*

Ice Hotel /Hôtel de Glace [GF] 75, Montée de l'Auberge, Pavillon Ukiuk, Sainte-Catherine-de-la-Jacques-Cartier 418/875-4522, 877/505-0423 *sometimes getting put on ice isn't a bad thing—check it out before it melts away, 9 km E of Québec City in Montmorency Falls Park (Jan-March only)*

PUBLICATIONS

2B 514/521-3873 *English-language LGBT publication covering Québec*

MEN'S CLUBS

Bloc 225 [PC] 225 St-Jean (at Turnbull) 418/523-2562, 877/523-2562 *24hrs*

Sauna Backboys [V] 264 rue de la Couronne (at Prince Edward) 418/521-6686, 877/523-6686 *24hrs*

Sauna/ Hotel Hippocampe [★V] 31 rue McMahon (at Ste-Angèle) 418/692-1521, 888/388-1521 *24hrs, bar, also small hotel*

EROTICA

Importation André Dubois [TG,WC] 46 côte de la Montagne (at Frontenac Castle) 418/692-0264

CRUISY AREAS

Rue St-Denis [AYOR]

St-Alphonse-de-Granby

ACCOMMODATIONS

Bain de Nature [MO,SW,N,GO] 127 rue Lussier 450/375-4765 *B&B & free-form camping, beautiful small lake, all meals included, hot tub, day visitors welcome*

St-François-du-Lac

ACCOMMODATIONS

Domaine Emeraude [MO,F,SW,N,GO] 450/568-3634 *seasonal, cabins, camping, RV spots & rental condos, also restaurant & bar*

St-Georges-de-Beauce

BARS

Le Planet [GS,NH] 8450 Blvd Lacroix 418/228-1322 *2pm-3am, till 10pm Sun, clsd Mon-Tue*

St-Hubert

MEN'S CLUBS

3481 Sauna [MO] 3481 Montee St-Hubert 450/462-3481 *24hrs*

Ste-Julienne

ACCOMMODATIONS

Camping de la Fierté [MO,SW,N,18+] 2905 Montée Hamilton 450/834-2888 *theme wknds summers, tent & RV spots, cabin, also bar/ restaurant/ rec hall*

Ste-Marthe

ACCOMMODATIONS

Camping Plein Bois [MO,D,SW,N,WI,GO] 550 chemin St-Henri 450/459-4646, 888/459-4646 *seasonal, DJ Fri-Sat, also restaurant & bar, volleyball, 350 campsites & 200 trailer sites*

SASKATCHEWAN

Provincewide

■PUBLICATIONS

Perceptions 306/244-1930 *covers the Canadian prairies*

Ravenscrag

■ACCOMMODATIONS

Spring Valley Guest Ranch [★GS,F,NS,GO] 306/295-4124 *1913 character home, also cabin, full brkfst*

Regina

■INFO LINES & SERVICES

The Gay & Lesbian Community of Regina 2070 Broad St (at Victoria) 306/569-1995 *7am-3pm*

■NIGHTCLUBS

The OUTside [MW,D] 2070 Broad St (at Victoria, at Gay Center) 306/569-1995 *7pm-3am*

■RESTAURANTS

Abstractions Cafe [E] 2161 Rose St 306/352-5374 *9am-6pm, from 11am Sat, clsd Sun*

The Creek in Cathedral Bistro 3414 13th Ave 306/352-4448 *lunch & dinner, clsd Sun*

■CRUISY AREAS

Douglas Park [AYOR]

Wascana Park [AYOR] at College Dr & Lorne St

Saskatoon

■INFO LINES & SERVICES

Avenue Community Centre 201-320 21st St W 306/665-1224, 800/358-1833 *10am-5pm, till 9pm Wed-Fri, 4:30pm-9:30pm Sat*

Circle of Choice Gay/ Lesbian AA 505 10th St E (at Grace Westminster United Church) 306/665-6727 *8pm Wed*

■NIGHTCLUBS

302 Lounge [MW,D] 302 Pacific Ave 306/665-6863 *7am-2am, till 3am Fri-Sat, clsd Sun-Tue*

Diva's [MW,D,DS,K,WI,PC] 220 3rd Ave S #110 (alley entrance) 306/665-0100 *8pm-2am, till 5am Sat, clsd Mon-Tue*

■RESTAURANTS

2nd Ave Grill 10-123 2nd Ave S 306/244-9899 *11am-10pm, till 11pm Fri-Sat*

The Berry Barn 830 Valley Rd 306/978-9797 *open daily, seasonal, home-style eatery w/ views of river*

The Ivy Dining & Lounge 24th St E & Ontario Ave 306/384-4444 *lunch & dinner Mon-Fri, dinner only Sat-Sun*

Prairie Ink 3130 8th St E 306/955-3579 *9am-10pm, till 11pm Fri-Sat, till 6pm Sun, also bookstore*

■ENTERTAINMENT & RECREATION

AKA Gallery 424 20th St W 306/652-0044 *noon-6pm, till 4pm Sat, clsd Sun-Mon, contemporary art & performance*

■BOOKSTORES

Turning the Tide 525 11th St E 306/955-9900 *noon-8pm, till 10pm Th-Sat, Saskatoon's alternative bookstore*

■RETAIL SHOPS

The Trading Post 226 2nd Ave S 306/653-1769 *10am-5:30pm, clsd Sun, clothing*

■CRUISY AREAS

Lakewood Park [AYOR] *nights*

Caribbean

BAHAMAS

Nassau

■ NIGHTCLUBS

Club Waterloo [GF,D,F,E,SW] E Bay St
(1/2 mile E of Paradise Island Bridge)
242/393-7324 *4pm-close, indoor/outdoor complex*

BARBADOS

Bridgetown

■ RESTAURANTS

The Waterfront Cafe [E] The
Careenage **246/427-0093** *10am-midnight, clsd Sun, also bar*

BRITISH VIRGIN ISLANDS

Tortola

■ ACCOMMODATIONS

Fort Recovery Villa Beach Resort
[GF,SW,WC] Road Town, Tortola
284/495-4467, 800/367-8455 (wait for ring) *grand home on beach & private beachfront villas*

DOMINICAN REPUBLIC

Boca Chica

■ ACCOMMODATIONS

Costalunga [GF] 3 Av del Sur
809/523-6883 *closest beach to Santo Domingo, also restaurant*

Puerto Plata

■ ACCOMMODATIONS

Tropix Hotel [GF,SW,GO]
809/571-2291 *garden setting near center of town & beach, full brkfst*

Santiago

■ BARS

Monaco Bar [MW,D] 40 Av 27 de
Febrero, Santo Domingo
809/226-1589

Santo Domingo

■ ACCOMMODATIONS

Caribe Colonial Hotel [GF,WI] Isabel
Catolica 159 **809/688-7799** *boutique hotel*

Foreigners Club Hotel
[MW,NS,WI,WC,GO] 102 Calle Canela (at
Estrelleta) **809/689-3017**

Hotel Aida [GF] Calle El Conde 464
809/685-7692 *near gay bars*

■ BARS

Bar Friends [M,AYOR] 10 Calle Povorin
809/689-7572 *buggarones (hustlers)*

Click [W,K] 3 Vicente Celestino Duarte
(Zona Colonial) **829/449-5154**

Colonial Bar & Disco [M,D,K] 109
Mella Ave (nr Calle Arzobispo Nouel)
809/205-1970 *open Th-Sun*

Esedeku [MW,F] **809/869-6322**
8pm-close, from 5pm Sun, clsd Mon

Fogoo Discotec [M,D,DS] 67 Calle
Arzobispo Nouel (btw Espaillat &
Santome) **809/205-1970**

Jay Dee's [M,NH,S,V] Jose Reyes 10,
Zona Colonial **809/335-5905**

■ NIGHTCLUBS

Pure Disco Club [GS,D] 365 George
Washington Ave (at Hotel Meliá)
809/221-6666 *open till 6am, no shorts or flip flops*

Sunev Bar & Lounge [M] 203 Calle 19
de Marzo (nr Calle El Conde) *open Th-Sun*

■ RESTAURANTS

El Conuco 152 Casimiro de Moya
(behind Jaragua Hotel) **809/686-0129**
touristy local landmark

Green Light Cuisine 20 Heriberto
Pieter, Naco **809/732-7719** *sandwiches & salads, fresh & light*

Mamajuana 451 Avenida Roberto
Pastoriza **809/547-1019**

Onno's Bar 157 Calle Hostos (at El
Conde) **809/689-1183** *DJ on the wknds*

Dominican Republic • CARIBBEAN

ENTERTAINMENT & RECREATION

Parque Duarte Calle Duarte (at Calle Padre Billini) *Th-Sun nights, this park is the gathering place for young gay Dominicans*

MEN'S CLUBS

Apolo Spa 108 Calle Arzobispo Noue (btw 19 de Marzo & Calle Duarte) **829/787-2010**

EROTICA

Cine Lido [AYOR] 342 Avenida Mella **809/682-8082** *6:30pm-10:30pm*

CRUISY AREAS

Avenida el Conde [AYOR] *pedestrian mall*

DUTCH & FRENCH WEST INDIES

Aruba

ACCOMMODATIONS

Little David Guest House [M,SW,N,GO] Seroe Blanco 56L, Oranjestad **297/583-8288**

BARS

Jimmy's Place [★MW,NH,D,F] Windstraat 32, Oranjestad **297/582-2550** *5pm-2am, till 4am Fri-Sat, from 8pm Mon*

The Paddock [GS,NH,F] LG Smith Blvd #13, Oranjestad **297/583-2334, 297/583-2606** *10am-2am*

RESTAURANTS

Cafe the Plaza Seaport Marketplace, Oranjestad **297/583-8826** *8am-1am, patio*

CRUISY AREAS

Eagle Beach [AYOR] btwn La Quinta Resort & Dutch Village Hotel, Oranjestad *afternoons*

Barbados

ACCOMMODATIONS

Gemini House B&B [GF,WI] 70 Plover Court, Inch Marlow, Christ Church **246/428-7221**

Inchcape Seaside Villas [GF,WI] **246/428-7006**

Curaçao

INFO LINES & SERVICES

Pink House Charlottestraat 6, Willemstad **5999/462-6616** *LGBT community center, health & rights organization; also events*

ACCOMMODATIONS

The Avila Beach Hotel [GF] 130 Penstraat, Willemstad **800/747-8162**

Floris Suite Hotel [M,SW,WI,WC,GO] Piscadera Bay **5999/462-6111**

Kura Hulanda [GF] Langestraat 8, Willemstad **888/264-3106 , 5999/434-7700** *also Jacob's Bar*

Papagayo Beach Resort [GF] Willemstad **800/652-2962** (from US), **5999/747-4333**

BARS

Grand Cafe De Heeren [GS,E] Zuikertuintjeweg 1 **5999/736-0491** *9am-1am, till 2:30am Th-Fri, clsd Sun, also restaurant*

Mundo Bizarro [GF,E] Nieuwestraat 12 (in the Pietermaai quarter) **5999/461-6767** *weird & wonderful eatery & café*

NIGHTCLUBS

Bermuda Disco [GF,D] Scharlooweg 72-76 (at the Waaigat, behind the movies), Willemstad **5999/461-4685** *10pm-4am, popular Fri-Sat*

Cabana Beach [GF,D] at Seaquarium Beach **599/946-5158** *open Wed-Sat, also restaurant*

Tu Tu Tango [GF] Plasa Mundo Merced, Punda **5999/465-4633** *11pm-4am, more gay Fri, also restaurant*

RESTAURANTS

Mambo Beach [GF] Bapor Kibra, Seaquarium Beach **5999/461-8999** *9am-midnight, till 4am Sat, full bar, more gay Sat*

O Mundo Zuikertuintje Shopping Mall, Willemstad *lunch & dinner, also gay party 2nd Sat*

ENTERTAINMENT & RECREATION

Cas Abao Beach [GF] *popular local beach*

Dolphin Academy Curaçao Sea Aquarium, Bapor Kibra z/n (east of Willemstad, at Sea Aquarium Park) **5999/465-8900, 5999/465-8300** *swim w/ dolphins!*

Jan Thiel Beach *good people-watching*

Museum Kura Hulanda Klipstraat 9, Willemstad **5999/434-7765** *African history & culture, Antillean art*

Saba

■ACCOMMODATIONS

Juliana's Hotel [GS,SW,WI] Windwardside **599/416-2269, 888/289-5708**

Shearwater Resort [GF,SW,WI,GO] Cliff Side (Booby Hill) **589/416-2498**

■RESTAURANTS

Rainforest Restaurant Windwardside **599/416-3888, 599/416-5507** *brkfst, lunch & dinner, full bar*

Restaurant Eden The Road (Windwardside), Windwardside **599/416-2539** *5:30pm-9:30pm*

St Barthélémy

■ACCOMMODATIONS

Hotel le Village St-Jean [GF,SW] St-Jean Hill **590–590/27–61–39, 800/651-8366** *hotel & cottages*

Hotel Normandie [GF,WI] Quartier Lorient **590–590/27–61–66**

Hotel St-Barth Isle De France [GF,F] Plage des Flamands **508/528-7727, 800/421-3396** *ultraluxe hotel*

■NIGHTCLUBS

Le Sélect [GF] Gustavia **590–590/27–86–87** *more gay after 11pm*

■RESTAURANTS

Le Grain de Sel Grand Saline Beach **590/524-605** *lunch & dinner, clsd Mon, relaxing setting, ideal before & after sunbathing*

■ENTERTAINMENT & RECREATION

Anse Gouverneur St-Jean Beach [N]

Anse Grande Saline Beach [N] *gay section on the left side of Saline*

Orient Beach [N] *gay beach*

St Maarten

■ACCOMMODATIONS

Blue Ocean Villas [GF] **352/505-2805** *private villa rentals*

Holland House [GF] 43 Front St, Philipsburg **599/542-2572** *on the beach, restaurant, bar*

■RESTAURANTS

Cheri's Cafe [★D,E,WC] Rhine Rd #45 (Maho Reef) **599/54-53-361** *11am-1:30am, clsd Tue, full bar, live music, touristy*

St Martin

■ACCOMMODATIONS

Villa Rainbow [MO,SW,NS,WI,GO] Pic Paradis **590/690-766-235** *stone villa w/ view of Caribbean*

■BARS

Tantra [GS] Rhine Road, Maho Bay, Marigot (at the Marina Royale) **599/545-2861** *11pm-close Wed, Fri-Sat*

■RESTAURANTS

L' Escapade [R] 94 Blvd de Grand Case **590–590/87–75–04** *French*

Le Pressoir 30 Blvd de Grand Case **590–590/87–76–62** *dinner nightly, clsd Sun*

■ENTERTAINMENT & RECREATION

Orient Beach [GF,N] on the northeast side of the island

■CRUISY AREAS

Cupecoy Beach [AYOR] park at established lot w/ blue & white "Cupecoy Beach" sign (near French border) *gay beach, take a friend & avoid if beach is secluded*

JAMAICA

Montego Bay

▪ACCOMMODATIONS

Half Moon [GF,SW] 877/956-625,
866/648-6951 *upscale resort*

Negril

▪ACCOMMODATIONS

Seagrape Villas [GS] The Cliffs, West
End Rd 831/625-1255 (US#)

Ocho Rios

▪ACCOMMODATIONS

Golden Clouds Villa [GF,SW,WC,GO]
North Coast Rd, Oracabessa
941/922-9191, 888/625-6007
private estate, full brkfst, fully staffed

Port Antonio

▪ACCOMMODATIONS

Hotel Mocking Bird Hill
[GF,F,SW,WC,GO] 876/993-7267,
876/993-7134

Westmoreland

▪ACCOMMODATIONS

Moun Tambrin Retreat [GS,F,SW,NS]
set in the mtns 28 miles from Montego
Bay 876/437-4353

MARTINIQUE

Les Trois Ilets

▪ACCOMMODATIONS

Le Carbet B&B [M,N,GO] 18 rue des
Alamandas (at Anse Mitan)
596/596-66-0331

PUERTO RICO

Please Note: For those with rusty or
no Spanish, "carretera" means
"highway" and "calle" means
"street."

Baja Sucia

▪ENTERTAINMENT &
RECREATION

Playa Sucia/ La Playuela S of Cabo
Rojo Nat'l Wildlife Refuge, Guanica
beautiful, secluded beach

Bayamon

▪BARS

Start Night Club [MW,DS] 31 Ongay St
(behind Clendo lab) 787/536-3579
open Th-Sat

Boqueron

▪BARS

El Schamar Bar [GS,DS] at corner of
Muñoz Rivera & Jose de Diego 787/
851-0542 *11am-midnight, also hotel*

Sunset Sunrise [GS,OC] 65 Calle
Barbosa 787/255-1478 *10am-close*

▪RESTAURANTS

**The Fish Net & Roberto's Villa
Playera** Calle de Diego 787/254-3163
best seafood in town

Camuy

▪BARS

Distortion [MW,D,SW] Carr 119 Norte,
KM 7.6 (Barrio Membrio)
787/614-3404 *10pm Sat only*

Ceiba

▪ACCOMMODATIONS

Ceiba Country Inn [GF,WI,GO]
Carretera 977 787/885-0471,
888/560-2816 *dramatic ocean views*

For more resources and the latest updates

DAMR⬤N
Online
www.damron.com

Guanica

■ ENTERTAINMENT & RECREATION

Gilligan's Island take Rd 333 to Copamarina Resort, then take ferry to island **787/821-5706 (ferry info)** *beautiful beach located in a biosphere on Southern coast of PR*

Ponce

■ BARS

Wejele's Cafe [MW,NH] 8 Leon St **787/603-8095** *9pm-3am Wed-Sat*

Rincon

■ ACCOMMODATIONS

Horned Dorset Primavera Hotel [GS,SW] Apartado 1132 **800/633-1857**

Lemontree Oceanfront Cottages [GS,NS,WI,WC] Carr 429, km 4.1 (at Carr 115) **787/823-6452, 888/418-8733**

San Juan

■ INFO LINES & SERVICES

Centro Communitario LGBTT/ LGBT Community Center 37 Calle Mayaguez **787/294-9850** *1pm-10pm, clsd wknds, resources, events, AIDS testing; also cyber cafe*

■ ACCOMMODATIONS

Andalucia Guesthouse & Vacation Rentals [M,WI,GO] 2011 McLeary Ave (at San Miguel St, Ocean Park) **787/309-3373**

At Wind Chimes Inn [GF,SW,NS,WI,WC] 1750 McLeary Ave, Condado (at Taft) **787/727-4153, 800/946-3244**

Casa del Caribe Guest House [GF,NS,WI] Calle Caribe 57, Condado (at Magdalena) **787/722-7139, 877/722-7139**

La Concha [GS] 1077 Ashford Ave, Condado **787/721-7500** *retro urban showcase & architectural landmark*

Coqui del Mar Guesthouse [GF,GO] 2218 Calle General del Valle (at General Patton, Ocean Park) **787/220-4204**

Hotel El Convento [GF,SW,WI] Calle Cristo 100, Old San Juan (btwn Caleta de las Monjas & Calle Sol) **787/723-9020, 800/468-2779**

Miramar Hotel [GF,WI] 606 Ave Ponce de Leon (at Miramar) **787/977-1000** *also restaurant & bar*

Numero Uno on the Beach [GS,SW,WC] Calle Santa Ana 1, Ocean Park (near Calle Italia) **787/726-5010, 866/726-5010** *also Pamela's restaurant & bar*

Ocean Hostal Playero [GS,NS,WI] 1853 McLeary Ave, Condado (at Calle Atlantic Pl) **787/728-8119** *budget accommodations, great beach location, also vegetarian restaurant*

The San Juan Water & Beach Club Hotel [GF,SW,NS,WI,WC] 2 Tartak St (Isla Verde), Carolina **787/728-3666, 888/265-6699** *boutique hotel on beach, restaurant & lounge*

■ BARS

Angelu's Cafe [W,NH] Calle Eleanor Roosevelt 239, Hato Rey *clsd Sun-Mon*

Atlantic Beach Bar [GS,AYOR] 1 Calle Vendig, Condado **787/721-6900** *10am-2am, less gay now, great beach location*

Batucada [GF,NH,K] 15 Ave Carlos Chardon, Hato Rey **787/993-1291** *Fri-Sun, sports bar & grill*

Club Hype San Juan [GS,D] 1204 Ponce de Leon (at RH Todd Ave) *10pm-5am, clsd Sun-Tue*

Heaven and Hell [MW,D] 365 Ave Jose de Diego (at Ponce de Leon), Santurce **917/544-7374** *10pm-5am Th-Sat, 2 levels with different ambience*

Rabanal Petit Club [M,NH] 1700 Ave Ponce de Leon (at Hotel San Jorge), Santurce **787/390-0336** *9pm-close Wed-Sun*

Splash [★M] Av Condado 6 (at Condado Inn) **787/721-7145** *1pm-close, near beach*

Tia Maria's [MW,NH] 326 Ave Jose de Diego, Parada 22 (at Ponce de León), Santurce **787/724-4011** *noon-2am, also liquor shop*

Puerto Rico • CARIBBEAN

VIP Bar [★M,NH,MR-L,TG,E,DS,S,YC] Calle Condado 613 (btwn Calle del Carmen & Av Ponce de León), Santurce **787/722-5509** *9pm-5am, leather & bear crowd Th, drag & bingo Sun*

■NIGHTCLUBS

Circo Bar [M,D,K,DS] Calle Condado 650, Parada 18, Santurce **787/725-9676** *9pm-5am, beware of the neighborhood*

Club Babylon [MO,D,DS,S] Marginal San Agustin, 65 de Infanteria, Rio Piedras *10pm-close Wed-Sun, theme nights*

Kali [GF] 1407 Ashford Ave, Condado **787/721-5104** *popular after-hrs club, dress code, also lounge & restaurant*

Kenny's Country Club [M,D] take PR-1 toward Caguas (23.6 KM) *9:30pm Sat only, 15 min outside of San Juan*

Krash Klub [★MW,D,DS,S,V,GO] Av Ponce de León 1257 (btwn Calles Villamil & Labra), Santurce **787/722-1131** *10pm-4am, clsd Sun-Mon*

Metro Lounge [MW,D,S] Av Roosevelt 1367 (Hato Rey) **787/447-5253** *Th-Sun*

■CAFES

Cafe Berlin [★] Calle San Francisco 407, Plaza Colón, Old San Juan (btwn Calles Norzagary & O'Donnel) **787/722-5205** *11am-11pm, espresso bar*

Kasalta Bakery 1966 McLeary Ave (at Teniente Matta) **787/727-7340** *6am-10pm, bakery & deli*

■RESTAURANTS

Aguaviva [WC] 364 Calle La Fortaleza, Old San Juan **787/722-0665** *dinner nightly, fresh seafood & ceviche*

Ajili Mojili 1052 Ashford Ave, Condado (at Aguadilla) **787/725-9195** *local specialties, live music, great ambiance*

Al Dente 309 Calle Recinto S, Old San Juan **787/723-7303** *lunch & dinner, clsd Sun, Italian, also wine bar*

Bebo's Cafe 1600 Calle Loiza (at Del Parque) **787/268-5087** *cheap & delicious, cafeteria-style Puerto Rican favorites*

Cafe Puerto Rico 208 O'Donnell, Old San Juan **787/724-2281** *noon-11pm, great mofongo, patio*

La Casita Blanca 351 Calle Tapia (off Ave Eduardo Conde, near Laguna Los Corozas) **787/726-5501** *11am-4pm, till 6pm Th, till 9pm Fri-Sat, amazing local cuisine, best reached by car, no English spoken, beware of neighborhood*

Colombo [WI] 1024 Ashford Ave (at Aguadilla St) **787/725-1212** *8am-3am, American, also bar*

Dieguito & Markito's [K] Kiosk 44 in Luquillo **787/355-0875** *2pm-9pm, open late wknds, also bar*

Dragonfly 364 S Fortaleza St, Old San Juan (across from Parrot Club) **787/977-3886** *opens 5:30pm daily, full bar*

Fleria 1754 Calle Loiza, Santurce **787/268-0010** *lunch & dinner, clsd Sun-Mon, Greek*

El Jibarito Calle Sol 280 **787/725-8375** *Puerto Rican/ criolla, also bar*

Oceano Restaurant & Lounge 2 Calle Vendig, Condado **787/724-6400** *great location on the beach, Sun gay party*

The Parrot Club [E] Calle Fortaleza 363, Old San Juan (btwn Plaza Colón & Callejón de la Capilla) **787/725-7370** *lunch & dinner, chic Nuevo Latino bistro & bar*

Perla 1077 Ashford Ave, at La Concha Resort, Condado **787/721-7500** *enjoy an upscale dining experience inside a gigantic conch shell*

Pura Vida [WI] 1853 McLeary Ave, Condado (at Calle Atlantic Pl) **787/728-8119** *noon-10pm, vegetarian*

Sarushe's 1025 Ave Jesus T Piñero **787/948-0548** *4pm-2:30am, from 8am Sat, clsd Sun-Tue, tapas*

Vidy's Cafe [K] Ave Universidad 104 (Rio Piedras) **787/767-3062** *10am-1am, plenty veggie*

■ENTERTAINMENT &
RECREATION

Atlantic Beach in front of Atlantic Beach Hotel *very gay-friendly beach*

Nuyorican Cafe San Francisco 312 (by El Callejon) 787/977-1276, 787/366-5074 *live music & arts venue*

Ocean Park Beach [GS] E of Condado *adult-oriented (less kids)*

La Placita/ Plaza del Mercado Santurce *open-air market by day, street-party by night; lots of bars & restaurants*

■PUBLICATIONS

Conexion G 787/607-3939 *LGBT paper, in Spanish*

■GYMS & HEALTH CLUBS

Muscle Factory Avenida Ashford (at Vendig, Condado) **787/721-0717**

■CRUISY AREAS

Parque Central [AYOR] at Interstate PR-1 & PR-2 *popular evenings*

La Playita [AYOR] Av Muñoz Rivera (in front of capitol bldg in Old San Juan) *afternoons*

Scenic Overlook [AYOR] off Muñoz Rivera Dr *observation parking area near capitol bldg*

Las Uvas [AYOR] E of Condado (at Ocean Park Beach, W of Calle Yardley Pl) *mixed gay/ straight by day, cruisy by night*

Vieques Island

■ACCOMMODATIONS

Bravo! [GS,SW,GO] North Shore Rd (at Lighthouse) 787/741-1128

Casa de Amistad [GS,SW,WI,GO] 27 Benitez Castano 787/741-3758

Crow's Nest Inn [GF,SW,NS] 787/741-0033, 877/276-9763 *restaurant*

Inn on the Blue Horizon [GF,SW,F,NS,WI] 787/741-3318

TRINIDAD & TOBAGO

Tobago

■ACCOMMODATIONS

Grafton Beach Resort [GF,F,SW] 868/639-0191, 888/790-5264

Kariwak Village Hotel & Holistic Haven [GF,F,SW,WI,WC] Store Bay Local Rd, Crown Point 868/639-8442, 868/639-8545 *holistic hotel*

US VIRGIN ISLANDS

St Croix

■ACCOMMODATIONS

King Christian Hotel [GF,F,SW] 59 Kings Wharf, Christiansted 340/773-6330, 800/524-2012 *also restaurant*

The Palms at Pelican Cove [MW,F,SW] 4126 La Grande Princesse 340/778-8920, 888/790-5264 *beachfront resort*

Sand Castle on the Beach [★MW,SW,WI,GO] 127 Smithfield, Frederiksted 340/772-1205, 800/524-2018 *gay resort (from rooms to beachfront villas), also restaurant & bar*

St John

■ACCOMMODATIONS

Gallows Point Suite Resort [GF,F,SW,WC] Cruz Bay 340/776-6434, 800/323-7229 *beachfront resort*

Hillcrest Guest House [GF,NS,WI] 340/776-6774, 340/998-8388

St John Inn [GF,SW,NS,WI] 800/666-7688, 340/693-8688

■RESTAURANTS

Asolare Rte 20, Cruz Bay 340/779-4747 *5:30pm-9:30pm, Asian/ French fusion, hip & elegant*

■ENTERTAINMENT &
RECREATION

Salomon Bay *20-minute hike on Salomon Beach Trail*

St Thomas

■ACCOMMODATIONS

Hotel 1829 [GF,F,SW] Government Hill
340/776-1829, 800/524-2002

Magen's Point Resort [GF,SW,WC]
6200 Magen's Bay Rd 340/777-6000,
877/850-4465

Pavilions & Pools Hotel [GF,SW] 6400
Estate Smith Bay 340/775-6110,
800/524-2001 *1-bdrm villas each w/
own private swimming pool*

■RESTAURANTS

Mafolie Hotel & Restaurant 7091
Estate Mafolie 340/774-2790 *great
place for lunch w/ a view*

Oceana Restaurant & Wine Bar
Historic Pointe at Villa Olga
340/774-4262 *on the water's edge*

Virgilio's 18 Dronningens Gade
340/776-4920 *great Italian, full bar*

■ENTERTAINMENT & RECREATION

Beach at Emerald Beach Resort up
hill (near airport runway) *walking
distance from cruise ship dock*

Little Magens Beach *gay nude beach,
near main beach at Magens Bay*

Morning Star Beach *popular gay
beach*

Mexico

MEXICO

**Please Note: Mexican cities are
often divided into districts or
"Colonias," which we abbreviate as
"Col." Please use these when giving
addresses for directions.**

Acapulco

■ACCOMMODATIONS

Casa Condesa [M,SW] Bella Vista 125
52-744/484-1616, 800/816-4817
(US & Canada) *full brkfst*

Hotel Boca Chica [GF,F,SW] Punta
Caletilla (Fraccionamiento las Playas)
800/337-4685

Hotel Encanto [GF,F,SW,WI] Jacques
Cousteau 51 (Fraccionamiento Brisas
Marques) 52-744/446-7101

Las Brisas [GF,SW,WC] Carretera
Escenica 5255 52-744/469-6900,
866/221-2961 (US#) *luxury resort,*

■BARS

Picante [★GS,D,S,AYOR,$] Privada Piedra
Picuda 16 (behind Demas)
52-744/484-2209 *9pm-5am, popular
male dancers, hustlers*

■NIGHTCLUBS

Baby 'O [GS,D] 52-744/484-7474
10:30pm-5am, till midnight Sun

Cabaré-Tito Beach [MW,D] Privada de
Piedra Picuda 17 PA (nr Torres Gemelas)
52-744/484-7146 *6pm-3am, from
4pm Th-Sat*

Demas Factory/ Pink [★MO,D,S,$] Ave
de los Deportes #10
52-744/484-1800 *10:30pm-3am*

Relax [★MW,D,DS,S,V,YC] Calle Lomas
de Mar 4 (Zona Dorada)
52-744/482-0421 *10pm-late, clsd
Mon-Wed, [DS,S] wknds*

■RESTAURANTS

100% Natural Av Costera Miguel
Alemán 200 (near Acapulco Plaza)
52-744/485-3982 *24hrs, fast
(healthy) food, plenty veggie*

Becco al Mare 52-744/446-7402
lunch & dinner, Italian, nice views

Beto's Restaurant [MW] Av Costera
Miguel Alemán 99 (at Condesa Beach)
52-744/484-0473 *11am-midnight,
full bar, seafood, palapas*

El Cabrito Av Costera Miguel Alemán
1480 (near Convention Center)
52-744/484-7711 *2pm-midnight, till
11pm Sun*

Carlos & Charlie's [E] Blvd de las
Naciones #1813 (in La Isla Shopping
Village) 52-744/462-2104 *lunch &
dinner*

Kookaburra 3 Fracc (at Marina Las
Brisas) 52-744/446-6039 *lunch &
dinner, int'l, expensive*

La Cabaña de Caleta Playa Caleta Lado Oriente s/n (Fracc. las Playas) **52-744/469-8553, 52-744/469-7919** *9am-9pm, seafood, right on Playa Caleta, great magaritas*

La Tortuga [GO] Calle Lomas del Mar 5 **52-744/484-6985** *noon-midnight, clsd Mon, full bar, patio*

Shu **52-744/462-2001** *Japanese*

Su Casa Angel & Shelly Av Anahuac 110 **52-744/484-1261, 52-744/484-4350**

Suntory de Acapulco Costera Miguel Alemán 36 **52-744/484-8088** *2pm-midnight, Japanese, gardens*

El Zorrito's Av Costera Miguel Alemán (at Anton de Alaminos) **52-744/485-3735** *traditional Mexican, several locations along Costera, some all night*

CRUISY AREAS

Playa Condesa & Beto's Beach near Hotel Fiesta Americana *cruisy by the rocks, at sundown*

Plaza Alvarez/ Zócalo [AYOR] *hustlers (chichifos)*

San Diego Fort [AYOR] along the Costera

Aguascalientes

NIGHTCLUBS

Mandiles [MW,D] Av Lopez Mateos Poniente 730 W (btwn Agucate & Chabacano) **52-449/153-281** *10pm-3am Fri-Sat only*

CRUISY AREAS

Plaza Principal [AYOR]

Cabo San Lucas

ACCOMMODATIONS

Cabo Villas Beach Resort [GF,SW] Callejon del Pescador s/n (Col. El Medano) **52-624/143-9199** *resort on Medano Beach*

Solmar Suites [GF,SW] Av Solmar 1 **800/344-3349, 310/459-9861 (US#)** *oceanfront suites at southern-most tip*

NIGHTCLUBS

Las Varitas [GF,D,E] Calle Vallentin Gomez Farias (at Camino Viejo a San Jose) **52-624/143-9999** *9pm-3am, clsd Mon, rock 'n' roll bar*

RESTAURANTS

Mi Casa [R] Av Cabo San Lucas (at Lazarus Cardenas) **52-624/143-1933** *clsd Sun, lunch & dinner, great chicken mole*

Cancún

see also Cozumel & Playa del Carmen

ACCOMMODATIONS

Rancho Sak Ol [GF] Puerto Morelos **52-998/871-0181** *beachfront palapa-style B&B, 30 minutes from Cancún*

BARS

11:11 Snack Bar Lounge [MW] Avenida Tulum, El Centro (M22 M5 Lotes 33 y 35) **52-044/998-1352** *near Karamba Bar*

Picante Bar [★M,D,S,S,YC] Av Tulúm 20, Centro (E of Av Uxmal, next to Plaza Galerías) *9pm-5am, hustlers, [DS,S] Wed-Sat*

Risky Times [GS,AYOR] Av Tulúm (at Av Coba) **52-998/884-7503** *24hrs, rowdy after-hours, best after 4am*

NIGHTCLUBS

Karamba [★MW,D,K,DS,S] Av Tulúm 9 (Azucenas 2nd flr, SM 22) **52-998/884-0032** *10:30pm-close, clsd Mon, go-go boys Fri*

RESTAURANTS

100% Natural Sunyaxchen 62 **52-998/884-0102** *healthy fast food*

Perico's Av Yaxhilan 61 **52-998/884-3152** *noon-1am, traditional Mexican served up w/ huge theatrical flare*

ENTERTAINMENT & RECREATION

Chichén Itza *the must-see Mayan ruin 125 miles from Cancún*

Playa Delfines in the Hotel Zone (next to Hilton's beach) *gay beach*

Cancún • MEXICO

CRUISY AREAS

Avenida Tulúm [AYOR] Centro *take a stroll & take your pick, late*

El Mirador (Ruinas del Rei) [AYOR] next to Hilton Hotel (near the lighthouse)

Parque de las Palapas [AYOR] opposite Cinema Blanquita *near the Cine Blanquita*

Playa Delfines [AYOR] at S end of hotel zone *afternoons, beware cops (!) back in the bushes*

Chihuahua

ACCOMMODATIONS

Hacienda Huiyochi [MW] Copper Canyon 51-1/625-121-8101

Ciudad Juárez

see also El Paso, Texas, USA

BARS

Bananas [S,AYOR] Ramon Corona & Ignacio Pena 52-656/222-5557 *till 2am, nude dancers, beware hustlers outside*

Club La Escondida [GS,NH] Calle Ignacio de la Peña 366 W

Club Olímpico [★M,NH,P] Av Lerdo 210 S (city center) 52-656/612-5742 *noon-2am*

NIGHTCLUBS

G&G Disco [M,D,S,V,$] Av Lincoln 1252, Córdoba-Américas *9pm-3am, strippers wknds*

MEN'S CLUBS

Baños Roma Calle Ignacio Mejía 881 E (at Calle Constitución) 52-656/612-7732 *9am-9pm*

CRUISY AREAS

Plaza de la Constitución [AYOR] Plaza Hidalgo

Copala

ACCOMMODATIONS

La Caracola [GS,SW,WI] Antelmo Ventura 68 (2 1/2 hrs from Acapulco) 52-741/101-3047

Cordoba

BARS

Salon Bar El Metro [MW,D] Av 7 no. 117-C (btwn Calles 1 & 3)

CRUISY AREAS

Mercado Juárez [AYOR] btwn Calles 7 & 9

Sidewalk Cafes [AYOR] El Portal Zevallos

Cozumel

see also Cancún & Playa del Carmen

ACCOMMODATIONS

Flamingo Hotel [GF] Calle 6 Norte #81 (at Ave 5) 954/351-9236, 800/806-1601

Cuernavaca

ACCOMMODATIONS

Casa del Angel [GS,NS,GO] Calle Clavel 18, Col. Satelite (at Begonia) 52-777/512-6775

Las Mañanitas [GF,SW] Ricardo Linares 107 52-777/312-8982 & 314-1466, 888/413-9199 (US only)

La Nuestra [GS,SW,NS,WI,GO] Calle Mesalina 18 (at Calle Neptuno) 52-777/315-2272, 404/806-9694

BARS

Barecito [MW,F,GO] Comonfort 17 (at Morrow) 52-777/314-1425

La Casa del Dictador [M,D] Jacarandas 4 (at Av Emiliano Zapata) 52-777/317-3186, 52-777/317-2377 *wknds only, garden*

NIGHTCLUBS

Oxygen [M,D,F,E,DS,S,V,18+,YC] Av Vincente Guerrero 1303 (near Sam's Club) 52-777/317-2714 *10pm-close, Fri-Sat only*

RESTAURANTS

La India Bonita Dwight Morrow 15 (btwn Morelos & Matamoros) 52-777/312-5021 *9am-9pm, till 5pm Sun-Mon*

La Maga [E] Calle Morrow #9 Altos **52-777/310-0432** *clsd Sun, popular lunch buffet, plenty veggie*

Marco Polo Calle Hidalgo 30 (in front of cathedral, 2nd flr) **52-777/312-3484, 52-777/318-4032** *1pm-close, Italian (pasta & pizza), overlooking cathedral*

▪ENTERTAINMENT & RECREATION

Diego Rivera Murals Plaza de Museo (in Cuauhnáhuac Regional Museum)

▪MEN'S CLUBS

Banos San Carlos Amado Nervo 111 (Col. Carolina) **52-777/317-2796** *6am-8am, clsd Sun*

Tepoz Spa [MO,18+,SW] Carretera San Andres de la Cal #69 (at Col. Carolina), Tepoztlan, Morelos **739/395-8457, 505/990-7522 (US)** *11am-9:30pm Sat-Sun only, also apt rental*

▪CRUISY AREAS

Mercado [AYOR] *Sun*

Plaza Morelos [AYOR]

Zócalo [AYOR] *also adjacent bar, Fri-Sat only*

Ensenada

▪NIGHTCLUBS

Sublime [M,D] Plaza Blanca , 3rd Fl **52-646/128-8798** *9pm-close*

▪RESTAURANTS

Casamar [★] Blvd Costero 987 **52-646/174-0417** *8am-10:30pm, seafood, also bar*

Guadalajara

▪ACCOMMODATIONS

Casa Alebrijes Hotel [M,WI,GO] Libertad 1016, Zona Centro **52-33/3614-5232** *boutique hotel in historic center, two blocks from gay nightlife area*

Casa de las Flores B&B [GF,WI] Santos Degollado 175, Tlaquepaque **52-33/3659-3186, 888/582-4896** *15 minutes from Guadalajara*

Casa Rayon [GS,WI,GO] Calle Rayon 179 (at Lopez Cotilla) **619/798-0568 (US#)**

Casa Venezuela [GS,NS,WI,GO] Calle Venezuela 459 (at Col. Americana) **52-33/3826-6590, 832/519-1904 (US#)** *B&B in 100-year-old colonial house, full brkfst*

Escape B&B [MO,WI] Enrique Gonzalez Martinez 446 **52-33/1596-6017**

Hostel Lit [GF,WI] Degollado 413 **52-33/1200-5055**

Hotel San Francisco [GF,F] Degollado 267 **52-33/3613-3256**

Old Guadalajara B&B [GS,NS,GO] Belén 236 (Centro Histórico) **52-33/3613-9958**

Orchid House B&B [GS,GO] Juan de Ojeda 75 (at Ave La Paz) **52-33/3335-19 21**

La Perla B&B [GS,NS,WI,GO] Prado 128, Col. Americana (Vallarta y Lopez Cotilla) **52-33/3825-1948**

La Villa del Ensueño [GS,NS] Florida St 305, Tlaquepaque **52-33/3635-8792**

▪BARS

Arizona's Bar Saloon [MO,B,DS,S] Av La Paz 1985 (at Av Chapultepec, Zona Rosa) **52-33/3826-3743** *11pm-3am, clsd Mon*

California's [M] Pedro Moreno 652 (at 8 de Julio, Col. Centro) **52-33/3614-3221** *6pm-3am, Mexican cantina bar*

Caudillos Bar [★M,D,F,YC] Calle Prisciliano Sánchez 305, Centro (at Ocampo) **52-33/3613-5445** *5pm-3am, dancing from 9pm, friendly bar, also restaurant*

El Ciervo [M,D] 20 de Noviembre 797 (at Los Angeles, Sector Reforma) **52-33/3619-6765** *cruisy*

Club YeYe [MW,V,F] Prisciliano Sánchez 395 (Zona Centro) **52-33/1337-5253** *5pm-3am, chic video lounge*

Condado [MO,CW] Colon 434 (btwn Leandro Valle & Nueva Galicia) *6pm-3am Wed-Sun*

Dona Diabla [GS,E] Colon 530 *7pm-3am Wed-Sun*

Equilibrio Restaurant & Bar Ocampo 293 (at Miguel Blanco)

Guadalajara • MEXICO

Maskaras [MW,NH,F,E] Calle Maestranza 238 (at Prisciliano Sánchez) **52-33/3614-8103** *noon-3am, colorful atmosphere, live music*

La Minerva [M,K,S] 8 de Julio #73 **52-33/3613-5167** *theme nights*

Voltio [MO,L,B,S] Mexicaltzingo 1521 (Av Enrique Diaz de Leon) *theme nights*

▉ NIGHTCLUBS

7 Sins [M,D] Pedro Moreno 532 (at Donato Guerra, Zona Centro) **52-33/3658-0713**

Babel [M,D] Morelos 741 *Fri-Sat only*

Black Cherry Grand [M,D] Popocatepetl 40 (at Adolfo Lopez Mateos Sur) **52-33/3647-9024** *10pm-5am Sat only*

El Botanero [M,D,F,K,DS,YC,$] Calle Javier Mina 1348 (at Calle 54, Sector Libertad) **52-33/3643-0545** *6pm-3am, till 1am Sun, clsd Mon-Tue, T-dance Sun*

Circus [★MW,D,E,DS] Galeana 277 (at Prisciliano Sánchez, Centro Histórico) **52-33/3613-0299** *9pm-5am*

Mónica's [★M,D,DS,S,YC,$] Av Álvaro Obregón 1713 (btwn Calles 68 & 70, Sector Libertad; no sign, look for canopy under a big palm tree) **52-33/3643-9544** *9pm-5am, clsd Mon-Tue, packed after midnight, [DS,S] wknds, take a taxi to & from*

Om Club [M,D] Ocampo 270 **52-33/3121-9547** *9am-4pm Th-Sat, 5pm-10pm Sun*

Velvett [MW,D] **52-33/3830-4165** *9pm-5am*

▉ CAFES

Dolce Veele [MW,WI] Enrique González Martínez 177 **52-33/1523-9593** *4pm-1am*

Queer Nation López Cotilla 611 *5pm-midnight, clsd Sun, souvenirs*

Vida Caffe [MW] Av Hidalgo 907 **52-33/1181-1834** *4:30pm-close*

▉ RESTAURANTS

Sanborns [WI] Av 16 de Septiembre 127 **52-33/3613-6264** *many locations*

▉ PUBLICATIONS

GAYGDL *online magazine at www.gaygdl.com*

Urbana Revista *gay lifestyle magazine w/ bars & clubs for Guadalajara & Puerto Vallarta*

▉ GYMS & HEALTH CLUBS

Renacer Day Spa [★MO] Amado Nervo 106 (Col. Ladrón de Guevara) **52-33/3616-4441 or 4442** *noon-9pm, European-style day spa*

▉ MEN'S CLUBS

La Academia [★PC] Prisciliano Sánchez 484 (btwn Donato Guerra & Enrique González Martínez) **52-33/3124-1154**

Baños Guadalajara Federalismo Sur #634 **52-33/3826-4149** *open till 8pm, till 3pm Sun, bar, popular afternoons*

Baños La Fuente Calle Manuel Acuña #1107 (btwn Nicolas Romero & Gregoria Davila) **52-33/3826-3618** *clsd Sun*

Banos Santa Terecita Andres Teram #462 (btwn Manuel Acuna & Herrara y Cairo Sts, Col. Santa Terecita) **52-33/3825-1464** *open daily, popular evenings, till 3pm Sun, four steam rooms*

Riilax [MO] Venustiano Carranza 313 (at Angulo) **52-33/3331-1062**

▉ EROTICA

Bite Garibaldi #1389-B **52-33/1661-4016**

▉ CRUISY AREAS

Parque Revolución [AYOR] Av Juárez at Av Federalismo

Plaza Tapatía [AYOR] near Degollado Theater *days*

Isla Mujeres

▉ ACCOMMODATIONS

Casa Sirena [GF,GO] Av Miguel Hidalgo, Centro (at Bravo y Allende)]

La Paz

▥ACCOMMODATIONS

La Casa Mexicana Inn [GS,NS,WI,WC] Calle Nicolas Bravo 106 (btwn Madero & Mutualismo) **52-612/125-2748** *open Nov-June*

Hotel Mediterrane [GS,F,NS,WI,GO] Allende 36 (at Malecón) **52-612/125-1195** *sundeck, also bar & restaurant*

▥BARS

Cafe La Pazta [GS,NH,YC,GO] Allende 36 (at Hotel Mediterrane) **52-612/125-1195** *7am-11pm*

▥NIGHTCLUBS

Las Varitas [GF,D,E] Calle Independencia 111 (at Malecón) **52-612/123-1590** *9pm-3am, clsd Mon, rock 'n' roll bar*

▥CRUISY AREAS

Malecón (Seawall) [AYOR] *afternoon & early evening*

León

▥BARS

G*bar [M,YC] Madero 226 (at Gante, Centro Histórico) **52-477/740-8863** *6pm-2am, café-bar w/ terrace*

▥NIGHTCLUBS

La Madame [M,D,DS] Blvd A López Mateos 1709 Oriente (in front of Torre Banamex) **52-477/763-3086** *10pm-3am, clsd Mon-Wed, go-go boys*

Nation [GS,D] **52-477/716-3695**

Manzanillo

▥ACCOMMODATIONS

Las Hadas [GF,SW] Av Vista Hermosa s/n (Fracc. Península de Santiago) **52-314/331-0101, 888/559-4329** *great resort & location*

Red Tree Melaque Inn [GF,SW,NS,WI,GO] Primaveras 32 (30 miles N of Manzanillo), Melaque-Villa Obregon **52-315/355-8917, 480/389-5786 (US)** *bungalows, near ocean*

▥CRUISY AREAS

Santiago Beach [AYOR]

Mazatlán

▥ACCOMMODATIONS

El Cid Resort [GF,SW] 866/306-6113, 52-669/913-3333

Hotel Los Sábalos [GF,SW] Av Playa Gaviotas 100 (Zona Dorada) **52-669/983-5333, 800/528-8760 (US#)** *resort, also popular Joe's Oyster Bar*

Old Mazatlan Inn [GF,SW,WI,GO] **52-520/366-8487, 866/385-2945**

The Pueblo Bonito Emerald Bay [GF,SW] Ave Ernesto Coppel Compaña 201 **52-669/989-0525, 800/990-8250** *also piano bar*

▥BARS

La Alemana [GS] Calle Zaragoza 16 (at Benito Juarez & Serdan) *sports bar*

Pepe Toro [★M,D,DS,S] Av de las Garzas 18 (1 block W of Av Camarón Sábalo, Zona Dorada) **52-669/914-4176** *9:30pm-4am, clsd Mon-Th*

Vitrolas Bar [MW,F,K,DS,S] Heriberto Frías 1608 (in Centro Historico) **52-669/985-2221** *3pm-1am, clsd Mon, lunch menu, [DS,S] Sun*

▥RESTAURANTS

Panamá Restaurant & Pastelería [GS] at Avs de las Garzas & Camarón Sábalo (Zona Dorada) **52-669/913-6977**

Roca Mar [★] Av del Mar (at Calle Isla de Lobos, Zona Costera) **52-669/981-6008** *till 2am, seafood, full bar*

▥MEN'S CLUBS

Baños Juan Carlos [AYOR] Calle Genaro Estrada 712 (btwn Benito Juarez & Arquiles Serdan) **52-669/981-7205** *sleazy, busy after 5pm, closes early*

Mérida

▥ACCOMMODATIONS

Angeles de Mérida [GF,SW,NS] Calle 74-A, #494-A (at Calle 57 & Calle 59) **52-999/923-8163** *restored 18th-c home, full brkfst, spa services available*

Los Arcos B&B [GF,SW,GO] Calle 66 **52-999/928-0214**

Mérida • MEXICO

Casa Ana B&B [GF,SW,NS] Calle 52 #469 (btwn 51 & 53) **52-999/924-0005**

La Casa Lorenzo [GF,SW,WI,GO] Calle 41 #516 A (btwn 62 & 64) **52-999/139-0423 , 866/515-4105**

Casa San Juan B&B [GS,NS,WC,GO] 545-A Calle 62 (btwn Calle 69 & Calle 71) **52-999/986-2937, 866/979-6753**

Casa Santiago B&B [GS,SW,NS,WI,WC,GO] Calle 63 #562 (btwn Calles 70 & 72) **52-999/928-9375**

Gran Hotel [GF,F] Calle 60 #496 (nr Parque Cepeda Peraza) **52-999/924-7730 & 923-6963**

Las Arecas Guesthouse [GF,GO] Calle 59 #541 (btwn Calle 66 & Calle 68) **52-999/928-3626** *guesthouse, full brkfst*

Posada Santiago Guesthouse [GS,SW,NS,WI,WC,GO] Calle 57 No 552 (between Calle 66 & 68, Centro Historico) **52-999/928-4258**

■BARS

El Establo [★GF,D,F] Calle 60 #482 (btwn Calle 56 & 58) **52-999/924-2289** *popular w/ tourists & locals*

■NIGHTCLUBS

Angeluz [M,D] *all taxi drivers know where it is located, near Pride Disco*

Pride Disco [M,D,S] Campeche A (200 meters del Puente de Ulman), Anillo Periferico **52-999/946-4401** *south of town, take a taxi*

Scalibur [M,D,S] **52-999/108-2046** *from 11pm, also wknd T-dance from 2pm, difficult to find but worth the ride*

■RESTAURANTS

Cafe La Habana Calle 59 #511-A (at Calle 62) **52-999/928-6502** *24hrs, also bar & café*

Cafeteria Pop [BW] Calle 57 (btwn Calle 60 & 62) **52-999/928-6163** *brkfst, lunch & "light dinner"*

La Bella Época Calle 60 #447 (upstairs in the Hotel del Parque) **52-99/928-1928** *4pm-1am, Yucatécan, try for a balcony table*

■MEN'S CLUBS

La Banana Azul [M,WI,NS,GO] 514 Calle 70 (btwn 65 & 67, 3 blocks from Parque Santiago) **52-999/923-3957** *steam room, massage, gym, friendly*

■CRUISY AREAS

Calle 60 [AYOR] btwn the Zócalo & Santa Lucia park

Santa Lucia Park [AYOR] *late afternoons & evenings*

Zócalo [AYOR] *near corner of Calle 60 & 61*

Mexicali

■BARS

La Linterna [M,NH,OC,AYOR] Blvd Juárez (btwn Calles Azueta & Altamirano) *1pm-1am, hustlers*

El Rey de Copas [MW,NH] Av Baja California (at Av Tuxtla Gutierrez, Pueblo Nuevo) *open till 3am*

El Taurino [★MW,D] Av Juan de Zuazua 480 (near Jose Morelos) *1pm-2am, clsd Mon, cruisy*

■NIGHTCLUBS

Mirage Disco [★D] Av Lerdo #430 (Zona Centro) **52-686/214-1285** *6pm-2am Wed-Sun*

■MEN'S CLUBS

Baños San Jose [GS] Av Juan de Zuazua 475 (enter rear) *7am-8pm*

■CRUISY AREAS

Chapultepec Park [AYOR] *afternoons*

Mexico City

Note: M°=Metro station

Note: Mexico City is divided into "Zonas" (ie, Zona Rosa) & "Colonias" (abbreviated here as "Col."). Remember to use these when giving addresses to taxi drivers.

■INFO LINES & SERVICES

Cálamo (LGBT AA) Av de Chapultepec 465, desd 202 (Col. Juárez) **52-55/5574-1210** *8pm Mon-Fri, 7pm Sat, 6pm Sun*

Centro Cultural de la Diversidad Sexual Colima 267 (Col. Roma Norte) **52-55/5514-2565, 52-55/1450-9511** *Mexico City's LGBT center, also cafe*

Jovenes La Villa AA Calle 521 #248 (nr Ave 510) **52-55/2603-7696**

◼ACCOMMODATIONS

6M9 Guesthouse [MO,SW,WI,GO] Marsella 69 (at Havre) **52-55/5208-8347** *in gay area*

Best Western Majestic Hotel [GF,WC] Ave Madero 73, Col. Centro **52-55/5521-8600, 800/528-1234** *on the Zócalo Plaza, rooftop restaurant*

Condesa Haus [GF,WI,GO] Cuernavaca 142 (at Campeche) **52-55/5256-2494, 310/622-4825** (US#)

Hostal Central Historico Regina [GF,F,WI] 5 de Febrero #53 (Col. Centro) **52-55/5709-4192**

Hotel Casa Blanca [GF,F,SW] Lafragua 7 (Col. Tabacalera) **52-55/5096-4500, 800/905-2905** *also restaurant & bar*

Hotel Gillow [GF,F,WI] Isabel la Católica 17 (Col. Centro) **52-55/5518-1440, 52-55/5510-2636**

Hotel Polanco [GF] Edgar Allan Poe 8 (Col. Polanco) **52-55/5280-8082, 800/221-9044**

Hotel Principado [GF] Londres 42 (Col Juarez) **52-55/5533-2944**

El Patio 77 [GF,WI] Icazbalceta 77 (Col. San Rafael) **52-55/5455-0332, 52-55/5592-8452** *eco-friendly B&B*

The Red Tree House [GF] Culiacan 6 (Col Condesa) **52-55/5584-3829** *stylish B&B*

Valentina [GF] Amberes 27, Col. Juárez (Zona Rosa) **52-55/5080-4500** *small boutique hotel*

W Mexico City [GF,WI] Campos Eliseos 252 **52-55/9138-1800** *in trendy Polanco, 2 restaurants & bar*

◼BARS

42 Bar Amberes 4 (Zona Rosa) **52-55/5208-0352**

Bar Lili [MW,NH] Calle 65 #7 (Col. Puebla) **52-55/4551-0414**

Black Out [GS] Amberes 11 (Zona Rosa) **52-55/5511-9247** *upscale lounge, also restaurant*

Boy Bar [M] Amberes 14 (Zona Rosa) **52-55/5511-3915, 52-55/5207-5591** *10pm-close Fri-Sat only*

Cafeína [GF,D] Nuevo Leon 73 (in Condesa) **52-55/5212-0090** *7pm-4am, 6pm-10pm Sun, co-owned by Diego Luna of Y Tu Mama También fame*

El Celo [M,NH,D,F,S,$] Calle Londres 104 (Zona Rosa) **52-55/5514-4766** *5pm-close, clsd Mon*

Enigma [MW,D,S,$] Calle Morelia 111, Col. Roma (4 blocks from Mº Niños Héroes, Zona Rosa) **52-55/5207-7367** *9pm-3:30am, 6pm-2am Sun, clsd Mon, go-go boys*

La Gayta/ Pussy Bar [MW,NH,YC] Amberes 18 (Zona Rosa) **52-551/055-5873**

Lipstick [GS,DS,V] Amberes 1 (at Paseo de la Reforma, Zona Rosa) **52-55/5514-4920** *clsd Sun, lounge, more gay Fri-Sat*

El Marrakech Salón [MW,NH] Republica de Cuba 18 (Col. Centro)

Oasis [M,DS,$] República de Cuba 2 (Centro Historico) **52-55/5511-9740** *3pm-1am, till 3am Fri-Sat*

Papi Fun Bar [MW,NH,YC] Amberes 18 (Zona Rosa) **52-55/5208-3755**

Pride Restbar Alfonso Reyes 281 (Col. Condesa) **52-55/5516-2368**

El Taller/ El Almacen [MO,D,B,L,S,V] Av Florencia 37-A, Zona Rosa (basement, no sign so look for big nuts & bolts above door) **52-55/5207-0727** *5pm-3am, clsd Mon, cruisy leather/ levi crowd, also sex shop*

Tom's Leather Bar [★M,B,L,S,V,$] Av Insurgentes 357 (Col. Condesa) **55-84/5564-0728** *9pm-4am, clsd Mon*

Viena Bar [★M] República de Cuba 3 (Centro Historico) **52-55/5512-0929** *11am-11pm, clsd Mon-Tue, beer bar*

Mexico City • MEXICO

NIGHTCLUBS

Butterflies [★MW,D,DS,S,$] Calle Izazaga 9 (at Av Lazaro Cárdenas S, Centro Historico) **52-55/5761-1861** 9pm-3am, till 4:30am Fri-Sat, clsd Mon, 2 flrs, lavish drag shows Fri-Sat

Cabaré-Tito Fusion [MW,18+] Londres 77 (Zona Rosa) **52-55/5511-1613** open 4pm, clsd Mon-Tue, drag shows Th

Cabaré-Tito Neón [MW,D,DS,S] Calle Londres 161, Local 20-A, Plaza del Angel (Zona Rosa) **52-55/5514-9455** 6pm-close

Club 24 [M,D] Santa María la Ribera # 24 Del Cuauhtémoc **52-55/2198-2580** 9am-4am Fri-Sat only

Envy [GS,D] Av Las Palmas 500 (Sierra Gamon)

Hibrido [MW,D,S] Calle Londres 161, Plaza del Angel, 2nd flr (Zona Rosa) **52-55/5511-1197** Th-Sun

Ken Club [M,D] Medellin 65, Roma Norte (at Ixchel) **52-55/4612-1755** Th & Sat only

Liverpool 100 [M,D] Liverpool 100 (Col. Juarez) **52-55/5208-4507** 9pm-close Wed, Fri-Sat only

Living [★M,D,DS,S] Bucareli 144 (Col. Juarez) **52-55/5512-7281** 10pm-close Fri-Sat only, theme nights

Nicho [MO,B] Calle Londres 182 open 8pm, clsd Sun

CAFES

B Gay B Proud [F] Amberes 12-B (Zona Rosa)

Coffee Station Londres 167-A (Zona Rosa) **52-55/5525-2705** clsd Mon-Tue

RESTAURANTS

12:30 Amberes 13 (Zona Rosa) **52-55/5514-5971** popular before-clubbing hangout

La Antigua Cortesana Chiapas 173-A (Col. Roma) **52-55/5584-4678** 1pm-11pm, till midnight Fri-Sat, till 7pm Sun, popular Mexican cuisine, also bar

Cafe 22 [E] Montes de Oca 22 (Col. Condesa) **52-55/5212-1533** 6pm-2am, Mexican & Italian, also shows

El Cardenal Calle de Palma 23 **52-55/5521-8815** incredible pastries

Casa Merlos Victoriano Zepeda 80 (at Observatoria) **52-55/5277-4360** traditional poblano food, definitely try the molé

Cote Sud Orizaba 87 (Col. Roma) **52-55/5219-2981** 8am-11pm, till midnight Fri, 10am-6pm Sun, French/tapas

Fonda San Ángel Plaza San Jacinto 3, Col. San Ángel (across from Bazar San Ángel) **52-55/5550-1641 & 1942** popular after 7pm Fri-Sat, classic Mexican dishes

Ixchel Medellín 65, Roma Norte **52-55/5208-4055**

Ligaya Nuevo Leon 68 (in Condesa) **52-55/5286-6268** nouvelle Mexican, dinner nightly, outdoor seating

La Nueva Opera [P] Ave Cinco de Mayo 10 (Centro Historico) **52-55/5512-8959** 1pm-midnight, clsd Sun, legendary cantina since Pancho Villa fired a bullet into the ceiling

Sanborns Madera 4 (in Casa de los Azulejos) **52-55/5518-6676** often cruisy, especially in magazine/news-stand section

Xel-Ha **52-55/5553-5968** traditional cuisine of the Yucatan

ENTERTAINMENT & RECREATION

El Hábito [S] Madrid 13 (Coyacán District) **52-55/5659-1139** avant-garde theater & bar

Museo de Arte Carrillo Gil Av Revolución 1608 (Col San Angel) **52-55/5550-6260, 52-55/5550-3983** 10am-6pm, clsd Mon, contemporary art

Museo de Frida Kahlo Calle Londres 247 (Coyacán) **52-55/5554-5999** 10am-5:45pm, clsd Mon, also garden & café

Museo Templo Mayor Calle Seminario 8 (at República de Guatemala, enter on plaza, near Cathedral) **52-55/4040-5600** 9am-5pm, clsd Mon, artifacts from the central Aztec temple at Tenochtitlán

▥BOOKSTORES

El Armario Abierto Agustín Melgar 25 (Col. Condesa) **52-55/5286-0895** *Mexico's only bookstore specializing in sexuality, some LGBT titles*

▥RETAIL SHOPS

Rainbowland Estrasburgo 31 (Zona Rosa) **52-55/5525-9066**

Roshell Lorenzo Boturini 440 **52-55/5768-1317** *drag emporium, hair styling, also monthly shows & events*

▥PUBLICATIONS

Ser Gay **52-55/1450-9511** *quarterly magazine, covers all Mexico nightlife*

▥GYMS & HEALTH CLUBS

Club San Francisco [M] Calle Rio Pánuco 207 (Col. Cuauhtémoc) **52-55/5525-0936**

QI Amsterdam 317 (in Condesa) **52-55/5574-5095** *gym w/ spa*

▥MEN'S CLUBS

Baños Finisterre [AYOR] Manuel Maria Contreras 11, Col. San Rafael (4 blocks W of M° San Cosme) **52-55/5555-3543** *traditional bathhouse where men go, hang out & get a massage; not "anything goes" like in US or Europe*

Baños San Juan [F,AYOR] Calle López 120 (N of M° Salto de Agua, in Centro Historico) **52-55/5521-3376** *also salon*

Baños Señorial [AYOR] Calle Isabel la Católica 92 (Centro Historico) **52-55/5709-0732, 52-55/5709-3120**

La Casita I [AYOR,18+] Viaducto Miguel Alemán 72, Col. Algarín (near Bolivar— no sign/ number on door) **52-55/5519-8842** *24hrs, gym equipment, porn shop*

La Casita II [AYOR,18+] Insurgentes S 228 (Col. Roma) **52-55/5514-4639, 52-55/5514-4591** *24hrs*

So Do Me [★] **52-55/5250-6653** *noon-10pm, till 1am Fri, 24hrs wknds*

La Toalla Obregon [AYOR,18+] Álvaro Obregón 259 (Col. Roma) **52-55/5511-0686** *24hrs*

La Toalla Valley [AYOR,18+] Cda. Sánchez Azcona 1724 (Col. del Valle) **52-55/5534-9399** *7am-11pm*

▥CRUISY AREAS

Alameda Central [AYOR] W side of park (Centro Historico) *afternoons & early evenings, dangerous later*

Bosque de Chapultepec [AYOR] either side of gate to monument (Zona Rosa) *afternoons*

Zona Rosa [AYOR] *nights, anywhere & everywhere, but especially Calle Florencia btwn Reforma & Liverpool, also Calles Génova, Hamburgo & Londres*

Monterrey

▥ACCOMMODATIONS

Holiday Inn Monterrey Centro [GF,SW] Av Padre Mier 194 N (at Garibaldi, Centro) **52-81/8228-6000** *also restaurant, near Zona Rosa*

▥BARS

Akbal [GS] Abasolo 870B, 2nd flr, Casa del Maíz **52-81/1257-2986** *more gay Sun*

Casa de Lola [M,D,K] **52-81/8343-6210** *Th-Sat only*

▥NIGHTCLUBS

Baby Shower [MW,D,S,V] Ocampo 433 Puente (btwn Rayon & Aldama Centro) **52-81/8881-5632** *9pm-close, clsd Mon-Tue*

Bizù Disco [M,DS] 1355 Miguel Hidalgo y Costilla **52-81/8994-4676**

Parking [M,D] Allende 120 Ote (btwn Juarez & Guerrero) **52-81/8343-2624** *10pm-close Wed-Sat*

Vongole & Between Bar [M,DS] 2121 Eugenio Garza Sada Ave **52-81/8358-7035**

▥MEN'S CLUBS

Baños Orientales Calle Hidalgo 310 Oriente, Guadalupe **52-81/8367-2843** *8am-10pm, till 3pm Sun, hustlers*

Sparta Sauna Gym 107 Álvaro Obregón **52-81/8342-2770** *noon-midnight, clsd Sun*

Monterrey • MEXICO

STIC Baños de Vapor & Spa Av de los Héroes 47 (at Av Francisco I Madero) **52-81/8375-7690** 6am-10pm, till 2pm Sun

▓CRUISY AREAS

Avenida Juárez [AYOR] btwn Calle Matamoros & Calle Padre Mier (Centro) part of "El Circuito," hustlers

Plaza Hidalgo [AYOR] Zona Rosa late afternoons & early evenings

Morelia

▓ACCOMMODATIONS

Hotel de la Soledad [GF,WI] Ignacio Zaragoza 90 **52-443/312-1888** in converted convent, also restaurant & bar

▓BARS

Beered [M,B] Vicente Barrozo 44 (at Félix Ireta) **52-44/3155-1481**

▓NIGHTCLUBS

Con la Rojas [M,D,$] Calle Aldama 343 (Centro) **52-443/312-1578** 10pm-2:30am, clsd Sun-Tue

Mamá no lo sabe [M,K] Aldama 116 (at García Obeso) **52-44/3189-9447** 10pm-3am

▓RESTAURANTS

Fonda Las Mercedes [★] Calle Leon Guzmán 47 **52-443/312-6113 &** 313-3222 inside beautiful colonial home

▓MEN'S CLUBS

Baños Mintzicuri Calle Vasco de Quiroga 227 (enter through the Hotel Mintzicuri) **52-443/312-0664** gay area through door marked "Ruso General"

Baños Valladolid Eduardo Ruiz 605 **52-44/3312-9985** 7am-8pm, till 2pm Sun

▓EROTICA

Cine Arcadia Eduardo Ruiz 870

▓CRUISY AREAS

Escalinatas de Santa María [AYOR]

Oaxaca

▓ACCOMMODATIONS

El Camino Real Oaxaca [GF,F,SW] Calle 5 de Mayo 300 **52-951/501-6100, 800/722-6466** restored 16th-c convent

Casa Adobe B&B [GS,WI,GO] Independencia 801 (at Matamoros), Tlalixtac de Cabrera **52-951/517-7268** 15 minutes from center of Oaxaca

La Casa de Don Pablo Hostel [GS,NS] Melchor Ocampo 412, Centro (at Rayon St) **52-951/516-8384**

Casa Machaya Oaxaca B&B [GF] Sierra Nevada 164, Col. Loma Linda **52/951-1328203**

Casa Sol Zipolite [M,SW,WI,GO] 6 Arco Iris, Col. Arroyo Tres **52-95/8100-0462** 300 meters from famous Playa Zipolite

Posada Arigalan [GS,WI] **52-958/111-5801, 956/280-2165 (US)**

▓NIGHTCLUBS

Club Privado 502 (aka El Número) [GS,D,K,PC,$] Calle Porfirio Díaz 502 (Centro, ring to enter) 10pm-close, clsd Sun-Tue

La Costa [M,D,S] Av 16 de Septiembre #517 (Col. Cinco Señores) **52-951/511-2908** wknds only 9pm-close

Elefante [GS,D] 20 de Noviembre **52-951/164-8637**

Gavana Dance Club [GS] Calzada Porfirio Diaz #216 (Col. Reforma) 9pm-close Th-Sat

▓CAFES

B Proud [WI] Morelos 1107-A open 9am & 4pm Sun

▓RESTAURANTS

El Asador Vasco [★] Portal de Flores 10-A (Centro) **52-951/514-4755** great views & authentic Oaxacan cuisine (can you say ¡mole!)

Casa Crespo Allende 107 **52-951/516-0918** lunch & dinner, also cooking classes

▓MEN'S CLUBS

Baños del Jardin Melchor Ocampo 509
52-951/516-5668

Banos La Fuente [MO] 20 de
Noviembre #1021 (near Periferico)
52-958/516-5668 *open till 8pm, 2
steam rms, friendly*

Baños La Fuente Calle 20 de
Noviembre **52-951/516-5668**

▓CRUISY AREAS

Parque Alemeda & Zócalo [AYOR]
early evenings

Playa del Carmen

see also Cancún & Cozumel

▓ACCOMMODATIONS

Acanto Boutique Hotel [GF,SW,NS,WI]
16th St N (btwn 5th Ave & the beach)
631/882-1986

Aventura Mexicana Hotel [GF,SW,N]
Av 10 (at Calle 24) **52-984/873-1876,
800/455-3417**

Hotel Copa Cabana [GS,WI,WC] 5ta Av
Norte **52-984/873-0218**

**Hotel Playa del Carmen & OM
Lounge** [GS,WI,GO] Calle 12 Norte con
1.ra privada, n.195 **52-984/147-0949**

Luna Blue Hotel & Bar [GS,WI] Calle
26 (at 5th Av) **415/839-8541**

Reina Roja Hotel [GS,SW,WI] 22 Street
(btwn 5th & 10th Ave)
52-984/877-3800

▓NIGHTCLUBS

Playa 69 [M,D,GO] Av 5 (btwn Calle 4 &
Calle 6, ground flr) *9pm-4am wknds,
cruisy*

Playa Palms [GS,SW] 1st Avenue Bis
(btwn 12 & 14th N St)
52-984/803-3908, 888/676-4431

▓RESTAURANTS

100% Natural Av 5 (btwn 10th &
12th) **52-984/73-2242** *vegetarian*

▓ENTERTAINMENT &
RECREATION

Playa Loves You Tours Estrella de Mar
137 **52-198/4110-0939** *tours especially for the LGBT Community in the SE
part of the Mexican Caribbean*

Puebla

▓BARS

La Cigarra [M,S,V] Ave 5 Poniente 538
(at Calle 7, Centro) **52-222/246-6356**
6pm-3am, beer bar

Franco's Bule Bar [M,E,DS,S] 5 Oriente
402 (Los Sapos) **52-222/232-3409**
10pm-3am, till 6am Th-Sat, clsd Mon

▓NIGHTCLUBS

Garotos [GF,D,$] 22 Orient E 602 (close
to Blvd 5 de Mayo, Xenenetla)
52-222/242-4232 *9pm-3am Fri-Sat
only*

▓MEN'S CLUBS

Baños Las Termas [MO,V,PC] Av 5 de
Mayo 2810, Centro **52-222/232-9562**
*8am-8pm, open later wknds, till 3pm
Sun, clsd Mon, 3 floors, gym, sauna,
popular afternoons*

Baños Las Termas Calle 5 de Mayo
2810 52-222/232-9562

▓CRUISY AREAS

Zócalo/ Main Park [AYOR] at cathedral
late evenings

Puerto Vallarta

▓INFO LINES & SERVICES

Community Center GLBT SETAC 427
Constitucion (at Manuel M Diéguez)
52-322/224-1974 *AA meetings,
movie nights, HIV testing and Spanish
classes*

▓ACCOMMODATIONS

Abbey Hotel [MO,SW] Pulpito 138 (at
Olas Altas) **52-322/222-4488** *also
restaurant & lounge*

Amaca Hotel [M,SW,WI] 583 Pino
Suarez (at Pulpito) **52-322/223-0272**
boutique hotel, also Sky Bar

Blue Chairs Beach Resort
[MW,SW,WI,WC] **52-322/222-5040,
888/302-3662**

Boana Torre Malibu Condo Hotel
[GS,F,SW,GO] Calle Amapas 325
**52-322/222-0999,
52-322/222-6695** *near gay beach*

Puerto Vallarta • MEXICO

Casa Cúpula [MW,SW,NS,WI,WC,GO] Callejon de la Igualdad 129, Col. Amapas 52-322/223-2484, 866/352-2511

Casa de las Flores [GO] Calle Santa Barbara #359 510/763 - 3913 (US#), 52-322/120-5242

Casa Fantasía [GS,SW,NS,WC,GO] Pinot Suarez 203, Col. Emiliano Zapata (near the Rio Cuale) 52-322/223-2444 *B&B made up of 3 haciendas, terrace*

Hotel Emperador [GS,WI] Amapas 114 52-322/222-1767, 800/523-1158 *located right on "Los muertos" beach*

Hotel Mercurio [MW,SW,WI,GO] 52-322/222-4793, 866/388-2689 *gay/ lesbian hotel in Vallarta's Gayborhood, 1 1/2 blocks from beach*

Hotelito Desconocido [GS,SW] Playon de Mismaloya, La Cruz de Loreto, Tomatlán 52-33/3611-3013, 800/851-1143 *eco-resort on the beach, 60 miles S of Puerto Vallarta, sauna*

El Panorama [GS,SW,WI,GO] Oceano Atlantico 82, La Penita 52-327/274-3499, 888/246-1369

The San Franciscan Resort & Gym [GS,SW,WI] Calle Pilitas #213 (at Playa Los Muertos) 52-322/222-6473 x0

Vallarta Cora [MO,SW,N,GO] Calle Pilitas 174 (at Playa Los Muertos) 52-322/222-6058

Villa Safari Condo [GS,SW,NS,GO] Francisca Rodriguez 203 269/469-0468 (US #)

Villas David B&B [MO,SW,NS,WI,GO] Calle Galeana 348 (at Calle Miramar) 877/832-3315 (US#), 52-322/223-0315

■ BARS

Los Amigos Bar [MW,NH] Calle Venustiano Carranza 237 (upstairs, next to Paco's Ranch) 52-322/222-7802 *6pm-4am, Mexican cantina, patio*

Amor Bar [MW] Lazaro Cardenas 271 52-322/222-7427 *9pm-4am, martini lounge*

Anonimo [M,NH] Rodolfo Gomez 157 *6pm-2am*

Apaches [GS,F,GO] Olas Altas 439 (at Rodriguez) 52-322/222-4004 *5pm-2am, till 1am Sun-Mon, classy cocktail bar, martinis & margaritas, tapas*

Blue Sunset Rooftop Bar [M,F,K,DS] Los Muertos Beach (at Blue Chairs Resort) *10am-midnight*

CC Slaughter's [M,D] Lazaro Cardenas 254 Emiliano (Zapata) 52-322/222-3412

Divas [MW,NH] 388 Francisco L Madero (E of Insurgentes) 52-322/135-0336 *2pm-2am*

Freedom [GS] 266 Ignacio Vallarta 52-322/188-2124

Frida [GS,B,F,GO] 301-A Insurgentes (at Venustiano Carranza) 52-322/223-3668 *1pm-2am, from 7pm Mon-Tue, Mexican cantina, more gay later in evening*

Garbo [M,E,P,GO,18+] Pulpito 142 (at Olas Altas) 52-322/223-5753 *6pm-2am, upscale martini lounge, live music*

Hot Frida's [GS,F] 155 Francisca Rodriguez, 2nd fl (at Olas Altas) 52-322/181-4556 *clsd Wed*

Los Equipales Grill [MW,F,GO] 315A Basillo Badillo

La Noche [MW] Lázaro Cárdenas 257 (Zona Romantica) 52-322/222-3364 *7pm-2am*

The Palm/ Viva [M,D,C] Olas Altas 508 (at Rodolfo Gomez) 52-322/223-4818 *4pm-4am*

Reinas [M,NH] Lazaro Cardenas 361 52-322/125-9532 *5pm-2am*

Sama [MW,NH,18+] Olas Altas 510 (at Rodolfo Gomez) 52-322/223-3182 *4:30pm-2am, small martini bar w/ side-walk seating*

Vallarta Cora Bar [★M,F] Calle Pilitas 174 (at Vallarta Cora hotel) 52-322/222-6234 *3pm-11pm, pool-side bar*

Wet Dreams [MO,S] Lazaro Cardenas 312 (Col. Emiliano Zapata) 52-322/222-8112 *8pm-2am, strip-pers*

◾NIGHTCLUBS

Antropology [MO,DS,S,YC,$] Calle Morelos 101, Plaza Río (at Plaza Rio Cuale) **52-322/306-1058** *9pm-4am, strippers*

Industry [M,D] Venustiano Carranza 200 *4pm-6am*

Koko Home [★M,D] Venustiano Carranza #290 (at Col. Emiliano Zapata) *Sat only*

No Borders [MW,NH] 221 Libertad **52-322/136-8775** *1pm-2am, rooftop patio*

Paco's Ranch [★M,D,DS,GO,$] 237 Ignacio Vallarta **52-322/222-1899** *9pm-6am, also rooftop terrace*

◾CAFES

A Page in the Sun 179 Plaza Lázaro Cárdenas (in Zona Romantica) **52-322/222-3608** *7am-11pm, coffee shop & English bookstore*

Cafe San Angel [F] Olas Altas 449 (at Francisco Rodreguez) **52-322/223-1273** *7am-1am*

The Coffee Cup [GO] Rodolfo Gómez 146-A (at Olas Altas) **52-322/222-8584** *7am-10pm, clsd Sun in summer*

CyberSmoothie [WI] Rodolfo Gómez 111 **52-322/223-4784** *9am-9:30pm*

Dee's Coffee Company [WI] **52-322/222-1197** *7am-10pm, home-made pastries*

Fuego Calle Amapas 147 (at Calle Pulpito) **52-322/222-2114** *8am-10pm, clsd Sun, Asian, also bar*

Uncommon Grounds Buddha Lounge [F] Lazaro Cardenas 625 **52-322/223-3834** *5pm-close, clsd Mon-Tue, also aromatherapy & gifts*

Xocodiva Rodolfo Gomez 118 **52-322/113-0352** *artisinal chocolate*

◾RESTAURANTS

El Arrayan [GO] Allende #344 (at El Centro) **52-322/222-7195** *6pm-11pm, clsd Tue*

The Blue Shrimp Olas Altas 366 (Zona Romantica) **52-322/222-4246** *11am-midnight*

El Brujo [★] Venustiano Carranza 510 (at Naranjo) **52-322/223-3026** *1pm-9:30pm, clsd Mon, Mexican/ seafood, worth the wait*

Cafe Bohemio [★MW,GO] Rodolfo Gómez 127 (at Olas Altas) **44-322/134-2436** *5pm-2am, clsd Sun, open-air cafe, late-evening happy hour*

Cafe de Olla [★] Calle Basilio Badillo 168 **52-322/223-1626** *10am-11pm, clsd Tue, Mexican, wait list an hour*

Cafe des Artistes [★R] Calle Guadalupe Sánchez 740 (at Leona Vicario) **52-322/222-3228** *6pm-11:30pm, upscale French w/ a Mexican twist*

Chez Elena [GO] Matamoros 520, Centro (at Los Quatro Vientos Hotel) **52-322/222-0161** *6pm-11pm, seasonal, garden restaurant, also rooftop bar*

Daiquiri Dick's [★] Olas Altas 314 (on Playa Los Muertos) **310/697-3799** *8:30am-11:30pm & 5:30pm-11pm, clsd Tue & clsd Sept*

De Santos [D] 771 Morelos **52-322/221-3090** *5pm-4am, chic Mediterranean, also dance club*

El Dorado Pulpito 102, Playa de los Muertos **52-322/222-4124** *beach club & restaurant, evening shows*

Le Bistro Jazz Cafe [GO] Isla Rio Cuale 16-A (on the island, at the East Bridge) **52-322/222-0283** *9am-midnight, clsd Sun*

Lido Beach Club Malecon 1 Esq Abedul (Col. Emiliano Zapata) **813/855-0190** *10am-6pm*

Memo's Casa de los Hotcakes [★] Calle Basilio Badillo 289 **52-322/222-6272** *8am-2pm, long lines for cheap & good brkfst*

Mezzogiorno Ristorante Italiano Avenida del Pacifico 33 (North Beach Bucerias Nayarit) **52-329/298-0350** *6pm-11pm (clsd Mon off-season)*

La Palapa Pulpito 103, Col. Emiliano Zapata 52-322/222-5225 brkfst, lunch & dinner, beachside dining

La Piazzetta Rodolfo Gomez #143 (at Olas Atlas, Romantic Zone) 52-322/222-0650 4pm-11pm, Italian

Planeta Vegetariano Iturbide 270 (Centro) 52-322/222-3073 8am-10pm, clsd Sun, buffet-style

Red Cabbage [GO] Calle Rivera del Rio 204-A (at Basilio Badillo) 52-322/223-0411 5pm-11pm, on Rio Cuale w/ great kitschy decor

The Swedes/ Crows Nest Bar [MW,GO] Púlpito 154 (at Olas Altas) 52-322/223-2353 Swedish/ European, also bar upstairs

Trio [★E] Guerrero 264 (Centro) 52-322/222-2196 6pm-midnight, clsd Sun

▥ ENTERTAINMENT & RECREATION

Boana Tours Calle Amapas 325 (at Casa Boana Torre Malibu) 52-322/222-0999, 52-322/222-6695 horseback tours daily

Diana's Cruise the Bay Tour [MW,F] meet at Los Muertos pier 9:30am-5pm Th, open bar

Ocean Friendly [GF] Paseo del Marlin 510-103, Col. Aralias 52-322/225-3774, 044-322/294-0385 (cell) whale-watching tours, Dec 15-March 31

Playa Los Muertos/ Playa del Sol [★] S of Rio Cuale the gay beach, now spans "Blue Chairs" & "Green Chairs"

▥ RETAIL SHOPS

La Rosa de Cristal [GO] Insurgentes 272 (at Cardenas) 52-322/222-5698 10am-8pm, local handicrafts blown-glass items

▥ PUBLICATIONS

Urbana Revista 52-333/844-6471 gay lifestyle magazine

▥ GYMS & HEALTH CLUBS

Acqua Day Spa & Gym Calle Constitución 450 (F Rodriguez) 52-322/223-5270 7am-9pm, till 5pm Sat, clsd Sun

▥ EROTICA

The Closet Lazaro Cardenas 230 52-322/223-3030 noon-9pm

Condom House Lazaro Cardenas 239 52-322/126-7722 noon-9pm, clsd Sun

▥ CRUISY AREAS

Malecón (Seawall) [AYOR] facing Calle Morelos (esp near benches across from Presidencia Municipal at Iturbide) evenings

Playa Los Muertos [AYOR] near green chairs at The Beach Café & further S by the rocks afternoons

Plaza Caracol Mall [AYOR]

Querétaro

▥ NIGHTCLUBS

Con la Rojas [M,D,$] Ave Constituyentes Pte 42A (Centro) 52-442/212-4795 10pm-2:30am, clsd Sun-Wed

▥ CRUISY AREAS

Alameda Parque [AYOR]

El Jardín Guerrero [AYOR] 3 blks from Centro Historico

Plaza de Armas [AYOR]

Zócalo/ Obregón Plaza [AYOR]

San Jose del Cabo

▥ ACCOMMODATIONS

El Encanto Inn [GF,SW] 210/858-6649, 52-614/142-0388

One & Only Palmilla [GF,SW] Apartado Postal 52, 23400 52-624/146-7000, 866/829-2977 (US#) upscale resort

▥ RESTAURANTS

Voila Bistro & Catering [★] 1705 Comonfort (Plaza Paulina) 52-624/130-7569 noon-10pm, from 4pm Sun, Mexican w/ French twist, full bar, patio

San Miguel de Allende

ACCOMMODATIONS

Casa de Sierra Nevada [GF,SW] Calle Hospicio 42 (Centro)
52-415/152-7040, 800/701-1561

Casa Schuck Boutique B&B [GF,SW,WI] Garita 3, Centro
52-415/152-6618, 937/684-4092

Dos Casas [GF] Calle Quebrada 101 (Guanajuato) **52-415/154-4073**

Las Terrazas San Miguel [GS,NS,WI,GO] Santo Domingo 3
52-415/152-5028, 707/534-1833 (US#) *4 rental homes*

RESTAURANTS

La Azotea Umaran 6
52-415/152-4977 *delicious tapas and drinks*

Mezzanine Bistro [GO] Cuna de Allende 11 (at Hotel Vista Hermosa)
52-415/152-2799

Tepic

MEN'S CLUBS

Banos America Jesus Garcia #37 (Fraccionamiento Simancas)
52-311/213-3747 *6am-10pm, till 3pm Sun, two steam rms, bar, popular afternoons*

Tijuana

BARS

Arco Iris Taberna [GS,F,GO] Av Pacifico 395 **52-664/631-8290** *beach bar w/ a great deck overlooking the new Malacon*

DF [M,NH,OC] Plaza Santa Cecilia 781 (btwn 1st Str & Ave Revolución) *open late*

El Ranchero Bar [★M,NH,D,F,AYOR] Plaza Santa Cecilia 769 (btwn Calles 1, 2, Revolución & Constitución)
52-664/685-2800 *1pm-late, cruisy cantina, hustlers, use caution in bathrooms*

El Taurino Bar [M,NH,S] Av Niños Héroes 189 (at Calles 1 & Constitución)
52-664/685-2478 *3pm-2am, till 5am Fri-Sat, cruisy, hustlers*

Tenampa Cantina [GF] Articulo 123 (at Revolución, by Hotel Cecilia)

Villa Garcia [M,D] Plaza Santa Cecilia 751 (next to El Ranchero) *10am-late, small dance flr, cruisy*

NIGHTCLUBS

Club Fusion [M,D,K,DS] Calle Larroque 213 **52-664/345-8817** *8pm-3am Fri-Sun*

Los Equipales [MW,D,DS,YC] Calle 7/ Galeana 2024 (at Av Revolución)
52-664/688-3006 *9pm-3am, clsd Mon-Tue*

Extasis [★M,D,S,$] Larroque 213 (in Plaza Viva Tijuana, next to the border)
52-664/682-8339 *8pm-late, clsd Mon-Wed, go-go boys, more women Th*

Mike's Disco [MW,D,DS,V,18+] Av Revolución 1220 (at Calle 6A)
52-664/685-3534 *8pm-5am, till 3am Th, clsd Wed*

Premier [M,S] Av Revolución (btwn 1st & Coahuila) *7pm-3am, clsd Mon-Tue*

Sin Tabu [GS] Av Sanchez Taboada 10291-7 **52-664/681-8138**

Terraza 9 [GF,D] Calle 5a (at Av Revolución) **52-664/685-3534** *5pm-2am, till 5am Fri-Sat, clsd Mon*

CAFES

D'Luna Cafe Calle 8 #8380
52-664/321-9735

MEN'S CLUBS

Banos Vica Gustavo Díaz Ordaz 1535
52-664/622-0386

Todos Santos

ACCOMMODATIONS

The Todos Santos Inn [GS,SW,NS,GO] Calle Legaspi #33 (Topete)
52-612/145-0040 *colonial inn w/ bar*

Tulúm

ACCOMMODATIONS

Adonis Tulum Riviera Maya Gay Resort & Spa [M,SW] Carretera Tulum Boca Paila Km 3.8 **800/233-5162, 52-984/871-1000**

Casa de las Olas [GF,WI] 10.km Tulum Beach Rd **52-984/807-3909**

Tulúm • MEXICO

EcoTulum Resorts & Spa [GF,WI]
Carretera Tulum Ruinas Km 5
54-115/5918-6400, 877/301-4666

Om Tulum [GF,WI] Caraterra Ruinas
Punta -Allen Km 9.5
521-98/4114-0538

Posada Luna del Sur [GF] Calle Luna
Sur 5 52-984/871-2984

Veracruz

■ACCOMMODATIONS

Hotel Villa del Mar [GF,SW] Blvd
Miguel Ávila Camacho 2431 (across
street from Playa del Mar beach)
52-229/989-6500

■ENTERTAINMENT & RECREATION

San Juan de Ulua Fortress 9am-
4:30pm, clsd Mon, impressive early colo-
nial-era floating fortress

Veracruz Aquarium Blvd Avila
Camacho (at Xicolencat)
52-229/932-7984 10am-7pm, one of
the largest & best in the world; don't
miss it!

■MEN'S CLUBS

Baños El Edén [AYOR] Miguel Hidalgo
1113 (Centro) 52-229/932-3360 buy
tickets at rear counter of music store

■CRUISY AREAS

Plaza de Armas/ Zócalo [AYOR]

Waterfront & Av República [AYOR]

Zacatecas

■ACCOMMODATIONS

Quinta Real Zacatecas [GF] Av Ignacio
Rayón 434 (Col. Centro)
52-492/1105-1010, 866/621-9288
5-star hotel built into grandstand of
bullfighting ring

■CRUISY AREAS

Av Juárez [AYOR] E from Av Hidalgo for
2 blks

Zihuatanejo

■ACCOMMODATIONS

Hotel Las Palmas [GF,SW] Calle de
Aeropuerto (at lot 5)
52-755/557-0634, 888/527-7256

■NIGHTCLUBS

Mydori Disco Bar [MW,D,DS,S] Calle La
Laja s/n (Col. Centro)
52-755/104-5670 8pm-4am

Tequila Town [★GF,K,V] Cuauhtemoc 3
(Col Centro) 52-755/553-8587 8pm-
4am, more gay after 11pm

Central America

COSTA RICA

Alajuela

■BARS

Rick's Bar & Restaurant [MW] 500
mts Este Casino Fiesta, carretera
Heredia, en Río Segundo de Alajuela
506-2/441-3213 6pm-close, from
4pm Sun

Chirripó Nat'l Park

■ACCOMMODATIONS

Monte Azul [GS,F,GO] Contiguo al
puente de Chucuyo, Chimirol
506/2742-5222

Escaleras

■ACCOMMODATIONS

Paradise Costa Rica [GS,SW,NS,GO]
800/708-4552 vacation villas

Guanacaste

■ACCOMMODATIONS

Villa Decary [GF,GO] Nuevo Arenal,
5717 Tilaran 506-2/694-4330,
800/556-0505 (from US & Canada)
former coffee farm overlooking Lake
Arenal

Manuel Antonio, Quepos

■ACCOMMODATIONS

Casa Antonio [MW,GO] Enter at
Arboleda Hotel 506/8639-1085

Casa de Frutas [GS,GO]
506-8/825-3257 (cell),
800/936-9622 luxury villa in Tulemar
Gardens

Casa Mono Titi [GF,SW,NS,WI,GO] in the hills **800/282-3680** *vacation home, near beaches & bars*

Casa Romano [GS,SW,WI,WC,GO] **404/290-6919** *near gay beach*

Casitas Eclipse [GS] KM 5 Manuel Antonio Rd **506-2/777-0408** *detached casitas*

Costa Verde [GS,SW,GO] **506-2/777-0584, 866/854-7958 (from US & Canada)**

Gaia Hotel & Reserve [GF,SW,WI,GO] km 2.7 Carretera Quepos a Manuel Antonio **506-2/777-9797, 800/226-2515** *boutique hotel, surrounded by wildlife refuge, full brkfst*

Hotel Parador [GF,SW,WI] **506-2/777-1414, 877/506-1414** *large luxury resort*

Hotel Villa Roca [M,SW,NS,WC,GO] **506-2/777-1349**

Las Aguas Resort [M,SW,WI,GO] **813/784-7930 (US#), 506-2/296-1880**

La Mansion Inn [GS,F,SW,GO] **506-2/777-3489, 800/360-2071**

La Posada [GF,SW,GO] **506-2/777-1446**

Si Como No [GF,SW,WC] **506-2/777-0777, 888/742-6667** *25-acre wildlife refuge, also spa*

◼ BARS

Tutu/ Gato Negro [★GS] KM 5 Manuel Antonio Rd (at Casitas Eclipse) **506-2/777-0408**

◼ NIGHTCLUBS

Liquid Lounge [M,D,DS] **506-2/777-5158** *9pm-3am Tue & Th-Sun*

◼ RESTAURANTS

El Barba Roja [★] Carretera al Parque Nacional **506-2/777-0331** *7am-10pm, from 4pm Mon, American, great sunset location*

El Gran Escape & Fish Head Bar Quepos Centro **506-2/777-0395** *brkfst, lunch, dinner, clsd Tue, seafood, full bar*

La Hacienda Restaurante [E] Plaza Yara **506-2/777-3473** *10:30am-10:30pm*

Rico Tico [★E] in Hotel Si Como No *brkfst, lunch & dinner, Tex/ Mex, includes use of pool bar*

◼ ENTERTAINMENT & RECREATION

La Playita N end of Playa Espadilla (w/ a steep hike over rocks) *the gay beach (impassable 2 hours before & after high tide)*

Osa Peninsula

◼ ACCOMMODATIONS

Blue Osa Yoga Sanctuary & Spa [GS,SW,NS,WI,GO] **506/8704-7006** *all meals included*

Pavones

◼ ACCOMMODATIONS

Casa Siempre Domingo B & B [GS,SW,WI,GO] **506/2776-2185**

Playa Sámara

◼ ACCOMMODATIONS

Casitas LazDívaz [GS,WI,WC,GO] **506/2656-0295**

Puerto Viejo de Limon

◼ ACCOMMODATIONS

Banana Azul [M,WI,GO] 200 meters N of Perla Negra Hotel **506-2/750-2035, 506-2/351-4582 (cell)**

Puntarenas

◼ CRUISY AREAS

Beach [AYOR]

San José

◼ ACCOMMODATIONS

Colours Oasis Resort [MW,F,E,SW,WI,GO] El Triangulo Noroeste, Blvd Rohrmoser (200 meters before end of blvd) **506-2/296-1880, 866/517-4390 (US & Canada)** *full brkfst*

Hotel El Mirador [M,SW] Bello Horizonte, Escazú **506/2289-3981**

Costa Rica • CENTRAL AMERICA

Hotel Kekoldi [GS,WI,GO] Av 9 (btwn Calles 5 & 7, Barrio Amón) **506-2/248-0804, 786/221-9011 (from US)**

Secret Garden B&B [GS,WI,GO] **506-2/224-1837**

▓BARS

Bar Al Despiste [GS,K] in front of Mudanzas Mundiales (W of Universal Zapote) **506-2/234-5956** *6pm-2am, 5pm-10pm Sun, clsd Mon*

Buenas Vibraciones [MW,GO] Ave 14 (btw Calle 7 & 9, in Paseo de los Estudiantes) **506-2/223-4573**

Casa Vieja [MW,F] 400 metros al este de la capilla religiosa de Montserrat, Alajuela **506/2440-8525** *6pm-2am, noon-midnight Sun*

Zona Rosa [MW,D,K] 250m norte del Correo Central

▓NIGHTCLUBS

La Avispa [MW,D] 834 Calle 1 (pink house btwn Avs 8 & 10) **506-2/223-5343** *9pm-2am, popular T-dance from 5pm Sun, clsd Mon-Wed*

Azotea [GS,D] Uruca, de Capris 300 Norte (Plaza Rohrmoser) **506-2/220-2506**

El Bochinche [MW,D,V] Calle 11 (btwn Avs 10 & 12, Paseo de los Etudiantes), San Pedro **506-2/221-0500** *7pm-2am, till 5pm Fri-Sat, clsd Sun-Tue, also full restaurant, Mexican, dancing/DJ after 10pm*

Club Energy [MW,D,F] Paseo Colon (near 30th, by Pizza Hut) **506/2223-7594** *from 7:30pm Th-Sun, also restaurant*

Club Oh! [GS,D] Calle 2 (btwn Avs 14 & 16) **506-22/221-9341** *9pm-close Fri-Sat, take taxi to avoid bad area*

Club Oh [M,D] Calle 2 (btwn Ave 14 & 16) **506-2/221-9341** *9pm-2am Fri-Sat*

Puchos [M,DS,S] Calle 11 & Av 8 (knock to enter) **506-2/256-1147, 506-2/222-7967** *8pm-2:30am, clsd Sun*

▓RESTAURANTS

Ankara [E] San José de la Montaña (Heredia, San Antonio de Belén, S of church) **50/8326 6646** *clsd Mon-Tue, live music*

Cafe Mundo [GO] Av 9 & Calle 15 (200 meters E of parking lot for INS, Barrio Amón) **506-2/222-6190** *11am-11pm, 5pm-midnight Sat, clsd Sun, garden seating, bar*

La Cocina de Leña [R] in El Pueblo complex **506-2/255-1360** *11am-11pm, 5 minutes from downtown*

Machu Picchu Calle 32 (btwn Aves 1 & 3) **506-2/283-3679** *Peruvian*

Mirador Ram Luna from center of Aserrí, go 4 kilometers on the road toward Tabarca, Aserrí **506-2/230-3060** *dinner nightly, lunch & dinner wknds, clsd Mon, hillside restaurant w/ amazing views*

Olio [★] Escalante, Bario California (N of Baselman's, San Pedro/ Los Yoses) **506-2/281-0541** *lunch & dinner, clsd Sun, Spanish, also full bar*

Vishnu Vegetarian Restaurant [★] Av 1 (btwn Calles 3 & 1) **506-2/256-6063** *8am-9:30pm*

▓ENTERTAINMENT & RECREATION

Gay Tours Costa Rica **506-2/305-8044** *daily events & excursions, Nov-April*

Mercado Central/ Central Market Central Avenida (btwn Calles 6 & 8) *bustling market selling food, clothing, souvenirs & more*

▓MEN'S CLUBS

Oasis Spa [MO] Avenida 4 (at Calle 20) **506/8824-8511, 506/8648-9504** *professional massage*

Paris Sauna corner of Calle 7 & Av 7 (1 block from Morazan Park) **506-2/258-7254** *noon-2am, till 4am Fri-Sat*

Sauna Hispalis [★V] Av 2 #1762 (E of the Plaza de la Democracia, btwn Calles 17 & 19) **506-2/256-9540** *noon-1am, [N] Wed*

■CRUISY AREAS

Parque La Sabana [AYOR] next to Municipal Stadium (btwn airport & San José) *evenings & wknds*

Parque Nacional [AYOR] N of Av 1 (btwn Calles 15 & 19)

Plaza de la Cultura [★AYOR] in front of the Nat'l Theater (btwn Calles 3 & 5) *late afternoons & early evenings*

San Ramon

■ACCOMMODATIONS

Angel Valley Farm B&B [GS,NS,WI,WC] 200m N & 300m E of Iglesia de Los Angeles (at Autopista to Arenal Volcano) 506-2/456-4084, 910/805-0149 (US#) *full brkfst*

Santa Clara

■ACCOMMODATIONS

Tree Houses Hotel Costa Rica [GS,NS,GO] 506-2/475-6507 *private treehouses in canopy of trees on wildlife refuge*

Tamarindo

■ACCOMMODATIONS

Cala Luna Hotel & Villas [GF,SW] Playa Langosta (at Playa Tamarindo) 506-2/653-0214, 800/503-5202

Hotel Sueño del Mar [GF,SW,NS,WI] Playa Langosta 506-2/653-0284 *private hacienda on the beach, full brkfst*

South America

ARGENTINA

Buenos Aires

■INFO LINES & SERVICES

Comunidad Homosexual Argentina Tomas Liberti 1080 54-11/4361-6382

Pink Point Avenida de Mayo 1370, 10th flr (at Palacio Barolo) 54-11/4382-8227 *LGBT tourist info*

■ACCOMMODATIONS

1555 Malabia House [GF,WI] Malabia 1555, Palermo Viejo (at Honduras) 54-11/4833-2410

Bayres B&B [M,GO] Av Córdoba 5842 (in Palermo) 54-11/4772-3877

The Cocker [GF,WI,GO] Av Juan de Garay 458 (at Defensa) 54-1/4362-8451

Don Sancho Youth Hostel [GS,WI] Constitucion 4062 (at Boedo) 54-11/4923-1422 *full brkfst, some shared baths, hot tub*

Faena Hotel & Universe [GS,WI] 445 Martha Salotti St 54-11/4010-9000 *luxury hotel, live shows at The Universe*

Home Hotel [GF,WI,SW] Honduras 5860 54-11/4778-1008 *boutique hotel*

Hotel Axel [MW,F,WI] Venezuela 649 54-11/4136-9393 *luxury gay hotel, pool parties*

Hotel Intercontinental Buenos Aires [GF,WI] Moreno 809 888/424-6835 (US#), 54-11/4340-7100

Hotel Vitrum [GF] 5641 Gorriti 54-1/4776-5030 *stylish boutique hotel*

Lugar Gay B&B [MO,WI,GO] Defensa 1120 54-11/4300-4747

Palermo Viejo B&B [GS,NS,WI,GO] Niceto Vega 4629 (at Av Scalabrini Ortiz) 54-11/4773-6012 *near shopping & gay nightlife*

Solar Soler B&B [GF,NS] Soler 5676 (at Bonpland) 54-11/4776-3065

Telmho Hotel Boutique [GF,WI] 1086 Defensa St (at Humberto Primo) 54-11/4116-5467

■BARS

Bach Bar [MW,E,K,V] Antonio Cabrera 4390 54-11/5184-0137

Bulnes Class [MW,D] Bulnes 1250 (Palermo) 54-11/4861-7492 *from 7pm Th & 11pm Fri-Sat*

Cero Consecuencia [MW] Cabrera 3769 *10pm-close, clsd Mon-Tue*

Flux Bar [MW,D] Marcelo T de Alvear 980 (at 9 de Julio) 54-11/5252-0258 *7pm-close, from 8pm wknds, clsd Sun*

Inside [M,F,E,S,OC] Bartolomé Mitre 1571 54-11/4372-5439 *[S] wknds*

Argentina • SOUTH AMERICA

Kadu [MO,L,18+] Sánchez de Bustamante 1633 *9pm-4am Wed & Fri-Sun, leather/ fetish bar, theme nights w/ strict dress code & entry times*

KM Zero [MW,D,DS,S,V] Av Santa Fe 2516 **54-11/4822-7530**

Mundo Bizarro [GF,F] 1222 Serrano **54-11/4773-1967** *1950s American-style cocktail lounge*

Shangay [M,D] Guemes 151 (Ramos Mejia) **54-1/5151-5788**

Sitges [★MW] Córdoba 4119 **54-11/4861-3763** *10:30pm-4am, till 6am Fri-Sat, clsd Mon-Tue*

Zoom [M,L,B$] Uriburu 1018 **54-11/4827-4828** *noon-3am, maze, lounge, cruisy*

▓NIGHTCLUBS

Ambar La Fox [MW,D] Av Federico Lacroze 3455 (at Alvarez Thomas, at El Teatro) *Sat only, young, alternative mixed crowd*

Amerika [M,D] Gascón 1040 (at Cordoba) **54-11/4865-4416** *darkroom*

Angel's Viamonte 2168 *midnight-7am Th-Sat*

Bahrein [GS,D,F] Lavalle 345 *6pm-7am Wed & Fri, from 10pm Sat, from midnight Tue*

Club 69 [GS,D,DS] Niceto Vega 5510 (btwn Humboldt & Fitzroy, Palermo) **54-11/4779-9396** *11:30pm Th only, over-the-top theme parties*

Club Namunkura [MW,D,TG] Niceto Vega 5699 (Palermo, at Club M) *1st Fri only*

Cocoliche [GS,D] Rivadavia 878

Contramano [MO,D,B] Rodriguez Peña 1082 (at Av Santa Fe) *midnight-close, from 7pm Sun, clsd Mon-Tue, hustlers*

Fiesta Dorothy [MW,D] Alsina 940 (near Plaza de Mayo, at Palacio Alsina) **54-11/4334-0097, 54-11/4334-0098** *huge dance bi-monthly dance party*

Fiesta Eyeliner [MW,D,A,DS] Sarmiento 1272 (at Salon Real) *monthly queer/ alternative dance party, check web for dates*

Fiesta Oliver [MW,D] Cordoba 543 (at Sub Club) *1am Fri only (Fri night)*

Fiesta Plop [MW,D] Av Federico Lacroze 3455 (at Alvarez Thomas, at El Teatro) *Fri only, young, alternative mixed crowd*

Fiesta Puerca [M,D] Federico Lacroze (at Alvarez Thomas)

Glam [★M,D] Cabrera 3046 **54-11/4963-2521** *midnight-close wknds, darkroom, patio*

Human [M,D] Av Costanera Norte Rafael Obligado (at Av Sarmiento, at Mandalay Complex) *midnight Fri only, huge dance party*

Juana [MW,D] 775 Av 44 **54-1/557-6807** *from 11:30pm Fri-Sat only*

Pacha [GF,D] Av Costanera y Pampa **54-11/4788-4280**

Rheo [M,D] Marcelino Freyre S/N, Arco 17 (at Crobar) **54-1/3430-2711** *midnight Sat only*

Sub Club [MW,D] Cordoba 543 *Fri-Sat only*

▓CAFES

Gout Cafe [GO] Juncal 2124 **54-11/4825-8330** *sandwiches, pastries*

Pride Cafe [E] Balcarce 869 (in San Telmo) **54-11/4300-6435** *10am-10pm, live show Th night*

Pure Vida Reconquista 516 (btwn Tucuman & Lavalle) **54-11/4393-0093** *8:30am-7pm, 10am-5:30pm Sat, clsd Sun, juice bar, food served, plenty veggie*

▓RESTAURANTS

Arevalito Arevalo 1478 **54-11/4776-4252** *9am-midnight, vegetarian*

Bar 6 Armenia 1676 **54-11/4833-6807** *8am-9:30pm, from 1pm wknds*

Bio Humbolt 2192 (Palermo Viejo) **54-11/4774-3880** *lunch & dinner, vegetarian, organic market*

La Cabana [★] Alicia Moreau de Justo 380 **54-11/4314-3710** *brkfst, lunch & dinner, upscale steak house*

Casa Cruz 1658 Uriarte
54-11/4833-1112 *8:30pm-3am, later Fri-Sat, upscale, trendy restaurant, also bar*

Cumana [★] Rodriguez Pena 1149 (at Arenales) 54-11/4813-9207 *regional cuisine*

El Palacio de la Papa Frita [★] Lavalle 735 (at Maipu)
54-11/4393-5849 *also Av Corrientes 1612, 11/4374-8063*

Filo San Martin 975
54-11/4311-0312, 54-11/4311-1871 *8pm-close*

Lobby Nicaragua 5944
54-11/4770-9335 *8am-1am, till 8pm Sun-Mon, wine bar, cafe & restaurant*

Mark's Deli & Coffeehouse [★] El Salvador 4107 (in Palermo)
54-11/4832-6244

Milion [★] Parana 1048
54-11/4815-9925 *swank lounge/ restaurant spread over 3-flr mansion, garden*

Naturaleza Sabia Balcarce 958 (at Carlos Calvo) 54-11/4300-6454 *clsd Mon, vegetarian*

Rave [★] Gorriti 5092
54-11/4833-7832

Sucre Sucre 676 54-11/4782-9082 *upscale contemporary*

Verde Llama Jorge Newbery 3623
54-11/4554-7467 *11am-6pm, till midnight Th-Sat, organic vegetarian cafe*

▪ENTERTAINMENT & RECREATION

Casa Brandon [F] Luis Maria Drago 236 (at Lavalleja) 54-11/4858-0610 *LGBT events, dance parties, poetry readings, art & more*

Espanol al Sur [GF,GO] Pichincha 1031 #2 (at Carlos Calvo)
54-11/4942-9582,
54-11/6449-5447 *Spanish language & tango classes*

La Marshall Maipu 444
54-11/4912-9043 *8:30pm Wed, exclusively gay tango lessons*

Museo Evita Peron Lafinur 2988 (in Palermo) 54-11/4807-9433 *2pm-7:30pm, clsd Mon*

Out And About Pub Crawl [MW]
54-1/5817-6678 *make new friends on a tour of the local gay bars*

Private Gay Tours *custom gay tours of BA*

▪BOOKSTORES

Otras Letras Soler 4796, Palermo
54-1/2060-2942 *2pm-8pm, from 3pm Sat, clsd Sun, LGBT books & culture*

▪PUBLICATIONS

Actitud www.agmagazine.info

G-Maps Buenos Aires Franklin 1463, Florida Oeste 54-11/4730-0729 *free pocket-size gay map of Buenos Aires*

The Ronda *gay pocket guide w/ local listings (www.theronda.com.ar)*

▪MEN'S CLUBS

A Full Spa [MO,V,GO] Viamonte 1770 (at Av Callao) 54-11/4371-7263 *noon-3am, 24hrs wknds*

Energy Spa [MO] Bravard 1105 (at Av Angel Gallardo, Villa Crespo)
54-1/4854-5625

Grupo Los Fiesteros [MO] *bi-weekly sex parties, grupolosfiesteros.com.ar*

Homo Sapiens [MO] Gascon 956
54-11/4862-6519

Nagasaki [MO] Aguero 427
54-11/4866-6335

Sauna Unikus Av Pueyrredón 1180 (near Calle Mansilla)
54-11/4961-7792

Tom's [MO,V] Viamonte 638, in basement 54-11/4322-4404

▪EROTICA

American Top Video Av Cabildo 2230 (Galeria Las Vegas) 54-11/4781-5343 *clsd Sun*

Box Laprida 1423 (at Santa Fe) *2pm-6am*

Cine ABC Esmeralda 506 (at the Microcentro)

Eden Av Santa Fe 1833 (gal Bozzini, B Norte)

Argentina • SOUTH AMERICA

Emporium [M] Cerrito 842 (btwn Marcelo T Alvear & Santa Fe) *sex store, also dark room, cruisy*

Ideal Suipacha 378

Multicine Lavalle 750

▓CRUISY AREAS

Avenida Santa Fe [AYOR] btwn Callao & Coronel Diaz

Bosques de Palermo [AYOR] Figueroa Alcorta & Dorrego St

Plaza Las Heras [AYOR] Coronel Dias & Av Las Heras

BRAZIL

Rio de Janeiro

Note: M°=Metro station

▓INFO LINES & SERVICES

Grupo Arco-Iris Rio de Janeiro Rua do Senado 230 **55–21/2222–7286** *1pm-7pm, till 11pm Sat, clsd Sun, LGBT community center*

Rainbow Kiosk/ Quiosque [★MW,DS] Atlantic Av (in front of Copacabana Palace Hotel) **55–21/2275–1641**

▓ACCOMMODATIONS

Casa Cool Beans [GS,SW,WI,GO] Rua Laurinda Santos Lobo 136 **55–21/2262–0552**

Casa Dois Gatos [M,SW,WI,GO] Rua Rosalina Terra 6, Cabo Frio **561/282–0023, 55–22/2645–5806** *free transportation from Rio airport*

Ipanema Plaza [GS,SW] Rua Farme Amoedo (at Rua Prudente de Morais) **55–21/3687–2000** *near gay beach, rooftop pool, also restaurant*

MyRioCondo.com [GS,WI,GO] 3150 Avenida Atlantica, Apt 901 (Copacabana) **215/847–2397 (US#)**

Rio Penthouse [GF] **55–21/2541–3882** *beachfront apts & penthouse suites*

▓BARS

Melt [GF,F,E] Rua Rita Ludolf 47 **55–21/2249–9309** *lounge, also restaurant*

TV Bar [M,NH] Av Nossa Senhora de Copacabana 1417 **55–21/2267–1663** *10pm-5am, 9pm-3am Sun, clsd Mon-Wed*

▓NIGHTCLUBS

Boite 1140 [MW,D,DS] 1140 Rua Capitao Menezes **55–21/7830–8867** *11pm-5am Th-Sun*

Le Boy [★MW,D,S,YC] Rua Raul Pompeia 102 (Copacabana) **55–21/2513–4993** *11pm-close, clsd Mon, also sauna*

Casa da Matriz [GS,D,18+] Rua Henrique de Novaes 107 **54–11/2226–9691, 54–11/2266–1014** *11pm-close, clsd Tue*

Cine Ideal [GS,D] Rua da Carioca 64 **55–21/2252–3460** *huge club w/ visting big-name DJs*

La Cueva [M,D,B,L] Rua Miguel Lemos 51 (Copacabana) **55–21/2267–1364**

Fosfobox [GS,D] Rua Siqueira Campos 143 **55–21/2548–7498** *open Th-Sun, underground techno*

Galeria Cafe [GS,D] Rua Teixeira de Melo 31 (Ipanema) **55–21/2523–8250** *10:30pm-close, clsd Sun-Tue, also gallery*

Papa G [MW,D,DS] 42 Almerinda Freitas **55–21/2450–1253**

Turma OK [M,DS] 43 Rua do Resende **55–21/2210–0965**

Up Turn [MW,D,F] 2000 Av das Americas **55–21/3387–7957** *patio*

The Week [GF,D] 154 Rua Sacadura Cabral **55–21/2253–1020**

▓CAFES

Cafeína Rua Farme de Amoedo 43 (Ipanema) **55–21/2521–2194** *8am-11:30pm*

Copa Cafe Av Atlantica 3056 **55–21/2235–2947**

Expresso Carioca Rua Farme de Amoedo 76 **55–21/2267–8604**

■RESTAURANTS

Bar d'Hotel Av Delfim Moreira 696 (2nd flr, inside Marina All Suites Hotel, Leblon) **55–21/2172-1112** *Mediterranean, food served all day, bar till late, see & be seen*

Boox Rua Br Torre 368 (in Ipanema) **55–21/2522-3730** *upscale restaurant & nightclub*

Cafe del Mar [GF] Av Atlantica 1910 **55–21/7857-8681** *upscale lounge*

Caroline Cafe 10 Rua JJ Seabra **55–21/2540-0705** *steak & burgers, full bar*

Gringo Cafe Rua Barao da Torre 240 **55–21/3813-3972** *American classics*

Maxim's Av Atlantica 1850 **55–21/2255-7444**

Pizzaria Guanabara 1228 Ave Ataulfo de Paiva, Leblon **55–21/2294-0797**

To Nem Ai [MW] Rua Farme de Amoedo 57 **55–21/2247-8403** *popular bar w/ outdoor seating*

Via Sete **55–21/2512-8100** *noon-midnight, plenty veggie*

Zero Zero [★GS,D,F] Av Padre Leonel Franca 240 (inside planetarium) **55–21/2540-8041** *gay night Sun, upscale restaurant & nightclub*

■ENTERTAINMENT & RECREATION

Copacabana Beach at Rua Rodolfo Dantas *gay across from Copacabana Palace Hotel*

Farme de Amoedo/ Farme Gay Beach across from Rua Farme de Amoedo *see & be seen at this popular gay beach*

Ipanema Beach *E of Rua Farme Amoedo*

■PUBLICATIONS

Rio For Partiers **55–21/2523-9857** *great guide book*

■MEN'S CLUBS

Bonsucesso Sauna Rua Bonsucesso 252 **55–21/2260-9385** *1pm-10pm, till 11pm wknds*

Club 117 Rua Cándido Mendes 117 (Gloria) **55–21/2252-0160** *clsd Mon, large sauna, steam, escorts*

Club 29 Rua Professor Alfredo Gomes 29 **55–21/2286-6380** *1pm-4am, bathhouse, cybercafe*

Copacabana Sauna [B] Rua Dias da Rocha 83 **55–21/2235-5563** *popular w/ bears*

Estação Rua Tonelero 217 (Copacabana) **55–21/2547-9953** *3pm-close*

Gayligola [M,V] Rua Ubaldino do Amaral 50 (downtown) **55–21/9259-5625, 55–21/2224-6144**

Nuovo Spazio [DS,18+] Rua Santo Amaro 18 (at Rua Catete) **55–21/2222-7319** *3pm-midnight, clsd Sun, also bar, theme nights*

Point 202 Rua Siqueira Campos 202 **55–21/3816-1757** *3pm-1am, also bar, massage, shows*

Projeto SB Rua 19 de Fevereiro 162 (M° Botafogo) **55–21/2244-4263, 55–21/2541-8698** *also internet cafe*

Rio G Spa Rua Teixeira de Melo 16 (at Prudente de Moraes) **55–21/2523-5092** *3pm-midnight, also bar, darkroom, massage*

Studio 64 [MO] Rua Redentor 64 **55–21/2523-5670, 55–21/2513-4229**

Termas Catete [MO,V] Rua Correia Dutra 34 **55–21/2265-5478** *darkrooms, cabins*

Termas Kabalk [MO,V] Rua Santa Luiza 459 (near Varnhagem Square) **55–21/2572-6210** *3pm-11pm, bar, darkroom, very clean*

Termas Leblon [MO] Rua Barao da Torre 522 (at Rua Garcia d'Avila, Ipanema) **55–21/2287-3762** *sauna, mature crowd*

■EROTICA

Cinema Iris Rua Caroica 49 **55–21/262-1729** *historic adult theater*

■CRUISY AREAS

Avenida Copacabana & Av Atlantica

Barra Beach *across street from beach; look for flags & go past building into woods*

CHILE

Santiago

Note: M°=Metro station

■INFO LINES & SERVICES

Acciongay - Corporacion Chilena de Prevencion del SIDA San Ignacio 165 56-32/672-0000, 56-32/755-285 *AIDS info, testing & workshops*

■ACCOMMODATIONS

The Aubrey Hotel [GF] Constitución 299-317, Bellavista 56-2/940-2800 *hip boutique hotel*

Casa Moro [MW,GO] Corte Suprema 177 (Departamento B) 56-2/696-9499 *full brkfst*

Hotel Maury [M] Tarapaca 1112 56-2/672-5859

Lastarria Hotel [GF] Coronel Santiago Bueras 188 56-2/840-3700 *luxury boutique hotel*

Le Reve Hotel [GF] Orrego Luco 023, Providencia 56-2/757-6000, 56-2/757-6011 *luxury boutique hotel*

■BARS

Bar 105 Bombero Nuñez 105 56-2/403-2990 *9pm-late Th-Sat*

Bar de Willy [MW,E,S] Av 11 de Septiembre 2214 (Común Providencia) 56-2/381-1806 *10pm-4am, till 5am wknds, strippers on 1st flr*

El Closet [MW,K] Santa Filomena 138 (at Bombero Nuñez)

Farinelli [F,E,DS,S] Bombero Nuñez 68 (Recoleta) 56-2/732-8966 *5pm-2am, also hotel*

Pub Friend's [MW,E,DS] Bombero Nuñez 365 (at Dominica, barrio Bellavista) 56-2/777-3979 *9:30pm-4am, till 5am Fri-Sat*

Vox Populi [M,F] Ernesto Pinto Lagarrigue 364 (Bellavista) 56-2/671-1267 *9:30pm-3am, clsd Sun-Mon, also restaurant, garden patio*

■NIGHTCLUBS

Blondie [GS,D,A] Alameda 2879, loc 104 56-2/681-7793 *theme nights*

Bokhara Discoteque [★M,D,F,DS,S] Pio Nono 430 (at Constitución, barrio Bellavista) 56-2/732-1050, 56-2/735-1271 *10pm-6am, till 7am wknds, darkroom*

Bunker [MW,D,F,E] Bombero Nuñez 159 (Bellavista) 56-2/738-2301, 56-2/738-2314 *11pm-close Fri-Sat*

Club Ignorancia Ernesto Pinto Lagarrigue 282 56-2/8216-3857

Club Principe [M,D] Pio Nono 398 56-2/777-6381

Fausto [M,D,DS] Av Sta Maria 832 56-2/777-1041

Nueva Cero [M,D,DS] Euclides 1204 par 2 Gran Avenida

■CAFES

Tavelli [★] Andrés de Fuenzalida 34 (Providencia) 56-2/231-5830 *8:30am-10pm, from 9:30am Sat*

■RESTAURANTS

Ali Baba 102 Santa Filomena (Barrio Bellavista, Recoleta) 56-2/732-7036 *Middle Eastern*

Capricho Español [MW] Purisima 65 (barrio Bellavista) 56-2/777-7674 *dinner only, Spanish, full bar*

Santo Remedio [D] 152 Roman Diaz, Providencia 56-2/235-0984 *6:30pm-close, from 10:30pm wknds, global, full bar*

El Toro Loreto 33 56-2/737-5937 *noon-midnight*

■MEN'S CLUBS

Baños 282 Bellavista 282 56-2/777-1709

Banos Metro [MO,V] Almirante Montt 471 56-2/633-1321 *1pm-midnight, also cafe, darkroom*

Sauna Mi Tiempo [V] Bombero Nuñez 230 56-2/735-3949 *2pm-midnight, 24hrs wknds, cafe, darkroom*

■EROTICA

Sex Shop Amsterdam

Sex Shop Multivariedades Paseo Las Palmas 2225, Local 111

■CRUISY AREAS

Paseo Las Palmas [AYOR] in Providencia neighborhood

Plaza de Armas [AYOR]

Europe

AUSTRIA

Vienna

▓ INFO LINES & SERVICES

Gay & Lesbian AA 43-1/799-5599, 43-665/490-5603 (English)

Hosi Zentrum Heumuhlgasse 14 43-1/216-6604 *LGBT political organization, groups & events, cafe, news magazine*

Rosa Lila Villa Linke Wienzeile 102 (near Hofmühlgasse, U4-Pilgramgasse) 43-1/586-8150 (women), 43-1/585-4343 (men) *LGBT center, info, gay city maps, also cafe-bar*

▓ ACCOMMODATIONS

Altstadt [GF,WI] Kirchengasse 41 43-1/522-6666

Arcotel Wimberger [GF] Neubaugürtel 34-36 (at Goldschlagstr) 43-1/521-650 *4-star hotel, restaurant & bar on premises*

Art Hotel [GF] Brandmayergasse 7-9 43-1/544-5108 *modern, art-filled hotel*

Boutique Hotel Stadthalle [GS] Hackengasse 20 43-1/982-4272 *eco-friendly boutique hotel*

Designapartment Vienna [GF,WI,GO] Glockengasse 25/ 9 43-650/592-8941

Gay At Home [MW,GO] 43-1/586-1200 *rental apts around Vienna*

Le Méridien Wien [GF,SW] Opernring 13-15 43-1/588-900, 800/543-4300 *sauna, hot tub, also restaurant & bar*

Pension Wild [M,F,GO] Lange Gasse 10 (off Lerchenfelder Str) 43-1/406-5174

Das Tyrol [GF] Mariahilfer Str 15 43-1/587-5415 *small luxury hotel*

▓ BARS

Alte Lampe [★M,P,OC] Heumühlgasse 13 (at Rechte Weinzeile, U4-Kettenbrückengasse) 43-1/587-3454 8pm-1am, clsd Mon-Tue, piano bar wknds, Vienna's oldest gay bar

Cafe Cheri [M,F] Franzensg 2 43-650/208-1471 10pm-4am, also cafe

Cafe Savoy [★MW,F] Linke Wienzeile 36 (at Köstlergasse) 43-1/581-1557 8am-2am, upscale cafe-bar

Eagle Bar [★M,L,V] Blümelgasse 1 (at Gumpendorfer Str, U3-Neubaugasse) 43-1/587-2661 9pm-4am, darkroom, also sex shop

Felixx [MW,F,WI] Gumpendorferstr 5 43-1/920-4714 7pm-3am, from 10am Sat, 7pm-1am Sun

Goldener Spiegel [★M,F,YC] Linke Wienzeile 46 (enter on Stiegengasse, U4-Kettenbrückengasse) 43-1/586-6608 7pm-2am, hustlers

Losch [MO,L] Fünfhuasgasse 1 (at Sechshauserstr) 43-1/895-9979 from 10pm Fri-Sat, also Sun in winter, call for events, leather/ uniform/ fetish club, strict dress code, 3 flrs

Mango Bar [★M,YC,GO] Laimgrubengasse 3 (U4-Kettenbrückengasse) 43-1/920-4714 9pm-4am

Merandy Lounge [MW,D] Mollardgasse 17 7pm-2am Th, 8pm-6am Fri-Sat

Peter's Operncafé Hartauer [GS,F] Riemergasse 9 (at Singer) 43-1/512-8981 6pm-2am, clsd Sun-Mon, terrace

Red Carpet [MW,D,YC] Magdalenenstr 2 43-1/676-782-2966 theme nights

Schik [MW,WI] Schikanedergasse 5 7pm-2am, till 4am Fri-Sat, clsd Sun

Sling [M,L] Kettenbrückengasse 4 (at Grüngasse, U4-Kettenbrückengasse) 43-1/586-2362 3pm-4am, darkroom, private rooms, sling, erotic shop, "piss cinema"

Studio 67 [GS,D] Gumpendorferstr 67 43-1/966-7182 10am-4am Th-Sat, upscale lounge & dance club

Le Swing [M,TG,V,$] Hannovergasse 5 (at Wallensteinstr) 43-1/332-1670 gay 9pm-2am Tue only for Transnight, also sauna

Village Bar [★M,YC] Stiegengasse 8 (near Naschmarkt) 43-1/676-3848977 8pm-3am

Wiener Freiheit [MW,D,TG,F,V] Schönbrunner Str 25 (U4-Kettenbrückengasse) 43-1/931-9111 8pm-midnight, clsd Sun-Mon, 3 flrs, disco 10pm-4am Fri-Sat

X Bar [M] Mariahilfer Str 45 (enter on Stiegengasse, U3-Neubaugasse) 43-1/009-2251 4pm-2am, 6pm-midnight Sun

NIGHTCLUBS

BallCanCan [MW,D] Schwarzenberg Platz 10 (at Ost Klub) monthly queer Balkan club

Heaven Gay Night [★M,D,TG,S,YC] 43-1/523-3063 10pm-6am Sat

Inside Bar [M,D,V] Schikanedergasse 12 43-1/581-2184 8pm-4am

Meat Market [MW,D] queer electro dance party, check local listings

Pitbull [M,D,B,L] Zieglergasse 26 (at Club Pi) 10pm 2nd Fri only

Queer Beat [M,D] Landstr Hauptstr 38 (at the Viper Room) 2nd & 4th Sat only

Up! [M,D] Mariahilfer Str 3 (at Lutz Club) 2nd Fri only, uplifting house music

Why Not? [M,D,S,V] Tiefer Graben 22 (at Wipplinger, U-Schottentor) 43-1/925-3024 10pm-close Fri-Sat & before public holidays, darkroom

CAFES

Bakul Margaretenstr 58 9am-2am, also guesthouse

Cafe Berg [★MW,F,YC] Berggasse 8 (at Wasagasse, U2-Schottentor) 43-1/319-5720 10am-1am, cafe-bar

Cafe Central Herrengasse 14 (at Strauchgasse) 43-1/533-3763 7:30am-10pm, from 10am Sun & public holidays, "world's most famous coffee-house"

Cafe Raimann [M] Schönbrunner Straße 285 43-1/813-5767 8am-2am, till midnight Sat, clsd wknds & holidays

Cafe Rifugio [M] Schönbrunner Str 10 43-699/1138-0250 10am-10pm

Cafe Standard Margaretenstr 63 43-1/581-0586 8am-midnight, from 11am wknds

Cafe Stein [GF,F] Währinger Str 6-8 (near U-Schottentor) 43-1/319-7241 7am-1am, from 9am Sun, internet access, terrace

Das Möbel Burggasse 10 (Spittelberg) 43-1/524-9497 10am-1am, trendy, internet, also art gallery

Point of Sale [WI] Schleifmuhlgasse 12 43-1/941-6397 7am-1am, cafe & deli, also vegan items, also bar

SMart Cafe [GS,F] Kostlergasse 9 43-1/585-7165 6pm-2am, till 4am Fri-Sat, clsd Sun-Mon, S/M & fetish cafe

RESTAURANTS

Andino [GS,E] Münzwardeingasse 2 (U4-Pilgramgasse) 43-1/587-6125 11am-2am, from 10am Sat, 11am-midnight Sun, Latin American, full bar

Aux Gazelles Rahlgasse 5 43-1/585-6645 French/ Moroccan restaurant 6pm-midnight; Arabian-style lounge, cafe & deli 11am-2am; also Turkish steam baths noon-10pm

Bin Im Leo [BW] Servitengasse 14 43-1/391-7763 4pm-midnight, from noon wknds, plenty veggie

Cafe-Restaurant Willendorf [MW] Linke Wienzeile 102 (near Hofmuhlgasse, U4-Pilgramgasse) 43-1/587-1789 6pm-2am, food served till midnight, plenty veggie, full bar, terrace

Halle Museumsquartier 1 43-1/523-7001 10am-2am, modern bistro, artsy crowd

Kantine Porzellangasse 19 43-1/319-5918 6pm-2am, Thai

Motto [★R] Schönbrunner Str 30 (enter on Rüdigergasse) 43-1/587-0672 6pm-2am, till 4am Fri-Sat, trendy, also bar, patio

Santo Spirito [E] Kumpfgasse 7 43-1/512-9998 6pm-11pm, bar till 2am, classical music

Schon Schön Lindengasse 53 (Ecke Andreasgasse) lunch & dinner, fashionable restaurant, also bar; also clothing & hair salon

Sly & Arny Lothringerstrasse 22 43-1/405-0458 lunch Mon-Fri, dinner nightly, bar till late

Stöger Rampersdorffergasse 63
43-1/544-7596 11am-midnight, clsd
Sun, from 5pm Mon, Viennese

Zum Roten Elefanten
Gumpendorferstrasse 2
43-1/966-8008 lunch & dinner, open
late Fri-Sat, clsd Sun (lunch only in
summer)

■ENTERTAINMENT &
RECREATION

Haus der Musik/ House of Music [F]
Seilerstätte 30 **43-1/516-4810**
10am-10pm, interactive museum of
sound, also cafe

Kunsthistorisches Museum Maria
Theresien-Platz (enter Heldenplatz)
43-1/525-240 10am-6pm, till 9pm
Th, clsd Mon, not to be missed

■BOOKSTORES

American Discount Rechte Wienzeile
5 (at Paniglgasse) **43-1/587-5772**
9:30am-6:30pm, till 5pm Sat, clsd Sun,
int'l magazines & books; also
Neubaugasse 39, 43-1/523-37-07

Löwenherz Berggasse 8 (next to Cafe
Berg, enter on Wasagasse, U2-
Schottentor) **43-1/317-2982** 10am-
7pm, till 8pm Fri, till 6pm Sat, clsd Sun,
LGBT, large selection of English titles

■PUBLICATIONS

Vienna Gay Guide **43-1/789-1000**
city map & guide

Xtra www.xtra-news.at

■MEN'S CLUBS

Apollo City Sauna [SW,V]
Wimbergergasse 34
43-699/811-65200 bar, darkroom,
gym equipment

Hard On [MO,L] Hamburgerstr 4
43-1/0681108-55105 fetish club;
hangout for LMC (Leather & Motorbike
Community)

Kaiserbründl [F,V,SW] Weihburggasse
18-20 (at Grünangergasse, U1-
Stephansplatz) **43-1/513-3293** 2pm-
midnight, till 2am Fri-Sat, 3 flrs, 2 bars,
darkroom maze, gym equipment

Kino Labyrinth [M,TG,V] Favoritenstr
164 **43-1/920-4088** [MO] Wed, gay &
[TG] Fri, darkrooms, cabins, huge cruising
area

Sauna Frisco [F,V] Schönbrunner Str 28
43-1/920-2488 3pm-midnight, 24hrs
wknds, private rooms, full bar

Sport Sauna [★F,V,YC] Lange Gasse 10
(at Pension Wild, U2-Lerchenfelderstr)
43-1/406-7156 3pm-1am, 24hrs
wknds, bar, gym equipment

■EROTICA

Art-X Percostr 3 **43-1/25804-4413**
erotic supermarket, clsd Sun

Man for Man [V] Hamburgerstr 8 (at
Rechte Wienzeile, U-
Kettenbrückengasse) **43-1/585-2064**
books, toys, videos, DVDs, private rooms

Sexworld XXL Store [GS,V] Mariahilfer
Str 49 **43-1/587-6656** clsd Sun,
cabins, darkroom, cruisy, special gay
section

Spartacus XXL Store Mariahilfer Str
49 (enter through Sexworld)
43-1/587-6656 clsd Sun, toys,
leather, books, videos, DVDs

Tiberius [WC] Lindengasse 2 (at
Stiftgasse, U3-Neubaugasse)
43-1/522-0474 clsd Sun, designer
fetish-wear

Wiscot Center Lerchenfelder Gürtel 45
43-1/402-7822

■CRUISY AREAS

Rathauspark [AYOR] evenings only

Schweizer Garten [AYOR] next to
Südbahnhof

CZECH REPUBLIC

Prague (Praha)

Note: M°=Metro station

**Prague is divided into 10 city
districts: Praha—1, Praha—2, etc.**

Praha—Overview

■ACCOMMODATIONS

Apartments in Prague [GS,WI,WC]
420/775-588-508, 303/800-0858

Praha—1

Gay Hotel Prague [★M,WI] Jecna 12
420/602-455-127 also bar/ cafe

Hotel Metropol [GS] Narodni 33 (at Na
Perstyne) 420/246-022-100

Czech Republic • *EUROPE*

The ICON Boutique Hotel [★GS,F,WI,WC] V Jame 6 (at Vodickova) **420/221-634-100**

The Palace Road Hotel Prague [GS,WI] Nerudova 7 (at Malostranske Namesti) **420/257-531-941**

▥ BARS

Café Bar Flirt [M,D,B,F,K] Martinská 5/419 **420/224-248-592** *cafe open 10am-4am, bar open 10pm-2am Fri-Sat, bears meet 7pm Wed*

Friends Bar [★M,NH,D,V,WI] Bartolomejská 11 **420/226-211-920** *7pm-6am*

K.U. Bar [GS,D,E] Rytirská 13 (at Perlová, near Oldtown Square) **420/724-695-910** *7pm-4am, upscale & trendy*

Silwer Cafe & Bar [GS,D,WI] **420/222-212-702** *10am-2am*

Tingl Tangl [MW,D,F,C,DS] Karolíny Svetlé 12 (at Konviktska) **420/224-238-278** *11am-10pm, [C] 9pm-5am Wed & Fri-Sat, also restaurant*

U Rudolfa [M,BW,OC] Mezibranská 3 **420/605-872-492** *2pm-2am, from 4pm wknds*

▥ NIGHTCLUBS

Escape Club [MO,D,F,S,$] V Jame 8 (off Wenceslas Square) **420/774-873-411** *9pm-4am, go-go boys, also hustlers*

Stage [M,D,F,K] Stepanska 23 (at Reznicka) **420/252-548-683** *cafe/ restaurant from 4pm, nightclub opens 9pm; karaoke Tue*

▥ CAFES

Cafe Cafe [WI] Rytirská 10 (at Perlová, near Oldtown Square) **420/224-210-597** *10am-11pm*

Cafe Erra [F] Konviktská 11 **420/222-220-568** *10am-midnight, salads, sandwiches & entrées*

Cafe Louvre [GS,F,NS] Národni 22 (M° Narodni Trida) **420/224-930-949** *9am-11:30pm, the favorite hangout of Albert Einstein & Franz Kafka*

Cafe Muzeum [★] Mezibranska 19 **420/222-221-312** *10am-11pm, from 1pm wknds*

Kafirna U Ceského Pána [★M,F] Kozi 13, Stare Mesto **420/222-328-283** *1pm-11pm, small bar popular w/ locals*

Q Cafe Opatovická 166/12 **420/776-856-361** *noon-midnight*

Vertigo Havelská 4 (at Perlová) **420/744-744-256** *cafe & restaurant, also [GF] nightclub, theme nights, DJs*

▥ RESTAURANTS

Campanulla Cafe Restaurant Velkoprevorske namesti 4 **420/257-217-736** *set in the beautiful garden of The Grand Priory of Bohemia Palace*

Farrango Dusni 15 **420/224-815-996** *4pm-midnight, clsd Sun, Thai*

Lehka Hlava Borsov 2/280 **420/222-220-665** *noon-11:30pm, vegetarian*

Maitrea Tynska 6/1064 (nr Old Town Square) **420/221-711-631** *noon-11:30pm, vegetarian*

Noi [GO] Ujezd 19 **420/257-311-411** *11am-1am, Thai*

Petrinské Terasy [GO] Seminarská Zahrada 393, Malá Strana **420/257-320-688** *noon-11pm, in a former monastery, great view*

Restaurant Dlouhá Dlouhá 23 (basement) **420/222-329-853** *11am-11pm, good seafood*

Staromestska Restaurace Staromestske namesti 19 **420/224-213-015** *11am-midnight, local Czech specialties*

▥ ENTERTAINMENT & RECREATION

NoD Gallery/ Roxy Dlouhá 33 *experimental theater, dance & performance; also cafe & live music venue*

Sex Machines Museum Melantrichova 18 **420/227-186-260** *10am-11pm*

▥ BOOKSTORES

Globe [E,F] Patrossova 6 **420/224-934-203** *English-language bookstore*

MEN'S CLUBS

Sauna Babylonia [★WI] Martinská 6
(at Na Perstyne) **420/224-232-304**
2pm-3am, gym equipment, bar

EROTICA

Erotic City Zitna 43
420/737-221-264

Praha—2

ACCOMMODATIONS

Balbin Penzion [GF,WI] Balbinova 26
(near Wenceslas Square)
420/222-250-660

Heaven Accommodations [★]
Gorazdova 11 (at Trojanova)
420/602-455-127 *also bar/ cafe,
erotica store*

Prague Saints [MW,GO] Polska 32
(office location) (at Trebizkeho, at Saints
Bar) **420/775-152-041,**
420/775-152-042 *apts in gay
Vinohrady district*

BARS

Angels Cafe [MW,WI] Vinohradská 30
*6pm-midnight, from 2pm Sat, 11am-
10pm Sun, cafe & lounge*

Charmisma Cafe [MW]
420/773-927-774 *5pm-2am, clsd
Sun*

Fan Fan Club [M,K,L] Dittrichova 5 (at
Trojanova) **420/776-360-698** *5pm-
2am, Czech leathermen every 3rd Sat*

Feno Man Club [M,D,F,WI] Blanická 28
(at Vinohradska) **420/603-740-263**

JampaDampa [★W,D,K] V Tunich 10 (at
Zitna) **420/603-260-678** *2pm-2am,
4pm-6am Fri-Sat, clsd Sun*

Klub 21 [MW,F,YC] Rimska 21 (at
Balbinova) **420/222-364-720** *7pm-
close, clsd Sun, cellar bar/ gallery, mostly
Czechs*

Klub Strelec [GF,B] Anglicka 2
420/224-941-446 *5pm-2am, till
midnight Sun, more bears on Wed & Sat*

Saints [MW] Polska 32 (at Trebizkeho)
420/222-250-326 *7pm-2am, till 4am
wknds*

NIGHTCLUBS

Lollypop [M,D] Belehradska 120,
Vinohrady (at Radost FX)
420/224-254-776,
420/603-193-711 *huge, bi-monthly
gay party*

On [MW,D,V] Vinohradska 40 (at
Blanicka) **420/222-520-630,**
420/776-360-698 (cell) *noon-5am,
3 levels, darkroom*

Termix [★MW,D,K] Trebizskeho 4 (at
Vinohradska) **420/222-710-462**
9pm-5am, clsd Mon-Tue

CAFES

Alex Bistro [WI] Jecna 4
420/224-919-125 *8am-10pm, from
9am Sat-Sun, till 5pm Sun, Italian &
Czech*

RESTAURANTS

Celebrity Cafe Vinohradska 40 (in
Vinohrady) **420/222-511-343** *8am-
2am, noon-3am Sat, noon-midnight
Sun, also bar*

Radost FX Belehradska 120, Vinohrady
420/224-254-776,
420/603-193-711 *fabulous wknd
brunch, vegetarian cafe, also nightclub
[GF] w/ popular bi-monthly gay party
Lollypop*

Sahara Cafe & Lounge [E] Namesti
Miru 6 **420/222-514-987** *11am-
midnight*

MEN'S CLUBS

Sauna Marco [★V] Lublanská 17,
Vinohrady (at Wenzigova)
420/224-262-833 *2pm-3am, also
bar, small but popular*

EROTICA

Heaven [★] Gorazdova 11
420/224-912-282 *cinema, toys,
magazines, DVDs, darkroom, also bar &
accommodations*

Czech Republic • EUROPE

Praha—3

■ BARS

Club Temple [★M,D,DS,S,V,AYOR]
Seifertova 3 (at Pribenicka)
420/222-710-773 *7pm-4am,
hustlers, also sex shop, rent boys & hotel*

Latimerie Club Cafe [MW,DS] Slezska
74 (at Nitranska) **420/224-252-049**
4pm-close

Piano Bar [MW,F,OC] Milesovská 10 (at
Ondrickova) **420/775-727-496**
5pm-close, mostly Czech

■ CAFES

Blaze Husitska 43 **420/777-102-028**
5pm-close, live music, art & more

■ RESTAURANTS

Restaurant Mozaika Nitranská 13
420/224-253-011 *contemporary take
on international cuisine*

■ ENTERTAINMENT & RECREATION

TV Tower Mahlerovy sady 1
420/724-251-286 *get a bird's-eye
view of the city from the top of this
tower*

■ MEN'S CLUBS

Alcatraz [MO,L,V,S] Borivojova 58 (off
Seifertova, in Zizhkov)
420/222-711-458 *9pm-6am, clsd
Mon, S/M club, theme nights*

Praha—5

■ ACCOMMODATIONS

Andel's Hotel [GF] Stroupeznickeho 21
(at Pizenska) **420/296-889-688**
restaurant & bar

■ MEN'S CLUBS

Drake's [MO,F,WI] Zborovska 50 (at
Petrinska) **420/257-326-828** *24hrs,
darkroom, maze, sex shop*

Praha—6

■ CRUISY AREAS

Sarka Lake [AYOR] by metro to
Dejvicka & tram 26 to end station *nude
bathing, summers*

Praha—7

■ NIGHTCLUBS

OMG/ Oh My Gay Party [M,D] U
Pruhonu 3 (at Mecca) *3rd Sat only*

■ CAFES

Duhova Cajovna [MW,F,WI] Milada
Horáková 73 (at Ovenecka)
420/775-269-699 *3pm-midnight,
"Rainbow Tearoom"*

Praha—8

■ ACCOMMODATIONS

Hotel Villa Mansland Prague
[M,F,SW,WI,GO] Stepnicná 9, Liben (at Na
Malem Klinu) **420/286-884-405,
420/777-839-733**

■ MEN'S CLUBS

Sauna David [WI] Sokolovská 44, Karlin
(at Vitkova) **420/222-317-869** *9am-
11pm, from 11am wknds*

Sauna Labyrint [★MO] Pernerova 4 (at
Peckova) *2pm-7am, sauna, steam room,
dark room, also bar*

Praha—10

■ ACCOMMODATIONS

Arco Guest House [M,WI,GO] Donská
176/13 **420/271-740-734**

Rainbow Inn [MO,SW,WI,GO] Zernovská
1195/2 (at Prubezna)
420/776-496-877

Ron's Rainbow Guest House
[GS,WI,GO] Bulharska 4 (at Finská)
**420/271-725-664,
420/731-165-022** (cell)

■ MEN'S CLUBS

Sauna Bonbon Cernomorska 6 (at
Charkovska) **420/777-146-068** *3pm-
1am, till 2am Fri-Sun*

Praha—11

■ CRUISY AREAS

Seberak Lake [AYOR] *from endstation
in Seberak, go to opposite side of lake to
nude beach, summers*

DENMARK

Copenhagen

■ INFO LINES & SERVICES

Kafe Knud Skindergade 21 45/3332-5861 4pm-10pm Tue & Th only, HIV resource center, cafe open Tue & Th only

Sabaah Onkel Dannys Plads 1 community center for LGBT ethnic minorities

Wonderful Copenhagen Convention & Visitors Bureau Vesterbrogade 4A 45/7022-2442 (tourist info)

■ ACCOMMODATIONS

Carstens Guesthouse [MW,WI,GO] Christians Brygge 28, 5th flr 45/3314-9107, 45/4050-9107 (cell) B&B, hostel & apts, 5 minutes from gay area

Copenhagen Admiral Hotel [GF] Toldbodgade 24-28 45/3374-1414

First Hotel Kong Frederik [GF] Vester Voldgade 25 45/3312-5902

First Hotel Skt. Petri [GF,F,WI,WC] Krystalgade 22 45/3345-9100

First Hotel Twentyseven [GF] Løngangstræde 27 45/7027-5627

Hotel Fox [GS,NS] Jarmers Plads 3 45/3395-7755, 45/3313-3000 artistic rooms, central location, roof terrace; also lounge & restaurant

Hotel Kong Arthur [GF] Norre Sogade 11 45/3311-1212

Hotel Windsor [M,GO] Frederiksborggade 30, 1360 45/3311-0830 near gay scene, shared baths

Radisson Blu Royal Hotel [GF] Hammerichsgade 1 45/3342-6000

The Square [GF] Rådhuspladsen 14 45/3338-1200

■ BARS

Amigo Bar [MW,NH,K] Schønbergsgade 4, Frederiksberg 45 5/3321-4915 10pm-6am

Cafe Intime [GF,P] Allegade 25, Frederiksberg 45/3834-1958 6pm-2am, cafe-bar

Can-Can [M,NH] Mikkel Bryggers Gade 11 45/3311-5010 2pm-2am, till 5am Fri-Sat

Centralhjørnet [M,WI] Kattesundet 18 45/3311-8549 noon-2am

Cosy Bar [★M] Studiestræde 24 (in Latin Quarter) 45/3312-7427 10pm-6am, till 8am Fri-Sat

Heaven [★MW,F] Radhuspladsen 75 45/3333-0806 10am-2am, till 5am wknds, bar/ cafe by day, nightclub late [MO]

Masken [★MW,F,WI] Studiestræde 33 45/3391-0937 2pm-3am, till 5am Fri-Sat

Men's Bar [MO,L] Teglgårdsstræde 3 45/3312-7303 3pm-2am, popular brunch 1st Sun

Never Mind [M] Nørre Voldgade 2 45/3311-8886 10pm-6am

Oscar Bar Cafe [★M,F,WI] Radhuspladsen 77 45/3312-0999 noon-2am, great happy hour

■ NIGHTCLUBS

Bear Aware [M,D] bear parties, check local listings for dates

Christopher Club [MW,D] Knabrostræde 3 midnight-5am Fri-Sat only

SLM (Scandinavian Leather Men)Copenhagen [MO,L,PC] 17-C Lavendelstraede (in back building) 45/3332-0601 10pm-close Fri-Sat, strict dress code; also 4pm-10pm 2nd Sun (no dress code)

■ CAFES

Jernbanecafeen [WI] 7am-2am, patio

■ RESTAURANTS

Jailhouse Restaurant & Bar [★M,B,F] Studiestraede 12 45/3315-2255 3pm-2am, till 5am Fri-Sat

Laekkerier Borgergade 17F 8:30am-5pm, till 10pm Th, from 10am wknds, organic take-out

Luna's Diner Vesterbrogade 42 45/3322-4757 10am-midnight, till 1am Fri-Sat

Tight Hyskenstraede 10 45/3311-0900 5pm-10pm, from noon wknds, Canadian, French & Australian

■ENTERTAINMENT & RECREATION

Amager Strandpark *beach 5 km from city center*

Bellevue Beach *mostly gay beach, left end is nude*

Kifak Staldgade 8 *venue for LGBT special events*

Tisvildeleje Beach N of the city (take S-train to Hillerød, then local train to beach) *gay beach*

Warehouse 9 Bygning 66 (enter from parking lot in front of Oksnehallen, in the meatpacking district) 45/3322-2847 *queer art, music, performance & more*

■PUBLICATIONS

Out & About 45/4093-1977

■MEN'S CLUBS

Amigo Sauna [★V] Studiestræde 31 45/3315-2028 *sauna, steam, tanning, cabins, mazes*

Body Bio [M,TG,V] Kingosgade 7 *cabins, sauna, cruisy; mostly gay men, but open to all genders*

Copenhagen Gay Center [V] Istedgade 34–36 (behind erotica shop) 45/33–220–300 *2-flr sauna, tanning*

■EROTICA

EP-video Kattesundet 10 45/3311-6406

Men's Shop Viktoriagade 24 45/3325-4475 *magazines, books, toys, leather/ rubber gear, videos*

■CRUISY AREAS

Ørstedsparken [AYOR] btwn Nørre voldgade & Nørre farimagsgade *mainly at night*

Utterslev Mose [AYOR] off hwy toward Farum

Zigøjnerpladsen (Gypsy Square) [AYOR] near Arillerivej & Lossepladsvej

ENGLAND

London

London is divided into 6 regions:
London—Overview
London—Central
London—West
London—North
London—East
London—South

London—Overview

■NIGHTCLUBS

Torture Garden 44–020/7700–1441 *the worlds largest fetish/ body art club; visit www.torturegarden.com for events*

■PUBLICATIONS

Boyz 44–020/7025–6100 *newspaper w/ extensive club & event listings*

Gay Times 44–020/7424–7400 *glorious gay glossy*

The Pink Paper 44–020/7424–7400 *free LGBT newspaper*

London—Central

London—Central includes Soho, Covent Garden, Bloomsbury, Mayfair, Westminster, Pimlico & Belgravia

■ACCOMMODATIONS

Dover Hotel [GF,WI] 42/44 Belgrave Rd 44–020/7821–9085

Fitz B&B [MW,NS,WI,GO] 15 Colville Place (btwn Charlotte & Whitfield) 44–(0)78/3437–2866

George Hotel [GF] 58–60 Cartwright Gardens (N of Russell Square) 44–020/7387–8777

Hazlitt's [GF,WI] 6 Frith St (Soho Sq) 44–020/7434–1771

Lincoln House [★GS,WI,WC] 33 Gloucester Pl, Marble Arch (at Baker St) 44–20/7486–7630 *B&B, full brkfst*

Marble Arch Inn [GF] 49-50 Upper Berkeley St 44–020/7723–7888

Z Hotel [GS,WI] 17 Moor St 44–020/3551–3700 *great Soho location*

■BARS

Note: "Pub hours" usually means 11am–11pm Mon–Sat and noon–3pm & 7pm–10:30pm Sun

79 CXR [★M,D,WC] 79 Charing Cross Rd (Soho) 44-020/7734-0783 *1pm–3am, till 11pm Sun, 2 flrs, cruisy*

The Admiral Duncan [★MW,NH,TG] 54 Old Compton St (Soho) 44-020/7437-5300 *pub hours*

Bar Soho [GS] 23-25 Old Compton St (at Frith St) 44-020/7439-0439 *noon–1am, till 3am Fri-Sat, from 2pm Sun*

Circa [M,D] 62 Frith St 44-020/7734-6826 *4pm–1am*

City of Quebec [M,NH,OC] 12 Old Quebec St (at Marble Arch) 44-020/7629-6159 *pub hours*

Compton's of Soho [★M,F,WC] 51-53 Old Compton St (at Dean St) 44-020/7479-7961 *noon–midnight, till 10:30pm Sun, cruisy*

Dog & Duck [GS,NH,F] 18 Bateman St (at Frith St) 44-020/7494-0697 *10am–11:30pm*

Duke of Wellington [GS,F] 77 Wardour (Soho) 44-020/7439-1274 *pub hours*

The Edge [★MW,D,F,WC] 11 Soho Square (at Oxford St) 44-020/7439-1313 *noon–1am, till 10:30pm Sun*

The Escape [★M,D,V] 10-A Brewer St (at Rupert) 44-020/7734-3040 *5pm–3am, clsd Sun-Mon, theme nights*

Freedom Bar [MW,D,F,YC] 66 Wardour St (off Old Compton St) 44-020/7734-0071 *4pm–3am, from 2pm Fri-Sat, 2pm-11:30pm Sun*

Friendly Society [MW,YC] 79 Wardour St (the basement at Old Compton, enter Tisbury Ct) 44-020/7434-3805 *4pm–11pm, till 10:30pm Sun*

G-A-Y Bar [MW,F,V] 30 Old Compton St (at Frith) 44-020/7494-2756 *noon–midnight*

Green Carnation [★MW,D,F] 4-5 Greek St (Soho Sq) 44-020/8123-4267 *4pm-2am, inspired by the time & life of Oscar Wilde*

Halfway to Heaven [M,NH,K,C,OC,GO] 7 Duncannon St (at Charing Cross, West End) 44-020/7321-2791 *noon-11pm, clsd Sun*

King's Arms Soho [M,NH,B,F,K,V] 23 Poland St (at Noel, Soho) 44-020/7734-5907 *noon-11pm, till 1am Fri-Sat, 1pm-midnight Sun, popular bear hangout*

Ku Bar/ Ku Klub [MW,K,YC,WI] 30 Lisle St (Leicester Sq) 44-020/7437-4303 *noon-3am, till 10:30pm Sun, also Soho bar at 25 Frith St*

Madam JoJo's [M,E,C] 8-10 Brewer St (at Rupert) 44-020/7734-3040 *Tranny Shack Wed*

The New Bloomsbury Set [GS] 76 Marchmont St (at Tavistock Pl) 44-020/7383-3084 *4pm-11pm, 2pm-10:30pm Sun*

The Retro Bar [MW,NH,D,K] 2 George Ct (at Strand) 44-020/7321-2811 *pub hours*

Rupert Street [★MW,F,WC] 50 Rupert St (off Brewer) 44-020/7292-7141 *pub hours, upscale "fashiony-types"*

Star at Night [MW,D,F,E] 22 Great Chapel St (at Hollen St) 44-020/7494-2488 *6pm-11:30pm, clsd Sun-Mon*

Vault 139 [M] 139-143 Whitfield St (Warren St) 44-020/7388-5500 *4pm-1am, from 1pm Sun, theme nights/dress codes*

The Village Soho [★M,F,18+,YC] 81 Wardour St (at Old Compton) 44-020/7478-0530 *4pm-1am, till 11:30pm Sun*

The Yard [★M,F,E,YC,WC] 57 Rupert St (off Brewer) 44-020/7437-2652, 871/426-2243 *pub hours*

■NIGHTCLUBS

G-A-Y Club [★M,D,E,YC,$] Under the Arches, Villers St (at Heaven) 44-020/7734-6963 *11pm-3am*

Heaven [★M,D] 9 The Arches (off Villiers St) 44-020/7930-2020 *the mother of all London gay clubs, call for hours/ events*

KU Bar Frith St [M,D] 25 Frith St (at Old Compton St, Soho) 44-020/7287-7986 *noon-11pm, till midnight wknds, 3 floors*

Profile/ Lo Profile [M,D] 84-86 Wardour St (at Peter St) 44-020/7734-3444 *bar/ restaurant upstairs, hip basement club downstairs wknds*

Room Service [M,D] 12-13 Greek St (at Miabella) *10pm Th only*

The Shadow Lounge [M,D,PC] 5-7 Brewer St (Soho) 44-020/7317-9270 *10pm-3am, clsd Sun*

▪CAFES

Balans Cafe [★MW] 34 Old Compton St 44-020/7439-3309 *24hrs, terrace*

Caffe Nero 43 Frith St 44-020/7434-3887 *cruisy cafe*

Flat White 17 Berwick St 44-020/7734-0370 *8am-7pm, 9am-6pm wknds, Australian-style cafe*

LJ Coffee House 3 Winnett St (at Rupert) 44-020/7434-1174 *7:30am-7pm, 10am-8pm Sat, from 1pm Sun, cozy cafe, lovely street views*

Milk Bar [WC] 3 Bateman St 44-020/7287-4796 *8am-7pm, till 5pm wknds*

▪RESTAURANTS

Cha Cha Moon 15-21 Ganton St 44-020/7297-9800 *noon-11pm, till 10pm Sun, inexpensive Chinese*

Food for Thought [BYOB] 31 Neal St, downstairs (Covent Garden) 44-020/7836-0239 *noon-8:30pm, till 5:30pm Sun, vegetarian*

The Gay Hussar [WC] 2 Greek St (on Soho Square) 44-020/7437-0973 *lunch & dinner, clsd Sun, Hungarian*

Mildred's [★] 45 Lexington 44-020/7494-1634 *noon-11pm, clsd Sun*

Nusa Dua 11-12 Dean St (Oxford Circus) 44-020/7437-3559 *Indonesian*

Randall & Aubin 16 Brewer St (at Walkers Court) 44-020/7287-4447 *noon-11pm, casual French, good people-watching*

Wagamama Noodle Bar [NS] 10-A Lexington St 44-020/7292-0990 *noon-11pm, Japanese; many locations throughout city*

▪BOOKSTORES

Gay's the Word 66 Marchmont St (near Russell Square) 44-020/7278-7654 *10am-6:30pm, 2pm-6pm Sun, LGBT*

▪RETAIL SHOPS

Gimme Gimme 4 Tisbury Court (Soho) 44-020/7287-4526 *noon-8pm, clsd Sun, gift & card shop for the LGBT community*

Prowler Soho [★] 5-7 Brewer St (behind Village Soho bar) 44-020/7734-4031 *11am-10pm, noon-8pm Sun, large gay dept store*

▪GYMS & HEALTH CLUBS

Soho Athletic Club [★M] 12 Macklin St (at Drury Ln, Covent Garden) 44-020/7242-1290

Sweatbox [GO] 1-2 Ramilies St, Soho 44-020/3214-6014

▪MEN'S CLUBS

The Sauna Bar Covent Garden [F] 29 Endell St (at Betterton) 44-020/7836-2236 *also bar*

Saunabar Portsea [MO] 2 Portsea Pl (at Connaught St, Marble Arch) 44-020/7402-3385

▪EROTICA

Clone Zone Soho 64 Old Compton St (at Whitcomb) 44-020/7287-1619

RoB London [WC] 24/25 Wells St (near Berwick St) 44-020/7073-1010 *leather/ fetish shop*

Soho Cinemas [V] 7-12 Walkers Court (off Brewer St, Soho) 44-020/7439-0835

London—West

London—West includes Earl's Court, Kensington, Chelsea & Bayswater

■ACCOMMODATIONS

Cardiff Hotel [GF,WI] 5, 7, 9 Norfolk Sq (Hyde Park) **44-020/7723-9068** *B&B hotel in 3 Victorian townhouses, some share baths*

Millennium Bailey's Hotel [GF] 140 Gloucester Rd (at Old Brompton Rd, Kensington) **44-020/7373-6000** *also restaurant & bar*

Myhotel Chelsea [GF] 35 Ixworth Place (at Elystan St, Chelsea) **44-020/7225-7500, 44-020/7637-2000**

Parkwood Hotel [GF,WI] 4 Stanhope Pl (Marble Arch) **44-020/7402-2241** *full brkfst*

■BARS

Queen's Head [M,NH,F,OC] 27 Tryon St (btwn King's Rd & Sloane Ave, Chelsea) **44-020/7589-0262** *pub hours, professional crowd*

Richmond Arms [MW,D,K,C,DS] 20 The Square (at Princes, Richmond) **44-020/8940-2118** *pub hours, professional crowd*

Ted's Place [M,D,TG,K,DS,V,PC] 305-A North End Rd (at Lillie Rd, Earl's Ct) **44-020/7385-9359** *7pm-midnight, men-only Mon-Wed & Fri, TV/TG from 8pm Th & 6pm Sun, darkroom, cruisy*

West Five (W5) [MW,C,P] 6 Popes Ln (South Ealing) **44-020/8579-3266** *7pm-close, clsd Mon-Tue*

■RESTAURANTS

The Churchill Arms 119 Kensington Church St **44-020/7727-4242** *inexpensive, fantastic Thai, also pub*

The Gate 51 Queen Caroline St, Hammersmith *lunch & dinner, clsd Sun, vegetarian*

Star of India 154 Old Brompton Rd **44-020/737-2901** *lunch & dinner, upscale*

■ENTERTAINMENT & RECREATION

Walking Tour of Gay SOHO 56 Old Compton St (at Admiral Duncan Pub) **44-020/7437-6063** *2pm Sun*

■RETAIL SHOPS

Adonis Art Gallery 1b Coleherne Rd **44-020/3417-0238** *gay art*

Clone Zone [GO] 266 Old Brompton Rd (Earl's Court) **44-020/7373-0598** *11:30am-8pm, 11am-6pm Sun; also Soho location, 64 Old Compton St*

London—North

London—North includes Paddington, Regents Park, Camden, St Pancras & Islington

■ACCOMMODATIONS

Ambassadors Bloomsbury [GF,WI,WC] 12 Upper Woburn Pl (at Euston Rd, Bloomsbury) **44-020/7693-5400**

Ossian Guesthouse [GF] 20 Ossian Rd (at Mt Pleasant Villas, Crouch Hill) **44-020/8340-4331**

The Royal Park Hotel [GF,WI] 3 Westbourne Terr (Hyde Park) **44-020/7479-6600**

■BARS

The Black Cap [★MW,D,TG,F,K,C] 171 Camden High St (Camden Town) **44-020/7485-0538** *noon-2am, till-3am Fri-Sat*

G-A-Y Late [M] 5 Goslett Yard (Camden Town) *11pm-3am*

The George Music Bar [M,TG,K,C,GO] 114 Twickenham Rd (Isleworth) **44-020/8560-1456** *5pm-close, from noon wknds, cabaret*

King William IV (KW) [★MW,F] 77 Hampstead High St (Hampstead) **44-020/7435-5747** *pub hours, beer garden*

■NIGHTCLUBS

Central Station [★MW,D,TG,F,C,DS,S,V,WI] 37 Wharfdale Rd (King's Cross) **44-020/7278-3294** *noon-1pm, complex includes B&B, terrace*

Club Kali [★MW,D,MR-A,TG,E,$] 1 Dartmouth Park Hill (at The Dome) **44-020/7272-8153 (Dome #)** *10pm-3am 3rd Fri, South Asian music*

Dream Bags Jaquar Shoes [MW,D] 32-36 Kingsland Rd **44-020/7729-5830** *noon-1am, jam-packed club in a former shoe shop*

East Bloc [M,D] 217 City Rd (at Shepherdess Walk, Old Street) **44-020/7253-0367** *10:30pm-6am Fri-Sat only, electro dance club in funky basement space*

Egg [GS,D] 200 York Way (Kings Cross) **44-020/7871-1111** *10pm-6am Sat, until late afternoon Sun*

Habibi London [MW,D] 85 Charterhouse St (Farringdon, at Raduno) *10:30pm last Fri only, Middle Eastern*

■**RESTAURANTS**

Manna [R] 4 Erskine Rd (at Ainger Rd, Camden) **44-020/7722-8028** *lunch Tue-Sun, dinner nightly, vegetarian*

Providors/ Tapa Room 109 Marylebone High St (at New Cavendish St) **44-020/7935-6175** *lunch & dinner, Asian fusion*

■**ENTERTAINMENT & RECREATION**

Rosemary Branch Theatre [GS,F] 2 Shepperton Rd **44-020/7704-2730 (bar), 44-020/7704-6665 (theatre)** *also restaurant & bar, many gay-themed plays*

■**MEN'S CLUBS**

Pants [MO,V] 37 Wharfdale Rd (King's Cross, at the Underground Club (below Central Station bar)) **44-020/7278-3294** *1pm-6pm, clsd Wed & Sun*

Paradise Spa 17 Crouch Hill **44-020/7263-9675**

Underground Club [★MO] 37 Wharfdale Rd (King's Cross, below Central Station bar) **44-020/7278-3294** *sex parties, theme nights, check web for events*

■**EROTICA**

Regulation 17a St Albans Pl (Islington Green) **44-020/7226-0665** *fetish gear & toys "made to measure"*

■**CRUISY AREAS**

Clapham Common [AYOR] *west side of the common near to the south circular road in the wooded area*

Earls Court Graveyard *summers, watch out for the bobbies*

Hampstead Heath [★AYOR]

Highgate Hill take Archway Tube *male sun bathing area at the Highgate Ponds*

London—East

London—East includes City, Tower, Clerkenwell & Shoreditch

■**ACCOMMODATIONS**

Andaz Liverpool Street [GS,F] 40 Liverpool St (near Bishopsgate, at Liverpool Street Station) **44-020/7961-1234**

The Hoxton [GF,SW,WI] 81 Great Eastern St **44-020/7550-1000**

■**BARS**

Bar Music Hall [GF,D,E,F] 134 Curtain Rd (Shoreditch) **44-020/7729-7216** *11am-midnight, till 3am Fri-Sat*

Bethnal Green Working Men's Club [MW,DS,C,TG] 42-44 Pollard Row (at Squirries St, Bethnal Green) **44-020/7739-7170** *performance art & cabaret*

BJ's White Swan [M,D,TG,F,WC] 556 Commercial Rd (near Bromley St) **44-020/7780-9870** *9pm-close, from 6pm Sun, clsd Mon*

Dalston Superstore [GS,NH,F,D,WI] 117 Kingsland High St (at Sandringham Rd) **44-020/7254 2273** *noon-2am*

Joiners Arms [M,E] 116 Hackney Rd **44-020/7739-9854** *5pm-2am, till 4am Fri-Sat, theme nights, live bands*

The Macbeth [GS,E,WI] 70 Hoxton St (at Crondall St, Old St) **44-020/ 7749-0600** *8pm-1am*

The Old Ship [MW,NH,C,WC] 17 Barnes St (Stepney) **44-020/7790-4082** *from 4pm Mon, from 7pm Wed-Sat, from 6pm Sun, clsd Tue*

The Victoria [GS,E] 186 Hoe St 44-020/8521-7611 *more gay 2nd & last Sat*

NIGHTCLUBS

Backstreet [MO,L,PC] Wentworth Mews, Burdett Rd (at Mile End Rd, Bow) 44-020/8980-8557, 44-020/8980-7880 *10pm-2am, till 3am Fri-Sat, till 1am Sun, clsd Mon-Wed, strict leather/ rubber dress code*

Kaos at Stunners [GS,TG,D,PC] 566 Cable St (at Butcher Row, Cable St Studios, Limehouse) *monthy parties, check www.kaoslondon.com*

Pelucas y Tacones [MW,D,A] 6 Shoreditch High St (at Concrete/ Pizza East) *9pm-2am 2nd Sat only*

Unskinny Bop [W,D,E] 42-44 Pollard Row (Bethnal Green Club) *9pm 3rd Fri only*

Way Out Club [MW,D,TG,S,PC,$] 9 Crosswall (at Charlie's) 44-(0)77/7815-7290 *9pm-4am Sat only, TV/TS & their friends*

CAFES

Pogo Cafe 76 Clarence Rd 44-020/8533-1214 *12:30pm-9pm, from 11am Sun, vegan, volunteer-run, events*

RESTAURANTS

Bistrotheque 23-27 Waderson St 44-020/8983-7900 *expensive & glamorous, also cabaret shows after dinner*

Bonds Restaurant & Bar 5 Threadneedle St 44-020/7657-8090 *hrs vary, European*

Cafe Spice Namaste 16 Prescott St 44-020/7488-9242 *lunch Mon-Fri, dinner nightly, clsd Sun, Indian*

Canteen [★] 2 Crispin Pl (Spitalfields) 44-(0)84/5686-1122 *place to be for brkfst*

Hoxton Square Bar & Kitchen [★E] 2-4 Hoxton Square 44-020/9613-1171 *great dark spot for brkfst*

Les Trois Garçons [R] 1 Club Row (at Bethnal, Shoreditch) 44-020/7613-1924 *6pm-midnight, clsd Sun*

Lounge Lover [R,WC] 44-020/7012-1234 *fancy Japanese cuisine in a posh lounge*

Royal Oak 73 Columbia Rd (at Hackney Rd, Old St) 44-020/7729-2220 *4pm-11pm, from noon Fri-Sun*

Saf 63-97 Barkers Building, High Street (in Kensington, at Wholefoods Market) 44-020/7368-4555 *lunch & dinner, also bar till midnight, upscale vegan/ raw food*

MEN'S CLUBS

Chariots Limehouse [F,V] 574 Commercial Rd (near Limehouse tube) 44-020/7247-5333 *24hrs*

Chariots Shoreditch [★SW,F,V] 1 Fairchild St (Shoreditch) 44-020/7247-5333

E15 Club 6 Leytonstone Rd 44-020/8555-5455 *11am-11pm*

EROTICA

Expectations 75 Great Eastern St (Shoreditch) 44-020/7739-0292 *rubber store*

London—South

London—South includes Southwark, Lambeth, Kennington, Vauxhall, Battersea, Lewisham & Greenwich

ACCOMMODATIONS

Griffin House [MW,WI,GO] 22 Stockwell Green 44-020/7096-3332 *2 rental apts near Vauxhall Gay Village & West End*

BARS

Bar Code [M,D,E,YC] 69 Goding St, Arch 69, Albert Embankment (Vauxhall) 44-020/7582-4180 *4pm-1am, till 5am Fri, & 7am Sat, from 5pm Sun*

Battersea Barge [GF,F,E,C,GO] Riverside Walk Nine Elms Ln (Vauxhall) 44-020/7498-0004 *call for events, cabaret, comedy on the Thames River!*

The Bird in Hand [MW,NH,K] 291 Sydenham Rd, Croydon 44-020/8683-3104 *5pm-midnight, from 2pm Sun*

The Cambria [GS,E,F] 40 Kemerton Rd 44-020/7737-3676 *noon-11pm, till 1am Fri-Sat*

The Eagle London [M,L] 349 Kennington Ln (Vauxhall) 44-020/7793-0903 *9pm-close, from 8pm Sun*

George & Dragon [MW,C] 2 Blackheath Hill (Greenwich) 44-020/8691-3764 *8pm-2am, till 4am Fri-Sat*

Kazbar [MW,TG,V] 50 Clapham High St (Clapham) 44-020/7622-0070 *5pm-midnight, till 1am Fri-Sat, from 1pm Sun*

The Little Apple [MW,D,TG,F,WC] 98 Kennington Ln 44-020/7735-2039 *noon-midnight, till 3am Sat, terrace*

Prince of Greenwich [M,NH,F,DS] 72 Royal Hill (Greenwich) *noon-11pm*

The Star & Garter [MW,K,WI,WC] 227 High St (Bromley) 44-020/8466-7733 *pub hours*

The Two Brewers [MW,D,K,C] 114 Clapham High St (Clapham) 44-020/7819-9539

Two8Six [MW,D,F,C,PC] 286 Lewisham High St 44-020/8690-7648 *noon-3am, till 1am Sun-Mon*

■NIGHTCLUBS

Black Sheep Bar [GS,D,A] 68 High St (at S Norwood Hill, Croydon) 44-020/8680-2233

Bootylicious [MW,MR] 1 Nine Elms (at Club Colosseum) *11pm 3rd Sat, popular black gay club*

Exilio [MW,D,MR-L] St Thomas St (at Guy's Bar) 44-(0)79/3137-4391 *9:30pm-2:30am Sat*

Fire [GS,D,$] 47B S Lambeth Rd (Vauxhall) 44-020/3242-0040 *after-hours, Sat mornings & Sun afternoons*

Hard On [MO,D,PC] 66 Albert Embankment (at Union, in Vauxhall) 44-020/7533 402 985 *3rd Sat only, fetish party, strict dress code*

The Hoist [M,L] Railway Arch 47b&tc, S Lambeth Rd (Vauxhall) 44-020/7735-9972 *S/M club w/ strict dress code, theme nights*

Horse Meat Disco [MW,D,TG] 349 Kennington Ln (at the Eagle) 44-020/7793-0903 *8pm Sun only, popular queer dance party*

Onyx [M,D] 65 Albert Embankment (Vauxhall) *London's hottest Friday night party*

Popstarz [★MW,D,$] 100 Tinworth St (at Hidden bar, Vauxhall) 44-020/7240-1900 *10pm-6am Fri, 4 rooms*

Royal Vauxhall Tavern [M,D,TG,F,WC] 372 Kennington Ln (Vauxhall) 44-020/7820-1222 *8pm-late, 9pm-3am Fri-Sat, 2pm-midnight Sun*

Union Club [M,D] 66 Albert Embankment (Vauxhall) 44-020/7278-3294 *cruise mazes, dark corners, popular Fri*

Urban Desi [MW,D,MR-A] 100 Tinworth St (at Hidden) 44-020/7820-6613 *11pm-5am 2nd Sat, South Asian*

XXL [MO,D,B] 1 Invicta Plaza (South Bank, at Pulse) 44-(0)78/7261-0981 *10pm-6am Sat, till 3am Wed, "one club fits all"*

■CAFES

Glow Lounge [WI] 6 Cavendish Parade (Clapham Common S Side) 44-020/8673-4471 *noon-11pm, 9:30am-1am Fri-Sat, 10am-7pm Sun*

■ENTERTAINMENT & RECREATION

Oval Theatre Cafe Bar [F] 52-54 Kennington Oval 44-020/7582-0080 *6pm-11pm Tue-Sat (cafe), inquire about current theatre & art*

■GYMS & HEALTH CLUBS

Paris Gymnasium [MO] 73 Goding St (behind Vauxhall Tavern, Vauxhall) 44-020/7735-8989

■MEN'S CLUBS

Chariots Streatham 292 Streatham High Rd (at Babington Rd, enter rear) 44-020/8696-0929 *24hrs wknds*

Chariots Vauxhall [F,V] Rail Arches 63-64 (Albert Embankment) 44-020/7247-5333

Chariots Waterloo 101 Lower Marsh (at Waterloo Rd) 44-020/7401-8484 *24hrs*

The Locker Room [V] 8 Cleaver St (Kennington) 44-020/7735-6064 *24hrs wknds*

Pleasuredrome [F,V,NS] 124 Cornwall Rd (at Alaska St, Waterloo) 44–020/7633–9194 *24hrs*

Star Steam [V] 38 Lavender Hill (Battersea) 44–020/7924–2269 *noon-8pm, clsd Mon*

Steamworks [V] 309 New Cross Rd 44–020/8694–0606 *24hrs wknds*

■CRUISY AREAS

Hyde Park [AYOR] *Southeast cornor of Hyde Park in the Rose Garden*

FRANCE

Paris

Note: M°=Métro station

Paris is divided by arrondissements (city districts); 01=1st arrondissement, 02=2nd arrondissement, etc

Paris—Overview

Note: When phoning Paris from the US, dial the country code + the city code + the local phone number

■INFO LINES & SERVICES

Centre Gai et Lesbien 63 rue Beaubourg 33–1/4357–2147 *drop-in evenings, many groups/ events*

Gay AA 7 rue Auguste Vacquerie (at St George's Anglican) 33–1/4634–5965 *7:30pm Tue, see calendar for other times*

■ACCOMMODATIONS

Gay Accommodation Paris [GO] 271, rue du Faubourg Saint Antoine 33–1/4348–1382 *studios for rent in central Paris*

Marais Flats/ Studios [GO] 20 rue Pierre Lescot 33–6/3256–5727 (European daytime only)

■PUBLICATIONS

Têtu 33–1/5680–2080 *stylish & intelligent LGBT monthly (en français)*

Paris—01

■ACCOMMODATIONS

Hotel Louvre Richelieu [GS,NS,WI] 51 rue de Richelieu (M° Palais-Royal) 33–1/4297–4620

Hotel Louvre Saint-Honoré [GS,WI,WC] 141 rue Saint-Honoré (at rue du Louvre) 33–1/4296–2323

■BARS

Le Banana Cafe [★MW,D,E,P,S,YC,WC] 13–15 rue de la Ferronnerie (near rue St-Denis, M° Châtelet) 33–1/4233–3531 *6pm-dawn, go-go boys Th-Sat terrace*

Bar du Kent'z [M] 2-4 rue Vauvilliers (M° Chatelet-Les Halles) 33–1/4221–0116 *1920s style cocktail lounge*

Le Tropic Cafe [MW,D,TG,F,YC,WC] 66 rue des Lombards (M° Châtelet) 33–1/4013–9262 *4pm-5am, tapas, terrace*

Wolf [M,B,V] 37 rue des Lombards (M° Châtelet) 33–1/4028–0252 *5pm-2am*

■NIGHTCLUBS

Le Club 18 [★M,D,YC,PC,$] 18 rue du Beaujolais (at rue Vivienne, M° Palais-Royal) 33–1/4297–5213 *Wed, Fri-Sat only*

Le Klub [GS,E,MR,$] 14 rue St-Denis (at rue des Lombards, M° Châtelet) 33–1/4508–9625 *8pm-11pm, till 6am Fri-Sat, clsd Wed & Sun, rock & electro club*

■RESTAURANTS

L' Amazonial [MW,C,DS,WC] 3 rue Ste-Opportune (at rue Ferronnerie, M° Châtelet) 33–1/4233–5313 *lunch & dinner, brunch wknds, Brazilian/ int'l, heated terrace*

Au Diable des Lombards 64 rue des Lombards (at rue St-Denis, M° Châtelet) 33–1/4233–8184 *8am-1am, American, full bar, terrace*

Marc Mitonne [E,C] 60 rue de l'Arbre-Sec (M° Les Halles) 33–1/4261–5316 *6pm-2am, clsd Sun-Mon*

La Poule au Pot 9 rue Vauvilliers (M° Les Halles) 33–1/4236–3296 *7pm-5am, clsd Mon & Aug, bistro, French*

Le Velvet 43 rue Saint Honore *Thai restaurant & small gay bar*

France • *EUROPE*

▌ENTERTAINMENT & RECREATION

Forum des Halles 101 Porte Berger (M° Châtelet-Les Halles) **33-1/4476-9656** *underground sports/ entertainment complex w/ museums, theater, shops, clubs, cafes & more*

▌GYMS & HEALTH CLUBS

Club Med Gym [GS] 147 rue St-Honoré (M° Louvre) **33-1/4020-0303** *day passes available, many locations throughout city*

▌MEN'S CLUBS

The Hole Next [MO] 87 rue St Honoré (at rue du Roule, M° Chatelet-Les Halles)

Til't [V] 41 rue Ste-Anne (near av de l'Opera, M° Pyramides) **33-1/4296-0743** *noon-7am, bar*

Le Transfert [MO] 3 rue de la Sourdiere (M° Tuileries) *10:30pm-daybreak, open 4pm-10pm some wknds*

▌EROTICA

Boxxman 2 rue de la Cossonnerie (M° Châtelet) **33-1/4221-4702** *videos, toys & fetish gear, also sex club, internet access*

▌CRUISY AREAS

Quai des Tuileries [AYOR] on bank of The Seine (M° Louvre) *aka Tata Beach*

Paris—02

▌BARS

Alex's [M,NH,OC] 2 rue de Marivaux (at boul des Italiens) **33-1/4296-4079** *6pm-close, friendly neighborhood bar, snacks served*

L' Impact [MO,N,V] 18 rue Grenéta (M° Châtelet) **33-1/4221-9424** *8pm-3am, 10pm-6am Fri-Sat, from 3pm Sun, 100% naked, backroom, theme nights, free brkfst wknds*

▌NIGHTCLUBS

Chez Carmen [GS,D] 53 rue Vivienne *after-hours club*

Rex Club [GF,D,E,$] 5 blvd Poissonière (M° Bonne Nouvelle) **33-1/4236-1096** *call for events, clsd August*

▌CAFES

Stuart Friendly [F] 16 rue Marie Stuart **33-1/4233-2400** *noon-11pm, till midnight Fri-Sat, till 5:30pm Sun, "straight-friendly" cafe*

▌RESTAURANTS

Le Lezard Cafe 32 rue Etienne Marcel **33-1/4233-2273** *full bar, terrace year round*

Le Loup Blanc [★MW] 42 rue Tiquetonne (M° Etienne-Marcel) **33-1/4013-0835** *7:30pm-midnight, till 1am Sat, also brunch 11am-4:30pm Sun*

▌RETAIL SHOPS

Galerie au Bonheur du Jour 11 rue Chabanais **33-1/4296-5864** *2:30pm-7:30pm, clsd Sun-Mon, gay art*

▌MEN'S CLUBS

Euro Men's Club [V,SW,OC] 10 rue St-Marc (M° Bourse) **33-1/4233-9263** *1pm-9pm*

Paris—03

▌ACCOMMODATIONS

➤Absolu Living [MW,GO] 236 rue St Martin **33-1/4454-9700** *fully furnished apts in central Paris, short & long-term stays*

Adorable Apartment in Paris [★GF,NS,GO] (M° Rambuteau) **415/287-0306 (US#)**

Hôtel du Vieux Saule [GF] 6 rue de Picardie **33-1/4272-0114**

Hotel Jules & Jim [GS,GO] 11 rue des Gravilliers **33-1/4454-1313**

▌BARS

Le CUD Club [★M,D,YC] 12 rue des Haudriettes **33-1/4277-4412** *11pm-6am, till 7am wknds*

Le Dépôt [MO,D,S,YC,$] 10 rue aux Ours (btwn bd de Sébastopol & rue St-Martin, M° Rambuteau) **33-1/4454-9696** *2pm-8am, huge cruise bar on 3 flrs, big backroom*

Le Duplex [MW,NH,S,WI] 25 rue Michel-Le-Comte (at rue Beaubourg, M° Rambuteau) **33-1/4272-8086** *8pm-2am, till 4am Fri-Sat*

One Way [M,NH,B,L,F,V,OC] 28 rue Charlot (at rue des 4 Fils, M° République) 33-1/4887-4610 5pm-2am, cruisy, darkroom, tapas

Snax Kfé [M,F] 182 rue Saint Martin (M° Rambuteau) 33-1/4027-8933 10am-2am, from 3:30pm Sat, clsd Sun

Le Tango/ La Boite à Frissons [★MW,F] 13 rue au Maire (M° Arts-et-Métiers) 33-1/4272-1778 10:30pm-5am, clsd Mon

RESTAURANTS

La Fontaine Gourmande 11 rue Charlot 33-1/4278-7240 lunch Tue-Fri & dinner Tue-Sun, French

MEN'S CLUBS

The Glove [L] 34 rue Charlot (M° St-Sebastien-Froissard) 33-1/4887-3136 from 10:30pm, 4:30pm-9pm Sun, clsd Mon-Wed, leather/ rubber/ uniform, also bar, brkfst wknds

Sun City [SW] 62 Blvd de Sébastopol (M° Rambuteau) 33-1/4274-3141 noon-6am, cruise bar & sauna, swimming, gym, private cabins

EROTICA

Rex 42 rue de Poitou (at rue Charlot, M° St-Sébastien-Froissard) 33-1/4277-5857 1pm-8pm, clsd Sun, leather & S/M accessories

Paris—04

ACCOMMODATIONS

Historic Rentals [GF,NS,WI] 800/537-5408 (US#) 1-bdrm apt

Hôtel Beaubourg [GS,WI] 11 rue Simon le Franc (btwn rue Beaubourg & rue du Temple, M° Hôtel-de-Ville) 33-1/4274-3424 next to Centre Pompidou

Hôtel de la Bretonnerie [GF] 22 rue Ste-Croix-de-la-Bretonnerie (M° Hôtel-de-Ville) 33-1/4887-7763

Hôtel du Vieux Marais [GF,WI] 8 rue du Plâtre (M° Hôtel-de-Ville) 33-1/4278-4722 centrally located

Paris At Home [MW,WI,GO] 33-06/1991-5828 B&B & apts

France • EUROPE

■ **BARS**

Au Mange Disque [M] 15 rue de la Reynie (at Boule de Sebastopol) 33-1/4804-7817 11am-2am, from 5pm Sun-Mon

Bears' Den [MO,D,B,V] 6 rue des Lombards (at rue St-Martin, M° Hôtel-de-Ville) 33-1/4271-0820 4pm-2am, till 4am Fri-Sat, T-dance Sun, darkroom, terrace

Le Carrefour [M,NH] 8 rue des Archives (at rue de la Verrerie) 33-1/4029-9005 6am-2am, good location & terrace

Cox [★M,D,V] 15 rue des Archives (at rue Ste-Croix-de-la-Bretonnerie, M° Hôtel-de-Ville) 33-1/4272-0800 5:30pm-2am, from 4:30pm Fri-Sun, terrace

Dandy's Cafe [M] 9 rue Nicolas Flamel 33-1/4271-4582 2pm-2am

L' Enchanteur [MW,K] 15 rue Michel Lecomte (M° Rambuteau) 33-1/4804-0238 6pm-6am, clsd Mon

Le Feeling [MW,NH,YC] 43 rue Ste-Croix-de-la-Bretonnerie (M° Hôtel-de-Ville) 33-1/4804-7003 3pm-2am

Les Filles de Paris [GS,D,E,C,K] 57 rue Quincampoix 33-1/4271-7220 10pm-5am Wed-Sat, clsd Sun-Mon, burlesque & drag shows

Le Freedj [MW,D] 35 rue Ste-Croix-de-la-Bretonnerie (at rue du Temple, M° Hôtel-de-Ville) 33-1/4029-4440 6pm-4am

Full Metal [M,L] 40 rue des Blancs-Manteaux (M° Rambuteau) 33-1/4272-3005 5pm-4am, till 6am Fri-Sat, from 3pm Sun, well-stocked "hard backroom bar," theme parties, dress code

Gossip Cafe [MW,F] 16 rue des Lombards (at bd de Sébastopol, M° Châtelet) 33-1/4271-3683 2pm-6am

L' Imprevu Cafe [M,NH,F] 9 rue Quincampoix 33-1/4278-2350 3pm-2am, from 1pm Sun, low key cafe/ bar

Les Jacasses [W] 5 rue des Ecouffes (M° St Paul) 33-1/4271-1551 5pm-2am

Krash [★MO,L,V] 12 rue Simon Lefranc (at rue du Renard, M° Rambuteau) 33-1/5041-1326 3pm-5am, till 7am Fri-Sat, sex bar

Le Mic-Man [M,NH,V] 24 rue Geoffroy-l'Angevin (at rue Beaubourg, M° Rambuteau) 33-1/4274-3980 noon-2am, open later wknds, friendly bar w/ cruisy cave downstairs

Morgan Bar [MW,D,WI] 25 rue du Roi de Sicile 33-1/4277-0666

L' Oiseau Bariolé [MW] 16 rue Saint-Croix-de-la-Bretonnerie (M° Hotel de Ville) 33-1/4272-3712 5pm-close, quiet

Okawa [★GS,F,C,P,YC] 40 rue Vieille du Temple (at rue Ste-Croix-de-la-Bretonnerie, M° Hôtel-de-Ville) 33-1/4804-3069 10am-2am, till 4am Fri-Sat, trendy cafe-bar in 12th- & 13th-c caves

L' Open Cafe [★MW,F] 17 rue des Archives (at rue Ste-Croix-de-la-Bretonnerie, M° Hôtel-de-Ville) 11am-2am, till 4am Fri-Sat, sidewalk cafe-bar

La Perle [GS] 78 rue Vieille du Temple 33-1/4272-6993 Parisian hipster dive bar

Le Pur Bar/ Titi's Bar [MW,NH] 12 rue de Plâtre (btwn rue du Temple & rue des Archives, M° Hôtel-de-Ville) 33-1/4887-0259 5pm-2am, cafe-bar

Quetzal [★M,NH,S,WI] 10 rue de la Verrerie (at rue des Archives, M° Hôtel-de-Ville) 33-1/4887-9907 5pm-5am, cruise bar, darkroom, terrace

Le Raidd [M,D,S] 23 rue du Temple (M° Hotel de ville) 33-1/4277-0488 5pm-5am

Secteur X [MO] 49 rue des Blancs-Manteaux (at rue du Temple, M° Rambuteau) 33-1-09/5039-5085 5pm-2am, cruisy, back room

Sly Bar [M,NH,D] 22 rue des Lombards 33-1/8253-2781

Les Souffleurs [MW,D,YC] 7 rue de la Verrerie (M° Hôtel-de-Ville) 33-1/6421-8133 artsy, younger crowd

Le Spyce [★M,D] 23 rue Ste-Croix de la Bretonnerie 6pm-close

Le Voulez-Vous [MW,F] 18 rue du Temple (M° Hôtel-de-Ville) 33-1/4459-3857 *11am-2am, lounge & restaurant, terrace*

Yono [M,D,E,F] 37 rue Vieille du Temple 33-1/4274-3165 *6pm-2am, 4:30pm-11pm Sun, clsd Mon, cozy basement bar*

Ze Baar [M,NH,F] 41 rue des Blancs Manteaux (at rue du Temple) 33-1/4271-7508 *5pm-2am, also restaurant*

CAFES

La Fronde 33 rue des Archives 33-1/4272-2734

Jul's Cafe 20 rue du Plâtre 33-1/4271-3039 *5pm-2am, also bar*

Le Kofi du Marais [MW] 54 rue Ste-Croix-de-la-Bretonnerie (M° Hôtel de Ville) 33-1/4887-4871 *7pm-midnight, clsd Sun*

RESTAURANTS

4 Pat [D] 4 rue St Merri 33-1/4277-2545 *noon-2am, Italian menu*

Les Agités 15 rue de la Reynie (at Boule de Sebastopol) 33-1/8389-5309 *7pm-2am, clsd Sun-Mon*

Le Chant des Voyelles 4 rue des Lombards (M° Châtelet) 33-1/4277-7707 *lunch & dinner, traditional French, terrace*

Etamine Cafe 13 rue des Ecouffes (at rue des Rosiers, M° Hotel de Ville) 33-1/4478-0962 *noon-midnight, clsd Mon, also bar*

Le Gai Moulin [MW] 10 rue St-Merri (at rue du Temple, M° Hôtel-de-Ville) 33-1/4887-0600 *noon-2am*

HD Diner 6-8 Square Ste-Croix de la Bretonnerie 33-1/4277-6934 *11am-midnight, 50's style diner*

La Pas-Sage-Oblige 29 rue du Bourg-Tibourg (M° Hôtel-de-Ville) 33-1/4041-9503 *lunch & dinner, vegetarian*

Les Piétons 8 rue des Lombards (M° Châtelet) 33-1/4887-8287 *noon-2am, Spanish/ tapas, also bar*

Who's 14 rue Saint Merri (M° Rambuteau) 33-1/4272-7597 *noon-6am*

Woo Bar 3 rue Pierre au Lard (M° Rambuteau) 33-1/4272-7597 *noon-6am*

ENTERTAINMENT & RECREATION

Gay Beach E end of Ile St-Louis *sunbathing*

BOOKSTORES

Les Mots à la Bouche 6 rue Ste-Croix-de-la-Bretonnerie (near rue du Vieille du Temple, M° Hôtel-de-Ville) 33-1/4278-8830 *11am-11pm, 1pm-9pm Sun, LGBT, English titles*

RETAIL SHOPS

Bow 5 rue St Merri 33-1/4278-0189 *menswear*

Boy'z Bazaar Collections 5 rue Ste-Croix-de-la-Bretonnerie (at rue Vieille du Temple, M° Hôtel-de-Ville) 33-1/4271-9400 *noon-8:30pm, till 10pm Fri-Sat, clubwear to drag to leather*

Sweetman 17 blvd de Raspail 33-8/4277-1137 *10:30am-7pm, clsd Sun, men's underwear & more*

EROTICA

BMC Store 21 rue des Lombards 33-1/4027-9809 *videos, DVDs, toys*

IEM Marais 16 rue Ste-Croix-de-la-Bretonnerie (M° Hôtel-de-Ville) 33-1/4274-0161 *leather, latex, uniforms & fetish gear*

Menstore 8 Square Ste-Croix de la Bretonnerie 33-1/4454-5115

RoB Paris 8 Square Ste-Croix de la Bretonnerie 33-1/4454-5116 *clsd Sun, leather/ fetish*

CRUISY AREAS

Square du Pont de Sully [AYOR] at the end of Ile St-Louis (M° Sully-Morland) *along the side paths at night*

Paris—05

■RESTAURANTS

Le Petit Prince [★] 12 rue de Lanneau (M° Maubert-Mutualité) **33-1/4354-7726** *7:30pm-midnight, French*

■ENTERTAINMENT & RECREATION

Open-Air Sculpture Museum Quai Saint-Bernard *along the Seine btwn the Jardin des Plantes & the Institut du Monde Arabe*

Paris—06

■ACCOMMODATIONS

The Hotel Luxembourg Parc [GS] 42 rue de Vaugirard **33-1/5310-3650**

Paris—07

■CRUISY AREAS

Champs de Mars [AYOR] (M° Pont-de-l'Alma)

Paris—08

■ACCOMMODATIONS

François 1er [GF,WI] 7 rue Magellan **33-1/4723-4404** *boutique hotel near les Champs-Elysées, also bar*

■BARS

Le Day Off [MW,NH,F] 10 rue de l'Isly (M° Gare-St-Lazare) **33-1/4522-8790**

■NIGHTCLUBS

Escualita [M,D,TG] 128 rue de la Boetie (at Club "MadaM") *midnight Sun only, fabulous tranny dance party, all are welcome*

Le Queen [★GS,D,TG,DS,YC,$] 102 av des Champs-Élysées (btwn rue Washington & rue de Berri, M° Georges-V) **33-8/5389-0890** *midnight-dawn, more gay Sun*

■MEN'S CLUBS

Steel Club [S,V] 23 rue de Penthièvre (off Champs d'Elysées, M° Miromesnil) **33-1/4561-9028** *noon-1am, maze, theme nights, also bar*

■EROTICA

Vidéovision 62 rue de Rome (M° Europe) **33-1/4522-5735** *clsd Sun*

Paris—09

■ACCOMMODATIONS

The Grand [GF,WI] 2 rue Scribe **33-1/4007-3232, 888/424-6835 (US#)** *ultraluxe art deco hotel*

■BARS

Mec Zone [M,L,V] 27 rue Turgot (M° Anvers) **33-1/4082-9418** *9pm-5am, 2pm-6am wknds, cruisy, theme nights, darkroom*

Rosa Bonheur [GF] 1 rue Botzaris **33-1/4200-0045** *more gay Sun, arrive before 6pm to avoid the line*

■NIGHTCLUBS

Blacks Blancs Beurs/ KELMA T-Dance [M,D,MR] 11 Place Pigalle (at Folies Pigalle) **33-1/4205-7300** (info-line) *10pm-5am Sun only, R&B & Arabic dance music, check www.kelma.org for location*

Folies Pigalle [GS,D,MR,$] 11 place Pigalle (M° Pigalle) **33-1/4878-5525, 33-1/4280-1203** (BBB info line) *midnight-dawn*

■MEN'S CLUBS

IDM [★V,WI] 4 rue du Faubourg-Montmartre (at bd St-Martin, M° Grand-Blvds) **33-1/4523-1003** *full gym, jacuzzi, bar*

Paris—10

■BARS

Cafe Moustache [M,NH,F,B,V] 138 rue du Faubourg St-Martin (at bd de Magenta, M° Gare-de-l'Est) **33-1/4607-7270** *4pm-2am, dark-room, patio*

■MEN'S CLUBS

Key West Sauna [★SW] 141 rue Lafayette (M° Gare-du-Nord) **33-1/4526-3174** *noon-1am, till 2am Fri-Sat*

■EROTICA

Concorde 27 Blvd de Magenta **33-1/4249-1172** *also at 6 rue du Dahomey*

CRUISY AREAS

Canal St-Martin Jean-Jaurès [AYOR] (M° Jaurès) *on the quais btwn the Jean-Jaurès & Louis-Blanc bridges*

Paris—11

ACCOMMODATIONS

Le 20 Prieure Hotel [GS,WI] 20 rue du Grand Prieuré 33-1/4700-7414

Le General Hotel [GF,WI,WC] 5/7 rue Rampon 33-1/4700-4157

HI Matic [GF,WI,WC, GO] 71 rue de Charonne *a new urban eco-logding concept*

Hôtel Beaumarchais [GS,WI] 3 rue Oberkampf (btwn bd Beaumarchais & bd Voltaire, M° Filles-du-Calvaire) 33-1/5336-8686

BARS

Le Bataclan [GF,E] 50 blvd Voltaire (at Bataclan club, M° Saint Ambroise) 33-1/4314-0030 *live music venue, more gay for the Follivores & Crazyvores*

Follivores/ Crazyvores [MW,D] 50 blvd Voltaire (M° Saint Ambroise) 33-1/4314-0030 *monthly sing-along dance parties; Follivores is 1960s-1990s French pop, Crazyvores is English-speaking; kitsch factor very high!*

In Out [GS,D,YC] 241 rue du Fbg St Antoine 33-9/5241-0037 *5pm-2am, clsd Sun*

NIGHTCLUBS

Les Disquaires [GS,D,E] 6 rue des Taillandiers (M° Bastille) 33-1/4021-9460 *dance bar, live bands*

Scream [M,D,18+] 18 rue du Faubourg-du-Temple (M° République, at Gibus Club) 33-1/4700-7888 *Sat only*

CAFES

Cannibale Café [WI] 93 Rue Jean-Pierre Timbaud 33-1/4929-0040 *an old-fashioned Parisian café in Belleville*

Le Pause Cafe [F] 41 rue de Charonne 33-1/4806-8033 *8am-2am, 9am-8pm Sun*

RESTAURANTS

Le Tabarin [MW,P] 3 rue Amelot 33-1/4807-1522 *lunch Sun-Fri, dinner Sun-Sat, full bar*

ENTERTAINMENT & RECREATION

L' ArtiShow 3 cite Souzy 33-1/4002-1803 *cabaret, also lunch & dinner served*

BOOKSTORES

Violette & Co [GO] 102 rue de Charonne (at boulevard Voltaire, M° Charonne) 33-1/4372-1607 *11am-8pm, 2pm-7pm Sun, clsd Mon, LGBT & feminist, English titles, lesbian-owned*

MEN'S CLUBS

Boys Video Club 8 rue de Nice (M° Charonne) 33-9/5392-5586 *11am-2am, gloryholes, video rooms, bar*

Bunker [V] 150 rue St-Maur (M° Goncourt) 33-1/5336-7887 *4pm-2am, till 3:30am Fri, till 4:30am Sat, till 1am Sun*

Entre Deux Eaux [MO] 45 rue de la Folie Mericourt (at rue Oberkampf) 33-1/4357-7646 *naked sex club for men, theme nights*

Paris—12

GYMS & HEALTH CLUBS

Atlantide [GS,TG,V] 13 rue Parrot (M° Gare de Lyon) 33-1/4342-2243 *women & transgender welcome, cabins, tanning, also bar*

CRUISY AREAS

Bois de Vincennes [AYOR]

Paris—13

CRUISY AREAS

Quai d'Austerlitz [AYOR]

Les Sablières [AYOR] *along the quai d'Austerlitz, from library to blvds Perijheriques, at night only*

France • *Europe*

Paris—14

▪ENTERTAINMENT & RECREATION

Friday Night Fever [GS] Place Raoul Dautry (btwn Montparnasse office tower & Montparnasse train station) 10pm-1am Fri (weather permitting), meet 9:30pm, rollerblading

▪GYMS & HEALTH CLUBS

Amphibi [GS,TG] 73 rue Hallé (at rue Bézout, M° Alesia) **33-1/4047-5090** sauna where everyone is welcome: gay, straight, bisexual, transgendered

▪MEN'S CLUBS

Les Bains d' Odessa [MO,SW,WI] 5 rue d'Odessa **33-1/4047-8343** noon-10pm, also bar

Paris—15

▪ACCOMMODATIONS

Platine Hotel [GS,WI,WC] 20 rue Ingénieur Robert Keller **33-1/4571-1515** Marilyn Monroe & '50s theme; 15 minute walk to the Seine & the Eiffel Tower

▪BARS

Mix [GS,D,$] 24 rue de l'Arrivée **33-1/5680-3737** open Th & Sat only

▪NIGHTCLUBS

Le Red Light [GS,D] 34 rue du Depart (M° Montparnasse-Bienvenue) **33-1/4279-9453** midnight-5am

▪MEN'S CLUBS

Le Steamer [MO] 5 rue du Dr Jacquemarie Clemenceau **33-1/4250-3649** 1pm-midnight, from 3pm wknds, also bar

Paris—16

▪ACCOMMODATIONS

Keppler [GF,WI] 10 rue Keppler **33-1/4720-6505** near major tourist stops, also bar

▪CRUISY AREAS

Bois de Boulogne [AYOR] (M° Porte Dauphine)

Paris—17

▪RESTAURANTS

Sans Gêne 112 rue Legendre **33-1/4627-6782** 5pm-2am, Sun brunch, clsd Mon, also bar

▪MEN'S CLUBS

King Sauna [★] 21 rue Bridaine (near place de Clichy, M° Rome) **33-1/4294-1910** 1pm-7am, bar

Paris—18

▪BARS

Karambole Cafe [GS,F] 10 rue Hegesippe Moreau (M° Place de Clichy or La Fourche) **33-1/4293-3068** 9am-2am, from 6pm Sat, clsd Sun, artsy cafe by day, DJs by night

Le Tagada Bar [M,F] 40 rue Trois-Frères (M° Abesses) **33-1/4255-9556** 6pm-2am, clsd Mon

▪NIGHTCLUBS

Beardrop [MO,D,B] 75 rue des Martyrs (at Le Divan du Monde club) monthly bear party

▪ENTERTAINMENT & RECREATION

Michou [F] 80 rue des Martyrs (at Blvd de Clichy, M° Pigalle) **33-1/4606-1604** infamous drag cabaret, dinner show

▪MEN'S CLUBS

Sauna Mykonos 71 rue des Martyrs **33-1/4252-1546** noon-11:30pm

Paris—19

▪ACCOMMODATIONS

Friendlyfrenchy's Gay B&B [M,WI] 38 ave Jean Jaures (at rue Michelet) **33-1/4354-3764**

▪CAFES

Cafe Cherie [GS,E,WI] 44 Blvd de la Villette (M° Belleville) **33-1/4202-0205** 8am-2am, live music & DJs starting at 10pm

Paris—20

▪ACCOMMODATIONS

Mama Shelter [GS,WI] 109 rue de Bagnolet **33-1/ 4348-4848**

■ENTERTAINMENT & RECREATION

Père Lachaise Cemetery bd de Ménilmontant (M° Père-Lachaise) *perhaps the world's most famous resting place, where lie such notables as Chopin, Oscar Wilde, Sarah Bernhardt, Isadora Duncan, Gertrude Stein & Jim Morrison*

■MEN'S CLUBS

Le Riad [SW,V] 184 rue des Pyrénnées (M° Gambetta) **33-1/4797-2552**

GERMANY

Berlin

Berlin is divided into 5 regions:
Berlin–Overview
Berlin–Kreuzberg
Berlin–Prenzlauer Berg-Mitte
Berlin–Schöneberg-Tiergarten
Berlin–Outer

Berlin—Overview

■INFO LINES & SERVICES

Gay AA for English Speakers at Mann-O-Meter **49-30/787-5188** *5pm Tue, also Gay AA 8pm Th*

Mann-O-Meter Bülowstr 106 (at Nollendorfplatz) **49-30/216-8008** *5pm-10pm, gay center, cafe and B&B referral service*

Sonntags Club Greifenhagener Str 28 (S/U-Schönhauser Allee) **49-30/449-7590** *info line 10am-6pm, LGBT info, also cafe-bar open 5pm-midnight*

■RESTAURANTS

Paris Bar Kantstrasse152 **49-30/313-8052** *bistro & bar*

■ENTERTAINMENT & RECREATION

Fritz Music Tour **49-30/3087-5633** *visit the haunts of David Bowie, Nina Hagen, Iggy Pop & Rammstein, among other popular musical acts*

The Jewish Museum Berlin Lindenstr 9-14 **49-30/2599-3300** *10am-8pm, till 10pm Mon*

Schwules (Gay) Museum U6/U7 Mehringdamm 61 **49-30/6959-9050** *2pm-6pm, till 7pm Sat, clsd Tue, guided tours 5pm Sat (in German)*

■PUBLICATIONS

Blu **49-30/443-1980** *free monthly gay magazine*

Siegessäule **49-30/235-5390** *free monthly LGBT city magazine (in German), awesome maps*

Berlin—Kreuzberg

■ACCOMMODATIONS

Hotel Transit [GF] Hagelberger Straße 53-54 **49-30/789-0470** *hotel in restored 19th-c factory*

The Mövenpick Hotel [GF,F] **49-30/230-060** *convenient location, space-agey bar*

■BARS

Barbie Bar [MW] Mehringdamm 77 (at Kreuzbergstr) **49-30/6956-8610** *3pm-close, lounge, terrace*

Bierhimmel [GS,YC] Oranienstr 183 (U-Kottbusser Tor) **49-30/615-3122** *9am-3am, from 1pm wknds*

Galander [GS] Grossbeerenstr 54 (nr Mehringdamm) **49-30/2850-9030** *6pm-2am*

Mobel Olfe [★MW] Reichenbergerstrasse 177 (at Skalitzer) **49-30/2327-4690** *8pm-close Tue-Sun*

Pork at Ficken 3000 [M,D,L,V,YC] Urbanstr 70 (at Hermannplatz) **49-30/6950-7335** *10pm Sun, cruisy, large darkroom*

Rauschgold [MW] Mehringdamm 62 (U-Mehringdamm) **49-30/7895-2668** *8pm-close*

Roses [★MW,TG,YC] Oranienstr 187 (at Kottbusser Tor) **49-30/615-6570** *10pm-close*

Sofia [MW] *open 9am, from 11am Sat & 8pm Sun*

■NIGHTCLUBS

SchwuZ (SchwulenZentrum) [★M,D,E,WC] Mehringdamm 61 (enter through Café Sundstroem) **49-30/629-088** *from 11pm Fri-Sat*

Serene Bar [MW,D] Schwiebusser Str 2 49-30/6904-1580

SO 36 [★GS,D,TG,S,V,YC,WC] Oranienstr 190 (at Kottbusser Tor) **49-30/6140-1306,** **49-30/6140-1307** *theme nights, also live music venue*

▇CAFES

Drama Mehringdamm 63 49-30/6746-9562 *opens 2pm, also bar & terrace*

Melitta Sundström [MW,WC] Mehringdamm 61 (at Gneisenaustr, U-Mehringdamm) **49-30/692-4414** *10am-11pm, terrace, also gay bookstore*

Sudblock [★MW,E] Admiralstrasse 1-2 *10am-7pm*

▇RESTAURANTS

Amrit Oranienstr 202 49-30/612-5550 *noon-1am, Indian*

Kaiserstein Mehringdamm 80 49-30/7889-5887 *9am-1am*

Little Otik [GO] Graefestrasse 71 49-30/5036-2301 *7pm-11pm, clsd Sun-Tue*

Locus [★MW] Marheinekeplatz 4 49-30/691-5637 *10am-1:30am, Mexican, full bar*

Restaurant Z Friesenstr 12 49-30/692-2716 *5pm-1am, Greek/ Mediterranean*

▇ENTERTAINMENT & RECREATION

Galerie Studio St.St. Sandersstrasse 26 (Neukoelln area) *4pm-7pm Tue & 4pm-mightnight Fri-Sat, a mix of living room, cabaret and gallery/pub*

▇MEN'S CLUBS

Böse Buben Sachsendamm 76-77 49-30/6270-5610 *4pm Wed, from 9pm Fri-Sat*

Triebwerk [M,L,V,WC] Urbanstr 64 (at Leinestr, U-Hermannplatz) 49-30/6950-5203 *10pm-close, cruise bar w/ darkroom*

▇SEX CLUBS

Club Culture Houze [GS] Görlitzer Str 71 (off Skalitzer Str) **49-30/6170-9669** *gay male theme nights Mon, Th & Sun, open to all other nights*

Berlin—Prenzlauer Berg-Mitte

▇ACCOMMODATIONS

Arte Luise Kunsthotel [GF] Luisenstr 19 (Mitte) 49-30/284-480 *near River Spree*

Le Moustache [M] Gartenstr 4 (at Rosenthaler Platz, U-Oranienburger Tor) 49-30/281-7277 *also Moustache Bar open 9pm-3am, clsd Sun-Tue*

Schall & Rauch Pension [MW] Gleimstr 23 (at Schönhauser Allee) 49-30/339-723 *also bar & restaurant*

▇BARS

Bärenhöhle [M,B,BW,WI] Schönhauser Allee 90 49-30/4473-6553 *4pm-6am, from 8pm Sat, from 6pm Sun*

Besenkammer Bar [MW] Rathausstr 1 (at Alexanderplatz, under the S-Bahn bridge) 49-30/242-4083 *24hrs, tiny "beer bar"*

Betty F* ** [MW,NH] Mulackstrasse 13 (at Gormannstrasse)

Cafe Amsterdam [GS,TG,F,YC,WC] Gleimstr 24 (at Schönhauser Allee) **49-30/448-0792, 49-30/231-6796** *9am-3am, till 5am Fri-Sat, terrace, also pension*

Cocks [M] Greifenhagener Strasse 33 (at Wisbyer Str) **49-152/2941-6510** *10pm-close, from 8pm Wed & Sun, cruisy*

DarkRoom [MO,L] Rodenbergstr 23 (at Schönhauser Allee) 49-30/444-9321 *10pm-6am, uniform bar, darkroom, theme parties wknds*

Flax [M,D,F,K] Chodowieckistr 41 (off Greifswalder Str) **49-30/4404-6988, 49-30/441-9856** *5pm-2am, brunch from 10am Sun, clsd Mon*

Greifbar [MO,L,V] Wichertstr 10 (at Greifenhagener Str, S/U-Schönhauser Allee) 49-30/444-0828 *10pm-6am, darkroom*

Grosse Freiheit 114 [MO] Boxhagener Str 114 (in Friedrichshain) 49-30/2977-6713 *10pm-4am, clsd Mon, darkroom*

Marietta [MW] Stargarder Str 13 49-30/4372-0646 *10am-2am, till 4am Sat-Sun*

Perle [MW] Sredzkistrasse 64 *7pm-close, clsd Sun-Mon*

Privatleben [MW] Rhinowerstr 12 (at Gleimstra) 49-30/4320-5851 *from 6pm, small friendly bar*

Reingold [GS,F,E,GO] Novalisstr 11 (U-Oranienburger Str) 49-30/4985-3450 *from 7pm, clsd Sun-Mon, more gay Th*

Sanatorium 23 [GS] Frankfurter Allee 23 49-30/4202-1193 *from 3pm, cafe/bar, also guesthouse*

Schoppenstube [M,D] Schönhauser Allee 44 (at Eberswalder Str) 49-30/442-8204 *9pm-close, from 10pm Fri-Sun, clsd Mon, terrace*

Sharon Stonewall [MW,WI] Kleinen Präsidentenstr 3 (at Hackeschen Market) 49-30/2408-5502 *8pm-2am, till 4:30am Fri-Sat, clsd Mon*

Stahlrohr [MO] Paul Robeson Strasse 50 49-70/803-7691 *10pm-close, sex parties*

Zum Schmutzigen Hobby/ Nina's Bar [MW,D,DS,TG,V] Revalerstrasse 99 *6pm-close*

◼NIGHTCLUBS

Berghain [★MW,D,E] Am Wrietzener Bahnhof (off Strasse der Pariser Kommune, near Ostbahnhof station) 49-30/2936-0210 *converted power station is now dance club*

Chantals House of Shame [MW,D] *11pm Th*

GMF [M,D,DS] Alexanderstrasse 7 (at Week End, U-Alexanderplatz) 49-30/2809-5396 *Sun only 11pm-close*

Irrenhouse [MW,D,DS,TG] Am Friedrichshain 33 (at Geburtstagsklub) *3rd Sat, Nina Queer's monthly drag party*

KitKat Club [GS,D,C] Kopenickerstrasse 76 (enter on Bruckenstrasse) 49-30/2173-6841 *8pm-close Th, 11pm-8am Fri-Sat, also S/M club*

Klub International [M,D,$] Karl-Marx-Allee 33 (at Kino International, U-Schillingstr) 49-30/2475-6011 *11pm-close 1st Sat*

Spy Club [MW,D] Friedrichstr/ Unter den Linden (at Cookies) 49-30/2809-5396 *last Sat only*

◼CAFES

Café Berger [★WI] Senefelderstr 4 (btwn Helmholtzplatz and Kollwitz area) 49-30/4320-5851 *10am-7pm*

The Kosher Classroom Kollwitzstrasse 83 49-30/4404-8641 *8am-2am, great brkfst*

November [MW] Husemannstr 15 (at Sredzkistr) 49-30/442-8425 *10am-2am, cafe-bar, terrace, brkfst buffet wknds*

◼RESTAURANTS

Anda Lucia Savignyplatz 2 49-30/5471-0271 *6pm-10pm, tapas bar*

The Kosher Classroom Auguststrasse 11-13 49-30/3300-6070 *traditional Jewish cuisine, vegan meals and specialties from the sea*

Rice Queen Danziger Str 13 (U-Eberswalder Str) 49-30/4404-5800 *5pm-11pm, from 2pm wknds, Asian fusion*

Schall & Rauch Wirtshaus [MW] Gleimstr 23 (at Schönhauser Allee) 49-30/443-3970 *10am-close*

Thüringer Stuben Stargarder Str 28 (at Dunckerstr, S/U-Schönhauser Allee) 49-30/4463-3339 *4pm-1am, from noon Sun, full bar*

◼MEN'S CLUBS

Gate Sauna [F,V,WI] Hannah Arendtstrasse 6 (U-Mohrenstr) 49-30/229-9430 *24hrs wknds, also bar*

Lab.oratory [MO] Am Wrietzener Bahnhof (downstairs at Berghain nightclub) *hardcore sex club*

Treibhaus Sauna [F,V,YC] Schönhauser Allee 132 (U-Eberswalder Str) 49-30/448-4503 *24hrs wknds, also bar*

Germany • EUROPE

EROTICA

Blackstyle Seelower Str 5 (S/U-Schönhauser Allee) 49-30/4468-8595 clsd Sun, latex & rubber wear

Duplexx Schönhauser Allee 131 (U-Eberswalder Str) 49-30/4849-4200 videos, cruisy

Leathers [V] Schliemannstr 38 (U-Eberswalder Str) 49-30/442-7786 noon-8pm

XXL Schönhauser Alle 98 49-30/3289-8222 large cruising cinema

CRUISY AREAS

Volkspark Friedrichshain [AYOR] (at Märchenbrunnen, in Friedrichshain)

Berlin—Schöneberg-Tiergarten

ACCOMMODATIONS

Arco Hotel [GS,WC,GO] Geisbergstr 30 (at Ansbacherstr, U-Wittenbergplatz) 49-30/235-1480 centrally located

Art-Hotel Connection [MO,L,WI,WC,GO] Fuggerstr 33 (corner Welser Str, near U-Wittenbergplatz) 49-30/2102-18800 also special "fantasy" apt for kink & S/M types

Axel Hotel Berlin [M,WI] Lietzenburger Str 13/15 49-30/2100-2893

Bananas Berlin [M,WI,GO] Geisbergstr 41 49-30/2196-1768 central location in a quiet area

Berlin B&B [MW,WI,GO] apt rentals, 2 locations

Hotel California [GF] Kurfürstendamm 35 (at Knesebeckstr, U-Uhlandstr) 49-30/880-120 cafe/bar

Hotel Hansablick [GF,WI] Flotowstr 6 (at Bachstr, off Str des 17 Juni) 49-30/390-4800

Hotel Zu Hause [GS,WI,GO] Kleiststrasse 35 (at Eisenacher Str) 49-30/2362-6522

RoB Play 'n Stay Leather Apartments [MO,GO] Fuggerstr 19 (behind RoB Berlin shop) 49-30/2196-7400 in the heart of Berlin's gay scene, playroom

Tom's Hotel [M] Motzstr 19 (at Eisenacherstr, U-Nollendorfplatz) 49-30/2196-6604

BARS

Ajpnia eV [MO] Eisenacher Str 23 (U-Eisenacher Str) 49-30/2191-8881 sex parties

Blond [GS,F,WI] Eisenacher Str 3a (at Fuggerstr, U-Nollendorfplatz) 49-30/6640-3947 10am-2am

Blue Boy Bar [M,V] Eisenacher Str 3a (at Fuggerstr, U-Nollendorfplatz) 49-30/218-7498 24hrs, ring bell, hustlers; also Fugger-Eck [GS,NH], 1pm-6am, clsd Sun, terrace

Bull [★MO,L,V] Kleiststr 35 (at Eisenacherstr, U-Nollendorfplatz) 49-30/9608-5760 24hrs, darkroom, very cruisy

CDL [MO] Hohenstauffenstr 58 49-30/3266-7855 open 7pm, from 9pm Fri-Sat, from 3pm Sun, sex club

Eldorado [M,F,E] Motzstr 20 (U-Nollendorfplatz) 49-30/8431-6901 24hrs, terrace

Hafen [★M,TG,S,YC] Motzstr 19 (at Eisenacher, U-Nollendorfplatz) 49-30/211-4118 8pm-close

HarDie's Kneipe [M,NH,F,OC] Ansbacherstr 29 (in Winterplatz) 49-30/2363-9841 noon-midnight, till 2am wknds

Heile Welt [★MW] Motzstrasse 5 49-30/2191-7507 6pm-4am

Incognito [MW,TG] Hohenstauffenstr 53 (off Luther Str, U-Viktoria Luise Platz) 49-30/2191-6300 6pm-4am

Kumpelnest 3000 [GF,D,TG,YC] Lützowstr 23 (at Potsdamer Str, U-Kurfürstenstr) 49-30/261-6918 5pm-5am, till 8am Fri-Sat, popular wknds

Mutschmann's [MO,L] Martin-Luther-Str 19 (at Motzstr, U-Nollendorfplatz) 49-30/2191-9640 10pm-close, from 11pm Fri-Sat, clsd Sun-Mon, darkroom

Neues Ufer [MW,OC] Hauptstrasse 157 (U-Bahn Kleistpark) 49-30/7895-7900 11am-2am, clsd wknds, city's oldest gay bar

New Action [★MO,L] Kleistsr 35 (at Eisenacherstr, U-Nollendorfplatz) *10pm-5am, till 7am Fri-Sat, from 5pm Sun, fetish/ cruise bar*

Pinocchio Musikcafe [M] Fuggerstr 3 (at Schönhauser Allee, U-Nollendorfplatz) **49-30/2362-0333** *2pm-2am, till 4am wknds*

Prinz Knecht [★M] Fuggerstr 33 (U-Nollendorfplatz) **49-30/236-27444** *3pm-2am*

Reizbar [M] Motzstr 30 (Kalckreuthstr) **49-30/2363-7981** *9pm-close, from 8pm Tue, clsd Mon*

Scheune [★MO,L,V] Motzstr 25 (at Nollendorfplatz) **49-30/213-8580** *9pm-7am, till 9am Fri-Sat, uniform bar, theme nights*

Storks [M,F] Kleistrasse 7 **49-30/2362-4700** *10pm-late, 24hrs wknds*

Tabasco [M,F,AYOR] Fuggerstr 3 (at Schönhauser Allee, U-Nollendorfplatz) **49-30/214-2636** *6pm-6am, 24hrs wknds, hustlers*

Tom's Bar [★MO,L,V] Motzstr 19 (at Eisenacherstr, U-Nollendorfplatz) **49-30/213-4570** *10pm-6am, open later Fri-Sat, very cruisy, downstairs maze*

Tramps [M,NH,B,L] Eisenacher Str 6 (atFuggerstr) *24hrs*

Vielharmonie [M,F] **49-30/3064-7302** *6pm-close*

Woof [M,B] Fuggerstr 37 (at Ansbacherstr) **49-30/2360-7870** *10pm-4am, 9pm-2am Sun*

▪NIGHTCLUBS

Connection [★MO,D,L,V,$] Fuggerstr 33 (at Art-Hotel Connection) **49-30/218-1432** *11pm-close Fri-Sat only, cruisy, darkroom; also sex shop & cinema*

Propaganda [M,D,DS] Nollendorfplatz 5 (at Goya Theater) *2nd Sat only*

▪CAFES

Cafe Berio [★WC] Maaßenstr 7 (at Winterfeldtstr, U-Nollendorfplatz) **49-30/216-1946** *7am-midnight, from 8am wknds, brkfst all day, terrace, also bar*

Cafe Savigny Grolmanstr 53–54 (at Savignyplatz) **49-30/4470-8386** *9am-midnight, full bar, terrace*

PositHiv Cafe [WC] **49-30/216-8654** *3pm-11pm, from 6pm Sat, clsd Mon, PWA's & their friends*

▪RESTAURANTS

Café des Artistes Fuggerstr 35 **49-30/2363-5249** *noon-midnight, great food and nice staff*

Diodata Goltzstrasse 51 **49-30/2191-7884** *11am-11pm, 10am-3pm Sun, Viennese*

Fritz & Co Wittenbergplatz *organic snack bar, look for the rainbow flags*

Gnadenbrot Martin-Luther-Str 20a **49-30/2196-1786** *3pm-1am, cheap & good*

More [★] Motzstrasse 28 (at Martin-Lutherstrasse) **49-30/2363-5702** *9am-midnight*

Sissi Motzstr 34 **49-30/2101-8101** *great Austrian food, terrace & location*

▪ENTERTAINMENT & RECREATION

Xenon Kino Kolonmenstr 5-6 **49-30/7800-1530** *gay & lesbian cinema*

▪BOOKSTORES

Bruno's [GO] Bülowstrasse 106 (U-Nollendorfplatz) **49-30/6150-0385**

Prinz Eisenherz Buchladen [WC] Lietzenburger Str 9 A (at Welserstr) **49-30/313-9936** *10am-8pm, clsd Sun, LGBT books, magazines, DVDs "in all languages"*

▪MEN'S CLUBS

Apollo Sauna [F,V] Kurfürstenstr 101 (in Charlottenburg, U-Wittenbergplatz) **49-30/213-2424**

▪EROTICA

Beate Uhse International Joachimstaler Str 4 (at Kantstr, at Erotic Museum) **49-30/886-0666**

City Men Fuggerstr 26 **49-30/218-2959**

The Jaxx Club [V] Motzstr 19 (U-Nollendorfplatz) **49-30/213-8103**

Germany • EUROPE

Mazeworld Kurfürstenstr 79 (at Keithstr) **49-30/4405-0540** *noon-5am*

Pool Berlin [V] Schaperstr 11 (at Joachimsthaler Str, in Wilmersdorf, U-Kurfürstendamm) **49-30/214-1989** *clsd Sun, gay emporium*

RoB Berlin Fuggerstr 19 **49-30/2196-7400** *clsd Sun, leather/fetish shop*

■**CRUISY AREAS**

Tiergarten [AYOR] along Str de 17 Juni (near the Siegessäule monument)

Berlin—Outer

■**ACCOMMODATIONS**

Charlottenburger Hof [GF,F] Stuttgarter Platz 14 (at Wilmersdorfer Str) **49-30/329-070** *also bar*

Hotel Kronprinz Berlin [GF,WC] Kronprinzendamm 1 (at Kurfürstendamm, in Halensee) **49-30/896-030**

■**BARS**

Himmelreich [MW] Simon Dach Str 36 (off Warschauer Str, in Friedrichshain, U-Frankfurter Tor) **49-30/2936-9292** *from 7pm Mon-Fri, 2pm-close wknds*

Monster Ronsons [★MW,K] Warschauerstr 34 **49-30/8975-1327** *7pm-4am*

Silver Future [MW] Weserstr 206 (Neukölln) **49-30/7563-4987** *2pm-2am, till 3am Th-Sat*

■**NIGHTCLUBS**

Die Busche [★MW,D,S,$] Warschauer Platz 18 **49-30/296-0800** *10pm-5am, till 7am Fri-Sat, clsd Tue & Th, terrace*

■**CAFES**

Schrader's [GO] Malplaquetstr 16b (at Utrechter Str, Wedding) **49-30/4508-2663** *also bar*

■**RESTAURANTS**

Cafe Rix Karl-Marx-Str 141 (in Neükolln) **49-30/686-9020** *9am-midnight, till 1am Fri-Sat, Mediterranean, also bar*

Kurhaus Korsakow Grunbergerstrasse 81 (in Friedrichshain) **49-30/5473-7786** *5pm-close, from 9am wknds, clsd Mon*

■**CRUISY AREAS**

Volkspark Wilmersdorf [AYOR]

IRELAND

Dublin

■**INFO LINES & SERVICES**

AA 105 Capel St (at Outhouse) **353-1/873-4999** *6pm Tue & 7:45pm Fri*

Gay Switchboard Dublin **353-1/872-1055** *6:30pm-9:30pm, 4pm-6pm wknds*

Outhouse 105 Capel St **353-1/873-4999** *LGBT community center, cafe, library, meetings*

■**ACCOMMODATIONS**

The Arlington Hotel Temple Bar [GS] 16 Lord Edward St **353-1/670-8777** *conveniently located with restaurant & bar*

The Clarence [GF,WI,WC] 6-8 Wellington Quay **353-1/407-0800** *owned by Bono & The Edge of U2*

The Dylan [★GS] Eastmoreland Place **353-1/660-3000** *restaurant & bar*

Fitzwilliam Hotel [GF] St Stephen's Green **353-1/478-7000**

Inn On the Liffey [MW,WI,GO] 21 Upper Ormond Quay **353-1/677-0828**

The Merchant House [GS,WI,GO] 8 Eustace St (Temple Bar Area) **353-1/633-4477** *free access to Basic Instincts Cruise Zone*

Waterloo House [GS,F] 8-10 Waterloo Rd **353-1/660-1888** *restaurant & bar*

■**BARS**

Bears Upstairs [M,B] Capel St (at Jack Nealon's Pub) *1st Sat 9pm*

The Dragon [MW,D] 64-45 S Great Georges St **353-1/478-1590** *8pm-3am, clsd Sun, Tue & Wed*

Front Lounge [★MW,D,TG,K] 33 Parliament St **353-1/670-4112** *noon-11:30pm, till 2am Sat*

The George aka Bridies
[★MW,D,K,DS,E] 87 S Great George St
353-1/677-6943 *12:30pm-2:30am,
till 11:30pm Mon-Tue*

Honeypot & Bears Upstairs [M,B]
check www.dublinbears.ie for events

Panti Bar [MW,D,F,DS,WC] 7-8 Capel St
353-1/874-0710 *5pm-close, theme
nights*

▪NIGHTCLUBS

Mother [MW,D] Exchange St (at Copper
Alley, Arlington Hotel) *10:30pm Sat only*

Nimhneach [GS] *fetish & BDSM party,
strict dress code, see www.nimhneach.ie
for dates and location*

Prhomo [MW,D] 6 Wicklow St (at Base
Ba) *10:30pm Th only*

▪CAFES

3Fe 54 Middle Abbey St (Twisted Pepper
Bldg) 353-1/661-9329 *10am-7pm,
noon-6pm Sun, run by barista champion*

**Irish Film Institute Bar &
Restaurant** 6 Eustace St (in Temple
Bar) 353-1/679-5744 *lunch & dinner,
next to independent cinema*

Lovinspoon Cafe 13 N Frederick St
353-1/804-7604 *7am-6pm, clsd Sun
(except summers)*

▪RESTAURANTS

Brasserie Sixty6 [WI] 66 S Great
Georges St 353-1/400-5878 *lunch,
dinner, brkfst wknds*

La Cave 28 S Anne St
353-1/679-4409 *12:30pm-close,
from 6pm Sun, French*

The Chameleon 1 Lower Fownes St
353-1/671-0362 *5pm-11pm, from
3pm Sun, clsd Mon, Indonesian*

Cornucopia 19 Wicklow
353-1/677-7583 *8:30am-9pm, till
10:30pm Sat, from noon Sun, affordable
vegetarian*

DavyByrnes 21 Duke St
353-1/677-5217 *11am-11pm,
famous pub frequented by James Joyce*

L' Ecrivain [P,R] 109A Lower Baggot St
353-1/661-1919 *lunch Mon-Fri,
dinner Mon-Sat, clsd Sun*

Eden Meeting House Square (entrance
on Sycamore) 353-1/670-5372 *lunch
& dinner, wknd brunch, patio dining*

F.X. Buckley 2 Crow St
353-1/671-1248 *5:30pm-close, steak
& seafood*

Fire Restaurant Mansion House,
Dawson St 353-1/676-7200 *5:30pm-
close, noon-3pm jazz lunch Sat, clsd Sun*

Gruel 68A Dame St 353-1/670-7119
lunch & dinner

Odessa [★DS] 14 Dame Court
353-1/670-7634 *also nightclub*

Shack 24 E Essex St 353-1/679-0043
lunch & dinner

Town Bar & Grill 21 Kildare St
353-1/662-4800 *lunch & dinner, Sun
brunch, Italian*

Trocadero 4 Saint Andrew St
353-1/677-5545 *5pm-midnight, clsd
Sun*

The Winding Stair Restaurant [YC]
40 Lower Ormond Quay
353-1/872-7320 *lunch & dinner,
Irish, also bookshop*

▪ENTERTAINMENT &
RECREATION

Irish Queer Archive 2 Kildare St
(National Library of Ireland)

▪BOOKSTORES

Chapters Bookstore Ivy House, Parnell
St 353-1/872-3297

The Winding Stair Bookshop 40
Lower Ormond Quay 353-1/872-7320
*10am-6pm, till 7pm Th-Sat, from noon
Sun, also restaurant*

▪PUBLICATIONS

GCN (Gay Community News) Unit 2
Scarlet Row, Essex St W, Temple Bar, 8
353-1/671-0939, 353-1/671-9076
*monthly LGBT newspaper, many
resources*

▪MEN'S CLUBS

The Boilerhouse [★F,V] 12 Crane Ln
353-1/677-3130 *noon-6am, 24hrs
wknds*

The Dock Sauna [WI] 21 Upper
Ormond Quay (at the Inn On the Liffey)
353-1/677 0828 *10am-4am, 24hrs
wknds; also gay B&B*

ITALY

Rome

Note: M°=Metro station

INFO LINES & SERVICES

Circolo di Cultura Omosessual Mario Mieli Via Efeso 2a (M° San Paolo) **800/110-611** *4pm-7pm Mon-Fri, switchboard, meetings & discussion groups*

Gay Help Line 800/713-713 *4pm-8pm, clsd Sun*

ACCOMMODATIONS

58 Le Real de Luxe [GS,NS,WI,WC] Via Cavour 58, 4th flr (near Colosseum) **39-06/482-3566, 0039/347-182-9387 (cell)** *B&B inn a few steps from Colosseum*

Albergo Del Sole al Pantheon [GF] Piazza della Rotonda 63 **39-06/678-0441**

Ares Rooms [GF] Via Domenichino 7 **39-06/474-4525, 39-340/278-1248 (cell)** *some shared baths*

B&B In And Out Rome [GS,NS,WI,WC,GO] Via Arco del Monte (at Viale Trastevere) **39-339/784-0653**

Best Place [MW,R] Via Turati 13 **39-329/213-2320**

Claridge Hotel [GF] Via Liegi 62 **39-06/845-441** *near Borghese park, gym w/ sauna & Turkish bath*

Daphne Veneto [GF,NS] Via di San Basilio 55 **39-06/8745-0086** *cozy inn in heart of historical Rome; also Daphne Trevi at Via degli Avignonesi 20*

Discover Roma [MW] Via Castelfidardo 50 **39-06/4470-3154**

Domus Valeria B&B [MW,WI,GO] Via del Babuino 96, Apt 14 (Spanish Square) **39-339/232-6540**

Franklin [GF] Via Rodi 29 **39-06/3903-0165** *music-themed hotel w/ CD library*

Gayopen B&B [GS,GO] Via dello Statuto 44, Apt 18 (at Via Merulana, Piazza Vittorio) **39-06/482-0013** *full brkfst*

Hotel Altavilla [GF] Via Principe Amedeo 9 **39-06/474-1186**

Hotel Edera [GF,WI] Via A Poliziano 75 **39-06/7045-3888**

Hotel Labelle [MW] Via Cavour 310 **39-06/679-4750** *near the Roman Forum*

Hotel Malu [GF,WI] Via Principe Amedeo 85/a **39-06/9603-1250** *near Termini Station*

Hotel Scott House [GF] Via Gioberti 30 **39-06/446-5379**

Hotel Welcome Piram [MW] Via Amendola 7 **39-06/4890-1248** *hot tubs*

Nicolas Inn [GF,NS,WI] Via Cavour 295 (at Via dei Serpenti) **39-06/9761-8483, 39-338/937-8387** *near the Colosseum & Roman Forum*

Pensione Ottaviano [GF] Via Ottaviano 6 **39-06/3973-8138** *in quiet area near St Peter's Square, hostel*

The Rainbow B&B [MW,WI] Viale Giulio Cesare 151 **39-06/347-507-0344 (cell), 39-06/348-3343689**

Relais Conte di Cavour de Luxe B&B [GF,WI] Via Farini 16 (at Via Cavour) **39-06/482-1638** *great location*

Relais le Clarisse [GS,NS,WI,GO] Via Cardinale Merry del Val 20 (at Viale Trastevere) **39-06/5833-4437** *on historic site in central Rome*

Scalinata di Spagna [GS,NS,WI] Piazza Trinità dei Monti 17 (M° Piazza di Spagna) **39-06/6994-0896, 39-06/679-3006 (booking #)** *roof garden*

Valadier [GF,WI] Via della Fontanella 15 **39-06/361-1998** *2 restaurants & piano bar*

BARS

Coming Out [★MW,TG,F,E,K,V,GO] Via San Giovanni in Laterano 8 (near Colosseum) **39-06/700-9871** *7:30pm-2am*

Garbo [MW,F,GO] Vicolo di Santa Margherita 1a (in Trastevere, Tram 8) **39-06/581-2766, 39-34/9815-1446** *10pm-3am, clsd Mon, cocktail bar*

Gate/ Frequency [MO,D,NS,V] Via Tuscolana, 378/380 **39-06/7840-335, 39-340/693-9719** *10pm-3am, till 4am Fri-Sat, sex club, naked bear parties*

Il Giardino dei Ciliegi [MW,F,E] Via dei Fienaroli 4 **39-06/580-3423** *5pm-2am, from 1pm Sun, tea salon & bar*

Hangar [★M,D,L,S,V,YC] Via In Selci 69 (M° Cavour) **39-06/488-1397** *10:30pm-2am, clsd Tue, cruisy, dark room*

Skyline [M,L,F,S,V,PC] Via Pontremoli 36 **39-06/700-9431** *10:30pm-3am, till 4am Fri-Sat, clsd Mon, 2-floor American bar, backroom, darkroom, monthly sex parties*

▓NIGHTCLUBS

L' Alibi [★MW,D,S,YC] Via di Monte Testaccio 40-44 (M° Piramide) **39-06/574-3448** *11pm-4am, clsd Mon-Tue, theme nights, rooftop garden in summer*

Amigdala [MW,D] Via delle Conce 14 (at Rising Love) *Sat only, check site for dates,www.amigdalaqueer.it*

Il Diavolo Dentro [M,L,N] Largo Itri 23-24 **39-392/490-7271** *11pm-5am Fri-Sat, 6pm-3am Sun, clsd Mon-Th & month of August*

Frutta e Verdura [MW,D] Via Placido Zurla 68-70 (in Casilina) **39-347/244-6721 (English), 39-348/879-7063 (Italian)** *4:30am-10am Sun & public holiday evenings, darkroom*

Gorgeous [M,D] Via del Commercio 36 (at Alpheus) **39-06/574-7826** *11pm-5am Sat*

Muccassassina [★MW,D,S,YC,$] via di Portonaccio 212 (at Qube) **39-06/541-3985** *10:30pm-5am Fri only (Sept-June)*

▓CAFES

Oppio Caffè [★MW,F,E] Via delle Terme di Tito 72 **39-06/474-5262, 39-347/510-8594 (cell)** *brkfst, lunch & dinner, open 24hrs in Aug, full bar, terrace w/ great view*

▓RESTAURANTS

Asino Cotto Ristorante [R,GO] Via dei Vascellari 38 (in Travestere, Tram 8) **39-06/589-8985** *lunch & dinner, clsd Mon, creative gourmet Mediterranean*

La Carbonara Via Panisperna 214 **39-06/482-5176** *lunch & dinner, clsd Sun, classic Roman cuisine since 1906*

Città in Fiore [MW] Via Cavour 269 **39-06/482-4874** *lunch Th-Mon, dinner nightly, Chinese*

Ditirambo Piazza della Cancelleria 74-75 (near Campo dei Fiori) **39-06/687-1626**

La Focaccia Via della Pace 11 **39-06/6880-3312** *11am-2am, pizza*

Gelateria San Crispino Via Panetteria 42 (near Trevi Fountain) **39-06/679-3924** *noon-12:30am, till 1:30am Fri-Sat, clsd Tue, gelato!*

Mater Matuta [★] Via Milano 47 (basement) **39-06/4782-5746** *lunch Mon-Fri, dinner nightly, also wine bar*

Osteria del Pegno [WC] Vicolo Montevecchio 8 (Plaza Navona) **39-06/6880-7025** *lunch & dinner, clsd Wed winter, large pizza selection*

Ristorante da Dino Via dei Mille 10 (at Piazza Indipendenza) **39-06/491-425** *clsd Wed*

La Taverna di Edoardo II [MW,WC] Vicolo Margana 14 **39-06/6994-2419** *7:30pm-midnight, clsd Tue, full bar*

▓ENTERTAINMENT & RECREATION

Gay Village **39-06/753-8396** *gay summer festival*

▓RETAIL SHOPS

Hydra II [L] Via Urbana 139 **39-06/489-7773** *leather, vinyl, clubwear, western, vintage & more*

Souvenir Rainbow via San Giovanni in Laterano 26 **39-06/7720-4593** *9am-9pm, gay gifts*

Gyms & Health Clubs

Roman Sport Center [GS] Via del Galoppatoio 33 **39-06/320-1667**

Men's Clubs

Apollion Sauna [V] Via Mecenate 59a (at Via Carlo Botta, M° Piazza Vittorio) **39-06/482-5389** *gym equipment, bar*

EMC-Europa Multiclub [V,YC,SW,PC] Via Aureliana 40 (M° Repubblica) **39-06/482-3650** *1pm-midnight, 24hrs wknds, fountain whirlpool, gym & bar*

Gate [MO] **39-392/795-9441** *theme nights, bear parties*

K Sex Club [L,V,PC] Via Amato Amati 6-8 (at Via Dulceri), Casilina **39-06/2170-1268, 39-349/587-6731** *10pm-4am, S/M club & bar, maze, darkroom*

Mediterraneo Sauna [F,V,PC] Via Pasquale Villari 3 (btwn Via Merulana & Via Labicana, M° Manzoni) **39-06/7720-5934** *3 flrs, full bar, jacuzzi, maze*

Erotica

Alcova Piazza Sforza Cesarini 27 (at Corso Vittorio Emanuele II) **39-06/686-4118** *fetish shop*

Cruisy Areas

Colosseo Quadrato [AYOR] (near Palazzo della Civiltà del Lavoro park)

Monte Caprino Park [AYOR] Capidoglio Hill

Villa Borghese [AYOR] (in front of the Architecture Academy)

Travel Agents

Through Eternity Tours Italy [GO] Via Astura 2/B **39-06/700-9336, 212/288-2208 (US#)** *walking tours of Rome*

Netherlands

Amsterdam

Amsterdam is divided into 5 regions:
Amsterdam—Overview
Amsterdam—Centrum
Amsterdam—Jordaan
Amsterdam—Rembrandtplein
Amsterdam—Outer

Amsterdam—Overview

Info Lines & Services

COC-Amsterdam Rozenstraat 14 (at Prinsengracht, in the Jordaan) **31-20/626-3087** *info line 10am-5pm, also cafe 8pm-11:30pm Wed-Fri*

Gay/ Lesbian Switchboard **31-20/623-6565** *noon-10pm, 4pm-8pm wknds, English spoken*

Pink Point Westermarkt (Raadhuisstraat & Keizersgracht, in the Jordaan by Homomonument) **31-20/428-1070** *10am-6pm; info on Homomonument & general LGBT info; friendly volunteers; queer souvenirs & gifts*

Nightclubs

Fuckin' Pop Queers/ Ultrasexi/ Multisexi [MW,D,TG,A] *monthly queer dance parties at different clubs around the city, check web for details*

Rapido/ Celebrate [M,D] *popular monthly dance parties, check clubrapido.com for dates & locations*

UNK [MW,D] Admiraal de Ruijterweg 56 B (at Club 8) **31-20/685-1703** *4th Sat only, electro/ queer dance party*

Entertainment & Recreation

The Anne Frank House Prinsengracht 263-267 (in the Jordaan) **31-20/556-7105 (recorded info), 31-20/556-7100** *the final hiding place of Amsterdam's most famous resident*

Boom Chicago Leidseplein 12 (Leidseplein Theater) **31-20/423-0101 (tickets)** *English-language improv comedy; distributes free Boom! guide*

Gay and Lesbian History Walks
31-20/628-689-775 *mention Damron & you get 10% off*

Homomonument Westermarkt (in the Jordaan) *moving sculptural tribute to lesbians & gays killed by Nazis*

MacBike Stationsplein 12 (next to Centraal Station) 31-20/620-0985 *rental bikes & map for self-guided tour of Amsterdam's gay points of interest*

The van Gogh Museum [WC] Paulus Potterstr 7 (on the Museumplein) 31-20/570-5200 *under renovations, check www.vangoghmuseum.nl for updates*

■PUBLICATIONS

Gay News Amsterdam
31-20/679-1556 *bilingual paper, extensive listings*

Gay & Night 31-20/788-1360 *free monthly bilingual entertainment paper w/ club listings*

Amsterdam—Centrum

■ACCOMMODATIONS

Amsterdam B&B Barangay
[GS,NS,WI,GO] 31-6/2504-5432 *near tourist attractions*

Amsterdam Central B&B [MW,WI,GO] Oudebrugsteeg 6-II (at Warmoesstraat) 31-62/445-7593 *in 16th-c guesthouse, also apts, full brkfst*

Anco Hotel-Bar [MO,L,N,NS,WI,GO] OZ Voorburgwal 55 (across from the Oude Kerk) 31-20/624-1126 *1640 canal house, also bar*

Crowne Plaza Amsterdam City Centre [GF,F,SW,WI,WC] NZ Voorburgwal 5 31-20/620-0500, 877/227-6963 (US#)

Mauro Mansion [GS] Geldersekade 16 (at OZ Kolk)

NH City Centre Hotel [GF,WI,WC] Spuistraat 288-292 31-20/420-4545

NH Grand Hotel Krasnapolsky [GF,WI,WC] Dam 9 (at Warmoesstraat) 31-20/554-9111

Palace B&B [GS,NS,WI,GO] Spuistraat 224 31-6/3169-3878 *1794 bldg w/ indoor garden*

Victoria Hotel Amsterdam
[GF,SW,WI,NS,WC] Damrak 1-5 (opposite Centraal Station) 31-20/623-4255, 800/777-1700 (US#)

Winston Hotel [GF] Warmoesstraat 129 31-20/623-1380 *hipster hotel w/ alt-rock bar & decor*

■BARS

Argos [★MO,L] Warmoesstraat 95 (at Oudekerksplein) 31-20/622-6595 *10pm-3am, till 4am Fri-Sat, popular darkroom, strict dress code, theme nights*

De Barderij [M,NH,OC] Zeedijk 14 (at OZ Kolk) 31-20/420-5132 *noon-1am, till 3am Fri-Sat, large brown café*

Boys Club 21 [MO,S] Spuistraat 21 31-20/622-8828 *noon-2am, boys' house (escorts) w/ full bar & live strip shows*

Cafe Mandje [GS] Zeedijk 63 (at Stormsteeg) 31-20/622-5375 *originally opened in 1927 as Amsterdam's first gay bar by dyke-on-bike Bet van Beeren*

Cozy Bar [M,NH,D] Sint Jacobsstraat 8 31-20/420-8321

The Cuckoo's Nest [MO,LV,18+] NZ Kolk 6 (at NZ Voorburgwal) 31-20/627-1752 *1pm-1am, till 2am Fri-Sat, cruisy, large play cellar*

De Engel Next Door [M] Zeedijk 23-25 (at OZ Kolk) 31-20/427-6381 *1pm-1am, till 3am Fri-Sat, clsd Mon-Tue*

De Engel van Amsterdam [M] Zeedijk 21 (at OZ Kolk) 31-20/427-6381 *1pm-1am, till 3am Fri-Sat, patio*

Dirty Dick's [MO,L] Warmoesstraat 86 (at Oudebrugsteeg) 31-20/627-8634 *4pm-3am, till 4am Fri-Sat, very cruisy, darkroom*

Getto [★MW,F,K] Warmoesstraat 51 (at Niezel) 31-20/421-5151 *4pm-1am, from 7pm Tue, 1pm-midnight Sun, clsd Mon, also restaurant, Sun brunch, live DJs*

Prik [MW,F] Spuistraat 109 31-20/320-0002 *4pm-1am, till 3am Fri-Sat, patio*

Queen's Head [M,D,S] Zeedijk 20 (off Nieuwmarkt) 31-20/420-2475 *4pm-1am, till 3am Fri-Sat, bingo Tue*

The Web [★MO,B,L,F,V] St Jacobsstraat 6 (btwn Nieuwendijk & NZ Voorburgwal) **31-20/623-6758** *1pm-1am, till 2am Fri-Sat, darkroom, [B] Sat, rooftop patio*

■NIGHTCLUBS

Club Fuxxx [★MO,D,S,V] Warmoesstraat 96 **31-20/456-45-879** *11pm-4am, till 5am Fri-Sat, cruisy darkroom*

Club Stereo [GS,D,E] Jonge Roelensteeg 4 (at Kalvertstraat) **31-20/770-4037** *7pm-1am, till 3am Fri-Sat*

■CAFES

Dampkring Haarlemmerstraat 44 **31-20/638-0705** *smoking coffeeshop*

Gary's Late Night [★] TT Vasumweg 260 **31-20/637-3643** *noon-3am, till 4am Fri-Sat, fresh muffins & bagels*

Puccini Bomboni [★] Staalstraat 17 **31-20/626-5474** *If you love chocolate, do we have a cafe for you!*

■RESTAURANTS

Cafe de Jaren [GS,V] Nieuwe Doelenstraat 20-22 **31-20/625-5771** *10am-1am, full bar, terrace*

Cafe de Schutter Voetboogstraat 13-15 (upstairs) **31-20/622-4608** *noon-1am, till 3am Fri-Sat, popular local hangout, plenty veggie, full bar, terrace*

Cafe Latei [WI] Zeedijk 143 (in Red Light District) **31-20/625-7485** *8am-5pm, from 9am Sat, from 11am Sun, Indian food*

Greenwoods Singel 103 (near Dam Square) **31-20/623-7071** *English-style brkfast & tea snacks*

Hemelse Modder [★WC,GO] Oude Waal 11 **31-20/624-3203** *6pm-10pm, popular w/ lesbians & gay men, full bar*

Krua Thai [WC] Staalstraat 22 **31-20/622-9533** *5pm-10:30pm*

Het Land Van Walem [WC,GO] Keizersgracht 449 **31-20/625-3544** *lunch & dinner, int'l, local crowd, canalside terrace*

Maoz Muntplein 1 **31-20/420-7435** *11am-1am, till 3am wknds, vegetarian*

't Sluisje [★MW,TG,DS] Torensteeg 1 **31-20/624-0813** *6pm-close, clsd Mon-Tue, steak house, full bar, drag shows nightly, cash only*

Song Kwae Kloveniersburgwal 14 (near Nieuwmarkt & Chinatown) **31-20/624-2568** *1pm-10:30pm, Thai, full bar, terrace*

■BOOKSTORES

The American Book Center [WC] Spui 12 **31-20/625-5537** *10am-8pm, till 9pm Th, 11am-6:30pm Sun, large LGBT section*

Boekhandel Vrolijk Gay & Lesbian Bookshop [★] Paleisstraat 135 (at Spuistraat, near Dam Square) **31-20/623-5142** *10am-6pm, 11am-6pm Mon, 10am-5pm Sat, from 1pm Sun*

■RETAIL SHOPS

Gays & Gadgets Spuistraat 44 **31-20/330-1461** *gifts, gadgets, clothing, cards*

Magic Mushroom Spuistraat 249 **31-20/427-5765** *11am-7pm, till 8pm Fri-Sat, "smartshop": magic mushrooms & more; also Singel 524*

Sissy Boy Kalverstraat 199 **31-20/638-9305** *French & Dutch designers duke it out on the racks*

■GYMS & HEALTH CLUBS

Splash Looiersgracht 26-30 **31-20/624-8404** *gym & wellness center*

■EROTICA

4men Spuistraat 21 **31-20/625-8797** *cinema, darkroom, all-day ticket, private cabin, large sexshop*

Adonis [V] Warmoesstraat 92 **31-20/627-2959** *10am-1am, till 3am wknds*

Alfa Blue Nieuwendijk 26 **31-20/627-1664** *porn store & video theater*

Black Body [WC] Spuistraat 44 **31-20/626-2553** *clsd Sun, rubber clothing specialists, also leather, toys, DVDs & more*

Christine Le Duc Spui 6 **31-20/624-8265**

Condomerie Het Gulden Vlies Warmoesstraat 141 **31–20/627–4174** *11am-6pm, clsd Sun, condoms in every size or color or configuration*

DeMask Zeedijk 64 **31–20/423–3090** *11am-7pm, clsd Sun, rubber & leather clothing*

Drake's of LA [★] Damrak 61 **31–20/627–9544** *videos & magazines, video cabins, cinema upstairs*

Mr B [WC] Warmoesstraat 89 **31–20/788–3060** *leather & rubber, also tattoo & piercing*

RoB Accessories Warmoesstraat 71 **31–20/428–3000** *leather, rubber, toys*

Le Salon Nieuwendijk 20-22 (near the Spui) **31–20/622–6565** *sex supermarket, cinema*

Amsterdam—Jordaan

■ACCOMMODATIONS

Chic and Basic Amsterdam [GF,NS,WI] Herengracht 13-19 (at Brouwersgr) **31–20/522–2345** *"the quiet hotel," full brkfst*

The Dylan [GF,WI] Keizersgracht 384 (at Runstraat) **31–20/530–2010** *also restaurant*

Hotel Acacia [GF,WI] Lindengracht 251 (at Lijnbaansgr) **31–20/622–1460** *"homey hotel in heart of Jordaan*

Hotel Pulitzer [GF,F,WI] Prinsengracht 315-331 (at Reestraat) **31–20/523–5235**

Hotel Rembrandt Centrum [GS] Herengracht 255 (at Hartenstraat) **31–20/622–1727** *canalside hotel near Dam Square*

Maes B&B [★GS,NS,WI,GO] Herenstraat 26 (at Keizersgr) **31–20/427–5165** *renovated 18th-c home btwn 2 canals*

Marnixkade Canalview Apartments [MW,NS,WI,GO] **31–6/1012–1296**

Sunhead of 1617 [GS,NS,WI,GO] Herengracht 152 (at Leliegracht & Raadshuisstraat) **31–20/626–1809** *full brkfst*

■BARS

Cafe de Gijs [GF,TG] Lindengracht 249 (at Lijnbaansgr) **31–20/638–0740, 31–6/2537–3674** *4pm-1am, 1st Wed of month social gathering for transvestites & transsexuals, from 6pm*

■NIGHTCLUBS

Jet Lounge [★GS,D,E] Groen van Prinstererstraat 41 (3 blks W of Westerpark) **31–20/684–1126** *6pm-1am, till 3am Fri-Sat, clsd Sun-Mon*

de Trut [★MW,D,YC] Bilderdijkstraat 165 (at Kinkerstraat) **31–20/612–3524** *11pm-4am Sun only, hip underground party in legalized squat, doors close when it's full (btwn 11:30pm-midnight) so come early*

■CAFES

Cafe 't Smalle Egelantiersgracht 12 **31–20/623–9617** *10am-1am, till 2am wknds, brown cafe, full bar, outdoor seating*

Lab111 [E] Arie Biemondstrat 111 **31–20/616–9994** *noon-1am, till 3am Fri-Sat*

■RESTAURANTS

Bojo [★] Lange Leidsedwarsstraat 49-51 (near Leidseplein) **31–20/622–7434** *11am-9pm, from 4:30pm wknds, Indonesian*

De Bolhoed Prinsengracht 60 (at Tuinstr) **31–20/626–1803** *vegetarian/ vegan*

Burger's Patio 2e Tuindwarsstr 12 **31–20/623–6854** *6pm-1am, Italian, plenty veggie*

Foodism Oude Leliestraat 8 **31–20/627–6464** *noon-10pm, till 6pm wknds, great soups & sandwiches, funky & fun*

Freud [E] Spaarndammerstraat 424 **31–20/688–5548** *lunch & dinner, clsd Sun-Mon*

Granada [E] Leidsekruisstraat 13 **31–20/625–1073** *5pm-close, Spanish, tapas, also bar*

De Vliegende Schotel Nieuwe Leliestraat 162 **31–20/625–2041** *4pm-11:30p, vegetarian/ vegan*

Netherlands • *EUROPE*

■ENTERTAINMENT & RECREATION

De Looier Art & Antiques Market Elandsgracht 109 31–20/624–9038, 31–20/427–4990 *11am-5pm, clsd Fri*

■RETAIL SHOPS

Dare to Wear Buiten Oranjestraat 15 31–20/686–8679 *piercing, jewelry & accessories*

House of Tattoos Haarlemmerdijk 130c 31–20/330–9046 *11am-6pm, from 1pm Sun, great tattoos, great people*

■SEX CLUBS

Sameplace [GS,TG,D] Nassaukade 120 31–20/475–1981 *[MO] Mon night only, theme nights, darkroom*

Amsterdam— Rembrandtplein

■ACCOMMODATIONS

Amsterdam House [GF] 's Gravelandseveer 7 (at Kloveniersburgwal) 31–20/626–2577 (office), 31–20/624–6607 (hotel) *hotel, apts & houseboats*

Dikker & Thijs Fenice Hotel [GF] Prinsengracht 444 (at Leidsestraat) 31–20/620–1212 *great location, restaurant & bar*

Eden Hotel [GF,WI,WC] Amstel 144 31–20/530–7878 *3-star hotel over-looking Amstel River, brasserie*

Hotel Amistad & Apts [★M,NS,WI,WC,GO] Kerkstraat 42 (at Leidsestraat) 31–20/624–8074

Hotel de l'Europe [GF,SW,WI] Nieuwe Doelenstraat 2-8 31–20/531–1777 *grand hotel on the River Amstel*

Hotel Monopole [GF] Amstel 60 (at Kloveniersburgwal) 31–20/624–6271 *also Cafe Rouge*

Hotel Orlando [GF,GO] Prinsengracht 1099 (at Amstel River) 31–20/638–6915

Hotel The Golden Bear [★MW,B,OC,WI,GO] Kerkstraat 37 (at Leidsestraat) 31–20/624–4785

Hotel Waterfront [GF] Singel 458 (at Koningsplein) 31–20/421–6621

ITC Hotel [MW,WI,GO] Prinsengracht 1051 (at Utrechtsestraat) 31–20/623–0230, 31–20/623–1711 *18th-c canal house, great location, also bar & lounge*

Seven Bridges [★GF] Reguliersgracht 31 (at KeizersGracht) 31–20/623–1329 *small & so elegant, canalside, view of 7 bridges (surprise!), brkfst brought to you*

■BARS

Amstel Fifty Four [M,NH] Amstel 54 (at Kloveniersburgwal) 31–20/623–4254 *5pm-1am, till 3am Fri-Sat, classic brown cafe gone gay*

Bump [MW,D] Kerkstraat 23 *5pm-1am, till 3am wknds, clsd weekdays*

Cafe Dwarsliggertje [M,NH] Reguliersdwarsstraat 105 *2pm-1am, till 3am wknds*

Cafe Mon Ami [M,NH,OC] Amstelstraat 34 (at Amstel) 31–20/626–2243 *5pm-1am, till 3am Fri-Sat, clsd Mon*

Cafe Rouge [M,NH] Amstel 60 (at Kloveniersburgwal) 31–20/420–9881 *4pm-1am, till 3am wknds*

Chez Rene [MW,GO] Amstel 50 (at Kloveniersburgwal) 31–20/420–3388 *8pm-3am, till 4am Fri-Sat*

Entre Nous [M,NH] Halvemaansteeg 14 (at Reguliersbreestr) 31–20/623–1700 *9pm-3am, till 4am Fri-Sat*

Eve [★GS,D,F,YC] Reguliersdwarsstraat 44 (at Geelvinckssteeg) 31–20/689–7070 *4pm-1am, till 3am Fri-Sat, also restaurant*

Habibi Ana [MW,MR,E] Lange Leidsedwarsstraat 93 31–06/2192–1686 *7pm-1am, till 3am Fri-Sat, clsd Mon-Tue, Arabian clientele, Arabian & int'l music, bellydancing shows wknds*

Hot Spot Cafe [M,NH] Amstel 102 (at Bakkersstr) 31–20/622–8335 *9pm-3am, from 8pm Fri-Sun*

Lellebel [★M,NH,TG,F,K,DS] Utrechtsestraat 4 31–20/427–5139 *8pm-3am, till 4am Fri-Sat, drag bar, very trans-friendly*

Ludwig [M,D] Reguliersdwarsstraat 37 (at St Jorisstraat) **31-20/625-3661** *7pm-1am, till 3am Fri-Sat, clsd Mon-Tue, terrace*

Mankind [MW,F,WI] Weteringstraat 60 (at Weteringschans) **31-20/638-4755** *noon-11pm, clsd Sun, cafe-bar, canal-side terrace*

Le Montmartre [★M,NH,YC] Halvemaansteeg 17 (at Reguliersbreestr) **31-20/625-5565** *5pm-1am, till 4am Fri-Sat, very Dutch*

Music Box [MO,AYOR] Paardenstraat 9 (near Rembrandtplein) **31-20/620-4110** *9pm-2am, till 3am Fri-Sat, clsd Mon, hustlers*

NYX [M,D] Reguliersdwarsstraat 42 **31-20/638-5700** *11pm-4am Th-Fri, till 9am first Sat of the month*

Reality [M,NH,MR-L] Reguliersdwarsstraat 129 **31-20/639-3012** *8pm-3am, till 4am Fri-Sat, Surinamese*

Soho [★MW,D,YC] Reguliersdwarsstraat 36 (at St Jorisstraat) **31-20/422-3312** *5pm-3am, till 4am Fri-Sat, British pub 1st flr, lounge upstairs, happy hour 10pm-11pm*

Spijker [★MO,NH,L,V] Kerkstraat 4 (at Leidsegracht) **31-20/341-7366** *4pm-1am, till 3am Fri-Sat, darkroom*

Sultana [MW,D] Reguliersdwarsstraat 21 *7pm-3am, from 4pm Th-Sat, snacks, drinks, hookah-smoking (shisha)*

Taboo [MW,NH] Reguliersdwarsstraat 45 **31-20/775-3963** *5pm-3am, from 4pm wknds*

Het Wapen van Londen [★M,YC] Amstel 14 (at Vijzelstraat) **31-6/1539-5317** *4pm-1am, till 2am Fri-Sat, clsd Mon, cafe-bar, terrace*

▪NIGHTCLUBS

Church [MO,D] Kerkstraat 52 (at Leidsestraat) *clsd Mon, theme nights w/ dress code, open to all on Th for Blue party*

Club Roque [MW,D] Amstel 178 (at Wagenstraat) **31-20/421-0900** *11pm-5am, clsd Sun-Tue*

Studio 80 [GS,D] Rembrandtplein 17 (at Amstelstraat) **31-20/521-8333** *9pm-5am Th-Sat*

▪CAFES

Betty, Too Reguliersdwarsstraat 29 (at Leidsestraat) *10am-1am, occasional gay events*

Happy Feelings Kerkstr 51 **31-20/423-1936** *smoking coffeeshop*

Lunchroom [GO] Reguliersdwarsstr 31 (at Koningsplein) **31-20/622-9958** *10am-7pm, terrace open in summer*

The Other Side [M,GO] Reguliersdwarsstr 6 (at Koningsplein) **31-72/625-5141** *11am-1am, gay smoking coffeeshop*

▪RESTAURANTS

Garlic Queen [R] Reguliersdwarsstr 27 **31-20/422-6426** *6pm-close, clsd Mon-Tue, even the desserts are made w/ garlic!*

Golden Temple [NS] Utrechtsestr 126 **31-20/626-8560** *5pm-9:30pm, vegetarian & vegan*

De Huyschkaemer Utrechtsestraat 137 **31-20/627-0575** *noon-1am, till 3am wknds*

Rose's Cantina [★] Reguliersdwarsstr 40 (near Rembrandtplein) **31-20/625-9797** *5pm-11pm, Tex-Mex, full bar*

Saturnino [GO] Reguliersdwarsstr 5 **31-20/639-0102** *noon-midnight, Italian, full bar*

▪MEN'S CLUBS

Thermos [★SW,F,WI] Raamstraat 33 (at Raamplein) **31-20/623-9158** *noon-8am, cruisy sauna on 5 flrs, also bar & cafe*

▪EROTICA

B1 Cinema Reguliersbreestraat 4 **31-20/623-9546** *9am-midnight, from noon Sun*

The Bronx Kerkstraat 53-55 (near Leidseplein) **31-20/623-1548** *huge gay shop for sex supplies & cinema*

Amsterdam—Outer

■ACCOMMODATIONS

Amsterdam B&B [GF,NS,WI,GO] Roeterstraat 18 (at Nieuwe Achtergracht) 31–20/624–0174 *powered by green energy*

Between Art & Kitsch [GF,WI] Ruysdaelkade 75-2 (at Daniel Stalpertstraat) 31–20/679–0485 *near museums*

Blue Moon B&B [GS,WI,GO] Weteringschans 123A (at Weteringstraat) 31–20/428–8800

The Collector B&B [GF,WI,GO] De Lairessestr 46 hs (in museum area) 31–6/1101–0105 (cell), 31–20/673–6779 *full brkfst*

Freeland Hotel [GF,WI,GO] Marnixstraat 386 (at Leidsegracht) 31–20/622–7511 *full brkfst*

Hemp Hotel Frederiksplein 15 (at Achtergracht) 31–20/625–4425 *only in Amsterdam: sleep on a hemp mattress, eat a hemp roll for brkfst or drink hemp beer in the Hemp Temple bar*

Hotel Arena [★GF,WI] Gravesandestraat 51 (at Mauritskade) 31–20/850–2400 *hotel in former orphanage, popular nightclub in restored chapel*

Hotel Kap [GS,GO] Den Texstraat 5 31–20/624–5908 *bikes available to rent, also self-catering apt*

Hotel Rembrandt [GF,NS] Plantage Middenlaan 17 (at Plantage Parklaan) 31–20/627–2714 *beautiful brkfst rm w/ 17th-c art, near Rembrandtplein*

Lloyd Hotel [★GF,F,WI] Oostelijke Handelskade 34 31–20/561–3636, 31–20/561–3604 *hip hotel for all budgets in cool Eastern Harbor area*

NL Hotel [GS,WI,GO] Nassaukade 368 (at B Toussaintstraat) 31–20/689–0030

Prinsen Hotel [GF] Vondelstraat 36-38 (near Leidseplein) 31–20/616–2323

■NIGHTCLUBS

Melkweg [GS,E] Lijnbaansgracht 234 (at Leidseplein) 31–20/531–8181 *popular live-music venue, also restaurant/ cafe, cinema, theater*

■RESTAURANTS

An Weteringschans 76 (in Museum Quarter) 31–20/624–4672 *dinner only, clsd Sun-Mon, Japanese, full bar, patio, cash only*

De Peper Overtoom 301 31–20/412–2954 *7pm-close Sun, Tue & Th-Fri, sliding scale, volunteer-run vegan cafe, also monthly queer parties*

De Waaghals Frans Halsstraat 29 31–20/679–9609 *5pm-9:30pm, clsd Mon, vegetarian*

■CRUISY AREAS

Oosterpark [AYOR] at Linnaeusstr (behind the Tropenmuseum)

Sarphatipark [AYOR] *near baseball field*

Vondelpark [AYOR] at Vondelstr *in the rose garden*

Westerpark [AYOR] *at night, N of lake*

SCOTLAND

Edinburgh

■INFO LINES & SERVICES

LGBT Centre for Health & Wellbeing 9 Howe St 44–0131/523–1100

■ACCOMMODATIONS

94DR [GS,WI,GO] 94 Dalkeith Rd 44–131/662–9286 *guesthouse central location*

Alva House [M,NS,GO] 45 Alva Pl 44–0845/257–1475 *near gay bars & nightlife*

Ardmor House [★MW,NS,WC,GO] 74 Pilrig St (at Leith Walk) 44–0131/554–4944 *Victorian in city center near gay life*

Averon Guest House [GF,NS] 44 Gilmore Pl 44–0131/229–9932 *comfortable guesthouse in city center*

Ayden Guest House [GS,NS,WI,GO] 70 Pilrig St 44–0131/554–2187 *in-house chef cooks fabulous brkfst*

Garlands [GS,NS,WI,GO] 48 Pilrig St (off Leith Walk) 44–0131/554–4205 *Georgian town house, full brkfst*

Sheraton Grand Hotel and Spa
[GF,SW] 1 Festival Sq
44-131/229-9131

Six Mary's Place Guest House [GF,NS]
Raeburn Pl (Stockbridge)
44-0131/332-8965 *vegetarian brkfst*

Tigerlily [GF,WI] 125 George St
44-131/225-5005

Village Apartments [MO,GO] 5
Broughton Market
44-0131/556-5094

The Witchery by the Castle [GF]
Castlehill (The Royal Mile)
44-0131/225.5613 *theatrical suites
at the gates of Edinburgh castle*

■ BARS

The Auld Hoose [GS,NH,F] 23-25 St
Leonards St **44-0131/668-2934**
11:30am-1am, from 12:30pm Sun

Cafe Habana [MW,WI] 22 Greenside Pl
44-0131/558-1270 *1pm-1am, theme
nights, popular pre-clubbing*

Cafe Nom de Plume [F] 60 Broughton
St **44-0131/478-1372** *11am-11pm,
till 1am Fri-Sat*

CC Bloom's [M,S,D,GO] 23 Greenside Pl
(at Leith Walk) **44-0131/556-9331**
6pm-3am, from 7pm Sun, theme nights

Deep Blue [★MW,F,GO] 1 Barony St
(below Blue Moon)
44-0131/556-2788 *4pm-1am*

Frenchies Bar [MW,NH] 89 Rose Street
Lane N **44-0131/225-6967** *2pm-
1am*

Newtown Bar [MW,D,F,WI] 26-B Dublin
St **44-0131/538-7775** *noon-1am, till
2am Fri-Sat*

Planet [★MW,F] 6 Baxter's Pl (at Leith
Walk) **44-0131/556-5551** *4pm-1am*

Priscilla's [M,K,C,DS] 17 Albert Pl (Leith
Walk) **44-0798/659-1695** *noon-1am,
from 5pm Sun*

The Regent [M,F,WI] 2 Montrose
Terrace **44-0131/661-8198** *11am-
1am, from 12:30pm Sun*

The Street [GS,D,F] 2 Picardy Pl
44-0131/556-4272 *4pm-1am, from
noon wknds, patio*

Theatre Royal Bar [GF] 25-27
Greenside Pl **44-0131/557-2142**
noon-midnight, clsd Sun

■ NIGHTCLUBS

DV8 Fetish Club [GS,PC] 258 Morrison
St (in Spiders Web basement)
44-0131/228-1949

GHQ [M,D] 4 Picardy Pl
44-0131/550-1780 *9pm-3am, fashionable gay crowd, theme nights*

Luvely [GS,D] Faith Nighclub, 207
Cowgate **44-0131/557-4656**
10:30pm-5am 1st Sat only

■ CAFES

Blue Moon [★MW,F,GO] 1 Barony St
44-0131/556-2788 *11am-midnight,
from 10am wknds*

Cafe Lucia 13-29 Nicolson St (next to
Edinburgh Festival Theatre)
44-0131/662-1112 *10am-10pm*

Filmhouse Cafe [BW] 88 Lothian Rd
44-0131/229-5932,
44-0131/228-2688 (cinema) *10am-
11:30pm, till 12:30am Fri-Sat, also
cinema*

■ RESTAURANTS

Black Bo's Vegetarian Restaurant
57/61 Blackfriars St
44-0131/557-6136 *6pm-10pm, also
bar till 1am*

Henderson's [BW] 94 Hanover St
44-0131/225.2131 *organic vegetarian, also deli & cafe*

Tower Restaurant & Terrace [WC]
National Museum of Scotland,
Chambers St (at George IV Brigde)
44-0131/225-3003 *lunch & dinner,
panoramic views of Edinburgh's castle &
historic skyline*

Valvona & Crolla [★] 19 Elm Row
44-0131/556-6066 *clsd Sun, oldest
Italian deli in Scotland*

■ ENTERTAINMENT &
RECREATION

The Luvvies *LGBT community theatre
company*

■ BOOKSTORES

Bobbie's Bookshop 220 Morrison St
44-0131/538-7069 *10am-5pm, clsd
Sun*

Word Power Books 43-45 W Nicolson St **44-0131/662-9112** *10am-6pm, noon-5pm Sun, independent & radical, events*

■RETAIL SHOPS

Q Store 5 Barony St
44-0131/477-4756

■NATIONAL PUBLICATIONS

ScotsGay 44-0131/539-0666

■MEN'S CLUBS

No 18 18 Albert Pl
44-0131/553-3222 *noon-10pm, till 11pm Fri-Sun, sauna club*

Steamworks [SW] 5 Broughton Market (btwn Barony & Dublin)
44-0131/477-3567 *11am-11pm, steamroom, sauna, labyrinth, massage, cafe lounge, internet*

■EROTICA

Leather & Lace 8 Drummond St
44-0131/557-9413 *10am-9pm, from noon Sun, toys, clothing & videos*

SPAIN

Barcelona

Note: M°=Metro station

■INFO LINES & SERVICES

Casal Lambda Verdaguer y Callis 10 (M° Drassanes) **34/93-319-5550** *5pm-9pm, community center & cafe, archives & library, also publish magazine*

Col-Lectiu Gai de Barcelona (CGB)
34/934-534-125 *staffed 7pm-9pm Mon-Sat, also publishess Info Gai*

Coordinadora Gai Lesbiana Vicant d'Hongria 156, E-08014
34/900-601-601 *7pm-9pm Mon-Fri, 6pm-8pm Sat*

■ACCOMMODATIONS

Agua Alegre [GS] c/ Roger de Lluria 47 (M° Catalunya) **34/93-487-8032**

Barcelona City Centre [M,WI,GO]
34/653-900-039 *in Eixample District*

California Hotel [GS] Rauric 14 (at Ferran, M° Liceu) **34/93-317-7766**

Casa de Billy Barcelona [GS,NS,WI,GO] Rambla Catalunya 85, Piso 5, Puerta 1 (at Mallorca) **34/93-426-3048** *shared baths, full brkfst*

Catalonia Diagonal Centro
[GF,F,WI,WC] Balmes 142-146
34/93-415-9090

Catalonia Portal de l'Àngel
[GF,SW,WI] Avenida Portal de L'Angel 17
34/93-318-4141

Central Town Rooms & Apartments [M,WC,GO] Ronda San Pau 51
34/93-442-7057, 24/670-260-298 *guesthouse*

Éos [MW,GO] Gran Via de los Corts Catalanes 575 (M° Universitat)
34/93-451-8772, 34/617-931-439 *B&B in gay district*

Fashion House [MW] Bruc 13 Principal
34/63-790-4044 *shared baths*

GayStay BCN [M,WI,GO] C / Piquer 15, Pral 3 (at Carrer de Mata)
34/676-145-909

HCC Regente [GF,SW,WI,WC] Rambla de Catalunya 76 **34/93-487-5989**

HCC Taber [GF,WI] Arago 256
34/93-487-3887

Hostal Absolut Centro [M,GO] Casanova 72 (at Balmes)
34/649-550-238 *hostel, some shared baths*

Hostal Baires [GF] **34/93-319-7774** *in Barrio Gótico*

Hostal Que Tal [M] Mallorca 290 (at Bruch) **34/93-459-2366**

Hotel Axel [MW,SW,WI,WC] Aribau 33 (at Consell de Cent) **34/93-323-9393** *full brkfst, rooftop bar*

Hotel Catalonia Fira [GF,SW,WI] Av. Gran Via N 50 (Plaza Europa)
34/93-236-0000 *new 4-star hotel in the heart of old Barcelona*

Hotel Colon [GF] Avenida Catedral 7
34/93-301-1404

Hotel Majestic Barcelona [GF,SW,WC] Paseo de Gracia 68 (in city center)
34/93-488-1717 *5-star hotel, rooftop pool*

Room Mate Emma [GF,WI] Carrer Rosselló 205 **34/932-385-606**

■BARS

Aire/ Sala Diana [GS,D,F,S,YC] Valencia 236 (btwn Enriq. Granados & c/ Balmes) **34/93-451-8462**

Al Maximo [MW,NH] Assaonadora 25

Átame [M,E,DS] Consell de Cent 257 (at M° Universidad) **34/93-454-9273** 7pm-2:30am

Bacon Bear Bar [M,B] Casanova 64 (M° Urgell) 6pm-3am, theme nights

El Balcon des Aquiles [M,NH] Lleo 9 7pm-3am

Bar Plata [M] Consejo de Ciento 233 (at Urgell) 5pm-3am

La Base [M,L,N] Carme 27 **34/933-017-396** 10pm-3am, till 5am Fri-Sat, leather & fetish, naked party Wed & Sat

Berlin Dark [M,L] Pasage Prunera 18 (at de la Font Honrada) 10pm-3am Tue-Sun, also Berlin Day 5pm-9pm Mon-Fri

BimBamBum [M,D] Casanova 48 11pm-3am, clsd Mon-Tue

Black Bull [M] Muntaner 64 **34/934-515 -104** 8pm-2:30am

Butch Bear Barcelona [M,B] Diputació 206 (btwn Muntaner & Ariba) 10pm-3am Th-Sat

El Cangrejo [MW,D] Villarroel 86 10:30pm-3am, clsd Mon-Tue

La Chapelle [M] Muntaner 65 cafe by day

Chiringuito GayLorenzo [M] Ed Dulce Deseo de Lorenzo (Playa de la Mar Bella) summer beach bar

La Cueva [MW,DS] Calàbria 91 open 4pm, clsd Mon

Dacksy [MW,D] Consell de Cent 247 **34/934-519-925** 5pm-3am, trendy cocktail lounge

Lust [MW] Casanova 75 (at Consell de Cent) 9pm-2:30am, clsd Mon, pre-clubbing bar

La Madame [★GS,D] Ronda Sant Pere 19-21 (M° Urquinaona) **34/93-426-8444** from midnight Sun only

Moeem [MW] Muntaner 11 **34/659-229-033** 6pm-3am, cheap drinks

Museum Cafe & Club [M] Sepulveda 178 (at Urgell) 6:30pm-3am

Museum Retro [M] Urgell 106 11:30pm-3am Fri-Sat

New Chaps [M,L,S,V] Av Diagonal 365 (M° Diagonal) **34/93-215-5365** 9pm-3am, till 3:30am Fri-Sat, from 7pm Sun, darkroom

Nightberry [MO,S] Diputació 161 (M° Urgell) **34/934-543-805** 6pm-2:30am, till 3am Fri-Sat, darkroom & cabins

People Lounge [M,E,F] Villarroel 71 (M° Urgell) **34/93-451-5986** 7pm-3am

Punto BCN [★M,WC] Muntaner 63-65 (enter on Consejo de Ciento Yragón, M° Universitat) **34/93-453-6123** 6pm-2:30am, upscale cafe-bar

SkyBar [MW] Aribau 33 (at Hotel Axel) **34/93-323-9393** open to non-guests 9pm-1:30am Wed

Zelig [GS,D,F] **34/93-441-5622** 7pm-2am, till 3am wknds, clsd Mon

■NIGHTCLUBS

Arena Classic [★M,D,S,V,YC,$] Diputació 233 (at Balmes, M° Universitat) **34/93-487-8342** 12:30am-5am Fri-Sat only, Spanish music

Arena Dandy/ VIP [M,D,S,V,YC,$] Gran Via 593 (at Balmes, M° Universitat) **34/93-487-8342** 1am-6am Fri-Sat

Arena Sala Madre [★M,D,F,S,V,YC,$] Balmes 32 (at Diputació, M° Universitat) **34/93-487-8342** 12:30am-5am, clsd Mon (except in Aug), darkroom

Bitch@Priviledge [M,D] Calle de Tarragona 141-147 12:30am Sat only

Bubbleboys [M] 10pm-3am Th-Sat, gay pole-dance bar

Centrik Weekend Bar [M] Aribau 30 11pm-3am Fri-Sat

Martin's [MO,D,L,S,V] C/ de Béjar 87 **34/934-265-332** midnight-5am Sat only, small backroom

Metro [★M,D,LDS,VYC,$] Sepúlveda 185 (M° Universitat) 34/93-323-5227 midnight-5am, from 1am Mon

Souvenir Barcelona [★GS,D] Noi del Sucre 75 (Viladecans) after-hours club 6am-1pm Sat-Sun & holidays

■CAFES

La Concha del Barrio Chino [GS,D,TG] Guardia 14 (M° Liceu) 34/93-302-4118 4pm-3am

■RESTAURANTS

7 Portes Passeig d'Isabel II, 14 34/93-319-3033, 34/93-319-2950 1pm-1am, Catalan

El Berro Diputació 180 34/933-236-956 7am-3am, from 9am wknds, inexpensive diner-style restaurant, also bar

Botafumeiro [R] El Gran de Gràcia 81 34/93-218-4230, 34/93-217-9642 1pm-1am, Galician seafood, full bar

Castro [S] Casanova 85 (M° Urgell) 34/93-323-6784 1pm-4pm & 9pm-midnight, clsd Sun, Catalan, full bar

dDivine [MW,DS,R] Balmes 24 (M° Universitat) 34/93-317-2248 9:30pm-1am, clsd Sun-Tue, dinner show hosted by "Divine"

Eterna [MW,DS] Consell de Cent 127-129 (at Villarroel) 34/93-424-2526 1pm-4pm Mon-Fri, 9:30pm-midnight Th-Sat, clsd Sun

La Flauta Magica [WC] c/ de Banys Vells 18 (M° Jaume I) 34/93-268-4694 dinner nightly, vegetarian/ organic

Iurantia [R] Casanova 42 (M° Urgell) 34/93-454-7887 lunch Mon-Fri, dinner Mon-Sat, clsd Sun, pizzeria

Little Italy [E] Carrer del Rec 30 (near Passeig del Born) 34/93-319-7973 1pm-4pm & 9pm-midnight, live jazz

Madrid-Barcelona [★] Carrer d'Arago 282 (M° Passeig de Gracia) 34/93-215-7027 lunch & dinner, clsd Sun

Marquette Diputació 172 (M° Universitat) 34/93-162-3905 6pm-3am

Sazzerak 34/93-451-1138 full bar

Tafino 1pm-4pm Mon-Fri, 8:30pm-midnight Tue-Sat

Tu Sabes 34/615-999-282 7pm-midnight Th, 9pm-3am Fri-Sat

La Veronica Rambla de Raval 2-4 34/93-329-3303 1pm-1am, clsd Mon, popular pizzeria

■ENTERTAINMENT & RECREATION

Chernobyl Beach take the Metro to Sant Roc popular gay beach

Mar Bella popular gay beach

Museu Picasso Montcada 15-23 34/93-256-3000 early Picasso works

Parc Guell Mount Tibidado mosiacs & sculpture by Gaudi

Sant Sebastiàn popular gay beach

■BOOKSTORES

Antinous [WC] Josep Anselm Clavé 6 (btwn Las Ramblas & Ample, M° Drassanes) 34/93-301-9070 LGBT, books & gifts, also cafe

Cómplices Cervantes 2 (at Avinyó, M° Liceu) 34/93-412-7283 10:30am-8:30pm, from noon Sat, clsd Sun, LGBT, Spanish & English titles

Nosotr@s Casanova 56 (M° Urgell) 34/93-451-5134 LGBT

■RETAIL SHOPS

Ovlas C/ d'Aribau 31 34/93-268-7691 clothing, also cafe

■PUBLICATIONS

Gay Barcelona Av Roma 152 34/93-454-9100 monthly gay magazine

■MEN'S CLUBS

Bruch C/ Pau Claris 87 34/93-487-4814 11am-10pm

Buenos Aires Urgell 114 (at Consell de Cent) 34/93-323-8199 24hrs

Casanova [★,F.V] Casanova 57 (at Diputació, M° Universitat) 34/93-323-7860, 34/65-016-5078 24hrs, gym equipment, also bar

Condal [F,V,SW] Espolsasacs 1 (at Carrer Condal, M° Catalunya) 34/93-317-6817 24hrs

Corinto [★F,V] Pelayo 62 (at Rambla, M° Catalunya) **34/93-318-6422** *24hrs wknds*

Galilea Sauna [F,V,WI] Calabria 59 (M° Rocafort) **34/93-426-7905** *24hrs wknds*

Neron Urgell 185 **34/934-511-0 28**

Open Mind Arago 130 **34/934-510-479** *11pm-4am, till 7am Fri-Sat, clsd Mon-Tue, cruising, fetish and SM club*

Sauna Barcelona [V,SW,WI] Tuset 1 (at Av Diagonal) **34/93-200-7716** *24hrs wknds*

Thermas [SW] Diputación 46 (at Entenza, M° Rocafort) **34/93-325-9346** *24hrs, hustlers*

Trash Calle de la Mare de Déu del Remei 11 *10pm-3am, midnight-6am Fri-Sat, 7pm-2am Sun, clsd Mon-Tue, fetish club and playground*

■EROTICA

Blue Star [GS] Av Roma 153 (Edificio Torre Catalunya) **34/93-452-5890**

Boyberry Calàbria 96 (M° Rocafort) **34/93-426-2312**

Erotic Museum of Barcelona Ramblas 96 **34/93-318-9865**

Harmony Love **34/93-405-3300**

Kitsch Muntaner 17-19 (at Gran Vía) **34/93-453-2052**

Nostromo Diputació 208 (downstairs, M° Universitat) **34/93-451-3323** *video cabins, darkroom*

Sestienda Rauric 11 (at Farran, M° Liceu) **34/93-318-8676** *clsd Sun*

Skorpius Gran Vía 384-390 **34/93-423-4040**

Zeus Gay Shop Riera Alta 20 (M° Sant Antoni) **34/93-442-9795** *clsd Sun*

■CRUISY AREAS

Parc de Montjuïc [AYOR] btwn Avs del Estadio & Rius y Taulet *behind the archaeology museum, by the cascade*

Parc Sagrada Familia [AYOR]

Playa de la Mar Bella [AYOR] *on the beach & in the park*

Las Ramblas [AYOR]

Madrid

Note: M°=Metro station

■INFO LINES & SERVICES

COGAM (Colectivo de Lesbianas, Gays, Transexuales, y Bisexuales de Madrid) Puebla 9 (Bajo) **34/91-522-4517** *LGBT center, groups, library, also cafe-bar*

■ACCOMMODATIONS

Camino de Soto [GS,SW,WI,GO] Puente de la Reine 18, Soto del Real **34-66/744-1351**

Chueca Pension [MW,WI] Gravina 4 **34/91-523-1473** *hostel*

Hostal CasaChueca [MW,WI,GO] Calle San Bartolomé 4 (at San Marcos) **34/91-523-8127**

Hostal La Fontana [MW,WI] Valverde 6, 1° (M° Gran Vía) **34/91-521-8449, 34/91-523-1561**

Hostal la Zona [M,WI,GO] Calle Valverde 7, 1 & 2 (at Gran Vía) **34/91-521-9904** *full brkfst, private balconies*

Hostal Odesa [★M,WI] Calle Hortaleza 38, 3rd flr (at Perez Galdos) **34/91-521-0338, 34/91-521-5901**

Hostal Puerta del Sol [M,WI,WC,GO] Plaza Puerta del Sol 14, 4° (at Calle de Alcalá, M° Sol) **34/91-522-5126** *centrally located*

Hotel Catalonia Gaudí [GF,F,WI] Gran Vía 7-9 (at Alcalá) **34/91-531-2222** *4-star hotel in the heart of the city*

Hotel Urban Madrid [GF,SW,WI] Carrera de San Jerónimo 34 **34/91-787-7770** *upscale hotel w/ 3 restaurants*

Pensión Madrid House [GS,WI,GO] Barbieri 1 **34/651-387 535** *one block from Chueca Square*

■BARS

El 51 [★M] Hortaleza 51 (in Chueca) **34/91-521-2564** *6pm-3am, from 4pm wknds, upscale cocktail lounge*

A Noite [M,D,DS,S,V] Hortaleza 43 (M° Chueca) **34/91-531-0715** *9pm-6am, darkroom, hustlers*

Spain • EUROPE

Ambienta2 [MW,D,DS,E] 22 San Bartolome (at Figueroa) 34/606-939592 6pm-2am, till 2:30am wknds, from noon Sun, theme nights

The Angel [M,D,B] Calle Infantas 9 (at Hortaleza) 34/68-779-1452 noon-5:30am, till 6am Fri-Sat, clsd Mon-Tue

Attack Fun SX Bar [M,V] Calle de Lavapiés 12 (M° Tirso de Molina) 34/91-528-3860 9pm-late, clsd Mon, sex club, darkroom

Bar Lio [MW,K,DS,TG] Pelayo 58 7pm-2am

Bar Nike [M,NH,F,YC] Augusto Figueroa 22 (at Barbieri) 34/915-210-751 cafeteria-style local bar, popular before going out

Bear's Bar [★MO,B,L,V] Calle Pelayo 4 (M° Chueca, ring to enter) 34/91-521-7358 6pm-2:30am, till 3:30am wknds, clsd Mon, darkroom, cruisy

Bebop [M,NH,F] Plaza de Chueca 9 34/9152-19873 11am-3am, cafe/ bar

Black & White (Blanco y Negro) [★M,D,S] Libertad 34 (at Gravina, M° Chueca) 34/91-531-1141 8pm-5am, hustlers

The Cage [M,L] San Marcos 11 34/911-234-567 3pm-2am, from 5pm Sat-Sun

Copper [MO,D,L,N] Calle San Vincente Ferrer 34 (M° Tribunal) 2pm-3am, till 3:30am Fri-Sat, dress code, sling, darkroom

Cruising [★M,D,L,V,YC] Calle de Pérez Galdós 5 (M° Chueca) 34/91-521-5143 9pm-close, till 3:30am Fri-Sat, hustlers

Eagle Madrid [M,L,F,V,N,PC] Calle Pelayo 30 (M° Chueca) 34/91-524-1627 2pm-close, from 3pm wknds, theme nights, darkroom

Enfrente [M,B,L] Infantas 12 (M° Gran Vía) 34/68-779-1462 8pm-3am, DJs Th & Sun

Fu3l [M,B] San Marcos 16 (at Barbieri) 7pm-3:30am

Fulanita de Tal [W,D] Calle del Conde de Xiquena 2 (at Prim)

Gris [★MW,E] 10pm-3am, from 9pm Th-Sat, clsd Sun-Mon, reduced drink prices until 11:30pm

Hot Bar [M,B,L,V] Infantas 9 (M° Chueca, ring to enter) 1pm-3am, cruising in the basement

Leather [MO,D,L,S,V,OC] Pelayo 42 (at Gravina, M° Chueca) 34/91-308-1462 7pm-3pm [S] Th-Sat, darkroom

Liquid [M,D,V] Calle Barbieri 7 (M° Banco) 34/91-532-7428 9pm-close, good place to start the night

LL [★M,D,S,DS,V] Pelayo 11 (M° Chueca) 34/91-523-3121 5pm-close

Museo Chicote [★GS,F,E] Calle Gran Via 12 34/915-326-737 9pm-3am

The Paso [★M,V] Calle Costanilla de los Capuchinos 1 (M° Gran Vía) 34/91-522-0888 6pm-close

Picardias Pub [M,NH,S,V,OC] Calle de Pérez Galdós 8 (M° Chueca) 7pm-3am, darkroom

Rick's [★M,D,YC] Calle del Clavel 8 (at Infantas, M° Gran Vía, ring to enter) 34/91-531-9186 11pm-6am, open later Fri-Sat, 9pm-2am Sun

Rimmel [M,NH,V,YC] Calle de Luis de Góngora 2 (M° Chueca) 7pm-3am, darkroom, hustlers

El Rincón Guay [MW,NH,F,WI] Embajadores 62 (Lavapiés quarter) 34/914-683-769 9am-2am

Sacha's [MW,D,DS] Plaza de Chueca 1 (M° Chueca) 8pm-3am, terrace

Sixta [GS,GO] Calatrava 15 (M° La Latina) 34/913-663-018 10pm-2am, 3pm-midnight Sun, clsd Mon-Wed, packed on Sun afternoon

Studio 54 Madrid [MW,D,S] Barbieri 7 (btwn San Marcos & Infantas, M° Chueca) 34/615-126-807 11:30pm-3:30am, clsd Mon-Tue

Tántalo [M,WI] Libertad 14 34/915-213-127 6pm-2:30am

Truco [★W,D] Calle de Gravina 10 (at Plaza de Chueca) 34/91-532-8921 8pm-close, clsd Mon-Tue, dance bar, seasonal terrace

Why Not [M,D] San Bartolomé 6 (M° Gran Vía) 9pm-3am, till 5am Fri-Sat

NIGHTCLUBS

Bangalá [MO,MR,V,YC,N] Escuadra 1 (M° Antón Martin/Lavapiés) 9pm-2:30am, darkroom

Boite [GS,D] Calle Tetuan 27 (Plaza del Carmen) 34/91-522-9620 check listings for gay club nights

Cool [★GS,D] 34/91-542-3439 midnight-6am, more gay Sat

Dark Hole [GS,D] Pelayo 80-82 1am-6am Sat, gay goth club

Delirio [M,D,S] Libertad 28 (at Figueroa) 34/91-531-1870 11pm-5:30am, go-go boys Wed

Griffin's [★M,D,DS,E] Marqués de Valdeiglesias 6 (M° Banco de España) 34/91-522-2079 11pm-late

Heaven @ Madrid [★GF] 34/91-535-4417 12:30am-6am only, mixed metrosexual party

Joy Eslava [★GS,D,DS,S] Arenal 11 (M° Sol) 34/91-366-3733 11:30pm-6pm Sat only, fabulous crowd

Long Play [MW,D] Plaza de Vázquez de Mella 2 midnight-6am wknds only

Mad Hunter Club [M,D,B,L] Pelayo 80-82 midnight-5:30am Fri-Sat only

The Moon [GF,D] Aduana 21 34/91-522-3561 after-hours club

Ohm [★GS,D,S] Plaza de Callao 4 (at Sala Bash, M° Callao) 34/91-531-0132 midnight-close Fri-Sat

The Paw [M,N] Calatrava 29 (M° La Latina) 34/91-366-6093 7pm-late, Sun, sex club, darkroom, slings

Space of Sound [MW,D,S] Sala Macumba (at Estación de Chamartin) 34/90-249-9994 midnight-close Sun only

Strong Center [M,D,L,S,V,$] Trujillos 7 (M° Santo Domingo) 34/91-541-5415 7pm-3am, the main attraction is its enormous darkroom

Tábata [MW,D,YC,$] Vergara 12 (next to Teatro Real, M° Opera) 34/91-547-9735 11:30pm-late Wed-Sat

Week-end [★MW,D,A,$] Plaza de Callao 4 (at Ohm Club) 34/91-541-3500 midnight-6am Sun

CAFES

El Apolo Barco 18 34/915-210-830 8am-3pm & 6pm-2am, 10am-2am Sat, from 5pm Sun

Cafe Acuarela [MW] Gravina 10 (M° Chueca) 34/91-522-2143, 34/91-570-6907 3pm-3am, from 11am Sat-Sun, bohemian cafe-bar

Cafe Figueroa [MW] Augusto Figueroa 17 (at Hortaleza, M° Chueca) 34/91-521-1673 4pm-midnight, till 2:30am wknds, also bar

Cafe la Troje [MW] Pelayo 26 (at Figueroa, M° Chueca) 34/91-531-0535 5pm-2am, full bar

D'Mystic [★GS,F] Gravina 5 (M° Pelayo) 34/91-308-2460 9:30am-close, hip cafe-bar in Chueca area

Mama Inés [★] Hortaleza 22 (M° Chueca) 34/91-523-2333 10am-2am, sandwiches, pies

XXX Cafe [M,F,C] Clavel 2 (M° Gran Vía) 34/91-532-8415 1pm-1am, till 2:30am Fri-Sat

RESTAURANTS

Al Natural Zorrilla 11 (M° Sevilla) 34/91-369-4709 lunch & dinner, no dinner Sun, vegetarian

El Armario [MW,S] San Bartolomé 7 (btwn Figueroa & San Marcos, M° Chueca) 34/91-532-8377

Artemisa [MW] Ventura de la Vega 4 (at Zorrilla) 34/91-429-5092 vegetarian

Botin 34/91-366-4217 one of the oldest restaurants in the world

Colby 34/91-521-2554 9:30am-close, from 11:30am Sun

Divina La Cocina [MW] Colmenares 13 (at San Marcos, M° Chueca) 34/91-531-3765 lunch & dinner, elegant & trendy

Ecocentro Esquilache 2, 4, y 6 (at Pablo Iglesias, M° Ríos Rosas) 34/91-553-5502 open till midnight, vegetarian, natural foods, also shop, herbalist school

Spain • *EUROPE*

El Chambao Manuel Malasana 16 (at Calle de Monteleon) *tapas restaurant, also bar*

Gula Gula [★MW,E,DS,R] Gran Via 1 (M° Gran Via) **34/91–522–8764** *lunch & dinner, buffet/ salad bar*

Marsot Pelayo 6 (M° Chueca) **34/91–531–0726** *lunch & dinner*

Momo [NS,GO] Calle de la Libertad 8 **34/91–532–7162** *lunch & dinner, charming staff*

Moskada Francisco Silvela 71 (at General Oraa) **34/91–563–0630** *lunch Mon-Fri, dinner Mon-Sat, clsd Sun*

El Rincón de Pelayo [★MW] Pelayo 19 (M° Chueca) **34/91–521–8407** *lunch & dinner*

Sama-Sama San Bartolomé 23 (M° Chueca) **34/91–521–5547** *lunch & dinner, clsd Sun, Balinese decor*

Vegaviana Pelayo 35 **34/913–080–381** *lunch & dinner, clsd Sun-Mon, vegetarian*

■ BOOKSTORES

A Different Life Pelayo 30 (M° Chueca) **34/91–532–9652** *11am-10pm, LGBT, books, magazines, music, videos, sex shop downstairs*

Berkana Bookstore [WC] Hortaleza 64 **34/91–522–5599** *10:30am-9pm, from noon Sat-Sun, LGBT, ask for free gay map of Madrid*

■ PUBLICATIONS

Shangay Express **34/91–445–1741** *free bi-weekly gay paper, also publishes Shanguide*

■ GYMS & HEALTH CLUBS

Energy Gym [★] Hortaleza 19 (M° Gran Via, Chueca) **34/91–531–1029, 34/91–522–3073**

Gimnasio V35 Valverde 35 (M° Gran Via) **34/91–523–9352**

Holiday Gym Princesa [SW] Serrano Jover 3 (M° Argüelles) **34/91–547–4033** *central location*

■ MEN'S CLUBS

Adán [V,SW] San Bernardo 38 (M° Noviciado) **34/91–532–9138** *24hrs wknds, 3 flrs, darkroom, also bar, hustlers*

Alameda [SW] Alameda 20 (M° Atocha) **34/91–429–8745** *1pm-11pm, darkroom, also bar*

Comendadoras [★OC,V] Plaza Comendadoras 9 (at Calle de Montserrat, M° Noviciado) **34/91–532–8892** *24hrs, also bar*

Cristal [V,SW] Augusto Figueroa 17 (M° Tribunal y Gran Via) **34/91–531–4489** *3pm-3am, also bar*

Men [V] Pelayo 25 (M° Chueca) **34/91–531–2583** *3pm-8am, 24hrs wknds, bar*

Octopus [M,V,SW] Churruca 10 (at Apodaca, M° Tribunal/ Chueca) **34/91–183–2832** *3pm-midnight, darkroom, bar*

Odarko [MO,D] Loreto & Chicote 7 (at Ballesta, M° Callao) **34/91–522–9251** *10pm-close, from 6pm Sun, "pervy & fetish sex club in Madrid"*

Paraíso [★SW,V] Norte 15 (at San Vicente F, M° Noviciado) **34/91–522–4232, 34/91–531–9891** *noon-midnight, 24hrs wknds, gym equipment, also bar, darkroom*

Premium Sauna Calle Costanilla de los Ángeles 5 (enter Priora 2) **34/911–155–411** *3pm-11pm, from 3am wknds*

Sauna Center [D] Cuesta de Santo Domingo 1

Sauna Gran Via [M] Barco 6 **34/915–230–468**

Sauna Lavapiés Zurita 3 *24hrs*

Sauna Príncipe [F,V] Travesia de las Beatas 3 (M° Ópera) **34/91–559–5353, 34/91–548–2218** *2pm-midnight, also bar, darkroom*

Sauna Puerta de Toledo **34/913–659–095** *2pm-11pm*

Xtrem Sex Club Valverde 3 (at del Desengaño 2) *6pm-3am, from 2pm Sun*

■ EROTICA

Amantis Pelayo 46 **34/91–702–0510**

City Sex Store c/ Hortaleza, next to #18 (in Chueca) **34/91–181–2723** *open every day*

La Juguetería Travesia de San Mateo 12 **34–91/308–7269**

Play 34/91-523-0841 *10am-8pm*

SR [GO] Pelayo 7 (M° Chueca) 34/91-523-1964 *clsd Sun, fetish, military, leather*

■CRUISY AREAS

Casa de Campo [AYOR] *at night on top of hill—travel along only road going up from lake*

El Corte Ingles [AYOR] Puerta del Sol *large department store, men's lounge on 3rd & 5th flrs*

Parque del Campo de las Naciones [AYOR] *by the bridge leading to the auditorium*

Parque El Retiro [AYOR] (M° Atocha) *at night in garden around statue of fallen angel*

Plaza de Toros [AYOR] *car cruising at night*

Sitges

■ACCOMMODATIONS

Antonio's Guesthouse [MW,WI,GO] Passeig Vilanova 58 34/93-894-9207 *also apts*

Los Globos [MW,WI,WC,GO] Avda Ntra Sra de Montserrat 43 34/93-894-9374 *also bar*

Hotel Antemare [GF,SW] Verge de Montserrat 48-50 34/93-894-7000 *1 block from beach*

Hotel Liberty [★MW,NS,WI,WC,GO] Isla de Cuba 45 (at Artur Carbonell) 34/93-811-0872 *seasonal*

Hotel Renaixença [M] Illa de Cuba 13 , 08070 34/93-894-8375 *some shared baths, bar*

Hotel Romàntic [GS] Sant Isidre 33 34/93-894-8375 *full brkfst, some shared baths, seasonal, also bar*

Hotel Santa Maria [GS] Paseo de la Ribera 52 34/93-894-0999 *clean & modest, great restaurant*

Medium Sitges Park Hotel [GS,SW,WI,WC] Calle Jesus 16 34/938-940-205

Parrot's Hotel [MW,WI] Joan Tarrida 16 34/93-894-1350 *also bar, restaurant & sauna*

Pensión Espalter [M] Espalter 11 34/938-942-863 *also sauna*

San Sebastian Playa [GF,SW,NS,WC] Port Alegre 53 305/538-9697 (US#), 866/376-7831 (in US) *also bar/restaurant*

Sitges Royal Rooms [M,WI,GO] 34/64-998-1148

■BARS

Azul [★M,NH,V] Sant Bonaventura 10 34/93-894-7634 *9pm-3am*

B-Side [★M,F,S,V] San Gaudencio 7 34/61-799-0926 *10pm-3:30am, cafe-bar, darkroom*

Bears' Bar [M,B,V] Bonaire 17 34/93-894-6296 *10pm-3am (Fri-Sat only off-season), also rooms to rent*

Dark/ DSB [M] Bonaire 14 *5pm-3am, sleek lounge*

El Horno [★M,B,L,F,V] Joan Tarrida Ferratges 6 34/93-894-0909 *5:30pm-3am, darkroom*

La Locacola [M] Bonaire 35 *7pm-close*

Man [★M,L] Bonaventura 19 *10pm-3:30am, nightly underwear parties except Th*

Mojito & Co [M] Plaza Industrial 1 *5pm-3am, breezy lounge w/ outdoor seating*

Parrot's Pub [★MW,S] Plaza Industria 2 (at Primero de Mayo) 34/93-894-7881 *5pm-close, seasonal, patio, also restaurant*

Ruby's Terrace [M,E,DS] Joan Tarrida Ferratges 14

El Seven [M,D,S,V] Calle Nou 7 *10pm-3am (wknds only off-season), clsd Nov, terrace, darkroom*

XXL [★M,D,L,V] Joan Tarrida Ferratges 7 11pm-3:30am (wknds only off-season), darkroom

■NIGHTCLUBS

L' Atlántida [M] *gay beach party from midnight on Tue (summers)*

Bourbon's [★M,D,V,YC] Sant Bonaventura 13 34/93-894-3347 *10:30pm-3:30am (Sat only off-season), darkroom*

Spain • *EUROPE*

El Candil [★M,D,V,YC] Carreta 9 34/93-894-1632 *seasonal, 10pm-3am, till 3:30am Fri-Sat, darkroom*

Comodín [M,D,DS] Tacó 4 34/93-894-1698 *10pm-3am, darkroom*

Le Male à Bar [MO,D,F,V] Centro Comercial Oasis 28 *11pm-late (only wknds in winter), underwear parties Mon & Wed*

Mediterraneo [★M,D,YC] Sant Bonaventura 6 34/93-894-3347 *11pm-3:30am, patio*

Orek's [M,D,S,V] Bonaire 13 *10pm-3am (only Fri-Sat in winter), darkroom*

Organic [M,D,TG,S,$] Bonaire 15 34/93-894-2230 *opens 2:30am (wknds only off-season), singles party Th, darkroom*

Perfil [M,NH,D,DS,V] Espalter 7 34/656-376-791 (cell) *10:30pm-3am, darkroom, seasonal*

El Piano [MW,C,P] Bonaventura 37 34/93-814-6245 *10pm-3am*

Prinz [M,C,DS,S] Nou 4 34/93-894-6736 *11pm-3:30am*

Privilege [M,D] Bonaire 24 *11pm-3:30am, seasonal, darkroom*

Queenz [M,D,DS,C] Bonaire 17 *10pm-3:30am, seasonal*

Ricky's [GS] *midnight-6am, clsd Mon, more gay Fri*

Trailer [★M,D] Angel Vidal 36 *1am-6am, seasonal, foam parties in summer*

■CAFES

Cafe Al Fresco Carrer Major 33 34/93-811-3307 *9am-midnight*

Mont Roig Cafe [★WI] Marques de Montroig 11-13 34/93-894-8439 *9am-4am, patio, also full bar*

■RESTAURANTS

Air Coco [★R] Paseo Maritim 2 34/93-894-2445

Alma [MW,F] Tacó 16 34/93-894-6387 *8pm-close (clsd Tue-Wed off-season), French, terrace*

Beach House [GO] Sant Pau 34 34/93-894-9029 *brkfst & dinner, full bar*

El Celler Vell 34/93-811-1961 *dinner nightly, lunch Fri-Sun, clsd Wed*

Ma Maison [★MW] Bonaire 28 34/93-894-6054 *lunch & dinner, French, full bar, terrace*

Mezzanine Espalter 8 34/93-894-9940 *dinner only, French*

Pic Nic [WI] Paseo de la Ribera 34/93-811-0040 *in front of gay beach*

Sitthai Bonaire 29 34/938-111-6 58 *8pm-midnight, clsd Mon*

So Ca/ Southern California Sant Gaudenci 9 34/93-894-3046 *1pm-close, also bar*

El Trull [★MW] Mossèn Felix Clará 3 (off Major) 34/93-894-4705 *dinner only, clsd Wed, French/ int'l*

■ENTERTAINMENT & RECREATION

Gay Beach Party La Playa De La Bossa Rodona *midnight-6am Tue in season*

Gay Beach (Platja de la Bassa Rodona) *in front of Calipolis Hotel & Picnic cafe*

Playa De Las Balmins *turn left then pass a long beach strip & then climb a hill past a cemetery*

Playa del Muerto *exclusively gay beach 50 minutes walk from the center of Sitges, also beach bar*

■RETAIL SHOPS

Boyzone Sant Bonaventura 18 34/93-894-6466 *clubwear, swimwear*

Laguna Beach Shop Sant Josep 25 34/938-947-204 *10:30am-2pm, 5pm-9pm*

Oscar Marquès de Montroig 2 (at Plaza Industria) 34/93-894-1976 *designer clothing*

■MEN'S CLUBS

Parrots Sauna [MO] Joan Tarrida 16 34/93-894-1350

Sauna Sitges Espalter 11 34/93-894-2863 *4pm-10am, also bar & foam parties*

■EROTICA

The Mask 34/93-811-2214 *24hrs wknds*

CRUISY AREAS

Espigon Beach [AYOR] *beware of cops!*

L' Estanyol Beach [AYOR] *nights, go right, past gay beach—beware of cops!*

Gay Beach [AYOR] La Playa De La Bossa Rodona *in front of Calipolis Hotel & Picnic cafe (beware of cops!)*

Playa del Muerto [AYOR] *in woods near Terramar Hotel, daytime (beware of cops!)*

Asia

JAPAN

Tokyo

ACCOMMODATIONS

24 Kaikan [M,F,V] Shinjuku 2-13-1 81-3/3354-2424 *hotel & sauna; also Asakusa 2-29-16 (81-3/5827-2424) & Kita-Ueno 1-8-7 (81-3/3847-2424)*

Capitol Tokyu [GF] 10-3 Nagata-cho 2-chome (Chiyoda-ku) 81-3/3581-4511, 800/428-6598 *near the Diet*

Four Seasons Hotel [GF,SW,WC] 10-8 Sekiguchi 2-chome (Bunkyo-ku) 81-3/3943-2222 *surrounded by historic Japanese garden*

HI Tokyo Central Hostel [GF] 18F Central Plaza (1-1 Kagurakashi, Shinjuku-ku) 81-3/3235-1107 *11pm curfew*

Hotel Century Southern Tower [GF] 2-2-1 Yoyogi (Shibuya-ku) 81-3/5354-0111 *near gay district*

Hotel Sunroute Plaza Shinjuku [GF] 2-3-1 Yoyogi (Shibuya-ku) 81-3/3375-3211 *near gay district*

Keio Plaza Hotel [GF,SW] 2-2-1 Nishi Shinjuku 81-3/3344-0111 *restaurants & bars*

Park Hyatt [GF,SW] 3-7-1-2 Nishi Shinjuku 81-3/5322-1234 *luxury hotel featured in Lost in Translation; also restaurants & lounge*

Shinjuku Prince Hotel [GF,WI] 30-1 Kabuki-cho 1-chome (Shinjuku-ku) 81-3/3205-1111, 800/542-8686 (US)

Shinjuku Washington Hotel [GF] 3-2-9 Nishi-Shinjuku (Shinjuku-ku) 81-3/3343-3111

Tokyu Stay [GF] 5-9-8 Nishi Shinjuku 81-3/3370-1090 *great location*

BARS

Advocates [MW,YC] 1-F, Dai-7 Tenka Bldg (Shinjuku 2-18-1) 81-3/3358-3988 *6pm-4am, till 1am Sun, cafe-bar*

Alamas Cafe [MW,D] 1/F Garnet Bldg, Shinjuku 2-12-1 81-3/6457-4242 *6pm-2am, till 5am Fri-Sat, 3pm-midnight Sun*

The Annex [M,F,OC] 1/F Futami Bld (2-14-11 Shinjuku Ni-Cho) 81-3/3356-5029 *5pm-3am*

Arty Farty [★M,D,YC] 2F, #33 Kyutei Bldg (Shinjuku 2-11-7), Shinjuku-ku 81-3/5362-9720 *6pm-5am, from 7pm Fri, from 5pm wknds, till 3am Sun*

Base [M,B,YC] 10-16 Maruyamacho (Shibuya) 81-3/5728-1233 *a warm den for young bears*

Bravo! [M] 2F Shinbashi 2-9-17 81-3/3503-8805 *6pm-midnight, clsd Sun*

DNA [GS,NH] 81-3/3341-4445 *3pm-5am*

The Dock [★M,D] B1, Dai-2 Seiko Bldg (Shinjuku 2-18-5), Shinjuku-ku 81-3/3226-4006 *9pm-4am*

Fuji [M,K,OC] St Four Bldg, B104 (Shinjuku 2-12-16), Shinjuku-ku 81-3/3354-2707 *8pm-3am, till 5am wknds*

GB [★M] B1, Shinjuku Plaza Bldg (Shinjuku 2-12-3), Shinjuku-ku 81-3/3352-8972 *8pm-2am, till Fri-Sat*

Keivi [M,NH] 4F Yoshino Bldg, 17-10 Sakuragaoka 81-3/3496-0006 *6pm-midnight*

Kinsmen [MW] 2F Shinjuku 2-12-16 (near Shinjuku Sanchome Station) 81-3/3354-4949 *7pm-1am, till 3am Fri-Sat, clsd Mon*

Kusuo [M] 3F Sunflower Bldg (Shinjuku 2-17-1) 81-3/3354-5050 *8pm-4am, till 5am wknds*

Japan • ASIA

Lamp Post [M,P] 201 Yamahara Heights (Shinjuku 2-12-15) 81-3/3354-0436 *7pm-3am*

Magnum [M,B,L] 3-11-12, B1 Nagatani Teikueito Bld, Shinjuku 81-3/3358-5245 *9pm-3am, from 8pm Sun-Mon, till 5am Fri-Sat*

Mango Mango [M] 81-3/3464-3884 *7pm-5am*

Monsoon [M] Shimazaki Bldg 6F (2-14-9 Shinjuku) 81-3/3354-0470 *3pm-6am, small, inexpensive bar*

Poplar [M,OC] B1 St Four Bldg (Shinjuku 2-12-16) 81-3/3350-6929 *6pm-2am*

Shibuya 246 [MO,WI,GO] 3/F Tozaki Bldg, 2-7-4 Dougen-zaka Shibuya 81-3/6277-5023 *6pm-2am, till midnight Sun*

Tac's Knot [MW] 2F, Rm 202 (Shinjuku 3-11-12) 81-3/3341-9404 *8pm-2am, also art exhibitions*

Town House [M,K] Ginza 6 Shinbashi, Bldg 1-11-15 (Minato-ku) 81-3/3289-8558 *6pm-midnight, from 4pm Sat, clsd Sun*

Usagi [M] on lock U facing block V, 5th Fl (up the narrow stairs) *great balcony*

Warai-Tei [M,B] 301 Nakae Bldg III, 2F (2-15-13 Shinjuku) 81-3/3226-0830 *8pm-1am, till 5am Fri-Sat, special welcome for hearing-impaired gays*

Wordup Bar [M,D] 2-10-7 2F TOM Bld Shinjuku 81-3/3353-2466

■ NIGHTCLUBS

Agit [MW,K,GO] 81-3/3350-8083 *8pm-6am*

Arch [★MW,D,DS] B1F Hayakawa Bldg (Shinjuku 2-14-6) 81-3/3352-6297

Club Zinc [MW] Shinjuku 2-14-6 (across from Shinjuku Park) 81-3/3352-6297 *8pm-4am*

Dragon Men [M,D] 1F Stork Nagasaki (2-11-4 Shinjuku Ni-Chome) 81-3/3341-0606 *6pm-3am, till 5am Fri-Sat, cruisy*

Hijoguchi [GF,D] 1F (Shinjuku 2-12-16) 81-3/3341-5445 *8pm-5am, till 3am Sun*

Rehab Lounge [M,D] 81-3/3355-7833 *7pm-2am, till 3am Fri-Sat, popular happy hour 7pm-9pm*

Shangri-La [M,D] Yume no Shima, Koto ward (at Ageha, Studio Coast) 81-3/5534-2525

Warehouse [GS,D] Fukao Bldg B 1-4-5 (exit 7 Azabu Juban station) 81-3/6230 0343 *large underground club host Red gay nights*

Word Up Bar [M,D] 2-10-7 2F Tom Bldg (Shinjyuku) 81-3/3353-2466 *11pm-close*

■ RESTAURANTS

Angkor Wat 1-38-13 Yoyogi (Shibuya-ku) 81-3/3370-3019 *lunch & dinner, Cambodian*

Ban Thai 1-23-14 Kabuki-cho, 3rd flr (Shinjuku) 81-3/3207-0068 *lunch & dinner*

Chin-ya 1-3-4 Asukusa 81-3/3841-0010 *lunch & dinner, serving shabu-shabu & sukiyaki since 1880*

Edogin [★] 4-5-1 Tsukiji (Chuo-ku) 81-3/3543-4401 *11am-9:30pm, till 8pm Sun, sushi*

Gonpachi 1-13-11 Nishi Azabu, 1F, 2F (Minato-ku) 81-3/5771-0170 *11:30am-5am, multiple locations*

Kakiden 3-37-11 Shinjuku, 8th flr 81-3/3352-5121 *lunch & dinner, upscale Japanese*

Kitchen Five 4-2-15 Nishi-Azabu (Minato-ku) 81-3/3409-8835 *6pm-9:45pm, Mediterranean*

Las Chicas Jingumae 5-47-6 (off Shibuya), Shibuya-ku 81-3/3407-6865 *11:30am-11pm, English spoken*

Maisen 4-8-5 Jingu-mae (Shibuya-ku) 81-3/3470-0071 *specializes in tonkatsu*

Moti 3F Roppongi Hama Bldg (6-2-35 Roppongi) 81-3/3479-1939 *noon-10pm, Indian*

New York Grill [R] 3-7-1-2 Nishi Shinjuku (at Park Hyatt Hotel, 52nd flr) 81-3/5322-1234 *lunch & dinner*

The Pink Cow 1-3-18 Shibuya, Shibuya-ku (Villa Modernuna B-1, across from Aoyama Park Tower) 81-3/3406-5597 *5pm-late, clsd Mon*

Sasa-no-yuki 2-15-10 Negishi (Taito-ku) 81-3/3873-1145 *11am-9pm, clsd Mon, serving homemade tofu for 300 years*

Tenmatsu 1-6-1 Dogen-zaka (Shibuya-ku) 81-3/3462-2815 *tempura*

▓ RETAIL SHOPS

Isetan Men's 3-14-1 Shinjyuku 1-11-15 81-3/3352-1111 *popular place for men's fashion, cruisy*

▓ GYMS & HEALTH CLUBS

Shinjuku Tipness Kaleido Bldg 5-7F (Nishi-Shinjuku 7-1), Shinjuku-ku 81-3/3368-3531 *many locations throughout city*

▓ MEN'S CLUBS

24 Kaikan [M,F,V] Shinjuku 2-13-1 81-3/3354-2424 *24hrs, darkroom, sauna, restaurant, hotel; also Asakusa 2-29-16 & Kita-Ueno 1-8-7*

Babylon Tokyo [MO] Sendagaya Bldg 3F-5F (Sendagaya 5-30-9, near Yoyogi Station), Yoyogi 81-3/3359-7619 *3pm-1am, till 7am Fri-Sat, [N] Wed & Fri*

Gong 1 Yoyogi (Shibuya-ku) 81-3/3372-3955 *5pm-1am, from 3pm Sat-Sun*

HX [MO,YC] 1F, UI Bldg (Shinjuku 5-9-6) 81-3/3226-4448 *3pm-10am, 24hrs wknds*

Jinya 2-30-19 Toshima-ku (Ikebukuro) 81-3/3931-0186 *24hrs*

King of College 2F Sakagami Bldg (2-14-5, Shinjuku-ku) 81-3/3352-3930 *6am-10pm, rent boys*

Roppongi Jinya 2F Nakanomachi Mansion (3-3-25 Roppongi exit 3) 81-3/3589-2102 *behind bar called Lost Angels*

Treff 4F Fukutomi Bldg (Akasaka 2-13-4) 81-3/5563-0523 *wknds naked*

▓ CRUISY AREAS

Hibiya Park [AYOR] near Yurakucho Station

Shin Kiba Park [AYOR] near Shin Kiba Station

Ueno Park near Tokyo Metropolitan Festival Hall

Southeast Asia

▐ THAILAND

Bangkok

▓ INFO LINES & SERVICES

Gay AA 12/3 Silom Rd (at the Coffee Society) 66-2/231-8300 *7pm Th*

▓ ACCOMMODATIONS

Annow Silom Guesthouse [M,WI] 35/11 Soi Yommarat (at Saladaeng Rd, Silom) USA 66-2/636-2834

Aquarius Gentlemen's House [MO,F,GO,AYOR] 243 Soi Huthayana, Soi Suan Phlu, S Sathorn Rd 66-2/679-3180, 66-2/677-2174 *massage & more; also bar, roof garden*

Baan Saladaeng [GF,WI] 69/2 Soi Saladaeng 3, Saladaeng Rd (Silom, Bangrak) 66-2/2636-3038 *upscale, near gay scene*

The Babylon Bangkok [MO,SW,WI] 34 Soi Nandha, Sathon Soi 1, S Sathon Rd 66-2/679-7984 *also spa & saunas, foam party last Sat*

Bangkok Rama Place, City Resort & Hotel [GF,SW,WI,WC,GO] 1546 Pattanakarn Rd (in Suan-Luang District) 66-2/722-6602-10 *full brkfst, also restaurant*

Best Comfort Residential Hotel [M,SW,WI] 49 Soi Sukhumvit 19 (Wattana) 66-2/651-1310 *residential hotel in the heart of Bangkok*

D&D Inn [GF,SW] 68-70 Khaosan Rd (Phranakorn) 66-2/629-0526

Elephantstay [GS,GO] Royal Elephant Kraal & Village (74/1 M3 Tumbol Suanpik), Phra Nakhon Si Ayutthaya 66-81/668-7727, 66-87/116-3307 *live w/, care for & learn about elephants; near Lopburi River; 1 hour to Bangkok*

Furama Silom [GF,SW] 59 Silom Rd 66-2/237-0488 *also gym, restaurant & bar*

Heaven@4 Hotel [GS,WI] Sukhumvit Soi 4 66-2/656-9450 *also bar*

Hotel de Moc [GF,SW,WI,WC] 78 Prajatipatai Rd, Pra-Nakorn **66-2/282-2831-3, 66-2/629-2100-5**

Lub d [GF] 4 Decho Rd (Silom, Bangrak) **66-2/634-7999**

Luxx [GF,WI] 6/11 Decho Rd **66-2/635-8800** *style-conscious, minimalist design hotel, full brkfst*

Old Bangkok Inn [GF,NS] 607 Pra Sumen Rd (at Rajdamnern Ave, in Pra Nakhon) **66-2/629-1787** *environmentally-friendly hotel*

Omyim Lodge [GS,NS,WA,GO] 72-74 Naratiwat Rd Silom **66-2/635-0169** *also restaurant*

Pinnacle Hotel [GS] 17 Soi Ngam Duphli, Rama 4 Rd, Sathorn **66-2/287-0111**

Regency Park Hotel [GF,SW] 12/3 Sukhumvit 22, Soi Sainamthip **66-2/259-7420** *located in heart of Bangkok, full brkfst*

Sheraton Grande Sukhumvit [GF,SW,WI,WC] 250 Sukhumvit Rd **66-2/649-8888**

Tarntawan Place Hotel [MW,WI,WC] 119/ 5-10 Surawong Rd **66-2/238-2620** *centrally located, modern amenities, bar & lounge*

Wow Bangkok [GF,WI] 3/16 Sukhumvit Soi 31 **66-2/260-3560**

■ BARS

70's Bar [MW,D] 231/16 Sarasin (Chitlom) **66-2/253-4433** *retro lounge*

The Balcony Pub & Restaurant [★M,F,K] 86-88 Silom Soi 4 (off Silom Rd) **66-2/235-5891** *5:30pm-close*

Balls Sports Bar [M,F] Duangthawee Plaza, 894 Soi Pratoochai, Surawong Rd **66-2/637-0078** *5pm-1am*

Bearbie Bar [M,B,K] 82 Silom Soi 4, 2nd flr **66-2/632-8446** *7:30pm-1am, till 2am Fri-Sat*

Bed Supperclub [GS,D,F] 26 Soi Sukhumvit 11, Sukhumvit Rd, Klongtoey-nua, Wattana **66-2/651-3537** *7:30pm-close*

Blue Club [M,D] 3161 Ramkhamhaeng Rd (btwn Soi 81 & 83, 2nd floor, above Duan Chai) **66-2/732-2360** *mostly Thai*

Club Cafe [M] 8/5 Silom Soi 2 (Bang Rak) **66-86/978-5221** *3pm-3am*

Club Love Remix [GS,D,F,YC] Ramkhamhaeng Soi 89/2 **66-2/378-4345, 66-1/987-4946** *also restaurant*

@Diamond [M,NH,F] 10/17 Silom Soi 2/1 **66-2/234-0459** *6pm-2am*

E-Male [M,C,DS] 62-64 Ramkhamhaeng, Soi 24 **66-2/319-6772**

Expresso [M] 8/10-11 Silom Rd, Soi 2 (Bang Rak) *relaxed café-bar*

Finallé [M,D,C] Ramkhamhaeng Soi 89/2 **66-1/503-5398** *9pm-2am*

G.O.D. [M,D] **66-2/632-8033** *11pm-5am, "guys on display"*

Golden Cock [M] 39/27 Soi Rajanakarindra 1, Surawong Rd (Bang Rak) **66-2/236-3859** *1pm-1am*

Golden Dome [MW,C] 252/5 Ratchadapisek Rd Soi 18 (Huay Kwang) **66-2/692-8202** *shows nightly at 5pm, 7pm & 9pm*

JJ Park [GS,F,E] 8/3 Silom Rd, Soi 2 (Bang Rak) **66-2/235-1227** *10:30pm-2am, live music*

Jupiter 2002 Men's Club [M,S] Thaniya Soi 2 (in Suriwonges Hotel) **0-81/617-2163** *8pm-1am*

Maxi's Bar & Restaurant [M] 38/1-2 Soi Pratoochai Suriwong Rd **66-2/2266-4225** *6pm-2am*

MTV Remix [GS,D] Ramkhamhaeng Soi 24 **66-2/319-8340**

One Night Only [M,D] Silom Soi 4, 74-1 **66-89/499-0303** *6pm-3am, small bar on the first floor, big bar and lounge and outside area*

Tawan [★M,S] 2/2 Soi Thantawan, Silom Rd, Soi 6 (off Suriwong Rd) 66-2/634-5833 *8pm-1am, specializing in muscular go-go boys*

Telephone Pub & Restaurant [★MW,F,K,WI] 114/ 11 Silom Rd, Soi 4 66-2/234-3279 *6pm-1am, Skype videophones on all the tables*

NIGHTCLUBS

Disco Disco [M,D] 8/12-13 Silom Rd, Soi 2 (Bang Rak) 66-2/234-6151, 66-2/266-4029 *9pm-2am*

DJ Station [★MW,D] 8/6-8 Silom Rd, Soi 2 (Bang Rak) 66-02/266-4029 *10:30pm-2am*

Dream Boy [★M,S] 38/3-6 Duangthawee Plaza (at 38 Surawong Rd, Bang Rak) 66-2/233-2121 *8pm-2am, go-go boy shows nightly at 10:30pm & 12:30am*

G-Star [M,D] Ratchada Rd, Soi 8 (Din Daeng) 66-2/643-8792 *7pm-2am*

Happen [M,K] 8/14 Silom Soi 2 *8pm-late, busy after 11pm*

Ick [M,D,E] Ramkhamhaeng Soi 89/2 0-83/975-3778 *5pm-2am*

Pharaoh's Music Bar [GS,F,K] 104 Silom Soi 4 (above Sphinx) 66-2/234-7249 *7pm-2am*

X Boom [M,D,S] Soi Anuman Ratchathon, Suriwong, Bangkok *opens at 8pm but popular 'after-hours' place, go-go dancers*

CAFES

Bug & Bee 18 Silom Rd, Suriyawong (Bang Rak) 66-2/233-8118 *24hrs*

Coffee Society [F,WI] 12/3 Silom Rd (Suriyawong, Bang Rak) 66-2/235-9784 *24hrs, also art gallery*

Dick's Cafe Bangkok 894/7-8 Soi Pratuchai (Duangthawee Plaza, off Surawong Rd) 66-2/637-0078 *11am-2am, European-style cafe*

RESTAURANTS

Cabbages & Condoms 6 Soi 12 Sukhumvit Rd (at Birds & Bees Resort) 66-2/229-4611 *11am-10pm, Thai food w/ safe-sex education*

Coyote on Convent 1/2 Sivadon Bldg Convent (Silom Bangrak) 66-2/631-2325 *11am-midnight, Mexican*

Crêpes & Co 59/4 Langsuan Soi 1 (Ploenchit Rd, Lumpini) 66-2/653-3990 *9am-11pm, lounge, full bar*

Eat Me [E] Soi Pipat 2 (off Soi Convent) 66-2/238-0931 *3pm-1am, upscale, also gallery, live music*

Food Loft 1027 Ploenchit Rd, Lumpini, Pathumwan (Central Chisholm, 7th flr) 66-2/655-7777 *upscale int'l food*

Full Moon [GO] 144/2 Silom Soi 10 66-2/634-0766 *Thai food*

Indigo 6 Convent Rd (off Silom Rd) 66-2/235-3268 *noon-1am, clsd Sun, patio, full bar, French*

Loy Nava Dinner Cruises [R] 37 Charoen Nakorn Rd, Klongsan 66-2/437-4932 *traditional Thai cuisine on rice barge on Chao Phraya River*

Mali [GO] 43 Sathorn Soi 1 66-2/679-8693 *8am-11pm*

Mango Tree [★R] 37 Soi Tantawan (off Suriwong Rd) 66-2/236-2820 *traditional Thai food, live music nightly*

May Kaidee 111 Tanao Rd, Bang-lamphu (behind Burger King) 66-9/137-3173 *9am-11pm, innovative vegetarian; also 33 Samen Rd*

O...Ho... [GO] 2/8 Soi Sri Bumphen 66-2/286-5292 *9am-midnight, Thai & Western menu*

Once Upon a Time 32 Soi Petchaburi 17, Pratunam 66-2/252-8629 *11am-11pm, Thai*

Sphinx [★M,K] 100 Silom Soi 4 66-2/234-7249 *6pm-1am, Thai & Western, full bar, terrace*

Sweet Basil [★] 1 Srivieng Rd (Si Lom, Bang Rak) 66-02/234-1889 *11:30am-9pm, Vietnamese food*

■ENTERTAINMENT & RECREATION

Calypso Cabaret [MW,C,DS] 296 Phaya Thai Rd, Pathumwan (at Asia Hotel) **66-2/261-6355** *shows nightly at 8:15pm & 9:30pm*

Mambo [C] 59/28 Sathu-phararam 3 Rd **66-2/294-7381-2** *shows nightly at 7:15pm & 10pm*

■GYMS & HEALTH CLUBS

Hercules Health Club [M,F] 91/194 Siam Park City, Sukhapiban 2 Rd, Siam Park Ave (Bangkapi) **66-2/919-9603** *4pm-midnight; also restaurant & bar*

■MEN'S CLUBS

Adonis Massage [★] 44/11 Convent Rd (Silom) **66-2/236-7789** *1pm-11pm*

Albury Men's Club 66/2 Soi Sukhumvit 26 **66-2/255-8920** *1pm-11pm*

Aqua Spa Club [F] 11/5 Soi Sathorn 9 **66-2/286-5233** *2pm-midnight, massage, tarot readings*

Arena 2/F Silom Plaza **66-2/635-3645** *Thai massage*

Banana Club [F] 41/9 Sukhumvit Soi 11 **66-2/651-0002** *3 flrs, massage, also restaurant*

Body Club 4/24-25 Sukhumvit Soi 8 **66-89/171-9009** *noon-10pm*

Chakran [F,K,V,SW] 32 Soi Ari 4, Phaholyothin Soi 7, Phayathai **66-2/279-1359** *darkroom, gym, poolside bar*

Sauna Mania 35/2 Soi Pipat 2 (off Soi Convent, Silom) **66-2/817-4073** *3pm-2am, enter on 2nd flr*

V Club 7 [F] 32 Chakran Bldg, Soi Paholyothin 7 (Soi Ari 4) **66-02/279-3322** *2pm-midnight*

Australia

NEW SOUTH WALES

Sydney

■INFO LINES & SERVICES

The Gender Centre **61-2/9569-2366** *free services for transgender/ transsexual people & their partners/ friends/ families, also publishes magazine Polare*

Lesbian & Gay Counselling Service **61-2/8594-9596, 1-800/18-4527 (outside Sydney)** *5:30pm-10:30pm, info & support*

■ACCOMMODATIONS

Apartment Hotel East Sydney [GS,NS] 150 Liverpool St, E Sydney (at Oxford St) **61/404-793-159** *2-bdrm apts, terrace*

Brickfield Hill B&B Inn [GS,WI,GO] 403 Riley St (at Foveaux), Surry Hills **61-2/9211-4886** *in gay district, near beaches*

Chelsea Guest House [GS,NS,GO] 49 Womerah Ave (at Oswald Ln), Darlinghurst **61-2/9380-5994** *Victorian w/ courtyard*

Governors on Fitzroy B&B [M,WI,GO] 64 Fitzroy St (at Bourke), Surry Hills **61-2/9331-4652** *3 blocks from Oxford St, full brkfst, hot tub, shared baths, garden*

Hotel Stellar [MW,WI] 4 Wentworth Ave (at Oxford St) **61-2/9264-9754** *kitchenette in each room, also cafe & bar*

Kirketon Boutique Hotel [GF,WI] 229 Darlinghurst Rd (at Farrell Ave) **61-2/9332-2011, 800/332-920 (Australia only)** *also restaurant & bar*

Medusa [GF,WI] 267 Darlinghurst Rd (at Liverpool), Darlinghurst **61-2/9331-1000** *modern boutique hotel*

Nomads Westend [GF,NS,WC] 412 Pitt St (at Goulburn St) **61-2/9211-4588, 1800/013-186** *budget/ backpacker's accommodations*

Oasis on Flinders [MO,N,GO] 48 Flinders St (at Taylor), Darlinghurst **61-2/9331-8791** *gay naturist B&B*

Pensione Hotel [GF,WI] 631-635 George St (at Goulburn St) **61-2/9265-8888, 800/885-886** *also restaurant & bar*

Victoria Court Hotel Sydney [GF] 122 Victoria St (at Orwell, Potts Point) **61-2/9357-3200, 1800/630-505 (in Australia)**

◼ BARS

Bar Cleveland/ Hershey Bar [GS,D,F,A,YC] 433 Cleveland St (at Bourke), Surry Hills **61-2/9698-1908** *11am-4am, noon-midnight Sun, cocktail lounge, DJ*

The Beauchamp [★GS,NH,F,GO] 265 Oxford St (at S Dowling), Darlinghurst **61-2/9331-2575** *noon-2am*

Beresford Sundays [MW] 354 Bourke St (at Albion St), Surry Hills **61-2/9357-1111** *from noon Sun, fun in the sun*

The Colombian [★MW,D] 117-123 Oxford St (at Crown St), Darlinghurst **61-2/9360-2151** *9am-6am, trendy pub & cocktail bar, 2 levels, theme nights*

Green Park Hotel [GS] 360 Victoria St (at Liverpool), Darlinghurst **61-2/9380-5311** *10am-2am, noon-midnight Sun, very gay Sun, stylish bar*

The Imperial Hotel [MW,D,F,DS,S] 35 Erskineville Rd, Newtown **61-2/9519-9899**

The Oxford [★MW,D,F,E] 134 Oxford St (at Bourke St, Taylor Square), Darlinghurst **61-2/8324-5200** *10am-close, 3 bars*

The Palms On Oxford [★M,D] 124 Oxford St (at Bourke St, Taylor Square), Darlinghurst **61-2/9357-4166** *8pm-late, clsd Mon-Wed*

Phoenix Bar [GS,D,E,DS] 34 Oxford St (at Exchange Hotel), Darlinghurst **61-2/9331-2956** *10am-5am, till 7am Fri-Sun, clsd Mon-Tue, sweaty downstairs dance den, also 5 other bars in complex*

The Stonewall [★M,D,K,DS,S] 175 Oxford St (at Bourke), Darlinghurst **61-2/9360-1963** *noon-6am, from 9am wknds, 3 bars*

The Taxi Club [M,D,TG,F,K,DS,PC,$] 40-42 Flinders St (at Grosvenor Club), Darlinghurst **61-2/9331-4256** *noon-midnight, till 5am Th-Sat*

ZanziBar [GF,F] 323 King St (at Phillips St), Newtown **62-2/9519-1511**

◼ NIGHTCLUBS

ARQ [★M,D,F,DS,$] 16 Flinders St (at Taylor Square), Darlinghurst **61-2/9380-8700** *9pm-late Th-Sun, clsd Mon-Wed, drag shows Th*

The Black Boater [GS,D,F] 16 Wentworth Ave (at Lyons Ln, Surry Hills) **61-2/9267-6440** *check www.theblackboater.com for events*

Home [★GF,D,$] Tenancy 101, Cockle Bay Wharf (at Wheat Rd, Darling Harbour) **61-2/9266-0600** *open Fri-Sun, hosts Homesexual (www.homesexual.com.au)*

The Midnight Shift [★M,D,V] 85 Oxford St (at Riley), Darlinghurst **61-2/9358-3848** *10pm-late Fri-Sat, also Saddle Bar*

Nevermind [GS,D] 163 Oxford St, Darlinghurst *Fri-Sun only, cutting edge electronic music, theme nights*

Rising Day Club [M,D] 34 Oxford St (at Phoenix bar), Darlinghurst *recovery club starts at 4am Sat-Sun*

Slide [MW,D,F,E,C] 41 Oxford St (at Pelican) **61-2/8915-1899** *6pm-3am, 5pm-4am Fri, 7pm-4am Sat-Sun, clsd Mon-Tue*

Sly Fox [MW,D,K] 199 Enmore Rd, Enmore **61-2/9557-1016**

Tank [GS,D,A] 3 Bridge Ln (behind Establishment Hotel) **61-2/9240-3000** *10pm-6am Fri-Sat, check locally for next DTPM gay party Sun nights*

◼ CAFES

Cafe Sopra [★] 7 Danks St **61-2/9699-3174** *10am-3pm, from 8am Sat, clsd Mon, Italian vegetarian*

Victoire 285 Darling St **61-2/9818-5529** *great bread*

Sydney • AUSTRALIA

Vinyl Lounge Cafe [MW,F] 17 Elizabeth Bay Rd, Elizabeth Bay **61-2/9326-9224** *7am-4pm, from 8am wknds, clsd Mon, light menu, plenty veggie, cash only*

■ RESTAURANTS

Bentley Restaurant & Bar 320 Crown St (Surry Hills) **61-2/9332-2344** *noon-late, clsd Sun-Mon, tapas & small plates, excellent wine*

Bertoni Casalinga 281 Darling St **61-2/9818-5845** *6am-6pm, clsd Sat-Sun, Italian*

Betty's Soup Kitchen [MW] 84 Oxford St, Darlinghurst **61-2/9360-9698** *noon-10pm, till midnight Fri-Sat, healthy homecooking, plenty veggie*

Bills Surry Hills 359 Crown St (Surry Hills) **61-2/9360-4762** *7am-10pm, great ricotta pancakes*

Billy Kwong [★R,WC] 3/355 Crown St (Surry Hills) **61-2/9332-3300** *sustainable local & organic Chinese from 6pm daily*

Bird Cow Fish 500 Crown St (Surry Hills) **61-2/9380-4090** *lunch & dinner, bistro & espresso bar*

The Boathouse on Blackwattle Bay [R] End of Ferry Road (Glebe) **61-2/9518-9011** *lunch & dinner Tue-Sun, gourmet seafood, some veggie, great view*

Bright N Up 77 Oxford St, Darlinghurst **61-2/9361-3379** *4:30pm-midnight*

Chu Bay 312a Bourke St, Darlinghurst **61-2/9331-3386** *5:30pm-11pm, Vietnamese, some veggie*

Danks Street Depot 2 Danks St **61-2/9698-2201** *great brkfst*

Fu Manchu [NS] 249 Victoria St, Darlinghurst **61-2/9360-9424** *lunch & dinner, chic noodle bar, cash only*

Iku Wholefood Kitchen [NS] 25a Glebe Point Rd, Glebe **61-2/9692-8720, 800/732-962** *lunch & dinner, creative vegan/ macrobiotic fare, outdoor seating*

Kujin 41b Elizabeth Bay Rd, Elizabeth Bay **61-2/9331-6077** *lunch & dinner, clsd Mon, Japanese*

Last Drop Cafe 538 Marrickville Rd (Dulwich Hill) **61-2/9572-9800** *7:30am-5:30pm, till 4pm Sat, clsd Sun, Greek food, art gallery*

Pink Peppercorn [GO] 122 Oxford St (near Taylor Square), Darlinghurst **61-2/9360-9922** *6pm-11pm, Laotian & Thai*

Queen Victoria Hotel/ Razors Bistro 167 Enmore Rd, Enmore **61-2/9517-9685**

Sean's Panorama 270 Campbell Parade, Bondi Beach **61-2/9365-4924** *lunch Fri-Sun, dinner Wed-Sat, clsd Mon-Tue*

Thai Kanteen [★GO] 541 Military Rd, Mosman **61-2/9960-3282** *lunch Th-Sun, dinner nightly, modern Thai*

Thai Pothong [WC] 294 King St (Newtown) **61-2/9550-6277** *lunch & dinner, Thai*

■ ENTERTAINMENT & RECREATION

Bondi Beach Bondi Beach *Sydney's most popular beach, more gay at north end*

Lady Jane Beach/ Lady Bay Beach [M,N] Watsons Bay

Obelisk Beach [M,N] Middle Head Rd (at Chowder Bay Rd)

Sydney by Diva departs from Oxford Hotel (in Taylor Square), Darlinghurst **61-2/9310-0200** *tour Sydney w/ drag queen host*

Sydney Gay/ Lesbian Mardi Gras 94 Oxford St, Darlinghurst 2010 **61-2/9383-0900** *the wildest party under the rainbow on this planet (see www.mardigras.org.au)*

■ BOOKSTORES

The Bookshop Darlinghurst 207 Oxford St (near Darlinghurst Rd), Darlinghurst **61-2/9331-1103** *10am-10pm, Australia's oldest LGBT bookstore, staff happy to help w/ tourist info*

Gertrude & Alice 46 Hall St (Bondi Beach) **61-2/9130-5155** *secondhand books, also coffee shop*

■RETAIL SHOPS

Bang 4 Flinders St, Darlinghurst 61–2/9357–3362 *designer labels, clubwear*

House of Priscilla 47 Oxford St, Darlinghurst 61–2/9286–3023 *wigs, costumes & more*

■PUBLICATIONS

DNA 61–2/9764–0200, 888/263–2624 (US #) *monthly gay men's magazine*

SX Weekly 61–2/9360–8934 *free gay/ lesbian weekly*

Sydney Star Observer 61–2/8263–0500 *weekly newspaper w/ club & event listings*

■GYMS & HEALTH CLUBS

City Gym 107–113 Crown St, E Sydney 61–2/9360–6247 *day passes available*

Gold's Gym Sydney 58 Kippax St (level 1), Surry Hills 61–2/9211–2799 *5:30am-9pm, 8am-8pm Sat, till 6pm Sun*

TBC Gym 122 Lang Rd, #2205A (The Entertainment Quarter), Moore Park 61–2/9357–7416

■MEN'S CLUBS

Bodyline Spa & Sauna [★V] 10 Taylor St (off Flinders), Darlinghurst 61–2/9360–1006 *24hrs wknds*

Headquarters [V,NS,WI] 273 Crown St (at Goulburn, near Oxford), Darlinghurst 61–2/9331–6217 *24hrs, theme rooms, theme nights*

Ken's at Kensington [SW,NS,WI,18+] 83 Anzac Parade (at Ascot St, Kensington), Kensington 61–2/9662–1359 *24hrs wknds*

Kingsteam [F,WI] 38–42 Oxford St (next to Exchange Hotel), Darlinghurst 61–2/9360–3431, 61–2/8250–1818 (info line) *24hrs*

Signal [V,WI] at Riley & Arnold Sts (upstairs), Darlinghurst 61–2/9331–8830

Sydney City Steam [F,WI,GO] 357 Sussex St (Darling Harbour) 61–2/9267–6766 *24hrs wknds*

■SEX CLUBS

Aarows [MW,TG,18+] 17 Bridge St (at Pitt St), Rydalmere 61–2/9638–0553, 61–2/1300–062–541 *24hrs*

■EROTICA

Gay Exchange 44 Park St 61–2/9267–6812

House of Fetish 93 Oxford St, Darlinghurst 61–2/9380–9042

Pleasure Chest 161 Oxford St, Darlinghurst 61–2/9332–2667, 61–2/9356–3640 *24hrs; also 705 George St, Haymarket*

The Probe [S] 159 Oxford St, upstairs, Darlinghurst 61–2/9361–5924 *24hrs*

Sax Fetish [GO] 110a Oxford St (Taylor Square) 61–2/9331–6105

Toolshed 81 Oxford St, Darlinghurst 61–2/9332–2792

■CRUISY AREAS

Beare Park [AYOR] Ithaca Rd

Bondi Beach Pavilion [AYOR] Bondi Beach

Gunnamatta Park [AYOR] Cronulla

Lady Bay Beach [AYOR] at N tip of South Head, Cronulla

Loftus Oval [AYOR] Princes Hwy (Loftus), Cronulla *park*

Marks Park [AYOR] S end of Bondi Beach, Cronulla *head toward the cliffs, evenings*

Rushcutters Bay Park [AYOR] New Beach Rd

Sydney Park [AYOR] King St & Mitchell Rd, Newtown *behind Old Brick Works*

Tour Operators

CRUISES

Mostly Men

Atlantis Events 9200 Sunset Blvd, Ste 500, West Hollywood, CA 90069 310/859-8800, 800/628-5268 largest LGBT tour operator in the world • all-gay cruise, resort & tour vacations • www.atlantisevents.com

Pied Piper Tours 330 W 42nd St, Ste 1804, New York, NY 10036 212/239-2412, 800/874-7312 gay group cruises • www.gaygroupcruises.com

Gay/Lesbian

Aquafest 4801 Woodway #400-W, Houston, TX 77056 800/592-9058 LGBT groups mingle w/ mixed clientele on major cruise lines • www.aquafestcruises.com

Gayribbean Cruises Dallas, TX 877/560-8318 gay & lesbian group cruise organizer • fabulous destinations • annual Halloween cruise from Galveston, TX • www.gayribbeancruises.com

Port Yacht Charters 9 Belleview Ave, Port Washington, NY 11050 516/883-0998, 877/DO-A-BOAT custom charters worldwide, specializing in the Caribbean • commitment ceremonies • gourmet cuisine • www.portyachtcharters.com

R Family 5 Washington Ave, Nyack, NY 10960 917/522-0985 family-friendly vacations designed especially for the LGBT community • www.rfamilyvacations.com

Rainbow Charters 939 Kawaiki Pl, Honolulu, HI 96825 808/347-0235 gay & lesbian weddings • custom sailing cruises • whale-watching • snorkeling • sunset cruises • www.RainbowChartersHawaii.com

RSVP Vacations 800/328-7787 gay & lesbian cruise vacations • www.rsvpvacations.com

Sailing Affairs 58 E 1st St #6-B, New York City, NY 10003 917/453-6425 gay sailboat charters, day trips, sunset sails & sailing vacations on 47-foot Beneteau • East Coast, Caribbean, Europe & Mediterranean • www.sailingaffairs.com

LUXURY TOURS

Men Only

➤**Hanns Ebensten Travel, Inc** 626 Josephine Parker Dr #206, Key West, FL 33040 305/294-8174, 866/294-8174 worldwide adventures for the uncommon traveler • Peru, India, Morocco, South Africa, Greece, Turkey, Italy, Egypt & more • www.hetravel.com

Mostly Men

EuroPanache 410 Park Ave, 15th flr, New York City, NY 10022 888/600-6777 unique, elite vacation experiences w/ an appealing mix of themes • offices in New York, Paris & Sydney • www.europanache.com

Gay/Lesbian

DavidTravel 310 Dahlia Pl, Ste A, Corona del Mar, CA 92625-2821 949/723-0699 full-service travel agency & tour operator • small luxury group departures & customized travel for individuals & groups • milestone events, including honeymoons! • www.DavidTravel.com

Steele Luxury Travel New York City, NY 10011 646/688-2274 unique & top-rated travel experiences to exotic destinations worldwide • www.steeletravel.com

GREAT OUTDOORS ADVENTURES

Men Only

Adventure Bound Expeditions 711 Walnut St, Boulder, CO 80302 **303/449-0990, 877/440-0990** outdoor adventure worldwide • hiking, kayaking, safaris, wildlife viewing • www.adventureboundmen.com

Mostly Men

Saltyboys gay & naturist sailing cruises • www.saltyboys.com

Scuba Scotty Oakland, CA **760/974-6477** scuba instruction • local & exotic destinations • gay-owned • www.scubascotty.com

Touring Cairns Kewarra Beach, Cairns, QLD, Australia **61-7/0402-868080** rain forest tours in the Cairns hinterland • www.touringcairns.com.au

Gay/Lesbian

►**Alyson Adventures, Inc** 626 Josephine Parker Dr #206, Key West, FL 33040 **305/296-9935, 800/825-9766** award-winning adventure travel & active vacations • hiking, biking & multi-sport activities • www.AlysonAdventures.com

Out in Alaska 1819 Dimond Dr, Anchorage, AK 99507 **907/347-2214** adventure travel throughout Alaska for LGBT travelers • your best bet for a fun & authentic Alaska vacation! • www.outinalaska.com

HE TRAVEL
ALYSON ADVENTURES

Travel to the World's Hottest Places With the World's Hottest Men

866-294-8174
info@HEtravel.com
www.HEtravel.com

Adventures for Single Gay Men...
...And Curious Couples

OutWest Global Adventures PO Box 2050, Red Lodge, MT 59068 **406/446-1533,
800/743-0458** specializing in gay/ lesbian active & adventure travel • worldwide •
www.outwestadventures.com

Undersea Expeditions 758 Kapahulu Ave #100-1188, Honolulu, HI 96816
858/270-2900, 800/669-0310 gay & lesbian scuba adventures worldwide •
www.UnderseaX.com

Gay/Straight

GoNorth Alaska Adventure Travel Center 3500 Davis Rd, Fairbanks, AK 99709
907/479-7272, 855/236-7272 guided tours throughout Alaska & the Arctic • air
taxis & transportation • canoe & bike rentals • hostel accommodations & camping •
www.GoNorth-Alaska.com

Himalayan High Treks 241 Dolores St, San Francisco, CA 94103 **415/551-1005,
800/455-8735** experience indigenous Buddhist & Hindu cultures •
www.hightreks.com

Natural Habitat Adventures PO Box 3065, Boulder, CO 80307 **303/449-3711,
800/543-8917** up-close encounters w/ the world's most amazing wildlife in its
natural habitat • www.nathab.com

Open Eye Tours PO Box 324, Makawao, HI 96768 **808/572-3483** customized private
land tours of Maui & other islands • visit popular spots or places seldom seen, walking or not • sharing Maui's best-kept secrets since 1983 • www.openeyetours.com

Paddling South & Saddling South PO Box 827, Calistoga, CA 94515 **707/942-4550,
800/398-6200** horseback, mountain-biking & sea-kayak trips in Baja • also
women-only trips • call for complete calendar • www.tourbaja.com

Puffin Fishing Charters PO Box 606, Seward, AK 99664 **907/224-4653,
800/978-3346** guided charter fishing • almost 30 years of experience • halibut,
salmon & rockfish on vessels custom-built for Alaskan waters •
www.puffincharters.com

Voyageur North Outfitters 1829 E Sheridan, Ely, MN 55731 **218/365-3251,
800/848-5530** canoe outfitting & trips • www.vnorth.com

SPIRITUAL/HEALTH VACATIONS

Gay/Lesbian

Spirit Journeys 134 River Rd, New Milford, NJ 07646 **201/483-3111, 800/754-1875**
spiritual retreats, workshops & adventure trips throughout the US & abroad •
www.spiritjouneys.com

THEMATIC TOURS

Men Only

Travel Keys Tours PO Box 162266, Sacramento, CA 95816-2266 **916/452-5200** tours
of dungeons & castles in Europe • also antique tours (gay/straight)

Mostly Men

Coda International Tours, Inc 12794 Forest Hill Blvd #1A, West Palm Beach, FL 33414
561/791-9890, 888/677-2632 culturally focused travel programs • www.coda-
tours.com

Hawaii Gay Tours Honolulu, HI 96821 **808/234-9260** experience Hawaii as the locals
do • customizable tours • www.hawaiigaytours.com

Africa Outing 3 Alcyone Rd, Claremont, Capetown 7708, South Africa 27–21/671–4028 gay/ lesbian safaris & more • tours customized to your needs • www.afouting.com

Brazil Fiesta Visa Service 268 Bush St #3531, San Francisco, CA 94104 415/986–1134, 800/200–0582 expedited Brazilian visa service • www.brazilfiesta.net

CM by Carlos Melia 630 5th Ave #2207, 10011 New York City 917/754–5515 boutique gay travel to Argentina, Uruguay & New York City • all services tested by me • "Been There Done That" • www.carlosmelia.com

Gay 2 Afrika 201/360–0558 providing African travel arrangements to the gay & lesbian community • www.gay2afrika.com

Gay Bali Tours Jl. Braban No. 67, Seminyak, 80361 Bali, Indonesia 62–361/736–818, 62–361/788–6627 premier & professional tour operator permanently based in Bali • www.baligay.net

Gay Travel Brasil Rua Sergipe 57 C 201, 20271- 310 Rio de Janeiro, Brazil 55–21/3415–3126 gay & lesbian travel in Brazil & South America • www.gaytravelbrasil.com

Go Pink China Beijing, China 86/1366–124–6689 adding queer elements to city tours & national trips in China • www.gopinkchina.com

Going Your Way Tours 123 Ledgewood Rd #509, Groton, CT 06340 860/447–9180 upscale customized group & individual itineraries worldwide • www.goingyourwaytours.com

Kuyay Travel Puerto Rosales 46, 5550000 Puerto Varas, Los Lagos, Chile 56–65/438–990 gay-owned/run travel planner & tour host in Patagonia • www.gaypatagonia.com

MexGay Vacations 355 S Grand Ave #2450, Los Angeles, CA 90071 213/383–9491, 866/639–4299 specializing in gay travel to Mexico • www.mexgay.com

National Gay Pilots Association PO Box 7271, Dallas, TX 75209 214/336–0873 several annual gatherings • call for more info • www.ngpa.org

Pacific Ocean Holidays Honolulu, HI 808/923–2400 Hawaii vacation packages • www.gayhawaiivacations.com

Planetdwellers Shop 47 Elizabeth Bay Rd, Elizabeth Bay, NSW 2011, Australia 61–2/8667–3336 LGBT tours of Australia • come to OZ! • www.planetdwellers.com.au

Toto Tours 1326 W Albion Ave #3W, Chicago, IL 60626 773/274–8686, 800/565–1241 unique worldwide adventures for gay men, lesbians, their friends & adult family members • www.tototours.com

Venture Out 575 Pierce St #604, San Francisco, CA 94117 415/626–5678, 888/431–6789 high-end escorted tours for gay & lesbian travelers to countries around the world • www.venture-out.com

Winelovertours.com 123 Ledgewood Rd #509, Groton, CT 06340 860/861–2301 upscale group tours & individual itineraries for foodies & winelovers • www.winelovertours.com

Alaska Railroad 431 W 1st Ave, Anchorage, AK 99501 907/265–2494, 800/544–0552 (reservations) rail & tour packages • www.alaskarailroad.com

Aria Tours PO Box 159, Little Bridge St, Almonte, ON K0A 1A0, Canada 866/686–1288 luxury travel for opera & the arts to the most spectacular destinations in the world • www.ariatours.com

Brazil Ecojourneys Estrada Rozalia Paulina Ferreira 1132, Armação, 88063-555 Florianopolis, Brazil **55-48/3389-5619** lesbian-owned Brazil tour operator • www.brazilecojourneys.com

Ecotour Expeditions, Inc PO Box 128, Jamestown, RI 02835 **401/423-3377, 800/688-1822** small group boat tours of the Amazon & more • call for color catalog • www.naturetours.com

Heritage Tours Private Travel 121 W 27th St #1201, New York, NY 10001 **212/206-8400, 800/378-4555** custom private trips to Morocco, Spain, Portugal, Turkey, Southern & East Africa • www.HTprivatetravel.com

Holbrook Travel 3540 NW 13th St, Gainesville, FL 32609 **352/377-7111, 800/451-7111** natural history tours in Central America, South America & Africa • small groups • www.holbrooktravel.com

Lebtour.com 00961 Beirut, Lebanon **961-3/004-572** professional travel in Lebanon, Syria & Jordan • gay packages available • www.lebtour.com

Lima Tours Jr De la Union 1040, Lima, Peru **51-1/619-6900** personalized, gay-friendly tours to Peru • www.limatours.com.pe

New England Vacation Tours PO Box 560, West Dover, VT 05356 **802/464-2076, 800/742-7669** gay/ lesbian tours (including fall foliage) conducted by a mainstream tour operator • www.newenglandvacationtours.com

Pacha Tours 295 Madison Ave, 43rd flr, New York City, NY 10017 **800/722-4288** trips to Turkey & Greece • www.pachatours.com

Sublime Journeys Albrook Plaza, no. 31, Panama City, Panama **800/830-7142** progressive, diverse & extraordinary travel experiences in South & Central America • www.discoversublime.com

VIP Tours of New York 205 W 57th St, New York, NY 10019 **212/247-0366, 800/300-6203** private, custom-designed tours of New York • specializing in theater, architecture, gay life & more • www.viptoursny.com

Welcome Rajasthan Jaipur, Rajasthan 30216, India **91-141/220-5527 x107, 91-931/450-3423** tours & car rentals for Rajasthan, India • www.welcomerajasthan.com

Wild Rainbow African Safaris 308 Jones St, Ukiah, CA 95482 **707/467-9676** bespoke African safaris lead by Jody Cole • www.wildrainbowsafaris.com

CUSTOM TOURS

Gay/Lesbian

Costa Rica Experts 3166 N Lincoln Ave #424, Chicago, IL 60657 **773/935-1009, 800/827-9046** • www.costaricaexperts.com

Embassy Travel 927 N Kings Rd #311, West Hollywood, CA 90069 **323/656-0743** personalized tours to southern Africa & other worldwide destinations

Travel & Culture Dubai 302 Escape Tower Business Bay Sh. Zyed Rd, Dubai, United Arab Emirates **971/567-15-90-25** tours, safaris & hotel reservations in Dubai • www.dubai.travel-culture.com

Travel & Culture Pakistan 702 Panorama Center Office Plaza, 75530 Karachi, Pakistan **92-321/242-4778** tours, safaris & hotel reservations in Pakistan • www.travel-culture.com

Travel & Culture Sri Lanka 07-1B, E Tower, World Trade Ctr, Colombo, Sri Lanka **94/777-864-479** tours, safaris & hotel reservations in Sri Lanka • www.srilanka.travel-culture.com

VARIOUS TOURS

Mostly Men

Source Events PO Box 530988, Miami, FL 33153 **305/672-9779, 888/768-7238**
specializing in all-gay Windstar cruises • luxury adventures around the world •
www.sourceevents.com

Gay/Lesbian

Footprints 19 Madison Ave #300, Toronto, ON M5R 2S2, Canada **416/962-8111,
888/962-6211** custom-designed, private tours arranged to worldwide destinations
• www.footprintstravel.com

Friends of Dorothy Travel® 1177 California St #B, San Francisco, CA 94108
415/864-1600, 800/640-4918 unique gay & lesbian adventures • individual &
group arrangements • www.fodtravel.com

Out & About Travel 161 Federal St, Providence, RI 02903 **800/842-4753** full-service
travel agency specializing in gay & lesbian tours, cruises, adventure travel, ski trips,
honeymoons, customized packages & more • serving the GLBT community since
1999! • www.gaytravelpros.com

Postcard Destinations 188 Crystal St, Johnstown, PA 15906 **814/539-4999,
800/484-3250 x2621** purveyors of gay travel worldwide since 1985 • tours,
cruises, groups, customized trips, air, hotel • Italy/Germany/Spain specialists • gay-
owned • www.postcarddestinations.com

Zoom Vacations Chicago, IL **773/772-9666, 866/966-6822** takes gay group travel
to the next level • experience the best of a destination w/ surprises, insider events &
a sense of magic • www.zoomvacations.com

EVENTS

January 2013

6-13: Arosa Gay Ski Week *Arosa, Switzerland*
mostly men • 500 attendees • 41-21/566-7020 • **www.arosa-gayskiweek.com**

9-13: Utah Gay & Lesbian Ski Week *Salt Lake City, UT*
ski at Alta, Snowbird, Solitude, Brighton, Snow Basin & The Canyons •
877/429-6368 • **www.gayskiing.org**

13-20: Aspen Gay Ski Week *Aspen, CO*
LGBT • 3000+ attendees • 970/925-4123, 866/564-8398 • **www.gayskiweek.com**

13-Feb 3: Midsumma Festival *Melbourne, Australia*
arts, culture & community • LGBTQ • 61-3/9415-9819 • **www.midsumma.org.au**

17-21: Sin City Shootout *Las Vegas, NV*
3,000 LGBT athletes compete in softball, basketball, wrestling, body building & more
• LGBT • 5,000 attendees • 909/227-1794 • **www.sincityshootout.com**

23-27: Winter Rendezvous *Stowe, VT*
annual gay ski week • skiing, winter sports & entertainment • 587/445-7198 •
www.winterrendezvous.com

February 2013

3-10: WinterPRIDE: Whistler Gay Ski Week   *Whistler, BC, Canada*
annual gay/ lesbian ski week • parties for boys & girls! • top-notch DJs & venues •
popular destination 75 miles N of Vancouver • LGBT • 3,000+ attendees •
604/288-7218, 866/787-1966 • **www.gaywhistler.com**

10-March 3: Sydney Gay Mardi Gras   *Sydney, Australia*
extravagant season of festivities, arts & culture, culminating in the parade & world-
famous Mardi Gras party • 011-61-2/9383-0900 • **www.mardigras.org.au**

12: Mardi Gras   *New Orleans, LA*
mixed gay/ straight • 800/672-6124 • **www.neworleanscvb.com**

22-March 3: Telluride Gay Ski Week   *Telluride, CO*
214/695-2646 • **www.telluridegayskiweek.com**

March 2013

15-24: Winter Music Conference   *Miami, FL*
huge annual EDM conference • workshops, seminars & of course dance parties •
mixed gay/ straight • 100,000 attendees • **www.WinterMusicConference.com**

16-23: European Gay Ski Week   *Alpe d'Huez, France*
Europe's biggest gay ski week • mostly men (women welcome!) • 1,000 attendees •
44-020/7183 0823 (option 1) • **www.europeangayskiweek.com**

TBA: Chicago Takes Off   *Chicago, IL*
burlesque show to fight HIV/AIDS in the Chicagoland area • LGBT • 1,400 attendees
• 773/989-9400 • **www.chicagotakesoff.org**

TBA: Lake Tahoe WinterFest Gay & Lesbian Ski Week   *Lake Tahoe, NV*
world-class skiing • gay comedy • Lake Tahoe dinner/dance cruise • LGBT • 800
attendees • **www.LakeTahoeWinterfest.com**

TBA: OutBoard   *Steamboat Springs, CO*
annual lesbian/ gay snowboarding festival • 300+ attendees • 877/38-BOARD •
www.outboard.org

April 2013

21: AIDS Walk Miami   *Miami Beach, FL*
5K walk-a-thon fundraiser benefiting Care Resource • LGBT • 305/576-1234 •
www.aidswalkmiami.org

30: Queensday   *Amsterdam, Netherlands*
huge street festival to celebrate what was originally the birthday of the Queen
Mother • LGBT • **www.queensdayamsterdam.eu**

TBA: Boybutante Ball   *Athens, GA*
LGBT • 1,000+ attendees • **www.boybutante.org**

TBA: Philadelphia Black Gay Pride   *Philadelphia, PA*
a weekend of social & cultural activities • films, BBQ, spoken word, parties & more •
LGBT • 877/497-7247 • **www.phillyblackpride.org**

May 2013

2-5: Equality Forum *Philadelphia, PA*
largest nat'l & int'l LGBT civil rights summit w/ panels, parties & special events •
215/732-3378 x116 • **www.equalityforum.com**

3-5: Blatino Oasis *Palm Springs, CA*
pool parties, DJs & hot porn stars draw hot black & Latino men from across the
country • men only • **www.blatinooasis.com**

4: Down & Derby *Louisville, KY*
official LGBT event of the Kentucky Derby • LGBT • **www.louisvilledownand-
derby.com**

6-19: Int'l Dublin Gay Theatre Festival *Dublin, Ireland*
353-87/657-3732 • **www.gaytheatre.ie**

19: AIDS Walk New York *New York City, NY*
AIDS benefit • mixed gay/ straight • 212/807-9255 • **www.aidswalk.net**

19: Minnesota AIDS Walk *Minneapolis, MN*
enjoy a 10K walk from Minnehaha Park & raise money for MN AIDS Project • mixed
gay/ straight • 10,000 attendees • 612/373-2410 • **www.mnaidsproject.org**

22-27: Annual Gay Bowling Tournament *Tampa, FL*
check site for local tournaments throughout the year • **www.igbo.org**

**23-26: Int'l Association of Country Western Dance Clubs Annual
Convention** *Seattle, WA*
also semi-annual conventions in March (Fort Lauderdale, FL) & October (San
Francisco, CA) • LGBT • 400-600 attendees • **www.outcountrydance.com**

23-26: Mondo Homo Dirty South *Atlanta, GA*
queer-centric festival featuring music, dance, crafts, performance & more •
404/243-3476 • **www.mondohomo.com**

23-26: Pensacola Memorial Day Weekend *Pensacola, FL*
many parties on beaches & in bars • LGBT • 35,000+ attendees • 850/433-9491 •
www.memorialweekendpensacola.com

24-June 9: Spoleto Festival USA *Charleston, SC*
one of the continent's premier avant-garde cultural arts festivals • 140+ performances of dance, theater & music from around the world • mixed gay/ straight •
843/579-3100 (tickets), 843/722-2764 (office) • **www.spoletousa.org**

30-June 3: Gay Days Orlando *Orlando, FL*
including Gay Day at Disney • 7 days of parties & fun for boys & girls alike! • LGBT
• 407/896-8431 • **www.gaydays.com**

TBA: Splash: Houston Black Gay Pride *Houston, TX*
LGBT • 832/443-1016 • **www.houstonsplash.com**

June 2013

ongoing: LGBT Pride *Cross-country, USA*
celebrate yourself & attend one - or many - of the hundreds of Gay Pride parades
& festivities happening in cities around the world • **www.interpride.org**

ongoing: Music in the Mountains   *Grass Valley, CA*
  summer music festival • mixed gay/ straight • 530/265-6173 • www.musicinthe-mountains.org

ongoing: National Queer Arts Festival   *San Francisco, CA*
  performances & exhibitions in the San Francisco Bay Area highlighting artists from around the country • year-round events • LGBT • 415/935-5948 • www.QueerCulturalCenter.org

2: AIDS Walk Boston & 5K Run   *Boston, MA*
  mixed gay/ straight • 12,000 attendees • 617/424-9255 • www.aidswalkboston.org

2-8: AIDS LifeCycle   *San Francisco to Los Angeles, CA*
  bike from San Francisco to Los Angeles to raise money for HIV/AIDS services • 415/581-7077 • www.aidslifecycle.org

14-16: Black Gay Pride   *Memphis, TN*
  LGBT • 901/522-8459 • www.brothersunited.com

16: Unofficial Gay Day at Cedar Point   *Sandusky, OH*
  wear red to show your support on the unofficial Gay Day at this popular amusement park • mixed gay/ straight •

19-23: South Carolina Black Pride   *Columbia, SC*
  • www.southcarolinablackpride.com

29-30: San Francisco LGBT Pride Parade/ Celebration *San Francisco, CA*
  LGBT • 415/864-0831 • www.sfpride.org

30: REACH Pride T-Dance   *San Francisco, CA*
  high energy music & fantastic DJs • mostly men • 600+ attendees • 415/608-4765 • www.juiceboxpresents.com

TBA: Idapalooza Fruit Jam   *Dowelltown, TN*
  queer music festival in backwoods TN • camping • vegetarian feasts • 615/597-4409 • www.planetida.com

TBA: IGLFA World Championship   *TBA, Worldwide*
  Int'l Gay & Lesbian Football Association's annual soccer tournament • www.iglfa.org

TBA: Paris Circuit Party   *Paris, France*
  gay culture festival • film • performance • political discussions • dance parties & more • LGBT • www.pariscircuitparty.com

TBA: PDX Black Pride   *Portland, OR*
  films, workshops, parties & more • LGBT • pflagpdx.org

TBA: PrideFest   *Milwaukee, WI*
  celebrate LGBT pride at Henry W Maier Festival Park • 414/272-3378 • www.pride-fest.com

TBA: Windy City Black Pride   *Chicago, IL*
  a weekend of parties, seminars & more • LGBT • 888/922-7244 • www.windycity-blackpride.org

July 2013

3-7: At the Beach/ LA Black Pride Weekend   *Los Angeles, CA*
  celebrate a weekend of diversity & LGBT-QS/SGL pride at the beach & across Los Angeles • LGBT • 323/285-4225 • www.atbla.com

4–7: Int'l Gay Square Dance Clubs Convention *San Francisco, CA*
303/722-5276 • www.iagsdc.org

10–13: Black & White Men Together Convention *Columbus, OH*
mostly men • 100+ attendees • 800/NA4-BWMT • www.nabwmt.org

10–20: EuroPride 2013 *Marseille, France*
parties, politics, performance & more • there is something for everyone at this
massive celebration of gay pride • www.europride.info

13–14: Ride for AIDS Chicago *Chicago, IL*
2-day bike ride to fight HIV/ AIDS in the Chicagoland area • LGBT • 350 attendees •
773/989-9400 • www.rideforaids.org

14–21: IMEN Gathering *near Baltimore, MD*
all-inclusive summer camp for gay men • party naked w/ 300 guys for an entire
week • theme parties, pool parties & great food • airport transportation to/from
BWI • 603/841-5636 • www.imengonude.org

21: AIDS Walk San Francisco *San Francisco, CA*
mixed gay/ straight • 27,000+ attendees • 415/615-9255 • www.aidswalk.net

25–28: Triangle Black Pride *Raleigh-Durham, Chapel Hill, NC*
celebrate & honor the diversity of the African American LGBTQ community in the
Triangle • 919/233-2044 • triangleblackpride.org

27: Crape Myrtle Festival *Raleigh-Durham, Chapel Hill, NC*
yearlong fundraising events for HIV/LGBT concerns culminating in a grand gala the
last Saturday of July • mixed gay/ straight • 500+ attendees • 919/656-4205 •
www.crapemyrtlefest.com

TBA: Charlotte Black Gay Pride *Charlotte, NC*
art & performances, community forums, dance parties & more • 704/953-8813 •
www.charlotteblackgaypride.com

TBA: Hotter Than July Weekend *Detroit, MI*
the Midwest's oldest black same-gender-loving pride celebration • LGBT •
888/755-9165 • blackpridesociety.org

TBA: Miami Beach Bruthaz *Miami, FL*
lifestyle event for same-gender-loving men & women • hip hop party • rooftop
pool party • fashion show & more! • mostly men • miamibeachbruthaz.com

August 2013

3–11: OutGames *Antwerp, Belgium*
gay sport & cultural festival • LGBT • 32 475/541 247 • www.woga2013.org

3–4: GaymerCon *San Francisco, CA*
gaming & geek lifestyle convention w/ a focus on LGBT culture • www.gaymer-con.org

9–11: Fire Island Black Out (FIBO) *Fire Island, NY*
3-day beach event for the LGBT community & friends • all are invited to attend &
enjoy, regardless of race, gender or orientation • LGBT • 215/751-0808 •
www.fireislandblackout.com

10: AIDS Walk Colorado *Denver, CO*
303/962-5303 • www.aidswalkcolorado.org

15-18: Tropical Heat *Key West, FL*
naked pool party • dungeon & fetish party • 4 days of HOT male events! • men only
• **www.tropicalheatkw.com**

16-25: GNI (Gay Naturist Int'l) Gathering *Poconos, PA*
weeklong gathering of gay nudists • price includes food, beverages, lodging &
entertainment • workshops • men only • 800 attendees • 954/567-2700 •
www.gaynaturists.org

17: UK Black Pride *London, England*
44 020/8257 5358 • **www.ukblackpride.org.uk**

18-23: Provincetown Carnival *Provincetown, MA*
508/487-2313 • **www.ptown.org**

18-25: 'Camp' Camp *Porter, ME*
summer camp for LGBT adults • sports, pottery, theater, yoga & more • LGBT •
347/453-5257 • **www.campcamp.com**

26-31: National Gay Softball World Series *Washington, DC*
LGBT • 412/362-1247 • **www.gaysoftballworldseries.com**

28-Sept 2: Atlanta Black Pride Weekend *Atlanta, GA*
celebrate Black Pride over Labor Day weekend in Atlanta • LGBT • 678/799-8526 •
www.inthelifeatl.com

28-Sept 2: Southern Decadence *New Orleans, LA*
mostly men • 504/522-8049 • **www.southerndecadence.com**

29-Sept 2: Inferno Dominican Republic *Punta Cana, Dominican Republic*
the premier Labor Day pride celebration • deluxe, all-inclusive accommodations •
LGBT • 305/891-7536 • **www.infernodr.com**

29-Sept 9: West Coast Gathering *Malibu, CA*
swimming, parties, workshops & more with fellow gay male naturists • also Spring
Gathering near Nashville, TN in June • men only • 400 attendees • 877/683-4781 •
www.cmen.info

30-Sept 2: Splash Days *Austin, TX*
weekend of hot dance & lake parties in Austin over Labor Day Wknd • **www.splash-
days.com**

TBA: Black Pride NYC *New York City, NY*
multicultural LGBT festival w/ a wide array of entertainment, forums, workshops &
events • LGBT • **www.nycblackpride.com**

TBA: Blackout: Oakland Black & Brown Pride *Oakland, CA*
celebrate w/ a weekend of conferences, awards ceremonies & parties •
510/621-3553 • **www.facebook.com/pages/Oakland-BlackOUT-Black-LGBTQ-
Pride-Celebration/100659563311405?ref=ts**

TBA: Edinburgh Fringe Festival *Edinburgh, Scotland*
the largest arts festival in the world • dance, theater, music, comedy, events & more
• mixed gay/ straight • 44-131/226-0026 • **www.edfringe.com**

TBA: Gay Ski Week NZ *Queenstown, New Zealand*
64 21/83-4640 • **www.gayskiweekqt.com**

TBA: Northalsted Market Days *Chicago, IL*
a good ol' summer block party on Main St of Boys' Town, USA • LGBT •
773/883-0500 • **www.northalsted.com**

TBA: Rendezvous 2013   *Medicine Bow Nat'l Forest, WY*
5-day camping festival to celebrate LGBT pride • 400+ attendees • 307/778-7465 •
www.wyomingequality.org

TBA: St Louis Black Pride   *St Louis, MO*
314/531-2284 • **www.st-louisblackpride.org**

September 2013

15: Out in the Park   *Springfield, MA*
unofficial gay day at Six Flags New England • wear red to show your support •
LGBT • 1,000+ attendees • **www.outinthepark.info**

26-30: Dallas Black Pride   *Dallas, TX*
LGBT • 214/440-9300 • **dfwpridemovement.org**

27: Out On The Mountain   *Valencia, CA*
gay day at Six Flags Magic Mountain • LGBT • **www.outonthemountain.com**

TBA: Braking the Cycle   *Boston, MA to New York City, NY*
3-day fully-supported bike ride from Boston to New York • benefiting the HIV/AIDS
related services of the LGBT Community Center in NYC • mixed gay/ straight •
212/989-1111 • **www.brakingthecycle.org**

TBA: Gay Days Las Vegas   *Orlando, FL*
including Gay Day at Disney • 7 days of parties & fun for boys & girls alike! • LGBT
• 407/896-8431 • **www.gaydays.com**

TBA: Get Wet Weekend   *Curaçao, Netherlands Antilles, Caribbean*
discover the Caribbean Dutch Paradise of Curaçao! • gay/ lesbian • 599/9510-6479,
599/9510-6499 • **www.gaycuracao.com**

TBA: Howl Festival   *New York City, NY*
a cabaret from the underworld • outdoor murals • hip hop howl • all in Tompkins
Square Park • mixed gay/ straight • 212/243-3413 • **www.howlfestival.com**

TBA: Pink Season   *Hong Kong, China*
2-month festival featuring speakers, plays, dance parties, pageants & more • LGBT •
www.pinkseason.hk

TBA: Seattle AIDS Walk   *Seattle, WA*
mixed gay/ straight • 4,000+ attendees • 206/328-8979 •
www.SeattleAIDSWalk.org

October 2013

3-6: Prime Timers World Wide Convention   *Columbus, OH*
bi-annual event for older gay men and the youngsters who admire them •
614/885-0846 • **www.primetimersww.org**

4-6: Gay Days Anaheim   *Anaheim, CA*
"join 30,000 GLBT mouseketeers as we turn the happiest place in earth into the
gayest!" • **www.GayDaysAnaheim.com**

6: Castro Street Fair   *San Francisco, CA*
performance, arts & community groups street fair • co-founded by Harvey Milk •
415/841-1824 • **www.castrostreetfair.org**

11: National Coming Out Day — *Cross-country, USA*
check local listings for events in your area or visit www.hrc.com/ncop •
202/628-4160, 800/777-4723 • **www.hrc.org/comingout**

18-27: Fantasy Fest — *Key West, FL*
10 days of parties, costume contests, street fairs, masquerade balls & parades •
70,000 attendees • 305/296-1817 • **www.fantasyfest.net**

20: AIDS Walk Atlanta & 5k Run — *Atlanta, GA*
mixed gay/ straight • 10,000+ attendees • 404/876-9255 • **WWW.aidswalkat-lanta.com**

20: AIDS Walk LA — *Los Angeles, CA*
annual AIDS fundraiser in West Hollywood • mixed gay/ straight • 213/201-9255 •
www.aidswalk.net

20-27: Fantasia Fair — *Provincetown, MA*
a weeklong celebration of gender diversity • workshops, fashion show, cabaret,
banquets & more • **www.fantasiafair.org**

31-Nov 3: Sundance Stompede — *San Francisco, CA*
San Francisco's annual country/ western dance weekend • LGBT • 415/820-1403 •
www.stompede.com

TBA: Black Pride — *Nashville, TN*
gay/ lesbian • 615/974-2832, 800/845-4266x269 • **www.brothersunited.com**

TBA: Gaylaxicon — *Minneapolis, MN*
LGBT science fiction, fantasy, horror & gaming convention • **www.gaylaxi-con2013.org**

TBA: Glasgay! — *Glasgow, Scotland*
UK's largest lesbian & gay multi-arts festival • 44-141/552-7575 •
www.glasgay.com

TBA: Taiwan LGBT Pride — *Taipei, Taiwan*
• **www.twpride.org**

TBA: World Gay Rodeo Finals — *TBA, USA*
check w/ local chapters for events throughout the year in your area •
303/766-5630 • **www.igra.com**

November 2013

2-3: Greater Palm Springs Pride — *Palm Springs, CA*
free entertainment, dance parties, lots of people & a parade on Sunday •
760/416-8711 • **www.PSPride.org**

TBA: Transgender Film Festival — *San Francisco, CA*
films that promote the visibility of transgender & gender variant people •
www.trannyfest.com

December 2013

11-15: IAGLBC Annual Bridge Tournament — *Palm Springs, CA*
Int'l Association of Gay & Lesbian Bridge Clubs • **www.GayBridge.org**

31: Mummer's Strut — *Philadelphia, PA*
big New Year's Eve party • followed by New Year's Day Parade • mixed gay/ straight
• $40-50 • 215/336-3050 • **www.mummers.com**

TBA: Holly Folly   *Provincetown, MA*
lesbian/ gay holiday celebration • fabulous parties • holiday concert • open houses
• 1st wknd in December • www.ptown.org

FILM FESTIVALS

January 2013

31–Feb 10: Reelout Queer Film & Video Festival   *Kingston, ON, Canada*
celebrating the best of queer independent film & video • 613/549-7335 •
www.reelout.com

31–Feb 10: Zinegoak   *Bilbao, Spain*
LGBT film & performing arts festival • 34-94/415-6258 • www.zinegoak.com

February 2013

TBA: Mardi Gras Film Festival   *Sydney, Australia*
Sydney film festival corresponds with massive Mardi Gras event • 61-2/9332-4938
• www.queerscreen.com.au

March 2013

14–24: Melbourne Queer Film Festival   *Melbourne, Australia*
613/9662-4147 • www.mqff.com.au

TBA: Fusion   *Los Angeles, CA*
Los Angeles' LGBT people of color film festival • 213/480-7088 •
www.outfest.org/fusion.html

TBA: London Lesbian & Gay Film Festival   *London, England*
grab your tickets for the largest LGBT film fest in Europe • 44 (0)20/7928-3232 •
www.llgff.org.uk

TBA: Out at the Movies   *Canton, NY*
LGBT film festival for Northern New York • www.outatthemovies.org

TBA: Verzaubert Int'l Queer Film Festival   *Berlin, Germany*
screening in Berlin, Cologne, Frankfurt & Munich • also fall screening in November •
LGBT • 49-30/861-4532 • www.liebefilme.com

April 2013

5–14: Brisbane Queer Film Festival   *Brisbane, Australia*
61 7/3358 8600 • www.bqff.com.au

26–May 5: Miami Gay & Lesbian Film Festival   *Miami, FL*
305/751-6305 • www.MGLFF.com

TBA: Out in Africa   *Cape Town, South Africa*
the only film festival of its kind on the African continent • three 10-day festivals
throughout the year • also August & October • also in Johannesburg • 27 21/461
40 27 • www.oia.co.za

TBA: QFest   *St Louis, MO*
314/289-4152 • www.stlqfest.org

May 2013

2-12: Boston LGBT Film Festival   *Boston, MA*
617/369-3300 • www.bostonlgbtfilmfest.org

16-26: Inside Out: Toronto LGBT Film Festival   *Toronto, ON, Canada*
416/977-6847 • www.insideout.ca

29-June 2: FilmOut San Diego   *San Diego, CA*
LGBT film festival • 619/512-5157 • www.filmoutsandiego.com

31-June 8: Connecticut Gay & Lesbian Film Festival   *Hartford, CT*
gay & lesbian film festival at Cinestudio • 860/586-1136 • www.outfilmct.org

TBA: Fairy Tales Int'l LGBT Film Festival   *Calgary, AB, Canada*
403/244-1956 • www.fairytalesfilmfest.com

TBA: Honolulu Rainbow Film Festival   *Honolulu, HI*
808/675-8428 • www.hglcf.org

TBA: Out Takes LGBT Film Festival   *Wellington, New Zealand*
week-long festival in Auckland & Wellington • 64-4/972-6775 •
www.outtakes.org.nz

TBA: Translations: Transgender Film Festival   *Seattle, WA*
206/323-4274 • www.threedollarbillcinema.org

June 2013

8-15: TLVFest: The Tel Aviv LGBT Film Festival   *Tel Aviv, Israel*
films will also show in Jerusalem & Haifa • 972-52/875-7955 • www.tlvfest.com

19-23: Provincetown Int'l Film Festival   *Provincetown, MA*
mixed gay/ straight • 508/487-3456 • www.ptownfilmfest.org

20-30: Frameline: San Francisco Int'l
LGBT Film Festival   *San Francisco, CA*
get your tickets early for a slew of films about us • LGBT • 65,000+ attendees •
415/703-8650 • www.frameline.org

TBA: Identities Queer Film Festival   *Vienna, Austria*
43-1/524-6274 • www.identities.at/index/en/

TBA: Mix Milano Int'l LGBT Film Festival   *Milan, Italy*
• www.cinemagaylesbico.com

TBA: NewFest: New York LGBT Film Festival   *New York City, NY*
646/290-8136 • www.newfest.org

TBA: Rio Gay Film Festival   *Rio de Janeiro, Brazil*
LGBT • www.riofgc.com

July 2013

11-21: Outfest   *Los Angeles, CA*
Los Angeles' lesbian/ gay film & video festival in mid-July • 213/480-7088 •
www.outfest.org

11-22: Philadelphia QFest   *Philadelphia, PA*
267/765-9800 • www.qfest.com

TBA: Fire Island Film & Video Festival *Fire Island, NY*
- www.liglff.org

TBA: Mostra Lambda Barcelona *Barcelona, Spain*
LGBT film festival • www.cinemalambda.com

TBA: Tokyo Int'l Lesbian & Gay Film Festival *Tokyo, Japan*
- www.tokyo-lgff.org

August 2013

2-4: Gaze Dublin Int'l LGBT Film Festival *Dublin, Ireland*
0872/709700 • www.gaze.ie

6-11: Flickers: Rhode Island Int'l Film Festival *Providence, RI*
don't miss the Gay & Lesbian Film Fest • mixed gay/ straight • 401/861-4445 •
www.film-festival.org

15-25: Vancouver Queer Film & Video Festival *Vancouver, BC, Canada*
LGBT • 604/844-1615 • www.queerfilmfestival.ca

23-25: Birmingham Shout *Birmingham, AL*
LGBT film festival • 205/324-0888 • www.bhamshout.com

TBA: North Carolina Gay & Lesbian Film Festival *Durham, NC*
919/560-3030 (box office), 919/560-3040 • festivals.carolinatheatre.org/ncglff

September 2013

13-15: Q Film Festival *Long Beach, CA*
showcasing films of interest to the queer community • 562/434-4455 •
www.qfilmslongbeach.com

20-28: Queer Lisbon *Lisbon, Portugal*
Portugal's only LGBT film festival • 351 91/335-8603 • www.queerlisboa.pt

TBA: Fresno Reel Pride *Fresno, CA*
annual lesbian & gay film festival in central California • 559/999-7971 • www.reel-
pride.com

TBA: Milwaukee LGBT Film/ Video Festival *Milwaukee, WI*
414/229-4758 • www4.uwm.edu/psoa/film/lgbtfilmfestival/

TBA: Outflix *Memphis, TN*
LGBT film festival • www.outflixfestival.org

TBA: Southwest Gay & Lesbian Film Festival *Albuquerque, NM*
also in Santa Fe, NM • 505/243-1870 • www.swglff.com

October 2013

3-10: Out on Film *Atlanta, GA*
LGBT • 678/237-7206 • www.outonfilm.org

10-12: Sacramento Int'l Gay & Lesbian Film Festival *Sacramento, CA*
916/304-3456 • www.siglff.org

10-13: Q Cinema *Fort Worth, TX*
annual celebration of LGBT-themed movies • 817/723-4358 • www.qcinema.org

three
dollar bill
cinema

Coming to Seattle? Sit in the dark with us.

Keeping audiences entertained since 1996, Three Dollar Bill Cinema promotes and produces LGBT film events throughout the year, including free outdoor movies every summer, our Spring Film Series of vintage queer classics, the Seattle Lesbian & Gay Film Festival in October, and other unique events.

Check out our website or find us on Facebook and Twitter to see what's happening on your next visit to Seattle.

three
dollar bill
cinema

www.threedollarbillcinema.org

11-20: Reel Q Int'l Lesbian & Gay Film Festival *Pittsburgh, PA*
412/422-6776 • www.plgfs.org

17-27: Barcelona Int'l LGTIB Film Festival *Barcelona, Spain*
gay/ lesbian • 973/664-421 • www.barcelonafilmfestival.org

18-27: Mix *Copenhagen, Denmark*
45/2843-4217 • www.mixcopenhagen.dk

TBA: Austin Gay & Lesbian International Film Festival *Austin, TX*
512/302-9889 • www.agliff.org

TBA: Cheries-Cheris:
Paris Gay, Lesbian & Trans Film Festival *Paris, France*
• www.cheries-cheris.com

TBA: Hamburg Int'l Lesbian & Gay Film Festival *Hamburg, Germany*
49-40/348-0670 • www.lsf-hamburg.de

TBA: image+nation: Montréal
Int'l LGBT Film Festival *Montréal, QC, Canada*
LGBT • 514/285-4467 • www.image-nation.org

TBA: Madrid LGBT Film Festival *Madrid, Spain*
34-91/593-0540 • www.lesgaicinemad.com

TBA: Portland Lesbian & Gay Film Festival *Portland, OR*
• www.plgff.org

TBA: Reel Affirmations: The Nation's LGBT Film Festival *Washington, DC*
lesbian/ gay films • 202/349-7358 • www.reelaffirmations.org

TBA: Seattle Lesbian & Gay Film Festival *Seattle, WA*
see ad on p. 499 • 206/323-4274 • www.threedollarbillcinema.org

TBA: Tampa Bay Int'l Gay & Lesbian Film Festival *Tampa Bay, FL*
813/879-4220 • www.tiglff.com

November 2013

TBA: Hong Kong Lesbian/ Gay Film Festival *Hong Kong, China*
LGBT • 852/2311 8081 • www.hklgff.hk

TBA: Long Island Gay & Lesbian Film Festival *Huntington, NY*
• www.liglff.org

TBA: Mezipatra *Prague & Brno, Czech Republic*
Czech LGBT film festival • www.mezipatra.cz

TBA: Mix: New York Lesbian & Gay
Experimental Film Fest *New York City, NY*
film, videos, installations & media performances • write for info • 212/742-8880 •
www.mixnyc.org

TBA: Reeling: Chicago Lesbian & Gay Int'l Film Fest *Chicago, IL*
773/293-1447 • www.reelingfilmfestival.org

LEATHER, FETISH & BEARS

January 2013

11-14: Mid-Atlantic Leather Weekend   *Washington, DC*
LGBT • 703/863-7295 • www.leatherweekend.com

17-21: La Fiesta de Los Osos   *Tucson, AZ*
a winter bear gathering in the warmth of the desert sun • men only •
520/310-3485 • www.botop.com

25-27: Southwest Leather Conference   *Phoenix, AZ*
workshops, vendors & fetish ball • MASTER/slave, Bootblack & Daddy/boy contests •
LGBT • www.southwestleather.org

27-Feb 3: Beef Dip: Int'l Bear Week   *Puerto Vallarta, Mexico*
beach parties, pool parties & hot DJs • local tours • booze cruise • bring sunscreen!
• men only • 416/922-1018 • www.beefdip.com

February 2013

TBA: West Coast Rubber Weekend   *Palm Springs, CA*
hot weekend dedicated to rubber, spandex, dive gear, BDSM • men only •
760/880-7470 • www.westcoastrubber.com

March 2013

15-24: Washington State Leather Pride Week   *Seattle, WA*
• www.wsmlo.org

28-April 1: Easter 2013 Berlin   *Berlin, Germany*
annual leather & fetish weekend • German Mr Leather contest • 49 30/215 0099 •
www.blf.de

TBA: Sugarbear Weekend   *Montréal, QC, Canada*
Quebecois bear party with lots of maple syrup • men only • www.sugarbearweek-
end.com

April 2013

12-14: Rubbout   *Vancouver, BC, Canada*
annual party weekend of rubber & fetish for men • men only • 604/345-1357 •
www.rubbout.com

22-24: Rocky Mountain Olympus Leather   *Salt Lake City, UT*
leather competition • participants from Utah, Colorado, Wyoming, Idaho &
Montana • mixed gay/ straight • 200 attendees • 415/409-9447 • www.rocky-
mountainolympus.com

TBA: Mr LeatherMan Italy   *Rome, Italy*
hot weekend of leather events culminating in the election of Mr LeatherMan Italy •
Mr Rubber Italy contest in October • men only • www.lcroma.com

May 2013

2-6: Phurfest   *Phoenix, AZ*
let the fur fly in Phoenix • 602/370-3260 • www.phurfest.org

8-13: Beach Bear Weekend   *Fort Lauderdale, FL*
get to the beach for a long weekend of dance parties, cocktails and great food • oh, and bears! • www.beachbearweekend.com

17-19: Northwest Leather Celebration   *San Jose, CA*
host of the NW regional Master/slave contest • LGBT • www.northwestleathercelebration.com

23-27: Bear Pride   *Chicago, IL*
1,000+ attendees • 312/590-4485 • www.bearpride.org

24-27: International Mr Bootblack Contest   *Chicago, IL*
contest takes place during International Mr Leather weekend • 800/545-6753 • www.imrl.com

24-27: International Mr Leather   *Chicago, IL*
weekend of leather events, capped by contest Sunday, Black & Blue Ball on Monday • 800/545-6753 • www.imrl.com

June 2013

20-23: Southeast Leatherfest   *Atlanta, GA*
LGBT • www.seleatherfest.com

TBA: Bear Arabia Trip   *Lebanon, Jordan, and Syria*
visit Lebanon, Jordan & Syria with the bears of Arabia • also in Sept or Oct • 961 3/004572 • www.beararabia.org

TBA: Bears on the Beach   *Cairns, Queensland, Australia*
pool party • BBQ • dancing • tours & more • men only • 07/4059-1800 • www.turtlecove.com/gay-lesbian-beachfront-resort/bears-on-the-beach-2012/

TBA: Folsom Street East   *New York City, NY*
New York City's answer to the famous San Francisco fetish street fair • LGBT • www.folsomstreeteast.org

TBA: Southern HiBearnation   *Melbourne, Australia*
a week of furry fun down under, culminating in the Mr Australasia Bear Contest, bringing bears from Australia, New Zealand, Southeast Asia, the South Pacific & beyond • 500+ attendees • 0409/360-031 • www.southernhibearnation.com

July 2013

12-14: Thunder in the Mountains   *Denver, CO*
weekend of pansexual leather events & seminars • kinky comedy revue • talent show • LGBT • 800+ attendees • 303/698-1207 • www.thunderinthemountains.com

13-21: Bear Week Provincetown   *Provincetown, MA*
come to Provincetown for a relaxing week of parties & events • men only • www.ptownbears.org

17-21: TransCampOUT *Walton, WV*
presentations • games • auctions • outdoor dungeon • swimming • trans-oriented • everyone welcome regardless of sexual orientation or gender identity • LGBT • 971/295-6106 • **www.transcampout.org**

28: Up Your Alley Fair *San Francisco, CA*
local SM/ leather street fair held in Dore Alley, South-of-Market • thousands of local kinky men & women attend • 415/777-3247 • **www.folsomstreetevents.org**

TBA: International LeatherSIR/ Leatherboy *San Francisco, CA*
also Int'l Community BootBlack • check website for regional contest info • **www.leathersir.com**

August 2013

6-11: International Deaf Leather *Montreal, QC, Canada*
weekend of events, including Mr & Ms Deaf Leather Contest • **www.international-aldeafleather.org**

TBA: Lazy Bear Weekend *Russian River, CA*
no contests, no pageants, no frills—just fun! • FUNdraiser benefits AIDS charities in Northern California & beyond • check web for details • mostly men • **www.lazybearweekend.com**

TBA: Pantheon of Leather *Atlanta, GA*
annual leather/ SM/ fetish community service awards & int'l Mr & Ms Olympus Leather • mixed gay/ straight • **www.TheLeatherJournal.com/pantheon**

TBA: Southeast Black & Blue *Atlanta, GA*
SE Leather Sir, Leather Boy & Bootblack contests • also Mr SE Rubber contest • **www.southeastlsb.com**

TBA: Toronto Leather Pride *Toronto, ON, Canada*
hot parties all weekend • competitions • Leather Ball on Sat • mostly men • 416/515-1910 • **www.torontoleatherpride.ca**

September 2013

14-15: Folsom Europe *Berlin, Germany*
• **www.folsomeurope.info**

29: Folsom Street Fair *San Francisco, CA*
huge SM/ leather street fair, topping a week of kinky events • LGBT • thousands of local & visiting kinky men & women attendees • 415/777-3247 • **www.folsomstreetevents.org**

TBA: Burning Bear Weekend *Winnemucca, NV*
hot weekend of dinners, dances & more • proceeds benefit local charity • men only • **bearsandfriendsofwinnemucca.com**

TBA: Oktobearfest *Munich, Germany*
join the Munich bears • 49-176/6312-7540 • **www.oktobearfest.de**

October 2013

3-6: Mates Leather Weekend *Provincetown, MA*
four days/nights of events, including Fetish Party, Uniforms & Cigars, and First Mate Contest • 800/330-9413 • **www.matesleatherweekend.com**

10-13: OctobearFest   *Denver, CO*
men only • www.octobearfest.org

18-20: Bear Bust   *Orlando, FL*
hot bear weekend at Parliament House Resort • men only • www.bearbust.org

TBA: Leather Pride Amsterdam   *Amsterdam, Netherlands*
weekend of hot leather events • men only • www.get-ruff.com**November 2013**

1-3: Mr Int'l Rubber & Rubber Blowout   *Chicago, IL*
largest rubber event in US • market, parties • men only • www.MIRubber.com

1-3: Santa Clara County Leather Weekend   *San Jose, CA*
leather fellowship in the San Jose area • LGBT • www.SCCLeather.org

TBA: Bear Pride Week   *Cologne, Germany*
49-221/5481-9259 • www.bearscologne.de

CONFERENCES & RETREATS

January 2013

23-27: Creating Change Conference   *Baltimore, MD*
for lesbians, gays, bisexuals, transgender people & allies seeking positive & enduring political & social change • 2,500+ attendees • 617/492-6393 • www.creatingchange.org

March 2013

22-24: Together We Can   *Detroit, MI*
annual LGBT substance abuse conference • 248/838-9905 • www.twcdetroit.com

May 2013

23-26: Saints & Sinners   *New Orleans, LA*
LGBT writers & readers from around the country gather for a hot weekend of readings, panels & performance • 300 attendees • $100 • 504/581-1144 • www.sasfest.com

June 2013

TBA: Lambda Literary Awards   *New York City, NY*
the Lammies are the Oscars of LGBT writing & publishing • LGBT • 323/366-2104 • www.lambdaliterary.org

August 2013

1-4: Gender Odyssey   *Seattle, WA*
4 days of panels, workshops & meetings • entertainment & art • focus on transmen, transwomen & families with transgender children & teens • open to all • 206/306-8383 • www.genderodyssey.org

6-11: RAD Conference:
Rainbow Alliance of the Deaf   *Montréal, QC, Canada*
workshops • conferences • keynote speakers • social events • come celebrate deaf culture & identity • **www.rad.org**

22-25: **Nat'l Lesbian & Gay Journalists Assoc Convention**   *Boston, MA*
workshops • keynote speakers • entertainment • 202/588-9888 x10 • **www.nlgja.org**

September 2013

TBA: **Southern Comfort Conference**   *Atlanta, GA*
entertainers & leaders from the entire spectrum of the transgender community offering 5 days of learning, networking & fun • 702/336-1202 • **www.sccatl.org**

October 2013

TBA: **National LGBT MBA Conference**   *TBA, USA*
career fair & discussions of sexual orientation, gender & leadership in the workplace by MBA students & out Fortune 500 company leaders • LGBT • 800+ attendees • **www.reachingoutmba.org**

November 2013

TBA: **Transgender Leadership Summit**   *TBA, USA*
join transgender activists to help create a unified voice to advance the movement for transgender equality • 200+ attendees • 415/865-0176 • **www.transgender-lawcenter.org**

SPIRITUAL

February 2013

15-18: **PantheaCon**   *San Jose, CA*
pagan convention • mixed gay/ straight • 510/653-3244 • **www.pantheacon.com**

June 2013

16-23: **Pagan Spirit Gathering**   *TBA, USA*
summer solstice celebration • primitive camping • workshops • rituals • advance registration required • mixed gay/ straight • 608/924-2216 • **www.circlesanctuary.org/psg**

August 2013

TBA: **BC Witchcamp**   *near Vancouver, BC, Canada*
weeklong Wiccan intensive at Evans Lake • mixed gay/ straight • 250/598-9229 • **www.bcwitchcamp.ca**

THE CIRCUIT

January 2013

TBA: Sapphire Ball   *Philadelphia, PA*
benefit wknd for the LGBT community highlighted by Saturday night dance at Nat'l
Constitution Center • open to all lifestyles • mostly men • 267/514-2088 •
www.sapphirefund.org

February 2013

3-10: WinterPRIDE: Whistler Gay Ski Week   *Whistler, BC, Canada*
annual gay/lesbian ski week • top-notch DJs & venues • popular destination 75
miles N of Vancouver • LGBT • 3,000+ attendees • 604/288-7218, 866/787-1966 •
www.gaywhistler.com

16: Red Party Weekend   *Montréal, QC, Canada*
AIDS benefit dance • mostly men • 2500+ attendees • $50+ • 514/875-7026 •
www.bbcm.org

March 2013

6-11: Winter Party Festival   *Miami Beach, FL*
celebration & fundraiser for the LGBT community • 10,000 attendees •
305/571-1924 • **www.winterparty.org**

23: The Black Party   *New York City, NY*
also BPX: Black Party Expo March 23-25 • www.blackpartyexpo.com • LGBT • $100
• 212/674-8541 • **www.saintatlarge.com**

30: White Party   *Palm Springs, CA*
spectacular live performances • top-notch talent • cutting-edge lighting & special
effects • mostly men • 30,000 attendees • 323/782-9924 •
www.jeffreysanker.com

April 2013

4-7: Cherry Weekend   *Washington, DC*
703/389-1238 • **www.cherryfund.org**

26-29: Purple Party   *Dallas, TX*
a weekend of dance parties & social events benefiting AIDS Services of Dallas •
www.dallaspurpleparty.org

May 2013

23-27: Sizzle 2013   *Miami, FL*
Miami's original circuit event • 305/938-9612 • **www.sizzlemiami.com**

July 2013

3-7: Summer Camp   *Provincetown, MA*
celebrate the week of the 4th at the longest running circuit celebration in New
England • 508/487-9601 • **www.davidflower.com**

TBA: San Diego Pride Parties   *San Diego, CA*
a weekend of hot parties w/ big name DJs, including the Zoo Party at the world-
famous San Diego Zoo • mostly men • 800-4,000 attendees • $75-100 •
619/770-8322 • **www.billhardtpresents.com**

August 2013

8-18: Circuit   *Barcelona, Spain*
water park events • club nights • pool parties • films, discussions & more • gay/
lesbian • **www.circuitfestival.net**

21-24: XLSior Int'l Gay Festival   *Mykonos, Greece*
hot beach party at Elia beach in Mykonos, Greece • mostly men • **www.xlsiorfesti-
val.com**

31: Elysium Pool Party   *Mykonos, Greece*
huge, int'l gay party • 30/22890-23952 • **www.mykonos-
accommodation.com/salvation-gay-party-mykonos-2012.htm**

September 2013

28: Magnitude   *San Francisco, CA*
the official, hottest dance & play party of the Folsom Street Fair • mostly men •
415/777-3247 • **www.folsomstreetevents.org/magnitude**

29: Aftershock: Folsom Street Fair   *San Francisco, CA*
DJ Abel keeps the leather crowd going • 4am Sunday morning/ Saturday night,
after Magnitude • mostly men • **www.TheDISCOSF.com**

29: REAL BAD   *San Francisco, CA*
"Be Bad... Do Good" • annual fundraiser immediately following the Folsom Street
Fair • proceeds go directly to beneficiaries • mostly men • **www.realbad.org**

October 2013

9-15: Black & Blue Festival   *Montréal, QC, Canada*
North America's biggest & most innovative dance event & cultural festival • mostly
men • 25,000+ attendees • $60-100+ • 514/875-7026 • **www.bbcm.org**

24-27: Halloween in New Orleans   *New Orleans, LA*
mostly men • 5,000+ attendees • **www.halloweenneworleans.com**

November 2013

27-Dec 1: White Party Week   *Miami Beach, FL*
6 days of festivities capped by the annual White Party at Vizcaya • benefitting Care
Resource • LGBT • 305/576-1234 • **www.whiteparty.org**

December 2013

31: Metropolis New Year's Eve 2013   *San Francisco, CA*
12-hour dance marathon • largest gay New Year's party in San Francisco • mostly
men • **www.guspresents.com**

SAN FRANCISCO PRIDE

Come see
what makes us
the largest
annual gathering
of LGBT people
in the US

The
43rd annual
San Francisco
LGBT Pride
Celebration
& Parade®

June
29-30
2013

sfpride.org

Photo: Bill Weaver

FOLSOM STREET FAIR

®

The San Francisco Original

SUNDAY, SEPTEMBER 29TH, 2013

1984   XXX   2013

SAN FRANCISCO, CA, USA
FOLSOMSTREETFAIR.ORG

THE OFFICIAL SATURDAY NIGHT DANCE EVENT OF FOLSOM STREET FAIR®

MAGNITUDE®

Saturday, September 28th, 2013

San Francisco, CA, USA
FOLSOMSTREETFAIR.ORG

FOLSOM STREET FAIR

Sunday, September 29th, 2013

REAL BAD XXV

A GRGR:WEST PRODUCTION

FOLSOM WEEKEND | SAN FRANCISCO

SUNDAY • SEPTEMBER 29, 2013 • 7PM - 4AM

realbad.org

BE BAD...DO GOOD

100% of the net proceeds benefit grassroots HIV/AIDS and community organizations annually

STYLING: ATOM EDWARDS • PHOTO: MICHAEL SMITH • GRAPHIC DESIGN: KENSHI@KENSHIWESTOVER.com

MEET LOCAL GUYS

Meet hot guys wherever you're traveling...

FREE

To Set up a Mailbox
To Listen to Personal Ads
To Reply to Personal Ads

USE FREE CODE: Damron